THE GOD OF JESUS
IN LIGHT OF CHRISTIAN DOGMA

THE GOD OF JESUS
IN LIGHT OF CHRISTIAN DOGMA

— The Recovery of New Testament Theology —

KEGAN A. CHANDLER

Restoration Fellowship
McDonough, Georgia

Copyright © 2016 by Kegan A. Chandler

Published by Restoration Fellowship

Restoration Fellowship
http://www.restorationfellowship.org
McDonough, Georgia

Most Scripture quotations taken from the New American Standard Bible®,
Copyright © 1960, 1962, 1963, 1968, 1971, 1972, 1973, 1975, 1977, 1995 by The Lockman
Foundation. Used by permission. (www.Lockman.org)

Most concordance references taken from *Strong's Exhaustive Concordance*: New American Standard
Bible. Updated ed. La Habra: Lockman Foundation, 1995. Retrieved from
http://www.blueletterbible.org

Cover Design by Lauren M. Chandler
The cover displays a detail of the 13th century Christ Pantocrator icon from the Serbian monastery
on Mount Athos in Greece. It is set against the Great Isaiah Scroll from the Dead Sea Scrolls
collection located at the Shrine of the Book in Jerusalem.

All rights reserved. First Published 2016.
Printed in the United States of America

ISBN 10 0-9673249-3-9
ISBN 13 978-0-9673249-3-7

For my sons, my little teachers

"God is the God of truth! The love of truth, submission to the force of truth, the surrender of traditional views which will not stand the test of truth, is a sacred duty, an element of the fear of God."

— Franz Julius Delitzsch (1813-1890)

Sincere thanks are owed to my wife Lauren for her love and patience during my many late hours; to Michael and Hildy, my devoted parents, for their enduring support and direction; to Sarah for her invaluable help in poring over the manuscript; to Carlos, Barbara, Jesse, Pierre, Shaun, Tony, Talitha, Randy, Ric, Menashe, Nathan and many others for their encouragement and partnership in the work of faith.

Special thanks are also owed to Sir Anthony Buzzard for his personal guidance and dedication to the Gospel, without which this book may never have come to be.

CONTENTS

PART II: THE RECOVERY

FOREWORD

This book is not for the faint-hearted. Nor is it for those who are comfortable with the status quo. It is a challenge, and a radical one, to "what we have always believed." Because the Christian definition of God has been promoted so massively and for so long as a non-negotiable taken-for-granted, it appears to have become a taboo subject for investigation. Many complain about the poor state of the Church, but few seem brave enough to get at the heart of the possibility that there may be some deep-seated problems with where and how we got our creedal confessions. It was the very insightful late F.F. Bruce who wrote to me many years ago with these sage words: "Evangelical Protestants can be as much servants of tradition as Roman Catholics or Greek Orthodox Christians; only they do not realize that it is 'tradition.' People who adhere to sola scriptura (as they believe) often adhere in fact to a traditional school of interpretation of sola scriptura" (June 13, 1981). It is this tradition which Kegan Chandler sets out to confront.

It is very important to emphasize that Chandler is not an innovator. The author's wide research in the history of Christianity, as well as in the Bible, shows us that he has left no stone unturned in his search for liberating truth. He has found that other options for defining the Messiah in relation to God are available, but only to those who are willing to challenge what is known as "orthodoxy." Kegan's irenic, non-combative style is bound to ease any discomfort the reader might experience when faced with some of the shocking but unarguable facts about the origin of some of our most cherished beliefs about God, the God of Jesus, and the God of Scripture. Few in Church, that regular habit embraced by so many week by week, have studied enough about Church history to know whether there is a solid scriptural basis for some of our most cherished ideas about who God is—beliefs indeed in the absence of which, it is loudly proclaimed, a person cannot be saved.

Kegan has dealt in a penetrating manner with a hugely significant topic. The great central, creedal basis of our faith, the way in which we define the universe, our sense of what life is all about in terms of God's great plan revealed in

Jesus—this is the subject Chandler has engaged with an impressive intensity and conviction. Again, he is inventing nothing new. He has read widely and consulted many. His investigation leads him to a discovery of what might be called a conspiracy of silence over what may turn out to be an acute embarrassment to the Bible-reading community. The hard facts about the development of doctrine in post-biblical times cannot in fact be aligned with Jesus' own explicit approval of his very Jewish definition of God as the God of Israel. Jesus called this "the greatest commandment," but are we listening as the Shema ("Listen!") tells us to?

Kegan devotes the first half of his work to history and the second half to exegeting the Biblical texts. He leads us through four centuries of post-biblical, fierce argumentation about who God and Jesus are. The bitter struggles and infighting of those times were muted only by Church Council decisions eventually enforced by Roman emperors on pain of death. But did Jesus believe in the God they defined? If perhaps the facts show that he did not, are we suffering from an unconscious dishonesty when we claim to follow him? Can we risk believing things about God and the Son of God that Jesus did not believe, and do all this "in his name"?

No subject is more timely than the one addressed by our author. There are a billion Muslims and a billion Christians in addition to millions of Jews, for whom the question of defining God is sufficient to erect huge barriers between vast religious blocks (this is without mentioning the tragic denominational splits which characterize what we know as the Christian faith). "I wish above all," said Paul, "that you be perfectly united in one mind and judgment all saying the same thing." This book raises the startling possibility that those claiming the Bible as their inspiration may have in fact erected an almost impenetrable barrier, unnecessarily, between themselves and others keen to establish a relationship with the One God. Our author raises the fundamental question about how well professed claimants to Christianity are in fact following Jesus.

Mr. Chandler, writing at a level engaging for both scholar and layman, has invited us on a journey of discovery which may well revolutionize our perception of the universe. He proposes a more honest and original reading of sacred Scripture, Scripture which may persuade us to shed some of the paralyzing and often incomprehensible dogmas which time and tradition have caused us to embrace and hallow as truth.

Sir Anthony F. Buzzard
MA (Oxon.), MA Th., Hon. PhD

INTRODUCTION

"Follow me."
— Jesus of Nazareth

*John 1:43, 10:27, 12:26, 13:36, 21:19, 22, Luke 5:27, 9:59,
Mark 2:14, Matthew 4:19, 8:22, 9:9, 10:38*

OVER TWO THOUSAND YEARS AGO, a controversial young rabbi walked the sandy shores of Galilee. His birthplace, his childhood home and the lands of his ministry are well-known to archaeology. His deeds are also well-documented, recorded by a variety of eye witnesses and investigators and transmitted through the ages with unparalleled reverence. His supreme influence upon world culture is still felt today, as one cannot even describe our point in time without referencing his birth, nor can one travel any substantial distance in any Western country without encountering a building bearing his name. Two millennia later, children are still being named after his followers, public holidays are held in his honor, and a large portion of the planet's population still claims to be aligned with him and his teachings. Without doubt, Jesus of Nazareth is the most famous and influential person to ever live. But is it possible that the actual teachings of a man of such unmatched reputation have gone largely unrecognized by the world today? Could the most known man in the world also be the most unknown?

As long as mankind has put pen to paper, he has excelled at doing what even God cannot: changing the past. The history we have is only what certain well-placed individuals have chosen to write down, while the history we commonly know is only what other well-placed individuals have chosen to talk about. It is therefore the great labor of the historian to bring to light new perspectives on the past in a world that has grown dark with prejudice and cover-up.

Readers of the human story will be disappointed to find a wearisome breed of miscreants who dutifully trample even the most sacred and meaningful of things, religion notwithstanding. That the Christian religion has somehow emerged unscathed from the dark tumult of human history has yet to be proven. What will be proven is that while the Jesus of Christianity can be found far and wide, the Jesus of history has been a far more elusive subject. Yet the advent of the Information Age has now begun to pry open the dusty coffers of antiquity and allow, for those investigators willing to get their hands dirty, a chance at regaining many broken pieces of the Christian puzzle. With determination, a healthy dose of skepticism, and a little providence, the most neglected information concerning the evolution of sacred tradition might be pieced together to offer a new outlook on primitive Christianity and her famous founder; an unorthodox, unofficial, and unsanitized perspective of the faith of antiquity.

For centuries, the majority of Christian traditions have viewed Jesus of Nazareth less as a theologian and more as the object of theology himself. Countless millions of earnest believers have entertained religious notions *about* Jesus, but what about the religious notions *of* Jesus? Has consideration for the particular theology of Jesus, the first-century Jewish rabbi, all but gone by the wayside? One German philosopher gives voice to this concern as he audaciously wonders if modern mainstream Christianity "is not based on the imitation of Christ but on the imitation of the imitation, on legends of Christ, the myth of Christ, the dogma of Christ, the idealization of Christ?"[1] This book humbly endeavors to confront this anxiety and provide a window into the unsung past of not only the earliest Christian theology, but the Christian convention which evidently has, for lack of a better word, supplanted it.

History reveals that at an early stage, the chessboard of Christian theology transitioned from the confines of the biblical data to the nebulous realm of post-biblical speculation. Today we wonder how one even begins to bridge the chasm between the historical sayings of Christ and the philosophical teachings of modern Christians. Scholar A. E. Harvey once wrote of Jesus and "the

---

[1] Peter Slotterdijk, *Kritik der Zynischen Vernunft II* (Frankfurt am Main: Suhrkamp, 1983), p. 518.

constraints of history,"[2] but those boundaries seem ever exceeded by the popular metaphysical statements his would-be disciples make about him. The longer we repeat those statements, and the further away we get from the historical Jesus, the more dire our situation becomes. Indeed, the number of honest Christians being marooned by a progressively widening gap between facts and faith is only increasing. But what if those historical facts, returning to the forefront of Christian thought, were given a chance to form the foundation of faith and not simply a challenge to it? In this we discover the central question facing Christology today: is the man of history the God of dogma?

The aim of this book is to strike at the core of exactly what it means to be a Christian: following Christ. What if Jesus is found to have espoused radically divergent theology from the myriad churches which bear his name today? Would even the words of Christ prove ineffectual in breaking the prohibitions on those most essential questions: Who is Jesus? Who is God? And particularly, *how would Jesus answer these questions?* Surely no one who endeavors to follow Christ can afford to ignore his startling, unmistakable and brilliant opinion on these issues; an opinion which, though sitting plainly on the pages before us, has been quietly gathering dust in the corner of Christian thought, waiting to be revisited.

Kicking Jesus Out of Church

One cannot help but wonder what Jesus himself would think of today's Christians if he happened to stroll into any one of the major denominations' churches and take a seat in the pews. Would he agree with what they were saying? Would he even understand them? We would expect the subjects of their hymns, the language of their sermons, and the theological demands of their official statements of faith to be as familiar to him as his own words—after all, shouldn't this be the faith he founded? Doubtless every one of the more than 41,000 Christian denominations in existence today[3] would affirm that Jesus would be most welcome in their congregation. But would he really be as comfortable as they might hope? It is difficult to imagine any group of Christians, much less the mainstream Christian body, ever banning the words of Jesus, and in effect Jesus himself, from their church. But few chronicles are filled with more bizarre and tragic tales than Church history.

---

[2] A. E. Harvey, *Jesus and the Constraints of History* (London: Duckworth, 1982).

[3] Pew Research Cener. "Methodology for Estimating Christian Movements," Appendix B in "Global Christianity: A Report on the Size and Distribution of the World's Christian Population," *Pew Research Center Religion & Public Life Project*. December 19, 2011.

In 529 CE, the Christian emperor Justinian commissioned an unprecedented rewriting of Roman law. The *Corpus Juris Civilis,* commonly known as the Justinian Code, contained new Church-codified ordinances forbidding "Jewish language" in the empire's worship services. In particular, the core Jewish prayer and statement of faith known as the *Shema* was "totally banned."[4]

Shema, the Hebrew for "hear" or "listen," describes what is widely regarded as the quintessential creed of Judaism: *"Hear O' Israel, the LORD is our God, the LORD is one"* (Deuteronomy 6:4 NASB). Traditionally, the *Shema* has been the first confession every Jew learns when he is young, and the last thing prescribed for his lips when he dies; without question, this simple testimony about God has been paid more attention by the Jewish mind than any other Hebrew Scripture. But why ban this famous biblical statement from the Christian world? What contest could Christianity possibly entertain with the heart and soul of the very Jewish religion it claims to be founded upon? The implications of one particular Jewish mind's radical fixation on the *Shema* may only compound our questions.

In the twelfth chapter of the Gospel of Mark we witness a Jewish Torah-expert and Rabbi Jesus engaging in a theological discussion. Here the curious Jew, apparently liking what he has overheard from the young man's public debate, makes an important inquiry which he hopes will assist him in sizing up Jesus' theology:

> *One of the scribes came and heard them arguing, and recognizing that he had answered them well, asked him, "What commandment is the foremost of all?" Jesus answered: "The foremost is, 'Hear O Israel! The LORD our God is one Lord' "* (Mark 12:28-29 NASB).

Upon hearing this, the Jew becomes ecstatic; Jesus' citation of the *Shema* as the most important of all God's holy prescriptions is exactly what one would have expected from a good Jew. Perhaps this Jesus wasn't as blasphemous as his colleagues had claimed? Though offering many profound and even mysterious sayings, here was Jesus, clearly operating in the mainstream of Judaism! The happy Jew takes it upon himself to personally interpret Jesus' statement:

> *The scribe said to him, "Right, teacher; you have truly stated that he is one, and there is no one else besides him"* (v. 32).

---

[4] Meir Holder, *History of the Jewish People: From Yavneh to Pumbedisa* (New York: Mesorah Publications, 2004), p. 254.

Many Christians have been taught that the oneness of God advocated in the *Shema* is really a "compound unity of multiple Persons," namely, the Father, Son, and Holy Spirit of Christian Trinitarianism. It is said by Trinitarians that the *Shema*'s "oneness" actually relates to the "one substance" shared by all three Persons of the Trinity, and therefore the *Shema* potentially refers to a *collection* of multiple Persons.[5] But do we not witness an *exclusion* of plural identity in the scribe's interpretation of the *Shema*, that is, in his identification of the singular "*He* is God and there is no one else besides *him*"? Especially in response to Jesus' own affirmation that "*our* God" (his and the Jew's) is to be known as only "*one Lord*" (v. 29), and consequently not two or three additional referents?[6] By the very nature of the language, the thousands of singular personal pronouns the Jews had used to describe their deity in the Scriptures, it seems obvious that he was believed to be a single personality. Indeed, as one Oxford professor affirms, "for a Jew the word *God* could mean one person only."[7]

Yet we wonder if it ever entered the Jewish mind that God's oneness described in the *Shema* might actually refer to a *substance* or *essence* distributed amongst a party of individuals. Was theirs a *philosophical* monotheism? What does the exact language which the scribe uses in Mark 12 indicate? The great Samuel Clarke writes that the *"one"* (Greek: *"heis"*) describing God here means just *"One Person*, and furthermore the scribe's response in Mk 12:29ff using the singular *He* does not mean 'no other than his Substance, but *personally*, no other than *He.*' "[8] Respected New Testament scholars agree: "the word 'one' is

---

[5] Trinitarian Christianity has proposed that the Jewish God is actually "not a solitary unity but a composite unity" (D. Bloesch, *God the Almighty* (Downers Grove: IVP, 1995), p. 184). It is said that the reality of distinctions within the Godhead was yet to be understood by the Jews, and the final disclosure of a multi-Person God "was not explicitly and openly revealed till the days of Christ, because the Jews were prone to idolatry" (Pietro Galatino, *De Arcanis Catholicae Veritatis* (Ortona: Gershom Soncino, 1516), p. 41). In effect, the historical Jews are viewed as essentially having worshipped a triune God unawares, and the consistent prohibition of the Trinitarian idea within post-Christian Judaism is considered only the perpetuation of ignorance of their own God and Scriptures.

[6] One must ask whether or not more than one person (defined as "an individual" by *Webster's*) may occupy a singular magisterial epithet such as "Lord." As the biblical term "Lord" is reliably employed as an appropriate descriptor of such solitary personalities as Moses (Num 36:2), David (1 Chron 21:3) and Abraham (Gen 24:48), and the plural "lords" for multiple personalities (Gen 19:2), how should we view singular applications such as "*the Lord Yahweh*" (Amos 9:5)? See Isaiah 26:13: "*O LORD our God, other lords besides you have ruled over us, but your name alone we bring to remembrance.*"

[7] D. E. H. Whiteley, *The Theology of St. Paul* (Oxford: Blackwell, 1980), pp. 105-106.

[8] Samuel Clarke, *The Works* (London: John & Paul Knapton, 1738), p. 367.

masculine in gender, and therefore is personal, referring to a person."[9] Interestingly, even the modern *Amplified Bible*, a Trinitarian translation which intends to bring out all shades of meaning in the original text, actually translates "God is only one" as "God is *only one Person*" at Galatians 3:20.[10] So who is correct? Those who say the "one" refers to a *substance* or those who concede its reference to a *person?* What did the Jews really believe about the *Shema?*

As a contemporary Jewish theologian explains, the people of Israel chose Deuteronomy 6:4 as their central creed "in order to protect the oneness of God from every multiplication, watering down, or amalgamation with the rites of the surrounding world."[11] One respected commentary adds, "There was no real doubt as to the great commandment, the Shema was repeated daily by the Jews. It was the foundation text of their monotheism, which was not a speculative theory but a practical conviction."[12] That the oneness of Deuteronomy 6:4, as all first-century Jews would have understood it, actually provided for alternative interpretation or expansion should be unthinkable. According to the Jews themselves, "Judaism has always been rigorously *unitarian*,"[13] that is, they have believed that the one God is a certain personal entity, a single self. Indeed, even Trinitarian scholars have admitted that:

> the Jews, though they have had the Law above three thousand, and the Prophets above two thousand years amongst them, yet to this day they could never make [the Trinity] an article of faith; but they still assert that God is only one in person, as well as nature.[14]

---

[9] Kenneth S. Wuest, *Wuest's Word Studies from the Greek New Testament for the English Reader*, Vol. 1. (Grand Rapids: Eerdmans, 1973), p. 106.

[10] Galatians 3:20 reads: "*Now a mediator is not a mediator of one [heis], but God is one*" (KJV).

[11] Pinchas Lapide, *Jewish Monotheism and Christian Trinitarian Doctrine* (Philadelphia: Fortress Press, 1981), p. 27.

[12] Peake adds: "in this, Jesus stood in complete and conscious agreement with Pharisaism" (Arthur Samuel Peake, *A Commentary on the Bible* (New York: Thomas Nelson & Sons, 1920), p. 696). Professor Joseph Klausner from the Hebrew University confirms: "Like every Pharisaic Jew, [Jesus] believed in the absolute unity of God" (Joseph Klausner, *Jesus of Nazareth: His Life, Times, and Teachings* (New York: Bloch, 1989), p. 377).

[13] Kaufmann Kohler, Emil G. Hirsch, "Deism," *Jewish Encyclopedia.* 1906. Jewish Encylcopedia.com. Web. 14 August 2014.

[14] William Beveridge, *Private Thoughts Upon Religion and Upon Christian Life*, Part II (Literary Licensing LLC, 1829), p. 66. *Note:* The respected observations of Trinitarian scholar Emil Brunner reinforce the fact that: "Judaism [is] unitarian" (*Dogmatics,* Vol. 1, p. 205). Trinitarian Leonard Hodgson concurs: "the [Jewish] monotheism was then, as it still is, unitarian" (*Christian Faith and Practice*, p. 74). We are often pressured by apologists to discover in biblical Judaism a hibernating Trinitarian faith which has only yet to be grasped. However, the thousands of singular personal pronouns describing God in the Jewish scriptures constitute an unambiguous presentation of a

Therefore if Jesus, being the supposed progenitor of present-day Christianity, actually fundamentally disagreed with the Jew on the nature of God (as the modern Christian does), or if he possessed some novel and important information to interject (perhaps information regarding himself), this would have been a most opportune time for Jesus to live up to his reputation as the great revealer of God (Jn 1:18). We are constantly bombarded by apologists asserting that at this point in the narrative Jesus had already claimed deity.[15] Surely now, in a public debate in Jerusalem, he would explain the reality of their God and reveal himself as their very Creator as he purportedly had already done.[16] Indeed, for Jesus' listeners to ever acquire the necessary understanding that the concept of God's oneness (as both the patriarchs and the friendly scribe understood it) had been drastically updated, there would have to exist at least *some* degree of exposition. As the famed *Hasting's Encyclopedia of Religion and Ethics* reports, "Abraham, Moses and Elijah were all equally zealous monotheists, and in none of their successors was there any retrogression from the highest and purest form of unitarian belief."[17] Yet far from providing the Jews any new and requisite information, what we hear from Jesus has proven puzzling for some:

> *When Jesus saw that he had answered intelligently, he said to him, "You are not far from the kingdom of God." After that, no one would venture to ask him any more questions* (v. 34).

Incredibly, Jesus publicly recognizes that this deeply Jewish understanding of the *Shema* is an exercise in wisdom, not in misunderstanding or abuse of the Scriptures. Bishop N. T. Wright observes that "The answer that Jesus gave [in Mark 12:29] was thoroughly *noncontroversial...* the Shema was as central to Judaism as it is now."[18] The Jew and Jesus thus reveal a solid consensus not only

---

single self. While the greatest stress is placed on the Deity's strict unity in the Jewish Scriptures, no plurality within him is ever expressly taught, much less emphasized or made part of requisite belief.

[15] See Sue Bolin, "Jesus' Claims to be God – Yes, Jesus Said He is God." Probe Ministries. 1992. Web. 5 May 2014.

[16] It is often claimed that at this point in the Gospel narrative, Jesus has already communicated that he is the God of Israel though his famous *"I am"* statements, including John 8:58, which took place at the Temple during his debate over father Abraham with the Pharisees. If this is true, we would expect him to have no reservations reasserting this in his subsequent conversation with the friendly scribe.

[17] J. Hastings (ed.), "Judaism," *Hasting's Encyclopedia of Religion and Ethics*, Vol. VII (New York: Charles Scribner's Sons, 1915), p. 582.

[18] N. T. Wright, *Jesus and the Victory of God* (Minneapolis: Fortress Press, 1996), p. 305, emphasis added.

on the correct interpretation of the *Shema's* content, but on its primacy as the quintessential religious obligation. The respected *New Century Bible Commentary* thus perceives that by this affirmation, "Jesus stands foursquare within the orbit of Jewish piety."[19] In other words, Jesus was firmly "Jewish" in his theology.[20]

The question then begs to be asked: Why is it that the Jewish *Shema*, the Christ-identified focal point of God's instruction to mankind, has enjoyed so little importance or repetition throughout centuries of Christian institution? Worse than being ignored, Jesus' statement of faith was apparently found by the Christian leadership of 529 CE to be so offensive, threatening, and anti-Christian that they would outlaw it from the empire.

Evidently, "The Justinian Codex... recognized a total incongruity between the *Shema* of Deuteronomy and the Trinity Doctrine,"[21] and thus even uttering the creed of Jesus in the Christian world "was banned, as a denial of the Trinity."[22] The orthodox doctrine of the Trinity, the Christian tradition's most storied, controversial, and peculiar dogma and her greatest differentiator from her strictly unitarian Jewish and Muslim cousins, is still used as a litmus test for authentic Christianity by the most popular denominations. Yet we must wonder if by the ancient Catholic Church's standards Jesus himself would have failed the examination of common faith?

Though Jesus openly taught that God's singular Lordship comprised the necessary foundation and supreme requirement of his own devotion, the later Christians of the Roman era seemed quite determined to exclude not only his words, but anyone who dared repeat them. As historians recall, state inspectors roamed the land guaranteeing no one violated the prayer's prohibition, and even "guards were sent to the synagogue to prevent recitation of the *Shema* because its proclamation of God's unity was thought to impugn, if only implicitly, the Christian notion of the Trinity."[23] To even obliquely challenge any orthodox decree, much less one as critical as the official conception of God, would be to threaten not only the authority of the Church, but the imperial theocracy which it authorized. The Roman emperor had essentially bound himself up with the Triune God, acting not only as the guardian of orthodoxy, but as God's

---

[19] Hugh Anderson, *New Century Bible Commentary on Mark* (Grand Rapids: Eerdmans, 1981), p. 280.

[20] The 2001 *Word Biblical Commentary* surprisingly concludes that Jesus' teaching here is "*not specifically Christian*" (*WBC*, (Nashville: Thomas Nelson, 2001), p. 261).

[21] Standford Rives, *Did Calvin Murder Servetus?* (Charleston: BookSurge Publishers, 2008), p. 268.

[22] Hyam Macoby, *Antisemitism and Modernity* (London: Routledge, 2006), p. 20.

[23] W. D. Davies, Louis Finkelstein, *The Cambridge History of Judaism*, Vol. 4 (Cambridge: CUP, 1984), p. 17.

omnipotent viceroy on the earth.[24] Obviously, there could be no room in the Christian world for "the recitation of the *Shema,* whose clear declaration of the Oneness of God openly contradicted Christian doctrine."[25] But how could this even be possible? How is it that Christianity was ever able to arrive at a state in which Jesus' own words could not be spoken in church?

Out with the Old

Evidently, there occurred a shocking exchange of principles within the Christian heritage: the *Shema* appears to have been traded for a confession in the *Trinity* as the fundamental dogma of the Christ imitator. As the catechism of the Catholic Church states:

> The mystery of the Most Holy Trinity is the central mystery of the Christian faith and of Christian life... It is the most fundamental and essential teaching in the hierarchy of the truths of faith.[26]

While for centuries the doctrine has indeed been crucial to conventional Christianity, renowned Catholic scholar Hans Küng nevertheless reveals that "the doctrine of the Trinity is as central as it is disputed."[27] Indeed, despite the immense priority paid to the Trinitarian idea in common devotion, we readily discover remarkably candid admissions from many Trinitarian scholars, apologists, and Church authorities that this most distinctive and fundamental doctrine "is not directly and immediately in the Word of God,"[28] and "formed no part of the original message."[29] But is such a scandal even possible? Surely

---

[24] Some, in a minority view, even included the emperor as a sort of earthly emanation of the Trinity. See Steven Runciman, *The Byzantine Theocracy* (Cambridge: CUP, 2004), p. 24. Freeman observes that in the preceding years "Diocletian had perfected the process of the elevation of the emperor above his subjects, linking himself to a favoured pagan god, Jupiter. For Constantine, that god was Christian; in his *Life of Constantine* Eusebius describes the ideal of the Christian monarch, the mirror of God on earth—there are again shades of Platonism here" (Charles Freeman, *The Closing of the Western Mind: The Rise of Faith and Fall of Reason* (New York: Vintage Books, 2002), p. 252). Ambrosiaster of Rome (4th century) would thus write: "The King [emperor] bears the image of God, just as the bishop bears the image of Christ." Likewise, the orator Themistius (4th century) says: "The emperor is an emanation of that divine nature; he is providence nearer the earth" (Ibid.).

[25] Meir, p. 195.

[26] Catechism of the Catholic Church, I, 2, 234.

[27] Hans Küng, "Foreword," *Born Before All Time?* (New York: Crossroad, 1998), p. xix.

[28] The Catholic University of America, "Trinity," *New Catholic Encyclopedia* (New York: McGraw-Hill, 1967, Vol. XIV), p. 304.

[29] W. R. Matthews, *God in Christian Experience* (Whitefish: Kessinger Pub., 2010 [1930]), p. 180.

the doctrine of the Trinity has experienced more controversy and undergone more scrutiny than any other Christian idea in history. But what is the modern Bible student to do with such stunning charges as those from respected Trinitarian professors who reveal that "The Bible does not teach the doctrine of the Trinity. Neither the word 'trinity' itself nor such language as 'one-in-three,' 'three-in-one,' one 'essence' (or 'substance'), and three 'persons' is biblical language"?[30] Trinitarian Christopher B. Kaiser, Professor of Historical and Systematic Theology at Western Theological Seminary, even provides this stunning confession:

> The Church's doctrine of the Trinity would seem to be the farthest thing from [Jesus' and the writers of the New Testament's] minds, and today's reader may well wonder if it is even helpful to refer to such a dogma in order to grasp the theology of the New Testament. When the church speaks of the doctrine of the Trinity, it refers to the specific belief that God exists eternally in three distinct "persons" who are equal in deity and one in substance. In this form the doctrine is not found anywhere in the New Testament; it was not so clearly articulated until the late fourth century AD.[31]

If unqualified scriptural authority for the essential Christian philosophy is scarce at best and possibly non-existent, from what fount has the dogma drawn its daunting ecclesiastical influence? In 2014, *Charisma Magazine* published an admission from popular Trinitarian professor at Fuller Theological Seminary, Charles Peter Wagner: "We today believe in the Trinity not because of direct biblical revelation but because of majority votes in certain councils—in other words, by extra-biblical revelation."[32] Of course, many evangelicals today are quick to look down their noses at their Catholic cousins for accepting dogmas received by traditions and councils but not stated in Scripture. Yet how many non-Catholics realize that one of their most cherished articles falls directly into this category? The many Trinitarian academics who openly admit the dramatic absence of direct historical reconciliation for their most necessary tenet amongst the teachings of Jesus or the Apostolic Church only compound the mystery.

---

[30] Shirley C. Guthrie, *Christian Doctrine* (Louisville: Westminster John Knox, 1994), pp. 76-77.

[31] Christopher B. Kaiser, *The Doctrine of God* (Eugene: Wipf & Stock, 2001), p. 27.

[32] Peter C. Wagner, "But That's Not in the Word!" *Charisma Magazine*. 2 June 2014. Web. 19 December 2014.

One noted Protestant professor of theology at the University of Hull even remarks that:

> No responsible NT scholar would claim that the doctrine of the Trinity was taught by Jesus or preached by the earliest Christians or consciously held by any writer of the NT. It was in fact slowly worked out in the course of the first few centuries.[33]

That the doctrine of the Trinity was absent from the conversation of the earliest Christian community and is but the long-contested product of later ecclesiastical developments will be investigated in the coming chapters. Yet it is easy to find many respected Christian authorities openly noting that the theological spirit of the faith shifted out of the world of Judaism and into the world of Greek philosophy at a very early stage. Renowned Bible scholar James Strong, author of the authoritative *Strong's Concordance*, writes that:

> Towards the end of the 1st century, and during the 2nd, many learned men came over both from [Hellenistic Judaism] and paganism to Christianity. These brought with them into the Christian schools of theology their Platonic ideas and phraseology.[34]

This shift evidently bolstered the production of creedal rules of faith which would have been quite indecipherable to the first Christians. Specifically, in regard to the doctrine of the Trinity, we find even Trinitarian theologians admitting that "St. Paul did not know it, and would have been unable to understand the meaning of the terms used in the theological formula on which the Church ultimately agreed."[35] If this is true, then how do modern Christian sects assert a direct theological link to the Apostolic Church while defining their central requirements through linguistic and philosophical modes which the Apostles would have found wholly unintelligible? Is it not possible to describe Apostolic belief using only the theological language of the Apostles? The same question must also be posed for the language and personal theology of Jesus, a teacher who seemingly failed to relate the fundamental objects of Christian discipleship if the forms required by developed Christianity were communicated

---

[33] A. T. Hanson, *The Image of the Invisible God* (London: SCM Press, 1982), p. 87.
[34] James Strong, John McClintock, "Trinity," *Cyclopaedia of Biblical, Theological, and Ecclesiastical Literature,* Vol. 10 (New York: Harper, 1891), p. 553.
[35] Matthews, *God in Christian Experience*, p. 180.

through the "Platonic ideas and phraseology" introduced in later centuries. If it is therefore true that Greek philosophy still dictates the terms of the Christian faith, then the implications for accepted piety, namely that the principal subjects of the New Testament have been made to dance to music played by decidedly pagan instruments, are rightly alarming.

Our Premise

For centuries there has occurred within the sphere of Christian apologetics an ongoing epidemic of what we might call *historical activism,* a subtle work of omission which selectively emphasizes only those moments and figures most critical to the mission of the party evangelist. The most popular and "official" story of church history is, of course, a sweeping and noble narrative. It is the tale of a great Trinitarian faith emanating out of the Apostolic age and surviving beneath the protection of the Catholic bishops, until bands of troublesome marauders appeared to waylay the true and original doctrine with sudden innovations. This beautifully sterilized image thrives in the books and lecture halls of the most respected Christian establishments today, but the white-washing appears to have begun at a very early stage. Much of the history of orthodox dogma has been learned from the polemical writings of such figures as Athanasius (d. 373 CE), or Eusebius of Caesarea (d. 339 CE), whose portrait of Church history has been discovered by scholars to be more like a Picasso than a Da Vinci, an abstract caricature of history seen through the eyes of a political survivalist.[36] As modern historians have noted, "Few areas of church history have been so completely rewritten in the past twenty years" as the theological controversies of the fourth century which moved to define Christian truth.[37] We might credit both the arrival of the modern era, with its increasing

---

[36] Historians from all eras have challenged the bias of Eusebius' accounts, finding him largely interested in the appeasement of the State. Socrates Scholasticus, from the 5th century, described Eusebius' work as "rhetorical finish" meant for the "praises of the emperor" rather than the "accurate statement of fact" (*Socrates' Church History*, Book I, Ch. 1). The great Edward Gibbon observed that Eusebius had "suppressed all that could tend to the disgrace of religion" (*Decline and Fall*, Vol. 2 (New York: Collier, 1876), p. 676), and one scholar even goes so far as to say that "Eusebius was the first thoroughly dishonest and unfair historian in ancient times" (Jakob Burckhardt, quoted in Robert L. Wilken, *The Myth of Christian Beginnings* (Eugene: Wipf and Stock, 1971), p. 57). Other scholars have characterized Eusebius as "a political propagandist" (Erik Peterson, *Der Monotheismus* (Munich, 1951), p. 91), and as "the great publicist of the first Christian emperor" (Robert A. Markus, "The Roman Empire in Early Christian Historiography," *The Downside Review*, Vol. 81, No. 265 (Downside: College of St. Gregory, 1963), p. 343), and finally as a "political theologian" (Hans Eger, "Kaiser und Kirche," *Zeitschrift für die neutestamentliche Wissenschaft*, Vol. 38 (Berlin: Degruyter, 1939), p. 115).

[37] Freeman, *Closing of the Western Mind,* p. 163.

spirit of academic latitude, and archaeological discoveries like the Nag Hammadi Codices and the Dead Sea Scrolls of Qumran, for advancing a new perspective of early Christianity—one without a monolithic orthodox structure, without a towering doctrine of the Trinity, and most importantly, one with a Jesus firmly rooted in the monotheistic traditions of Judaism which later Christianity came to reject.

If today we wish to better understand the theology of Jesus and the New Testament authors, we must first learn how they, as real historical persons in a real religious context, viewed God, and furthermore how they anticipated their own literature to be received. Did the Apostles have a Trinitarian background? Did their historical milieu foster the requisite philosophical concepts by which they could have recognized Jesus as one "Person" of a poly-personal "triune" being? If there was one thing the writers' Jewish environment should have cemented for them, it was their idea of God. If we discover that the Trinitarian concept was completely foreign to their background, and if it is also true that they themselves did not announce such a novelty, can we assert their belief in it without falling into speculation? What we do know is that the earliest Jewish disciples already had a concrete religious framework of their own through which they viewed the coming of Jesus Christ. Could re-acquiring that same theology help us to better understand Jesus in our own time? Could the Bible actually present enough information on its own to prove the beloved and mystifying creeds of the fourth century *radically unnecessary?*

Throughout the course of this book, we will observe, as many Trinitarian scholars have already disclosed, that because the New Testament does not clearly set forth any triune God, the developed Trinitarian system is built squarely upon *inference*.[38] It is essentially a theory constructed on what is *not said* in the Bible, and a theory which could not exist without a parallel metaphysical framework that is fundamentally alien to it. Our premise in this regard is that the biblical interpretations of later Christian orthodoxy would never have been arrived at from the Jewish Scriptures and the inherited Jewish worldview of the Apostles alone. Those metaphysical interpretations were expressly and only facilitated by external philosophies grafted onto the biblical writings by later religious synthesizers. This process resulted in a grand transformation of the

---

[38] Trinitarian academics have long explained that the doctrine is not plainly expressed anywhere in the biblical documents, but is deduced only through implications: "It needs to be emphasized that this is a doctrine that is not explicitly stated either in the Old or New Testaments, but it is implicit in both" (J. Hampton Keathley, "The Trinity (Triunity) of God." *Bible.org.* 18 May 2004. Web. 23 October 2015).

original faith of the first Jewish believers in Jesus. As it has been observed, "What we call Christianity is a vast ocean into which flow a number of spiritual currents of distant and various origin—certain religions, that is to say, of Asia and of Europe, the great ideas of Greek wisdom, and especially those of Platonism."[39] But in viewing the deeply Jewish documents of the New Testament, we wonder why the later Christians so earnestly preferred a *Gentile* lens? Furthermore, why did they feel the need to so tirelessly speculate about how to best fill in missing theological data if the Apostles themselves expressed no such discontent? Was anything fundamental really omitted from their writings to begin with?

Ultimately, it will be demonstrated that the orthodox dogma about God is primarily the product of unnecessary problem-solving. The philosophers of the late Roman Empire were attempting to unravel two non-issues: First, Christianity's implications for Greek philosophy. If the Jesus movement were to succeed amongst the academics, it needed, in their view, to be able to mesh with the established intellectual systems of their age, or to outperform them philosophically. Without raising questions about their piety or intentions, we may easily recognize how advantageous such a reconciliation was. Second, they were attempting to solve what they supposed were inconsistencies between the Old and New Testaments. In the record of the Jesus incident they had perceived the incarnation of a second divine being, or wanted to, and the event needed to make sense in light of a monotheism which had always distinguished the biblical community from the surrounding pagans. Admittedly, the solutions they constructed were often ingenious. However, as we will see, the problems for which they were created did not really exist. The apparent discrepancies encountered by the Gentile philosophers were only misunderstandings enabled by their separation from the Jewish worldview, while the conclusions they ultimately formed were enabled only by their Platonic, and even *Gnostic*, saturation. These two stumbling blocks, the Jewish disconnect and the infatuation with Hellenistic formulae, were evidently enough to skew the religious mind of the early Christians so that they not only mishandled the original faith, but created an entirely new one.

For those who prefer a roadmap of their journey, the aforementioned ideas will be demonstrated in two parts: the first part of this book will be primarily concerned with the evolutionary history of orthodox theology, its interchange

---

[39] H. F. Amiel, quoted in L. L. Paine, *The Ethnic Trinities and Their Relations to the Christian Trinity* (New York: Houghton, Mifflin and Co., 1901), p. 199.

with historical Platonic and Gnostic thought, and some of its early ecclesiastical challenges. The second half will focus on biblical interpretation in light of the dogma's arguments. It is hoped that through this in-depth interrogation of what has become the trademark of Christian orthodoxy, a more comprehensive portrait of Jesus' historical theology may be uncovered.

A Call to Unity Around Jesus

For centuries the world has experienced life alongside a fractured Christianity. Civilization has waited patiently for Christians to absolve their differences and unite beneath the one they all claim to follow, yet that unity is more distant now than when the seeds of dissention were first sown in the all-too-distant past. That the peace of the Apostolic faith was disturbed at a very early stage by costly internal clashes over Trinitarian principles is not disputed; what must be determined is the nature and extent of the injury. As has been said, the doctrine of the Trinity "had its birth and growth in the blood of thousands and thousands of martyrs."[40] But what was really purchased at so great a price? H.G. Wells wrote in *The Outline of History* that "We shall see presently how later on all Christendom was torn by disputes about the Trinity," a fact which becomes all the more disheartening if Wells is also correct that "There is no evidence that the apostles of Jesus ever heard of a Trinity, at any rate from him."[41]

Upon proof of these allegations, we can confidently assume that the root cause of Christendom's present brokenness lies not in political corruption, an epidemic divorce rate, or greed, but in what appears to be a tragic detachment from the teachings of Christ. Incredibly, this separation is precisely what some of the most respected evangelicals have already admitted. The renowned Presbyterian Dr. James Kennedy writes: "Many people today think that the essence of Christianity is Jesus' teaching, but that is not so... Christianity centers *not* in the teachings of Jesus, but in the person of Jesus as Incarnate God who came into the world."[42] Dr. Harold O.J. Brown concurs: "Christianity is *not* belief in Jesus' teaching, but what is taught *about* him... The appeal... 'to believe

---

[40] Thomas Jefferson, Letter to theologian James Smith, December 8, 1822.

[41] H. G. Wells, *The Outline of History: Being a Plain History of Life and Mankind* (London: The Waverley Book Company, 1920), p. 284.

[42] James Kennedy, "How I Know Jesus is God," *Truths that Transform*. James Kennedy Ministries, 11 November, 1998. Web. 15 December 2015, emphasis added.

as Jesus believed,' rather than to believe in Jesus, is a dramatic transformation of the fundamental nature of Christianity."[43]

We must ask ourselves why mainstream Christianity has not only been largely uninterested in what the historical Jesus actually taught, but views "believing as Jesus believed" as a major departure from the religion. Does this not reveal an understanding that what Jesus actually taught contradicts what the inherited system teaches about him? How aware is the Christian public of this discrepancy? If the large majority of modern denominations have unknowingly embraced post-biblical ideologies which have severed Jesus from his own theology, the consequences could be nothing less than earth-shattering. We should not be surprised at the recent state of the faith.

Ultimately, the bonds of beloved custom may prove inexorable for many. As Dr. Jason BeDuhn remarks, "Age adds a certain sanctity to things. It starts to seem that it has always been that way, and that any change is a dangerous innovation... [But] the success of numbers or of time does not guarantee truth."[44] Might the testimony of Jesus of Nazareth, long taken for granted, ignite a comprehensive reconsideration of the faith of millions? As long as the Scriptures are chained to the pulpit of denominational convention, the world may never get the chance. Yet we must assert that it is only through a mass exodus out of the realm of Christian dogma and into the land of Scriptural truth that the fragmented Body of Christ can ever be mended.

Concerning the pronounced emphasis which Jesus placed on the *Shema* in Mark 12, one Christian scholar offers an alarming observation: "Jesus' affirmation of the Shema is neither remarkable nor specifically Christian."[45] However, the fact that Jesus publicly demonstrates "non-Christian" theology should be more than remarkable, if not downright distressing for the modern disciple endeavoring to imitate him. But asking why the Jesus of the New Testament does not sound "specifically Christian" is perhaps not as pertinent a question as asking why today's Christians do not sound like Christ? If it really is true that Christendom has done away with Christianity without being quite aware of it,[46] then as J.W. Bowman once so pointedly remarked, "The Church cannot

---

[43] Harold Brown, *Heresies* (Peabody: Hendrickson, 1984), p. 13, emphasis added.

[44] Jason David BeDuhn, *Truth in Translation: Accuracy and Bias in English Versions of the New Testament* (Lanham, University Press of America, 2003), p. xiv, xv.

[45] Craig Evans, *Word Biblical Commentary, Mark 34b* (Nashville: Thomas Nelson, 2001), p. 261.

[46] Søren Kierkegaard, *Time Magazine*, Dec. 16, 1946, p. 64.

indefinitely continue to believe about Jesus what he did not know to be true about himself."[47]

To discover and defend the God whom Jesus preached must be the solemn obligation of anyone who would follow him. It is to this God that Jesus dedicated his time, his energy, and his greatest love. Every student seeking discipleship of the Nazarene must be willing, despite any cost, to pursue that same God with equally fervent devotion.

---

[47] John Wick Bowman, *The Intention of Jesus* (London: SCM Press, 1945), p. 108.

PART I

THE ECLIPSE

On the History of Orthodox Theology
and Some of its Early Challenges

"The true criticism of dogma is its history."
– David Friederich Strauss

*"We believe the doctrine of a triune God because we have received it by
tradition, though not mentioned at all in Scripture."*
– Cardinal Stanislaus Hosius

1

THE UNFINISHED REFORMATION

"The Reformer is always right about what's wrong. However, he's often wrong about what is right."

— *G. K. Chesterton*

T HE FIRST SIX HUNDRED YEARS of the Church of Jesus Christ were incredibly perilous. The many competing doctrines concerning Christ's identity tossed the Church about like a ship on a raging ocean; wave after wave of debate smashing and splintering the members and tragically drowning many of them. Rivals were exiled, books were burned, heretics were executed, and the theology of Jesus fell deeper and deeper into confusion. Horrifying accounts of Christian brutality can be found in many periods of Church history, such as the Inquisition or the Crusades, but the raging storm of Christian-on-Christian violence of the fifth-and-sixth-century debates has yet to be outdone.[48]

---

[48] John Philip Jenkins, *Jesus Wars: How Four Patriarchs, Three Queens, and Two Emperors Decided What Christians Would Believe For the Next 1,500 Years* (New York: HarperOne, 2011), p. xxi.

When the dust of the first six hundred years had settled, Christianity resembled a religion fundamentally different than the humble movement that began in the first century. Once a heavily persecuted and decidedly fringe sect of Judaism that operated in local synagogues and house churches, Christianity was now the authorized state religion of the most powerful government in human history. From its principles, to its rituals, to its operational organization; no aspect of the original Christian religion remained unaffected. It was through the era's contentious ecclesiastical collaborations, which instituted creedal verdicts as rules of faith, that Christianity experienced a dramatic shift not only in theology, but in attitude and ethics. By some tragic stroke, Christians had gone from being the admirable victims of brutal religious intolerance, to terrible authoritarians in their own right who burned their theological opponents at the stake. It is in the progress of the Christian religion from infancy to influence that we find the most ironic and tragic of human histories: a persecuted people who, when suddenly thrust into power, demonstrated a shocking lapse in memory and compassion. Indeed, no sooner had the scars healed on the backs of the Church's elected leadership than they cracked the same whips across the shoulders of myriad theological dissenters. If the spread of primitive Christianity among the pagans of the first century owed any success to the startling love and compassion which Christians showed one another, how detrimental was the equally startling hatred and bigotry fostered by the later synodic era to the persistence of the original Christian religion?

The great tempest of intra-Christian bloodshed in the early centuries revolved primarily around disagreements over a variety of doctrinal developments concerning the identity of Jesus of Nazareth. Somehow, the person of Jesus, having inspired the most intrepid strength and unity amongst Christians in the earliest eras of Roman persecution, was disastrously transformed into a political lightning rod invoking the darkest behaviors of men. The peculiar doctrinal evolutions surrounding him, formulations operated on by myriad theological doctors over hundreds of years, would eventually translate Christian theology from a courageous choice for potential converts, into a partisan compulsion backed by the spears of emperors. Many of these most extraordinary theological speculations have maintained their hold on Christendom to this day. The most profound theological export of Christianity's tumultuous transition from obscurity to officialdom was certainly the doctrine of the Trinity.

The Christian Trinity

Roughly three hundred years after the resurrection and ascension of Christ, the Roman emperor Constantine (c. 272-337 CE) initiated a series of councils with the intention of unifying the various dissenting Christian factions in the Roman Empire. After decades of vicious deliberation and political upheaval, by 381 CE, it was determined, by the authority of the State, that every true Christian must confess the following:

> *God exists eternally as "three hypostases (persons) and one ousia (substance);"*
> *God the Father, God the Son, and God the Holy Spirit.*[49]

> *Jesus Christ [is] the only-begotten Son of God, eternally begotten of the Father, Light from Light, true God from true God, begotten not made, of one being with the Father... he came down from heaven, was incarnate of the Holy Spirit and the virgin Mary, and became fully human.*[50]

By 451 CE, the following confession was added:

> *Jesus Christ is to us one and the same Son, the self-same perfect in Godhead, the self-same perfect in Manhood; truly God and truly Man; the self-same of a rational soul and body; co-essential with the Father according to the Godhead, the self-same co-essential with us according to the Manhood... acknowledged in two natures unconfusedly, unchangeably, indivisibly, inseparably; the difference of the natures being in no way removed because of the union, but rather the properties of each nature being preserved, and (both) concurring into one Person and one hypostasis; not as though he were parted or divided into two Persons, but one and the self-same son and only-begotten God.*[51]

And around 500 CE:

> *Whosoever will be saved [must] worship one God in Trinity, and Trinity in unity; neither confounding the Persons; nor dividing the substance. For there is one Person of the Father; another of the Son; and another of the Holy Spirit... So the Father is God; the Son is God; and the Holy Spirit is God. And yet they are not three*

---

[49] The Cappadocian Trinitarian formula, circa 381 CE.
[50] An excerpt from the updated Niceno-Constantinopolitan Creed, 381 CE.
[51] Excerpt from the Chalcedonian Confession achieved at the Council of Chalcedon in 451 CE.

Gods; but one God... He therefore that will be saved, let him think thus of the Trinity.[52]

Christians today often make the mistake of assuming that there is only one doctrine of the Trinity, and that all legitimate Christians are, and always have been, insisting upon the same thing. The truth is that while there may be official sets of words which allegedly express the doctrine, there is to this day no universally agreed upon meaning of those words. Trinitarian Christianity has, in fact, been historically far more diverse than it would have the world believe. Orthodox theologians have battled for centuries over not only the Bible's teaching regarding the Trinity, but over what the Trinitarian creeds themselves actually teach. The creedal instruction to simply *"think thus of the Trinity,"* has proven more than difficult for the majority of Christians. This is a serious problem, especially if, as the creeds declare, *salvation hangs on one's proper thinking of these things.*

Today, many apologists assert that the doctrine of the Trinity, or their interpretation of it, is obviously implied by the Scriptures. But history exposes this illusion: if the biblical documents plainly teach Trinitarianism then why did the Christian Church argue so violently, and for so long, over whether this was really the case? Why has the debate over the wording and intention of the creeds which describe this allegedly obvious Trinitarianism not ceased to this day? In light of this diversity, we will focus our attention on the creedal framework itself, how it came into being, what some of the early believers first meant by it, and how it ever managed to characterize the religion of the historical Jesus.

Regardless of the problem of interpretation, the Catholic Church has decreed and maintained the above creedal statements as the framework of "orthodoxy" since at least the fifth century. Interestingly, these statements are still considered orthodox by the overwhelmingly large majority of Protestant Christian groups. This is worth noting, especially in light of the opinions of such noteworthy scholars as Emil Brunner, one of the most influential Protestant theologians of the last century, who states with surprising candor, "Certainly, it cannot be denied that not only the word 'Trinity,' but even the explicit idea of the Trinity is absent from the apostolic witness to the faith." Brunner further demands of his colleagues: "We must honestly admit that the doctrine of the Trinity did not form part of the early Christian—New Testament—message."[53]

---

[52] Excerpt from the Athanasian Creed, c. 500 CE.
[53] Emil Brunner, *Dogmatics,* Vol. 1 (London: Lutterworth Press, 1949), p. 205.

Yet this still seems difficult to believe; how could so many devou̱
theologians have *passed over* the theology of Jesus in favor of a message ̱
professed or endorsed?

Without doubt, the average Western churchgoer has had little to no exposure to the historical legacy of non-Trinitarian Christianity. Many Christians today are scarcely aware that any Christology outside the Catholic system might be Scripturally defensible; neither are they aware that the historical Christian sects advocating the tri-personal nature of God actually maintained the minority camp for decades at a time. One encyclopedia confirms that historically "the Trinitarians and the Unitarians continued to confront each other, the latter at the beginning of the third century still forming the large majority."[54] Evidently, it would require decades of controversy for the doctrine of the Trinity to finally wrestle its much-contested place in orthodoxy.

The rancorous historical battles over the dogma are often explained, by those supporting their outcomes, as being but the sparks generated by countless heresies arising to challenge a long-accepted core of faith inherited from the earliest Christians. But in the wake of modern scholarship and archaeology, this "official version" of Church history has crumbled. The rise and dominance of "the orthodox faith" was in fact a much more convoluted and painful business than popular histories have permitted. Furthermore, as we examine the developing doctrine of the Trinity's protracted demand for successive episcopal tournaments to elucidate even its most basic precepts, we may observe, as both historians and apologists have recognized, that "much of the defense of the Trinity as a 'revealed' doctrine, is really an evasion of the objections that can be brought against it."[55] Many Christian students have therefore, in light of recent scholarship and the unprecedented rise in access to religious materials, courageously questioned if the dogma's place in orthodoxy is really well-deserved.

Orthodoxy and Protestantism

Orthodox is a word composed of the Greek *orthos* meaning "right" and *doxa* meaning "opinion." In essence, the word describes a state of belief which adheres to what is generally accepted as true in society. Belief in anything other than what is socially accepted is known as *heterodoxy*, or different opinion. It is

---

[54] Encyclopedia Britannica, Inc., "Trinity," *Encyclopedia Britannica*, Vol. 27 (Chicago: Encyclopedia Britannica, Inc., 1956), p. 2941.

[55] Cyril C. Richardson, *The Doctrine of the Trinity: A Clarification of What it Attempts to Express* (Nashville, TN: Abingdon Press, 1958), p. 16.

word that we derive the most popular verbal device for winning
nts throughout Church history: *heresy.*[56]

The truth is that it is just as common for Christians to be branded *heretics*
today as it was a thousand years ago, though the consequences of carrying this
title now result in decidedly less bodily harm. Many Christians who are unwilling
to endure theological arguments which diverge from the inherited creedal
statements will sometimes admit to subscribing to the proposition that "God
guided the councils,"[57] that is to say that the doctrinal conclusions of the
councils of the early Catholic Church were arrived at by the prompting of the
Holy Spirit. However, the startling revelation of history is that the present
positions of Christian orthodoxy concerning God and Jesus were actually
deemed *unorthodox* for decades at a time by the very same council system. •This
information, perhaps unknown to the student who has been taught that the
Council of Nicaea (325 CE) was a unified and decisive effort to finalize Christian
truth, will be covered in the coming chapters.

For many Christians, great assurance is placed in doctrines like the Trinity
due to a belief in the preeminence of the orthodox councils; but those in
Protestant or evangelical traditions, more than others, find themselves in an odd
predicament. For them the conclusions of the old Roman synods are
authoritative, but only to a certain point. The common Protestant claims a
dutiful subscription to early Catholic decisions, but suddenly begins to assert the
error of Catholic fiat during the era preceding Martin Luther's challenge. But
what prevented conciliar blunder before this point? Indeed it must be asked
how so many Protestants and evangelicals today, though proudly never assenting
to the doctrinal authority of any present-day bishops, happily submit to the
pronouncements made by those same bishops' offices 1600 years removed? The
matter is rarely, if ever, addressed publicly.

In reality, a pick-and-choose approach has been employed when determining
which councils, and even which decisions made by those councils, are valid.
Some Protestants will accept at least the seven so-called "ecumenical" councils as
authoritative, and some accept many more than that. Most disconcerting is the
fact that a great deal of today's evangelicals who claim and demand adherence to
"orthodox" theology actually stand in direct opposition to many of the orthodox
council decrees. For example, the same council which affirmed the divine nature

---

[56] In Christendom the word heresy as describing a "false teaching" came into common usage
after Irenaeus' 2nd-century work *On the Detection and Overthrow of the So-Called Gnosis*, popularly
known as *Against Heresies*. See n. 91 on p. 37.

[57] Willis C. Newman, *You Can Believe the Bible* (Willis Newman, 2010), p. 97.

of Christ also concluded that Mary was the "*Theotokos*" or "Mother of God" and not just the mother of the human Jesus.[58] The council also determined that it was *God* who actually suffered on the cross, and not just the human nature.[59] Furthermore, the councils also concluded that any military service, even becoming a chaplain,[60] was forbidden for the true Christian.[61] These are all conclusions with which most evangelical and Protestant communities today sharply disagree, and yet the Canons of the councils read: "if anyone should in any way attempt to set aside the orders made by the holy Synod… they shall be excommunicated."[62] While one may often hear the arguments of the evangelical littered with accusations of *heresy* against Christians who do not align with their denominational theology, how many realize that they might also be anathematized as heretics themselves? As Stefan Zweig rightly stated in his book on heresy in the Reformation: "In and by itself, the very notion of a 'heretic' is absurd as far as a Protestant Church is concerned, since Protestants demand that everyone shall have the right of interpretation."[63] Statistically speaking, today's Protestants have happily exercised such latitude, even to the point where the majority have quit Trinitarianism altogether.

---

[58] As Catholics have pointed out: "[Protestants] are sometimes horrified when the Virgin Mary is referred to as the Mother of God… To avoid this conclusion, Fundamentalists often assert that Mary… only carried Christ's human nature. This assertion reinvents a heresy from the fifth century known as Nestorianism… [But] women do not give birth to human natures; they give birth to persons. Mary thus carried and gave birth to the person of Jesus Christ, and the person she gave birth to was God" ("Mary: Mother of God," Catholic Answers. Web. 28 December 2014).

[59] Council of Ephesus, 431 CE. Nestorius held that the divine nature (God the Word) had not suffered, but Cyril, in his twelve anathemas against him, declared: "If anyone does not confess that the Word of God suffered in the flesh and was crucified in the flesh and tasted death in the flesh and became the first born of the dead, although as God he is life and life-giving. Let him be anathema" (*Third Epistle to Nestorius*).

[60] The Council of Chalcedon declares in its 7th Canon that clergy "shall not accept military service nor any secular dignity," and if they "do not repent… they shall be anathematized."

[61] The Council of Nicaea in 325 CE, famous for its declaration of Christ's consubstantiality with the Father, also affirmed that military service is forbidden for the Christian in Canon 12. If a military man wanted to convert, he would first have to do penitence for ten years, which was even more than the penitence of seven years required for someone who denied Christ under persecution. Emperor Constantine, having presided over Nicaea, knew that Christians could not serve in his military, and thus knew that emperors, being military commanders, could not be Christians. This may be why he forewent baptism until he was on his deathbed. Later, Ambrose's critique of Emperor Theodosius I (d. 395 CE) provided the fuel for Augustine's systematized "Just War" theory. In the medieval era, Aquinas (d. 1274 CE) further re-shaped Christian-thinking about conditional military participation. For a brief history of this evolution see Wim Smit, *Just War and Terrorism* (Leuven: Peeters, 2005), pp. 108-122.

[62] See Canon 6 of the Council of Ephesus, 431 CE.

[63] Stefan Zweig, Eden Paul Cedar Paul. *The Right to Heresy: Castellio Against Calvin*. Boston: The Beacon Press, 1951. Web. 9 May 2014. <http://www.gospeltruth.net/heresy/heresy_chap6.htm>

In October of 2014, major Trinitarian organizations LifeWay Ministries and Ligonier Ministries conducted a survey of evangelical Christians in the United States. The results, which they said were "disappointing," demonstrated that "most American evangelicals hold views condemned as heretical by some of the most important councils of the early church."[64] The poll found that while almost all evangelicals say they believe in the Trinity (96%) and that Jesus is fully human and fully divine (88%), nearly a quarter (22%) said God the Father is more divine than Jesus, and nine percent weren't sure. Sixteen percent said that Jesus was the first *creature* created by God, while another eleven percent were unsure. As the surveyors noted, "No doubt, phrases like '*only begotten Son*' (John 3:16) and '*firstborn of all creation*' (Col. 1:15) have led others in history to hold these views, too... The idea [is] known as Arianism." The survey furthermore discovered that while most say they affirm the Trinity, *more than half* (51%) actually said that the Holy Spirit is a force, not a personal being. Seven percent weren't sure.

Incredibly, most evangelicals tend towards Arianism, a form of non-Trinitarian Christianity. While outwardly professing the Trinity, most do not actually believe in it, or likely even know what it is. Due to their rejection of the "third Person of the Trinity," more than half of all evangelicals in America are by definition not Trinitarians. As there are approximately 60 million Christians who identify as evangelicals in the United States alone, these statistics represent a vast amount of doubt, denial, and confusion on what is commonly said to be the happily-agreed-upon foundation and litmus test of the true Christian faith. The claim of Christian unity on the matter is therefore a façade. Despite the confidence of many that the doctrine is agreed upon by all legitimate Christians, one Baptist authority admits that it is still:

> a widely disputed doctrine, which has provoked discussion throughout all the centuries of the church's existence... Yet many are unsure of the exact meaning of their belief [and] it is still one of the most misunderstood and disputed doctrines.[65]

Another Catholic scholar correctly perceives that far from being settled:

> a fundamental crisis over plausibility and acceptance of the church's Christology still exists today. Incomprehensibility,

---

[64] Kevin P. Emmert, "New Poll Finds Evangelical's Favorite Heresies," *Christianity Today*. 28 October 2014. Web. 14 November 2014.

[65] Millard J. Erickson, *God in Three Persons: A Contemporary Interpretation of the Trinity* (Grand Rapids: Baker Publishing Group, 1995), pp. 11-12.

complexity and remoteness from life and the Bible are today
the themes of a crisis of belief.[66]

Despite the muddle, if the evangelicals surveyed in the aforementioned study, who do not truly adhere to the doctrine, were challenged to formally abandon it and to publicly admit their break with "orthodoxy," many would shudder at the thought. Yet how much of the dogmatic attachment within these circles comes from an affection for received tradition, social pressure, or downright misconception, rather than by direct and personal conviction from the Scriptures?

In a related 2014 research report, *seventy percent* of Christians said they do not recite or use any of the historical Christian creeds in personal discipleship, and more than thirty percent said there is *little value* in even studying or reciting creeds and catechisms.[67] Incredibly, the same creeds which define the Trinity, the statements by which one supposedly proves one's Christian legitimacy, are scarcely discussed. While the creeds may appear in the official laws of congregations, paying them any real mind is not the practice of the vast majority of believers. All of this is important because it demonstrates that a great many devoted Christians are already on bad terms with the "official" dogma about God. They have neglected the authority of the orthodox councils on these issues, either by consciously doubting some critical aspect of the doctrines themselves, or by simply ignoring the councils' opinions and primacy. While establishment Christianity may find this "disappointing," those Christians who have knowingly rejected Catholic prerogative in defining their personal beliefs may recognize an opportunity for education and reform on a grand scale.

The famous 1689 Baptist confession of faith states that Scripture is "the supreme judge, by which all controversies of religion are to be determined, *and all decrees of councils*, opinions of ancient writers, doctrines of men, and private spirits, are to be examined."[68] Many of the original Protestant leaders were inspired towards reformation upon recognizing various testimonies of Scripture which flew in the face of official edicts from Rome. *The Westminster Confession of Faith*, a famous standard set forth by Reformed Christianity, has this to say about the authority of the councils:

---

[66] Karl Josef Kuschel, *Born Before All Time?* (New York: Crossroad, 1998), p. 59.

[67] Ligonier Ministries, "The State of Theology," Ligonier Ministries. 2014. Web. 20 December 2014.

[68] See http://www.reformed.org/documents/index.html, emphasis added.

IV. All synods or councils, since the apostles' times, whether general or particular, may err; and many have erred. Therefore they are not to be made the rule of faith, or practice; but to be used as a help in both.[69]

> — *Chapter XXXI, Of Synods and Councils,*
> *Westminster Confession of Faith, 1646*

How many Reformed Christians today are aware that one of their most cherished foundational documents states that many of the councils *have* erred in their deliverance of the rule of faith? If it is admitted that the councils and synods have been mistaken, the question naturally arises: how widespread was the error? If the framers of the Reformed tradition are correct and the orthodox councils are not free from doctrinal error and should only be used as a guide of sorts, to what extent can they really be trusted? How do today's Reformed Christians know which particular edicts to accept or reject? If not aligning oneself with orthodox decree is a damnable offense, the non-Catholic seems constantly to tread a slippery slope.[70]

The Protestant Perpetuation

A healthy question for today's Protestants is this: *What exactly are you protesting?* Martin Luther's original conflagration was born out of an internal rejection of what was then universally accepted as Christian orthodoxy. Those who filed in behind the unlikely German revolutionary likewise sought to free themselves from the orthodox Roman system and reacquire the Scriptural standard for a faith which they deemed had, at that point, been widely discarded. Another healthy question for the modern Protestant is this: was the Reformation ever complete, or is there still reforming yet undone?

Today's Protestants will sometimes reveal great pride in their heritage as a group who believe they have successfully cast off "unscriptural" Roman dogma. The original Protestants had loudly claimed Luther's famous *"Sola Scriptura!"*

---

[69] "Westminster Confession of Faith, 31, 4" Center for Reformed Theology and Apologetics. Web. 23 September 2014.

[70] The Reformed Westminster Confession is still affirmed by many branches of the Presbyterian denomination today. In regard to the Confession, the Presbyterian Church in America demands that "Officers in the Presbyterian Church in America take a vow to 'sincerely receive and adopt' these confessional documents." But do they really adopt this mantra—that the councils were replete with error and should not be used as a rule of faith? Or do they continue to marginalize other Christians who do not fully adhere to orthodox council decrees with charges of heresy? See "Westminster Confession of Faith," Administrative Committee PCA. 2015. Web. 14 January 2015.

(Scripture alone) as their battle cry. Yet Luther's followers appear to have been unable (or unwilling) to purge themselves of Rome's designs completely. As has been said, "Truth is the cry of all, but the game of the few."[71] Some of Rome's most spectacular machinations still abide in the heart of the Protestant and the Catholic alike. Renowned Catholic scholar Graham Greene makes this observation of Protestants today:

> Our opponents sometimes claim that no belief should be held dogmatically which is not explicitly stated in Scripture... But the Protestant churches have themselves accepted such dogmas as the Trinity, for which there is no such precise authority in the Gospels.[72]

The Reformers of the 16th century challenged the authority of many Catholic decrees based on a lack of Scriptural support, yet curiously the doctrine of the Trinity remained largely untouched by the most well-known Protestant leaders. One encyclopedia recognizes that even though "the doctrine is not found in its fully developed form in the Scripture... at the time of the Reformation the Protestant Church took over the doctrine of the Trinity without serious examination."[73] Luther, Calvin, Melanchthon and others appear to have wholly "by-passed it [rather] than made it the subject of their own theological reflection."[74] But why did this dogma not receive the same scrutiny as, say, the Catholic doctrines of transubstantiation or the primacy of the Pope? Was the Trinity considered so beloved or foundational that it need not be held to the same standard of textual endorsement? We naturally wonder if Protestant traditions today are still staving off the inevitable confrontation with the biblical data. On this issue, one modern scholar offers an enlightening observation:

> Protestant forms of Christianity, following the motto of *sola scriptura*, insist that all legitimate Christian beliefs (and practices) must be found in, or at least based on, the Bible. That's a very clear and admirable principle. The problem is that Protestant Christianity was not born in a historical vacuum, and does not go back directly to the time that the

---

[71] George Berkeley, *Siris*, 1744.

[72] Graham Greene, "Assumption of Mary," *Life Magazine*, 30 October 1950, p. 51.

[73] Frank Moore Colby, Talcott Williams (ed.), *New International Encyclopedia*, Vol. XXII (New York: Dodd, Mead and Company, 1916), p. 477.

[74] Brunner, p. 205.

Bible was written. Protestantism was and is a reformation of an already fully developed form of Christianity: Catholicism. When the Protestant Reformation occurred just five hundred years ago, it did not re-invent Christianity from scratch, but carried over many of the doctrines that had developed within Catholicism over the course of the previous thousand years and more. In this sense, one might argue that the Protestant Reformation is incomplete, that it did not fully realize the high ideals that were set for it.

For the doctrines that Protestantism inherited to be considered true, they had to be found in the Bible. And precisely because they were considered true already, there was and is tremendous pressure to read those truths back into the Bible, whether or not they are actually there... Protestant Christians don't like to imagine themselves building too much beyond what the Bible spells out for itself. So even if most, if not all of the ideas and concepts held by modern Protestant Christians can be found, at least implied, somewhere in the Bible, there is a pressure (conscious or unconscious) to build up those ideas and concepts within the biblical text, to paraphrase or expand on what the Bible does say in the direction of what modern readers want and need it to say.[75]

The defense of an inherited faith is indeed a praiseworthy and worthwhile venture. Yet while it may be an anchor to the meek in a chaotic world, it can swiftly become the pretext of the radical. There is always a tendency for the partisan to view the unflinching preservation of his faith as increasingly honorable as the arguments mount against it, and soon the temptation to fiddle with the facts to assist the greater good becomes real. Of course, to bring untruth into favor is never honorable. But surely to speak the truth, though it bankrupt beloved faith, is always honorable, and by the Christian God always required.

Historically, however, Protestants appear to have largely shied away from investigating the biblical documents with too critical an eye. In the popular evangelical publication *Christianity Today*, a 2015 article admits: "The academic study of the Bible has a well-earned reputation for hurling students and scholars

---

[75] BeDuhn, pp. 163-164.

alike beyond the safe boundaries of orthodox faith."[76] Reflecting on this, scholar James F. McGrath concludes that "many evangelicals fear engaging in scholarship precisely because, when done honestly, it can lead to conclusions that one set out hoping to avoid drawing."[77] For the ordinary Christian, pitting the inherited strictures of orthodoxy against the historical and biblical data is just expected to be too costly. This is clearly a failure at the pastoral level to instill much confidence in Christian dogma. The fact that more than half of evangelicals who claim to believe in the Trinity are not actually Trinitarians demonstrates that they are not even being taught the alleged fundamentals of the faith. We might understand why the layman wishes to avoid academic investigation of the Bible; the Trinity doctrine has never made much sense to him, and digging too deeply may only confirm his doubts and force him into difficult situations. But why has evangelical leadership avoided even educating their communities about this hallmark of Christian thought? Do concerns over ambiguity go straight to the top? Some Trinitarian churches even require their ministers to teach on the doctrine of the Trinity at least one Sunday each year,[78] and one former minister and professor at Pittsburgh Theological Seminary admits that:

> Many pastors dread Trinity Sunday. They hope it falls on a Memorial Day weekend or graduation Sunday, even Mother's Day—anything so they don't have to talk about the Trinity. After all, what is the Trinity anyway? And what good is it?[79]

The official dogma about God has long generated a serious hesitancy on behalf of laymen and clergy alike. Far from a brilliant revelation to be trumpeted and explored, it has often remained, for the majority, a relic to be adored from afar. To come too close to the altar would be to risk perceiving in too vivid

---

[76] Andrew Byers, "Dispatches from the Wondrous, Terrifying World of Biblical Scholarship," *Christianity Today*. 28 December 2015. Web. 12 January 2016.

[77] James F. McGrath, "More on Mark's Christology," Exploring Our Matrix. 18 January 2016. Web. 28 January 2016.

[78] "Trinity Sunday" is usually celebrated after the Day of Pentecost in liturgical Western churches, and actually on the Day of Pentecost in Eastern churches. It is, as one Episcopal minister has called it, "the dread of all preachers, the bane of all seminarians" (Susan Sloan, "Trinity Sunday," 26 May 2013, St. Stephen's Episcopal Church, Huntsville, AL). One evangelical professor at Biola University adds: "Preachers apparently dread Trinity Sunday, and (that being the case) who knows what congregations think?" (Fred Sanders, "The Trinity: Yes, A Doctrine About God," The Scriptorium Daily. 3 June 2012. Web. 28 January 2016).

[79] Teresa Stricklen, as quoted by Ronald J. Allen, *Preaching is Believing: The Sermon as Theological Reflection* (London: Westminster John Knox Press, 2002), p. 91

detail the tarnish of inconsistency. But is God really to blame for this remoteness of the Christian God from Christian life? Did not the original Protestants seek to overcome a dogmatism which stifled self-determination? Surely a spirit of inquiry must be the essential companion of Protestantism. But the silencing power of enshrined dogma, when wielded by a guardian class, traverses all denominational bounds. Throughout Church history, both Catholic and Protestant, a concern for the preservation of doctrine has largely prevailed over concerns about vagueness, freedom of thought, and even human life.

The Dark Reformation

There were, unknown to many, thousands of courageous Reformation-era contenders who did arise to challenge the Catholic doctrine of the Trinity. These Christian thinkers might be more well-known today had they and their books survived the incredible zeal of their Reformer companions, a zeal which tragically proved no less violent than their Catholic forebears. But history often obscures those events which are most disgraceful to a particular group of people. As John Quincy Adams so rightly observed, "The public history of all countries, and all ages, is but a sort of mask, richly colored. The interior working of the machinery must be foul."[80] That the present religious systems have much to gain from the exclusion of many scandalous occurrences should go without saying. But it is not simply the exclusion, but the choice inclusion and exaltation of certain subjects, which clouds our apprehension of the past. Certainly every group of people maintains their own heroes and villains, but one's ability to produce private and unrestricted distinctions between heroism and villainy can be severely compromised when much of the larger picture is left draped in shadows. Specifically, a broader perspective of Church antiquity may provide an avenue by which the modern Christian might better exercise his own authority as a free agent of human history. The examples of those Christians whom the orthodox record has disowned are surely just as valuable in forming judgments as the ones who survived to write the books.

Suffice it to say, many Protestants today have had little to no education on the darker history of the Protestant Reformation of the 16th century. Yet we expect that upon the embrace of sudden power even the noblest of insurrectionists may command, with despotic passion, the same intolerance which prompted their revolt. Indeed, the torch of the revolutionary has always

---

[80] John Quincy Adams, November 9, 1832, quoted in Robert Nowlan, *The American Presidents, Washington to Tyler* (Jefferson: McFarland, 2012), p. 251.

been an unwieldy thing; while setting fire to the errors of tyranny, he may easily ignite within himself a hubris or a paranoia which compels him to heap upon the pyre of revolution his own friends. However unpalatable to their present-day successors, history reveals that the original Protestants proved just as bloodthirsty as the Catholics in their defense of their updated marque of orthodoxy. As Gibbon recalls:

> The Reformers were ambitious of succeeding tyrants whom they had dethroned. They imposed with equal rigor their creeds and confessions; they asserted the right of the magistrate to punish heretics with death. The nature of the tiger was the same.[81]

The violence began in Switzerland. Felix Manz, a brilliant young theologian and co-founder of the first Anabaptist congregation in that country became the first martyr of the Reformation to be killed by his fellow Protestants. Manz had been a former student of the famous reformer Ulrich Zwingli, but when Manz challenged Zwingli on the nature of the Eucharist, and when he later denied the practice of infant baptism, he quickly found himself on the wrong side of Protestantism. The Protestant council in Zurich had outlawed adult re-baptism, but Manz held that there was no biblical warrant for the baptism of infants and refused to recant. Thus, since he was evidently so desirous of rebaptism, the Protestants obliged him and drowned him in the River Limmat.[82] The murder of Manz would set the stage for a sordid stretch of Christian history wherein countless devoted Protestants chose biblical testimony over orthodox decree and so surrendered their lives.

Though scores of devoted Christians found death at the hands of their fellows, the martyrdom of Michael Servetus in 1553 for denying the doctrine of the Trinity was perhaps the crowning episode in the unsung saga of reformer-on-reformer violence. Servetus was a Spanish theologian, a respected cartographer, a brilliant mathematician and a pioneering physician credited with the discovery of the pulmonary circulation of the blood. Despite his respectability, however, his unorthodox theology proved intolerable. In their treatment of Servetus, the reformers, particularly John Calvin, demonstrated that their dogmatism for the Roman councils' decisions had lost no fervor. It was

---

[81] Edward Gibbon, *The Decline and Fall of the Roman Empire*, Vol. 6 (London: Metheun & Co., 1902 [1776-1789]), p. 127.

[82] Alister E. McGrath, *Christianity's Dangerous Idea: The Protestant Revolution: A History from the Sixteenth Century to the Twenty-First* (New York: HarperOne, 2007), p. 71.

out of his desire to defend orthodoxy (and his own public assertions), that John Calvin had his colleague and one-time friend arrested as a heretic, convicted and burned to death.[83] Servetus, having dared to deny the orthodox doctrine of the Trinity,[84] was trapped and handed over to the Catholic authorities by Calvin, and so strong was Calvin's reaction to Servetus' ideas that during his trial Calvin said that he hoped "for the death penalty."[85] Though faced with painful execution, Servetus refused to recant his beliefs and ultimately:

> the Council of Two Hundred ordered Servetus "to be led to Champel and burned there alive on the next day together with his books." Only two charges were mentioned in his sentencing—anti-trinitarianism and anti-pedobaptism. The law under which Servetus was condemned was the Codex of Justinian that prescribed the death penalty for the denial of the Trinity.[86]

Learning of his sentence, Servetus pleaded with Calvin to be mercifully beheaded, fearing he might not remain faithful under torture. But Servetus was ordered to be burned with green wood to prolong the suffering, and sulfur was placed on Servetus' head so that when the flames finally reached high enough, the sulfur would ignite and burn his head with even greater intensity.[87] Yet throughout his ordeal, he did not recant. Calvin would afterwards unremorsefully instruct others to follow in his bloody footsteps: "Do not fail to rid the country of those scoundrels, who stir up the people to revolt against us. Such monsters should be exterminated, as I have exterminated Michael Servetus the Spaniard."[88] Calvin and others perpetuated the Roman Church's ignoble history of refutation not by argument alone, but by execution. One historian writes:

---

[83] Elgin Sylvester Moyer, *The Wycliffe Biographical Dictionary of the Church* (Illinois: Moody Press, 1982), p. 366.

[84] Merrick Whitcomb (ed.), *"The Complaint of Nicholas de la Fontaine Against Servetus, 14 August, 1553,"* in *Period of the later reformation* in *Translations and Reprints from the Original Sources of European History*, Vol. 3 (Philadelphia: University of Pennsylvania History Department, 1898-1912), no. 3.

[85] Walter Nigg, *The Heretics* (New York: Alfred A. Knopf, Inc., 1962), p. 328.

[86] Ken Westby, "Michael Servetus Murdered by John Calvin," *Kingdom Ready.* 9 July 2012. Web. 19 November 2014. This was the same law introduced in 529 CE which also forbade the utterance of the *"Shema"* creed preached by Jesus (Mark 12:29).

[87] Ibid.

[88] Merrick Whitcomb (ed.), "Calvin to the Marquis Paet, high chamberlain to the King of Navarre, 1561," *Period of the later reformation in Translations and Reprints from the Original Sources of European History*, Vol. 3 (Philadelphia: University of Pennsylvania History Department, 1898-1912), no. 3.

Just as earlier Catholic popes and cardinals attacked heretics out of fear that heresy would destroy the Church, the new Protestant leaders attacked their "heretics" (Catholics and Protestants putting forth heretical views) with equal ferocity for the same reasons. Just as the Catholic Inquisition led to abuses, so too did the Protestant versions of "cleansings" in the name of God. To the Protestant leaders, the greatest heresy was denial of the Trinity, just as to the Catholic Inquisition the greatest heresy was any challenge to the trinity of God, pope and inquisitor.[89]

French reformer Sebastian Castellio,[90] condemning Calvin's excessive treatment of Servetus, rightly stated, "To kill a man is not to defend a doctrine, but to kill a man."[91] The great mystery of the Reformation is why the Protestant leadership felt such violent zeal was necessary to defend the Trinity doctrine; indeed why invoke the power of the state to enforce what should be an obvious and scripturally healthy view? We might ask this question of the majority Christian party throughout every era of Church history, and at every step remind ourselves that "it is error alone which needs the support of government. Truth can stand by itself."[92]

Today's Christians should agree, however, that no amount of zeal, violent or peaceful, is appropriate when applied to the defense of assertions which are unscriptural. Are modern Protestants prepared to once again confront their doctrinal heritage, to resume the old call of *"Sola Scriptura"* should the challenge

---

[89] Michael Thomsett, *The Inquisition: A History* (Jefferson: McFarland, 2010), p. 205.

[90] Castellio was once a close friend of Calvin before the martyrdom of Servetus. Castellio became one of the first Reformers to advocate for religious tolerance and freedom of conscience. He was a man of incredible intellect and talent, and Voltaire spoke of his relation to Calvin in this way: "We can measure the virulence of this tyranny by the persecution to which Castellio was exposed at Calvin's instance—although Castellio was a far greater scholar than Calvin, whose jealousy drove him out of Geneva" (Zweig, *The Right to Heresy*, p. 89).

[91] Earl Morse Wilbur, *A History of Unitarianism, Socinianism and its Antecedents* (Boston: Beacon Press, 1946, 1972), p. 203. Castellio adds: "What do we really mean by the term heretic? Whom are we entitled to call a heretic, without being unjust? ... I do not believe that all those who are termed heretics are really heretics... The appellation has today become so abusive, so terrifying, carries with it such an atmosphere of opprobrium, that whenever a man wishes to rid himself of a private enemy, he finds that the most convenient way is to accuse this foe of heresy. As soon as others hear the dreaded name, they are filled with such overwhelming fear that they stop their ears, and blindly assail, not only the alleged heretic, but also those who venture to say a word in his favour" (Zweig, *The Right to Heresy*, p. 89).

[92] Thomas Jefferson, *Notes on Virginia*.

present itself?   Catholics, on the other hand, have had no qualms about the acceptance of doctrines received outside of Scripture.   The mouths of Church leadership, such as the Pope, have long been considered founts of policy no less authoritative than the pages of the Bible.[93]   Regardless of one's stance on this issue, it is remarkable to note that many in staunchly anti-Catholic circles who have been historically critical of such processes may have unknowingly adopted a strikingly similar standard.

A Doctrine of the Earliest Church?

Many biblical passages have long been championed by Trinitarianism as substantiating an Apostolic legacy for the dogma. However, none of the most widely cited passages, even such favorites as the Gospel of John's prologue, actually produce a single instance of the developed *Trinitarian* doctrine.   The great "proof-texts" must therefore be acknowledged as only qualification for particular doctrinal principles, while the larger dogma itself is derived only from inference.   It is often alleged that the Old Testament "*seems* to contain *references that foreshadow* this doctrine,"[94] and that in the New Testament it is "plainly *implied*."[95]   Some have even gone so far as to say that "The Trinity is an unfathomable yet unmistakable doctrine in Scripture."[96]   However, as one Baptist scholar recognizes, many "passages have been seen on closer study to be applicable only under the greatest strain."[97]

Nearly all of the most popular proofs come from John's Gospel.   The apologist rarely tries to substantiate the doctrine from the earlier Synoptics, with a host of modern scholars even affirming that Matthew, Mark and Luke simply do not teach the pre-existence or deity of Christ.[98]   More "liberal" scholarship

---

[93] "When, in the exercise of his office as shepherd and teacher of all Christians, in virtue of his supreme apostolic authority, [the Pope] defines a doctrine concerning faith or morals to be held by the whole Church" (First Vatican Council, First Dogmatic Constitution of the Church, Ch. 4, 9).

[94] Jack Cottrell, *What the Bible Says About God the Redeemer* (Eugene: Wipf and Stock Publishers, 1987), p. 133, emphasis added.

[95] John Richardson Illingworth, quoted in: Alister McGrath, *Christian Theology: An Introduction.* (Oxford: Blackwell Publishing, 2011), p. 236, emphasis added.

[96] John F. MacArthur, *New Testament Commentary on 1-3 John* (Chicago: Moody Publishers, 2007), p. 162.

[97] Erickson, *God in Three Persons*, pp. 108-109.

[98] See A.T. Hanson, "Two Consciousnesses: The Modern Version of Chalcedon," *Scottish Journal of Theology*, 37 (1984), p. 478. See also Dale Moody, *The Word of Truth* (Grand Rapids: Eerdmans, 1981), p. 393; James Dunn, *Christology in the Making* (Grand Rapids: Eerdmans, 1980), p. 89; James F. McGrath, "More on Mark's Christology," Exploring Our Matrix. 18 January 2016. Web. 28 January 2016; Adela Yarbro Collins, John Joseph Collins, *King and Messiah as Son of God: Divine,*

often concludes that John simply diverges from the Synoptic portrait of Jesus, and that Jesus was not thought of or portrayed as God until this later writing,[99] while more "conservative" scholarship argues that the Synoptics must somewhere contain hints and subtleties that do allow for consistency with John. Yet we wonder if there is a third option: could neither the Synoptics *nor* John actually teach Trinitarian principles? Could the perceived inconsistency between them be only the result of trying to force the Gospels to harmonize with ideas projected backwards from fourth-century scholarship? Despite the great Trinitarian appropriation of John's Gospel, J. A. T. Robinson reveals that:

> John is as undeviating a witness as any in the NT to the fundamental tenet of Judaism, of unitary monotheism (cf. Rom. 3:30; James 2:19). There is one, true and only God (John 5:44; 17:3): everything else is idols (1 John 5:21). In fact nowhere is the Jewishness of John, which has emerged in all recent study, more clear.[100]

If this is true, we wonder how many of the great Johannine texts viewed as "implying" the deity of Christ might stand in this light because of honest misunderstanding? Interestingly, we find that *misunderstanding Jesus* is actually a major theme of the Gospel of John. Episodes involving his audience's misinterpretation of his sayings occur in at least fifteen out of the twenty-one chapters.[101] Might contemporary audiences be missing his intentions now, just as so many did in his own time?

Regarding modern proof-texting, we recognize how easy it is for idiomatic transmission between cultures to fail. For example, when an Englishman reports that an endeavor was a "total bomb" he means it was a success. However, an American listener understands it to be a complete failure. When an Englishman says he wants to "table an issue" because it is a "moot point," he means he wants to actively discuss it because the point is open to debate; the American hears that

---

Human, and Angelic Messianic Figures in Biblical and Related Literature (Grand Rapids: Eerdmans, 2008), p. 209.

[99] Bart Ehrman, *How Jesus Became God: The Exaltation of a Jewish Preacher from Galilee* (New York: HarperOne, 2014), p. 44.

[100] J. A. T. Robinson, "The Fourth Gospel and the Church's Doctrine of the Trinity," *Twelve More New Testament Studies*, p. 175.

[101] See John 2:19-22, 3:4-13, 4:31-34, 6:51-61, 71, 7:33-36, 8:18-19, 21-22, 27, 33-34, 38-44, 51-52, 56-58, 9:39-41, 10:1-6, 26-36, 11:11-14, 11:23-25, 12:16, 32-34, 40, 13:6-12, 27-29, 33-37, 14:2-5, 7-11, 16:16-18, 16:25-29, 20:9, 21:22-23. See also Matthew 13:10-17, 13:34-36, 15:11-20, 16: 5-12, 27:46-47; Mark 4:10-13, 33-34; Luke 2:50, 9:45, 18:34. See also Proverbs 28:5; Isaiah 6:9.

the issue is irrelevant. We wonder then, if meaning can be so easily lost even between concurrent cultures sharing the same language, how easy might it be to misinterpret the phraseology employed by the ancient personalities of the New Testament? Later portions of this book will examine in detail how far the power of culture separation, tradition, and translation bias have gone in influencing modern Christians' apprehension of authentic biblical opinion. It may seem shocking for today's Trinitarians to hear other Christians confirm that Jesus never really claimed to be the God of Israel, but a thorough investigation of language, Church history, and traditional exegetical methodologies will reveal a disquieting justification for their skepticism. The opinions of Trinitarian scholars from all eras regarding the dogma's precarious scriptural foundation only tip the scales further.

As Martin Luther himself rightly stated, "It is indeed true that the name 'Trinity' is nowhere to be found in the Holy Scriptures, but has been conceived and invented by man."[102] While the Trinitarian tradition provides incessant assurance of the peculiar and essential "oneness" enjoyed by their triad's divine members, this unique oneness being the sole object which constitutes any distinction from pagan polytheism, it is striking that "In Scripture there is yet no single term by which the Three Divine Persons are denoted together."[103] Evidently, it was not until the 2nd and 3rd centuries that the term "trinity" would surface in context with Christianity. The writings of Theophilus of Antioch (d. 183 CE), the first Christian we find employing the word (Latin: *trinitas*, Greek: *trias*), do not, however, utilize the term in the same sense as later orthodoxy. Rather, Theophilus uses the word as a *plural referring term*, and writes that "the three days before the luminaries were created are types of the trinity; God, his Word, and his Wisdom."[104] As scholars like Dr. Dale Tuggy have explained, "Theophilus does not use [trinity] to mean 'three-in-one', but rather simply uses it to indicate that there were three things before man, God and His Word and His Wisdom'... [and was referring to] a 'trinity,' triad or threesome, but not a triune or tripersonal God."[105] Beyond this occurrence, the word "trinity" can be found in the theological commentary of the third-century Latin theologian

---

[102] Martin Luther, *Complete Sermons of Martin Luther,* Vol. 2 (Grand Rapids: Baker Books, 2000), pp. 406-407.

[103] George Joyce, "The Blessed Trinity," *The Catholic Encyclopedia,* Vol. 15 (New York: Robert Appleton Company, 1912), p. 47.

[104] Theophilus, *Apology to Autolycus*, 2.

[105] Dale Tuggy, "History of Trinitarian Doctrines," *Stanford Encyclopedia of Philosophy,* 2013.

Tertullian (160-225 CE).[106] However, as we will see in the coming chapters, Tertullian's conceptions differed greatly from the later Trinitarian doctrine which would be solidified only after centuries of arduous debate within the Roman synodic program.

It is often claimed by apologists that there existed a steady stream of Trinitarianism emanating out of the Apostolic era and maintained in some sense throughout the second and third centuries of the Church until heretics arose to challenge it. But one scholar observes a shift in the way we are able to look at Church history today:

> The classical understanding of the relationship of orthodoxy
> and heresy remained unchallenged, for the most part, until the
> modern period... Did Jesus and his disciples teach an
> orthodoxy that was transmitted to the churches of the second
> and third centuries? The answer... as now known, is probably
> No. Scholars who first propounded [this] answer engaged in
> daring, even risky, historical work. But their conclusions are
> now so widely held as to be virtually commonplace.[107]

In our own historical investigation, we will likewise give a tempered consideration to the progress of the ante-Nicene faith. During this careful survey of the writings of Tertullian, Irenaeus, Justin Martyr, Origen and others, it will be revealed that they were by no means committed Trinitarians.[108] Indeed, we should not forget that "the word Trinity is not found in the Bible... [because] it did not find a place formally in the theology of the church *until the fourth century*."[109] Hundreds of years after Jesus walked the earth, the first foundational components of this Christian philosophy would be authorized by the Roman government at the Council of Nicaea in 325 CE. Still decades later, the broader doctrine would be generally solidified (381 CE), further solidified (451 CE) and ultimately deemed necessary for salvation as the Athanasian Creed (c. 500 CE) demonstrates.

---

[106] See Tertullian, *Against Praxeas*, 2.

[107] Bart D. Ehrman, *Lost Christianities: The Battles for Scripture and the Faiths We Never Knew* (New York: OUP, 2003), pp. 168-169.

[108] Our forthcoming survey of the Church Fathers will demonstrate that despite any Trinitarian-sounding language, they do not exhibit the necessary qualities of Trinitarianism, that is, the essential co-eternality and co-equality amongst the three Persons, but present what we would call Subordinationist and even unitarian theology.

[109] R. A. Finlayson, "Trinity," *Illustrated Bible Dictionary,* Vol. 3 (Westmont: IVP, Tyndale House Publishers, 1980), p. 1597, emphasis added.

What then preceded the progressive elaboration and institution of the orthodox model? History reveals a variety of rival Christologies occupying the debates of the pre-Nicene Christians, yet the majority appears to have maintained, even throughout the period of escalating Platonic synthesis in the second and third centuries, an anchor to the traditional unitarian monotheism of the Jews. As one distinguished mind has noted:

> No historical fact is better established, than that the doctrine of
> one God, pure and uncompounded, was that of the early ages
> of Christianity; and was among the efficacious doctrines which
> gave it triumph over the polytheism of the ancients... Nor was
> the unity of the Supreme Being ousted from the Christian
> creed by the force of reason, but by the sword of civil
> government.[110]

Historically speaking, any emphasis institutionalized Christianity places on the well-established fact that in terms of global evangelism, "the Gospel gained its first and most decisive triumph without any formulated Trinitarian doctrine,"[111] has hardly been adequate.

A fair question arises when reviewing the doctrine's developmental history: Who was the first Trinitarian? Was it John the Baptist? Perhaps Paul of Tarsus? Or is it really, as history attests, that the first Trinitarians rose out of the various Greco-Roman philosophers of the later Church? If the Apostles in the first century had believed in the Trinity, they certainly do not seem too interested in explaining its principles, much less mentioning it. Nowhere do they expound on the tri-personal nature of God or the deity of Christ the way the Christians of the later centuries do. Alongside the loud, voluminous fixation of the later Catholics, the Apostolic silence is deafening. Why, if the doctrine is so essential to Christianity, and if unbelief in it assures damnation according to the Athanasian Creed, do we not find it plainly set forth in the pages of the Bible? Indeed, it would seem that, according to even Catholic sources, "among the Apostolic Fathers, there had been nothing even remotely approaching such a mentality or perspective."[112] The *Dictionary of the Bible* by John L. McKenzie,

---

[110] Thomas Jefferson, *Letter to Theologian James Smith*, December 8, 1822.
[111] Matthews, *God in Christian Experience*, p. 180.
[112] "Trinity," *The New Catholic Encyclopedia*, p. 299.

bearing the Catholic Church's official seals of approval,[113] reads thus concerning the Trinitarian doctrine:

> The trinity of God is defined by the Church as the belief that in God are three persons who subsist in one nature. That belief as so defined was reached only in the 4th and 5th centuries AD and hence is not explicitly and formally a biblical belief.[114]

McKenzie, the premier Bible scholar of the mid-twentieth century, has provided a startlingly candid observation. Are the modern apologists diligently arguing for the Apostolic origins of the Trinity aware of such reflections within high-ranking Christian scholarship? The *New Catholic Encyclopedia* likewise reveals that discussions of the Trinity within a first-century context are acutely *anachronistic:*

> It is difficult in the second half of the 20th century to offer a clear, objective and straightforward account of the revelation, doctrinal evolution, and the theological elaboration of the Mystery of the Trinity... Historians of dogma and systematic theologians [recognize] that when one does speak of an unqualified Trinitarianism, one has moved from the period of Christian origins to, say, the last quadrant of the 4th century. It was only then that what might be called the definitive Trinitarian dogma "One God in three Persons" became thoroughly assimilated into Christian life and thought... it was the product of three centuries of development.[115]

Of course, it is not only Catholic scholarship which acknowledges the three-in-one God's development outside the borders of Holy Writ; the opinion of experts from all corners of Christendom is resoundingly lucid. Bruce Metzger, one of the 20th century's most respected and influential scholars on the New Testament, makes an astute observation:

---

[113] The accreditation in the books opening pages contains 'Nihil Obstat' signed by John B. Amber, S.J., Archdiocesan Censor and 'Imprimatur' signed by Cletus F. O'Donnell, J. C. D., Vicar General, Archdiocese of Chicago February 18, 1965: "The Nihil Obstat and Imprimatur are official declarations that a book or pamphlet is free of doctrinal or moral error."

[114] John L. McKenzie, *Dictionary of the Bible* (New York: Touchstone, 1995), p. 899.

[115] Thomas Carson, *The New Catholic Encyclopedia,* Vol. XIV (Farmington Hills: Gale, 2003), p. 295.

Because the Trinity is such an important part of later Christian doctrine, it is striking that the term does not appear in the New Testament. Likewise, the developed concept of three coequal partners in the Godhead found in later creedal formulations cannot be clearly detected within the confines of the canon... While the New Testament writers say a great deal about God, Jesus, and the Spirit of each, no New Testament writer expounds on the relationship among the three in the detail that later Christian writers do.[116]

Famed Trinitarian professor Charles Ryrie, in his popular book *Basic Theology,* likewise concedes that the doctrine is nowhere to be found in Scripture. While many of his fellow evangelicals are often heard criticizing Catholic dogmas over a lack of scriptural justification, somehow the Trinity's absence in no way, for Ryrie, invalidates its authority and primacy. He argues:

But many doctrines are accepted by evangelicals as being clearly taught in the Scripture for which there are no proof texts. The doctrine of the Trinity furnishes the best example of this. It is fair to say that the Bible does not clearly teach the doctrine of the Trinity.[117]

Ryrie furthermore illuminates the fact that evangelicals actually teach and accept *many* doctrines without biblical support, "prov[ing] the fallacy of concluding that if something is not proof texted in the Bible we cannot clearly teach the results... If that were so, I could never teach the doctrine of the Trinity or the deity of Christ or the deity of the Holy Spirit."[118] While some theologians are disposed to overlooking the lack of scriptural precedent, acclaimed Trinitarian theologian Millard J. Erickson asks all the right questions in his book *God in Three Persons*:

It is claimed that the doctrine of the Trinity is a very important, crucial, and even basic doctrine. If that is indeed the case, should it not be somewhere more clearly, directly, and explicitly stated in the Bible? If this is the doctrine that

---

[116] Bruce Metzger, Michael Coogan, *The Oxford Companion to the Bible* (Oxford: OUP, 1993), p. 782.

[117] Charles C. Ryrie, *Basic Theology: A Popular Systematic Guide to Understanding Biblical Truth* (Chicago: Moody Publishers, 1999), p. 89.

[118] Ibid., p. 90.

especially constitutes Christianity's uniqueness, as over against unitarian monotheism on the one hand, and polytheism on the other hand, how can it be only implied in the biblical revelation? In response to the complaint that a number of portions of the Bible are ambiguous or unclear, we often hear a statement something like, "It is the peripheral matters that are hazy or which there seem to be conflicting biblical materials. The core beliefs are clearly and unequivocally revealed." This argument would appear to fail us with respect to the doctrine of the Trinity, however. For here is a seemingly crucial matter where the Scriptures do not speak loudly and clearly. Little direct response can be made to this charge. It is unlikely that any text of Scripture can be shown to teach the doctrine of the Trinity in a clear, direct, and unmistakable fashion.[119]

All of these observations return us to our earlier question: Who was the first Trinitarian? Modern scholarship presses us to wonder if the most storied, controversial, and allegedly fundamental of all Christian doctrines is in fact an out-of-place artifact which sincere and dedicated believers remain determined to insert into the world of the New Testament writers. If it is true that the doctrine "is not found in any document or relic belonging to the church of the first three centuries," and that "letters, art, usage, theology, worship, creed, hymn, chant, doxology, ascription, commemorative rite, and festive observances... are, as regards this doctrine, an absolute blank,"[120] how should the Christian respond to the frequent popular claims that the doctrine is Apostolic or taught by the New Testament church? Brunner exposes our dilemma:

> When we turn to the problem of the doctrine of the Trinity we are confronted by a peculiarly contradictory situation. On the one hand, the history of Christian theology and of dogma teaches us to regard the dogma of the Trinity as the distinctive element of the Christian idea of God, that which distinguishes it from the Idea of God in Judaism and in Islam, and indeed, in all forms of rational Theism, Judaism, Islam and Rational Theism are Unitarian. On the other hand, we must honestly

---

[119] Erickson, *God in Three Persons,* pp. 108-109.
[120] Alvan Lamson, Ezra Abbot, *The Church of the First Three Centuries* (Toronto: University of Tornoto Libraries, 1875), pp. 466-467.

admit that the doctrine of the Trinity did not form part of the early Christian—New Testament—message.[121]

A respect for history must enjoy a certain dominance in this investigation. Evidence that the Christian Trinity was "a conception at which the age had not yet arrived"[122] has long been appreciated by historians. In the coming chapters it will be demonstrated that the concept of the Trinity is indeed an out-of-place artifact not only in the earliest period of the Church, but also in the generations of fiercely monotheistic Hebrews whose detailed history of direct encounters with God we would expect to comprise the foundation of Christian understanding. Despite the frequent problematic presentations of such famous passages as Genesis 1:26 ("*Let us make man…*") as evidence of the Trinity in the Hebrew Scriptures, Christian scholarship universally agrees that "the doctrine of the Holy Trinity is not taught in the OT."[123] Even throughout the post-Easter chronicles of early Jewish and Christian debate, the Old Testament has not proven an easily recruited supporter of the doctrine's tenets. The lack of any documentation of arguments in the New Testament Church over the nature of God is likewise troubling. The Apostolic community saw fierce debates concerning a variety of important matters, from diet, to circumcision, to baptism and more. Where are the debates over any of the radical principles of the Trinity? After all, the Jews are and always have been intensely monotheistic. To avoid inviting the objection of the Trinitarian who assures us of his maintenance of said monotheism, we will appeal to such respected Trinitarian theologians as Leonard Hodgson who clarifies that "the [Jewish] monotheism was then, as it is still, unitarian."[124] Historically speaking, the Jews have consistently criticized orthodox Christianity of violating the Hebrew Scriptures by suggesting that the one God of Israel is actually a multiplicity of Persons. If copious documentation exists of the historical debates between Jews and Christians during the post-Apostolic period, why do we not also encounter in the New Testament even a hint of conflict over that most necessary of subjects, the identity of God? Could it be because the Christians who walked and talked with Jesus and the Apostles

---

[121] Brunner, p. 205.

[122] Ibid., p. 467.

[123] "Trinity," *New Catholic Encyclopedia*, p. 306. Trinitarian scholars from all ages have admitted: "It is evident, that, from the authorities of the Old Testament, sufficient and clear proof cannot be drawn either for the Trinity, or for a plurality of divine persons" (Bishop Tostat, *De Sanct. Trin.*, p. 14 as quoted by Wilson, *Uni. Princ.*, (1888), p. 344). See also Gordon J. Wenham, *Word Biblical Commentary on Genesis* (Nashville: Word Books, 1987), pp. 27-28.

[124] Leonard Hodgson, *Christian Faith and Practice, Seven Lectures* (Oxford: Blackwell, 1952), p. 74.

had never heard of the Trinity? If they did believe it, is it possible that they simply didn't speak about what should have been the core of their religion? As one writer emphasizes, if fifteen New Testament chapters were written to persuade the Jews of an update to their view of the Law of Moses:

> Shouldn't we find at least one or two [chapters] explaining the change in how God would be viewed from now on? But not a single verse suggests the Jew change his view of God... The Bible has many verses which "teach" justification, "teach" repentance, "teach" baptism, "teach" the resurrection, but not one verse in the entire Bible "teaches" the doctrine of the Trinity. No verse describes, explains it, or defines it. And no verse tells us to believe it.[125]

As Erickson likewise wondered, where is the historical discussion of the Trinitarian theology which supposedly distinguished the early Christians from their unitarian Jewish cousins on the one hand and their polytheistic pagan neighbors on the other? The striking absence of such critical exposition should be enough to tempt every serious Bible student into deeper investigation. Ultimately, as one scholar notes, considering the developmental history of orthodoxy and contrasting it with the biblical data actually:

> leads us away from the classical notion that orthodoxy is rooted in the apostles' teaching as accurately preserved in the New Testament Gospels and to the realization that the doctrines of orthodox Christianity must have developed at a time later than the historical Jesus and his apostles.[126]

The Authority of Tradition

What do Ptolemy's geocentric model, Aristotle's law of motion, and Hippocrates-Galen's Humoralism all share in common?[127] Each were widely accepted classical dogmas propagated by famous Greek philosophers, and each also, largely due to the prominence of their developers, maintained their place in

---

[125] Robert A. Wagoner, *The Great Debate Regarding the Father, Son & Holy Spirit* (Santa Ana, 1997), p. 12.

[126] Ehrman, *Lost Christianities,* p. 170.

[127] Geocentricism is the belief that the earth is at the center of the galaxy. Aristotle's law of motion held that an object will *not* continue in motion unless acted upon by an outside force. Humoralism is the belief that the body's health is governed by the balance of four "humors": blood, phlegm, yellow bile, and black bile.

accepted convention for thousands of years after their progenitors died. Lastly, they are all doctrines which modernity has proven false. The legacy of Humoralism is particularly relevant to this study:

> Galen's influence was so great that even after Western Europeans started making dissections in the thirteenth century, scholars often assimilated findings into the Galenic model that otherwise might have thrown Galen's accuracy into doubt. Over time, however, Classical medical theory came to be superseded by increasing emphasis on scientific experimental methods in the 16th and 17th centuries. Nevertheless, the Hippocratic-Galenic practice of bloodletting was practiced into the 19th century, despite its empirical ineffectiveness and riskiness.[128]

Similar histories can be found following Ptolemy's geocentric cosmology and Aristotle's law of motion, which were not widely considered disproven until 1543 and 1687 respectively.[129] In each of these cases we find that the prominence and authority ascribed to these philosophers actually severely retarded progress in the fields of astronomy, physics, and medicine. Might the field of Christian theology also have suffered a similar phenomenon? We must boldly ask whether the peculiar Trinitarian framework of the Greek and Latin Fathers has truly served to advance the world towards a rational and defensible concept of God, or whether it has perpetuated a systematic tradition dependent on spiritual mystery and faith in dogma. The legacy of Humoralism and its blood-letting certainly provides a fascinating parallel. For centuries, untold amounts of harm were perpetuated by "orthodox" medicine despite their ability to adopt alternative practices based on new perspective. While the myriad Christians beneath the rule of the ancient Catholic Church were effectively kept from private interpretation of the Scriptures in their own languages, Christians today enjoy an unprecedented freedom of access not only to the Scriptures, but to historical, cultural and linguistic information quite beyond the reach of their forebears. Certainly there was much literal bloodshed over the doctrine of the

---

[128] World Public Library, "Ancient Greek Medicine," World Heritage Encyclopedia. 26 July 2014. Web. 12 September 2014.

[129] See Nicholas Copernicus' "On the Revolutions of the Celestial Spheres," and Sir Isaac Newton's "Laws of Motion."

Trinity throughout antiquity and even into the 1700s,[130] but is Christianity still "letting blood" in light of modern scholarship and better manuscripts? When will the priority entertained by the ecclesiastical authorities of antiquity prove unsustainable for the modern Christian who carries with him tools for biblical study which the ancient philosophers could have only dreamed of?

What is certain is that the modern student cannot afford, in light of the forthcoming evidence, to continue to address the Bible's content through the prism of fourth-century learning. Nevertheless we find many authorities not only admitting to this very practice, but extoling it as virtue. Anglican priest and professor Peter Toon happily confesses, "I am a theologian, who is committed to the Faith expressed in the Nicene Creed from the fourth century. I approach and expound the Scriptures within this creedal and doctrinal framework."[131] While Professor Toon's spirit of loyalty is appreciated, we would hope that the best and brightest Christian minds would find themselves obligated only to the accurate elucidation of the Bible's content, to establishing the genuinely biblical worldview, despite any implications for Faith. After all, should not the Bible be the source of Christian faith standards? Is this not what is routinely claimed by so many churches today? To say that the Bible has become more the source of ammunition in the defense of a certain pre-existing doctrinal framework, the very framework so loudly celebrated by Toon and others, is to effectively reveal the lamentable state of present-day Catholic and Protestant exegesis. Indeed when historical documents, like the first-century New Testament writings, are deliberately and only considered in the light of creeds and doctrines "from the fourth century," we fear the worst about the state of Christian thought. We can only wonder what progress historical and philological integrity might effect upon the general faith, were such items awarded even half the love and attention as the standards expressed by the conciliar creeds. At present, a passion for legacy appears to have seriously skewed the explanatory energies of much of Christian theology. We find so many of our most trusted biblical interpreters admitting:

---

[130] The last year recorded in which anyone was officially prosecuted and executed by the English state for rejection of the Trinity doctrine was 1697. The last jail sentence for blasphemy in Britain occurred in 1922. See T. B. Howell, "Proceedings Against Thomas Aikenhead for Blasphemy," *A complete collection of state trials and proceedings for high treason and other crimes and misdemeanors from the earliest period to 1783,* Vol. 13 (London: Longman, Hurst, Rees, Orme and Brown, 1816).

[131] Peter Toon, *Our Triune God: A Biblical Portrait of the Trinity* (Vancouver: Regent College Publishing, 1996), p. 10.

"We are *hopelessly committed* to the Chalcedonian formulation."[132] But what about a hopeless commitment to the worldview of the historical Jesus? To the faith and formulae of the Bible, *Chalcedonian or not?* Such virtue seems always out of reach for the theologian, as long as "orthodox" dogma, with its daunting legacy, looms like a shadow over the Christian mind.

A Warning

In light of the widespread academic commitment to orthodox tradition, every Christian student should consider our earlier question: *was the Reformation ever complete, or is there still reforming yet undone?* Many mainstream Protestants seem confident enough in the accomplishments of their Reformation-era predecessors that they no longer feel the need to be actively on watch to protect themselves from unbiblical dogma. However, maintaining *"the faith once delivered to the saints"* (Jude 1:3) should be a full time endeavor for both scholar and layman alike. Paul himself cautioned the young Christian faith at the end of his ministry:

> *I know that after my departure savage wolves will come in among you, not sparing the flock; and from among your own selves men will arise, speaking perverse things, to draw away the disciples after them. Therefore be on the alert, remembering that night and day for a period of three years I did not cease to admonish each one with tears.*

(Acts 20:29-31)

The Apostles warned with great urgency that the ink of their writings would have barely begun to dry before disruptive teachings would enter in. Apparently they would arise from within the Church herself, and even her very members would not be spared. Paul reveals that he was explicitly warned by God that members of the Christian movement would produce and promulgate erroneous and detrimental policies: *"But the Spirit explicitly says that in later times some will fall away from the faith, paying attention to deceitful spirits and doctrines of demons"* (1 Tim 4:1 NIV). The surety with which Paul admonished the Church about the days after the Apostolic departure is both tragic and terrifying:

> *For the time will come when they will not endure sound doctrine; but wanting to have their ears tickled, they will accumulate for themselves*

---

[132] R. Douglas Geivett, Timothy R. Phillips, Dennis L. Okholm, Alister E. McGrath, Clark H. Pinnock, John Hick, W. Gary Phillips, *Four Views on Salvation in a Pluralistic World* (Grand Rapids: Zondervan, 1996), p. 74, emphasis added.

*teachers in accordance to their own desires, and will turn away their ears
from the truth and will turn aside to myths.*
(2 Timothy 4:3-4)

What sort of myths or persuasive teachings could arise to challenge the power and success of the Apostolic testimony? Evidently, Paul located the threat within the popular philosophies of his day:

*See to it that no one takes you captive through philosophy and empty
deception, according to the tradition of men, according to the elementary
principles of the world, rather than according to Christ.*
(Colossians 2:8)

Remembering that during the time of Paul's writing to the Colossians "the *Greek* philosophy prevailed much in the regions around Colossae,"[133] our culprit begins to reveal itself. But could these Hellenizing influences operate so subtly and compellingly that even many of the early Christians would succumb, individuals no more than one or two generations removed from the Apostles? The Apostle John, writing at the end of the first century, appears to have already witnessed the birth pains of this adversity in his own lifetime: *"They went out from us, but they were not really of us… but they went out so that it would be shown that they are all not of us"* (1 John 2:19). If the external influences Paul warned about were then powerful enough to persuade even the students of the early Church, how much stronger might the persuasion be among persons so linguistically, culturally and temporally detached as the disciples of our present day? Professor Anthony Buzzard, recalling the original charge of Jude 1:3 to defend Apostolic belief, writes, "If earnest effort was required to preserve the faith then, how much more so two thousand years later!"[134]

The task before us then, in the first half of this book, is to determine whether the integrity of the theology of Jesus has been widely and disastrously compromised despite all warnings. If such a transformation has occurred, how did it happen? If it really is true that orthodox Trinitarianism was absent among the Apostles, then when did the belief that Jesus of Nazareth is a co-equal, co-eternal, co-essential member of a multiplicity of divine Persons become not only

---

[133] Albert Barnes, *Notes on the Bible*, Baker Books, 1834. Web. 5 January 2015. <http://www.sacred-texts.com/bib/cmt/barnes/col002.htm>, emphasis added.
[134] Anthony F. Buzzard, *Our Fathers Who Aren't In Heaven: The Forgotten Christianity of Jesus the Jew* (McDonough: Restoration Fellowship, 1995), p. 202.

orthodox, but necessary for salvation? Is this really what Jesus personally believed and taught?

We shall presently observe how the ancients studiously engrafted sophistications "from the jargon of Plato, of Aristotle and other mystics"[135] upon Christianity, so that in its present form it hardly resembles the original devotion of the magnificent preacher. Yet we are inclined to assume, in regard to the future of the Christian faith, the contagious optimism of Thomas Jefferson:

> The genuine and simple religion of Jesus will one day be restored: such as it was preached and practiced by himself. Very soon after his death it became muffled up in mysteries, and has been ever since kept in concealment from the vulgar eye. To penetrate and dissipate these clouds of darkness, the general mind must be strengthened by education.[136]

It is precisely such an education we endeavor to procure, of both the history of orthodoxy and the Scriptural methodology required to rediscover the God of Jesus. As we move now to revisit the ancient evolutionary history of Christian dogma, the words of a great German historian prepare us for the coming trial: "We shall have to learn to detach from the forms of our Christian belief some things which by habit and custom people have supposed to be closely connected with its innermost being."[137]

---

[135] Thomas Jefferson, *Letter to Dr. Waterhouse*, 1815.
[136] Thomas Jefferson, *Letter to Van der Kemp*, 1820.
[137] Adolf von Harnack, quoted by Agnes Zahn-Harnack, *Adolf von Harnack* (Berlin: Tempelhof & Bott, 1936), p. 80.

2

THE ROOTS OF THE TREE

*He shall break the obelisks of
Heliopolis, which is in the land of
Egypt, and the temples of the gods of
Egypt he shall burn with fire.*
— *Jeremiah 43:13*

TRINITARIAN VOICES OFTEN PORTRAY THE CONCEPT of the three-in-one God as a purely heavenly disclosure, and some insist that this is the only justification for its peculiarity. Distinguished Trinitarian A. W. Tozer affirms, "The fact that it cannot be satisfactorily explained, instead of being against it, is in its favor. Such a truth had to be revealed; no one could have imagined it."[138] Baptist scholar Millard Erickson agrees:

> The Trinity must be divinely revealed, not humanly constructed. It is so absurd from a human standpoint that no one would have invented it. We do not hold the doctrine of the Trinity because it is self-evident or logically cogent.[139]

Evidently absurdity, illogicality and obscurity are the hallmarks of divine and certified truth. Of course, this argument that the doctrine's lack of reasonableness demonstrates its sure origin in God is a proposition which seems

---

[138] A. W. Tozer, *The Knowledge of the Holy* (New York: HarperOne, 1961), p. 23.
[139] Millard J. Erickson, *Christian Theology* (Grand Rapids: Baker Book House. 1998), p. 367.

to effect more questions for orthodox Christianity than confidence. In normal thinking, obscurity is a sign of a theory's weakness. But of course Trinitarianism has never, by admission, been overly concerned with normal thinking.[140]

While it is argued by Tozer and Erickson that the notion of the triune God cannot be the product of any historical philosophy's influence upon the age-long brooding of theologians, students of history and religion are immediately forced to wonder about the various world faiths which have expressed strikingly similar beliefs. Many of the essential constructions of the Catholic developers, and even many of the precise locutions which describe them, are found explicitly in the various religions of history. The Mesopotamian cultures, the Hindus, the ancient Irish, the Greeks, the Egyptians; each bore their own remarkable trinitarian theology which, though varying systematically, devotedly described a single God mysteriously comprised of three unique personalities.[141] One historian writes:

> It is an undoubted fact that more or less all over the world the deities are in triads... in some mystical way, the triad of three persons is one... they are one in the same individual being. The [Christian Trinitarian] definition of Athanasius,[142] who lived in Egypt, applies to the trinities of all heathen religions.[143]

We are forced to ask, in light of Erickson's claim that "no one would have invented it," if these other religions were divinely revealed by God as well? If

---

[140] Lord Francis Bacon, a Trinitarian, writes, "A Christian is one that believes things his reason cannot comprehend" (*Works*, Vol. 2. (London: D. Midwinter, 1753), p. 372). Another Trinitarian writes, "These are notions which may well puzzle our reason in conceiving how they agree, but should not stagger our faith in assenting that they are true; upon which we should meditate, not with hope to comprehend, but with dispositions to admire, veiling our faces in the presence, and prostrating our reason at the feet of wisdom so far transcending us" (Isaac Barrow, *Defence of the Blessed Trinity; in Works*, Vol. 2 (New York: John C. Riker, 1845), p. 150).

[141] The ancient Babylonians "recognized the doctrine of a trinity, or three persons in one god—as appears from a composite god with three heads forming part of their mythology, and the use of the equilateral triangle, also, as an emblem of such trinity in unity" (Thomas Dennis Rock, *The Mystical Woman and the Cities of the Nations* (Whitefish: Kessinger Publishing, 1867), pp. 22-23). A 3,000 year old Hindu text describes a worshipper praying to the Hindu Trinity: "O' ye three Lords! Know that I recognize only one God. Inform me, therefore, which of you is the true divinity, that I may address to him alone my adorations." Brahma, Vishnu, and Shiva reply, "Learn, O' devotee, that there is no real distinction between us... The single being appears under three forms... but he is one" (Marie Sinclair, *Old Truths in a New Light* (London: Chapman and Hall, 1876), p. 383).

[142] Athanasius is often considered the hero of the proto-Trinitarian party during the Council of Nicaea in 325 CE. His vigorous (and often violent) efforts paved the way for the Catholic Church's acceptance of first a doctrine of "consubstantiality" between the Father and the Son, and later, a Trinitarian definition of God. This information will be covered in the following chapters.

[143] James Bonwick, *Egyptian Belief and Modern Thought* (London: C. Kegan Paul & Co., 1878), p. 396.

not, because the exact forms do not always equate, then how close to the orthodox definitions of the fourth century would the pagans need to have come before any relationship or influence was at the very least suspected? Despite any Trinitarian claims of a new and exclusive revelation, of a dogma descending from heaven untouched by the outside world, we must not forget that:

> The law of historical evolution is universal and knows no break in its line of continuity. This is a first principle of the scientific or historical method. It holds true as well in the history of religion, as in that of nature or of human life, in its practical, social or intellectual movements. Otherwise there could be no *history* of religion... The relations of the Ethnic trinities to the Christian dogma have a plain historical foundation... No historical breach occurs [with Christian Trinitarianism], but the old evolution moves on in the ordinary historical channels.[144]

Nevertheless, the inevitable protest of modern Trinitarians is to be anticipated when the issue of historical precedence is raised, namely the objection that *"these pagan religions of the ancient world were mostly tri-theistic and do not align with Christian Trinitarianism which asserts only one God in three persons; the similarities in no way prove the same substance."* But proving that orthodoxy merely inherited its doctrine directly from previous religions is neither our goal nor belief. Rather, it is to be shown that several of the world's theologies lent their *principles* to a compromised Christian posterity, which, after centuries, gathered the choicest of their milieu's traditional philosophies and subsumed them into an evolving Christian faith. The result was a pliable Christianity which began interpreting the subjects of the Bible through the lens of a worldview wholly alien to it. This is much different than just saying, "the doctrine of the Trinity (as expressed by the Catholic Church) *is* pagan." No, it is not that simple. The doctrine is certainly Christian, at least in the sense that it was produced by historical Christians upon reading the Scriptures. Our attention is focused on *how* they read these Scriptures and what historic or contiguous religious elements may have empowered those interpretations.

We will now move to demonstrate not only the serial influence of the world's religious thought upon the later Christian doctors, but also the precise formulas of those religions extant in the doctrines of the Church, and even the

---

[144] L. L. Paine, *The Ethnic Trinities and Their Relations to the Christian Trinity* (New York: Houghton, Mifflin and Co., 1901), pp. 191-192.

public citation by Catholic authorities of those same external philosophies as justification for the establishment of rules of faith.

Out of Africa

Historically speaking, far from achieving any great novelty for orthodox Christianity, the "three-in-one Godhead" only presses Trinitarianism into a startlingly close alignment with various unsavory sources, particularly the world of Greek philosophy. As Erickson reveals, "the specific metaphysical vehicle used to express the classical doctrine of the Trinity as originally formulated was a Greek metaphysics that was viable in that time but no longer makes a great deal of sense to most persons today."[145] We should not then preclude the fact that the Greek and Latin Church Fathers who composed the conjectural formula of faith were specialists who, regardless of their virtue, were predisposed to the philosophies which defined their civilizations. Greek philosophy, particularly Platonism,[146] had long dominated the world by the time of the Church's genesis. But many of the Greek principles may not have been completely unique. Much may be owed, by even the most inventive and illustrious of the Greeks, to the religious mind of ancient Egypt. Indeed historians have long acknowledged that "many of the pagan tenets, invented by the Egyptians and idealized by Plato, were retained as being worthy of belief" by the later Christian synthesizers.[147]

It is true that within ancient Egyptian theology we observe a fixation on the idea of a divine trinity. One scholar reports:

> The *Hymn to Amun* decreed that "No god came into being before him (Amun)" and that "All gods are three: Amun, Re and Ptah, and there is no second to them. Hidden is his name as Amun, he is Re in face, and his body is Ptah"... This is a statement of trinity, the three chief gods of Egypt subsumed into one of them, Amun. Clearly, the concept of organic unity within plurality got an extraordinary boost with this

---

[145] Erickson, *God in Three Persons*, p. 211.

[146] Platonism refers primarily to the philosophical systems of Plato (d. 347 BC), and in a modern sense, to the system that confirms the reality of abstract objects. Platonism experienced various colorful stages of evolution: Arcesilaus introduced skepticism in the third century BCE, Antiochus introduced stoicism in 90 BCE and what is known as *Middle Platonism*. Later, in the 3rd century CE, Plotinus introduced mysticism and ushered in *Neoplatonism*. It is Neoplatonism, along with the parallel Gnosticism, which is uniformly recognized by scholars as having the most significant and direct influence upon the Christian philosophers of the Catholic Church. See W. R. Inge, "The Permanent Influence of Neoplatonism upon Christianity," *The American Journal of Theology*, Vol. 4, No. 2 (Chicago: The University of Chicago Press, 1900), pp. 238-244.

[147] Edward Gibbon, *History of Christianity* (New York: Peter Eckler, 1891), p. xvi.

formulation. Theologically, in a crude form it came strikingly close to the later Christian form of plural Trinitarian monotheism.[148]

Expert on Egyptian religion, Siegfried Morenz likewise recognizes that:

> the trinity was a major preoccupation of Egyptian theologians... Three gods combined and treated as a single being, addressed in the singular. In this way the spiritual force of the Egyptian religion shows a direct link with Christian theology.[149]

This point has been historically utilized, effectively or not, by myriad critics of the Christian Trinity. It is nevertheless more difficult to say that Christianity simply borrowed an intact Trinity model directly from the Egyptians. As far as an expressed tri-unity is concerned, the influence of Egypt on orthodoxy seems of a more remote character. While the comparison may be striking, we will not spend time attempting to unequivocally establish the similarities between the Egyptian Trinity and the orthodox Trinity as anything more than that. There is another more fundamental, more palpable strain of philosophy emanating out of Egypt and projected through the Hellenic ages which enables the most critical components of orthodox Christology: the doctrine of the immortal, transmigrating soul.

The Seed of the Soul

The ancient notion of the transmigrating soul unquestionably forms the metaphysical backbone of the present Trinitarian Christology; it is the philosophical framework which facilitates the doctrines of the dual natures, pre-existence, and the Incarnation. According to the ancient Greek historians, the genesis of this notion, which so characterized the Grecian worldview, was in Egyptian theology.[150] One German Egyptologist confirms that:

---

[148] Simson Najovits, *Egypt, Trunk of the Tree,* Vol. 2 (New York: Algora Publishing, 2004), pp. 83-84.

[149] Siegfried Morenz, *Egyptian Religion* (New York: Cornell, 1992 [1973]), p. 255. Other features of Egyptian religion are noteworthy in this regard, such as the demi-god status ascribed to the Egyptian Pharaoh who "from the very moment of his accession to the throne could bear the title 'Son of God.' Indeed a twofold nature, true God and true man, had already been attributed to the Pharaoh, son of a virgin mother and a divine father" (Kuschel, p. 236).

[150] Herodotus claims that the Egyptians were the first to develop the idea of the transmigrating soul. He writes: "The Egyptians were the first who maintained the following doctrine, too, that

The [immortal soul] doctrine influenced the systems of Greek philosophers; it made itself felt in the teachings of the Gnostics; we find traces of it in the writings of Christian apologists and the older fathers of the Church, and through their agency it has affected the thoughts and opinions in our own time.[151]

This concept is certainly the enduring thread running through the whole spectrum of world religion. We might say that the primitive Egyptian idea of the immortal, transmigrating soul was a planted seed, a spiritual germ which, upon being cultivated by myriad industrious minds for centuries, sprouted and became a great tree supporting a vibrant outgrowth in a hundred directions; the Egyptians, the Platonists, the Gnostics, and the Christians each making their home in its branches. Yet we wonder, if this doctrine-seed about the soul was discovered to be acutely divergent from and antagonistic to the worldview of the Jewish Bible, if the surrounding religious infra-structure would not eventually collapse?

The widespread doctrine of the immortal soul is primarily characterized by a *distinction* between the soul, or the person, and their flesh, or bodily nature. Both the ancient Egyptians and the Greeks considered the soul to be an indestructible substance which had transmigrated from a pre-existent state in the heavens to come down and take on a human nature on the earth.[152] It is already easy to see how this worldview is important to orthodox Christology. But we wonder if it is important to the Bible?

The *International Standard Bible Encyclopedia* reveals that "the Greek, Platonic idea that the body dies, yet the soul is immortal... is utterly contrary to the Israelite consciousness and is nowhere found in the Old Testament."[153] The *Jewish Encyclopedia* similarly reports:

---

the human soul is immortal, and at the death of the body enters into some other living thing then coming to birth; and after passing through all creatures of land, sea, and air, it enters once more into a human body at birth, a cycle which it completes in three thousand years. There are Greeks who have used this doctrine, some earlier and some later, as if it were their own; I know their names, but do not record them" (*Histories*, 2, 123).

[151] Alfred Wiedemann, *The Ancient Egyptian Doctrine of the Immortality of the Soul* (London: H. Grevel & Co., 1895), p. viii.

[152] Gerald Massey, *Ancient Egypt, the Light of the World* (London: T. Fisher Unwin, 1907), p. 137.

[153] Geoffery W. Bromley (ed.), "Death," *International Standard Bible Encyclopedia,* Vol. I (Grand Rapids: Eerdmans, 1960), p. 812.

The belief that the soul continues in existence after the dissolution of the body is… speculation… nowhere expressly taught in Holy Scripture. As long as the soul was conceived to be merely a breath ("nefesh"), and inseparably connected, if not identified with [fleshly matter], no real substance could be ascribed to it.[154]

In the Hebrew Bible, God is not viewed as having imbued the empty body of Adam with a pre-existing soul. Rather, Genesis 2:7 says, "*And the LORD God formed man of dust of the ground, and breathed into his nostrils the breath of life; and man became a living soul.*" Here Adam *himself* is a soul. "Hence," as even mainline evangelical authorities recognize, "in Scripture, *spirit* and *soul* are interchangeably used with *body* for human nature in general, not as though indicating three separate entities, but as denoting a parallelism which brings out the full personality of man."[155] We will presently observe how the contrasting doctrine of the distinct, transmigrating soul progressed in conjunction with other ancient Egyptian and Greek beliefs until it ultimately enabled the Trinitarian interpretation of the Bible's content.

The Personal Soul and Incarnation of Egypt

First we must take a moment to analyze the Egyptian concept of the immortal soul in some detail. The primary feature of interest in this doctrine is its distinction between the humanity (the physical properties) and the "Ba" or

---

[154] Kaufmann Kohler, "Immortality of the Soul," *Jewish Encyclopedia*, 1941, pp. 564, 566.

[155] James Orr, John L. Nuelsen, Edgar Y. Mullins (ed.), *The International Standard Bible Encyclopedia*, Vol. IV (Chicago: The Howard-Severance Company, 1915), p. 2497. The passage continues, "Soul and body are threatened with destruction (Mt 10:28); body without spirit is a corpse (Jas 2:26); soul and spirit are interchangeably united: '*Stand fast in one spirit, with one soul striving,*' etc. (Phil 1:27)." This eliminates the popular belief of many Christians in a conscious life as a disembodied immortal soul in either heaven or hell upon death. Rather, in the biblical worldview, humans are either resurrected at the Last Judgment by new spirit being breathed into their dust, or they are destroyed permanently in the lake of fire (Dan 12:2-3; Jn 5:28ff; Ezk 37:12ff). For an introduction to these matters, see Anthony Buzzard, *Our Fathers Who Aren't in Heaven* (Restoration Fellowship, 2001). It may be important to note the sometimes interchangeable use of spirit and soul terminology as a reference to mankind in the NT. See the *English Standard Version Bible*'s footnote on 1 Thessalonians 5:23: "Spirit, soul, and body represent the entirety of [a person]. It seems unlikely that this is a tripartite division of human nature into body, soul and spirit, where 'spirit' and 'soul' would refer to different parts; more likely Paul is simply using several terms of emphasis [in 1 Thess 5:23]. For similar ways of expressing the totality of [a person] see Matt. 10:28; Mark 12:30; 1 Cor. 7:34."

the soul (the spiritual properties).[156] To the Egyptian theologians, the body was a bony framework inhabited by a pre-existent *spirit-man*.[157] At death, only the earthly being, that is, the bodily nature, perished, while the spirit-man endured.[158] This evacuated soul would, at the moment of expiration, participate in an incredible out-of-body journey, a return to the divine from whence it came.[159] As we will soon see, this correlates with both the later Platonic and Gnostic views of the afterlife and human destiny. Of course, it also corresponds to today's popular Christian belief in the soul's transmigration to heaven immediately after death.

Another feature of the Egyptian belief is relevant to our study: the gods themselves, including the Supreme God, were each believed to have their own divine soul, or, we might venture to say, substantial *God-nature*. In some eras we even find that gods and pharaohs were the only ones thought to have immortal souls at all.[160] Most incredibly, we also encounter a developed, functional model in which an immortal God-soul could unite with a human being, that is, a model of divine Incarnation.

---

[156] "There exists a philosophic explanation of the distinction between Personalities (souls) and Persons, such as that contained in the Platonic Ideas. But the Egyptian was incapable of abstract thought, and was reduced to forming a purely concrete conception of this individuality... he endowed it with a material form completely corresponding to that of the man, exactly resembling him, his second self, his Double, his Doppelganger... the Personality accompanies the Person" (Wiedemann, p. 11, 13).

[157] "The soul was called BA... the meaning of the word seems to be something like 'sublime,' 'noble,' 'mighty.' The BA dwelt in the KA, and seems to have had the power of becoming corporeal or incorporeal at will; it had both substance and form... [It was] attached to the body in some remarkable way... it may be defined as an abstract individuality or personality which was endowed with all his characteristic attributes" (Wallis Budge, *Of the Future Life: Egyptian Religion* (New York: Kensington Publishing Corp, 1997), pp. 189-190). By the time of Amenophis III, about 1500 BCE, "the Egyptians had carried the idea still further... the Ka could live without the body, but the body could not live without the Ka... After a man's death his Ka became his Personality proper" (Wiedemann, p. 13,15-16, 19).

[158] See Ernst Von Bergmann, *Der Sarkophag des Panchemisis*, Vol. I (Vienna, 1883), p. 22; Vol. II, p. 74 et seq.

[159] The spiritual properties of a man had once "found their common home in his living body; but only leaving it at his death each set out alone to find its own way to the gods... they again became one with him, and so entered into the company of the blessed, or even of the gods" (Wiedemann, p. 10).

[160] "In Predynastic and Early dynastic times, the pharaoh's divinity was also exemplified by the fact that only the gods and the pharaoh had souls and only the pharaoh had the privilege of afterlife immortality. And throughout Egyptian history, the pharaoh alone was the governor of the *maat* principle of cosmic order..." (Najovits, p. 153). We wonder at this principle's relation to the later divine "logos" envisioned by the Greek philosophers, which they said was the governing Ideas that brought order to the chaotic universe.

We find that "the Egyptians invented a system of divine kingship... The human pharaoh became a god in addition to being a representative and a mediator between the gods and man."[161] However, far from undergoing a mere deification, a unilateral change of his own nature, "the pharaoh was believed to be an *incarnation* of the Sun god Amun-Re."[162] The Egyptians were as industrious in their mystical thinking here as anywhere else and even provide a fairly systematic explanation of this doctrine: there had first occurred a "transmission of Amun-Re's Ka into the body of the pharaoh... Amun-Re then intertwined himself with the new pharaoh and the divine Ka souls which flowed in his body were transmitted to his pharaoh/son."[163] Modern scholars have recognized this event as yielding a "dual nature" view of the pharaoh.[164] What's more, the God Amun-Re was even called "the Father," while his incarnation in the human pharaoh was considered Horus, "the Son."[165] Upon the death of the human Son, it was said that the divine soul would return to heaven to be reunited with the Father.[166] As scholars have confirmed:

> there is no doubt that the claims of the pharaoh to divine status were taken seriously in ancient Egypt, in the sense that he was not regarded as an ordinary mortal. While the most explicit claims of divine birth date from the New Kingdom period, the affirmation that the king is "son of Re" persists down to the Ptolemaic period. The title "son of Re" bespoke a special kinship with the divine, both in origin and in ultimate destiny after death.[167]

In the second half of this book we will contrast these ideas with both the Incarnation tradition of Christianity and the notion of divine kingship found in the Israelite religion. But at this early stage we may already recognize that the

---

[161] Ibid., p. 152.

[162] Paul Flux, *Ancient Egypt* (Oxford: Reed Educational and Professional Publishing, 2001), p. 17, emphasis added.

[163] Najovits, pp. 154-155.

[164] Adela Yarbro Collins, John Joseph Collins, *King and Messiah as Son of God: Divine, Human, and Angelic Messianic Figures in Biblical and Related Literature* (Grand Rapids: Eerdmans, 2008), p. 9.

[165] See Kuschel, p. 236. Indeed, "at least from about Pharaoh Radjedef's (Djedefra) time (c. 2566-2558 BC), the Pharaoh was not only Horus but he had no human father, his father being the god Amun-Re who magically impregnated the royal wife" (Najovits, pp. 154-155).

[166] "The rulers of Egypt, first the kings and later the pharaohs, were gods as well as men who ruled by divine right. Each king was 'the son of god,' who at the point of death became one with his father, a god in a cosmic Heaven" (Christopher Knight, Robert Lomas, *The Hiram Key: Pharaohs, Freemasons and the Discovery of the Secret Scrolls of Jesus* (Vancouver: Fairwinds Press, 2001), p. 100).

[167] Collins, *King and Messiah as Son of God*, p. 7.

incarnation of the supreme Egyptian God, with its ontological union of the human and divine properties and the resulting entity's subsequent recognition as "the Son of God," bears a striking resemblance to the arrangement of later Christianity. But why did such a doctrine of incarnation arise in ancient Egypt? Perhaps, as one scholar speculates, "They may have consciously exploited man's yearning for the gods to come into the human domain, for a superhuman presence among humans, an immanent god-man who could lead, reassure and comfort."[168] As we will observe later, Egypt's notion of divine kingship would reverberate through the later imperial cults of ancient Greece and Rome.[169] Nevertheless, despite any parallels to developed Christianity, we doubt that the Egyptian theology would be considered divinely-revealed by modern Trinitarians. Similarities or no, we will stick to our primary cause and focus our attention on the transmission of the golden-thread notion of the pre-existent soul into the world of the Greeks, and from there into the world of the Gnostics and the orthodox Christians. The litany of philosophers who will assist this progression is long and varied, yet we routinely find the influence of several esteemed speculators powering the evolutionary engine of Christian dogma more than others. These personalities and their methods we will now review, as briskly and equitably as we may.

The Athenian Sage

The Greek philosopher Plato (427-347 BCE) is without doubt one of the most influential figures in Western history. Long has the lofty mind of the Athenian remained the venerable treasure of a horde of admirers and imitators. The Church Fathers of the first few centuries of Christianity demonstrated their mania for the religion of Plato, and to this day the majority of Christians hold the usually unattributed philosophical property of the Athenian as fundamental to their worldview.

Certainly one of Plato's most enduring and distinctive doctrines is the immortality and transmigration of the soul. Precisely how or when the immortal soul came to be taken up in the minds of the Greek people is not quite clear.

---

[168] Najovits, p. 153.

[169] "Alexander was the first Greek to claim that he had actually been born the son of a god. He failed to convince the Greeks, but in Egypt the Ptolemies were more successful in assuming divinity. They made use of the tradition that the pharaoh was the son of the god Amun" (Freeman, p. 40). After his death, like the Roman emperors who followed him, Alexander became the object of cult worship. See L. Cerfaux, J. Tondriau, *Le culte des souverains* (Tournai: Desclee, 1957), p. 202.

While the records of cultic transmission between Egypt and Greece routinely identify Egypt as the place of origin,[170] time has a tendency to blur such things. The further we get from the moment of meeting between the most remote cultures, the more their various streams of belief seem to merge into the same river, flowing through time. Yet Martin Bernal, professor of Near Eastern Studies at Cornell University, asserts that the transmission of religious thought from Africa to ancient Greece is actually quite clear:

> We find the survival of Egyptian religion both within Christianity and outside it in heretical sects like those of the Gnostics, and in the Hermetic tradition that was frankly pagan... Greek civilization and philosophy derived from Egypt... the chief ways in which they had been transmitted were through Egyptian colonizations of Greece and later Greek study in Egypt.[171]

Indeed, the Hermetic tradition, which will come to play a role in fourth-century Christian development, was especially focused on the relationship between Egyptian religion and Platonism.[172] The Hermeticists were not the only ones to assert this link, however. Some ancient historians have even reported that Plato himself personally visited Egypt to study its unique mystical theology. Later Christian philosopher Clement of Alexandria (150-215 CE) wrote that after the execution of his master Socrates, Plato absconded to Egypt where he studied for thirteen years under the Horite priest Sechnuphis.[173] Though several ancient sources record such a direct encounter of Plato with the doctrines of the Egyptians, modern scholarship is somewhat divided on this record. Some doubt the authenticity of the reports about the Athenian's African holiday for various

---

[170] Miguel Jauregui, *Orphism and Christianity in Late Antiquity* (Berlin: Walter de Gruyter, 2010), p. 51.

[171] Martin Bernal, *Black Athena Writes Back* (London: Duke University Press, 2001), p. 121, emphasis added. Interestingly, yet another scholar has recognized this progression, the precise historic-religious trail we endeavor to follow—from the Egyptians, to the Greeks, to the post-Christian Gnostics, and ultimately to orthodox Christianity.

[172] For an analysis of fourth-century Hermetic readings of Plato, see Pier Franco Beatrice, "The Word 'Homoousios' From Hellenism to Christianity," *Church History*, Vol. 71, No. 2 (Cambridge: Cambridge University Press, 2002), pp. 243-272.

[173] "And it is well known that Plato is found perpetually celebrating the [Egyptians], remembering that both himself and Pythagoras learned the most and noblest of their dogmas among the barbarians. Wherefore he also called the races of the [Egyptians], 'races of barbarian philosophers,' ...who were said to make the soul immortal" (Clement of Alexandria, *Stromata*, 1, 15).

reasons,[174] nevertheless, whether directly or indirectly, Plato encountered Egyptian thought. Regarding the doctrine of the immortal soul, another route of entry into the Hellenistic world, and thus into the mind of Plato, was through the permeation of the Orphic cult.

Sometime between 700 and 600 BCE there arrived in Greece a mystic religious movement from Egypt called Orphicism.[175] The cult claimed to have as its founder and prophet the Orpheus of Greek legend.[176] One notion fundamental to the Orphicists was the ability of the human soul to move into and out of the body, particularly upon death. The Orphic movement demonstrated as much of an obsession over the afterlife as their Egyptian forebears,[177] and the distinction between soul and body was therefore just as crucial. It is also here that a dualistic view of the material body as evil, and the soul as good or divine, first enters into Greek thinking. Thus the conquest of the flesh became a foremost function of most Western philosophy and a requirement for the soul's discharge from its material bondage.[178]

That Plato received many of his doctrines from Orphicism is well documented. One encyclopedia reports that Plato was led to the doctrine of the

---

[174] It is thought by some that because Plato does not himself mention his time in Egypt that it did not occur. See Eduard Zeller, *Plato and the Older Academy* (London: Longmans, Green, and Co., 1888), p. 23. However, the first century BCE Greek historian Strabo says that he was actually shown the house in Heliopolis where Plato had stayed with Eudoxus for thirteen years. Plato is said by him to have stayed at Heliopolis until he persuaded the priests to communicate some of their astronomical lore to him. At any rate, they kept the greater part of their mysteries to themselves (Strabo, *Geography*, 17, 1, 29). Diogenes Laertius, in the third century CE also reports that Plato went to Egypt to study with Egyptian theologians. Nevertheless, the precise academic intermingling between the teachers of Greece and the teachers of Egypt is still hotly debated to this day. See Martin Bernal, *Black Athena* (Brunswick: Rutger University Press, 1987), and the follow up *Black Athena Writes Back* (Durham: Duke University Press, 2001), in contrast to Mary R. Lefkowitz, *Not Out of Africa* (New York: Basic Books, 1997).

[175] Will Durant, *The Story of Civilization Vol. 2: The Life of Greece* (New York: Simon & Schuster, 1966), pp. 188-192.

[176] Clement of Alexandria, in the third century, would later write that Jesus Christ was the new and "higher Orpheus" (Lamson, p. 179). Representations of Jesus as Orpheus were prevalent in Christian art from late antiquity, particularly in Christian catacomb murals.

[177] "In the Orphic Mysteries of ancient Greece, the same [Egyptian] teaching is found... With the dead, the Orphics deposited engraved metal plates containing instructions for the descent into Hades. These instructions closely resemble those of the [Egyptian] *Book of the Dead*" (Katherine Tingley (ed.), *The Theosophical Path*, Vol. XXI (Point Loma: New Century Corporation, 1921), p. 436).

[178] Ibid. The Orphic religion exhibited several other familiar advancements. After death, the soul would be judged and sent down to Hades to face eternal punishment if guilty, or to lives of better station if found to be pure. One variation of the Orphic cult even provided that eternal punishment could be abated by the individual's relatives after death; a spiritual precursor perhaps to the Catholic doctrines regarding purgatory.

immortal soul explicitly "through Orphic and Elusinian mysteries in which Babylonian and Egyptian views were strangely blended,"[179] and Bertrand Russell confirms that "Orphic elements entered into the philosophy of Plato, and from Plato into most later philosophy that was in any degree religious."[180] Plato's ultimate audience would prove broad: Jews, Christians, Gnostics—many branches of world religion have, knowingly or unknowingly, vigorously perpetuated his views. But Plato's teaching on the soul is not the only system which would directly enable the biblical interpretations of later Christian orthodoxy; his unique visions of God and Creation would play key and undeniable roles.

The Demiurge and the Logos

The thrust of Plato's other most pertinent lessons are as follows. Plato taught that all matter was inherently imperfect. Matter was imperfect because it experienced change, and anything that was perfect would not need to be modified—any change from perfection could only be change for the worse. The universe was thus arranged in levels, with the lowest or most liable to change principles at the bottom, like our world, and the highest, most unchanging at the top. Furthermore, Plato taught that all human souls had previously existed in a higher, more perfect sphere of life where they once had all knowledge. Upon incarnating into human forms in this world, all but a residual, innate knowledge had dissipated; humanity was forced to learn all over again.

For Plato, because there still existed an underlying order beneath the outwardly chaotic world (an order which the philosophers would call a "logos"), that meant that it was built by a rational, orderly principle. In his *The Republic*, Plato calls this highest principle "The Good" (which some have called "a God").[181] In another work, *The Timaeus*, Plato introduced another divine figure which he called the "Demiurge" (or "Craftsman"). This Demiurge was a high, but seemingly limited god (perhaps beneath "The Good"), who manufactured our cosmos as a model of a perfect mathematical order in the heavens.[182] Plato himself is not exactly clear on whether or not The Good and the Demiurge are

---

[179] *Jewish Encyclopedia,* pp. 564, 566.

[180] Bertrand Russell, *History of Western Philosophy* (New York: Simon & Schuster, 2008 [1946]), p. 19.

[181] The place of "God" in Plato is still controversial amongst scholars. Plato does not explicitly connect the idea of "the Good" with "a God" per say, and some would rather connect his "Ideas" (Nous) with such a notion. Nevertheless, he does maintain a place for personal divinities, especially in his concept of the Demiurge or "Craftsman" who made our universe.

[182] Plato, *Timaeus*, 40c.

one and the same, or if they are distinct entities. Later Platonists, of course, would clarify this matter. Even later, Plato's unique Demiurge figure would experience an important transformation in the age of the Hellenistic Jews into an *angel*, and this angel, by the Platonizing Christians, into *the Son of God.*

The idea of the divine "logos" would become an important concept for later Christianity. This term, which bears no direct equivalent in English, is usually translated "word" or "reason," but may also be translated "account," "principle," "plan," or "formula."[183] The first philosopher we find speaking of the "logos" is Heraclitus (c. 535–c. 475 BCE), who describes it as the principle of the cosmos which organizes the universe, an eternal blueprint behind the scenes holding together the hectic, ever-changing creation.[184] The later Stoic philosophers conceived of the "logos" as the animating principle which gave life to all beings, dwelling both in the world and in each human soul. By the era of Socrates (d. 399 BCE) and Plato, "logos" had become a well-established term for the faculty of human reason. Plato's student Aristotle (384–322 BC) further defined it along these lines.

Whether Plato or his fellow Greeks had ever regarded the "logos" as having a real and independent substance is of no real matter. Some of Plato's later admirers, particularly those in the Alexandrian schools, would certainly portray the "logos" as a distinct and rational entity, a real person.[185] Later, others would identify this personal logos entity with Plato's Demiurge figure, and ultimately, in the Christian era, this demiurgic logos-creator would be identified by many Church Fathers as *Jesus of Nazareth.*

All of this is not to say that in Plato we should find a proto-Christian, rather that the early Church Fathers, who were so publicly enamored with Plato,[186] demonstrated a brilliant knack for synthesis. There had occurred within the Alexandrian schools a re-examination of Platonism in light of the Bible, and an active process of reconciliation took place. Plato's musings opened a lively hunting ground in which the Christian philosophers:

> found hidden meanings and connections with the Jewish and
> Christian Scriptures, and out of them they elicited doctrines
> quite at variance with the spirit of Plato. Believing that he was

---

[183] See Calvert Watkins, "Appendix I: Indo-European Roots," *The American Heritage Dictionary of the English Language* (Boston: Houghton Mifflin, 2000).

[184] See Robert Audi, "Heraclitus," *Cambridge Dictionary of Philosophy* (New York: CUP, 1999).

[185] See Lamson, Abbot, *The Church of the First Three Centuries*, p. 66.

[186] For example, Eusebius of Caesarea calls Plato "the only Greek who has attained the porch of [Christian] truth" (*Praep. Evang.* 13, 14), and Augustine describes, "the utterance of Plato, the most pure and bright in all philosophy, scattering the clouds of error" (*Contra Acad.*, 3, 18).

inspired by the Holy Ghost, or had received his wisdom from Moses, they seemed to find in his writings the Christian Trinity, the Word, the Church, the creation of the world in a Jewish sense, as they really found the personality of God or of mind, and the immortality of the soul. All religions and philosophies met and mingled in the schools of Alexandria, and the Neo-Platonists had a method of interpretation which could elicit any meaning out of any words.[187]

Whether the original spirit of Plato's discourses remained with the Church Fathers or not is inconsequential to the fact that the Fathers did not consider their Platonic worldview compromised by the advent of Christianity.[188] Plato had provided a necessary metaphysical frame within which the brilliant converts to Christianity might paint a picture of a glorious new religion which married the transcendent moral philosophy of the New Testament with the beloved academic fashions of their time.

Further Platonic Evolutions

During the era of Middle Platonism (c. 90 BCE–200 CE), Plato's teachings afforded significant elaboration by his later students. The first-century philosopher Plutarch (c. 45–120 CE) gains our attention for his syncretistic efforts. Plutarch believed that "all religions are essentially one in spirit and aim, and that a common truth underlies all the diversified forms of religious faith."[189] His most interesting work came from his contemplation of Plato's Demiurge figure and his own fixation on the Egyptian religion. Plutarch explains that Plato himself was already "adopting into his system chiefly the religious notions of the Egyptians,"[190] and so he viewed his own efforts as simply a continuation of the master's work. In his *De Iside et Osride*, Plutarch interprets the ancient Egyptian myth of Isis and Osiris as a Demiurgic account, and links it directly to Plato's

---

[187] Benjamin Jowett, *The Dialogues of Plato* (New York: Charles Scribner's Sons, 1911), pp. 455-456. W. R. Inge writes, "There is a fine saying in Clement of Alexandria, that, that the truth is like a river, which receives tributaries from every side. But the river of speculative theology at Alexandria was like the Nile delta in which it flourished... so that he would be a very learned or a very confident man who should attempt to define precisely the obligations of [an Alexandrian] Jew, Christian, and Greek to each other... at Alexandria there was too much interchange of thought for it to be possible to label each doctrine with the name of a nationality or creed" (Inge, p. 328).

[188] See Clement of Alexandria's recognition of the Trinity in Plato in *Strom.*, 103, 1.

[189] Paine, *The Ethnic Trinities*, p. 138.

[190] Ibid., p. 140.

Demiurge narrative in the *Timaeus* (the later Valentinian Gnostic myth of Sophia would also follow in this tradition).[191] Plutarch up to this point had identified Plato's Demiurge figure as identical to the The Good, or the Supreme God,[192] yet there was still a problem: if this one God was perfect and thus did not change, how could he suddenly go from a state of *not creating* to suddenly *creating*, which required him to change? If he were truly good, how could he build a world which was full of imperfection and evil? Furthermore, if the Demiurge modeled our imperfect world after a perfect world in the heavens, who made the perfect world? Was it not another, higher God? Other Platonists had the answer: the Demiurge who created the world was indeed a distinct *second god*.[193]

Numenius (2nd century CE) taught that in order to manage the universe, and because God could not by nature create the world himself, God had generated this lesser principle from his own essence. The Demiurge then acted as a sort of buffer between God and creation, a mediator. Numenius furthermore posited that if there were two gods, then there had to be a *third* principle: the spiritual universe which the second had made. There were then three principles of reality, a trinity of the "First God, the Demiurge, and the World-Soul."[194] The First God was characterized by his mind, goodness, and self-existence. He did not himself create, but delegated all creation to the Demiurge, who existed in a subordinate position to him, as did the World-Soul, which was the spiritual substance that related to the created world. These three principles were said to be both distinct and "one."[195]

This thinking would have monumental impact on Platonic philosophy in the succeeding generation, particularly on Plotinus (204-270 CE), the so-called founder of the school of Neoplatonism.[196] As we will later see, Plotinus translated Numenius' divine principles into "hypostases" (existences, realities),

---

[191] See Carl Sean O'Brien, *The Demiurge in Ancient Thought: Secondary Gods and Divine Mediators* (Cambridge: CUP, 2015), pp. 83-116.

[192] Israel Gallarte, Lautaro Lanzillotta, *Plutarch in the Religious and Philosophical Discourse of Late Antiquity* (Leiden: Koninklije Brill, 2012), p. 80.

[193] Svetla Griffin, Pauliina Remes, *The Routledge Handbook of Neoplatonism* (London: Routledge, 2014), p. 49.

[194] O'Brien, p. 154.

[195] Robbert M. van den Berg, "God the Creator, God the Creation: Numenius' Interpretation of Genesis 1:2 (frg. 30)," *The Creation of Heaven and Earth: Re-interpreations of Genesis 1 in the Context of Judaism, Ancient Philosophy, Christianity, and Modern Physics* (Leiden: Brill, 2005), pp. 109-123.

[196] A native of Egypt, Plotinus relocated to Rome in 244 CE where he taught for ten years. His successors include the famed Porphyry (234-305 CE) and Proclus (412-485 CE). The formal Neoplatonic tradition continued until just after Emperor Justinian I shuttered the Platonic Academy in Athens in 529 CE. Its principles lived on, however, in the speculative philosophy of orthodox Christianity.

and it is this divine triad of the Platonists, combined with the Greek model of the migrating soul, which more readily and directly prepared the way for the production of the later Christian Trinity than any particularly Egyptian notion. Interestingly, the most immediate conduit for this transference of Greek thought into Christianity was actually Greek thought's earlier transference into the world of Judaism.

Judaism and Plato

The most prevalent Judaism, even through the times of Christ, maintained a starkly divergent outlook on the nature of humanity from the Greeks. For the Hebrews, the soul was not an immortal spark concealed in the body and awaiting a joyous return to the divine upon death. According their Scriptures, the living soul was *the whole man* (Gen 2:7). Death had always meant a silencing, an end to the thoughts and works of a man, a descent into a world of nothing.[197] It was to them a great and unconscious sleep.[198] The hope for the common Jew of the first century was not a transcendent life as a disembodied soul in the heavens, but a future *resurrection* of the whole man by God, a return from death to life in a renewed material existence. The prophet Daniel had explained to them, *"Many of those who sleep in the dust of the earth shall awake, some to everlasting life, and some to shame and everlasting contempt"* (Dan 12:2). The dead, then, at the moment of resuscitation, were "sleeping," not in a higher spiritual realm, but "in the dust of the earth." The promised destiny of the Jewish faithful was not trans-material. In 2 Maccabees, a Jew about to be martyred by Greek tyrants holds out his arms and says, *"God gave these to me. But his laws mean more to me than my hands, and I know God will give them back to me again"* (7:11).[199] Of course the Jewish rabbi Jesus

---

[197] Many verses in the Hebrew Scriptures provide clarity on the state of the dead: *"For in death there is no remembrance of thee: in the grave who shall give thee thanks?"* (Ps 6:3-5); *"The dead praise not the LORD, neither any that go down in silence"* (Ps 115:17); *"In that very day his thoughts perish"* (Ps 146:4); *"For the living know that they shall die, but the dead know not any thing, neither have they any more reward; for the memory of them is forgotten. Also their love, and their hatred, and their envy, is now perished"* (Ecc 9:5-6). See also Acts 2:29, 34: *"David, he is both dead and buried, and his grave is with us to this day. For David did not ascend into the heavens…"*

[198] Death is constantly described by both Old and New Testaments as a sleep; in other words, a state of unconsciousness much different from the immediate and conscious transmigration of the soul taught by the Egyptians and the Platonists: *"I sleep the sleep of death"* (Ps 13:3); *"So man lieth down… they shall not awake, nor be raised out of their sleep"* (Job 14:12); *"Lazarus sleeps, but I go, that I may wake him out of sleep… Then Jesus said to them plainly, Lazarus is dead"* (Jn 11:11-14); *"But now Christ has been raised from the dead, the first fruits of those who are asleep"* (1 Cor 15:20).

[199] The events depicted in 2 Maccabees take place between 180 and 161 BCE. The author claims to be abridging a history by Jason of Cyrene, who wrote five books on the Maccabean revolt around 100 BCE. See 2 Maccabees 2:24.

continued to emphasize this full resurrection from the dead, a sudden reconstruction of life out of unconscious sleep: *"An hour is coming, in which all who are in their graves will hear his voice, and will come forth; those who did the good deeds to a resurrection of life, those who committed the evil deeds to a resurrection of judgment"* (Jn 5:28-29). This was therefore the precise hope of the earliest Jewish Christians as well, that *"he who raised the Messiah Jesus from the dead will give life to your mortal bodies also"* (Rom 8:11). N. T. Wright thus concludes that "the early Christian hope for bodily resurrection is clearly Jewish in origin, there being no possible pagan antecedent."[200]

While the Jews, including the first Christians, faithfully awaited their bodily reconstitution from the grave, the doctrine of the migrating, unconditionally immortal soul introduced to the Jews by the Greeks was duly viewed as a major departure from the faith. One Jewish source confirms, "The belief in a continuous life of the soul... was discouraged and suppressed by prophet and lawgiver as antagonistic to the belief in YHWH, the God of life."[201] We must therefore agree with the abundance of scholarship which concludes that:

> The belief in the immortality of the soul came to the Jews from contact with Greek thought and chiefly through the philosophy of Plato, its principal exponent, who was led to it through Orphic... and Egyptian views.[202]

Indeed, while we find that some later mystical Jewish works, such as *The Prayer of Joseph* (1st-3rd century CE), and *Slavonic Enoch* (late 1st century CE), suggest some kind of pre-existence and incarnation of the soul,[203] we may readily observe that it was only under the prevailing Greek influence that these notions took any hold in Judaism, and, as we will see, at a later stage and on the fringe.[204]

In the aftermath of Alexander's conquests, Platonism had irreversibly permeated the religions of the Eastern Mediterranean. By the late 4th-century BCE, as Hellenizing forces reached Palestine, and as the Jews of the Diaspora began to assimilate in the great centers of Alexandria and Antioch, Greek metaphysics were already coming into direct contact, and conflict, with Judaism. It was at this time that a new and lasting struggle ignited among the Jewish

---

[200] N. T. Wright, "The Resurrection of Resurrection," *Bible Review*, Vol. 16, No. 4 (Biblical Archaeology Society, 2000).

[201] "Immortality of the Soul," *Jewish Encyclopedia*, pp. 564-566.

[202] Ibid.

[203] See *Slavonic Enoch* 23:5

[204] Kuschel, p. 184.

people over how their faith should adapt to a domineering Greco-Roman influence. All the way through the second-century CE, the Jews found themselves increasingly divided: the "Hellenizing" Jews embraced religious syncretism, while the traditionalists rejected it and saw the former as adulterous compromisers. Again, it was only after this Hellenizing segment of Judaism encountered and cooperated with Greek philosophy that the Platonic models of pre-existence, transmigration, and incarnation were applied to the biblical stories and granted new life as Jewish mythology. Indeed, scholars have observed that "already in Second Temple Judaism, Hellenistic Jewish writers had *captured* these Greco-Roman metamorphosis ideas."[205]   The Jews of the Diaspora were especially diligent in appropriating "alien elements" and "pressing Gentile thought into the service of Jewish faith."[206]   But an important question in our larger study is this: were the New Testament Apostles Hellenizers? Did they view their world and the coming of the Messiah into that world through a philosophical, Platonic lens? Was Jesus himself an innovative syncretist or a traditionalist? We will soon pursue these questions and more. But for now we may confirm that long before the time of Jesus, there had already been a serious socio-cultural and religious battle raging between the Greek and Jewish worlds, an old struggle that would characterize the entire life of the Christian religion from its conception to our present day.

Philo the Jew and the Logos Angel

One Jewish mind from the first century CE, a man of about fifty years old at the time of Christ's crucifixion, would demonstrate an exceptional passion for Platonism, and his enduring syncretistic spirit would extend beyond the Jewish fringe in which he flourished and into early Christianity. Arguably, more than any other theologian, the industrious syncretistic activity of the Middle Platonist Philo of Alexandria (c. 15 BCE – 50 CE) would grease the theological tracks for the persistent fusion of Plato and Christ.

As a boy, Philo's wealthy family enrolled him in a Greek gymnasium where he learned the arts, mathematics and philosophy. He developed an enthusiasm for Greek drama and athletics, particularly boxing. Later in life, however, we find Philo drawn towards asceticism. He writes favorably of the austerity of the Essenes, a Jewish monastic community often associated with the Dead Sea

---

[205] Simon S. Lee, *Jesus' Transfiguration and the Believer's Transformation* (Tubingen: Mohr Siebeck, 2009), p. 28, emphasis added.

[206] Gerald van Groningen, citing Wilson, *First Century Gnosticism: Its Origin and Motifs* (Leiden: Brill, 1967), pp. 62-63.

Scrolls.[207] The older Philo appears torn between the virtues of the philosopher's life and the duties of Roman aristocracy.[208] One moment Philo is found debating rival interpretations of Plato, the next he is representing the needs of Jews in the empire before Caligula.[209] In every respect, the life of Philo displays a unique intersection of the Jewish and Gentile worlds, and his religious thought is no exception.

As a philosopher, Philo openly endeavored to harmonize Greek philosophy with Judaism. Perhaps the greatest of all Hellenizing Jews, he represents a confluence of biblical content with a broader Platonic frame of reference than is encountered in most early Hellenic Jewish writers. Philo's home of Alexandria was, after all, the most vivacious intellectual spot on planet Earth, and, as noted earlier, "All religions and philosophies met and mingled in the schools of Alexandria."[210] It was within this diverse, academically competitive melting pot that Philo diligently produced a system of biblical justification for the philosophical worldview and "interpreted Hebrew Scripture along Platonic lines, [ultimately] exercising an immense influence on developing Christianity."[211]

It was for his non-traditional views, and for his insistence upon the brilliance of his own Platonic, Stoic reinterpretation of the Bible, that the mainstream Jewish community rejected him. Indeed, Philo's works may not have been preserved at all had it not been for the Gentile Church Fathers' infatuation with them. The *Jewish Encyclopedia* recalls that:

> Philo included in his philosophy both Greek wisdom and
> Hebrew religion, which he sought to fuse and harmonize by
> means of the art of allegory that he had learned from the

---

[207] See Philo, *Every Good Man is Free*, XII, 75-87, XIII, 88-91. Until the 1990s, virtually every scholar believed the Essene sect (2nd century BCE—1st century CE) had written the Dead Sea Scrolls discovered in Qumran in 1946. Some have challenged this long-standing hypothesis and suggest that the scrolls were actually written in Jerusalem before being transferred to the caves of Qumran to avoid the Roman siege of 70 CE. See Norman Golb, *Who Wrote the Dead Sea Scrolls?* (New York: Charles Scribner's Sons, 1995).

[208] Philo is thought by some to have experienced an "identity crisis" of sorts. Dissatisfied by the worldly affairs of Alexandria, he may have even joined the Egyptian Jewish sect called the Therapeutae before being called to attend to the needs of his countrymen. See Matt Stefon (ed.), *Judaism: History, Belief, and Practice* (New York: Rosen Publishing, 2012), p. 312.

[209] Due to his education, Philo was nominated to lead a group of Jewish ambassadors to Rome around 40 CE. Philo petitioned the emperor to defend the rights of Jews suffering in Alexandria, and condemned Caligula's plan to construct a statue of himself in the Jewish temple as a provocation to war. After their diplomatic efforts failed, Philo is said to have encouraged his fellows that God would not allow Caligula to go unpunished. Months later, the emperor was assassinated by his own soldiers.

[210] Jowett, p. 456.

[211] Edward Moore, "Middle Platonism," *Internet Encyclopedia of Philosophy*. Web. 16 May 2014.

Stoics. His work was not accepted by contemporary Judaism. *"The sophists of literalness,"* as he calls them (*De Somniis*, i. 16-17), *"opened their eyes superciliously"* when he explained to them the marvels of his exegesis... Philo was all the more enthusiastically received by the early Christians, some of whom saw in him a Christian... The Church Fathers have preserved most of Philo's works that are now extant.[212]

What were some of the Platonic doctrines that the Jews rejected as being incompatible with the biblical faith, but the Christian philosophers happily embraced? Of course, Philo had readily adopted Plato's immortal soul, proclaiming that upon death, the soul would enjoy "a higher existence, immortal and uncreated."[213] But Philo's most important and most elaborated-upon doctrine was his own unique view of the logos. He blended the Greek logos and the Demiurgic accounts of the earlier Platonists with the creation narrative of the Hebrew Bible, and it is in this synchronism that we find the catalyst for the introduction of Plato directly into the bloodstream of the infant Christian faith.

As we saw earlier, by Philo's day the term logos had long been in the conversation of the Greeks, at least since the fifth century BCE. Again, the logos had taken on a variety of meanings over time; first as the principle of order or divine knowledge in the universe by Heraclitus, then as the animating principle permeating the created world by the Stoics, then as the inner reasonable discourse of man by Aristotle. Yet the actual Greek word "logos" meant "a plea," "an opinion," "an expectation," "word," "speech," "account," "reason," and more. Thus in the *Septuagint*, the Greek translation of the Hebrew Bible produced by the Jews between the 3rd to the 1st centuries BCE, the Greek word "logos" was used to translate the Hebrew "davar" (word). The translation seems appropriate; the term was rightly used of the Jewish God's pronouncements (Gen 1:3, 6, 9), God's action (Zech 5:1-4), and the messages which he communicated to his prophets (Jer 1:4-19). But of course, the Jews translating into Greek were using the word differently than the Platonists.[214] We must emphasize that "logos" was used by the Jews in the *Septuagint* to describe

---

[212] C. H. Toy, C. Siegfried, J. Z. Lauterbach, "Philo Judaeus," *Jewish Encyclopedia*, 1906.

[213] Philo, *On the Giants*, 14.

[214] Scholars have reported that "the [Jewish] authors of the *Septuagint* version and the Platonists employed the same term (logos) to express totally different views: the former intending by it simply a mode of action in the Deity; the latter, a real being, his agent and minister in executing his will" (Lamson, Abbot, p. 68).

God's activity.[215]   But the Hellenizing Philo appears to have seen something more.

In the Greek and Jewish usage of "logos," Philo perceived a brilliant connection between two parallel religions. He set out to prove that the logos of Platonism and the "word" by which the God of Israel spoke the universe into being were one and the same.[216]   He not only ultimately confirmed this observation for himself, but elaborated further.   For Philo, the logos was complex; it was at once the sum of God's reason, and also, ostensibly, a *person*.[217] Some scholars have even reported that "Philo was the first, we believe, who attributed to the logos a permanent personal subsistence; thus proceeding one step beyond Plato."[218]   Evidently, his logos was not only God's rational order, but a powerful, divine entity, a mediator between God and mankind.[219] O'Brien writes that Philo's logos "is more than a mere tool or knife used by God in creation. It is a mediating entity, which functions as a co-Creator and plays an active role in the universe after genesis."[220] Philo even identified this being as *"an angel."*[221] This figure was, he claimed, the very same *"angel of the Lord"* mentioned in the Hebrew Bible (Gen 16:7-14, Ex 3:2-4, Jdg 2:1-3), and "the chief messenger,"[222] the "First-born Son of God," and the eldest of all the angelic beings.[223] Yet Philo also believed this angel to be in some sense a "hypostatization" (individualization) of God's own reason.[224]   Considering

---

[215] Marian Hillar, "Philo of Alexandria," *Internet Encyclopedia of Philosophy*. Web. 10 August 2015.

[216] O'Brien notes a parallel between the early Middle Platonist Plutarch, as he worked to find Platonism in the Egyptian Isis and Osiris myth, and the later Middle Platonist Philo, as he worked to locate Platonism in the Jewish Bible: "In recounting the myth of Isis and Osiris, the philosophical doctrines are expounded, at times, in a confusing manner, as various details of the myth have to be included. One might compare Plutarch's situation to that of Philo, who also has to deal with a creative religious myth (that of the *Pentateuch*). There is, however, an important distinction between the cases. Plutarch was under no compulsion to use this myth in order to expound philosophy; he does so, because it evidently interests him, and he presumably viewed it as containing philosophical truth (to some degree). Philo attempts to expound another generational account, the *Pentateuch*, in philosophical language; as a pious Jew, it represents the core of his belief and he could not simply ignore it, as Plutarch could with the Isis myth" (O'Brien, pp. 83-116).

[217] There is today still much debate over "whether Philo's Logos is a Person or an abstraction" (Stewart Salmond, *Critic. Review of Theo. & Phil. Lit.,* Vol. 13. (Edinburgh: T &T Clark, 1903), p. 2).

[218] Lamson, Abbot, p. 68.

[219] O'Brien, p. 43.

[220] Ibid., p. 45.

[221] Philo, *De Somniis.* 1, 228-239; *De Cherubim.* 1-3; *Cher.* 3 and 35; *Mut.* 87; *Deus* 182.

[222] Philo, *Her.* 205.

[223] Hillar, *IEP*. The Hermetic work *Poimandres* likewise features a demiurgic Logos entity called "the son of God." For Hermeticism's link to Alexandrian Judaism and affinity with the work of Philo, see Dragos Giulea, *Pre-Nicene Christology in Paschal Contexts* (Leiden: Brill, 2014), pp. 68-72.

[224] Ibid.

Philo's sweeping, mystical style, it is possible that he himself never determined whether or not the logos was completely and only a distinct personal being, or only a personified expression of the one God.[225] Regardless, Philo's "idea that the logos is begotten by God, and is his 'first-born'... whether directly from him or not, comes into Christian thinking."[226] One encyclopedia recognizes the thread tying Plato to Philo, and ultimately to the personal logos Christology and Trinity of the later Christian philosophers:

> Inspired by the *Timaeus* of Plato, Philo read the Jewish Bible as teaching that God created the cosmos by his Word (*logos*), the first-born son of God. Alternately, or via further emanation from this Word, God creates by means of his creative power and his royal power, conceived of both as his powers, and yet as agents distinct from him... Another influence [on the later Christians] may have been Neopythagorean Middle Platonist Numenius (fl. 150), who posited a triad of gods, calling them alternately, Father, Creator, and Creature.[227]

In the philosophies of both Philo and Numenius, the logos is "related to [the highest Deity] as the light to the sun, being at the same time different and inseparable from him."[228] As we will soon observe, influential Christian figures like Justin Martyr (d. 165 CE) would also describe the relationship between God and the logos (to him the pre-existing Jesus) as "light from the sun, fire from fire, speaker and his speech."[229] It is easy to see how in Philo the later Platonizing Christians discovered the perfect conduit for a new pluralistic exegesis, an agile and even brilliant validation for bringing the Bible up to speed with modern academics. Without question, Philo's pioneering methods were fundamental to developing concepts for future Hellenistic interpretation of

---

[225] Certainly Philo's logos was convoluted. Scholars are still divided on whether or not his logos was really a person. As Heuser reports, "Indeed, it is very problematic just what Philo's logos is. There were too many philosophies at work upon the Alexandrian to result in anything definite. However, the dominant notion of the logos in Philo seems to be that of the Stoic, half-abstract and half-concrete entity, intervening between Creator and creation, the Unbegotten and the begotten... Just what sort of a being this intermediary logos is, we cannot say" (Herman Joseph Heuser, *The American Ecclesiastical Review*, Vol. 54 (Philadelphia: The Dolphin Press, 1916), p. 229).

[226] Richardson, p. 34.

[227] Dale Tuggy, "History of Trinitarian Doctrines." *Stanford Encyclopedia of Philosophy*. Stanford University. Web. 8 Aug 2014.

[228] Eduard Zeller, *Outlines of the History of Greek Philosophy* (New York: Henry Holt and Company, 1889), p. 815.

[229] Tuggy, *Stanford Encyclopedia of Philosophy*.

Hebrew thought, especially by Clement of Alexandria, Justin Martyr, Tertullian, and Origen.[230] Indeed Justin Martyr would agree that the logos who created the world was a lesser, subordinate being, described as *an angel*, who had become incarnate as *the man Jesus Christ*. It is an unsung fact of Church history that the most well-known second and third century Church Fathers believed that Jesus had pre-existed, not eternally as the one true God himself, *but as a subordinate angelic being*, God's first creation. These theologians did not preach therefore a doctrine of three eternally co-equal Persons in one God, a doctrine which, according to the Trinitarian scholars consulted in the previous chapter, did not arrive as an object of faith until the fourth century CE. As Harnack observed, in Patristic studies "The subordination of Christ as a heavenly being to the Godhead, is seldom or never carefully emphasized, though it frequently comes plainly into prominence."[231]   An in-depth analysis of these widespread "Subordinationist" views of the most well-known Church Fathers leading up to the Council of Nicaea (325 CE), and therefore a demonstration that they were *not* committed Trinitarians will be offered in the coming chapters.

Justin Martyr and the Rise of Platonic Christianity

Briefly, and for the purposes of chronological organization, an account of the famous Justin Martyr (100-165 CE) and how he adapted the thus-far evolved Platonic philosophy into the Christian faith, is needed. Justin was, by his own account, a pagan Gentile born in Judea.[232] Being a pagan raised in a Jewish environment, the studious Justin provided the ideal juncture for several second-century faiths. In his famous *Dialogue with Trypho the Jew*, he describes his dissatisfaction with his own early, meandering education, during which he had sampled the various Greek philosophies of his day. He found most of the Greek systems uninspiring, until he finally settled on Platonism.[233] Later, around 132 CE, Justin made fateful contact with a Christian man, possibly a Syrian, who argued that the Jewish prophets were more reliable than the Greek philosophers.[234] Justin's investigation of this claim would ultimately turn him towards the Christian faith. By his own admission, however, his affection for the religion of Plato did not wane.

---

[230] Marian Hillar, "Philo of Alexandria (c. 20 BCE—40 CE)," *Internet Encyclopedia of Philosophy*. Web. 16 May 2014.

[231] Harnack, *History of Dogma*, Vol. 1 (1894), p. 193.

[232] Dawid Roqueah, *Justin Martyr and the Jews* (Leiden: Brill, 2001), p. 128.

[233] Justin Martyr, *Dialogue with Trypho the Jew*, 2, 8.

[234] Ibid.

Instead of renouncing Platonism, Justin elected to view Christianity and Plato as mutually complimentary, one justifying the other. Beyond being a matter of preference, however, this sort of syncretism may have been seen as necessary for survival. One historian reveals that Justin's situation was representative of the plight of the whole of burgeoning Christian academia:

> It was common for students in the Greek world to go from one school of philosophy to another, listening to debates and querying positions taken, and unless Christians were able to take part in such debates, Christianity was unlikely to achieve intellectual respectability. In a growing church, most Christians at any one time were converts, and there were many who had a traditional training in philosophy either before encountering Christianity or while waiting for baptism. Some kind of accommodation had to be made with Greek philosophy. The Christian Justin Martyr (c. 100-c. 165), a Platonist by training, was among the first to argue that Christianity could draw on both the scriptures and Greek philosophy and could even appropriate philosophy for its own ends. "Whatever good they [the philosophers] taught belongs to us Christians." He was echoed by Clement of Alexandria (c. 150-c. 215), who claimed that God had given philosophy to the Greeks as a "school-master" until the coming of the Lord as "a preparation which paved the way towards perfection in Christ."[235]

Justin's methodology resembled that of the earlier Philo, who had likewise perceived compatibility between Plato and Judaism. Though Justin declines to ever mention Philo by name (who would have been dead eighty years prior to Justin's conversion), we may readily detect the influence of his exegesis.[236] Scholars have noted, in regard to Philo's influence upon Gentile Christian leadership, that:

---

[235] Freeman, *Closing of the Western Mind,* pp. 142-143.

[236] Willis Shotwell, *The Biblical Exegesis of Justin Martyr* (London: SPCK, 1965), p. 115. For more on Philo's influence on the thought of Justin Martyr, see Demetrius Traketellis, *Pre-Existence of Christ in the Writings of Justin Martyr* (Scholars PR, 1976), p. 47, pp. 53-92; Alan Segal, *Two Powers in Heaven: Early Rabbinic Reports About Christianity and Gnosticism* (Leiden: Brill, 2002), p. 224. Compare also Justin's *Dialogue,* 56, 1 with Philo's *De Mutatione Nominum,* 15, and *Dialogue* 56.4,10 and *Moses,* I, 66.

Justin and the subsequent Fathers, we know, read Philo; and their thoughts and expressions often exhibit a remarkable coincidence with his. Indeed, so deeply are their writings imbued with his sentiments and spirit that without him, as Mosheim observes, they would often be "altogether unintelligible." No one who compares their sentiments in reference to the Logos with those entertained and expressed by him, can doubt, we think, that they must have been derived from a common source; and this could be no other than the doctrines of Plato, as explained by his later followers of the Alexandrian School.[237]

Accordingly, in Justin Martyr we discover the same Philonic identification of the logos as an angelic being, a subordinate divine entity used by God in the act of creation.[238] This being is likewise identified by him as the *"angel of the Lord"* in the Old Testament (Gen 16:13, 21:17, etc.),[239] and of course, Justin would ultimately identify this logos-angel as Jesus Christ, primarily, it would seem, through a Platonic reading of the Gospel of John's famous and controversial prologue.[240] The angel in the Old Testament was therefore said by Justin to be a "Christophany" or an early manifestation of the pre-incarnate Jesus. But was this pre-incarnate Christ the eternally existent supreme God to Justin? Was Justin a Trinitarian? Apparently not. Justin calls the Son "another god" who is "under the Creator of all things" and who is "also called an angel." Furthermore, he is "distinct from God, the Creator; distinct that is, in number, and not in mind."[241] It was through the agency of this pre-existent, lesser god that Yahweh had created the present material world; he was God's viceroy, the "minister to the Father's will… since he was begotten of the Father by an act of

---

[237] Lamson, Abbot. p. 69.

[238] Justin Martyr. *Dialogue with Trypho the Jew*. Ch. 2, 8.

[239] Ibid., 56.

[240] This still hotly debated passage is usually translated in the following way by Trinitarian Christians: *"In the beginning was the Word (logos), and the Word (logos) was with God, and the Word (logos) was God"* (John 1:1 NASB). In later portions of this book, we will discover the Jewish view of creation, as expressed by the Bible, which enables a more appropriate interpretation of John 1:1-14, that is, we will learn that the logos of God, as understood by the Jews (like John), should not be considered a distinct *Person*, as Philo and Justin perceived. By the end of this investigation, it should become clear that the whole system of Justin's (and also Trinitarianism's) personal Logos-Christology is severely weakened once John's logos is interpreted, not through the lens of the Greeks, but of the Jews, whose Scriptures are to be held above any pagan speculations as the standard of Christian belief.

[241] Justin Martyr, *Dialogue*, 56.

will."[242] This last quotation is interesting: Justin holds that the Son was begotten, not eternally by requirement of nature as the later Trinitarians would say, but by an act of the Father's will, that is, by another's personal choice. It follows that before the Father chose to beget him, there was no Son. Evidently, the Son only came to be, in Justin's view, when he was needed by the Father, perhaps for the act of creation. The Father on the other hand did not exist due to anyone's choice and was thus the only eternal God.

At this point we must stress that by all accounts, second-century Platonic Christianity, as exemplified by Justin, did not yet hold that Jesus was *co-equal* or *co-eternal* with the Father or the Holy Spirit. This was a much later development. Instead Justin consistently taught that for Christians, the Son was held "in the second place" to the "true God."[243] In this regard Justin is clearly representative of widespread second-century exegesis.[244] But exactly how prevalent were Justin's Christological views? Did all Christians in the second century believe that the man Jesus had first pre-existed in the heavens? Much more on the beliefs of Justin Martyr and other Church Fathers will be provided in the coming chapters, where we will discover that the most famous theologians of the second and third century were not yet Trinitarians, but only Hellenizers who still believed that the Father was the one true God, and that Jesus was a distinct and subordinate figure.

But we still wonder how Justin's vision of Jesus as a divine, pre-existent being ever came about in Christianity? Had the earliest Jewish disciples of Jesus ever imagined such a thing? Surely the Apostles were not Platonists? Exactly what those first Jewish Christians believed remains to be seen. But we can already detect a dramatic *shift* towards Platonism in the Christian theology of the second century. Historians have recognized that:

> From the second century... after the New Testament period—
> in the time of the Apostolic Fathers and the early Christian
> Apologists [like Justin], the spiritual climate *changed completely*...
> a fixation and gradual Hellenization of Christianity as a
> doctrine set in... From the second century on... [they

---

[242] Ibid., 61.

[243] Justin Martyr, *First Apology*, Ch. 13, 1.

[244] A. Lukyn Williams, *Justin Martyr: The Dialouge with Trypho*, (London, 1930), p. xiv; William Horbury, *Jews and Christians* (Edinburgh: Bloomsbury, 1998), p. 129; T. D. Barnes, *Tertullian* (Oxford, 1971), pp. 106-108.

delivered] Christianity over to philosophical, cosmological and speculative systems of thought.[245]

One historian thus concludes: "If there is one historical fact that is more assured to me than any other in the history of Christian theology, it is the fact that the Christian Trinitarian dogma, with its cardinal logos doctrine, is the direct lineal descendant of the Platonic dualistic idealism."[246] Indeed, the philosophers of this era who laid the groundwork for the later Trinity had confused New Testament Christology with Greek cosmology: the historical Jewish man Jesus was made an integral and transcendent utility of the Platonic world. This was probing, intellectualist conjecture, far removed from the Messianic Jewish framework of the New Testament, and the consequences of this peculiar activity have yet to be realized on a large scale. William Sanday, an Oxford theologian, attempted to smooth over the risky syncretism of the Platonizing Christians:

> Sooner or later, it was inevitable that Christianity should be brought into relation with the contemporary philosophy… Was it not a noble thought on the part of Justin which led him to see "seeds" of the Divine Logos at work in the Gentile thinkers of old, in men like Heraclitus and Socrates or Plato or Pythagoras, while the divine Word as a whole was incarnate in Christ?[247]

But Friedrich Loofs, professor of Church History at the University of Halle, recognized that the second-century Christians had, through their speculation, laid the foundation for the transformation of the original Jewish-Christian faith into a Hellenistic mystery. This was the precarious, pioneering work that paved the way for the eventual setting up of the eternal Jesus of the later creeds. Loofs reveals that:

> Their Christology affected the later development disastrously. By taking for granted the transfer of the concept of Son of God onto the pre-existing Christ, they were the cause of the Christological problem of the fourth century. They caused a shift in the point of departure of Christological thinking—away from the historical Christ and onto the issue of pre-existence.

---

[245] Kuschel recalling Harnack, pp. 43-51, emphasis added.
[246] Paine, *The Ethnic Trinities*, p. 202.
[247] William Sanday, *Christologies Ancient and Modern* (Oxford: OUP, 1910), p. 17.

They thus shifted away from the historical life of Jesus, putting it into the shadow and promoting instead the incarnation.[248]

A comparison between one New Testament text and a second-century Christian homily encapsulates the fundamental change experienced by Christianity in this period. In 1 Peter 1:20 we read that Christ *"was foreknown before the foundation of the world, but has appeared in these last times for the sake of you."* However, in an anonymous text known as 2 Clement, dating between 95-145 CE, we read: *"Christ… being first spirit, then became flesh."*[249] Here we observe a dramatic shift from Christ being previously "foreknown" by God, to Christ being previously a real spiritual being; the "appearance of Christ" in history became a metaphysical assumption of a human nature. Harnack writes that the vision of 2 Clement 9:5 is "the fundamental, theological and philosophical creed on which the whole Trinitarian and Christological speculations of the Church of the succeeding centuries are built, and it is thus the root of the orthodox system of dogmatics." The exchange between the New Testament and this later text represents "the history of the substitution of the historical Jesus by the pre-existing Christ."[250]

The divine Logos of the second-century Apologists like Justin would continue to siphon away the significance of the human Jesus until he nearly disappeared. However, we find that in some early Christian circles the disappearance of the human Jesus had already been achieved. Travelling several decades backwards from Justin's birth, we encounter another dynamic religious movement that had already been actively fusing Platonism and Christianity since even the last days of the New Testament Apostles—a movement which aggressively challenged the God of Judaism and threatened to destroy the infant Christian faith from within.

---

[248] Friedrich Loofs, *Guide to Studying the History of Dogma* (Niemeyer Verlag, 1951 [1890]), p. 97.

[249] "The document that goes under this misleading name is neither a letter nor a genuine work of Clement of Rome. It is an anonymous Christian sermon… written at some time before the middle of the second century; and while scholars differ widely on its place of origin, there are a number of indications that it stems from Egypt" (Cyril Richardson, *Early Christian Fathers* (New York: Simon & Schuster, 1995), p. 183).

[250] Harnack, *History of Dogma*, Vol. 1 (1894), p. 328.

3

ANOTHER JESUS

*"If a person comes and preaches some
other Jesus than the one we preached…
you put up with it easily enough!"*
— *Paul (2 Cor 11:4)*

T HE GREEKS WERE THE GREAT CHAMPIONS of the doctrine of
the immortal soul. Through their pervasive influence this notion, along
with the concept of the Demiurge, was rapidly assumed in various
religious groups beyond Greece. One family of thought particularly struck with
these doctrines was the early Christian Gnostic movement. "Gnosticism" is a
modern designation for a category of ancient religions that preached the soul's
salvation from the material world through the enlightenment of secret
knowledge. The origins of Gnosticism are still debated by scholars. Some have
speculated that it predates Christianity, with some even suggesting an origin in a
sector of dissatisfied Judaism.[251] But the discovery of the cache of Gnostic
literature in Nag Hammadi in 1945 has continued to propose revisions of pre-
Christian hypotheses.[252] Some scholars have even made the case that we should

---

[251] See Carl Smith, *No Longer Jews: The Search for Gnostic Origins* (Hendrickson Publishers, 2004).

[252] Hengel concludes that "there is no Gnostic redeemer myth in the sources which can be
demonstrated chronologically to be pre-Christian. This state of affairs should not be confused
with the real problem of a later Gnosticism standing apart from Christianity, as we find it, e.g. in
the Hermetica and in some of the Nag Hammadi writings. Gnosticism itself is first visible as a

abandon the category of "Gnosticism" altogether due to the cumbersome variety of sects which the label attempts to corral.[253] Others still find the category useful for describing "demiurgical" and basically dualistic forms of Christian and non-Christian movements.[254] Being well aware of the loose status of the terminology, we will continue to use the word "Gnostic" in this investigation for the purposes of comparison.[255]

But why is a consideration of Gnostic Christianity especially important to our analysis of Trinitarian evolution? The Greek and Latin Church Fathers tell us themselves that they are Platonists; that fact is already widely appreciated and has not concerned modern Christendom one iota. But all of the major Fathers whom Trinitarians hold in high esteem strongly condemn Gnostic Christology, as does the Apostle John in the New Testament. This is significant because, as we will see upon completion of our broader survey, the Christians we find utilizing some of the most peculiar metaphysical tenets of Trinitarianism in the first two centuries of the Church were, in fact, the Gnostics. Despite the historical condemnation of Gnosticism by the "proto-orthodox" tradition, it cannot now be denied that the Gnostic schools had "a far-reaching effect" on "the subsequent formation of Christian doctrine."[256] Indeed, much of later orthodox dogma really represents the consequences of proto-orthodoxy's early

---

spiritual movement at the end of the first century AD at the earliest, and only develops fully in the second century" (Martin Hengel, *The Son of God* (Eugene: Wipf & Stock, 1976), p. 34). See also J. M. Robinson, "Sethians and Johannine Thought," *The Rediscovery of Gnosticism,* Vol. 2 (Leiden: E.J. Brill, 1981), p. 662. The Nag Hammadi Library, a collection of twelve papyrus codices containing fifty-two Gnostic works written in Coptic, was found buried in jars the sands of Upper Egypt in 1945. The codices may have been hidden after Athanasius issued a ban on non-canonical literature in 367 CE. These works have lent considerable insight into the diverse nature of early Christianity, casting further doubt on the common narrative of a monolithic "orthodoxy" in the first few centuries of Christianity. Prior to their publication, scholarly understanding of Gnostic thought had been limited to the antagonistic heresiological writings of figures such as Irenaeus and Hippolytus.

[253] See Michael Williams, *Rethinking Gnosticism* (Princeton University Press, 1999).

[254] Dualism is usually cast as a fundamental feature of "Gnosticism." However, Valentinianism, the most influential form of Gnostic Christianity and a qualified monism, is an example of a major exception to that rule and may exemplify the difficulty of categorization.

[255] "[Williams'] recognition of gnostic diversity merely parallels the similar recognition by scholars of diversity in Judaism and Christianity. This recognition of diversity has led Jacob Neusner to suggest 'Judaisms' and Jonathan Z. Smith 'Christianities' as appropriate terms for these diverse religious movements. Perhaps we might also opt for 'gnosticisms' or 'gnostic religions' as a similar way of acknowledging the differences among religions of gnosis" (Willis Barnstone, Marvin Meyer, *The Gnostic Bible* (Boston: Shambhala, 2006), p. 14). Our usage of the word "Gnostic" seems also justified by the fact that, according to Irenaeus of Lyon, the Sethians described themselves as Gnostic. Here is "the historical basis for the use of Gnostic as a valid term of self-definition" (Ibid., p. 15).

[256] Rudolph, *Gnosis*, p. 369.

encounter with Gnosis. Christianity was likely able to retrace Gnostic theology in the fourth century only because it had been saturated in Gnostic concerns and sensibilities in the second and third. As we will see, this saturation was conveyed upon the wider Church primarily through the influence of the Alexandrian and Roman schools of Christianity. However, during this investigation we must keep in mind that exactly how early Gnosis affected later orthodoxy, and how it did not, is not always obvious. As scholar of Gnosticism Kurt Rudolph explains, "the connecting links often are 'subterranean' channels."[257] While there has certainly occurred a "retention of Gnostic positions in Christian theology," they were perpetuated only by "a kind of transformation (metamorphosis) of Gnostic ideas and traditions."[258] Many of mainstream Christianity's most treasured Christological ideas may in fact be owed to the Gnostics' early pressing of the historical Jesus through the pre-existing Platonic framework. Though most Christians have been taught that Gnostic thought is dangerous and heretical, the Jesus of orthodox Trinitarianism appears to have much more in common with the mystical Christ of Gnosticism than the apocalyptic Messiah-king of the Jews. To make matters worse, we have preserved for us in the New Testament evidence of a vehement opposition to Gnostic Christology by the early Church, an opposition accompanied by dire warnings against *antichrist*.

The Cosmic Jesus

The direct Apostolic conflict with the Gnostic movement is easily detected in the late first-century writings of the Apostle John.[259] Some have proposed that John even wrote his own Gospel between 80-90 CE[260] to battle the

---

[257] Ibid., p. 368.

[258] Ibid.

[259] Several Gnostic groups, which we do not have the space to examine here, arose among the Jews in the late first century CE. These factions included the Elkesaites, the Symmachians, the Gnostic-Ebionites, and others. For analysis of these movements, see Kurt Rudolph, *Gnosis: The Nature and History of Gnosticism* (Edinburgh: T & T Clark, 1983), p. 307; Harnack, *History of Dogma*, Vol. 1, Ch. VI, pp. 245-246, 301-317. The Church Fathers draw a great deal of attention to these groups, and loudly condemn them, but Klijin and Reinink demonstrate that their accounts of these Gnostic-Jewish-Christian factions "have little bearing on Jewish Christianity" (A. F. J. Klijn, G. J. Reinink, *Patristic Evidence for Jewish Christian Sects*, (Leiden: Brill, 1973), pp. 3-19, 52-67). The distinction between these groups and "Jewish Christianity" is both critical and undeniable. See Ray Pritz, *Nazarene Christianity* (Jerusalem: Hebrew University of Jerusalem Press, 1988). As Harnack notes, "The Jewish Christians took no considerable part in the Gnostic controversy, the epoch-making conflict which was raised within the pale of the larger Christendom" (Harnack, *History of Dogma*, Vol. 1, p. 290).

[260] For the early date see D. A. Carson, *The Gospel According to John* (Grand Rapids: Eerdmans, 1991), p. 86.

increasingly popular Gnostic theories,[261] but scholars are agreed that at least his complimentary epistles are supremely concerned with Gnostic refutation.[262]

But what did Gnostic Christians believe? What made them so dangerous? In essence, the various Christian Gnostic sects actively blended mystical Platonic, Egyptian, and eastern philosophies with Jewish and Christian teaching.[263] The Gnostics appear to have gathered from Plato the belief that the material, physical world was an inherently inferior plane created by a Demiurge, yet most of the Gnostic groups went one step further. While Plato had entertained a positive view of the Demiurge, the Gnostics believed this lesser creator was actually evil or incompetent, or both.[264] This was a serious break from the Platonic tradition. The Neoplatonists lambasted Gnostics as heretics who diverted too largely from Plato with their express hatred of the Demiurge and his material creation. Thus the Gnostics were viewed as heretical by both the Platonists and the earliest Christian community.[265]

---

[261] "But even if Irenaeus had not asserted that St. John wrote his Gospel against the Gnostics, and particularly against Cerinthus, the contents of the Gospel itself would lead to this conclusion. The speeches of Christ, which John has recorded, are selected with a totally different view from that of the three first evangelists... In the very choice of his expressions, such as 'light,' 'life,' etc. he had in view the philosophy of the Gnostics, who used or rather abused these terms... Unless John had an adversary to combat who made particular use of the words... he would not have thought it necessary" (J. D. Michaelis, quoted in Thomas Horne, *An Introduction to the Critical Study and Knowledge*, Vol. 2 (New York: Robert Carter, 1847), p. 316).

[262] Scholars have long confirmed that "it was the object of St. John in his Epistle to condemn certain doctrines of the Gnostics respecting Jesus Christ" (Ben David, *The Monthly Repository of Theology and General Literature*, Vol. 21 (Hackney: Sherwood, Gilbert, and Piper, 1826), p. 469).

[263] Some sects seem to have leaned more into Eastern-Asiatic traditions, while others appear to have embraced the revelations of the religious mind of the Alexandrian schools, like Platonism. The eastern-leaning sects likely favored Zoroastrianism, an ancient Persian religion which still enjoys millions of adherents today. In Zoroastrianism, two opposite divine forces were at work in the universe, "Progressive" and "Destructive." These forces were subjugated to a single supreme deity, Ahura Mazda, the divine embodiment of Wisdom. The dichotomy between good (spirit) and evil (matter) was a consistent theme in Gnostic thought. Of course, precisely which religious streams contributed to "Gnostic thought" and which did not, remains one of the greatest mysteries in the history of religion.

[264] This Creator god was wicked, ignorant, and even incapable of doing good. It was precisely his incompetence that landed the Gnostic soul in what he perceived to be bondage to the physical. This god was ultimately held responsible for the catastrophe in the Garden of Eden and in some Gnostic literature, such as the *Testimony of Truth*, Eve and the Serpent are even portrayed as heroes trying to outsmart the Creator. See Elaine Pagels, *The Gnostic Gospels* (New York: Vintage Books, 1979), pp. xiii-xxiii. The Valentinians are an exception here, as they are in many "Gnostic" matters, and view the Demiurge as a lesser, but still positive figure.

[265] See Plotinus, "Against the Gnostics," in *The Enneads*. Plotinus derides what he perceives as the foolishness of Gnostic escapism: "Furthermore, these teachers, in their contempt for this creation and this earth, proclaim that another earth has been made for them into which they are to enter when they depart. Now this new earth is the Reason-Form [the Logos] of our world. Why should they desire to live in the archetype of a world abhorrent to them?" (*Enneads*, 9, 5). Plotinus

The Gnostics held that the evil Demiurge creator was none other than Yahweh, the God of the Old Testament. Furthermore, since the world was created by the evil God of the Old Testament, all matter was inherently evil and should be shunned in pursuit of the immortal soul's liberation from the body through the illumination of spiritual knowledge (*gnosis*). The ultimate destiny of the enlightened Gnostic was a Platonic freedom from all matter and an existence as a bodiless being in a higher divine realm.[266]

The Gnostic vision of Jesus was certainly their most significant and infamous novelty. The fundamental Gnostic thesis was that Christ is by nature a spiritual being, even God.[267] Most Platonists, like Justin Martyr, drew a sharp distinction between the unchanging divine world and the changeable lower world, and could not conceive of the highest God coming down and uniting with humanity.[268] Thus for Justin, Christ was a demiurgical mediator between the worlds. But the Gnostics felt no such restriction. For them, Christ was actually an emanation of *the Supreme God*. This good God was directly opposed to the evil Demiurge creator, and had sent the Christ to travel down to our realm to save the human race from the Old Testament God's clutches. But this divine Christ, having not been created by the Demiurge, could not have actually come to them in material flesh (which would have been evil). The question for the Gnostics was, of course, how to account for the visible ministry of Jesus recorded in the Gospels. There were several ways in which the different schools attempted to solve this problem. The following represent the three major Gnostic Christologies which emerged before the middle of the second century:

1) *Docetism:* In this view, popularized by Marcion (85-160 CE), Christ was completely spiritual. The Savior only *seemed* to be in physical form, his image actually being a sort of phantasm. The docetic Jesus only appeared to suffer, only appeared to require food, only appeared to be crucified, since he was not truly a man, but a divine being clothed in the form of a man. This is by far the prevailing picture conjured by most popular considerations of Gnostic Christology.

---

ultimately challenges them that if they are so eager to leave this world, they should commit suicide. See Williams, *Rethinking Gnosticism*, pp. 134-135.

[266] Popular Christianity still propagates this notion in its teachings regarding man leaving the physical world and ascending to a higher spiritual plane upon death; i.e. "going to heaven." See Buzzard, *Our Fathers Who Aren't in Heaven*, 1999.

[267] Harnack, *History of Dogma*, Vol. 1 (1894), p. 193.

[268] See Broek, p. 197; Justin Martyr, *Dialouge with Trypho*, 60.

2) *Cerinthian possessionism:* In this view, popularized by Cerinthus (fl. 100 CE), the human "Jesus" and the divine "Christ" were two different entities. "Jesus" was not born of a virgin, but was the natural son of Mary and Joseph. "Christ" descended upon the man Jesus at his baptism and remained with him throughout his ministry. At the crucifixion, the Christ left Jesus so that the human being alone would experience death.

3) *Valentinianism:* The two school of Valentinus (100-160 CE) taught that Jesus descended from heaven with a special, uncorrupted human body. This Jesus was born through the virgin Mary, and was joined by the divine Christ either at birth or baptism. The human nature suffered pain and death, while the divine survived.[269]

Contrary to Gnostic teaching, the Apostle John held that the Creator of the Old Testament and Jesus were in perfect harmony, and that Jesus, by his very real humanity, was bound up with the material world God had created. To battle the Gnostics, John was forced to go back to the *beginning* and testify that even before Creation, God had a divine idea or wise plan for the world, an intention that was fully representative of his own goodness. In opposition to the Gnostic Christ who came to *change course* on the old Creator's program, John's Jesus is the very spiritual center of the Creator's objective for the world. That it was the wisdom and purpose of the Creator which finally became manifest in the person and work of Jesus Christ is likely what is explained in the famous prologue of John 1:1-5, 14.[270]

In his epistles, John writes against docetic Gnostic Christology, saying, "*every spirit that confesses that Jesus Christ has come in the flesh is of God... every spirit that does not confess that Jesus Christ has come in the flesh is not of God*" (1 Jn 4:2-3). John argued that Jesus truly came to them "*in sarx*" or "in the compass of humanity" or "as a human being."[271] In other words, John's position is that the real Jesus had

---

[269] This represents the school of "Western" Valentinianism, exhibited by Ptolemy and Heracleon. The Valentinian Christology was in reality free and diverse; the view of the "Eastern" school may even be considered partly docetic in the sense that there appears to be only one divine Christ who assumes a purely spiritual body and is born through the virgin.

[270] John's usage of the logos terminology will follow in the later half of this book.

[271] While the NASB translates "sarx" as "body" it also translates it as "man." One definition from *Thayer's Lexicon* reads: "a living creature... specifically, a man... human nature, the soul included." John's Christ comes merely in "a" flesh, that is, Jesus does not employ an impersonal

enjoyed material existence as a genuinely *human* entity and therefore was not the docetic emanation of the Gnostics. For John, the person of Jesus belonged unequivocally to the sphere of humanity.[272]

Despite the Apostolic effort, elements of the Gnostic Jesus appear to have lingered in the wider Christian world, especially in Alexandria, into the third century and beyond. We now know that a "philosophical interpretation" of the Christian religion was already thriving in Alexandria by the second century, and in the opinions of the most famous voices within that syncretistic milieu we may detect Gnostic artifacts. Clement of Alexandria (150-215 CE) and Origen (184-254 CE), though acknowledging Christ's corporeality, appear to shy away from a full and normative human experience. Origen taught that "the mortal quality of Jesus' body [was] ethereal and divine," and that the matter of his body would change form depending on who was looking at him.[273] The Gnostic Valentinus likewise said that "Christ's flesh was spiritual,"[274] and that Jesus "ate and drank, but did not defecate."[275] The Christian Clement also writes:

> it [is] ridiculous to suppose that the body demanded, as a body,
> the necessary aids for its maintenance. For He ate, not for the
> sake of the body, which had its continuance from a holy

---

body as a vehicle, as an abstraction attached to a divine person. Rather, the state in which the Jesus of history lived and operated was *"in the flesh,"* that is, as a real human being. Real humanity presupposes not an abstract flesh or experience, but real human personhood and psychology.

[272] We must emphasize that John does not use "sarx" as an encapsulation of anachronistic Trinitarian doctrine. We should draw no other conclusion from his polemic than the simple acknowledgment that Jesus was really a human being. In the Trinitarian Albert Barnes' classic notes on 1 Jn 4:2 we find an interesting struggle: Barnes first concludes that John was simply arguing *"that the Son of God was really a man."* This succinct and appropriate assessment is, however, immediately contradicted by Barnes' secondary speculation that John might have also been saying that a divine being *"actually assumed human nature in permanent union with the divine."* This is, of course, speculation. Later Barnes summarizes: *"The point of the remark made by the apostle is, that the acknowledgment was to be that Christ assumed human nature; that he was really a man as he appeared to be."* This is, again, correct. But Barnes once more feels the need to add, *"or that there was a real incarnation* [of a divine being]." Trinitarian commentators often feel the need to affix an additional polemic to John's doctrinal statement, though John himself only demands that Jesus be thought of as a real human being. There is nothing unequivocally demanded by the Apostle here regarding Incarnation, that is, of an additional divine nature being present alongside the human.

[273] Origen, *Against Celsus*, 3, 41. Origen says that Jesus' material body "at one time possesses a quality of which it is said 'He had not form or beauty,' and at another time a quality so glorious and striking and wonderful" that the Apostles fell on their faces (*Against Celsus*, 6, 77). Chadwick writes: "That this tradition had Gnostic origin is suggested by the [Gnostic text] *Acts of John*, 93, where St. John says, 'Sometimes when I would lay hold on him, I met with a material and solid body, and at other times, again, when I felt him, the substance was immaterial and as if it existed not at all' " (Henry Chadwick, *Origen: Contra Celsum* (Cambridge: CUP, 1980 [1953]), p. 390).

[274] Tertullian, *De Carne Christi*, 15, 1.

[275] Douglas Biow, *The Culture of Cleanliness* (London: Cornell University Press, 2006), p. 146.

power, but lest those in His company might happen to think otherwise of Him... He was in general dispassionate; and no movement of feeling penetrated Him, whether pleasure or pain.[276]

Of course, these ideas seem difficult to reconcile with the teaching of the New Testament, namely that Jesus was "*like his brethren in all things*" (Heb 2:17 NASB), "*fully human in every way*" (NIV), and "*a high priest who* [can] *sympathize with our weaknesses*" (Heb 4:15 NASB). Like the Gnostics' docetic Christ and the quasi-human figure of many Alexandrian Christians, so too does the later Trinitarian Jesus of fourth-century orthodoxy seem questionable in light of the New Testament description; his is an incomprehensible existence as a supreme being bearing multiple natures, minds, and wills—an otherworldly intelligence without beginning or end who lies not in the genuine peril of other men but is himself the very almighty God. We shall see in this and later chapters how from the first few centuries through the Reformation and into the modern era, Christianity has never resolved the contradiction of Christ's opposing natures in a way that has proven both ecumenically durable and able to avoid the pitfalls of Gnostic Christology.

Docetism in the Orthodox Jesus

First, we will consider the latent docetism in orthodoxy's view of Jesus' humanity. Orthodoxy teaches that the second Person of the Trinity, an eternally pre-existent God-the-Son, traveled down to earth to unite with "a human nature."[277] However, it is said that the human nature did not confer its own person; there were not two persons in Christ. The orthodox Council of Ephesus convened in 431 CE precisely to deal with this matter, and confirmed that Christ was only one person—one person with two natures. Because of this, Trinitarians have acknowledged that the Son simply took on an "*impersonal human nature*" at the Incarnation.[278] One modern Trinitarian scholar admits: "The humanity taken up into the person of the logos is, then, not a personal

---

[276] William A. Jugens, *The Faith of the Early Fathers*, Vol. 1. (Collegeville: The Liturgical Press, 1970), p. 184.

[277] Thomas Ridgley, *A Body of Divinity*, Vol. I (Philadelphia: William W. Woodward, 1814), pp. 288-289.

[278] A. E. Whatham, "The Psychology of the Incarnation," *The Church Eclectic*, Vol. 26 (Chicago: University of Chicago, 1898), pp. 822-824.

man but human nature without personal subsistence."[279] Christ is therefore not to be thought of as *a man*, but a personality-less abstraction united with God.

Saint Thomas Aquinas (1225-1274 CE), one of the most influential Trinitarian theologians of all time, wrote, in his reply to objections against the Incarnation, that the Logos "has not its [personality] from its human nature, but rather draws that human nature to its own subsistence or personality... Yes (Christ) is a person, but no other person than the person of the [Logos]."[280] Aquinas also reveals this understanding amongst the Trinity's developers: "And with this the sayings of some ancient Doctors agree, who have laid it down that the human nature in Christ is an instrument of His divinity, as the body is an instrument of the soul."[281] One scholar's important footnote on this comment reveals that this Trinitarian understanding "is founded rather upon a Platonic view of the relation between soul and body; which, considering the devotion of the ancient Fathers, of the Alexandrines particularly, to Plato, is not surprising."[282] But the ancient Trinitarians and the medieval Trinitarians like Aquinas are not the only ones to understand this; modern apologists like those at the popular Desiring God ministries, led by theologian John Piper, wholeheartedly agree:

> The kind of humanity Jesus took in the incarnation was impersonal. He did not add a human person to himself... His humanity is not only impersonal (anhypostasis), but it's also in-personal (that's what enhypostasis means), in that its personhood is in the personhood of the eternal second person of the Trinity. The fully divine Son is the person.[283]

Quite plainly, if we adhere to strict orthodoxy, then we must admit that *the human person* Jesus does not even exist—the "humanity" is only an abstraction that God's pre-existing substance entangles itself with. One judicious Professor of Divinity at Cambridge reveals the great danger in traveling down the road which orthodox Christology invariably leads—a subtle embrace of the docetic Jesus:

---

279 Heinrich Heppe, *Reformed Dogmatics* (Eugene: Wipf & Stock Publishers, 2007), p. 416
280 Thomas Aquinas, *Summa Contra Gentiles*, 4.
281 Ibid.
282 Joseph Rickaby, *Saint Thomas Aquinas' Of God and His Creatures: An Annotated Translation* (London: Burns & Oates, 1905), p. 373.
283 David Mathis, "Enhypostasis: What Kind of Flesh Did the Word Become?" Desiring God. 25 December 2010. Web. 27 July 2015.

The Christological concept of the preexistent divine Son reduces the real social and culturally conditioned personality of Jesus to the metaphysical abstraction "human nature"... Human nature, according to the classical Alexandrine tradition, was enhypostatized in the divine Person of the Son; it became the human nature of a divine personal subject... According to this Christology the eternal Son assumes a timeless human nature, or makes it timeless by making it his own; it is human nature which owes nothing essential to geographical circumstances; it corresponds to nothing in the actual concrete world; Jesus [in this view] has not, after all, really "come in the flesh."[284]

Buzzard's note on Lampe's conclusion is important: "I hardly need to point out that the learned professor's strictures imply that the traditional view of Jesus as having a divine personal center or ego united to an impersonal human nature ranks as the antichristian view condemned by John in 1 John 4:2 and 2 John 7."[285]

Indeed, John taught that the person named Jesus Christ was truly a human being,[286] and the Bible describes Jesus as plainly "*a man*" many times (Acts 2:22, John 8:40).[287] But note the careful wording of today's Trinitarian apologists: "Jesus Christ is God and *man*,"[288] that is, he is not *a* man. J. I. Packer confirms that in the orthodox Jesus we have "the union of Godhead and *manhood*."[289] We will allow the Trinitarian to spell it out further:

Jesus has not always been *man*. The fantastic miracle is that this eternal God became man at the Incarnation approximately 2,000 years ago. That's what the Incarnation was—God the

---

[284] Geoffery Lampe, *God as Spirit* (Norwich: SCM Press, 1977), p. 144.

[285] Anthony Buzzard, "What's in a Word?" Focus on the Kingdom. Web. 27 February 2015. <http://focusonthekingdom.org/articles/word.htm>.

[286] Jesus is described throughout the NT as "aner" (a male human being, a man), and "anthropos" (a man, one of the human race). Again, we recall Barnes' primary summary of 1 Jn 4:2 as intending "*that the Son of God was really a man.*" We must be careful to accept only what John provides, that is, only an acknowledgment of the Christ as a real human being, and even more careful to avoid inserting the dual-natured incarnational Christology of the Valentinian Gnostics into the mouth of the very Apostle who wrote to defeat the Gnostic view.

[287] Biblical statements in which Jesus is explicitly "a man" include: Luke 24:19, John 1:30, John 3:27, John 8:40, Acts 2:22, Acts 17:31, Romans 5:15, 1 Cor 15:21, 1 Cor 15:47, 1 Tim 2:5.

[288] Matt Perman, "How Can Jesus Be God and Man?" Desiring God. 5 October 2006. Web. 25 July 2015, emphasis added.

[289] J.I. Packer, *Knowing God* (Downers Grove: IVP, 1993), p. 53.

Son becoming *man*. But what exactly do we mean when we say that God the Son became man? We certainly do not mean that He turned into *a* man... Jesus did not give up any of His divine attributes at the Incarnation... [the Incarnation is God] taking *manhood* to Himself.[290]

The essence of the docetic Christology of the Gnostics was also that the Christ is *not* "*a* man" but God who took on the form of a man to himself. In the Cerinthian and Valentinian Christologies too, Christ is not "*a* man," but God who has eclipsed a human being and subjected his properties to his divine personal center while preserving a complete and functional human nature. All of these Gnostic Christologies align with Christian orthodoxy on this point: the divine Savior was not "*a* man" but God united with human qualities (either psychic or real).

John Against Cerinthus

The Apostle John's Christological polemics can certainly be taken as direct refutations of the docetic view. However, he may also aim to refute the "possessionism" of Cerinthus, which Cerinthus probably did not invent himself but came to be its champion.[291] Again, Cerinthus had taught that the Christ descended upon Jesus at his baptism: "Jesus Christ" was not one person, but two—"Jesus" had come in the flesh, but "Christ" had not come in the flesh. John appears to write against this distinction, saying: *"many deceivers have gone out into the world, those who do not acknowledge Jesus Christ as coming in the flesh. This is the deceiver and the antichrist"* (2 John 1:7). That Cerinthian Christology was the target, or an additional target of John here is reinforced by the historian Irenaeus, who mentions a personal conflict between John and Cerinthus.[292] John's writings, including his Gospel, were indeed thought by the Fathers to be specifically "an

---

[290] Perman, emphasis added.

[291] Hippolytus says that Cerinthus was first educated in Egyptian wisdom. Irenaeus appears to find his origins in Asia, however, and Irenaeus' story of Cerinthus' conflict with John takes place in Ephesus. See C. Wilfred Griggs, *Early Egyptian Christianity: From Its Origins to 451 CE* (Leiden: Brill, 2000), p. 47.

[292] See Irenaeus, *Against Heresies*, 3, 11, 1-2. According to Irenaeus, Polycarp related a story passed on to him by the Apostle John: John had once entered a bathhouse in Ephesus, and upon seeing that Cerinthus was inside, got up and rushed out of the building saying, "Let us fly, lest even the bath-house fall down, because Cerinthus, the enemy of truth, is within" (Ibid., 3, 3, 4).

antidote to this heresy,"[293] and there are reasons to appreciate this view. Consider John's explicit reason for the Fourth Gospel: *"these things have been written so that you may believe that Jesus is the Christ, the Son of God, and that believing you may have life in his name"* (John 20:31), and this aligns with sentiments in his anti-Gnostic epistle (1 John 5:13). For John, Jesus and the Christ are one and the same entity, and that entity is truly human.

When modern Christians think of Gnostic Christology, and John's argument against it, they often think of a pure docetism, which denied the humanity altogether. But the overarching concern of John is simply that the human person named "Jesus Christ" was being compromised by his association with a divine being, and this is accomplished by all of the Gnostic Christologies. What is especially noteworthy for our study is the fact that neither Cerinthus nor Valentinus denied the humanity of the Savior; the humanity dwelled alongside the divinity and played an important role in the salvific work. John writing against a Cerinthian vision, and therefore against a Christology which distinguishes between the truly human and the truly divine in the Savior, may have serious implications for orthodox Christianity.

The Valentinian Christ

It is in Valentinian Gnosticism where we find the most alarming connections to orthodox Christology. Valentinianism, the most popular and widespread of the Christian Gnostic schools, was founded by the brilliant and eloquent Gnostic teacher Valentinus (d. 160 CE) in the first half of the second century. Valentinus first studied in Egypt and left to teach in Rome around 136 CE,[294] and the influence of the large and diverse sect that learned from him (and which often elaborated far beyond his original vision) has yet to be adequately appreciated on a large scale. As modern scholars reveal, "far from being a local sect with limited appeal, Valentinian adherents *permeated* Christianity."[295] They were without doubt one of the most dangerous enemies of the proto-orthodox Christians, and Justin, Irenaeus, Hippolytus, and Tertullian each wrote spirited, almost desperate pleas to the Christian world to resist their theology. Hippolytus reports that there was actually a division among the Valentinians; they were evidently split into rough geographies of East and West, and Hippolytus informs us that this division of the schools was over the particulars of the incredible Valentinian

---

[293] J. B. Lightfoot, *The Apostolic Fathers, Part II: S. Ignatius, S. Polycarp* (London: Macmillan and Co., 1889), pp. 379-383.

[294] "Valentius (Gnostic)," *Encyclopedia Britannica*, 1911. Web. 29 September 2014.

[295] Griggs, p. 55, emphasis added.

Christology.[296] Valentinus himself, evidently resembling the "Eastern" view, had presented a different Gnostic Jesus. Again, in the docetism described thus far, the Christ did not actually have a real body, but only appeared to have one to the deficient intellects of those around him. In the Cerinthian view, Jesus, the real human son of Joseph and Mary, was temporarily possessed by God at his baptism. But in the system of Valentinus, the divine Christ *did* have a body, and this body had been born through the virgin Mary. One dictionary records that:

> It appears that Valentinus was only partly docetic. He conceded to Jesus the possession of a real body capable of really affecting the senses... [He argued] that if our Lord had not taken substance of flesh in the womb of the Virgin, he could not have been the real man who suffered hunger and thirst and weariness, who wept at the grave of Lazarus, who sweat drops of blood, from whose wounded side came forth blood and water.[297]

According to this family of Gnostic thought, "the Incarnation and contact with the physical body was real... they stressed the link between the divine and human elements in Christ."[298]

In the Eastern Valentinian view, the uniting of these elements began in the highest heaven: the angelic Aeons (powers of God) had collaboratively produced

---

[296] Hippolytus, *Refutation of All Heresies*, 6, 35. Modern scholars likewise often make a distinction between "Eastern" or "Asiatic" Valentinianism and "Italian" or "Western" Valentinianism. Kalvesmaki, in his 2008 article, challenged this geographical division on the basis of unreliable historical testimony (Joel Kalvesmaki, "Italian versus Eastern Valentinianism?" Vigilae Christianae, Vol. 62 (Leiden: Brill, 2008), pp. 79-89). Regardless, in this alleged "Eastern" version (apparently the older view), Christ had a spiritual, *pneumatic* body only. In the Western, Christ had both a spiritual and *psychic* body. The reasons for this distinction were soteriological: the Gnostics claimed to have pneumatic natures, while the non-Gnostic Christians had *psychic* natures—the non-Gnostics Christians required a *psychic* Jesus to rescue them on the cross. The Western branch thus believed Christians could be saved even without *gnosis,* but the *hylic* (material) peoples, non-Christians, were without redemption. See R. van den Broek, *Gnostic Religion in Antiquity* (Cambridge: CUP, 2013), pp. 193ff.

[297] William C. Piercy, Henry Wace (ed.), "Docetism," *A Dictionary of Christian Biography and Literature to the End of the Sixth Century A.D., with an Account of the Principal Sects and Heresies.* (Peabody: Hendrickson Publishers, 1999), p. 272. See also Valentinus, *Letter to Agathopus,* ap. Clem. Alex. *Strom.* III. 7, 451. There is an obvious and startling resemblance here to the orthodox presentation of Jesus; a bodily human nature that can suffer affixed to a divine and transcendent God.

[298] Piotr Ashwin-Siejkowski, *Clement of Alexandria on Trial* (Leiden: Brill, 2010), p. 108. One mysterious Gnostic work titled *Melchizedek* reveals that some Gnostics were using Jesus' eating and suffering as evidence against a purely docetic view. This demonstrates their "awareness of the alternative (docetic) models and teaching" that contrasted with their dual-nature view.

a new divine entity, Jesus, and sent him down through the heavens. As he descended into our world, the Aeon named Acamoth (the lower Sophia) gave him an uncorrupted human body that was "made in such a way that it was visible and tangible and could suffer."[299]

According to the Western Valentinians, however, it was actually the Demiurge (a more positive figure in this system) who constructed his human body. Eventually, this Jesus passed into and through the womb of the virgin "like water through a tube."[300] In the Western system, it was at the baptism of this specially-made human Jesus that the Demiurge clothed him with the divine Christ. While the human Jesus and the divine Christ were two distinct personalities, at the Incarnation it was the celestial ego, the one divine Person of Christ, who became the operative center of the two entities.[301] Both of these entities' natures were to exercise diverse and critical duties during the Savior's earthly life. Modern Gnostic historians recognize that:

> [Valentinian] understanding of his incarnation places great emphasis on both his human and divine nature. The human Jesus alone died on the cross since the divine transcends pain and death. This is distinctly different from "docetism." Valentinians never claimed that Jesus only appeared to suffer or that his body was an apparition.[302]

Indeed, Valentinian theologians describe Jesus as having come down precisely "in order to enter the cosmic region and share 'in human likeness' the 'weakness' of the human condition."[303] The parallels between the Valentinian Christology and what eventually manifested as orthodoxy two centuries later are striking: just as in later orthodoxy, the Valentinians had understood the suffering and death of Jesus as taking place in his humanity only,[304] and despite the survival of the divine person, it was only the divine person who qualified to make the redemption for sins.[305] The divine thus experienced the grief of death,

---

[299] Broek, *Gnostic Religion in Antiquity*, p. 194. The body the Son took on, though specially made, was still completely human and able to undergo the fullness of human experience. Ibid., p. 193.

[300] Irenaeus, *Against Heresies*, 1, 7, 2.

[301] J. L. Mosheim, *Historical Commentaries on the State of Christianity During the First Three Hundred and Twenty-Five Years,* Vol. 1 (New York: Converse, 1851), p. 467.

[302] David Brons, "The Role of Jesus in Valentinianism," The Gnostic Society Library. Web. 25 July 2015.

[303] Elaine Pagels, *The Gnostic Paul: Gnostic Exegesis of the Pauline Letters* (New York: Bloomsbury, 1992), p. 147.

[304] See Irenaeus, *Against Heresies*, 1, 7, 2.

[305] See *Interpretation of Knowledge* 12:29-31.

but not death itself.[306] Incredibly, the underlying framework of the Valentinian Christology closely resembles the basic position of modern Trinitarians today: Christ was a divine entity, a hypostasis of the Supreme God, who literally came down from heaven and enjoyed two complete natures; one by which he might exert all the miraculous and salvific prerogatives of the Supreme God, and the other yielding a true human experience and a body capable of hunger, pain, and death.

So what does all of this mean? Essentially, a widely influential heretical sect had promoted a highly developed doctrine of the dual natures of Jesus long before the ecumenical councils of the Catholic Church ever met. At every step, the comparison becomes more concerning: one Valentinian document declares that Christ was *"possessing the humanity and the divinity... originally from above... before this structure of the cosmos came into being,"*[307] while later orthodox Trinitarian statements also read that Christ was possessing *"divinity and humanity together"*[308] and was *"begotten of the Father before all worlds."*[309] Should we be alarmed by this harmony? The Apostle John denounced those who were arguing for (some form of) Christ's deity as *antichrist.*[310] Of course the modern Trinitarian affirms that John denies the deity of Jesus in the Gnostic sense, but claims John must have approved of it in the Trinitarian sense. Despite this speculation, however, the fact remains that John countered the Gnostic teaching about Jesus' deity with only a firm and unadorned assertion of his *humanity.*[311]

---

[306] In the work *Acts of John* (2nd century CE), probably edited by the Valentinian Leucius, Christ reveals: "What [non-Gnostic Christians] say of me, I did not endure, but what they do not say, those things I did suffer" (*Acts of John*, 101).

[307] *Treatise on the Resurrection (Letter to Rheginus)*, 44.

[308] *Second Epistle of St. Cyril to Nestorius*, Council of Ephesus, 431 CE.

[309] Niceno-Constantinopolitan Creed, 381 CE.

[310] See J. A. T. Robinson, *Twelve More New Testament Studies* (London: SCM Press, 1984), p. 142.

[311] See one scholar's extended argument on this point: "The doctrine of the divinity of Christ originated with the worst enemies of the gospel, as a specious plea for destroying the gospel itself... Some of the Gnostics allowed that Jesus was the Christ, but that he was a God in the empty form or the appearance of a man. These were called docetae... The other class, of which the leading men were Cerinthus and Simon, taught that Jesus was not the Christ; but that the Christ was *God*, which descended upon Jesus at his baptism, resided upon him during his ministry, and then fled off before his crucifixion... [the first group] taught that this God constituted the Christ, and rejected the man Jesus... The Cerinthians [and the Valentinians], then, maintained that Christ was *God*; John, that he was *the Son of God*. With this view he wrote his epistle... to prove that Jesus is the Son of God, in opposition to the Gnostics, who taught that Christ was God... John then wrote to prove that Christ was a real man, and wrote against those who taught his divinity. How then can it be that he does not condemn all doctrines whatever of Christ's divinity, when he calls those who taught his divinity *liars, false prophets,* and *antichrist?* ... [Trinitarians] affirm that John, while he denies the divinity of Christ in the Gnostic sense, asserts it in the orthodox sense. My position on the other hand is, that the apostle in affirming the *real* humanity of Christ,

But how could it be that Gnostic views were ever taken up as orthodox in the later Church? Were not the Gnostics publically and repeatedly condemned by the *real* Christians? Today, scholars have begun to shed light on the questionable (Gnostic) past of Alexandria, the empire's greatest academic center. We now realize that Egyptian Christianity in the second and third century was "very open and was characterized by a pluriformity of currents within the one Church."[312] It is interesting that there is no evidence whatsoever that Gnostic masters like Valentinus and Basilides were ever expelled from the Egyptian Church during their careers.[313] Indeed this should surprise us, because both Basilides and Valentinus openly taught the Gnostic doctrine of the inferior Demiurge, that the God of the Jewish Bible was not the highest God, a teaching which would have immediately repulsed the Christians of that region if they were not largely Gnosticized. Remembering how important the Alexandrians were in the laying down of Christology at Nicaea (325 CE), we already begin to wonder if we will discover in Alexandria a mediating party between the condemned Gnosticism and orthodox Christianity, a mediating party which could later reintroduce a reformulated Gnostic Jesus to the wider Christian world.

The Gnostic Cross and the Two Persons

We may further discover Gnostic Christology lingering in Christianity when we consider many modern Trinitarians' view of the crucifixion. Particularly in evangelical circles we often hear the claim that it was merely Christ's *humanity* that died on the cross. Popular Reformed theologian R. C. Sproul confirms that the Second Person of the Trinity was spared real death, and that we should "shrink in horror" from the idea that the divine entity died on the cross.[314] Other evangelical outlets agree: "death is something that is experienced only by the human nature… The Son, the second Person of the Trinity, left the body He temporarily inhabited on Earth, but His divine nature did not die, nor could it."[315] Indeed, this opinion has been rampant amongst evangelical scholars: "On

---

affirms his simple humanity, and in denying his divinity in *one* sense, denies it *every sense*" (Ben David, *The Monthly Repository of Theology and General Literature*, p. 469, emphasis added).

[312] Gilles Quispel, "Origen and Valentinian Gnosis," *Gnostica, Judaica, Catholica* (Leiden: Brill, 2008), p. 291, 293.

[313] Ibid.

[314] R. C. Sproul, "Did God Die on the Cross?" Ligonier Ministries. 14 April 2014. Web. 27 October 2014.

[315] "Did God Die?" Got Questions Ministries. Web. 16 December 2014.

the cross the divine spiritual nature left the body it had possessed."[316]   In this, Trinitarians have taken expressly to the Gnostic view, for according to both the Cerinthian and Valentinian Gnostics: "before Jesus died (since the divine cannot die), the Christ left him."[317]   This was why, according to their exegesis, the crucified Jesus cried out, *"My God, my God, why have you forsaken me?"* (Matt 27:46).

Both the Gnostics and the Trinitarians, with their distinction of humanity and divinity in the Savior, embark upon a dangerous question when it comes to the cross: Who died? Was it *the human nature* of Jesus that was destroyed, or the *person* of Jesus? As we have seen, the human nature owned by the Christ of orthodoxy is an abstraction owing nothing to the relatable world. Can such a thing pay for sins? Can it even *die?* The New Testament is clear that it was *"the Son of God"* that died (Rom 5:10, 8:32; Jn 3:16). Indeed, it is the self-sacrificial death of the *person* of Jesus that qualifies to make propitiation. But in both the docetic and the Valentinian Christologies, the divine Person does not truly expire; it is either a human image, or a distinguishable human person that perishes. Likewise in the Trinitarian view, the Person of the Son ultimately escapes destruction. If the Trinitarian Son of God does not ultimately survive the cross, then the Son is not proven to be immortal, co-eternal, and essential to the Godhead by nature; the orthodox Trinity itself is extinguished with his final breath. As Sproul agrees: "If God dies, everything dies with him. Obviously, then, God could not have perished on the cross."[318] But as Aquinas confirmed that the only person in the Trinitarian Jesus is the person of God, it is clear to us now that no one has even died on the cross at all.

This makes obvious and serious trouble for the atonement, and only edges orthodoxy into dangerous alignment with the Gnostics they condemn. Just as the Valentinian Christ experienced the grief of death, but did not actually die, Grudem concurs that the orthodox Christ *"somehow tasted something of what it was like* to go through death. The person of Christ *experienced* death."[319] As the Gnostic crucifixion was no real or meaningful death for the divine Person, but an illusion, so the Trinitarian vision too is only a sleight of hand, a substitution of the historical Son of God for an empty human nature—a reflection.

---

[316] Frederic Dan Huntington (ed.), *The Monthly Religious Magazine*, Vol. 15 (Boston: Leonard C. Bowles, 1856), p. 198.

[317] Ehrman, *Lost Christianities*, p. 15.

[318] Sproul, "Did God Die on the Cross?"

[319] Wayne Grudem, *Systematic Theology: An Introduction to Biblical Doctrine* (Downer's Grove: InterVarsity Press, 1994), p. 556.

Apologetically, modern Trinitarians have not been as successful as the Cerinthians and the Valentinians on this point. Evangelical arguments for the deity of Christ often feature the claim that *if Jesus were not God, his death could not have paid for sins.*[320] But according to the New Testament, God is *"immortal"* (1 Tim 6:16), and this simply means that whatever "dying" is, God cannot do it. Both the Gnostics and the Trinitarians know this, but the former prove the more reasonable by making "Christ" a different person than "Jesus." For the Gnostics, it is precisely because they believe in the deity of Christ that they are forced to keep the Christ from death and to confine that destruction to another entity. The evangelical's apology is conclusively spoiled here: he likewise keeps the Person of God from perishing, but at the same time asserts his perishing as necessary for human redemption. Thus the last resort of orthodoxy is found in that famous hymn: "'Tis *mystery* all! The immortal dies!"[321] But it is not merely the atonement that is cast into shadow here, but the entire Christian life. The historical fact that *"Christ died"* (Rom 14:9) is both the New Testament believer's motivation for today, and his hope for tomorrow: *"For if we believe that Jesus died and rose again even so God will bring with him those who have fallen asleep"* (1 Thess 4:14). But the salvific act of Jesus is made unintelligible, and unbelievable, so long as the person of Jesus is made immortal. In this, the Cerinthian and Valentinian model succeeds and the orthodox concept of the Incarnation is devoid of any practical religious meaning.

In the later history of the Church, the affirmation of the deity of Christ did not cease to beg for a "Valentinian" distinction of persons within the Savior. This is the conclusion which the Gnostic thesis, that Christ is by nature God, inevitably draws, and one which ecumenical Trinitarianism to this day has yet to adequately circumvent. As we will cover in detail later, orthodox rulings at the councils of Constantinople (381 CE, 680 CE) actually decreed that within Jesus dwelled not only the divine Person of the Logos, but also another *"rational human soul."* This meant that the Savior's human nature had retained a human mind and a human will, in addition to his divine mind and divine will. Nevertheless, they said, there was still only one person in Jesus—one divine Person. Of course, it is still very hard to see how a full human nature, a human

---

[320] "The most important reason that Jesus has to be God is that if He is not God, His death would not have been sufficient to pay the penalty for the sins of the world… Only God could pay such an infinite penalty. Only God could take on the sins of the world, die, and be resurrected" (S. Michael Houdmann, *Got Questions? Bible Questions Answered* (Bloomington: Westbow Press, 2014), p. 41).

[321] Charles Wesley, "And Can it Be," *Psalms and Hymns* (1738).

mind, and a human will do not constitute another human person in Jesus. For this reason, the notion that Christ had a human soul was resisted in the earlier phases of development. When Origen, in the third century, taught that Christ also had a human soul, he was accused by his contemporaries of preaching two Christs. This was, according to his critics, "the logical outcome of his thesis that the God-man possessed a human soul."[322] This great tension over the possibility of two persons in the Savior was never lost, even as Christ's human soul eventually won its way into orthodoxy. In response to this, the fourth-century "heretical" theologian Apollinaris was compelled to teach that Christ did *not* have a human rational soul (mind and will), but only a divine.[323] He realized the implications of the orthodox system: the two minds, two wills, and two natures in the Savior were, despite any sophistry, really two persons. Some evangelical authorities today have likewise realized this.[324] But Apollinaris, with his assertion of only one divine mind in Jesus, was condemned by the orthodox—the rational human soul was to remain alongside the divine in Christ. Thus the Valentinian Savior, composed of rational human and divine entities, would likewise survive, albeit in an orthodox guise.

Of course, Trinitarians will protest that they do not put two persons in Christ like the Valentinians. For example, evangelicals have pointed out that the orthodox Jesus "never speaks of himself as *We,* but always as *I.*"[325] But the Valentinian Christ, even with his two persons, also speaks as *"I"*. The division of both the Gnostic and orthodox Christs is subterranean. As Irenaeus said of the Valentinians, "Certainly they confess with their tongues the one Jesus Christ, but in their minds they divide him."[326] In both the orthodox and Valentinian Saviors

---

[322] J. N. D. Kelly, *Early Christian Doctrines* (Peabody: Prince Press, 2007 [1960]), p. 160.

[323] "Apollinaris believed that the incarnation of God in Jesus Christ could easily be explained by saying that he was a human body and soul (animating life force) without a human rational soul (mind, spirit); in Jesus Christ, Apollinaris argued, the place of a human rational soul or spirit was filled by the divine Logos/Word, the eternal Son of God, the second person of the Trinity" (Roger E. Olson, *The Mosaic Belief: Twenty Centuries of Unity & Diversity* (Downers Grove: InterVarsity Press, 2002), p. 239).

[324] See William Lane Craig, "Monotheletism," Reasonable Faith. 21 September 2008. Web. 20 July 2015.

[325] Perman argues: "by virtue of the union of the natures in one Person, the things that are true of and done by only one of Christ's natures are nonetheless true of and done by the Person of Christ. In other words, things which only one nature does can be considered to have been done by Christ himself. Likewise, things that are true of one nature but not the other are true of the Person of Christ as a whole. What this means, in simple terms, is that if there is something that only one of Christ's natures did, he can still say, 'I did it' " (Perman, "How Can Jesus Be God and Man?").

[326] Irenaeus, *Against Heresies*, 3, 16.

there are two souls, but only *one* ego dominates: the divine Person.[327]   As
Mosheim explains, the Gnostics evidently delegated the psychology of the Savior
to the divine out of fear that the dominance of the human mind could have led
Christ into temptation and sin.[328]   This same process, the celestial ego eclipsing
the human in order to complete the redemptive mission, also takes place in the
orthodox Jesus. If this is not the case, then Jesus did not really have to be divine
in order to be sinless; this common Trinitarian argument for the necessity of the
Incarnation is made useless by the fact that Jesus could have been a human being
without divine faculties and completed the saving work.[329]   In reality, the only
practical difference between Valentinian Gnosticism and orthodoxy on this point
of the two natures and two rational souls is the fact that the former's
presentation of two distinct persons is admitted and undeniable, while the latter's
is suspect and debatable.[330]

Ultimately, considering the Gnostic Savior, should we not worry at the hazy
recognition of this mystical figure propped upon the pedestal of popular
Christianity?   Rudolph makes an important observation regarding the
encroachment of the Gnostic Jesus upon the Christian mind of the second and
third centuries, and the dangerous affiliation which Gnosticism and orthodoxy
acquired through the later synodic enshrining of dogma:

> The early Christian fathers, foremost Irenaeus and Tertullian,
> strove hard to find forms which make intelligible, in a non-
> Gnostic sense, the prevailing division of the one Jesus Christ.
> Strictly speaking they did not succeed. Already [German
> historian Adolf] Harnack was forced to say: "*Who can maintain
> that the Church ever overcame the Gnostic doctrine of the two natures or
> the Valentinian docetism?*" Even the later councils of the Church
> which discussed the Christological problems in complicated,
> and nowadays hardly intelligible, definitions did not manage to
> do this; the unity of the Church foundered precisely on this...
> *It has often been forgotten* that Gnostic theologians saw Christ as

---

[327] J. L. Mosheim, *Historical Commentaries on the State of Christianity During the First Three Hundred and
Twenty-Five Years,* Vol. 1 (New York: Converse, 1851), p. 467.

[328] Ibid., pp. 465-471.

[329] See John Hick, *The Metaphor of God Incarnate* (London: Westminster John Knox Press, 2005
[1993]), pp. 58-60.

[330] "If Christ's human nature had its own proper will so that Christ literally had two wills, as the
Council affirmed, then there would be two person, one human and one divine... I cannot
understand how Christ's human nature could have a will of its own, distinct from the will of the
Second Person of the Trinity, and not be a person" (William Lane Craig, "Monotheletism").

"consubstantial" (homoousios) with the Father, before ecclesiastical theology established this as a principle, in order to preserve his full divinity.[331]

The Gnostic Homoousian

As the Gnostics had claimed that Jesus was a manifestation of the highest God, sent to rescue mankind from the clutches of the evil Creator, this meant that Jesus and the God of the Old Testament were effectively working against each other. In response, John would evidently write to provide the world with the teachings of Jesus which highlighted not only his genuine humanity, but his unity of purpose with the old God of Judaism (Jn 8:40, 54; 10:30). Yet the philosophers who quickly filled the Church in the Apostolic twilight, within less than a few years of John's writing, began to view his Gospel in a fundamentally different way, namely, that John presented a Christ who was not simply united with the Creator in divine purpose, but also in divine *substance*. Indeed, the later Christian theologians at the Council of Nicaea (325 CE) would agree upon a particular metaphysical word to define the relationship between God and his Son: "*homoousios*" or "same substance." But this term did not come to the Church from the teachings of Christ or any of his Apostles. The origin of this precise philosophical delineation appears, by all accounts, to have been the dreaded Gnostics themselves. Evidently, the Gnostic parties against whom John had struggled to preserve the faith would eventually provide the very doctrinal language that would prove that faith's undoing, and with his own Gospel as the catalyst![332] It is a largely forgotten fact that the "homoousian" definition was first in use, not by the earliest Christian community, but by various Gnostic sects

---

[331] Kurt Rudolph, *Gnosis: The Nature and History of Gnosticism* (New York: Harper & Row, 1983), p. 372, emphasis added.

[332] Surprisingly, the very Gospel that may have been written to stifle the contentions of the Gnostics, was largely commandeered by their later apologists. Groningen says that "the Gnostics made much use of the Gospel of John" (Gerard Groningen, *First Century Gnosticism: Its Origin and Motifs* (Leiden: Brill, 1967), p. 103). And E. F. Harrison also reveals that "Movements of doubtful orthodoxy began to spring up in the second century; they tended to favour whichever of the gospels was most congenial to their point of view. So Matthew became associated with the Ebionites, Luke with the followers of Marcion, and John with most of the Gnostic groups" (E. F. Harrison, *Introduction to the New Testament* (Grand Rapids: Eerdmans, 1964), p. 303). J. A. T. Robinson explains that "the stress in the Johannine epistles on Jesus come in the flesh must be seen as a reaction to the docetic impression his teaching evidently provoked. But the very fact that the reaction was so vehement suggests that this is genuinely a misrepresentation of his intention: indeed for him it is very 'antichrist' " (J.A.T. Robinson, *Twelve More New Testament Studies* (London: SCM Press, 1984), p. 142).

by at least the second century CE.[333] Scholarship is in *total agreement* that there is no tangible usage of it before the Gnostics.[334]

The Christians who agreed upon the word at the Council of Nicaea not only did not learn it from the New Testament, they likewise did not learn it from any "orthodox" Christian theologian. As Professor Pier Franco Beatrice explains, the outdated thesis that the word "homoousios" was merely the Greek equivalent of the Latin "una substantia," and that the introduction of the definition at Nicaea was only the adoption of the Western tradition of Tertullian is "definitely to be rejected."[335] Indeed, Tertullian had used the Latin "una substantia" in his own doctrines, but Tertullian actually uses the Latin "consubstantialis" or "consubstantivus" when translating the acutely Gnostic word "homoousios" in his writings against the Valentinians.[336] Furthermore, Tertullian had used the idea of divine substance in a material sense, but at Nicaea, consubstantiality was specifically interpreted in an immaterial sense.[337] Ultimately "there is no evidence at all of an 'orthodox' or 'Roman' interpretation of homoousios that would have anticipated the formula adopted at Nicaea."[338] As scholars reveal, "the early history of the Nicene homoousios shows us that the theologians of the church were probably made aware of this concept, and thus of the doctrine of emanation, *by the Gnostics*."[339]

The Nicene implementation of this Gnostic term was, arguably, the single most critical and controversial application of any theological word in the history of Christianity and remains the most fundamental tenet of orthodoxy to this

---

[333] Philip Schaff, *History of the Christian Church* (Grand Rapids: Eerdmans, 1985), p. 628. See also Victor I. Ezigbo, *Introducing Christian Theologies*, Vol. 1 (Eugene: Wipf & Stock, 2013), pp. 154-155.

[334] "It is conceded today that homoousios had the first phase of its theological history in Gnosticism" (Aloys Grillmeier, *Christ in Christian Tradition*, Vol. 1 (Atlanta: John Knox Press, 1975), p. 269). See also Adolf von Harnack, *History of Dogma*, Vol. 1 (Freiburg, 1893), pp. 284-285, n. 3; Vol. 2, pp. 232-234, n. 4; George Leonard Prestige, *God in Patristic Thought* (London: SPCK, 1952 [1936]), pp. 197-218. J. N. D. Kelly, *Early Christian Creeds* (London: Longman, 1972), pp. 240-262. Frauke Dinsen, *Homoousios, Die Geschichte des Begriffs bis zum Konzil von Konstantinopel* (Kiel, 1976), pp. 4-11; Robert W. Jensen, "The Triune God," *Christian Dogmatics,* Vol. 1 (Philadelphia: Fortress Press, 1984), p. 128. Beatrice also includes Ignacio Ortiz de Urbina, Luis M. Mendizabal, Emphrem Boularand, Frauke Dinsen, Christopher Stead and Aloys Grillmeier in his analysis of the consensus (Pier Franco Beatrice, "The Word 'Homoousios' from Hellenism to Christianity." The Free Library. 2002 American Society of Church History 12 Jun. 2016).

[335] Ibid.

[336] See Tertullian, *Against the Valentinians*, 18, which describes the Aeons or hypostases in God as "consubstantial beings."

[337] See Eusebius, *Life of Constantine*, 35.

[338] Beatrice, "Homoousios"

[339] Aloys Grillmeier, "Christ in Christian Tradition," *From the Apostolic Age to Chalcedon*, Vol. 1 (London: Mowbrays, 1975), p. 109, emphasis added.

day.[340] However, as we will discover later, the recommendation of this definition was first made at the Council of Nicaea, not by any established Christian theologian, but by Constantine the Great (d. 337 CE), an unbaptized Roman emperor.[341]

But how did the pre-Nicene Gnostics first use the term "homoousios"? Where did they learn it? As scholars explain, "the Gnostics evidently drew this word from their Egyptian and Hermetic sources, introducing it for the first time into the Christian lexicon."[342]   In other words, its origin is decidedly pagan. Scholars believe that it was used to indicate "identity of substance between generating and generated," and "to describe 'the relationship between beings compounded of kindred substance' and was 'used alongside notions of emanation.' "[343] We find the earliest Gnostic use of "homoousios" in Basilides (f. 117-138 CE), a popular teacher from Alexandria.[344]   Other Gnostics, such as the Valentinian Claudius Ptolemy (90-168 CE), can also be found using the term. Long before any orthodox councils adopted the word, Ptolemy wrote that "it is the nature of the good [God] to beget and bring forth that which is similar to it and *homoousios*."[345]   However, this was not the only pre-Nicene contact Christendom would have with this term.   A widely unknown fact of Church

---

[340] Today, Trinitarians confirm that this necessary word, and its origin, continues to place their faith in an awkward position. One Trinitarian admits that "it is odd to say that we have to confess a nonbiblical term in order to hold the Bible's teaching together, but confess that we do" (Jason Byassee, *Trinity: The God We Don't Know* (Nashville: Abingdon Press), Ch. 1). Source credit: Carlos Xavier (http://thehumanjesus.org).

[341] "The word homoousious (same substance) was inserted in the Nicene Creed solely by the personal order of Constantine" (Beatrice, "Homoousios"). After Nicaea, Eusebius of Caesarea wrote to his church: "[Constantine] ordered all to assent to subscribe to the teaching and to be in harmony with them, although only one word, 'homoousios,' was added, which he himself interpreted... And our emperor, most wise and pious, thought philosophically in this manner" Eusebius' letter quoted in Socrates' *Church History*, 1, 8.

[342] Beatirce, "Homoousios." For an analysis of the interchange between pre-Christian Egypt and Gnosticism, see Garth Fowden, *The Egyptian Hermes: A Historical Approach to the Late Pagan Mind* (Princeton: Princeton University Press, 1993) p. 113ff.

[343] Victor I. Ezigbo quoting first J. N. D. Kelly (*Early Christian Doctrines*, p. 232), then Lewis Ayres (*Nicaea and Its Legacy*, p. 93), in *Introducing Christian Theologies*, Vol. 1, p. 155.

[344] Miroslav Marcovich, *Patristic Texts & Studies*, 25. (Berlin: Gruyter, 1986), p. 290f. The later Christian Hippolytus of Rome (d. 235 CE), in an extensive criticism of Basilides, remarked that he was "struck with the doctrines of the Platonists," and in his relation of Basilides' teaching we actually detect remarkable ideas which would resemble later Christian thinking. Basilides spoke of a Seed of Sonship projected out of God, that is "*in every respect of the same substance* (homoousios)" as God. To this consubstantial Sonship, Basilides also equipped a soul (Hippolytus cites Plato's *Phaedrus* as Basilides' justification for this), and he called the affixed soul, "the Holy Spirit." See Hippolytus of Rome, *The Refutation of All Heresies*, Book VII.

[345] See Ptolemy's *Letter to Flora* as recalled by Epiphanius in *Panarion*, 33, 7:8.

history is that "homoousios" had already been *banned* by Christian councils before it ever came to be accepted in 325 CE at Nicaea.

The Synod of Antioch in 268 CE had met to deal with the bishop of Antioch, Paul of Samosata, who had claimed that the divine logos indwelt the human Jesus at his baptism. Paul had used the word "homoousios" to describe the relationship between the logos, which he viewed as an impersonal attribute, and God.[346] This term was seen as *alien* to Christianity. One encyclopedia reports: "It must be regarded as certain that the council rejected the term homoousios."[347] Ironically, the Council of Nicaea some fifty years later employed the very same language in its confession of faith about the relation of the Son to the Father.[348] This proved to be an embarrassing situation for Nicaea's supporters; the fact that the word had already been banned by the well-respected council at Antioch was repeatedly recalled by the Arians and other opponents of the Nicene Creed, in order to prove the unacceptability of the term. Despite the word's established ban, however, it would eventually be pressed into the service of orthodoxy.[349] But how did the later Christians at Nicaea use the term "homoousios?" How was it viewed by Emperor Constantine who personally resurrected the word and codified it into Christian and Roman law? One scholar writes that, having excluded any relationship between the Nicene "homoousios" and the preceding *Christian* tradition, Constantine's view of the term:

> came straight from Constantine's Hermetic [Gnostic] background… In the theological language of Egyptian paganism the word *homoousios* meant that the Nous-Father and the Logos-Son, who are two distinct beings, share the same perfection of the divine nature.[350]

Hermeticism, one of several pagan religions associated with the Emperor Constantine, was a mystical Gnostic tradition which blended the doctrines and

---

[346] Charles Joseph Hefele, *A History of the Christian Councils From the Original Documents,* Book II (Edinburgh: T & T Clark, 1894), p. 9.

[347] John Chapman, "Paul of Samosata," *Catholic Encyclopedia.*

[348] William G. Rusch, *Ecumenical Reception: Its Challenge and Opportunity* (Grand Rapids: Eerdmans, 2007), p. 18.

[349] Chapman, "Paul of Samosata," *Catholic Encyclopedia.*

[350] Pier Franco Beatrice, "The Word 'Homoousios' from Hellenism to Christianity," *Church History,* Vol. 71, No 2. (Cambridge: CUP, 2002), p. 243.

mythology of Greece and ancient Egypt.[351] Ultimately, "the use of 'homoousios' in the Hermetic tractate *Poimandres* for the common nature of Nous and his Son the Logos, [and] Constantine's knowledge of Hermeticism" evidences the lingering presence of Gnostic thought-forms at Nicaea.[352] As we will see in chapter five, we know that the original Nicene understanding of the term was Hermetic-Gnostic, since Constantine provided not only the word, but a philosophical explanation of the word to the council.[353] In this, we have once again encountered the phantoms of the Egyptian religion and the endless mystery cults it generated lurking in the hallowed halls of Christian orthodoxy.

Translating Gnosis

At this point we still wonder how any of the ideas of convicted "heretics" like the Gnostics could ever have come to be viewed as "orthodox" in the Church. Had not respected proto-orthodox authorities such as Irenaeus and Hippolytus loudly condemned the Gnostics of their day? The sanitization efforts of orthodox historians have long obscured the fact that Christianity in the second century was far more diverse, and far more *Gnostic*, than has commonly been believed.

By mid-century, Gnostic teaching had grown immensely popular in the academic hubs of the Roman Empire, particularly in Rome and Alexandria. Its riveting theology of inner knowledge and escapism offered a significant challenge to the proto-orthodox bishops who struggled to gain and maintain influence over the Church. The controversy surrounding Marcion of Sinope (c. 85-160 CE), a fascinating and powerful Gnostic leader,[354] provides an example

---

[351] The chief texts of the Hermetic tradition include *The Corpus Hermeticum* (2nd-3rd centuries CE), *the Emerald Tablet of Hermes* (manuscripts from 6th century CE), and *The Asclepius* (2nd-3rd centuries CE). For an introduction to this literature see Brian P. Copenhaver, *Hermetica: The Greek Corpus Hermeticum and the Latin Asclepius in a New English Translation, with Notes and Introduction* (Cambridge, 1992). Hereticism's mythical founder, Hermes Trismegistus ("Thrice Great"), was said to have been an Egyptian priest-king, who was called thus due to his own teachings of a divine Trinity. One 10th-century source states that he "was called Trismegistus on account of his praise of the Trinity, saying there is one divine nature in the Trinity" (*Suda*, Copenhaver, *Hermetica*, p. xli). In the Hermetic Gnostic tradition we detect other familiar principles; the *Corpus Hermeticum* says that Atum, the Sun god, was "unbegotten and came into being by spontaneous self-generation" (F. Daumas, "Atum," *Dictionary of Deities and Demons in the Bible* (Leiden: Brill, 1999), p. 119). Credit for notice of the above dictionary source goes to Carlos Xavier at http://thehumanjesus.org.

[352] Everett Ferguson, "Creeds, Councils, and Canons," *The Oxford Handbook of Early Christian Studies,* (Oxford: OUP, 2008), p. 432.

[353] Beatrice, "Homoousios"

[354] Philip Schaff called Marcion "the most earnest, the most practical, and the most dangerous among the Gnostics, full of energy and zeal for reforming, but restless, rough and eccentric"

of the difficulty experienced by the catholic fathers. Marcion, like many other Gnostics, taught a docetic Christ, rejected the God of the Jews as an evil Demiurge, and aggressively argued for the Christian elimination of the Old Testament.[355] His teachings were so influential that scholars have estimated that Marcionite churches far outnumbered proto-orthodox churches between 160-170 CE.[356] It is even possible that the majority of Christians in that era completely rejected the Hebrew Bible.[357] We may gain even further insight into how powerful Gnostic Christianity had become from the fact that, according to Tertullian, Valentinus himself was a strong candidate for bishop of Rome. In other words, a Gnostic nearly became Pope.[358]

In response to this phenomenon, prominent proto-orthodox bishops and teachers were forced to publicly confront the Gnostic arguments. Theologians such as Irenaeus of Lyon and Clement of Alexandria composed many spirited, polemical discourses against them. Around 180 CE, Irenaeus argued for the unacceptability of Gnostic Christianity, particularly Valentinianism, by tracing

---

(Philip Schaff, *History of the Christian Church*, Vol. 2 (New York: Scribner's), p. 483). Some scholars have distinguished Marcion's thought from Gnosticism, usually due to his failure to align with the standard Gnostic view of human beings as containing a "divine spark," a shard of God's own soul trapped in their alien matter (See Adolf von Harnack, *Marcion* (Darmstadt: W.B., 1996 [1921]), p. 196). Others have recognized an obvious parallel to Gnostic teaching (Sebastian Moll, *The Archheretic Marcion* (Tubingen: Mohr Siebeck, 2010), pp. 72-75). Of course, "the ancient heresiologists lumped Marcion together with the Gnostics, and it is not hard to see why" (Ibid., p. 74).

[355] Marcion famously rejected the Old Testament books, while gathering the letters of Paul and the writings of Luke into what has been described as the first "canon" of Scripture. For a modern reconstruction of his collection see Jason BeDuhn, *The First New Testament: Marcion's Scriptural Canon* (Salem: Polebridge Press, 2013). Marcion is often considered by scholars to be "the principal factor" in the establishment of a rival "orthodox" canon. See Hans von Campenhausen, "The Emergence of the Christian Bible," *Contributions to Historical Theology*, Vol. 39 (Tubingen: Mohr Siebeck, 1968). For a detailed analysis of this history, see Bruce M. Metzger, *The Canon of the New Testament: Its Origin, Development, and Significance* (Oxford: OUP, 1987).

[356] See John J. Clabeaux, "Marcion," *Anchor Bible Dictionary*, Vol. 4 (New York: Doubleday, 1992), p. 515.

[357] Tertullian's notice that "today" (in his time) there were more Christians who accepted the Old Testament than those who rejected it evidences a time when this was not the case, and a previously significant Marcionite population. See Tertullian, *Against Marcion*, 5, 20.

[358] See Tertullian, *Against the Valentinians*, 4; see also Bentley Layton, *The Gnostic Scriptures* (New York, 1987), p. 220. Rome in that era, like Alexandria, appears to have been much more tolerant of Gnostic teaching: "Aside from [two] individual literary denunciations by Justin and Irenaeus... there is no reliable evidence that Valentinus or the Valentinians were ever condemned by anything resembling an office of ecclesiastical authority in Rome" (Einar Thomassen, "Orthodoxy and Heresy in Second-Century Rome," *The Harvard Theological Review*, Vol. 97, No. 3 (Cambridge: CUP, 2004), p. 241).

its historical development through long genealogies which culminated in various unsavory characters of history.[359]

Clement (d. 215 CE), a pagan convert, was an influential theologian and head of the famous Catechetical School in Alexandria. A Platonist by training (and the one who had argued that Greek philosophy had originated in Egypt), Clement would also train (or at least influence) the renowned scholar Origen (184-253 CE). Like other proto-orthodox theologians, Clement did not share the negative Gnostic outlook on the created world or the Hebrew Scriptures. However, in Clement we may nevertheless detect evidence of a shadowy exchange between Gnosticism and proto-orthodoxy. As scholars have noted:

> Clement's philosophical and theological struggle with alternative hetero-Gnostic doctrines left a visible mark on his own thought... However, his comprehension of hetero-Gnosticism is as complex as his attitude towards Judaism and is far from being utterly negative.[360]

But how could such a respected Christian leader have possibly entertained an even obliquely favorable view of Gnostic doctrine? More than that, Clement has been discovered by recent scholarship to be "profoundly imbued" with the thought of his Gnostic adversaries.[361] Clement's environment is key to understanding the mechanics behind his subtle adoption of Gnostic ideas. As noted in the previous chapter, the city of Alexandria was the philosophical capital of the ancient world, and in that world, religious syncretism was in vogue. Clement himself once said that truth is like a river which receives tributaries from every side. But, as W. R. Inge writes:

> the river of speculative theology at Alexandria was like *the Nile delta*... so that he would be a very learned or a very confident man who should attempt to define precisely the obligations of [an Alexandrian] Jew, Christian, and Greek to each other... at Alexandria there was too much interchange of thought for it to be possible to label each doctrine with the name of a nationality or creed.[362]

---

[359] See Irenaeus, *Against Heresies* (also known as: *On the Detection and Overthrow of the So-Called Gnosis*). While Gnostic leaders often traced the source of their teaching back to the Apostle Paul, Irenaeus traced them back to Simon Magus, an antagonistic "sorcerer" from the NT (Acts 8:9-24).

[360] Piotr Ashwin-Siejkowski, *Clement of Alexandria* (New York: T & T Clark, 2008), p. 9.

[361] W. Barnstone, M. Meyer (ed.), *The Gnostic Bible* (London: Shambala, 2003), p. 307.

[362] Inge, p. 328, emphasis added.

This was the cloudy atmosphere in which Clement set out to challenge Gnosticism. Not surprisingly, modern scholars observe how Clement's extended public disputation with the Gnostics actually exposed their similarities.[363] Some even recognize direct parallels between Clementine and Valentinian exegesis of the Scriptures, and even Clement's "adaptation" of their interpretations in his own theology.[364] As Chadwick notes: "With the teachings of Basilides and more especially of Valentinus, Clement found himself in a fair degree of sympathy."[365]

Clement exemplifies a strain of Alexandrian Christianity which rejected most of the Gnostic views, but found their mystical Christology and speculative exegesis not entirely useless. There was evidently some advantageous property to extract, adapt, and rename "orthodox." Thus the Alexandrian apologists became embroiled in a "Crypto-Gnosticism"; they publicly denounced Gnostic thought while quietly permitting it in through the back door.[366] Camouflaged by both the ingenious syncretism of the philosophers and the public assurances of the heresiologists, the infiltration of Gnostic sensibilities into the most prominent proto-orthodox schools was achieved.

Clement concealed his tendencies well. He even described his true doctrine as being "covered over and hidden," and "kept for the husbandmen of faith, and nobody else."[367] The idea of *secret knowledge* was strong with Clement. Scholars have thus placed him "in the midst of the Gnostic milieu by accepting the tradition of secret gnosis."[368] He even touted a new vision of what he called *"Christian Gnosticism,"* to him a pure, true, and orthodox form of gnosis meant only for the elect.[369] For Clement, the "true gnostic" is a Christian who rejects all passion in favor of the divine knowledge that was in Christ, until his own soul is ultimately detached from the material realm and "assimilated to God, becoming truly angelic."[370] For Clement, this Gnostic return to the divine could

---

[363] See S. R. C. Lilla, *Clement of Alexandria: A Study in Christian Platonism and Gnosticism* (Oxford: OUP, 1971), pp. 162-163.

[364] See J. L. Kovacs, "Echoes of Valentinian Exegesis in Clement of Alexandria and Origen," *Origeniana Octava, Bib. Ephemeridum Theologicarum Lovaniensium* (Leuven: Peeters, 2004), pp. 317-329.

[365] Henry Chadwick, quoted in C. Wilfred Griggs, *Early Egyptian Christianity: From Its Origins to 451 CE* (Leiden: Brill, 1991), p. 60.

[366] Valentinus himself may have been the first orthodox "Crypto-Gnostic"; he was "the first one who transposed the principles of the so-called Gnostic heresy" (Irenaeus, quoted by Griggs, p. 54).

[367] Clement of Alexandria, *Stromata*, 1.

[368] Griggs, p. 59. This tradition would continue with Origen.

[369] Ibid., 6, 7, 494.

[370] Clement of Alexandria, *Stromata*, 7, 14, 547.

only be achieved by reaching a pureness of mind: *total impassibility* was the Gnostic's goal. The pre-existent Jesus himself, he claimed, "was impassible," and after assuming flesh, he "trained it to the condition of impassibility."[371] Just as the Gnostics Cerinthus and Ptolemy uniquely applied the Platonic ideal of impassivity to Jesus, teaching that Christ was free from the passions of life and unable to suffer or feel pain,[372] likewise Clement said that Christ "was in general dispassionate; and no movement of feeling penetrated him, whether pleasure or pain."[373] And just as Valentinus taught that Jesus' body received heavenly sustenance, Clement also said Christ only appeared to require food.[374] But again, Clement had cloaked his predispositions. As one historian explains, the "obscurity of his style prevented Clement from suffering condemnation like Origen in later centuries."[375] Another scholar suggests: "It is not impossible that he avoided rejection by the Church as a Gnostic primarily because Irenaeus wrote his polemic against the Gnostics before Clement's time."[376]

Interestingly, later Christians appear to have rediscovered Clement's heretical links. Photios of Constantinople (820-893 CE), the most prominent patriarch of the ninth century, eventually condemned the ancient Alexandrian as a heretic.[377] But Clement had already influenced the great Origen, and Origen had already influenced an entire generation of fourth-century Alexandrian philosophers, including Athanasius, the champion of Nicene orthodoxy. Was the damage already done? One voice highlights our anxiety on this point: "[How is one] to distinguish between the Christian Gnosticism which is orthodox, or comparatively orthodox, in Clement of Alexandria and Origen, and the Christian Gnosticism which is heretical in Basilides or in Valentinus?"[378] As one encyclopedia so appropriately demands: "we cannot omit the observation that the Christian Church in later centuries to a certain extent travelled again over

---

[371] Ibid., 7, 2, 525.

[372] For Ptolemy, see Irenaeus, *Against Heresies*, 1, 12; 2, 4; for notice of Cerinthus see 1, 26.

[373] Clement of Alexandria, *Stromata*, 6, 9, 71, 1.

[374] See n. 294 on p. 94.

[375] Chadwick, quoted in Griggs, *Early Egyptian Christianity*, p. 58. In the construction of his theological system, Origen "transposed the Gnostic (specifically Valentinian) myth of the soul with its descent and ascent into a Christian scheme in such a way that it was largely 'demythologized'; in spite of this, even in this form it was soon recognized to be heretical" (Rudolph, *Gnosis*, p. 369).

[376] Griggs, p. 58.

[377] For an account of Photios' accusations, see Piotr Ashwin-Siejkowski, *Clement of Alexandria: A Project of Christian Perfection* (New York: T & T Clark, 2008). "Clement often understated the Logos' humanity, especially when he compared incarnation to 'a dream' or described it as 'putting on the linen robe.' Here, Christ's body is compared to a linen cloth, which to later orthodox sensitivities, such as that of Photios, sounded dangerously vague" (Ibid., p. 100).

[378] Griggs, p. 60.

Gnostic ground in its sacramental theories and fully developed Christological speculations."[379]

We must emphasize that this subterranean Gnosticizing was by no means confined to Clement or his era. For example, the later Lucius Lactantius (c. 250-c. 325 CE), a highly educated theologian who became a chief religious advisor of Emperor Constantine, likewise "stood in the tradition of the 'philosophical Gnosis' of Alexandria."[380] As scholars reveal, Lactantius constructed his doctrines "in obvious dependence on the Gnostic, especially Hermetic, but clothed it, following Clement, at the same time in the dress of official theology."[381] As we will see in chapter five, Lactantius may have even personally played a decisive role in the establishment of Christian dogma at Nicaea.

In the Western half of the empire, Rome proved just as hospitable to Gnostic sensibilities as Alexandria. The Roman bishop Marius Victorinus, who died sometime after 355 CE, is significant not only for his presentation of the Christian God in terms of Neoplatonism and his great influence on Augustine of Hippo (d. 430 CE),[382] but for another reason largely unnoticed by earlier historical analysis. Modern scholarship now realizes that Victorinus used *Gnostic* texts to facilitate his own Trinitarian vision. Only since the 1990's have scholars been able to demonstrate how closely the "orthodox" Victorinus' work mirrors the Gnostic literature discovered at Nag Hammadi, sometimes word for word.[383] But how could such a respected member of the Church have done this? It has been suggested that Victorinus was "reading an explicitly Gnostic text, rejecting Gnosticism and, in the same instance, transforming some of its ideas into his own theories, adopting certain of its expressions."[384] During the embryonic stages of Nicene-Trinitarian development, some proto-orthodox bishops (both in Rome and Alexandria) evidently found Gnostic literature useful. Scholars have now noted "striking similarities" between Victorinus' and the Gnostic's

---

[379] "Valentinus and the Valentinians," *Encyclopedia Britannica*, Vol. 27, 1911.

[380] Rudolph, *Gnosis*, p. 370.

[381] Ibid.

[382] Alice E. Guinther, "Augustine and Victorinus: An Analysis of a Trinitarian Argument" (2015). *Undergraduate Honors Theses*. Paper 974. See also F. F. Bruce, "Marius Victorinus and His Works," *The Evangelical Quarterly*, Vol. 18 (1946), p. 140.

[383] Portions of Vicotrinus' apology parallel the Gnostic text known as *Zostrianos,* a 3rd-century CE document discovered in the Nag Hammadi Library. That book details an account of Zostrianos, a figure said to be an older relative of the Persian religious leader Zoroaster, the founder of Zoroastrianism. See "The Sermon of Zostrianos," in *The Gnostic Bible*, p. 215.

[384] Volker Henning Drecoll, "The Greek Text Behind the Parallel Sections in Zostrianos and Marius Victorinus," *Plato's Parmenides and Its Heritage*, Vol. 1 (Atlanta: Society of Biblical Literature, 2010), p. 210.

triad.[385]   One example can be found in an important Gnostic work called *The Gospel of the Egyptians,* which states of God: "Three powers came forth from him; they are the Father, the Mother, and the Son."[386]   Victorinus likewise clearly identifies the Holy Spirit as "the Mother" of Christ[387] and furthermore writes: "God is triple-powerful, he has three powers."[388]   The Gnostic keyword here is "*tridunamos*" (triple-power).[389]   Thus we find in Victorinus yet another "Crypto-Gnostic"; he presents his "very own specific theory of the Trinity which also includes Gnostic notions."[390]   Modern scholars, such as Rasimus, have now affixed a Gnostic background to the "orthodox" Victorinus.[391]   Likewise Abramowski emphasizes both Neoplatonic and Gnostic (especially Sethian Barbelo-Gnostic) thought in his writing, and Tommasi even detects his "direct knowledge" of Valentinianism.[392]   We must remember that in Rome, Gnostics were "highly assimilated" members of the Church (we recall that Valentinus was nearly made bishop there).   All of this may lead us to conclude that Marius Victorinus himself either belonged to or was heavily influenced by what Abramowski calls "a Crypto-Gnostic and Nicene circle in Rome."[393]   Could evidence of this circle confirm a compatibility or an association of Gnostic thought with Nicene Christianity?   Could this circle, and others like it in

---

[385] Gerald P. Boersma, *Augustine's Early Theology of Image* (Oxford: OUP, 2016), p. 63. See also Luise Abramowski, "Marius Victorinus, Porphyrius und die romischen Gnostiker," *Zeitschrift fur die neutestamentliche Wissenschaft*, Vol. 74 (1983), pp. 108-128.

[386] *Gospel of the Egyptians*, 1, 2. Modern Gnostic Reverend Steven Marshall reveals that the "Mother" was, and still is, known to be the person of "the Holy Spirit." See Steven Marshall, "A Homily for Trinity Sunday: Devotion to the Triune Deity," Meditations. Web. 19 September 2014. <http://gnosis.org/ecclesia/homily_Trinity.htm>.

[387] Victorinus, *Against the Arians*, 1, 56-58.

[388] Ibid., 4, 21.

[389] In addition to its usage in Gnostic religion, the term was also used intermittently in late Neoplatonic circles. Majercik highlights the use of the idea in both the Syrian Porphyry and in Coptic Gnostic literature. See Ruth Majercik, "The Existence-Life-Intellect Triad in Gnosticism and Neoplatonism," *The Classical Quarterly*, Vol. 42 (1992), pp. 475-488. At every turn we are struck by a link between Gnosticism, Neoplatonism, and developing orthodox Christianity.

[390] Ibid. See Victorinus, *Against the Arians*, 1, 49-50.

[391] Tuomas Rasimus, "Stoic Ingredients in the Neoplatonic Being-Life-Mind Triad: An Original Second-Century Gnostic Innovation?" in *Stoicism in Early Christianity* (Grand Rapids, 2010), pp. 257-273.

[392] Chiara O. Tommasi, "L'androginia di Cristo-Logos: Mario Vittorino tra platonismo e gnosi," *Cassiodorus*, Vol. 4 (1998), pp. 11-46.

[393] See Luise Abramowski, "Nicanismus und Gnosis im Rom Des Bischofs Liberius: der Fall des Marius Victorinus," *Zeitschrift fur Antikes Christentum*, Vol. 8, No. 3 (S.N., S.L., 2005), pp. 513-566.

Alexandria,[394] have paved the way for the later production of the orthodox Trinity after Nicaea?

That some of the most powerful supporters of Nicene theology in the fourth century were inundated with Gnostic sensibilities cannot be denied. Augustine of Hippo (d. 430 CE) provides the best example of this, and is in fact the greatest of all the "Crypto-Gnostics" of the fourth century. Augustine's voluminous and beloved writings certainly gave shape to the emerging doctrine of the Trinity, and his unique models would ultimately be taken up as orthodox in the West.[395] However, mostly lost in the public memory is Augustine's pre-conversion life as a student of the Gnostic prophet Mani.

Mani (216–274 CE) was an influential Persian mystic from Babylon. Born the son of a Gnostic father, at twelve years old Mani had experienced visions of a figure describing himself as Mani's "heavenly twin" who called upon Mani to preach the "true message" of Jesus Christ. He journeyed to modern Afghanistan where he studied Hinduism and Buddhism, and upon returning to Persia he claimed that he was the last messenger, the "Comforter" promised to the world by Jesus in John 14:26. Mani gained some significance in the royal court before his terrible martyrdom,[396] and the popular sect that followed in his footsteps stretched across the ancient world.[397]

---

[394] For notice of established "*Christian* Gnostics in Alexandria," see Birger A. Pearson, *Gnosticism, Judaism, and Egyptian Christianity* (Fortress Press, 2006), p. 200.

[395] Augustine was instrumental in the development of an additional point of Trinitarian doctrine represented by a phrase known as the "Filioque," which was added in the sixth century to some later forms of the Niceno-Constantinopolitan Creed of 381 CE. Essentially, the doctrine held that the Holy Spirit proceeded from both the Father *and* the Son. The addition of "and the Son" was a point of great controversy, especially between the Eastern and Western churches, as it was thought to have negative implications for the Father's function in the economy of the Trinity. The addition was ultimately accepted by the Pope in 1014 CE, but was rejected by the Oriental Orthodox and Eastern Orthodox Churches. Because Augustine was so influential in the formation of the "double-procession," in the Eastern churches it has always been viewed as a private speculation of Augustine and has never been accepted.

[396] Mani had joined the court of Shapur I, a tolerant Zoroastrian king. But one of the king's zealous successors, Bahram I, harshly persecuted Manichaeism and reportedly tortured and executed Mani, hanging his corpse in the city as a warning to his followers. The Manicheans of course saw Mani's death as reflecting the sacrificial death of Christ, who gave up his life for his friends. Later Mani would become an object of prayer and a god, even a "Buddha." See Majella Franzmann, *Jesus in the Manichaean Writings* (London: T & T Clark, 2003), pp. 25-26.

[397] Manichaeism thrived not only throughout the Middle East but as far as Rome and even China. When the Italian merchant traveler Marco Polo journeyed to China between 1271 and 1288 CE, he encountered a group of Chinese Manicheans in Fujian province, and recognized them as "neither Buddhist nor Zoroastrian, neither Christian nor Muslim." See Ronald Latham, *The Travels of Marco Polo* (London: Penguin Books, 1958), pp. 235-236.

Augustine studied for ten years as a "hearer" in this Manichean sect.[398] The complex teachings of the Gnostics were attractive to Augustine because, as he himself admits, he "craved, in excessive vanity, to be thought elegant and urbane."[399] Like other Gnostic groups, Manichaeism taught a highly-developed dualistic worldview, emphasizing the continuous battle between spiritual good and material evil. In the Manichean view, sex and procreation were seen as negative activities that trapped immortal souls in the bondage of inherited corruption. They held that humanity was *polluted* with evil from birth. This teaching had a considerable effect on the thinking of Augustine, who himself famously struggled with sexual desire.[400] We can easily see how liberating the Manichaean doctrine must have been for Augustine. His situation, they had explained, was the fault of his material state.

Eventually, Augustine was inspired by the conversion of the Neoplatonist (and Crypto-Gnostic) Marius Victorinus. He was baptized himself in 386 CE and soon began to exert great influence over the Western Church.[401] It is clear, however, that Augustine brought his Gnostic concerns with him when he converted. For example, the Manichean views of sex, procreation, sin, and election were adapted and preserved in his orthodox teaching.[402] Scholars

---

[398] Disciples were split into a hierarchy of "the elect" and "hearers," the latter group probably being based on the Buddhist "Sanga," or monastic assembly of ordained monks.

[399] Augustine, *Confessions*, 3, 1.

[400] In Augustine's celebrated work *Confessions*, we find that "sexual desire played a central role in Augustine's life. He referred to himself prior to his conversion to Catholic Christianity as a 'slave to lust' (*libidinis seruus*). He represented his conversion as a commitment to 'Continence' (*Continentia*), the female personification of sexual renunciation. Nevertheless, he experienced an ongoing struggle with his sexual passions even long after his conversion" (Mathew Kuefler, "Homosexuality: Augustine and the Christian Closet," *Why the Middle Ages Matter* (London: Routledge, 2012), p. 78.

[401] During his life as a Gnostic, Augustine had little regard for the Bible. To him the Scriptures lacked the beauty and complexity of Greek philosophy; they were "lowly in the hearing" and "undignified" and were only a "sort of aid to the growth of little ones" (Augustine, *Confessions*, 3, 5). But when Augustine moved to Milan in 384 CE, he heard Ambrose applying the Neoplatonic ideas of Plotinus to the interpretation of the Christian Scriptures. Intrigued, Augustine studied Neoplatonism himself, and became convinced that it was a superior philosophy to Manichaeism. Augustine then heard the moving story of the Neoplatonist Marius Victorinus, who had ultimately converted and been baptized as a Christian. Augustine was inspired. Two years after moving to Milan, and after a series of dramas involving his concubine, he was finally baptized by Ambrose.

[402] The Christian Augustine now defined the human desire for sex as the result and punishment of Adam and Eve's original disobedience, and held that their guilt polluted their progeny, contaminating mankind with evil from birth. Echoing his Gnostic past, Augustine's argument was that human procreation was how this transmission of bondage was being effected. See Kelly, p. 363. Thus in Augustine's Christian writings we still find not only a negative view towards procreation, but "[a] note of melancholy, of disgust, and even of brutality, towards [humanity]" (John Mahoney, "The Legacy of Augustine," *The Making of Moral Theology: A Study of the Roman*

confirm that Augustine's view of humanity "was a heritage of Gnosis which had not been fully overcome but was only *translated Gnosis.*"[403] While on the one hand publically condemning the radical Gnostic dualism of his former Manichean brothers, their thinking "continued to be alive within [Augustine's teachings on] mankind and its history as absolute separation of the called and the rejected."[404] Despite his public antagonism with the Manicheans, their worldview was still the energizing power behind much of Augustine's most characteristic thought, and experts on Gnosticism have long recognized this.[405] What is Augustine then if not a "Crypto-Gnostic" in the spirit of the earlier Clement and Victorinus? Through Augustine, a transformed Manichean worldview eventually came to soundly dominate later Christian thinking.[406] Gnostic theology is thus confirmed to be still enabling Christian doctrine all the way into the fourth century. The process of catholicizing Gnosis initiated at the

---

Catholic Tradition (OUP, 1987), p. 46). Scholar of Gnosticism Elaine Pagels reveals that "Augustine's theory of original sin not only proved politically expedient, since it persuaded many of his contemporaries that human beings universally need external government... but also offered an analysis of human nature that became, for better and worse, the heritage of all subsequent generations of western Christians and the major influence on their psychological and political thinking... During Augustine's own lifetime... various Christians objected to his radical theory, and others bitterly contested it; but within the next few generations, Christians who held to more traditional views of human freedom were themselves condemned as heretics" (Elaine Pagels, *Adam, Eve, and the Serpent: Sex and Politics in Early Christianity* (New York: Vintage, 1989), p. xxvi).

[403] Rudolph, *Gnosis,* p. 371.

[404] Ibid., p. 370.

[405] Augustine "appropriated this heritage most clearly in the impressive historical review of the two 'realms' (*civitates*), the devil's or that of the wicked (*civitas diabolic* or *impiorum*), and God's (*civitas Dei*), and thus shaped the Christian historical metaphysics of the Middle Ages. Other aspects of his teaching, too, cannot be understood without this heritage which is linked closely with the related late Platonic, such as the famous faith in predestination (grace and election), the role of the soul as being in the image of God and thus an immortal element and, above all, the concept of original sin. This latter is the result of man's fall from the divine original state brought about by his own guilt. Its position in Augustine's teaching is an echo of the Manichean idea of the fateful 'mixture' of light and darkness, spirit and matter, which necessarily determines human existence" (Ibid.).

[406] The Protestant Reformation of Luther and Calvin was a revival of Augustinianism, and today millions of Christians perpetuate Augustine's low view of humanity. Within the Protestant Reformation, "a renewed consideration of Augustine occupied all Western Christian denominations... Luther's Augustinian view of a will enslaved by original sin held the greatest sway within Protestantism for two centuries" (Anthony Kruppo, *Reason's Children* (Cranbury: Associated University Press, 2009), p. 110). Scholars confirm that "still today, in the important theological revival of our own time, the influence of Augustine is obviously one of the most potent and productive impulses at work" (Albert Cook Outler (trans.), *The Confessions of St. Augustine* (Mineola: Dover Publications, 2002 [1955]), p. vi).

beginning of the third century clearly reaches its zenith in Augustine. As Rudolph confirms, Augustine "was the last in the chain of development."[407]

Ultimately, as modern scholarship concludes, "it must have been just as possible to adopt Gnostic ideas in fourth-century Rome as it was during the [3rd century]."[408] It was the early assumption of these sensibilities, of the Gnostic thesis about the deity of Christ, which provided the fertile soil in which the eternal Jesus of Nicaea could be grown. Indeed, Professor Werner reveals that "A Gnostic theory was rejected, but sooner or later it was *annexed* by the Church to its own fundamental notions." It was with this background and formulae that "the Nicaean party at first entered into the debate with the Arians."[409] The entire Trinity theory surrounding the Nicene Jesus may in fact prove to be only the Catholic working-out of the original Gnostic thesis, and, as we will see, the Trinity may have only avoided defeat in the fourth century thanks to the timely resurrection of acutely Gnostic definitions.

The Gnostic Hypostases

It may come as no surprise that, according to ancient sources, the most fundamental orthodox delineation of God's triadic nature, *"three hypostases (persons),"* was already manufactured and in use by the Gnostic heretics before any of the Catholic councils had ever convened. This was pointed out during the Arian controversy by fourth century theologian Marcellus of Ancyra (d. 374 CE), who argued that this model had come directly from the teachings of Valentinus. Marcellus protested:

> These then teach three hypostases, just as Valentinus the heresiarch first invented in the book entitled by him *On the Three Natures*. For he was the first to invent three hypostases and three persons of the Father, Son and Holy Spirit, and he is discovered to have filched this from Hermes and Plato.[410]

---

[407] Ibid. Augustine's low view of humanity must have played a role in his Christology. Because humans are by nature polluted and incapable, Christ must have been fundamentally God. For Augustine it is the divine Person who is the "owner" and the "true life" of the human nature; the divine person "bears" or "acts through" a human person, or as has "put on" human nature like a garment (Allan Fitzgerald, John C. Cavadini (ed.), *Augustine Through the Ages: An Encyclopedia* (Grand Rapids: Eerdmans, 1999), p. 167). For Augustine, "while the human nature was real, the fact that it was born from a pure virgin preserved it from original sin; nor was it susceptible, despite the Gospel statements which seem to suggest the contrary, to human ignorance" (Kelly, p. 336).

[408] Drecoll, "Zostrianos and Marius Victorinus," p. 210.

[409] Martin Werner, quoted in Buzzard, *Jesus Was Not A Trinitarian*, p. 320, emphasis added.

[410] Marcellus, *On the Holy Church*, 9. See Logan, p. 393. Marcellus' citation of Valentinus, and his secondary notice of Plato and Hermes is interesting in the sense that these teachers did not view

Marcellus, who was ally of neither the unitarian Arians nor the proto-Trinitarians during the Arian controversy, was himself later anathematized for his rejection of the "three hypostases" model. Though Marcellus agreed that Christ was God (evidently in a Sabellian sense),[411] he rejected any theologian's multiplication of hypostases as Gnostic-pagan.[412]   Nevertheless, as one encyclopedia states, "this single Valentinian teaching came to be seen as orthodox, as it offered a useful middle ground between the Arian and Sabellian positions."[413]   But exactly what were these "hypostases" in the Valentinian system? Was the Gnostic teaching truly similar to later orthodoxy?

The meaning of the word "hypostasis" changed throughout philosophical history. Among the ancient Greeks, the term had first been synonymous with "ousia" (being, substance). The great Socrates had never used "hypostasis," but preferred "ousia"; Plato likewise never used "hypostasis." The Stoics were really the first to use the word and to them it meant substance or "objective reality." The Latin Stoics also used "hypostasis" and the Latin term "substantia" synonymously, indicating that the original Greek meaning was indeed synonymous with "ousia" (substance). In the third century CE, the word would eventually be used by Plotinus to describe the three principles of reality.

We find the earliest Christian use of the word actually in the Greek New Testament. The term is used several times to indicate *"assurance," "substance"* (in a non-technical sense), or *"reality."*[414]   For example, in Hebrews 11:1 we read: *"Now faith is a well-grounded assurance* (hypostasis) *of that for which we hope, and a conviction of the reality of things which we do not see"* (Heb 11:1). Once, in Hebrews 1:3,

---

"hypostasis" in the same way. For example, Valentinus' hypostases are personal and Platonism's are impersonal. Marcellus clearly targets *personal* hypostases with his primary citation of Valentinus. But in the eyes of Marcellus, a Sabellian who believed in only one hypostasis, both Arians, like his opponent Eusebius, and anti-Arians would be guilty of multiplying hypostases and applying Platonic language to distinct entities of the Father and Son. He detects in Eusebius in particular what he labels a Hermetic tendency to connect two divine beings through the sharing of nature.

[411] Sabellianism (also known as Modalism) was the doctrine that God is one Person who exists in the different modes or aspects of the Father, Son, and Holy Spirit. This theology, which denied any distinct personhood between the hypostases, was condemned by the Council of Antioch in 269 CE. Nevertheless, its presence remained strong throughout Church history. Today, Oneness Pentecostalism, a Modalist Christian movement, claims millions of adherents.

[412] John Arendzen, "Marcellus of Ancyra." *The Catholic Encyclopedia*, Vol. 9 (New York: Robert Appleton Company, 1910). Web. 29 Sep 2014.

[413] "Valentinus," *New World Encyclopedia*. 2008. Web. 29 Sep 2014.

[414] "In the fourth century… hypostasis was no longer synonymous with ousia… In Heb 11:1, which predates these developments, hypostasis may be translated 'substance' (in a nontechnical sense) or 'reality' " (James W. Thompson, *Paideia Commentaries on the New Testament: Hebrews* (Grand Rapids: Baker, 2008), p. 230).

the word is applied to God, and is used to describe God's one "being," or "substance."[415] As Pelikan explains, this New Testament usage of "hypostases" actually appears to be "biblical evidence *against* the formulation of one ousia and three hypostases."[416] Clearly, the early Jewish-Christian usage continued to be a synonym for "ousia," just as it had been with the Greeks. But if both the earliest Jewish Christians and the Greek philosophers used "hypostasis" to mean "substance" or "reality," how did the later Gentile Christians ever come to use "hypostasis" to mean *"person,"* as in Valentinus, and ultimately, as in orthodox Trinitarianism?

Orthodoxy, though obviously influenced by Neoplatonism, did not learn its view of "hypostasis" from Plotinus. Despite any personification language, it is clear that to Plotinus the word still did not mean "person." He continued to view the Platonic hypostases as merely the underlying principles beneath everything we experience.[417] Indeed, "To Plotinus, as to Plato and Aristotle, hypostasis meant the underlying essence or principle of things... To the 'One or Good' he would not allow even any hypostatic character... In the Plotinian vocabulary hypostasis did not mean an individual or a person... 'The One, Mind, Soul,' were in no sense persons."[418]

Thus we are pressed to conclude that the definition of "hypostasis" as *"person"* was provided by the Gnostics.[419] Indeed, it is the expressly *Gnostic* concept of "hypostasis" and the related concept of emanation that later orthodox Trinitarianism echoes. As scholars reveal:

> The concept of hypostasis has a particular importance in Gnosticism... according to the Gnostics, from preexisting principles... there gush forth a multiplicity of existences or

---

[415] Heb 1:3 receives a variety of treatments in English translations, but most obviously refer to the original meaning of "hypostasis" as a synonym for "ousia." The NASB translates the word at Heb 1:3 as "nature," however, others use "being" (ISV, CEB, NAB), "substance" (ASV, DARBY, DRA), and "essence" (AMP, LEB). The later Cappadocian usage is not represented anywhere in the NT. Interestingly, Heb 1:3 does appear to say that "God" has *one* "hypostasis." If this word meant "person" as it did to the fourth-century Cappadocians, then God would be only one person. But the (post KJV) English translators must revert to the classic meaning of "hypostasis" as "being" or "substance," and do so for this verse. Otherwise, the doctrine that God is *three* "hypostases" is damaged by this NT reference to the one "hypostasis" of "God" in Heb 1:3.

[416] Jaroslav Pelikan, *The Christian Tradition, Vol. 1* (Chicago: CUP, 1975), p. 129.

[417] See Kevin Corrigan, *Reading Plotinus: A Practical Introduction to Neoplatonism* (West Lafayette: Purdue University Press, 2005), pp. 23-26. See also Paine, *The Ethnic Trinities*, pp. 145-146.

[418] Paine, *The Ethnic Trinities*, p. 176, 184.

[419] Among the earliest uses of the word "hypostasis" in the Gentile Christian world was by the Syrian theologian (and later convert to Valentinism) Tatian (c. 120-180 CE), but at this stage it still meant "substance" as it did in Platonism and the New Testament.

hypostases… What defines the Gnostic hypostases is that they are in some way incarnate in a personal entity.[420]

For the Gnostics, the hypostases were not simply underlying principles or substances, they were distinct intellects or *persons*. As Tertullian explains in his writings against the Valentinians, "although they would have [the Deity] be alone, they assign to him *a second person* in himself and with himself."[421] Plotinus was especially frustrated by the Gnostic usage of "hypostases." According to him, the Gnostics were wrongly teaching that the different hypostases were different intellects within God.[422] He accuses the Gnostics of misusing Plato's writing "to proof text their notion of the hypostases while missing the plain meaning of the passage,"[423] and he regularly criticizes their abuse of Platonic language.[424] Plotinus ultimately argues against their plurality of persons in God in this way: "[We are not] warranted in affirming a plurality of intellectual principles… [this] would give us two beings."[425]

But the Gnostics saw things differently. In the Valentinian view, the Pleroma (fullness) of God was "unitary," it was the *one* divine being of God. But within this fullness dwelled distinct persons or intellects. As Tertullian explains, "Valentinus had included these *in the very essence* of the Deity."[426] The Gnostics had disagreed with Plotinus' critique of their doctrine; their "hypostases" were not different "beings," though the term "hypostasis" still referred to the one God. Incredibly, this is the same peculiar sense in which this language is employed by later orthodox Trinitarianism. As one scholar explains, though

---

[420] Giorgio Agamben, *The Use of Bodies* (Stanford: Stanford University Press, 2015), p. 140.

[421] Tertullian, *Against the Valentinians*, 7.

[422] Plotinus argues: "And the making of a plurality in the intelligible world, Being and Intellect and the maker different from Intellect, and Soul, is taken from the words in the *Timaeus*: for Plato says, 'The maker of this universe thought that it should contain all the forms that intelligence discerns contained in the Living Being that truly is.' But they did not understand, and took it to mean that there is one mind which contains in it in repose all realities, and another mind different from it which contemplates them, and another which plans… and they think that this is the maker according to Plato, being a long way from knowing who the maker is" (Plotinus, *Ennead* II, 9, 6, 14-24).

[423] Scott T. Carroll, "Gnosticism and the Classical Tradition," *Hellenization Revisited: Shaping a Christian Response Within the Greco-Roman World* (Lanham: University Press of America, 1994), p. 298.

[424] "For instance, Gnostics used imagery of the *individual human soul* [an individual intelligence or person] shredding its wings and falling, from Plato's *Phaedrus*, to describe the fall of *the world-soul* [the third hypostases of Neoplatonism]. Ignoring the original intention, Gnostics brazenly adopted a well-known term while radically transforming its meaning" (Ibid., emphasis added).

[425] Plotinus, *Ennead* II, 9. Interestingly, this resembles the argument of critics of the Christian Trinity, that three personal hypostases ultimately gives us three beings.

[426] Tertullian, *Against the Valentinians*, 4.

"hypostasis" had meant something quite different to earlier Christians, "it prevailed—in a definitive way only from the time of Athanasius [really, the time of the Cappadocians]—as a way to express the ontological relation implicit in the doctrine of the Trinity: 'one God in three hypostases'... the three hypostases or existences refer to one sole substance."[427]

Let us observe how closely the Gnostic hypostases really parallel the later Trinitarianism. According to Tertullian, the Gnostic God's Pleroma (fullness) was considered a single substance or essence.[428] Various principles or attributes existed within God's substance, particular characteristics such as *"felicity," "only-begotten," "self-existent,"* and *"faith,"* and these ultimately translated to personal hypostases. These hypostases were seen as "homoousios" (consubstantial) with one another.[429] Each were themselves manifestations of the fullness or the entirety of God,[430] and, as Professor O'Brien explains, the hypostases ultimately represent "modes of God."[431]

Similarly, in the view of the orthodox Cappadocians who produced the final Trinity formula, we find that: "Each of the divine hypostases is the substance or essence of the Godhead determined by its appropriate particularizing characteristic or identifying particularity... these particularizing characteristics are respectively *'paternity,' 'sonship,'* and *'sanctification.'* "[432] These hypostases were seen as "homoousios" (consubstantial) with one another. Each also bears the entire essence or fullness of God.[433] For the fourth-century Trinitarians, "the essence of their doctrine is that the one Godhead exists simultaneously in three modes of being, or hypostases... They come to be termed 'modes of coming to be'... 'mode[s] of existence.' "[434]

---

[427] Agamben, p. 140, brackets mine.

[428] Tertullian, *Against the Valentinians*, 4; 13.

[429] See Tertullian, *Against the Valentinians*, 12; 13; esp. 18, which describes the Aeons or hypostases in God as "consubstantial." See also Rudolph's observation that Gnostic theologians saw the hypostases of Christ and God as "consubstantial" before the Catholics (Rudolph, p. 372).

[430] "All the emanations of the father, therefore, are fullnesses [Pleromas], and all his emanations have their roots in the one who caused them all to grow from himself" (*Gospel of Truth*, trans. Barnstone, Meyer, p. 255).

[431] O'Brien, p. 216.

[432] Kelly, p. 267.

[433] In the orthodox system, each hypostasis is the bearer of the entire essence. Basil, one of the Cappadocian Fathers, writes: "Whatever the Father is, is also found in the Son. And whatever the Son is, is also found in the Father. The Son is found in His entirety within the Father and He respectively has the Father in His entirety within Him. Thus, the hypostasis of the Son is the image and the likeness by which the Father is recognized. And the hypostasis of the Father is recognized in the image of the Son" (Basil of Caesarea, *38th Letter*).

[434] Kelly, pp. 265-266.

Thus, in both the Gnostic and the orthodox view, it is the distinctiveness of the attributes within the divine substance that yields God's manifestation in personal hypostases without causing a division of being, and these hypostases are "homoousios" with one another, are in themselves the fullness of God, and are "modes" of God's being.

Another related Gnostic feature in orthodoxy is the concept of *emanation* or *procession* of the hypostases. Emanation differs from the idea of creation or formation. In this model, God projects manifestations of himself but is in no way diminished in quality or quantity. The Gnostics used the illustration of the sun and its rays: the sun was not diminished by its projection of the rays, and while the rays themselves were of the same essence, they were distinct from it.

It is often thought that orthodox Christianity learned emanation from the Neoplatonist Plotinus. However, modern scholars now recognize that even before the Neoplatonists, "a number of Gnostic thinkers were developing schemes by which a hierarchy of transcendental beings emanated from a single source by a process of dynamic emanation."[435] As John D. Turner reveals: "Although Plotinus has often been credited with being the first major philosopher to elaborate such a scheme, it is clear that similar models of dynamic emanation are beginning to develop in Gnostic thought, some of which chronologically precedes Plotinus."[436]

Irenaeus was indeed already condemning this concept as expressly Gnostic decades earlier.[437] However, we find that by the third century, the later Christian Tertullian had no problem "revising" this Gnostic theory for his own purposes, and even used the Valentinian term *"probola"* (procession) to describe it.[438] In his view, when the Son and Spirit emanated out from the Father, even though they contained less of the divine substance and were subordinate to God, they remained completely unsevered from their source.[439] Regarding his explicit use of Gnostic language and ideas, Tertullian advises his readers to "flinch not" and to "never mind heresy." He argues: "Truth must not therefore refrain from the use of such a term, and its reality and meaning, because heresy also employs

---

[435] John D. Turner, "Plotinus and the Gnostics: Opposed Heirs of Plato," *The Routledge Handbook of Neoplatonism* (London: Routledge, 2014), p. 58, emphasis added.

[436] Ibid., p. 53.

[437] George Balderston Kidd, *Christophany: Doctrine of the Manifestations of the Son of God Under the Economy of the Old Testament* (London: Ward and Co., 1852), p. 689.

[438] "Emanation," IEP.

[439] Frances Schussler Fiorenza, *Systematic Theology: Roman Catholic Perspectives* (Minneapolis: Fortress, 2011), p. 159. Tertullian's emanations remained connected, in opposition to the Gnostics, in *mind* to the Father.

it."[440] Ultimately, this adaptation ushered Gnostic emanationism into the conversations of the fourth century. As one encyclopedia reveals, "In the final establishment of the Trinitarian doctrine, the idea of emanation undoubtedly played a part, as in the emphasis laid upon the Son's being 'begotten, not made' (Nicene Creed), and the 'procession' of the Holy Ghost."[441]

In reality, much of what later became the "revealed" dogma of Christianity, today still widely viewed as descending from heaven upon the Church, should really be seen as a retreading of Gnostic waters, as a relapse into the inevitable side-effects of the old Gnostic thesis that Christ is by nature God. As we will see in chapter five, it is Origen, Athanasius, and the Gnosticized proto-orthodox tradition emanating out of Alexandria that would first endeavor to stitch these side-effects together into the theological super-structure of orthodoxy.

Trauma

As we have observed, and will continue to observe, the philosophical transformation of the Christian faith was achieved by the combined power of the influx of converted Platonists, the long and harrowing interchange with the Gnostics, and the great pressure to acclimate the Jewish faith of the New Testament to a wider religious world. Looking back, the eventual triumph of orthodoxy came at a serious price. The fact that Christianity's response to the Gnostic heresy included a great deal of compromise shows us how desperately that victory was won. As German historian Hans Blumenberg so pointedly recognized: "The Gnostic trauma of the first post-Christian centuries goes deeper than that of the bloody [Roman] persecutions."[442]

In the end, the decline of Gnosis, as a unique religious force, was achieved in the empire by a two-fold process: first, the Christian Church had adequately "adapted to its environment" and accepted "Gnostic concerns" and "the cultural heritage of antiquity" into its theological message.[443] Second, the orthodox party eventually employed the power of the state against Gnostic adherents resisting assimilation. But any account of the eventual "defeat" of Gnosis by the orthodox must include a *seizure* of Gnostic territory, a sacking of its stores, and, ultimately, a victorious return to the confines of catholicism with a train of Gnostic plunder. Even at this stage we are already able see that when the great Gnostic schools met their end in the era following Nicaea, their Christology was

---

[440] Tertullian, *Against Praxeas*, 8.
[441] "Emanation," IEP.
[442] H. Blumenberg, quoted in Rudolph, *Gnosis*, p. 368.
[443] Rudolph, *Gnosis*, p. 367.

by no means extinguished. Gnostic Christianity's unabashed separation of the human and the divine in Jesus was only muted and internalized; the "radical *form* of early [Gnostic] ideas about Christ was set aside, but not the consequences which are at its root."[444] Our wider study will reveal that the Gnostic Jesus was not eliminated, but was only *translated* into more palatable language and presented once again to the Church in an age far removed from his first controversy, an age when his memory had grown dim enough, and the unity of the Church had grown fragile enough, that he seemed to present a more reasonable and necessary solution than he once had. Indeed, time and circumstance had made the Gnostic Jesus unrecognizable, and he continues to go unnoticed today for the same reasons.

In conclusion, to recall Harnack, we ask who can now maintain that Christianity ever truly overcame the Valentinian doctrine of the two natures?[445] This was only one facet of the overarching philosophical, Platonic, metamorphosis of the Church. The pagan doctrines of the immortal soul, the transmigration and incarnation of the soul, the subsuming of impersonal human nature, the divine hypostases—without these what would be left of Christian orthodoxy? As one 16th-century reformer recognized, early Christianity was "weakened by Platonic philosophy" and "embraced Aristotle instead of Christ."[446] But the Reformation still appears drastically incomplete. Looking around at the most popular forms of Christianity today, we scarcely detect any practical difference between the hymns of the mainstream churches celebrating triadic mysteries and the numinous liturgy of the Gnostics. As Rudolph surmises: "One can almost say that Gnosis followed the Church like a shadow; the Church could never overcome it, its influence had gone too deep. By reason of their common history they remain two—hostile—sisters."[447]

In future chapters we will continue to investigate how the adoption of Gnostic theology was achieved in the wider Church, which Christians were responsible, and exactly how that process laid the groundwork for the establishment of dogma at Nicaea. But next we must turn back time once again and revisit the earliest period of Christian origins in order to introduce a wider view of the state of the Christian faith, and its relationship to Trinitarianism, leading up to the drama of the fourth century.

---

[444] Ibid., p. 372, emphasis added.

[445] Ibid.

[446] Melanchthon, quoted in Wilhelm Pauck, *Melanchthon and Bucer* (London: The Westminster Press, 1969), p. 23.

[447] Rudolph, *Gnosis*, p. 368.

4

STRUGGLE AND EVOLUTION:
THE TRANSITION TO GENTILE PHILOSOPHY

"Most human beings have an almost infinite
capacity for taking things for granted. That men
do not learn very much from the lessons of history
is the most important of all lessons of history."
— Aldous Huxley

S WE HAVE PREVIOUSLY OBSERVED IN DETAIL the evolution of Neoplatonic and Gnostic thought, we turn now to a broader narrative of Church history. In this chapter, an account of early Christianity from the departure of the Apostles up to the fourth century will be provided, with notices of some of the most famous and influential Church Fathers and their beliefs in relation to the established Trinitarian doctrine. The invaluable hindsight afforded by the modern student into this saga not only provides much needed clarity on the precise means of proliferation and adoption of Greek philosophical elements within Christian theology, it more importantly challenges many of the explanations offered by modern Trinitarian authorities regarding the historical doctrine of the Church.

It will presently be observed that the most prominent "catholic" Christianity of the first through the third centuries did not hold "orthodox" Trinitarian views. Indeed, for most of the Platonizing Church Fathers, Jesus was a kind of angelic being, a lesser god, a pre-existing divine entity distinct from and subordinate to the one God. It would not be until the fourth century when the long-standing subordinate-Christ view would be toppled in the empire, and only then after much contest. Despite the claims of modern apologists that a belief in the co-equal Trinity has always characterized Christian orthodoxy, history will demonstrate that this was simply not the case. From Christian beginnings through the fourth century, there were a number of contending theological options available to believers. Professor Bart Ehrman writes:

> To this extent, "orthodoxy," in the sense of a unified group advocating an apostolic doctrine accepted by the majority of Christians everywhere, simply did not exist in the second and third centuries… Beliefs that later came to be accepted as orthodox or heretical were competing interpretations of Christianity… Eventually one of these groups established itself as dominant, acquiring more converts than all the others, over-powering its opponents, and declaring itself the true faith. Once its victory was secured, it could call itself "orthodox" and marginalize the opposition parties as heretics. It then rewrote the history of the conflict, making its views and the people who held them appear to have been in the majority from apostolic times onwards… It is widely thought today that proto-orthodoxy was simply one of many competing interpretations of Christianity in the early church. It was neither a self-evident interpretation nor an original apostolic view. The apostles, for example, did not teach the Nicene Creed or anything like it.[448]

With the intention of recapturing the spirit of the most ancient Christian ideas, we will begin by raising the curtain on the period immediately following the deaths of the Apostles. In this remote era we discover one of the greatest and most unsung Christian struggles, one with the most dire, pervasive and lasting results for the religion of Jesus: the direct clash between the culture and mind of the Gentile converts with the first-century Christian Jews.

---

[448] Ehrman, *Lost Christianities*, p. 173. (Paraphrasing Walter Bauer's conclusions)

The Early Jewish Christians

The discovery of the Dead Sea Scrolls of Qumran in 1954 has continued to force serious revisions to beliefs about the relationship between "first-century Judaism" and "first-century Christianity." But, as one scholar has observed, the new data has not yet overwhelmed traditional presuppositions about their differences:

> Scholars continue to speak of "Christianity" in the first century of the Common Era—and to juxtapose Christianity and Judaism—as though these were distinct and different social phenomena. Such practice will become increasingly difficult as our sketch of the larger Jewish community continues to be revised by what we have learned from the DSS. What were taken to be distinctive features of the New Testament— distinctive in the sense that they manifest a "Christian" perspective over Judaism—turn up in the Qumran Scrolls. One of the greatest changes taking place is the relocation of the literature of the Palestinian Jesus Movement squarely within the larger Jewish community.[449]

In other words, the Dead Sea Scrolls have caused us to reconsider what it meant to be both Jewish *and* Christian in the first century. Jesus and his earliest followers evidently used both language and concepts found explicitly in Second Temple Jewish documents, language which post fourth-century Christianity has ever presented as evidence of a necessary shift towards Trinitarianism.[450] But there exists now, in the eyes of scholars, an unbroken theological legacy between the first Christians and their parent Judaism.[451] Thus, if we want to better understand the theology of the New Testament, we must look not only to first century Judaism, but also to the sects of "Jewish Christianity" that flourished in Palestine after the conclusion of the Book of Acts. Examining the beliefs of

---

[449] Donald H. Juel, "The Future of a Religious Past," *The Bible and the Dead Sea Scrolls,* Vol. 1 (Waco: Baylor University Press, 2006), p. 64.

[450] An in-depth analysis of Christ's sayings in the Gospels and how they compare to well-established concepts in late Second Temple Judaism will be undertaken in the second half of this book.

[451] For a recent and comprehensive analysis of this relationship, see James Dunn, *Neither Jew Nor Greek: A Contested Identity* (Grand Rapids: Eerdmans, 2015).

these two Jewish "bookends" on either side of the New Testament should help us realize what theological ideas really lie between them.

Unknown to most Christians, there has been preserved a great deal of useful information about the historical sects of "Jewish Christianity" that thrived in the late first century. One particular strain invites our study's acute consideration, principally in that it appears to have vigorously resisted the influx of Greek philosophical concepts into their community: the *Nazarenes*. The Nazarenes were, by all historical accounts, the immediate continuation of the Apostolic movement in the city of Jerusalem.[452] According to both the New Testament and later Christian sources, Christians were first known by the name "Nazarenes" before they began to be called "Christians" at Antioch (Acts 11:26).[453] Regarding the Jerusalem church at which they were headquartered, we find that:

> The first fifteen bishops of Jerusalem were all circumcised Jews; and the congregation over which they presided united the law of Moses with the doctrine of Christ. It was natural that the primitive tradition of a church which was founded only forty days after the death of Christ, and was governed almost as many years under the immediate inspection of his apostle, should be received as the standard of orthodoxy. The distant churches very frequently appealed to the authority of their venerable Parent, and relieved her distress by a liberal contribution of alms.[454]

Of all the groups asserting clerical and theological succession from the Apostles, the congregation in Jerusalem presents the most direct and obvious link. Specialists have confirmed that the earliest form of New Testament Christianity indeed shared many "fundamental" features with the Nazarenes,[455] and scholars have thus recognized "sufficient continuity between them for it to

---

[452] See B. Pixner, "Church of the Apostles Found on Mt. Zion," *Biblical Archaeology Review*, May/June 1990. See also Epiphanius, *Panarion*, 29, 7:7. For a detailed textual analysis of the historical sources, see Ray Pritz, *Nazarene Christianity* (Jerusalem: Hebrew University of Jerusalem Press, 1988).

[453] Epiphanius, *Panarion*, 29, 1:3. In the Qur'an, Christians are also called "Al-Naṣara."

[454] Gibbon, *Decline and Fall*, p. 453.

[455] See James Dunn, *Unity and Diversity in the New Testament: An Inquiry into the Character of Earliest Christianity* (London: SCM Press, 1990), pp. 240-243.

be legitimate to group them together under the single heading 'Jewish Christianity.' "[456]

What then of the Nazarene Christology? Might it better represent a view of Jesus in perfect harmony with the traditional monotheism of the Jews? We find them openly acknowledging Jesus as the Messiah, affirming his miraculous birth by the virgin Mary,[457] and far from considering Christ to be the one true God himself, "declar[ing] that God is one, and that his Son is Jesus Christ."[458] They evidently "did accept this title [Son of God] but did not understand it in the same way that later Nicene and Chalcedonian orthodoxy would."[459] The Messiah was, to them, a uniquely born and empowered human being, the prophesied seed of David.[460]

It may be important to note that scholars both ancient and modern have distinguished the Nazarenes from other related Jewish Christian groups such as the Ebionites, who may represent a closely related offshoot.[461] Some of these Ebionites evidently doubted the virgin birth, but the lack of information among many scholars of the first few centuries seems to have provided some difficulty in formally distinguishing the variations between the sectors of the Jewish Christians. However it is certain that unlike probably half of the Ebionites, the

---

[456] James F. McGrath, "Johannine Christianity – Jewish Christianity?" *Koinonia,* 8.1 (Butler University Libraries, 1996), p. 3; See also Carsten Colpe, "The Oldest Jewish-Christian Community," *Christian Beginnings* (Louisville: Westminster, 1993), p. 75; Gilles Quispel, "Qumran, John and Jewish Christianity," *John and Qumran* (London: Geoffery Chapman, 1972), pp. 137-140; Hans-Joachim Schoeps, *Theologie und Geschichte* (Tubingen: J.C.B. Mohr, 1949), p. 257. (Credit to McGrath for these sources)

[457] Jerome, *Letter 112 – Jerome to Augustine.* Concerning the Nazarenes he writes, *"They believe that Messiah, the Son of God, was born of the Virgin Mary."*

[458] Epiphanius, *Panarion* 29, 7, 2

[459] McGrath, "Johannine Christianity," p. 4.

[460] This Jewish expectation of a human messiah from the line of David, distinct from the one God, was derived from the widespread Messianic exegesis of Old Testament books such as Jeremiah and Zechariah (with their motif of the Davidic "Branch" figure – ie: Jer 30:8-9; Zech 6:12), and Ezekiel (with its motif of the subordinate, Davidic shepherd empowered by God to govern the nation – ie: Ezek 34:23-24). The DSS document 4QFlorilegium (4Q174) demonstrates how the "Son of David" prophecy of 2 Sam 7:14 was combined with the aforementioned passages to yield a Jewish expectation of a Messiah who was both called "the Son of David" and the "Son of God." Another DSS documents, 4Q246, explicitly speaks of the "Son of God... Son of the Most High." The parallel to Luke 1:35 is obvious. Further analysis of these Messianic titles and the Jewish expectations will be undertaken in this book's second half.

[461] See Richard Bauckham, *The Image of the Judeo-Christians in Ancient Jewish and Christian Literature* (Leiden: Brill, 2003), pp. 162-181. Pritz explains that "the writings of some of the Church Fathers from the third and fourth centuries and later... led to confusion and to the confounding of different sects under the name 'Ebionites' " (Pritz, p. 9). The historian Epiphanius (d. 403 CE), who "wrongly grouped the Nazarenes together with other sects," may provide the best example of this mistake (Ibid., p. 43).

Nazarenes accepted the virgin birth,[462] and "all reject his pre-existence and his divinity."[463]

Generally, we find the early Jewish Christians heartily refusing the encroaching Hellenistic influence of the Platonists and the blossoming Gnostics, and maintaining the classic unitary oneness of Jewish monotheism while embracing an authentically human Messiah who was not God himself, but God's supremely elevated servant. In other words, the advent of Jesus appears to have effected no change whatsoever upon their pre-existing Jewish theology. For them Jesus was a man divinely anointed by God at his baptism, and while he may have been conceived of in the mind or plan of God before all time, Jesus had experienced his literal, physical beginning not in a distant heavenly cosmos, but in the womb of a woman:

> They revered Jesus as the greatest of the prophets, endowed with supernatural virtue and power. They ascribed to his person and to his future reign all the predictions of the Hebrew oracles which relate to the spiritual and everlasting kingdom of the promised Messiah. Some of them might confess that he was born of a virgin; but they obstinately rejected the preceding existence.[464]

The Gnostics had certainly muddled the humanity of Christ. As we have seen, some had even said his humanity was only an illusion, while others said that though his body was real, the Savior was really the divine Person of God who had taken on a human being. In contrast to these views, the Nazarene Christians held vigorously to the real and unadulterated human life of Jesus, a humanity which their Hebrew forebears had always expected in the long-awaited agent of God. Ultimately, as James Dunn concludes, "Heretical Jewish Christianity [that is, the Nazarenes and the Ebionites] would appear to be not so very different from the faith of the first Jewish believers."[465]

But what happened to the Jerusalem Christians? Why did their Christology so severely recess in popularity? Several factors contribute to their eventual decline in prominence, but the primary source of these factors is unquestionably the jarringly rapid transformation, both in demographics and religious thought,

---

[462] Samuel Krauss, "Nazarenes," *Jewish Encyclopedia*. 1906. Web. 09 September 2014.

[463] John Arendzen, "Ebionites," *The Catholic Encyclopedia*, Vol. 5.

[464] Edward Gibbon, *The History of the Decline and Fall of the Roman Empire*, Vol. 1 (London: Penguin Books, 2005 [1890]), p. 774.

[465] Dunn, *Unity and Diversity*, p. 242.

from a Jewish to a Gentile Church. The Church at Jerusalem had enjoyed primacy as the seat of ecclesial authority for many years. However:

> When numerous and opulent societies were established in the great cities of the empire, in Antioch, Alexandria, Ephesus, Corinth, and Rome, the reverence which Jerusalem had inspired to all the Christian colonies insensibly diminished. The Jewish converts, or, as they were afterwards called, the Nazarenes, who had laid the foundations of the church, soon found themselves overwhelmed by the increasing multitudes that from all the various religions of polytheism enlisted under the banner of Christ.[466]

Not only do we see that Gentile wisdom had a profound effect on the waning of Jewish influence in the Church, the richness of the pagan world proved more than capable at aiming the attention of Christendom in alien directions. The original Christian movement, founded and governed by Jewish peasants and helmed by the courageous friends of a martyred rabbi, had exhibited a sagely modesty which surely contributed to its happy growth. Yet the monetary and philosophical wealth of the Gentile converts seems to have activated within their most publicly conspicuous affiliates a lingering secularism which repulsed them from the meekness of the Jewish pioneers and drew them expeditiously towards the great cities of the empire. However, the transference of influence away from Judea to Rome was far from passive; there had occurred an active and systematic takeover of the political operations of the faith:

> The Christian community in Rome was comparatively large and affluent. Moreover, located in the capital of the empire, it had inherited a tradition of administrative prowess from the state apparatus through a kind of trickle-down effect. Using the administrative skills of its leaders and its vast material resources, the church in Rome managed to exert influence over the other Christian communities. Among other things, the Roman Christians promoted a hierarchical structure, insisting that each church should have a single bishop. Given the right

---

[466] Gibbon, *Decline and Fall*, p. 453.

bishop, of course, certain theological views could then be preached and enforced.[467]

Thus the Jewish Christians' sway over matters both theological and political would progressively wane. Of course, it did not help that they were nearly annihilated by the Roman army.

Following Jerusalem's mid-century decline in popularity amongst the new Christians, we encounter a harrowing tale: Jewish revolts had cued the famous Roman siege and subsequent ransacking of Jerusalem. But the Nazarene Jews appear to have narrowly missed the rape of the holy city, having collectively absconded just months before the Roman holocaust. As the Christians of Jerusalem retreated on the Feast of Pentecost in 69 CE, it seems immediately obvious that they accomplished their survival by successfully heeding Christ's prophetic warning to flee Judea at the sign of invasion (Matt 24:16). The historian Epiphanius certainly agrees that "Christ told them to abandon Jerusalem and withdraw from it because of its coming siege. And they settled in Peraea for this reason."[468] Before the merciless hordes of Titus crushed their countrymen and finally took the city in 70 CE, "the Christian community had fled to Pella in Peraea, east of the Jordan (southeast of Jening), before the beginning of the siege."[469] The Jewish historian Josephus may also have recorded this event.[470] Even after the razing of the cultural and religious center of their civilization, the Nazarenes are said to have adhered to the national customs of their fathers and taken up residence in the churches of the East.[471]

The city of Pella became their headquarters for another sixty years from which they made frequent pilgrimages to Jerusalem, where they hoped to one day be permanently restored. However, the Romans, under Hadrian, further demolished their hopes by preventing Jews from approaching the city with military blockades. A sudden political shift eventually saw the election of a man named Marcus as their bishop, a minister of the Gentiles, and probably a native of one of the Latin provinces. Capitalizing on their desperation, Marcus persuaded many of them to renounce their practice of Mosaic law so as to purchase admission to Jerusalem from the Romans, integrating them further with the Catholic establishment of the Gentiles whose growing success and

---

[467] Ehrman, *Lost Christianities*, p. 175.

[468] Epiphanius, *Panarion*, 29, 7:8.

[469] See Adrian Fortescue, *The Catholic Encyclopedia*, Vol. VIII (New York: Robert Appleton Company, 1910), pp. 355-361.

[470] Josephus, *Wars of the Jews*, Book VI, Chapter V, Section 3, (Whiston, 1957), p. 825.

[471] See Jerome, *From Jerome to Augustine (AD 404); Letter 75 (Augustine) or 112 (Jerome).*

opulence weighed heavily on the scarcity of the Nazarenes. Yet not all of the Nazarenes followed Marcus. Soon, in the wake of this disruption, the Catholics began to lay upon those dissenters rabid accusations of *heresy*, a practice in which the Church would continuously improve. Historians recognize that:

> The church diverged in discipline and dogma more and more widely from its ancient form, till in the second century the Christians of Judea, who had faithfully followed the customs and tenets of the twelve apostles, were informed that they were heretics. During that interval a new religion had arisen. Christianity had conquered paganism, and paganism had corrupted Christianity... The single Deity of the Jews had been exchanged for the Trinity, which the Egyptians had invented, and which Plato had idealized into a philosophic system. The man who had said, *"Why callest thou me good? There is none good but one, that is God,"* had now himself been made a god, or the third part of one.[472]

One might expect such pressure to swiftly extinguish the Nazarenes' resolve and cause their remnants to liquefy into the Roman system or retreat back into the synagogues. However, the unsung annals of this dramatic Christian history yield a stunning fact: in spite of the world, the Nazarenes are found still thriving in the *fourth century*—even during the troublesome Council of Nicaea (325 CE). Epiphanius reveals that these later Nazarenes were, in fact, the very same Jewish converts who directly inherited their church from the Apostles in first-century Jerusalem.[473]

As Christendom crept through the mire of Greek philosophy towards what would eventually become orthodox Trinitarianism, we find that not only did the ecclesiastical presence of the Nazarenes persist into the fourth century, but so did the spirit of their Human Christology, even amongst many of the Gentile Church Fathers who fought to stem the prodigious tide of mystical Platonic and Gnostic philosophy. Indeed, in the later conciliar disputes, the names "Jew" and "Ebionite" were "hurled at those Christians who resisted the advancing Hellenizing of Christianity, with regard, for example, to the doctrine of God,

---

[472] William Winwood Reade, *The Martyrdom of Man* (New York: Peter Eckler, 1890), p. 235.
[473] Epiphanius, *Panarion*, 29, 5, 4 and 5, 6 and 7, 7.

eschatology, Christology, etc."[474] These persons will be discussed in both this and the following chapter.

Ultimately, it is clear that just prior to the second century, Jewish Christianity had been in "the comfortable majority, as it was in the first generation of disciples and in the end of the New Testament period."[475] However, comparing that New Testament community with post-first-century Jewish Christianity, scholars have concluded that "there is not much evidence that Jewish Christianity had changed radically." Thus it was the very faith of the earliest Palestinian Jesus movement that had been *superseded* by an overbearing, incompatible Gentile church. Indeed, "what *had* changed, obviously, was the social characteristics and environment of Christianity."[476] By the fourth century, this shift had driven an immovable wedge between "Judaism" and "Christianity" as two separate religions. Modern Trinitarian scholars have often attempted to reconcile orthodoxy with this hard fact; they have painted the "Catholic" Christianity that emerged out of the fourth century as compatible with the thought and organization of the first Jewish community. But this proposition has not rightly taken history into account. As Harnack writes, "historical observation, which reckons only with concrete quantities, can discover in Catholicism... no element which it would have to describe as Jewish Christian. It observes only a progressive Hellenizing."[477] This Hellenizing has, unquestionably, taken the primeval Jewish-Christian faith far beyond the boundaries of the Jewish world. It is now a square peg that cannot be pressed backwards into a circular hole.

Were the 2nd and 3rd Century Fathers Trinitarians?

Though historians find the orthodox doctrine of the Trinity absent until the fourth century, it is still popularly claimed by apologists that there has existed an unbroken stream of Trinitarianism emanating from the Apostolic church, and that only the terminology evolved within Christendom as they labored to accurately express in language what they had always believed. In this view, it was not until the Greek and Latin proto-orthodox Church Fathers, with their philosophical backgrounds, assumed the Jewish Christian religion that its true doctrines could have possibly been explicated. But if one were to discover the

---

[474] Harnack, *History of Dogma*, Vol. 1, 1894, Ch. VI, p. 292.

[475] Alan F. Segal, "Jewish Christianity," *Eusebius, Christianity, and Judaism* (Detroit: Wayne State University Press, 1992), p. 340.

[476] Ibid., emphasis added.

[477] Harnack, *History of Dogma*, Vol. 1, pp. 292-293.

most prominent Gentile Christians of the second and third centuries expressing explicitly non-Trinitarian sentiments, would that not be reason to esteem them as non-Trinitarians?

Justin Martyr, Irenaeus, Tertullian, and others are cited by mainstream apologists as examples of major Church Fathers who exhibited at least a primitive, under-developed, or "naïve" Trinitarianism.[478] We might assume this means that they simply did not have the finer points resolved, such as the relationship between the dual natures of Christ, or the two minds and wills of Christ (which would not be actively debated by the orthodox until the fourth and fifth centuries). Perhaps, at least, the foundations were present? The most fundamental components of Trinitarianism, including the eternal co-equality of three different God-persons, or at least the equal and identical status of the Father and the Son, should at least be present in some rudimentary form if this were the case. After all, wouldn't the Apostles who supposedly imparted their Trinitarianism to the Church Fathers at least be able to articulate such essentials? We should say that anything less than such a basic requirement should not be counted as fair evidence of Trinitarianism.

The most famous Church figures of the first three centuries should not therefore be cited as proof of the Trinitarian dogma's ecumenical acceptance, as they not only fail to espouse even the most fundamental Trinitarian requisites, but actually promote contrary, and often *unitarian* opinions. What these individuals actually represent is a proto-orthodox Gentile Christianity which actively Hellenized the faith, but not to the point where it had produced Trinitarianism, nor to the point where it had ceased entertaining the essentially unitarian view it was progressively moving away from. Some, like the Sabellians (Modalists), had said that God was one person, but he existed in different modes of the Father, Son, and Spirit. Others, the Subordinationists, whom we will presently investigate, had said that the Son was distinct and subjected to the one person of the Father. Indeed, these rival factions celebrated, incorporated, and viewed the Scriptures through an overtly Platonic worldview, as had Philo before them, but none of the "catholics" yet professed God's existence as three different co-equal, co-eternal, and divine individuals. As one encyclopedia aptly summarizes, "No theologian in the first three Christian centuries was a

---

[478] J. N. D. Kelly, *Early Christian Doctrines* (London: A&C Black, 1977), p. 90.

Trinitarian in the sense of believing that the one God is tripersonal, containing equally divine "persons," Father, Son, and Holy Spirit."[479]

Subordinationism

Subordinationism is the doctrine which posits that the Son is subordinate to God the Father in nature and being, and that the Son both takes his orders from and owes his existence to God. It is easy to see why this view was so popular in the early Church; evidence of Subordinationism within the biblical documents is widespread:

> *"… the Father is greater than I."* (John 14:28)

> *"My Father, who has given them to me, is greater than all."* (John 10:29)

> *"Truly, truly, I say to you, a slave is not greater than his master, nor is the one who is sent greater than the one who sent him."* (John 13:16)

> *"For just as the Father has life in himself, even so he gave to the Son also to have life in himself, and he gave him authority to execute judgment."* (John 5:26)

> *"But I want you to understand that Christ is the head of every man, and the man is the head of a woman, and God is the head of Christ."* (1 Cor 11:3)

> *"and you belong to Christ; and Christ belongs to God"* (1 Cor 3:23)

> *"But when [God] says, "All things are put in subjection to [Christ]," it is evident that he is excepted who put all things in subjection to him… When all things are subjected to him, then the Son himself will be subjected to the one who subjected all things to him, so that God may be all in all."* (1 Cor 15:27-28)

---

[479] Dale Tuggy, "History of Trinitarian Doctrines," *Stanford Encyclopedia of Philosophy*. 2013. Web. 22 December 2014.

"Then I said, Behold, I have come (in the scroll of the book it is written of me) to do your will, O God." (Hebrews 10:7)

"Father, if you are willing, take this cup from me; yet not my will, but yours be done." (Luke 22:42)

"Behold, my servant whom I have chosen; my beloved in whom my soul is well pleased; I will put my spirit upon him, and he shall proclaim justice to the Gentiles." (Matthew 12:18, Isaiah 42:1-4)

Some of the earliest Church records evidence no break with these views. For example, Clement I of Rome (45-101 CE), not to be confused with the later Clement of Alexandria, is often considered the first Pope (the second or third after Peter if one consults the Catholics), and tradition even has it that he was consecrated by Peter himself.[480] Clement presents himself as a committed Subordinationist, and even a unitarian. He writes: *"Let all the heathen know that thou [the Father] art God alone, and that Jesus Christ is thy Servant"* (59:4). For Clement, the only God is the one called the Father of Jesus, while the Christ clearly takes a place of subjection. Clement routinely distinguishes Christ from God: *"Have we not one God, and one Christ, and one spirit of grace (or love) poured out upon us?"* (46:6). His subordination of Jesus to the one God is unswerving: *"Jesus Christ was sent from God. So Christ is from God, and the apostles are from Christ: thus both came in proper order by the will of God"* (42:1-2).

Interestingly, what is lacking at this early stage is any mention of the Philonic logos angel used by God in creation, with whom later proto-orthodox Christians like Justin Martyr would become so enamored. Most conspicuously absent is the Trinitarian notion of the Father and Son's co-equality. Far from holding to the Demiurgic logos view of the Platonizers, Clement writes: *"By his almighty power he established the heavens... he called it into being by his command... With his holy and pure hands he also formed man"* (1 Clement 33). Here God himself is the sole creator; he has not employed a personal logos, an angel, or Jesus to execute his creation; it is by his own hand. One scholar writes: "In conclusion, one searches in vain in [Clement] for those views of the logos, as a personified attribute of the Father, which are so prominent in the writings of the philosophical converts to

---

[480] See John Chapman, "Pope St. Clement I," *The Catholic Encyclopedia*, 1908.

Christianity."[481] Neither of course, is there any Clementine statement of triune co-equality in the Godhead.

However, by the time of Justin Martyr in the second century, the logos-angel of Philo was growing popular amongst the Platonizing Christian philosophers, though most had ostensibly remained Subordinationist. As Subordinationists, they taught that while the Son may have pre-existed as the logos of God, and may be divine in some sense, he is not identical to the one true God. Neither is the Holy Spirit identified by these teachers as a third co-equal person of the One God, but was considered an even lesser creature, even subordinate to the Son. This very "Arian" faith which is so often erroneously said to have only arisen to challenge a long-standing Trinitarian orthodoxy in the fourth century, is much older than is popularly suggested. Regarding this common white-washing of history, the great Anglican bishop R. P. C. Hanson writes:

> The accounts of what happened which have come down to us were mostly written by those who belonged to the school of thought which eventually prevailed and have been deeply colored by that fact. The supporters of this view wanted their readers to think that orthodoxy on the subject under discussion had always existed and that the period was simply a story of the defense of that orthodoxy against heresy and error. But it ought to be obvious that his could not possibly have been the case.[482]

Even in the fourth century debates, Arius' teaching that Jesus was a subordinate being was able to be defended as "traditional," and by many he was seen as a committed theological conservative.[483] Even Constantine, in a letter to Arius and his bishop Alexander, observed that the controversy between them had not erupted over any "new" theology.[484] Indeed, historians now recognize that:

> Many of the earlier Church Fathers, including Justin Martyr, Clement and Origen—the last two Alexandrians themselves—

---

[481] Lamson, Abbot, p. 9.

[482] R. P. C. Hanson, *The Search for the Christian Doctrine of God: The Arian Controversy, 318-381* (Edinburgh: T & T Clark, 1988), pp. xviii-xix.

[483] Rowan Williams, "Arius: Heresy and Tradition," *The Journal of Roman Studies*, Vol. 79 (London: Society for the Promotion of Roman Studies, 1989), pp. 256-257. See Griggs, p. 145.

[484] Constantine wrote: "The cause of your difference has not been any of the leadership doctrines or precepts of the Divine Law, nor has any new heresy respecting the worship of God arisen among you" (quoted by Freeman in *The Closing of the Western Mind*, p. 166).

treated Jesus the Son as somehow derivative of the Father…
When Arius claimed that he was following "our faith from our
forefathers, which we have learnt from you," these were the
formidable theologians whose work he could draw on.[485]

Despite the contention of polemicists like Athanasius and Eusebius of
Caesarea, it appears that the proto-Trinitarian party's view was the more
revolutionary. As scholars reveal, the idea that Arius was the innovator is a
"legend."[486] However, this is not to say that the traditional "Arian" view (the
belief in a subordinate, pre-existent Logos-being) is necessarily the best
interpretation of the biblical data, but only to demonstrate the absence of an
assumed Trinitarianism and the continued, widespread presence of the view that
the Father is superior to the Son through the middle of the fourth century CE.
Bishop Hanson confirms that:

> with the exception of Athanasius, virtually every theologian,
> East and West, accepted some form of Subordinationism at
> least up to the year 355 CE; subordinationism might indeed,
> until the denouement of the controversy, have been described
> as accepted orthodoxy.[487]

It would not be until the Athanasian movement asserted the co-equality of
Father and Son and backed their view by the mandate of the Roman state that
the majority Subordinationism began to lose real political power. But even
before then, at the dawn of the third century, Subordinationism had been
challenged by another rival view: Sabellianism, also known as Modalism, a view
which battled not only the Platonic Subordinationists, but the unitarians who still
maintained the Christology of the Nazarene and Ebionite Jews.

Subordinationism Clashes with Sabellianism

In the late second century, a respectable and well-learned cobbler named
Theodotus (fl. 190 CE) enjoyed a sizeable following with a striking teaching that
echoed the Human Christology of the Jewish Christians of Jerusalem.
Theodotus said that the Father was the true God, and that Jesus was a man born
of the virgin Mary who had been empowered by God at his baptism to be the

---

[485] Freeman, *Closing of the Western Mind,* p. 165.
[486] Griggs, p. 245.
[487] Hanson, p. xix.

Messiah.[488]   Many Gentile intellectuals in the Church found an attractive rationality in his doctrine,[489] and a large number of the Christian bishops are thought to have followed in this or similar thinking.[490]   Yet there were those amongst the bishops who argued that Christ could be no "mere man."

One such hostile person was Pope Victor I (d. 199 CE). Victor, an ostensibly rash magistrate who had excommunicated all the eastern churches because they did not observe Easter at the same time that the western churches did,[491] appears to have taken to the influence of another man named Praxeas (fl. 190 CE).[492] This Praxeas had taught the strict unity of God (that God was one person), but that the Son was a *mode* of the one God, that the Father himself had come down and suffered to be crucified.[493] Ultimately Praxeas' teachings would influence the later Sabellius, who would carry on the view in the third century and have his name identified with it.[494]   Pope Victor I is thought to have "endeavored to strengthen" the Praxean view in Rome, and so came into conflict with the human Christ views of Theodotus the cobbler.[495] The dispute between Victor and the Theodotians was a scuffle between two essentially "unitary" views; Theodotus' God was one person, while Praxeas' God was one person in three modes. Ultimately, Victor excommunicated Theodotus around 190 CE, though it is still not known on precisely what grounds. Today some might assert that it was for Theodotus' unitarian teaching, but as Dr. Priestley notes:

> Theodotus having been excommunicated as a Unitarian is
> hardly consistent with that general prevalence of the Unitarian
> doctrine in the time of Tertullian, (which was also that of

---

[488] See Hippolytus, *The Refutation of All Heresies*, Ch. VII, 23.   Some scholars have disputed Hippolytus' account of Theodotus' belief in the virgin birth, seeing him as more of an Adoptionist (that God adopted Jesus to be his son at his baptism).   Hippolytus however, certainly saw in Theodotus an adherence to the virginal birth.   Nevertheless, Theodotus' view of God was indisputably unitarian and his view of Christ indisputably human and Subordinationist.

[489] Epiphanius reports that Theodotus and the "Theodotian sect" he founded, constantly appealed to Scripture to support their view of the human Jesus. Some of Theodotus' favorite texts included John 8:40: *"you seek to kill me, a man that has told you the truth that I heard from God,"* and Deuteronomy 18:15: *"Yahweh your God will raise up a prophet like me from among you, from your countrymen, you shall listen to him."* See Epiphanius, *Panarion*, 1, 9; 3, 1.

[490] Ehrman, *Lost Christianities*, pp. 152-155.

[491] Joseph Priestley, *The Theological Works of Joseph Priestley*, Vol. 6 (London: G. Smallfield, 1786), p. 505.

[492] John Chapman, "Praxeas," *The Catholic Encyclopedia*, Vol. 12 (New York: The Encyclopedia Press, 1911), p. 344.

[493] Tertullian, *Against Praxeas*, 1.

[494] Kenneth Latourette, *A History of Christianity*, Vol. 1 (New York: HarperCollins, 1875), pp. 144-146.

[495] Tertullian, *De Praescriptione*, Appendix.

Victor)… Theodotus… is said by the Unitarians to have been well received by Victor at first; so that it is very possible that the latter might have been instigated to what he did by some quarrel between them, of which we have no account… There is no instance, I believe, of any person having been excommunicated for being a Unitarian before Theodotus. Whereas, had the universal church been Trinitarian from the beginning, would not the first Unitarians… have been expelled from all Christian societies with horror?[496]

After Theodotus' excommunication, the Theodotian sect nevertheless endured independently in sizeable numbers into the late 3rd century.[497] But in confronting the Theodotians, along with several others who had held his views,[498] later members of Victor's party in Rome may have over-compensated. In the wake of Victor's death, Victor's successor, Pope Zephyrinus, tolerated and probably encouraged the Praxean Modalist heresy.[499] Though this Praxean view that Jesus was identical to God the Father had become strong in Rome, it came under heavy criticism, most famously by Tertullian in his celebrated work *Against Praxeas* (c. 213). Tertullian allied with the influential Hippolytus of Rome (170-235 CE), and the pair argued for the distinction and subordination of the Son to the Father in this way:

Why does Scripture say that God sent his son, rather than that he sent himself? How can anyone be his own father? To whom is Jesus speaking when he prays? How can Jesus talk about his going to the Father (John 20:17) if he *is* the Father? And is it really conceivable that God the Father was killed?[500]

Pope Zephyrinus came under harsh criticism from Hippolytus, who accused him of Modalism. The feud resulted in Hippolytus and his disciples fleeing from

---

[496] Priestley, *Works*, pp. 504-506.

[497] After both Theodotus and Victor's demise, the Theodotians continued under the leadership of yet another Theodotus (known as the Money Changer), and Asclepiodotus. The dispute between these elders and Victor's successor Zephyrinus evidently took its toll on the pope. Though Zephyrinus was not actually martyred, his mental suffering during his reign earned him a martyr's title.

[498] See Epiphanius, *Heresies*, 54; Eusebius, *Church History*, l, 5.

[499] C. Wordsworth, *St. Hippolytus and the Church of Rome* (Oxford: Rivingtons, 1880), p. 192.

[500] Ehrman, *Lost Christianities*, p. 153. See also Tertullian, *Against Praxeas*, and Hippolytus, *Against Noetus*.

communion with the pope and proclaiming themselves the true church in Rome.[501] Ultimately, Tertullian, Hippolytus and others vigorously defended the more traditional subordinate logos Christology[502] until the Praxean/Sabellian view eventually fell out of favor and was repeatedly condemned as heresy.[503] Thus the Father and the Son were, in the third century, viewed by the mainstream of Christendom as being distinct. Indeed, at this stage, Subordinationism still prevailed. And not only Subordinationism, but even the Human Christology of Theodotus continued to hold ground against the increasing Logos Christology, and was still able to publicly trace itself back to the times of the earliest Jewish Christians.

The history of Artemon (c. 230 CE) is useful in this regard. Artemon was a prominent and popular teacher in Rome who held to the Human Christology, Jesus' birth by a virgin, and the unitarian Godhead.[504] Artemon is worthy of notice especially in that he publicly claimed the authority of antiquity for his views, tracing them back to the first Christian community in Judea. Not only this, but Artemon and his allies furthermore claimed that the belief in a divine Christ had only begun to hold major sway over Christendom around the time of Pope Victor I and Zephyrinus (late second century). This date appears to align with our earlier notice of the success of Marcionite and Valentinian Christianity in the late second century. Between the powerful Gnostic, Crypto-Gnostic, and Sabellian influences emanating out of Rome and Alexandria in that era, it seems reasonable to agree with the Artemonites that this period marked the widespread drowning out of the human Jesus. Eusebius recalls:

---

[501] Burton Easton, *The Apostolic Tradition of Hippolytus* (Cambridge: CUP, 1934), pp. 21-22.

[502] Hippolytus exhibits similar views as Tertullian in the sense that the Logos of God was eternally divine, but did not yet become the person of the Son until it was willed by God later; thus there was no eternal generation of a co-equal Son. One source reports, "In Hippolytus, the Logos *becomes* personal first at the creation, and remains so henceforth to all eternity; but He *becomes* perfect as the Son of God first at the Incarnation... Moreover, Hippolytus assumes a relation of *strict subordination*" (John Dollinger, *Hippolytus and Callistus* (Edinburgh: T & T Clark, 1876), p. 202, emphasis added). Another explains: "[Hippolytus] believes that the Logos fully becomes the Son only when he assumes humanity. For instance, the polemicist writes: 'Now what Son of his own has God sent down through the flesh if not the Word, whom he addressed as Son in view of the fact that he was going to become such in the future?' " (Edgar G. Foster, *Angelomorphic Christology and the Exegesis of Psalm 8:5 in Tertullian's Adversus Praxean* (Lanham: University Press of America, 2005), p. 24).

[503] Sabellius, a Libyan priest, gave new rise to the Praxean/Modalist view during the opening of the third century, thus his name is so closely associated with the view today. After first enjoying the acceptance of Bishop Callistus, he was excommunicated by Callistus around 220 CE after Hippolytus turned the bishop's favor. Sabellius was again denounced by Dionysius around 260 CE. Once more Bishop Damascus condemned Sabellius in 380 CE.

[504] See Theodoretus, *Compendium of Heretical Accounts*, 2, 6. See also Lamson, Abbot, p. 225.

[the Artemonites] affirm that all the ancients, and the very Apostles, received and taught the same things which they now assert; and that the preaching of the truth was preserved till the times of Victor, who, from Peter, was the thirteenth Bishop of Rome; but, from the times of his successor Zephyrinus, the truth has been adulterated.[505]

Continuing, the orthodox Eusebius attempts to refute the Artemonite claims by citing the antiquity of those who held the personal Logos doctrine. However, he only goes back as far as Clement of Alexandria (late 2nd century CE) and Justin Martyr (c. 150 CE), and does not, or cannot, venture any further. But, as we will soon discover, even in Justin's time the Logos doctrine had not prevailed over all of Christianity, and many still held to the purely human Christology. In light of the history of the Nazarene Christians and others, Artemon's assertions seem substantiated. As one pair of historians notes, "Artemon's claim to hold the ancient doctrine has somewhat perplexed the advocates of the 'Logos doctrine.' It is to them an ugly fact, difficult to be disposed of."[506]

Regardless, as one scholar aptly summarizes, "While the forms of subordinationism varied, virtually all ante-Nicene theologians engaged in some form of it."[507] Again, it would not be until the fourth century that these views would be seriously threatened, when the proto-orthodox party "refined their categories and came to reject any notion of Christ's subordination to God."[508]

Having described the broader theological climate of the late second and third centuries, we will now pay careful consideration to several of the most prominent figures of those eras who are most often enlisted by apologists as devoted Trinitarians. We will investigate whether or not they still exhibited the traditional subordination of the Son, or whether they professed the necessary co-eternality and co-equality required to be Trinitarians. We will also continue to note in their opinions the lively perpetuation of the distinctive Platonic notions of the Demiurge and Philonic logos.

---

[505] Eusebius, *Church History*, 5, 28.

[506] Lamson, Abbot, p. 225.

[507] Thomas C. Pfizenmaier, *The Trinitarian Theology of Dr. Samuel Clarke* (Leiden: Brill, 1997), p. 91.

[508] Ehrman, *Lost Christianites*, p. 155.

Justin Martyr, a Committed Trinitarian?

Regarding the celebrated Justin Martyr (100-165 CE), it is sometimes claimed by apologists that: "Justin believed in a Father, Son, and Spirit as three distinct persons. All three of these persons were [the same] God."[509] But does Justin himself ever ascribe such a tri-personal nature to the one God? Does he view Jesus, the Father, and the Holy Spirit as the same single Deity? We do not find in Justin a committed Trinitarian, but only a Hellenizing Christian philosopher determined to synthesize the faith with Platonism, which he found the most worthwhile of all the Greek philosophic schools he dabbled in.

It is true that Justin, like many of the Fathers, used the term "God" (or "god") to describe Christ. However, we will soon observe that the classical application of the word was much broader than it is today. While Justin's employment of "God" to describe Jesus may generate confusion amongst some contemporary readers, Justin's other statements about Christ and the Father shed light on his actual faith. In his famous *Dialogue with Trypho the Jew* he writes: "We do not claim that our God is different from yours... The God of Abraham, and of Isaac, and of Jacob."[510] This is obviously a claim which modern Trinitarians would also make. However, in his first apology Justin elaborates:

> We worship the maker of this universe... Our teacher of these
> things is Jesus Christ... we reasonably worship him, having
> learned that he is the son of the true God himself, and holding
> him in the second place, and the prophetic spirit in the third,
> we will prove... we give to a crucified man a place second to
> the unchangeable and eternal God, the Creator of all.[511]

So far we have seen that Justin's God is the God of the Jews and that he is also the Father of Jesus. His mention of worshiping or honoring the Son and the Spirit in addition to "the true God" does not automatically make him a Trinitarian. The fact that he ranks them in degree demonstrates that he does not consider these subjects co-equal God, without which dogma there is no Trinitarianism. Justin is a Subordinationist; the Father takes precedence over the Son. It is also clear that unlike many evangelical Trinitarians today, Justin does not take the stance that religious honor is to be reserved for God alone. For Justin, God is:

---

[509] Robert Alan King, *Justin Martyr on the Trinity: God as Father, Son, and Spirit* (Casa Grande: King & Associates, 2011), p. 1.

[510] Justin Martyr, *Dialogue*, 11, 1.

[511] Justin Martyr, *First Apology*, 13, 1.

the most true God, the Father of righteousness and
temperance who is unmixed with evil, but we worship and
adore both him and the son who came from him and taught us
these things and the army of the other good angels who follow
him and are made like him and the prophetic spirit giving
honor and reason and truth.[512]

Here Justin is demonstrating the breadth of worship for the Christian. He
explains that alongside God, who is the Father, he also worships the Son, the
angels, and the prophetic spirit, though obviously not in the exact same way or
to the same degree as he worships the one God, the Father of Jesus, as he has
already ranked them by degree. Furthermore, after mentioning the Son, Justin
directly mentions "the *other* good angels... who are made like him." For Justin,
the Son was a divine spirit who was not the one God, but was the Logos of God,
a pre-incarnate angelic being who became a man:

> There exists and is mentioned in Scripture another God and
> Lord under the Creator of all things who is also called an
> Angel... [who also] appeared to Abraham, Jacob, and Moses,
> and is called God, [and] is distinct from God, the Creator;
> distinct, that is, in number, and not in mind.[513]

This Logos is said to be "another God" who is "under the Creator"; while
united with the one God in mind or purpose, this angelic incarnation is not the
Creator God. Justin even appears to abhor the idea that the Creator became
incarnate as a human being:

> No one with even the slightest intelligence would dare to assert
> that the Creator and Father of all things left His super-celestial
> realms to make himself visible in a little spot on earth.[514]

Though Justin calls Jesus "God" (theos), we know that Justin is not a
Trinitarian, because to him the Son exists outside the one true Godhead as a
secondary, lesser "god"—a person certainly not co-equal with the Father but a
separate divine being of lesser quality and honor. One scholar summarizes:

---

[512] Ibid., 6.
[513] Justin Martyr, *Dialogue,* 56.
[514] Ibid., 60.

The modern popular doctrine of the Trinity... derives no support from the language of Justin, and this observation may be extended to all the ante-Nicene Fathers; that is, to all Christian writers for three centuries after the birth of Christ. It is true, they speak of the Father, Son, and... holy Spirit, but not as co-equal, not as one numerical essence, not as Three in one, in any sense now admitted by Trinitarians. The very reverse is the fact.[515]

But we still wonder if Justin's view of Christ's pre-existence as a second divine being was the accepted view of all (non-Gnostic) Christians in his day? Delving a little deeper into Justin's conversation with Trypho the Jew yields interesting information. In *Dialogue* chapter 48, Trypho questions Justin's view of Christ's non-human pre-existence. He wonders how it is possible that Justin's Christ could be truly human and *born of man*, and yet had first existed as something else, and was therefore not *of man*. "It seems to be," Trypho protests, "entirely absurd and utterly impossible for proof."[516] We must here remember that the Jew had a very different idea of the soul than the Hellenizers. The traditional Jew was lacking the metaphysical system of Plato which enabled a divine nature or pre-existing person to unite with another abstract nature. Thus Trypho calls Justin's belief in Jesus' pre-existence "not merely paradoxical, but also foolish."[517] Surprisingly however, instead of simply providing Scripture to prove unequivocally that Christ did in fact pre-exist his humanity, Justin makes a remarkable series of statements which may help to shed light on the state of Christianity in his era. He begins by saying:

I know that the statement does appear to be paradoxical, especially to those of your race, who are ever unwilling to understand or to perform the requirements of God, but ready to perform those of your teachers.[518]

By this Justin appears to reveal that there was indeed no belief in literal pre-existence of the Messiah widely established among the Jews, no religious or philosophical frame of reference by which the incarnation of a heavenly being and unison with a human nature could have been perceived as anything but

---

[515] Lamson, Abbot, pp. 56-57.
[516] Justin Martyr, *Dialogue with Trypho,* 48.
[517] Ibid., 48, 1.
[518] Ibid., 48, 2.

nonsense. This seems historically correct; the traditional Jewish and Platonic worldviews were ever incompatible despite the fashions of any progressive Alexandrian exegetes. The Jews certainly were not then, and still to this day cannot be led by their scriptures to view the Messiah as a literally pre-existing divine being, but simply as a man.[519] Even Trypho himself says, "We Jews all expect that Christ will be a man of merely human origin... If this man appears to be the Christ, he must be considered to be a man of solely human birth."[520] Nevertheless, Justin continues to assert a heavenly pre-existence for the Messiah, yet he seems to do so tenuously:

> Now assuredly, Trypho, [the proof] that this man is the Christ of God does not fail, *though I be unable to prove that he existed formerly* as Son of the Maker of all things, being God [or "god"], and was born a man by the Virgin. But since I have certainly proved that this man is the Christ of God, whoever he be, *even if I do not prove that he pre-existed*, and submitted to be born a man of like passions with us, having a body, according to the Father's will; in this last matter alone is it just to say that I have erred, and not to deny that he is the Christ, *though it should appear that he was born man of men, and [nothing more] is proved [than this], that he has become Christ by election*. For there are some, my friends, of our race, who admit that he is Christ, *while holding him to be man of men*; with whom I do not agree, nor would I, even [if] most of those who have the same opinions as myself should say so.[521]

Justin's tactic here is revealing. He argues that the substance of proof lies in the fact that the man Jesus of Nazareth is the prophesied Messiah. Furthermore, the only matters which he has so far been able to prove, and quite possibly the *only* matters he can prove, are that Jesus was born of man, and that he is the

---

[519] The reformer Melanchthon writes, "The Jews... expected a Messiah that would be... only a man like the other prophets, though surpassing them in wisdom, virtue, and capacity to obtain and govern the whole world" (F. A. Cox, *Life of Melancthon* (London: Forgotten Books, 2013 [1815]), p. 120). A Trinitarian bishop agrees, "That the [Jews] should have expected their Messiah to have been very and perfect God, of one substance with the Father, is, I think, more than we are warranted in asserting" (Charles J. Blomfield, *Dissertation upon the Traditional Knowledge of a Promised Redeemer* (Cambridge: J. Smith, 1819), p. 98).

[520] Justin Martyr, *Dialogue with Trypho*, 49, 1.

[521] Ibid., 48, 2-4, emphasis added.

Christ, having been made the Christ by God's own choice.[522] If Justin could prove that Jesus met the requirements of being the Christ *without* proving that he pre-existed or had anything other than a human nature, then a preceding existence or a divine nature did not represent any specific Messianic requirement to Justin's Christianity. In other words, Jesus did not have to be identical to God to be authentically the Christ, and, when it comes to providing conclusive evidence of any pre-existence, Justin seems to interject some hesitancy.

Even more interesting perhaps is that Justin says there were those, even among his own, who did not believe in Christ's pre-existence as a divine being, but who held that Jesus was purely and originally human. Thus he reveals that in early non-Gnostic Gentile Christianity not all had accepted the burgeoning Logos-Christology which Justin and his philosophical movement had adapted from Philo. Justin certainly views those with the Human Christology as fellow Christians who properly accepted Jesus as the Christ sans pre-existence, and he clearly begs Trypho to join them in that confession. Of course Justin himself strongly believes in the pre-existence, and claims he would stick to it, even if the members of his faith who currently held his own beliefs were convinced to believe otherwise. Again, Justin seems to provide at least the possibility of reasonable Christian doubt of the pre-existence idea. But wouldn't Christ's pre-existence as eternal God have been a cornerstone of the Christian belief delivered to them by the Apostles, if the Apostles were indeed Trinitarians as some modern apologists claim? At the very least Justin does not appear to share the spirit of Athanasius and the later orthodox party of the fourth century who immediately consigned those who disagreed to the flames of anathema.

We will consider one scholar's astute summary of the possible inferences we may draw from Justin's revealing statements:

> The doctrine of Christ's divinity and pre-existence had at this
> period gained little footing among Christians, if it was not the
> invention of Justin himself, for we do not find him appealing
> to former writers on the subject, or even to the general opinion
> of Christians in his time, but only to his own sense, or
> interpretation, of the Scriptures... [Furthermore it is possible
> that] the diffidence with which Justin expresses his own

---

[522] Biblically speaking, Jesus was not the Christ by the result of deity incarnating into human flesh; he was not the Christ by virtue of nature. Rather, it was explicitly by God's decree. The Apostle Peter declared at Pentecost: "*Jesus of Nazareth was a man... having been exalted to the right hand of God... let all the house of Israel know for certain that <u>God has made him both Lord and Christ</u>—this Jesus whom you crucified*" (Acts 2:22ff).

opinion, and the doubt which he intimates whether he should be able to demonstrate that Christ pre-existed, and his asserting that in case of a failure in his proof, the Messiahship of Jesus would remain firm notwithstanding, are all indications that the doctrine of the Divinity and Pre-existence of the Messiah, was at that time accounted a novel and very precarious opinion.[523]

Recalling the influence of Philo, and knowing that many modern scholars trace the rise of Christian Gnosticism to Alexandria, it seems probable that both the Gnostics and Justin were drawing upon the earlier mystical Hellenistic Jewish ideas about pre-existence emanating out of Alexandria. Certainly what we would call "catholic" Christianity in Justin's time still contrasted sharply from "Gnostic" Christianity.[524] The school of Valentinus, who was born the same year as Justin, was characterized by a complete acceptance of Christ's pre-existence and deity as fundamental to the faith, but this was evidently not yet an indispensable requirement of all non-Gnostic believers. It is clear that in Justin's era non-Gnostic Christians were divided (to some measurable extent) over pre-existence. Some said the Christ was simply a man, agreeing with the Jews. Some said he was in some sense a heavenly being, agreeing with Justin. Combined with the growing numbers of Gnostic Christians in the mid-second century, the heavenly Christ opinion does appear to have taken a sizeable hold by Justin's twilight, or shortly after his death. Of course, the actual percentage of Christians which fell into each camp in Justin's era is probably impossible to know. What should be known, however, is that the ancient debate over Christ's pre-existence as God, or a lesser god, or as anything else, is still alive today.

In our own time there exists a vibrant undercurrent of Christianity still looking back on the skepticism of both the Jews and many early Christians and detecting wisdom in their wariness of policies which smack too much of the Platonic spirit, and smack too little of incontrovertible biblical proof. "It appears to me," concluded Trypho, "that they who assert that he was of human origin, and was anointed as the Christ only by [God's] choice, propose a doctrine

---

[523] William Christie, *Dissertations on the Unity of God in the Person of the Father* (Philadelphia: R. H. Small, 1828), pp. 210-211.

[524] Justin himself wrote against Marcion and other Gnostics, revealing that though they were being called "Christians" in the empire, their views sharply contrasted with theirs (*First Apology*, 15). After Justin's death, Tatian (d. 180 CE), one of Justin's closest pupils, caused a major scandal by later joining in the Valentinian theology.

much more credible than yours."[525] In the second half of this book, where we will dedicate no less than two chapters to the elucidation of the biblical view of pre-existence, we will encounter evidence which should make it difficult to disagree with Trypho's conclusion.

Irenaeus of Lyon

Irenaeus (130-202 CE), famous for his polemics against the Gnostics, was a disciple of Polycarp, who was a disciple of Papias, who was a disciple of John the Apostle. Like Justin Martyr, he is sometimes cited by modern apologists as an "early prominent Trinitarian teacher and theologian."[526] In one evangelical editorial we encounter the claim that "Irenaeus testified to the church's Trinitarian understanding of God's nature long before the councils of Nicaea (325) and Constantinople (381) produced their traditional confessional creed."[527] But did Irenaeus really entertain Trinitarian theology? Did he testify of three distinct entities' unity in one equal divinity as is claimed by some?[528] Irenaeus, in his celebrated *Against Heresies*, writes:

> Wherefore I do also call upon thee, LORD God of Abraham, and God of Isaac, and God of Jacob and Israel, who art *the Father of our Lord Jesus Christ*, the God who, through the abundance of Thy mercy, hast had a favour towards us, that we should know Thee, who hast made heaven and earth, who rulest over all, who art *the only and the true God*, above whom there is none other God; grant, by our Lord Jesus Christ, the governing power of the Holy Spirit; give to every reader of this book to know Thee, *that Thou art God alone*, to be strengthened in Thee, and to avoid every heretical, and godless, and impious doctrine.[529]

As in Justin, we see that for Irenaeus, God is an individual identity, the Father of Jesus, who is recognized as the only one who is true God. Irenaeus continues:

---

[525] Justin Martyr, *Dialogue with Trypho*, 49, 1.

[526] "The God Revealed in Jesus Christ: A Brief Introduction to Trinitarian Theology". Grace Communion International. Web. 04 November 2014. <http://www.gci.org/god/revealed>.

[527] Paul Koll, *Christian Odyssey*, April/May 2008. Grace Communion International.

[528] J. J. Lashier, *The Trinitarian Theology of Irenaeus of Lyons*. Marquette University. 2009. Web. 04 November 2014. See also Steven D. Cone, *An Ocean Vast of Blessing: A Theology of Grace* (Eugene: Wipf & Stock, 2014), p. 45.

[529] Irenaeus, *Against Heresies*, 3, 4, 4.

neither the prophets, nor the apostles, nor the Lord Christ in his own person, did acknowledge any other Lord or God, but the God and Lord supreme: the prophets and the apostles confessing the Father and the Son; but naming no other as God [*but the Father*], and confessing no other as Lord [*but Christ*]: and the Lord [*Christ*] himself handing down to his disciples, *that he, the Father, is the only God and Lord, who alone is God and ruler of all*—it is incumbent on us to follow, if we are their disciples indeed, their testimonies to this effect... [John the Baptist] did not declare to them another God... There is therefore *one and the same God, the Father of our Lord*, who also promised, through the prophets, that he would send his forerunner; and his salvation—that is, his Word—he caused to be made visible to all flesh, [*the Word*] himself being made incarnate.[530]

For Irenaeus, the Lord Jesus had handed down to them the doctrine that "he, the Father" is the only one who is God over all. It is clear that "the Father of our Lord" is the supreme God, even in light of any revelation brought by John the Baptist or by Jesus Christ. Certainly Irenaeus echoes Christ in this regard, who in John's Gospel describes his Father as *"the only true God"* (Jn 17:1-3). Concerning Christ, Irenaeus, like Justin, views the Word (Logos) as a secondary entity made incarnate, who is not identified as one-and-the-same as the one true God.

We know that Irenaeus argued extensively against the Gnostics. His greatest opponents were certainly the students of Valentinus.[531] Arguing against that school, Irenaeus writes:

even the Lord, the very Son of God, allowed that the Father alone knows the very day and hour of judgment, when he plainly declares, *"But of that day and that hour knows no man, neither the Son, but the Father only"*... the Son was not ashamed to ascribe the knowledge of that day to the Father only... For if anyone should inquire the reason why the Father, who has fellowship with the Son in all things, has been declared by the Lord alone to know the hour and the day [of judgment], he will

---

[530] Ibid., 9, 1.
[531] Ibid.

find at present no more suitable, or becoming, or safe reason than this (since, indeed, the Lord is the only true Master), that we may learn through him that *the Father is above all things.* For "*the Father,*" says he, "*is greater than I.*" [We should not] fall into the danger of starting the question whether there is a God above God.[532]

Irenaeus again demonstrates his belief that the Son is another, lesser entity than the Father, whom he believes alone is supreme over all, reserving things for himself that he does not share with any co-equal partners. Irenaeus' Christ is not an incarnation or an emanation of the good God as the Gnostics preached. Despite the Son's lofty status and his continuous fellowship and association with the God of all, he nevertheless consistently remains lacking in some ways in which the Father is sufficient, not only in some economic, hierarchical authority or primacy, but in the very privileges and property of God. Irenaeus' view is quite contrary to those modern apologists who have claimed that Irenaeus was a Trinitarian who devotedly taught three entities who were each divine and powerful to the same degree.

Again, while today much is made of Justin, Irenaeus, and other early Church Fathers' usage of the word "God" (theos) to describe Jesus, without doubt the word is proven to have been used classically in a much broader sense. For example, Christians are also called "God" (theos) alongside the Father and the Son by Irenaeus:

> There is none other called God by the Scriptures except the Father of all, and the Son, and those who possess the adoption.[533]

If Christians, as the sons of God (John 1:12), are also "God" to Irenaeus, we cannot assume that his usage of the word to describe the Christ means that he believes Jesus is one-and-the-same God with the Father or that he views Christ as "fully God" in any Trinitarian sense. Likewise, we should note the conspicuous absence of the Holy Spirit, the assumed third person of the Trinity which Irenaeus, as a supposed Trinitarian, should have also readily acknowledged here as "God."

---

[532] Ibid., 2, 28, 6-8.
[533] Irenaeus, *Against Heresies*, 4, Preface, 4. (Edited by Alexander Roberts & James Donaldson. American Edition, 1885)

Ultimately, for at least these two oft-cited Church Fathers, we find a clear acknowledgment of the Father of Jesus as the only supreme God, and his Son as an entity certainly not equal to the Father, but subordinate (as the Father is the only God "over all") and even inferior in the things pertaining to God (such as God's knowledge). Irenaeus and Justin's view of Christ as the Logos, a high and spiritual being existing with God before creation, proves not only their Subordinationism, but also their "Arianism." As "Arians," they therefore hold a unitarian, not a Trinitarian view of the Godhead. Again, this is not to say that their Arian Christological opinions are correct, but we hope to conclusively demonstrate a heritage of unitarian theology in light of an assumed Trinitarianism; a faith which, historically speaking, would not be established as orthodox until the fourth century.

Origen Adamantius

Origen (184-254 CE) was the greatest of the Alexandrian theologians, and one of the most industrious and influential Christian thinkers of all time.[534] He was a masterful philosopher who taught Plato and Philo's immortality and pre-existence of the soul (again the golden thread of the Egyptian-Greek soul doctrine continues to show itself), and entertained an array of mystical theories about the incarnation of angelic beings.[535] He even speculated that John the Baptist was an embodied angel who had known Jesus in a previous life.[536] Origen was familiar with a wide variety of disciplines; even the great Neoplatonists reluctantly admitted his philosophical prowess. But it was Origen's pioneering *Christian* theology, particularly his "eternal generation" of the Son (which we will cover in the next chapter), that immediately set the stage for the solidification of orthodoxy in the century after his death.

According to Eusebius, Origen had been a pupil of the famed Clement of Alexandria.[537] Eusebius reports that after the great Roman persecution of 202

---

[534] Boer notes that "Origen's mind was so productive that he was able to keep six secretaries occupied in writing out the thoughts that he lectured and dictated" (Harry R. Boer, *A Short History of the Early Church*, Grand Rapids: Eerdmans, 1976), p. 92).

[535] Due to Origen's insistence on the Platonic immortal soul, the proto-orthodox party that followed after him is thus thought to have completely discarded the belief in a bodily resurrection. See Outi Lehtipuu, *Debates Over the Resurrection of the Dead: Constructing Early Christian Identity* (Oxford: OUP, 2015), p. 130.

[536] Mark J. Edwards, "Origen," *Standford Encyclopedia of Philosophy*, 2014. Web. 03 December 2014. See also Origen, *Comm. John*, 2, 31, 186.

[537] Eusebius, *Church History*, 5, 3, 3. We cannot know for certain that the young Origen would have attended Clement's courses. Eusebius obviously makes this connection, though Clement's

CE, Origen took over the Catechetical School from Clement at eighteen years old.[538] The school was influential in Alexandria and its frequent clashes with the Gnostics living in that city were not lost on Origen. He himself followed in the tradition of Clement and publicly opposed them. But we wonder if he followed in Clement's tendency to commandeer and adapt Gnostic models as well?

Origen was certainly openly antagonistic towards the Valentinians in Alexandria. However, he recognized one thing in their theology that was seriously lacking in his own proto-orthodox circle: organization. Indeed, "the oldest Christian theological systems were those of the Christian Gnostics."[539] It had been through this sophistication that they had so effectively grown their adherents; the systems were their power. But in Origen's time there was no technically comparable, non-Gnostic philosophical Christian organism.[540] Thus Origen moved to systematize Christianity in his work *On First Principles*.

Origen lays out his divine triad in the manner of the Platonists. He even uses the "three hypostases" locution found in Plotinus, but calls the members "Father," "Christ," and "Holy Spirit." But Origen is not a Trinitarian. Contrary to later Cappadocian orthodoxy, he obviously uses the word "hypostasis" to mean "substance" or "being." Thus for him, the three members of the triad are not all the same being, or God; the Father, Son, and Spirit are three different substances.[541] The possibility of orthodox Trinitarianism for Origen is dashed further by his exhibition of clear Subordinationist views. Origen explicitly writes that: "we believe nothing to be uncreated but the Father."[542] Thus he structures the relationship between the Father and Christ in the manner of the second-

---

extant works seem to be aimed at more advanced students. Nevertheless, the influence of Clement over the Catechetical School is certain.

[538] Roelof van den Broek, *Studies in Gnosticism and Alexandrian Christianity* (Leiden: Brill, 1996), p. 198.

[539] Rudolph, *Gnosis,* p. 369.

[540] Edward Moore, "Origen," Internet Encyclopedia of Philosophy. Web. 13 March 2015.

[541] Ayres explains his usage further: "Origen's use of the term hypostasis opens a debate that continues throughout the fourth century: he used the term to indicate 'real existence'—as opposed to existence only in thought—but also as 'individual circumscribed existence'... In his *Against Celsus* Origen also speaks of Father and Son as two 'things in hypostasis, but one in like-mindedness, harmony, and identity of will'... Elsewhere, at *Commentary on John* 2.75, Origen writes that 'we are persuaded that there are three hypostases, the Father, the Son, and the Holy Spirit'... This is the only time Origen speaks of 'three hypostases' directly... Origen's intention here is not to describe the three hypostases as ontologically equal in all senses. He is primarily concerned to state that the three are equal in being distinct as individuals. The language of three hypostases evolves as part of a continuing attempt to describe the participation and hierarchy existing among the three that are most definitely three" (Lewis Ayres, *Nicaea and Its Legacy: An Approach to Fourth-Century Trinitarian Theology* (Oxford: OUP, 2004), p. 25).

[542] Origen, *Commentary on the Gospel of John,* 2, 6.

century Platonist Numenius—the Christ is a "second god" who was generated from the first,[543] though Origen repeatedly insists that the Son was different in substance than the Father.[544] For Origen, the Holy Spirit then "proceeds" from the Son in the manner of Plotinus' World-Soul. As in Plotinus, Origen's triad is hierarchical; the first principle is greater than the second and the second is greater than the third. Origen therefore exhibits the same Subordinationist hierarchy of Justin and other Fathers. He writes:

> The God and Father who holds all things together, reaches by his influence each one of these things that are, bestowing being upon each from what is His own. One of these things is the Son *who is less than the Father* and whose influence reaches to rational beings only, for He is *second* from the Father. *Still inferior is the Holy Spirit*, who penetrates only the saints; so that in this way the power of the Father *is greater than* that of the Son, but that of the Son is *more than* that of the Holy Spirit.[545]

It is also worth noting that scholars have noted "interesting" and "remarkable" parallels between heretical Gnostic thought and Origen's doctrine of the Son in his *On First Principles*.[546] As scholars remind us, "we must not forget how widespread were the Gnostic heresies in the Christian church in this period... Origen and his Alexandrian school formed a sort of *mediating position* between the church and the Gnostic parties. Origen himself was inclined to a free and tolerant speculation."[547] It is within this speculation that we may discover the true nature of his thought. Scholars such as Danielou, Butterworth, deFaye, and Griggs conclude that Origen's system "is in the same class with the Gnostic speculations of his time."[548] Furthermore, just as his predecessor Clement had adopted the tradition of secret gnosis, Origen "speaks of mysteries which may not be entrusted even to paper, including secrets of the Eternal Gospel, doctrines of angels and demons, and the history of the soul after death." As Griggs reveals, "these subjects happen to be the foci of recently found Gnostic texts which claim to contain secret doctrines or

---

[543] Origen, *Against Celsus,* 5,39, 5,61.
[544] Ibid., 8, 12.
[545] Origen, *On First Principles*, I, 8
[546] Broek, p. 129.
[547] Paine, *Ethnic Trinities,* p. 88.
[548] Griggs, p. 66.

mysteries."[549] Was Origen a Gnostic? Griggs reminds us that "not all Gnostics or Gnostic systems use every element associated with Gnosticism."[550] Soon we will investigate this association in detail and its implications for the myriad Nicene theologians who were influenced by Origen. But for now we may conclude that Origen, while a studious Platonist and a brilliant and innovative thinker, was far from "orthodox." Despite any advancement towards Trinitarian thinking, it was for his obviously Subordinationist views, amongst other intolerable things,[551] that the Catholic Church would ultimately deny Origen sainthood. Certain elements in his writings might be viewed as foreshadowing what would later become orthodox policy, yet one encyclopedia concludes that:

> however one accounts for these obscurities, it seems unlikely that Origen could have signed the Nicene Creed of 325, in which the Son is declared to be from the *ousia* of the Father, and therefore *homoousios* (of one essence, substance or nature) with him (c. *Comm. John* 20.18.157).[552]

In the next chapter, however, we will observe how Origen's enduring influence in the Alexandrian school of theology nevertheless served as the impetus for the most characteristic formulations of the emerging proto-orthodox party. In particular, we will examine the legacy of Origen's doctrine of the "eternal generation" of the Son at Nicaea.

Tertullian of Carthage

The ideas of Latin theologian Tertullian (160-225 CE), along with Origen, indeed laid the groundwork for the later Christian Trinitarianism that would be promoted by Athanasius and the famous Cappadocian Fathers. Interestingly, though we will see those later Trinitarians make use of ostensibly Valentinian notions in their formulae, "Valentinian Christianity was seen as one of the main enemies by proto-orthodox authors like Irenaeus and Tertullian."[553]

---

[549] Ibid.

[550] Ibid., p. 59.

[551] Origen infamously castrated himself, under the premise of tutoring women without misgivings. This left a sour taste in the mouths of many Catholics. Furthermore, his teachings regarding the pre-existence of human souls, and his suggestion of Universalism, that is, the universal reconciliation (salvation) of all beings to God, including the devil, contributed to his exclusion from the canon.

[552] Edwards, "Origen," *Stanford Encyclopedia of Philosophy.*

[553] Ehrman, *Lost Christianities,* p. 127.

Tertullian himself, like Origen, would also later be condemned as heretical by the very council system that sought to elaborate on some of his most successful contributions. Nevertheless, the influence his speculations have had on the development of the tri-personal Godhead of orthodoxy is substantial. This is not to say that Tertullian's usage of the Latin word *trinitas* (a translation of the Greek *trias*) is evidence of a developed orthodox Trinitarian doctrine before the third century. As a Trinitarian encyclopedia recommends: "Hasty conclusions cannot be drawn from its usage, for [Tertullian] does not apply the words to Trinitarian theology."[554]

Tertullian does differ from the other Christian speculators in that he seems to exhibit a distaste for angel-Christology. Though affirming that Christ could be called the "Angel of the Great Counsel," in that he held the office of messenger, Tertullian denied that Christ was an angel like Michael or Gabriel (*De Carne Christi*, 14).[555] Instead, Tertullian said that the Son was made of *a portion* of the same divine *material* as the Father. Taking after the philosophy of the Stoics, Tertullian believed that all real things were material, even God. The Son was made out of God's eternal and divine matter. This did not mean that the Son and the Father were numerically identical, or that they were co-equal. Tertullian writes:

> the Father is the *entire* [divine] substance, but the Son is a derivation and *portion* of the whole, as he himself acknowledges: "*My Father is greater than I.*" ... He who begets is one, and he who is begotten is another: He too, who sends is one, and he who is sent is another.[556]

As scholars have observed, "it is almost certain that Tertullian does not believe the Son or Holy Spirit possess divinity in its fullness. The Father is not simply the entire divine substance; He is the plenitude of divinity, whereas the Son is but a part."[557] Indeed, Tertullian "does not think the Son is fully God... [he] possesses a relative type of divinity, thereby making him dependent on the Father's absolute and unqualified ousia [substance]."[558]

---

[554] Michael O'Carroll, *Trinitas: A Theological Encyclopedia of the Holy Trinity* (Collegeville: Liturgical Press, 1987), p. 208

[555] Peter R. Carrell, *Jesus and the Angels: Angelology and the Christology of the Apocalypse of John* (Cambridge: CUP, 1997), p. 101.

[556] Tertullian, *Against Praxeas*, 9

[557] Edgar G. Foster, *Angelmorphic Christology and the Exegesis of Psalm 8:5 in Tertullian's Adversus Praxean* (Lanham: University Press of America, 2005), p. 72.

[558] Ibid., p. 73.

In other words, Tertullian believed that God took a piece of his eternal matter and *later* formed it into the Son. This is quite contrary to the Trinitarian tenet of the *eternality* of the person of the Son. This begetting (bringing forth) of the Son, for Tertullian, happened expressly *in time*. Tertullian writes:

> *Then*, as soon as God had willed to put forth into his own matter and form… he *first* brought forth the word itself… that everything might be made through the very word by which all had been planned and arranged, or rather already made, so far as God's thought was concerned.[559]

The personal logos was only truly *created* when the Father wished to carry out his plan for the formation of the cosmos: "This is the complete birth of the word, since it proceeds out of God. Having first been created by him as far as thought is concerned."[560] Before this time, the logos could not be called "Son," because the Father-Son relationship did not exist. All that had existed was God's relationship to that aspect of his own substance which he had foreknown as the logos. As we see in many other prominent theologians, such as the later Arius, Tertullian explicitly professed: *"There was a time when there was no Son and no sin, when God was neither Father nor Judge."*[561] Because the Son is dependent upon the Father for his existence and his substance, he is thus *subordinate* to him.

In the end, Tertullian, despite any Trinitarian-sounding language, clearly does not fit the bill of a Trinitarian. He subordinates the Son in essence, and does not assert the Son's eternal begetting. As *the New Catholic Encyclopedia* says:

> In not a few areas of theology, Tertullian's views are, of course, completely unacceptable. Thus, for example, his teaching on the Trinity reveals a subordination of Son to Father that in the later crass form of Arianism the Church rejected as heretical.[562]

---

[559] Tertullian, *Against Praxeas* 6, 6.

[560] Ibid., 6, 7.

[561] Tertullian, *Against Hermogenes*, 3, 18. The later Arians would famously repeat: "There was a time when the Son was not." See Socrates, "The Dispute of Arius with Alexander, his Bishop," *Church History*. This sentiment was repudiated by the "Crypto-Gnostic" Origen (*On First Principles*, 4, 4, 1), and by his Alexandrian successors at Nicaea in 325 CE. As Webb notes, "Tertullian is a kind of anti-Origen" (Stephen H. Webb, *Jesus Christ, Eternal God* (Oxford: OUP, 2012), p. 38).

[562] W. Le Saint, "Tertullian," *The New Catholic Encyclopedia*, Vol. 13 (Farmington Hills: Thompson Gale, 2003), p. 837. While modern Trinitarians may owe a degree of thanks to Tertullian's efforts to bridge the gap between Christianity and the Neoplatonism that dominated his time, he developed his proto-Trinitarian formula after converting to Montanism, for which, among his other obviously "heretical" theological reasonings, he would be denied canonization by the

Indeed, many more tumultuous decades would be required to finally arrive at what today is considered Trinitarianism.

Ignatius and the General Problem of Patristic Forgery

We should take a moment to note one more important aspect of this issue: the problem of *forgery*. Manuscript evidence has demonstrated that some writings of pre-Nicene Christians were corrupted by later sectarians, in hopes of historically substantiating their views. We will consider one early figure who suffered this unfortunate activity.

Ignatius of Antioch (d. 107 CE) was an early Christian who is said to have been a disciple of John, and who was publicly executed in the Coliseum of Rome. As the narrative goes, during his fateful journey towards his martyrdom, he wrote letters of encouragement to the churches. Within certain versions of Ignatius' letters one may find references to Christ's deity, his embodiment of God in the flesh, and so on. This has caused some modern apologists to cite him as evidence that the Trinitarian dogma traces back to the times directly following the deaths of the Apostles.[563] However, experts have uniformly concluded that all is not well with the letters of Ignatius.

The early date of Ignatius' writings evidently made him a prime candidate for appropriation. Through the comparison of various manuscripts scholars have determined that many unitarian-sounding phrases may have been exchanged for more Trinitarian-sounding phrases. One historian and expert on Ignatius reports that his original letters "were undoubtedly seen as [non-Trinitarian] by the [forger], who duly altered them and gave them a properly Trinitarian form."[564] For example, in one epistle we read "by the blood *of Christ*," while another version reads "by the blood *of God*."[565] Elsewhere, while one reads "by the will of God the Father, and of our Lord Jesus Christ *our Savior*," another says,

---

Catholic Church. Though revered for his early triadic formulations, he demonstrates not Trinitarian but something closer to Semi-Arian views.

[563] See Mark Hanson, "Tracing the Thread of Trinitarian Thought From Ignatius to Origen," Maranatha Baptist Seminary. 30 December 2011. Web. 15 December 2014. See also Edmund J. Fortman, *The Triune God: A Historical Study of the Doctrine of the Trinity* (Eugene: Wipf & Stock, 1999), pp. 38-40.

[564] Allen Brent, *Ignatius of Antioch* (New York: T & T Clark International, 2009), p. 87, 135.

[565] Ignatius, *Epistle to the Ephesians*, 1 (Short Recension vs. Long Recension). The phrase *"blood of Christ"* is certainly biblical language, appearing in 1 Cor 10:16, Eph 2:13, Heb 9:14, and 1 Peter 1:19, while 'blood of God' is entirely absent. We are pressed to say this language reflects a later tradition.

"the Father, and Jesus Christ, *our God*."[566] Of course, even these alleged corruptions of the text describing Christ as "God" do not prove Trinitarianism. No one is arguing that Jesus was not called "god" in the early centuries of Christianity. Yet it was, as we have seen, generally a term used in a secondary or derived sense, not as the one Supreme God.

Regardless, *The Catholic Encyclopedia* warns that of all the letters attributed to Ignatius, there are believed to be "seven genuine and six spurious letters." However, "even the genuine epistles were greatly interpolated to lend weight to the personal views of its [reviser]. For this reason they are incapable of bearing witness to the original form."[567] Protestant historian Phillip Schaff likewise confirms that: "the seven genuine also have not wholly escaped the hand of the forger."[568] All of this forces us to agree with historians of the following opinion:

> We pass over the Epistles ascribed to Ignatius with slight
> notice, regarding them as of too uncertain authorship, and too
> hopelessly corrupt to justify the use of them in connection
> with our present inquiry. As to the bearing of the Epistles…
> on the question of the belief of the old Christians on the
> subject of the Trinity, we shall not attempt to argue the
> question on the genuineness of the Ignatian letters… What is
> called the "testimony of antiquity" in their favor is too meagre,
> too loose, and not sufficiently early, and one of the pieces
> referred to of too suspicious a character to prove anything…[569]

The quest for doctrinal validation and proof of ecclesiastical continuity seems to have taken extremists in antiquity to irresponsible and unscrupulous ends.[570] These are, we must recognize, symptoms of the larger historical malaise

---

[566] Ibid.

[567] John Bonaventure O'Connor, "St. Ignatius of Antioch," *The Catholic Encyclopedia*, Vol. 7 (New York: Robert Appleton Company, 1910), p. 645.

[568] Phillip Schaff, *History of the Christian Church*, Vol. 2 (New York: Charles Scribner's Sons, 1910), p. 663. Because the Ignatian letters discuss church organization, Catholics and Anglicans have pointed to them to justify the establishment of the office of bishop. The Anglican bishop James Ussher (famous for his influential work in biblical chronology), argued that this was proof that the authority of the bishops could be traced back to the first-century. John Milton, the celebrated author behind *Paradise Lost*, himself a unitarian, argued that the letters were forgeries developed precisely to enforce the authority of the establishment. After much debate, it was Ussher himself who confirmed that six of the letters were indeed forgeries, and that even the legitimate ones had themselves been indeterminably corrupted. See Ehrman, *Lost Christianities*, pp. 137-141.

[569] Lamson, Abbot, p. 13.

[570] For more on this topic see Bart D. Ehrman's *The Orthodox Corruption of Scripture: The Effect of Early Christological Controversies on the Test of the New Testament* (Oxford: OUP, 1993).

which plagues the Christian dogma about God. We wonder how many Church Fathers' extant works have remained wholly untouched by the reviser's devious pen? We must ground ourselves in the sum of scholarship. As observed in chapter one, we cannot ignore the droves of historical and theological authorities who acknowledge that the Trinitarian system was not established until the fourth century, and the associated Christological particulars until the late fifth century CE. Certainly the musings of some of these second and third century Christians served to usher in the eventual Trinitarian delineations, being supported by the efforts of the Gnostics and Neoplatonists, but we cannot ignore the fact that these famous theologians were not devoted Trinitarians, nor were they Trinitarians who were simply having difficulty expressing what they believed. Rather, they were what we would call *Subordinationists*. The *Oxford Encyclopedia of the Early Church* justly rounds out our survey of the beliefs of these figures:

> Subordinationism: thus we call the tendency, strong in the theology of the 2nd and 3rd centuries, to consider Christ, as Son of God, inferior to the Father. Behind this tendency were gospel statements in which Christ himself stressed his inferiority (Jn 14: 28, Mk 10:18, 13:32, etc.) and it was developed especially by the Logos-Christology. This theology, partly under the influence of middle Platonism [i.e. Philo], considered Christ, logos and divine wisdom, as the means of liaison and mediation between the Father's position to him. When the conception of the Trinity was enlarged to include the Holy Spirit, as in Origen, this in turn was considered inferior to the Son. Subordinationist tendencies are evident especially in theologians like Justin, Tertullian, Origen and Novation; but even Irenaeus, to whom Trinitarian speculations are alien, commenting on John 14:28, has no difficulty in considering Christ inferior to the Father.[571]

As Hanson reveals, it was this theology of the second and third century apologists like Irenaeus, Tertullian, and Hippolytus that was ultimately "rejected" at the end of the fourth century. Orthodoxy's "evolution" committed a clear and serious "break with the past."[572]

---

[571] M. Simmonetti, "Subordinationism," *Oxford Encyclopedia of the Early Church*, Vol. 2 (OUP, 1992), p. 797.

[572] Hanson, p, 872.

Closing the Third Century

The most active work of ecclesiastical academia just before the opening of the fourth century was in contemplating the problems posed by the generation and relationship of multiple divine entities and the conflict of those entities with the spirit of biblical monotheism. As Gibbon notes:

> The suspense and fluctuation produced in the minds of the Christians by these opposite tendencies [plurality versus unity] may be observed in the writings of the theologians who flourished after the end of the apostolic age, and before the origin of the Arian controversy... They have delivered their conceptions in loose, inaccurate, and sometimes contradictory language.[573]

As the Hebrew God was being violently stretched against a backdrop of Hellenistic principle, so too were the minds of even the most rigorously educated. Converting the sacred religious thought of one culture into another was proving no easy task. It was the anxiety generated by possible incompatibility with the God of Israel that propelled the third-century Christians forward in vigorous pursuit of resolution. Would the theologians of the fourth century succeed in rectifying these daunting problems? What sort of faith would they lay down for subsequent Christian generations?

Countless denominations still subscribe to the creedal mandates of the assemblies of the fourth-and-fifth century Catholic Church. But are those Christians who repeat the creeds each week aware of the pervading influence of the mystery schools upon the worldviews of the orthodox contributors? The pagan aroma brewing in the council chambers as the Gentiles met to unify religion and empire evidently still flavors the faith today, so much so that if Christians were introduced to the Jewish faith of Jesus and the Apostles they would hardly identify the taste. But revisiting the theology of Jesus will prove difficult if the clouded air of establishment religious history is not somewhat dispersed. A confrontation with not only the theological conventions but the socio-political context surrounding the progress of dogma must take place.

---

[573] Ibid., p. 778.

5

NICAEA AND THE DAWN
OF A NEW FAITH

"All things are subject to interpretation;
whichever interpretation prevails at a
given time is a function of power and not
truth."

— *Friedrich Nietzsche*

EACH SUNDAY, CHRISTIANS DUTIFULLY RECITE the Nicene
Creed, the Athanasian Creed, and other beloved statements of faith. It is
assumed that the ancient synods which produced these statements are
thoroughly appreciated. Indeed, when such doctrines as the Trinity are
challenged today we often hear some reference to the primacy of the councils'
determinations. But how many of the faithful reciters of the creeds are able to
name a single contributor to those proceedings? Doubtless they are all familiar
with St. James, St. John, and St. Paul, but it is not the precise authority of the
Apostles which is routinely summoned by apologists to define and defend
orthodox doctrine. As reformer John Calvin's French Confession of Faith of
1559 states: "we confess that which has been established by the ancient councils,
and we detest all sects and heresies which were rejected by the holy doctors, such
as Saint Hilary, Saint Athanasius, Saint Ambrose and Saint Cyril."[574] Herein lies

the justification for Calvin's wanton murder of Michael Servetus for denying the doctrine of the Trinity, and the foundation for all similar persecutions. *Heresy*, that most dreaded of words defined by the imperial synods of ages past, still condemns such devoted persons to this day and precludes many scripturally-grounded theological submissions from the marketplace of Christian ideas. Today, the fire beneath the feet of the martyrs in the Roman and Reformation eras continues to burn in a social and spiritual sense.

But how were the standards which have enabled such persecutions put into place? Who was responsible for them? We cannot begin to understand the orthodox creeds and their anathemas, much less make a value judgement on their content, unless we first come to terms with the historical reality which produced them. If Martin Luther and the other Reformers made their famous break with accepted pietism upon recognizing political and unscriptural influence in the orthodox system, what would modern Christians do if the same influences were discovered thriving in the old councils which defined their most sacred beliefs? Would there not be some cause for reconsideration? There is no better place to begin our investigation of the orthodox creeds than in the period leading up to the infamous Council of Nicaea.

Christianity in the Early Fourth Century

As we have seen, prior to the council of 325 CE, division reigned in the world of Christian theology. Interestingly enough, after Nicaea the division was amplified tenfold. Modern defenders of the councils' authority often paint Nicaea as the decisive moment in Christian history when the Trinity won out over the "heresy" that Jesus isn't God, putting the heretics to rest forever by a resounding consensus of authentic disciples. Far from being the accepted theology of the Church at the opening of the fourth century, however, we find the blossoming proto-Trinitarian faith to be only one of many competing ideologies. Ostensibly, the prevailing view amongst most Christians in the Roman Empire was still that God was a single monolithic individual, not three co-equal and eternal Persons, and that Christ was in some sense distinct from and subordinate to the one true God.[575]

Yet we do find that the Christian empire at the opening of the fourth century was already deep in the throes of a new evolutionary phase; a slow but

---

[574] John Calvin, Henry Beveridge (trans.), *Calvin's Tracts* (Translation Society, Edinburgh: Calvin Translation Society, 1849).

[575] Encyclopedia Britannica, Inc., "Trinity," *Encyclopedia Britannica*, Vol. 27, p. 2941.

vivacious philosophical revolution initiated in the halls of the Alexandrian mystery schools, institutions whose high societal reputation inevitably delivered the conflict to the public arena. Fresh debate over the nature of the Deity was now permeating both chapel and marketplace. By 325, nearly three centuries of philosophical musing had effectively seeded the furthest reaches of Christendom with a variety of competing Christologies around which large factions fostered by prominent bishops were rapidly forming.[576] The unity of the faith, already ravaged by the great controversies with the Gnostic sects in the preceding centuries, was again in shambles.

At the onset of the fourth century two broad theological camps (though they were far from the only camps) had begun to emerge in the greater Roman Empire. These parties, though bearing seemingly endless offshoots and divisions in and of themselves, would effectively split the Roman world in two: the more unitarian-minded *"Arians"*, and the more Trinitarian-minded *anti-Arians* (from here we may interchangeably call the anti-Arians the *proto-orthodox* or the *Athanasians*). Yet the epic clash between these general groups had started in Alexandria. What began as a local theological dispute between episcopal rivals in that great city would suddenly escalate into an empire-wide conflict that would change the world forever.

Alexandrian Proto-Orthodox Christianity

At virtually every stage of our evolutionary journey towards orthodox dogma we have encountered the syncretism of the Alexandrians. We recall how difficult it was to tell rival philosophies apart in that city.[577] It will then be no great surprise that one of the most popular strains of Christianity to emanate from this academic melting pot, and the form that would ultimately come to dominate the rest of Christendom, exhibits the influences of both Gnosticism and Neoplatonism.

---

[576] Many Christian converts had evidently not found in the arguments of the Alexandrian philosophers much which offered practical assistance for the rigors of life in the late Roman Empire. In this regard, a human Christ who, regardless of any preceding existence, bore true limitations and nevertheless succeeded and ascended, was perhaps more attractive to the common Christian. Yet many sophisticated Romans (the philosophers, the aristocracy, and the wealthy) appear to have found the emerging God-Christ more compelling; an all-powerful being who descended from on high to reach down to a lowly rabble. The conflict intensified between these general, competing versions of Jesus: one who was himself the mysterious and all-powerful Yahweh, and one who enjoyed no access to supernatural power save what God might grant, who truly conquered desperate conditions and gained eminence.

[577] Inge, p. 328.

In the years prior to Nicaea, there appear to have been, generally, two kinds of Christians thriving in Alexandria: the Gnostics, whom we might call the extreme progressives, and the proto-orthodox Christians, themselves rife with Gnostic adaptations, who considered their version of the faith the "true philosophy" and who expressed the Christian religion in the language of the Platonists.[578] From the latter group sprang a vibrant movement intent on leading Alexandria into a more scripturally-grounded, ecclesiastical orientation, and these Christians vigorously pushed for the acceptance of their own views as "orthodox" by the opposing sects. Despite any inclination towards conservatism, however, for them "the philosophical (Platonic) interpretation of Christianity remained predominant."[579] The movement's meteoric rise may also have been arrived at in part via the manner in which it confronted its rivals. One scholar writes that this party "stifled its opposition, it claimed that its views had always been the majority position and that its rivals were, and always had been, 'heretics,' who willfully 'chose' to reject the 'true belief.' "[580]

What were these proto-orthodox Christians teaching in Alexandria? Their beliefs appear to have been the result of a massive amalgamation of Plotinian and Gnostic views, yet more directly, their foundation was the masterful Origen.

The great Origen had died around 254 CE, and left behind him in that vivacious philosophical milieu an unmatched wealth of speculative exegesis which would motivate Alexandrian Christianity for decades. The two most prominent fourth-century Alexandrians, Bishop Alexander I (d. 326 CE) and his pupil Athanasius (296-373 CE), were deeply Origenist.[581] Naturally, Origen's views had experienced some modification in the years after his death, but at its core, as Schaff notes, "the theology of Alexandria remained Origenist."[582] We will now focus on Origen's most peculiar advancement, the *eternal generation* of the Son, which would play such a critical role in the definitions of Alexander and Athanasius at Nicaea.

Though Origen was a Subordinationist (*On First Principles*, 1, 2, 23), he was also among the first of the proto-orthodox, if not the very first, to speculate that the generation of the Son was in a sense *eternal*.[583] As one Reformed scholar

---

[578] R. van den Broek, *Studies in Gnosticism and Alexandrian Christianity* (Leiden: Brill, 1996), p. 233.
[579] Ibid., p. 234.
[580] Bart D. Ehrman, *The New Testament: A Historical Introduction* (Oxford: OUP, 2011), p. 7.
[581] See Philip Schaff, Henry Wace, *A Select Library of Nicene and Post-Nicene Fathers of the Christian Church*, Vol. IV (New York: The Christian Literature Company, 1892), pp. lxvii-lxix.
[582] Ibid., p. lxviii.
[583] The schismatic Novation (200-258 CE), born two decades after Origen, caused great distress in the Church in the third century. He set himself up as the "antipope," and was considered a

reports, "The well-known teaching of the eternal generation of the Son *had its beginning with Origen.*"[584] Of course, it must be emphasized that while Origen had begun speaking of the Son's begetting as "eternal," to him it was evidently eternal in the sense that it was a *continuous* generation.[585] In fact, to Origen *all things* were continually generated; there was no time when God was not creating. Indeed, "with Origen all creation is eternal, that is, creative activity has neither beginning nor end."[586]

But why did Origen feel the need to speak this way? Here the Platonic spirit once again wafts to the forefront. Origen, as we recall, was a committed Platonist, and thus had difficulty in reconciling how a good God, eternally unchanging in the Platonic sense, could suddenly go from inactivity to creation. Origen therefore concluded that creation itself had no beginning. This view had clearly been gained from the Platonists:

> Not only does the Plotinian trinity exist by *eternal generation* but the world is equally eternal. The principle of progression which the terms generation or evolution would seem to involve is, with Plotinus, as he directly asserts, logical, *not chronological.*[587]

For Origen, the creative activity which produced both the Son and the created world was outside of time.[588] One historian confirms that:

---

heretic by the proto-orthodox bishops. His followers were among the groups banned by Constantine after Nicaea. Novation is thought by some to have also pioneered an early "eternal generation" scheme. He envisioned an ineffable procession of the Son, who was nevertheless said to mysteriously be "the second Person after the Father, less than the Father in that he is originated by the Father." See John Chapman, "Novation and Novationism," *The Catholic Encyclopedia*, Vol. 11 (New York: Robert Appleton Company, 1911). For a view favoring an eternal-generation doctrine for Novation, see James L. Papandrea, *Novation of Rome and the Culmination of Pre-Nicene Orthodoxy* (Eugene: Wipf & Stock, 2011), pp. 85-90. For the opinion that Novation did not have such a doctrine, see Ayres, *Nicaea and Its Legacy*, pp. 71-75.

[584] Boer, p. 92.

[585] Kevin Giles, *The Eternal Generation of the Son: Maintaining Orthodoxy in Trinitarian Theology* (Downer's Grove: IVP, 2012), p. 101.

[586] Ernest Belfort Bax, *A Handbook of the History of Philosophy for the Use of Students* (London: George Bell and Sons, 1888), p. 105.

[587] Paine, *The Ethnic Trinities*, p. 175, emphasis added.

[588] "It is easy to see to see, that, along with such speculations on the cosmogony, [Origen's] generation of the Son might be disengaged from the idea of time. We are willing that the doctrine of the eternal generation should stand on the ground on which Origen virtually put it; that is, eternity may be ascribed to the Son in the same sense in which it may be ascribed to the material creation, and only in that sense. This is not what modern Trinitarians mean" (Lamson, Abbot, p. 224).

[Origen,] who fixed no beginning to creation, but supposed it to be eternal, would far less fix any beginning [to the generation of the Son]. He strove to banish all notions of time from the conception of the generation of the Logos. It was necessary here, as he thought, to conceive of a timeless present, an eternal now... [Origen arrived at this view by his] philosophical education in the Platonic school.[589]

As hinted in the previous chapter, in addition to Origen's Platonic reasons for the Son's eternal generation, his system also appears tinged with Gnosticism.[590] More study is certainly needed in this area, but already we may be able to catch a glimpse of a great confluence of Platonic and Gnostic thought in Origen's generation of the Son.

Earlier Gnostics, like Valentinus and the writer of *Eugnostus*, had held that many "powers" dwell in God. As covered earlier, an important characteristic of Gnostic teaching was the idea that the Supreme God generates a divine realm or substance full of these powers called the "Pleroma." Each of these powers (divine hypostases called Aeons), produced other powers like themselves within the Pleroma, and the sum of these Aeons composed the fullness of God himself (Pleroma means "fullness").[591] Several of the highest powers were named Sophia (Wisdom), Aletheia (Truth), Logos (Word), and Zoe (Life). For the Valentinians especially, Jesus was not simply another Aeon produced by one of these powers within the Pleroma,[592] rather, he was a special emanation who

---

[589] August Neander, *History of the Christian Religion and Church* (London: Wiley & Putnam, 1854), p. 588.

[590] Not surprisingly however, we may also discern the idea of an eternal sonship already working amongst the Gnostics, and, interestingly, in the same *Tripartite Tractate* in which are discovered other favorite notions of both Origen and Athanasius. Though much study is still required in this area, several scholars have argued that the Gnostic *Tripartite Tractate* indeed already taught some form of the co-eternality of the Father and the Son before Origen or Athanasius. See H. Puech, Gilles Quispel, "Le quatrime ecrit gnostique du Codex Jung," *Vig. Chr.* 9. 1955, pp. 77-81 as quoted in Broek, p. 252.

[591] The word "pleroma" literally means "sum total, fullness, fulfillment, super abundance," and is used 18 times in the NT. Most famously, it is found in Col 2:9: "*For in [Jesus] all the fullness of Deity dwells in bodily form*" (NASB) or "*the fullness of the Godhead*" (KJV) or "*the fullness of God's nature*" (HCSB). Though this text is often employed by Trinitarians to prove that Jesus uniquely was fully God and fully man, Apostolic usage of "pleroma" becomes more clear when we consider John 1:16: "*Out of his fullness we have all received*," and Eph 3:19: "*that you may be filled up to all the fullness of God.*" This pleroma was to fill all Christians. Indeed, Jesus' disciples were to also become partakers in whatever "divinity" was in Christ. See also 2 Pet 1:4: "*so that you may become sharers in the divine nature.*"

[592] Irenaeus, *Against Heresies*, 1, 11, 1.

embodied every power of God; Jesus was himself a Pleroma.[593] Indeed, the "the whole Pleroma of Aeons" was represented in the Son.[594] Interestingly, Origen appears to take a similar view. For him, Jesus was an embodiment of all of the powers of God's Pleroma. As Professor Broek explains, "there can be no doubt that for Origen the Son is basically Wisdom [Sophia] and Truth [Aletheia], Word [Logos], and Life [Zoe]."[595] Obviously Origen has the Johannine language in mind, but Origen conceives of these names as not simply principles which Jesus represents, but as powers he truly embodies. These are the divine attributes that are inseparable from God and are always produced by him; the powers in Jesus are the very substance of the one Pleroma. Origen writes: "although in our mind they are regarded as many, yet in fact and substance they are one, and in them resides the 'fullness [Pleroma] of the Godhead' (Col 2:9)."[596] According to Origen, "Sophia, Aletheia, and Logos are the principal constituents of the Pleroma."[597] Interestingly, these "three powers are also part of the first stage of the Pleroma according to the Valentinians."[598] Furthermore, just as Origen writes that each of these powers were arranged by "Foreknowledge," the Gnostics likewise ascribe the entire race of these powers to the "Foreknowledge" of the Unbegotten.[599] Ultimately, to both Origen and the Valentinians, Jesus was the very manifestation of the divine powers of God's Pleroma, and just as it was foolish to think that Aletheia and Zoe had not always existed, the Son, who contained these essential attributes, must also be eternal. Origen writes:

> Whoever dares to say that "There was a time that the Son did
> not exist," should understand that he also will say that "Once

---

[593] "The Savior, in fact, was a bodily image of something unitary, namely the Pleroma" (*Tripartite Tractate,* 116-117). See also the *Gospel of Truth*: "All the emanations of the father, therefore, are fullnesses [Pleromas], and all his emanations have their roots in the one who caused them all to grow from himself" (trans. Barnstone, Meyer, p. 255).

[594] Irenaeus, *Against Heresies,* 1, 2, 6. Irenaeus explains the Gnostic reasoning from Scripture: "They moreover affirm that the Savior is shown to be derived from all the Aeons, and to be in himself everything by the following passage: 'Every male that opens the womb.' For he, being everything, opened the womb of the enthymesis of the suffering Aeon... And they state that it was clearly on this account that Paul said, 'And he himself is all things,' and again, 'All things are to him and of him are all things,' and further, 'In him dwells all the fullness of the Godhead;' and yet again, 'All things are gathered together by God in Christ.' Thus do they interpret these and any like passages to be found in Scripture" (Ibid., 1, 3, 4).

[595] Broek, p. 129.

[596] Ibid., p. 130.

[597] Ibid.

[598] Valentinus was likely drawing on earlier Platonic and/or Gnostic Alexandrian speculation for his model. As Broek suggests: "[Valentinus] was not the first nor the last to reason about God in this way, as is shown by Eugnostus and Origen. This explains why [Valentinus'] teaching was so readily accepted by so many Christians, both in Alexandria and abroad" (Broek, p. 130).

[599] Broek, p. 129.

Wisdom did not exist, and Logos did not exist, and Life did not exist," whereas we must believe that in all these the substance of God exists in perfection… in them is the Pleroma of divinity.[600]

Scholars have thus concluded that "Valentinian teachings about the eternal generation of the Son… were similar to those which Origen advocated."[601] And not only Valentinus' teaching, but perhaps more importantly his pupil Heracleon's Gnostic model of an eternal Trinity exhibits a dubious similarity to Origen's views.[602] But is this all a coincidence? Within modern scholarship, "a new stage has already begun, which pays full attention to Origen in so far as he is a Gnostic."[603] Though a serious student of Platonism, and a great opponent of the Gnostics, Quispel confirms that "even in his exegesis Origen is much more a Gnostic than a Platonist."[604] Indeed, the discovery of Nag Hammadi has helped to "narrow" the gap between Origen and Valentinianism.[605] But we must mention that the differences between them in regard to the Son's existence are significant. For example, Origen assigns the name Sophia (Wisdom) to a higher place in the Pleroma than the Valentinians. But we need not argue that Origen depended directly upon Valentinus; there is enough evidence to demonstrate that "both were making use of earlier Alexandrian speculations on the nature of

---

[600] Origen, *On First Principles*, 4, 4, 1. Interestingly, this statement which Origen argues against was the very standard of Tertullian (*Hermogenes*, 3, 18), and the Arians in the following century.

[601] Philip F. Esler, *The Early Christian World, Vol. I-II* (London: Routledge, 2000), p. 1016. See also Alan B. Scott, *Origen and the Life of the Stars* (Oxford: Clarendon Press, 1992).

[602] Quispel observes that Origen's eternal generation, though it is now considered an "essential" to orthodoxy, comes very "near" to Heracleon and Valentinus' teachings. He writes: "Heracleon and Origen have in common that their concept of God remains strictly personal, even if they use the Platonic categories to express his transcendence. Because God is Father in the real sense of the word, he is the eternal Father of the eternal Son. From their mutual love a third hypostasis is born… Therefore we may say that Heracleon teaches an ontological and eternal Trinity" (Quispel, "Origen," pp. 296-297).

[603] Ibid., p. 289.

[604] Quispel argues: "In [Origen's] spiritual world all kinds of happenings do take place, whereas among Plato's ideas nothing happens at all. Nor should we say that such a 'vertical' exegesis is necessarily Greek, because the Stoics too gave allegorical interpretations of Greek mythology. The later Jewish Cabbalists gave a very similar interpretation of the OT. More than alien influences it is a certain Gnostic mentality which produces these hermeneutics" (Ibid., p. 290). Vertical exegesis "treats the text as an isolated phenomenon. We take this text with just these few verses and plumb the depth that is there. 'Vertical' exegesis makes the assumption that each text is a meaning-world unto itself… a highly problematic assumption!" (R. Jensen, *Thinking in Story* (Lima: CSS Publishing Co., 1995 [1993]), p. 94). Interestingly, the Gnostic texts of Nag Hammadi reveal a relationship to the exegesis of Origen: "They are replete with allegorical interpretations of Scripture, especially of the first three chapters of Genesis, and address the fall of the soul, and the nature of the resurrection—all issues which were associated with 'Origenists' by their opponents" (Hugo Lundhaug, *The Monastic Origins of the Nag Hammadi Codices* (Tubingen: Mohr Siebeck, 2015), p. 242).

[605] Quispel, cited in Griggs, p. 64.

God."[606] This circle of Alexandrian thought clearly envisioned a transcendent but still personal God generating subsequent manifestations as separate hypostases.[607] This explains why Valentinus' Gnostic teaching about God "was so readily accepted by so many Christians, both in Alexandria and abroad"[608]— both the "heretical" Valentinus and the "catholic" Origen had drawn from a common well. Because of the complex relationship between the different traditions, "the majority of Christians… could not tell the difference between Valentinian and orthodox teaching."[609] The Valentinian and Origenist Christological speculations might be seen as different branches of the same syncretistic tree, a tree with roots stretching deep into Platonic, Hellenistic Jewish, and Sethian-Gnostic theory. Of course, in past analysis "it was usual to oppose the ideas of Origen to those of the Gnostics, [but] we now see that in the second half of the second century the transitions had become so gradual as to become almost unperceptible."[610] Origen himself ultimately represents both an updated and "catholicized" Gnosticism,[611] and despite his own public opposition to the heretics, it is possible to conclude with Quispel that "Origen is a *consummation* of Gnostic developments."[612] Other scholars, like Griggs, are already prepared to find in Origen yet another "Crypto-Gnostic" in the vein of Clement and the later Marius Victorinus.[613] The implications of such a conclusion may be serious: Origen was arguably the most important theologian for fourth-century orthodoxy and the Nicene doctrine of Jesus would scarcely have come to be without his important groundwork. Indeed, scholars have determined that:

> In designating the eternal origin of the Son as his "eternal generation," Origen firmly cemented this way of speaking of divine Father-Son self-differentiation in eternity into the Alexandrian theological tradition, and for that matter into

---

[606] Broek, p. 130.

[607] Ibid.

[608] Ibid.

[609] Elaine Pagels, *The Gnostic Gospels* (New York: Vintage Books, 1979), p. 32.

[610] Ibid. As Quispel concludes, "Within the school of Valentinus a certain evolution has taken place… There has been a way from Valentinus to Heracleon, and Heracleon to Origen. The transition is much more gradual than a phenomenological comparison can discern" (Ibid., p. 293). Indeed the Valentinians experienced as much an adaption as the proto-orthodox. Especially in the Western or Roman branch of Valentinianism, we find a Gnosticism much more sympathetic to non-Gnostics; Heracleon and Ptolemy for example even believed that the "catholics" could be saved outside of gaining Gnosis.

[611] Quispel, p. 297.

[612] Ibid., p. 270.

[613] Griggs, in Paul McKechnie's summary of his investigation, "pictures Origen as a semi- (or even crypto-) gnostic" (Paul McKechnie, *Prudentia*, Vol. 24, No. 1 (University of Auckland Bindery, 1992), p. 67).

historical orthodoxy. However, it would be for others to eliminate completely the Subordinationist elements of his theology.[614]

Evidently, the ones who would perform this purging of Origen's lingering Subordinationism would be Bishop Alexander and Athanasius. The late third to early fourth-century modification of Origen's scheme was to be expected. During Origen's time, proto-orthodox influences appear to have already swept in and "brought Egypt into line."[615] At the opening of the third century, the more conspicuous (Gnostic) elements in Alexandrian Christianity were in the process of being suppressed, and a more "uniformed" Christianity was being progressively "imposed."[616] Eventually, the Catholic leadership "invented an orthodox past for the Egyptian Church."[617] Looking back, we are pressed to wonder if the product of this catholicizing of a long-compromised Alexandrian Christianity can be seen in the Nicene theology of Bishop Alexander and Athanasius?

Reconciling Christianity's deeply Gnostic history with the new order set forth by Athanasius and his party, despite their imperial backing, would continue to prove problematic. Though the fourth century had focused acutely on Arianism, scholars are now asking if Gnosticism was "of more importance than Athanasius would like us to think?"[618] The Nicene theology's tumultuous rise to power certainly prompted a great whitewashing of orthodox involvement with Gnosis. As Constantine solidified the party's authority over the Church, their next task was to solidify their doctrinal standards in a way that would finally separate them from the pitfalls of Egyptian Christianity. In 367 CE, Athanasius launched a campaign against Gnostic literature. He ordered the complete destruction of Gnostic books, arguing, "For even if a useful word is found in them, it is still not good to trust them."[619] This fallout from Athanasius' "pressure towards orthodoxy" may have been why the Gnostic books of the

---

[614] Kevin Giles, *The Eternal Generation of the Son: Maintaining Orthodoxy in Trinitarian Theology* (Downer's Grove: IVP, 2012), p. 102.

[615] McKechnie's summary of Griggs, in *Prudentia*, Vol. 24, No. 1, p. 66.

[616] Griggs, p. 29. The diversity of interpretation survived in that milieu until the days of Bishop Demetrius of Alexandria (189-232 CE), whose reign accomplished an "infusion of stringently defined Christianity" (Ibid., p. 45).

[617] McKechnie's summary of Griggs, in *Prudentia*, Vol. 24, No. 1, p. 66.

[618] Ibid., p. 68.

[619] Athanasius, *Festal Letter 39*, 367 CE.

Nag Hammadi codices were buried in the sands of Egypt.[620] But it seems that many "useful words" had already been drawn from those heretical texts and employed in the construction of orthodox faith. Athanasius himself was certainly guilty of this, as one encyclopedia reveals that he "shared in some of the Gnostic errors... [in his tract] on the Incarnation, we meet the very same prominent [Gnostic] doctrine [of virginity] *spoken of as a characteristic of the Christian system*, and even including the Gnostic phrase[s]."[621] One modern scholar asks: "Was the fact that [Gnosticism] was dying out connected with the [Nag Hammadi] codices getting buried?"[622] But we wonder if it was truly dying out, or if it was only taking on new and sudden life in the mainstream of Christendom? Regardless, as scholars have observed, "orthodox doctrines were fashioned to serve the needs of temporal power... Athanasius of Alexandria... created a 'template' for orthodoxy: closing the canon, ascribing knowledge to Christ only, and embracing desert monasticism. Each of these steps served the political interests of institutional orthodoxy, enabling it to triumph over Gnosticism in a culture that had been highly eclectic and cosmopolitan."[623]

Despite the efforts of Athanasius to subdue overtly Gnostic influences, finally separating orthodoxy from Gnostic thought continued to prove difficult. For example, Athanasius lambasts those who "think that the evil is in their very nature, which is what the heretics assert."[624] As one scholar reminds us, "This was a teaching held by some Gnostic groups and also by Manichaeism."[625] But we have already seen how this teaching was taken up in orthodoxy through the former Manichean Gnostic Augustine. Even in the years shortly after Athanasius' death, distinguishing between "orthodox" and "heretical" thought is often difficult and at times impossible.

---

[620] David M. Gwynn, *Athanasius of Alexandria: Bishop, Theologian, Ascetic, Father* (Oxford: OUP, 2012), p. 156.

[621] Josh McClintock, James Strong, "Athanasius," *Cyclopaedia of Biblical, Theological, and Ecclesiastical Literature*, Vol. 1 (New York: Harper & Brothers, 1891), p. 508, emphasis his. "In some points [Athanasius] was 'weak like other men;' and the ascetic and monastic spirit received a strong impulse from his writings" (Ibid.). The Athanasian incline towards asceticism is emblematic of the general process of Christian amalgamation with Greek and Gnostic ideals. As Harnack notes, "the Christian religion was mixed up with the refined asceticism of a perishing civilization" (*History of Dogma*, Vol. 1 (1894), p. 330). Even into the late fifth and early sixth century, in the times of Pope Gregory, Harnack notes a regular appeal to a "declining civilization sunk in superstition and magic" (*History of Dogma*, Vol. 5 (1961), p. 262).

[622] McKechrie, p. 68.

[623] Mike Wilson, "Egypt: Shaping Gnosis for Christianity," *The Midwest Quarterly*, Vol. 44, No. 2 (Pittsburg: Pittsburg State University, 2003), p. 100.

[624] Gwynn, p. 151.

[625] Ibid.

Alexander, Athanasius, and the Nicene Jesus

That Alexander and his student Athanasius received the basis of their doctrines from Origen is clear, but it seems obvious that their Origenism had already been modified by their catholicizing Alexandrian predecessors by the time they received it. As Schaff confirms, "the theological training of Athanasius was... under the still predominant although modified influence of Origen."[626] In Alexander, "the combination of a fundamentally Origenist theology with ideas traceable to the Asiatic tradition is conspicuous."[627] The level of modification Origen's teaching experienced varied between the fourth-century theologians. Athanasius' own studious attention "was focused on God being always the Father of the Son; this implied, of course, that the Son was always the Son of the Father."[628] Thus he proceeded beyond Origen's eternal generation of the Son. To him, "eternal" did not mean generated continually with the rest of creation, but it meant that the Son should be thought of as uniquely and personally co-eternal with the Father in relation to time.

The period leading up to Nicaea represents a culmination of a long process of speculation about the Son's generation. During the early fourth century, "the orthodox advanced in their views, and began to say that his Sonship, as well as his existence, had been from all eternity. At first this idea was cautiously and timidly intimated... it was not universally prevalent at the time of the Nicene Council."[629] It was nevertheless the distinctive doctrine of Athanasius at Nicaea, which he relentlessly publicized.[630]

One scholar reveals that there was one circumstance which "contributed much to promote in the Church the growth of the idea of an *Eternal Generation*... the introduction into the current language of the Church of various comparisons from the external world... these illustrations were first used by enthusiasts not sanctioned by the General Church."[631] These "novel illustrations" of the generation of the Son from the Father include an example of "the sun, the ray, and the terminating point of the ray."[632] George Kidd recalls that in the second-century records of Irenaeus, the comparison of the sun and its

---

[626] Schaff, *A Select Library of Nicene and Post-Nicene Fathers*, p. xviii.

[627] Ibid.

[628] Broek, p. 252.

[629] George Balderston Kidd, *Christophany: Doctrine of the Manifestations of the Son of God Under the Economy of the Old Testament* (London: Ward and Co., 1852), pp. 689-690.

[630] At Nicaea, Athanasius' flagship argument was that the Son "began not his existence in time, but was before all ages *eternally* and incomprehensibly begotten of the Father" (Schaff, *A Select Library of Nicene and Post-Nicene Fathers*, Vol. 7, p. xlix, emphasis added).

[631] Kidd, p. 689, emphasis added.

[632] Ibid., quoting Kaye.

rays occurs three times. "But it is remarkable," says Kidd, "that it is never used by [Irenaeus] to illustrate his own view of the prolation of the Logos… but is quoted by him from the language of the Gnostic heretics he was refuting, who used it to explain the emanation of the Aeons which made so great a figure in their vain Theosophy, from the Primal Divinity… Irenaeus decidedly opposed such figures and analogies."[633] Though the earlier anti-Gnostics such as Irenaeus had condemned this model and emphasized the vanity of speculation, one scholar notes that: "This is the favorite illustration which the Fathers used for explaining the union of the Father and the Son: and though it is better not to pry too deeply into such subjects, it is perhaps the closest and plainest illustration which can be found."[634] The same scholar also recognizes that "the soaring mind of Athanasius, as well as the restless activity of Origen" did not adhere to Irenaeus' caution about Gnosticism.[635]

Origen, like the Gnostics, had evidently adopted the Platonic view that matter was not only inherently imperfect, but that it was even a disgusting pollution.[636] In *Against Celsus*, Origen addresses the question about why God had to put his Son's spirit into the virgin Mary, "*Since he already knew how to make men, he could have formed a body for this one also without having to thrust his own spirit into such foul pollution*"(6, 73). He concludes that the divine nature was not thrust into pollution in a way that he himself became polluted, arguing that we should not "*think that the rays of the sun are defiled by dung-heaps and stinking bodies.*"[637] Origen's Christ, emanating from God, was not contaminated by matter, but *illuminated* it, and remained unsullied by the mud (matter) that it touched.

But was Origen's placement of a transcendent Jesus into this Platonic scheme his own innovation? The Gnostics had already posited that the divine Christ was united with matter in such a way that he remained distinct and uncontaminated by it. One popular 3rd-century Gnostic work, *The Tripartite Tractate*, explicitly relates that the Savior united with human "*smallness,*" permitting himself "*to be conceived and born as an infant in body and soul,*" and yet that he did so without "*pollution*" (115:3-11, 15-17).[638] Origen certainly reflects this model, even in the same language. The identification of matter as pollution

---

[633] Kidd, *Doctrine of the Manifestations of the Son of God*, p. 689.

[634] Burton, quoted Ibid., pp. 689-690.

[635] Ibid., p. 691.

[636] "[the soul] departs stained with corporeal pollution, which was rendered natural to it, by its continual commerce and too intimate union with the body at a time when it was its constant companion… This pollution… is a gross, heavy, earthy, and visible mass" (Plato, *Phaedo*, 1).

[637] See H. Chadwick, *Origen: Contra Celsum* (Cambridge: CUP, 1980).

[638] *The Tripartite Tractate*, 115, 3-11. See also Sarah Iles Johnston, *Religions of the Ancient World: A Guide* (Cambridge: Belknap Press, 2004), p. 82.

affixed to the soul is obviously Platonic, but it is the peculiar association of this model with Jesus, and the presentation of Christ's emanation and exemption from that pollution, that is particularly Gnostic.[639] Thus it is under the dubious, Gnosticized influence of Origen that Athanasius also present the same Gnostic system, and again, in the same language.[640] Athanasius writes:

> *For if the Sun... as it circles in the heavens is not defiled* by approaching terrestrial bodies nor is destroyed by darkness, but rather illuminates and purifies them, much more the all-holy Word of God, maker of the Sun and Lord, *when he was known in the body was not polluted.*[641]

Ultimately, in Athanasius we find a perpetuation of an eerily Gnostic, untouchable divine being entering the womb from the outside. On Athanasius' Christological predilections, the president of the Catholic Theological Society of America provides this assessment:

> Jesus is not for Athanasius a human being like us. The actor in history is God, or the divine Word who was defined as consubstantial (homoousios) with the Father at Nicaea. In many passages one has the distinct impression that his body or flesh is an instrument through which a divine being, in effect God, is the subject or actor in history. By inference, then, Jesus is not a human being identical with all others, but a bodily form or vehicle in which the divine being, the Word, is the actor.[642]

Another scholar observes that:

> Athanasius got into enormous difficulties (as, it should be stressed, did most theologians) when he tried to make sense of a Jesus who is divine yet human. He created an elaborate

---

[639] "Some claim that Origen is more Platonic and philosophical than the Gnostics, but that argument becomes less tenable with the discovery of a fragmentary text from Plato's *Republic* as part of the Gnostic library from Nag Hammadi" (Griggs, p. 66).

[640] "The theological training of Athanasius was... under the still predominant although modified influence of Origen... In Alexander, the theological sponsor of the young Athanasius, the combination of a fundamentally Origenist theology with ideas traceable to the Asiatic tradition is conspicuous" (Philip Schaff, *Nicene and Post-Nicene Fathers*, Vol. IV (London: Parker & Company, 1892), p. lxviii).

[641] R. W. Thompson, *Athanasius, Contra Gentes and De Incarnatione* (Oxford, 1971), p. 177, emphasis added.

[642] Roger Haight, *Jesus: Symbol of God* (Maryknoll: Orbis Books, 1999), p. 222.

distinction between the human body of Jesus, which appears to suffer, as when on the cross, and the divine logos, which is somehow inside the human body but does not suffer. So, for instance, the mind of Jesus, which he allocated to the logos rather than to his body, could not feel anything and was not even subject to moral dilemmas.[643]

We are immediately reminded of the Gnostic Christological elements surviving in Clement and Origen: they had also envisioned a divine being who did not experience the fullness of human needs but appeared to. The young Athanasius would certainly get his chance to publicly advance his vision of Jesus as he dueled the traditional Subordinationists who refused to accept his blurring of the lines, both temporal and ontological, between the Father and the Son.

Athanasius is still often called by orthodox Christians the "Defender of the Faith" as he is widely viewed as having tirelessly protected the unvarnished, sanctimonious traditions of the Apostles from the intrusion of heretical systems. Yet none of his recently considered thought-forms, we must remind ourselves, find their origin in the Bible. The trademarks of Gnosticism are found dynamically coursing through his philosophical veins, as well as in those of other figures whom orthodox tradition now holds as guardians of the purest, most Apostolic faith.

We again recall modern scholar's detection of a "Crypto-Gnostic and Nicene circle in Rome."[644] Have we not already uncovered such a circle in Alexandria? Can we identify Alexander and Athanasius as its spiritual successors? Regardless, it should at least be plain that fourth-century "Alexandrian" Christianity had gone far beyond the Jewish faith of the earliest Christians. One scholar notes:

> The farther one moves from the Jewish-messianic roots of Christology, the more the humanity of Jesus fades. While some Jewish Christians consistently emphasized Jesus' full humanity and some Gnostic Christians equally consistently his full divinity, the proto-orthodox [of Alexandria] and many Gnostic Christians tried to have it both ways. On the orthodox side this led to a complicated doctrine of Christ's two

---

[643] Freeman, *Closing of the Western Mind,* p. 187.

[644] Abramowski, "Nicanismus und Gnosis," Zeitschrift fur Antikes Christentum, Vol. 8, No. 3 (S.N., S.L., 2005), pp. 513-566.

natures; one tried to work out a view that maintained a monotheistic stance while also doing justice to the divinity of Jesus. For a modern perception, neither the proto-orthodox nor the Gnostics assume a fully human being who is truly similar to all others.[645]

Setting the Stage for Nicaea

The great enemies of Athanasius and his party were the "Arians." This name has been used to describe them in most histories, but they were not really followers of Arius. The opposition consisted of a variety of Subordinationists; some of them certainly aligned with Arius' specific views, others were more deeply Origenist. In reality, they were only named "Arians" by Athanasius and other polemicists in hopes of discrediting their Subordinationist views as novel. From here, we may continue to use the traditional label "Arians" but we should not lose sight of the fact that they were not clinging to any innovation of Arius, but the traditional, majority view of the faith.

The man Arius (250-336 CE) was himself a Subordinationist presbyter from Libya who served in the church at Baucalis.[646] Arius first caught negative attention in Alexandria due to his strident rejection of his bishop's advancing doctrine of the eternal sonship of Christ. Though one of the most vocal, Arius was not the only dissenter on this point. He was "simply a die-hard conservative who was not afraid to challenge what he considered the innovations of his bishop, and who attracted a following merely on the grounds that he voiced what so many others felt about dangerous theological developments."[647] Even in Egypt, Alexander's doctrine was considered novel and precarious, and "most Egyptian Christians did not accept or understand the theology of the bishop."[648]

In opposition to Alexander, Arius loudly maintained that only the one God was truly eternal, and that he had *created* a Son, not eternally, but *in time,* before the creation of the world. Some of his chief proofs included passages like Colossians 1:15, which designates the Son as *"the firstborn of every creature,"* and from these texts Arius argued persuasively that the Son was first a pre-existent

---

[645] Heikki Raisanen, *The Rise of Christian Beliefs: The Thought World of Early Christians* (Minneapolis: Fortress Press, 2010), p. 225.

[646] Baucalis was the section of Alexandria where Mark the Evangelist was reportedly martyred. See Albert Birger Pearson, *Gnosticism and Christianity: In Roman and Coptic Egypt* (London: Continuum International Publishing Group, 2004), p. 105.

[647] Young, quoted in Griggs, p. 145.

[648] Ibid., p. 138.

angelic being who later became incarnate as the real man Jesus of Nazareth. Arius persistently taught that there was a time when the Son did not exist, and in this regard he was aligned with Tertullian and others.[649]   Diverging from Tertullian however, Arius also taught that God created Jesus out of nothing, being "made on our account, in order that God might create us by him, as by an instrument; nor would he ever have existed, unless God had wished to create us."[650]

Interestingly, even in the aftermath of Arius' first resistance, he nevertheless "continued in favor" with his bishop, who held him in "high esteem because of his speaking ability."[651]   Perhaps Alexander still found much in common between them.   Regardless, Arius' very public defiance became too controversial to ignore.   Alexander could not afford to appear weak.   Ancient Church historians agree that "Alexander took action against Arius only when forced to do so by the reports and criticisms of others."[652] Finally, in true proto-orthodox fashion, Alexander designed to compel everyone under his jurisdiction to sign a statement of faith in agreement with his views.   Of course, Arius refused.

Arius was swiftly excommunicated by Alexander around 320 CE.   However, Arius immediately appealed to another bishop, the famous Eusebius of Nicomedia, himself a Subordinationist.   Eusebius launched a successful campaign to have Arius reinstated, and soon another influential bishop from Caesarea, also named Eusebius, joined Arius' side in the scuffle.   Interestingly, this latter Eusebius is the same one who would later write against the Arians as heretics.   But at this stage, both Eusebiuses convened a council of bishops in Palestine and, in direct opposition to Alexander, *supported Arius*.[653]

As word of the controversy spread, Christians began to file in behind either the so-called "Arian" or anti-Arian groups.   Professor Richard E. Rubenstein describes what sort of Christians found themselves gathering in the general Arian and anti-Arian and camps around the time of Nicaea:

> [Those] for whom Christianity seemed a natural extension of
> and improvement on Judaism, tended to be Arians of one sort
> or another. By contrast, the strongest anti-Arians experienced
> their present as a sharp break with the past. It was they who

---

[649] Tertullian, *Against Hermogenes*, 3, 18.

[650] As quoted by Socrates Scholasticus, *Ecclesiastical Histories of Socrates Scholasticus,* 1, 6.

[651] Griggs, p. 120, citing Epiphanius and Sozomen.

[652] Ibid.

[653] Hanson, p. 135. See also Paul Foster, *Early Christian Thinkers: The Lives and Legacies of Twelve Key Figures* (London: Society for Promoting Christian Knowledge, 2010).

demanded, in effect, that Christianity be "updated" by blurring or even obliterating the long-accepted distinction between the Father and the Son. From the perspective of our own time, it may seem strange to think of Arian "heretics" as conservatives, but emphasizing Jesus' humanity and God's transcendent otherness never seemed heretical in the East.[654]

The proto-orthodox movement of Athanasius, at the time of Nicaea in 325 CE, was still certainly the minority camp.[655] Of course, today the roles have been reversed; now many Christians who consider themselves orthodox "consider Arianism obviously heretical, but during the first three centuries after Jesus' crucifixion, the idea that the Savior was separate from God and subordinate to Him was not particularly shocking."[656] The agitation between the widely held distinction of the Father and the Son and the budding demand for their radical eternal unity would prove the zenith controversy of a comprehensively troubled religion. The discord which erupted over the issue prior to 325 CE had already torn at the cultural fabric of the empire. It was a distress, it would seem, that only a Roman emperor had the power to soothe. Eventually, at Constantine's great "ecumenical" council,[657] the feverish clash of the Subordinationists and the Athanasian party would take center stage.

The Emperor's New Clothes

On October 27th, 312 CE, the decidedly pagan Emperor Constantine, having prayed for divine assistance in a crucial battle, saw a vision of a cross in the sky and heard a voice telling him to "conquer" by this sign.[658] Upon his dramatic victory, Constantine declared that it had been granted by the approving hand of the "Supreme Deity." From this day onward the Roman Empire would experience an incredible shift in its attitude towards Christianity. Constantine

---

[654] Richard E. Rubenstein, *When Jesus Became God: The Epic Fight Over Christ's Divinity in the Last Days of Rome* (New York: Harcourt Brace & Company, 1999), p. 74.

[655] Encyclopedia Britannica, Inc., "Trinity," *Encyclopedia Britannica*, Vol. 27, p. 2941.

[656] Rubenstein, p. 10.

[657] The first council ever called by Constantine was actually at Arles in 314 CE. Though Augustine of Hippo called Arles an ecumenical council, it has been largely forgotten in the shadow of Nicaea. See Karl Joseph von Hefele, *A History of the Councils of the Church* (Edinburgh: T & T Clark, 1871), p. 182.

[658] Baldwin H. Ward, *Pictorial History of the World's Great Religions* (New York: Gache Publishing Company, 1965), p. 72.

would not only legalize the faith, protecting Christians from harsh persecution,[659] but he would also lay the groundwork for its eventual proclamation as the state religion.[660] Constantine quickly anointed himself as Christianity's champion and sought to politically unify the quarreling Christian factions within his empire through the institution of official government-backed councils. The most famous of these convened at Nicaea in modern-day Turkey from May 20th to July 25th, 325 CE.

Constantine was a religious man, involved in both the pagan Sol Invictus and Hermetic (Gnostic) cults. He vigorously detested Judaism,[661] and his own conversion to Christianity remains questionable to this day.[662] Constantine's earliest interactions with the Church reveal both the controlling nature of his approach to Christianity, and his continuous and abysmal failure to understand it. One year after his decisive victory had turned him toward the Christian religion, Constantine issued the Edict of Milan which ordered toleration of not only Christianity, but all religions in the empire. But he quickly discovered that this decree was not enough to bring stability to the Christian world. In that era the faith was in the agonizing throes of the Donatist controversy; the churches of northern Africa were dividing over who was the "true Church."[663]

---

[659] Constantine's Edict of Milan in 313 CE not only established tolerance for Christianity but for all religions in the empire: "When you see that this has been granted to [Christians] by us, your Worship will know that we have also conceded to other religions the right of open and free observance of their worship for the sake of the peace of our times, that each one may have the free opportunity to worship as he pleases; this regulation is made that we may not seem to detract from any dignity of any religion" (Edict of Milan as recorded by Lactantius, *On the Deaths of the Persecutors*, Ch. 48).

[660] Theodosius' Edict of Thessalonica in 380 CE ordered all members of the empire to adopt the faith of the Roman and Alexandrian bishops over every other religion.

[661] W. H. C. Frend, *Rise of Christianity* (Philadelphia: Fortress Press, 1984), p. 499.

[662] The Christian faith of the historical Constantine is an enigma. He was clearly a sun-worshiping pagan before his vision of the "cross" in the sky. The confusion amongst historians arises when attempting to determine when, if ever, his conversion to Christianity took place. Ultimately, Constantine appears conflicted. At the same time of his Nicene convention, he was issuing coins from Antioch depicting himself alongside the sun god and carrying the legend "To the Sun, Companion of our Augustus." Constantine was of course not the only man in the council-chamber, but one should not shrug off his presence as inconsequential to the direction of the debates.

[663] In the late 3rd century CE, the Emperor Diocletian had severely persecuted the Church, especially in Northern Africa. During that difficult era, any Christians who renounced Christ or sacrificed to the pagan gods were spared by the government. While many Christians refused and were martyred, some denied Christ and retained their lives.   When the persecutions were over, some of the Christians who had endured the suffering refused to admit those who did not back into the Church. Donatus (d. 355 CE) held that sacraments given out by clergy who had renounced Christ were invalid. Those who agreed, the Donatists, held that they were the "true Church" since they were the only ones who held the "true Sacraments." The Donatist controversy

In 314, 315, and 316 CE, Constantine called his first Christian councils. He ordered the Donatists to unite with the rest of the Christians, and enforced his decrees using military power. But when the Donatists refused to give up their churches, violence ensued. Constantine's forces even slaughtered the Bishop of Sicilibba, the Bishop of Advocata, and many others.[664] Though in later years Constantine would ease his violent tendencies, he would continue to use strong-arm tactics to compel the Christians to unify. As we will soon see, despite his own edict of religious toleration, Constantine would later order the burning of dissident writings, confiscate property, and ban the meeting of Christian groups who did not contribute to his program of unification. Unity, above all else, was always the emperor's prize, and it is with this intention that he called the Council of Nicaea to order in 325 CE to settle the burgeoning "Arian controversy."

Constantine would personally oversee the proceedings at Nicaea and chaperone the bishops' discussions as a "significant member throughout the sessions of the council."[665] In tracing the early development of the doctrine of the Trinity, the hand of Constantine in these debates should not be ignored. After all, it was the emperor himself who would strategically propose controversial language for the Nicene Creed that would shake the Christian world to its core. For those modern Christians who trust in the absolute authority of the Roman council's decisions, there is often a tendency to downplay Constantine's role. However, the fact remains that:

> Constantine presided at the Council of Nicaea. He not only presided but exercised final authority. Today millions of Christians repeat the words of the Nicene Creed dictated at one crucial point the relation of the essence of the Father and the Son—not by episcopal wisdom but by an un-baptized layman.[666]

Constantine, ever the tactician, intentionally postponed baptism until just before his death, perhaps in order to continue solidifying his reign through martial and less-than-moral methods. Constantine's Christianity, which seems to have gone woefully neglected after Nicaea as he had his own wife and son

---

was never actually settled. It remained an issue all the way through the 7th century CE, when Christianity was finally destroyed in northern Africa by the Muslim invasion.

[664] Noel Lenski, *Constantine and the Cities: Imperial Authority and Civic Politics* (University of Pennsylvania Press, 2016), p. 80. See also Louis Duchesne, *Early History of the Christian Church*, Vol. 2 (New York: Longmans, Green and Co., 1920), pp. 85-95.

[665] Ward, *Pictorial History of the World's Great Religions*, p.73.

[666] Ross R. Holloway, *Constantine and Rome* (New Haven: Yale University Press, 2004), p. 15.

murdered,[667] should be considered in light of his willingness to spare no expense to accomplish his objectives. Otherwise Constantine seems perplexingly conflicted.

Regardless, it was under Constantine's leadership, three hundred years after the ascension of Christ, that the first authorization of Trinitarian principles would take place. Nicaea would provide not only a launching pad for future Trinitarian developments, but also for a long age of contention which would ultimately produce the dogmatic schisms of our present day.

Nicaea Revisited

Neither the Arians nor the proto-orthodox seem to have adequately represented the precise faith of the historical Jesus (though the Subordinationist Arians much more so), and certainly neither party had yet produced a complete reconciliation with the preceding Judaism. However, it seems that while the Subordinationist theologians could readily prove the distinction between the Son and the Father from Scripture, and the Athanasians could argue for passages they believed suggested their essential unity, the latter had the most difficulty in reconciling their belief with biblical monotheism.

The Athanasians were seriously compelled however by a certain passage in the fourth Gospel which to this day enjoys frequent citation. In John 10:30, Christ declares, *"the Father and I are one."* This the Athanasians took to mean that the Father and the Son's oneness was a unity of essence or nature.[668] They had evidently drawn upon the interpretations Tertullian, who had previously written that the words of Christ were "pointing to a unity of substance."[669] John 10:30 was thought to condemn both the Arian *and* Sabellian positions. If Jesus had intended by the word "one" to mean that he and the Father were one person (as the Sabellians taught), then he doubtless would have used the singular masculine Greek word "heis" (one person). However, Jesus uses "hen," meaning only "one thing." Interestingly, this word "heis" is exactly how Jesus describes God in Mark 12:29—God is "one," that is, *one person.* This stunning proof of Jesus'

---

[667] Patrick Guthrie, "The Execution of Crispus," *Phoenix,* 20: 4 (Classical Association of Canada, 1966), pp. 325–331.

[668] Athanasius, *Four Discourses Against the Arians,* Discourse III, Ch. 23, 4.

[669] See Tertullian, *Against Praxeas,* 25. "Recent scholarship on patristic exegesis has highlighted the role of Greco-Roman grammatical reading techniques in determining the meaning of the scriptural text... Unsurprisingly, Christian exegetes trained in these grammatical techniques applied them when reading Scripture" (Mark DelCogliano, "The Interpretation of John 10:30 in the Third Century," *Journal of Theological Interpretation,* Vol. XI (Winona Lake: Eisenbrauns, 2012), pp. 118-119).

unitary monotheism has yet to be appreciated by the mainstream. Nevertheless, the Athanasians continued to employ John 10:30 as their flagship argument.

Of course, the Arians found the Athanasian exegesis problematic. They argued against their "unity of substance" interpretation on the grounds that their opponents had not considered the passage in context, or the language's usage elsewhere in the Gospel. They pointed out that surrounding John 10:30 is an explanation by Christ that both he and the Father are responsible for protecting the sheep (believers). When he says, *"I and the Father are one,"* he is only explaining that both he and his Father are united in the common purpose of preserving the flock. This passage could be easily linked to John 17:20-30, where we find Jesus praying to God, asking that in the same way that he is one with God, his followers would also be one: *"That they may all be one, just as you, Father, are in me, and I in you, that they also may be in us, so that the world may believe that you have sent me"* (Jn 17:21). In repeatedly praying that his disciples *"would be one just as we are one"* (v. 22), and furthermore that they would also be *"one"* with Jesus and his Father (v. 23), Jesus made it clear that the unity in view was to be understood as one of mind, not substance.

So far, the Arian reasoning seems sound. Many Trinitarian commentators have agreed that this language certainly reflects a unity of purpose, not of essence, substance, or being.[670] Even John Calvin wrote that:

> The ancients made a wrong use of [John 10:30] to prove that Christ is…of the same essence with the Father. For Christ does not argue about the unity of substance, but about the agreement that he has with the Father.[671]

Baptist theologian George R. Beasley-Murray writes that "from earliest times it has been observed that Jesus says, *'I and the Father are one'* (Greek: *'hen'*), not *'heis'*, i.e., one in action, not in person."[672] Many scholars have agreed therefore that Jesus means that he and the Father have only a unity of purpose.[673]

---

[670] R. V. G. Tasker, *Tyndale NT Commentaries: John* (Downer's Grove, IVP, 1983), p. 136; J. N. Sanders, B. A. Mastin, *The Gospel According to John* (Randomhouse New Zealand, 1968), p. 258; J. H. Bernard, *A Critical and Exegetical Commentary on the Gospel According to St. John* (Edinburgh: T & T Clark, 1928), pp. 365-366; Kuschel, *Born Before All Time*, p. 170.

[671] John Calvin, *Commentary on John*, John 10:30.

[672] George R. Beasley-Murray, *World Bibilical Commentary*, Vol. 36 (New York: Thomas Nelson, 1999), p. 174.

[673] See Marianne Meye Thompson, *Dictionary of Jesus and the Gospels*, (Downer's Grove: IVP, 1992), p. 378; Warren Carter, *John: Storyteller, Interpreter, Evangelist* (Grand Rapids: Baker Academic, 2006), p. 53; Gail R. O'Day, *New Interpreter's Bible*, Vol. IX (Nashville: Abingdon Press, 1996), p. 677.

The Athanasian party's diligent attempts to demonstrate the agreement of their dogma of the Son's co-equal divinity with the faith of the Hebrews proved the most rigorous of all challenges—they constantly found themselves teetering on the edge of many Gods. How indeed might the theologians affirm, without at least some degree of reservation, that multiple divine individuals did *not* represent multiple divinities? This anxiety remains active amongst modern scholars. Trinitarian professor Shirley C. Guthrie Jr. reveals the tenacious worry of his tradition: "If we say that God is really present and at work in Jesus, how can we avoid saying that there are in fact two Gods—one 'up in heaven' and one who appeared down here on earth? The N.T. does not solve this problem."[674] Of course, in addition to not solving this problem, Guthrie should also recognize that the New Testament does not exactly present the problem either, as he himself states: "The doctrine of the Trinity is not found in the Bible."[675]

To complicate the Athanasians' tension with monotheism further, not only must the Son belong to the same Godhead as the Father, so too must a *third* consubstantial Person. Many of the Subordinationists of this era also believed in the real personhood of the Holy Spirit but regarded him as a unique creature outside the Godhead, or a form of high angel. However, at this time protracted arguments over the precise nature of the mysterious Holy Spirit were not at the forefront of the debate. While the Nicene Creed would move to solidify the relationship between Father and Son, the Holy Spirit was not made a point of debate until much later, and nothing was even "decided" about the Spirit until the First Council of Constantinople in 381 CE.[676] Indeed Nicaea's creedal determinations produced nothing concrete concerning the unity of three divine "Persons" of Trinitarianism. Christian theology required more than half a century of further debate and development to modify and sanction the regurgitated Gnostic and Neoplatonic system in which the relationship between Father, Son, and Holy Spirit could be described, as it is today, as one substance (ousia) and three persons (hypostases). But the first order of business at Nicaea was dealing with the relationship between the Father and the Son.

Athanasius' personal style throughout the controversy was bold and abrasive and often landed him beneath accusations of instigation and even murder.[677] It

---

[674] Guthrie, *Christian Doctrine*, pp. 78-80.

[675] Ibid.

[676] Kelly, p. 88.

[677] See Timothy D. Barnes, *Athanasius and Constantius: Theology and Politics in the Constantinian Empire* (Cambridge: Harvard University Press, 1993). Athanasius' personal history is sordid at best. He was charged with forcing his way into his bishopric after the death of his predecessor, defiling a

was no secret that he advocated even the use of violence against those he deemed dangerous to the Church.[678] Looking back, writes Griggs, "if Athanasius had been more like his predecessor [Alexander], that is to say, more conciliatory and less ruthless and violent toward any who disagreed with him, he might have avoided exile so many times, and the widening theological gulf of the fourth century might not have occurred."[679] But to Athanasius, those who denied that Christ was eternal God were even worse than the Christ-crucifying Jews.[680] Athanasius could not imagine how one could ever hope to be saved if he denied the very nature of the divine Savior.

Interestingly, while Athanasius was certainly the most vocal and demanding of belief in his doctrine, he can often be found exhibiting a strange candor, perhaps a byproduct of his youthful zeal. One historian recounts that:

> Athanasius himself has candidly confessed that whenever he forced his understanding to meditate on the divinity of the Logos, his toilsome and unavailing efforts recoiled on themselves; that the more he thought, the less he comprehended; and the more he wrote, the less capable was he of expressing his thoughts.[681]

Despite the many explanations and analogies put forth by orthodoxy over the centuries in hopes of soothing the jarring mental exercise of the Athanasian faith, a distinguished Trinitarian professor admits that "there is no way to overcome the paradox that we must think of God both as one and as a society. There simply is no way in human thought to compose this paradox."[682] Likewise we find such famous thinkers as Thomas Jefferson, with his typical refreshing bluntness, warning the student of Athanasius' bewildering cause:

> The Athanasian paradox that one is three, and three but one, is so incomprehensible to the human mind, that no candid man can say he has any idea of it, and how can he believe what presents no idea? He who thinks he does, only deceives

---

sacred altar, stealing Church grain away from the poor and sold it for personal gain, and even suppressing dissent through murder. While the truth behind each of these accusations may never be known, there is no doubt that Athanasius was well-known by all as an aggressive firebrand who would succeed by whatever means necessary.

[678] Roger E. Olson, *The Story of Christian Theology* (Wheaton: IVP, 1999), p. 172.

[679] Griggs, p. 138.

[680] Rubenstein, p. 9.

[681] Gibbon, p. 777.

[682] Richardson, p. 95.

himself. He proves, also, that man, once surrendering his reason, has no remaining guard against absurdities… and like a ship without a rudder, is the sport of every wind… [such faith] takes the helm from the hand of reason, and the mind becomes a wreck.[683]

The Greek philosophers certainly entertained, and even celebrated, an inability to perfectly realize the transcendent "Unknown God." But the latitude provided by the philosophical community was not offered by the Athanasians, who sought to cage the wandering curiosity of the disciple through the introduction of official creeds. Despite even Athanasius' own failure to mentally exercise the Trinitarian idea, it would become the unquestioned law for the Christian.

While the Arians urged consideration of the futility offered by the incomprehensible nature of the Athanasian system, and further "disclaimed the use of any terms or definitions which could not be found in the scriptures,"[684] the Athanasians seemed less aware of a need for both rational and textual qualification for their dogma. Athanasius, grown and well-trained by the Alexandrian schools, operated with such a honed mental elasticity, that the same Supreme, untouchable, and incomprehensible sense of mystery that had stimulated the Gnostics could be at the same time spiritually accepted without being cognitively appreciated. In fact it *must* be, against all directives of human faculty, that the Christ is fundamentally beyond us. How then could he benevolently reach down into the mire of the human condition and deposit any divine knowledge, much less atone for the sins of his lowly, floundering disciples? His works were too profound, his sayings too lofty, his piety and indomitable strength of character too extraordinary for any "mere man" to ever achieve; the Nazarene must, inexplicably, be God himself.

Their Arian opponents saw things differently, of course: Jesus Christ had exhibited such inspiring and significant obedience to God that he had been chosen (either before Creation or at his baptism) to carry out God's redemptive plan for mankind. Because of his faithful submission to God's will, even to the point of ultimate sacrifice, he had been granted lordly status over all Creation. To some he even had a mark of "divinity," though a divinity derived from, and lesser than that of his heavenly Father. Due to the complete agreement with

---

[683] Thomas Jefferson, Letter to the theologian James Smith, December 8, 1822.
[684] Gibbon, p. 782.

God which the Christ demonstrated during his life, he became a model of ideal faith and righteousness, his very same reward of immortality becoming attainable for all mankind. One historian summarizes the Arians' argument for Christ:

> From the Arian perspective, it was essential that Jesus *not* be God, since God, being perfect by nature, is inimitable. By contrast, Christ's transcendent virtue, achieved by repeated acts of will, is available (at least potentially) to the rest of us. Even though we may fall short of his impeccable standards, his triumph over egoism shows us how we also may become the Sons and Daughters of God.[685]

That Jesus must exhibit a distinction from God's superlative *otherness* was essential. How could men hope to follow Christ, their prescribed example, without being almighty God themselves? While Christ's superior knowledge of and intimacy with God and the critical nature of his commission certainly elevated him far beyond any other creature, he was nevertheless an individual whose power, even very existence, was wholly *derived*. The Arian understanding of Christian purpose and destiny hinged on this crucial point: what real hope was there for the Christian in regard to *living the life Christ lived* (1 John 2:3-6) if he were actually the Supreme God himself? This array of questions severely agitated the Athanasian position at Nicaea:

> How could an all-powerful, all-knowing, all-good Creator experience temptation, learn wisdom and grow in virtue? How could he suffer on the Cross and die the death of a human being? Surely, when Jesus cried out, *"My God, my God, why hast Thou forsaken me?"* he was not talking to himself! When he admitted that nobody knows the day and the hour of Judgment, *"not even the angels of heaven, nor the Son, but the Father only,"* he was not just being modest. And when he told the disciples that *"the Father is greater than I,"* he meant exactly what he said.[686]

The Politics of Faith

In determining Nicaea's ultimate outcome, the strength of each side's theological arguments and debating prowess may have contributed, yet we must

---

[685] Rubenstein, p. 56.
[686] Ibid., p. 8.

also take into account the immediate *political* context. Having recently battled his way to the highest seat of power in the mortal world, Emperor Constantine had no intention of letting his rule go to ruin over the sectarian quarrelling of his Christian subjects. Constantine himself expressed his fears that the bishops' quarrelling over Jesus would undermine his own divine appointment as God's chosen ruler of the world. He writes:

> I consider it absolutely contrary to the divine law that [God] would overlook such quarrels and contentions... whereby the Highest Divinity may perhaps be roused not only against the human race but also against myself, to whose care he has by his celestial will committed the government of all earthly things.[687]

The warring bishops must be made to unite in one direction or the other, and quickly. A clever strategist until his dying day, Constantine planned to bring this balance not only by forcing their consensus on doctrine (by the point of the sword if necessary), but by bringing them under his personal supervision. He lavished the bishops with incredible riches and positions of honor and awarded tax exemption to both them and their properties.[688] He skillfully led them into positions of dependency on his patronage, and himself into a position from which he might exert influence over Church decisions without serious objection. As bishop Hilary of Poitier observed of his fellows: "[Constantine] does not bring you liberty by casting you in prison, but treats you with respect within his palace and thus makes you his slave."[689]

Whether or not Constantine had any personal interest in the teachings of Jesus, it is undeniable that the prize of political order always proved Constantine's greatest motivator.[690] Many later Christians have praised Nicaea's result as a providential act of divine persuasion in favor of genuine Christian

---

[687] Quoted in M. Beard, J. North and S. Price, *Religions of Rome*, Vol. 1 (Cambridge, 1998), p. 367.

[688] "Once Constantine had provided tax exemption for Christian clergy, eventually including exemptions for church lands, it became imperative to tighten up the definition of 'Christian'... This explains why the emperors came to play such a large part in the determining of doctrine, although their roles varied: some had personal convictions to impose, others were more concerned to find formulations of doctrine around which consensus could be built. By the end of the century emperors were imposing doctrinal solutions that were backed by imperial edicts" (Freeman, *Closing of the Western Mind*, p. 179)

[689] Hilary, On the New Status of Bishops. Quoted by Freeman, *Closing of the Western Mind*, p. 202.

[690] Durant notes that the letter of Constantine to Alexander and Arius urging them to keep their doctrinal dispute from the public's ears "reveals Constantine's lack of theology, and the political purpose of his religious policy" (Will Durant, *The Story of Civilization: Caesar and Christ* (New York: Simon & Schuster, 1944), p. 659).

truth, with Martin Luther even naming Nicaea "the most sacred of all councils."[691] But one of Church history's most crucial unsung footnotes is the fact that Constantine went into the debate *with his mind already made up.*

Prior to the council, Constantine's trusted advisor, Bishop Hosius, had met with Alexander and his allies to plan their victory.[692] The Arians had taken the long way around to the site of the council, through Palestine and Syria, but Alexander had taken the fastest route by boat. Upon arrival he colluded with Hosius and they agreed to endorse a doctrine which would force the exile of Arius.[693] To Hosius, it was clear that Constantine should side with Alexander's party; Constantine's open distaste for Judaism might have helped to make that obvious. To Constantine, the Jews were "a hostile people" and a "nation of parricides" who "slew their Lord."[694] The God proposed by the Athanasians certainly offered a more complete severance with Judaism than the Arians. Furthermore, Constantine's (disputably former) participation in the Roman cult of Sol Invictus, which advocated the incorporation of many divinities into a single sun god, may have expedited his affirmation of a system which enthusiastically identified this Jesus Christ with the Supreme Being. Sol Invictus, Constantine's "personal patron deity,"[695] commanded a form of monotheistic worship which was able to conquer rival gods, not by eradicating their unique worship, but by subsuming it. The popularity of this deity was emblematic of a new era of paganism; Rome's polytheistic worldview had long been tolerant of the local deities of the territories the nation had conquered, and wisely allowed them to be easily absorbed into the Roman pantheon.[696] But in the pagan world things were already changing: monotheism was quickly being recognized as a useful tool for consolidating both cultural and political power, and the radical spread of Christianity's monotheism amongst the Roman subjects was certainly not lost on the emperor.[697] It may be argued that Constantine, who only five years prior to Nicaea had minted currency embossed with *"To Sol Invictus my*

---

[691] Gordon Rupp, *Luther's Progress to the Diet of Worms* (New York: Harper and Row Publishers, 1964), p. 66.

[692] Eusebius, *Life of Constantine,* 27-28.

[693] Photios' epitome of Philostorgius' *Church History,* 1, 7.

[694] Frend, p. 499.

[695] Elizabeth Marlowe, "Framing the Sun: The Arch of Constantine and the Roman Cityscape," *The Art Bulletin,* Vol. 88, No. 2, (College Art Association, 2006), pp. 223-242.

[696] Freeman, *Closing of the Western Mind,* p. 57.

[697] "By the second century AD it was increasingly commonplace to see the divine world as subject to one supreme god, with the other gods being either manifestations of his divinity or lesser divinities… It is possible even to go so far as to say that a belief in an overriding deity was, by this period, the most widespread belief of pagan religion" (Freeman. p. 69).

companion,"[698] perceived the peculiar brand of plural monotheism presented by the Athanasians as the best vehicle for compounding religion and power in his empire. One historian notes that:

> Caesars had habitually declared special sponsorship by gods, but in this era, the meaning of such piety was changing. The coming to the fore of Christian ideas was only part of a larger religious revolution, which our own simplistic notions of paganism fall short of explaining. For example, it is significant that Constantine's coins stated his devotion to the Unconquered Sun. Sol Invictus had already come to be understood, in a proclamation by the emperor Aurelian in 274, as *"the one universal Godhead... recognized under a thousand names."*[699]

The Athanasian presentation of Jesus' essential identification with the Godhead more readily facilitated Constantine's balancing act between the imperial traditions and his newfound Christian inclinations. Ultimately, we find that:

> [Constantine] agreed with Hosius that the dispute should be ended on terms favorable to [the Athanasians]. The question was how to accomplish this in such a way that the bishops did not leave Nicaea more seriously divided than they had been before they arrived.[700]

Interestingly, we find that during the debate, Eusebius of Caesarea, the same bishop who had originally sided with Arius in his early fights with Alexander, was instrumental in the production of a creed that at first seemed palatable to both the Arians and the Athanasians. It was thought that the ambiguity of the creed's language could accommodate both parties, so long as they privately interpreted it in their own ways. It appeared for a time that Christendom might continue in the diversity in which it had thrived for hundreds of years, but such an open-ended conclusion was not the emperor's aim. The faith must be completely united, and on the side of the Athanasians—Arius and his allies had to be ousted. Thus, during a critical point, Constantine personally suggested the council adopt the word *"homoousios"* ("same substance") to describe the

---

[698] Ibid., p. 160.

[699] James Carroll, *Constantine's Sword: The Church and the Jews* (New York: Houghton Mifflin Company, 2002), pp. 180-181, emphasis added.

[700] Rubenstein, pp. 71-72.

relationship between the Father and the Son. The word that Constantine so famously interjected was, as we have previously seen, by no means a biblical term or even a creation of Constantine's, but "had previously arisen in theological language, and occurs even in Origen and among the Gnostics."[701] As we discovered in chapter three, his use of "homoousios" was actually derived from the Hermetic Gnostic tractate *Poimandres*. In that expressly pagan work, Nous, the supreme God, was said to be consubstantial with his Son, the Logos, who proceeded from him as light from the sun. Again, this pagan work is the only text which made such specific use of this word and concept.[702]

But how was such a definition, which had no basis in Scripture, to be justified with the Christian bishops? Constantine, ostensibly qualifying before the assembly the identification of Jesus Christ as "God from God," and "of one substance with the Father," is recorded to have invoked a rather conspicuous pagan authority, saying:

> *Plato* himself… declared, with truth, a God exalted above every essence, but to him he added also a second, distinguishing them as two, though both possessing one perfection, and the being of the second Deity proceeding from the first.[703]

Constantine's citation of *Plato* as justification for the establishment of *Christian* doctrine should be concerning enough. But was it really Plato to whom the emperor appealed? We find that Constantine had provided not only the word "homoousios" but even a philosophical explanation of its usage.[704] However, his explanation "evidently has no relation at all with Plato's real doctrine. Neither is Numenius likely to have exerted any influence on Constantine's speech."[705] His understanding clearly originates in the Gnostic tradition of Heremeticism. As Beatrice reveals, "the Plato recalled by Constantine is just a name used to cover precisely the Egyptian and Hermetic theology of the 'consubstantiality' of the Logos-Son with the Nous-Father."[706]

---

[701] Philip Schaff, *History of the Christian Church* (Grand Rapids: Eerdmans, 1985), 3, 628.

[702] Beatrice, "Homoousios"

[703] Eusebius, *Oration of Constantine.*

[704] Eusebius recalls: "[Constantine] interpreted [homoousios] not in the sense of the affections of bodies, nor as if the Son subsisted from the Father, in the way of division, or any severance; for that the immaterial and intellectual and incorporeal nature could not be the subject of any corporeal affection, but that it became us to conceive of such things in a divine and ineffable manner. And such were the theological remarks of our most wise and most religious emperor" (Eusebius, *Life of Constantine*, 35).

[705] Beatrice, "Homoousios"

[706] Ibid.

Where did Constantine learn to read Plato this way? Constantine's close religious advisor, Lucius Lactantius, the Christian Crypto-Gnostic mentioned in chapter three, had likely assisted Constantine here. Beatrice postulates that "in the years of the outbreak of the Arian controversy, Lactantius might have played *a decisive role* in influencing Constantine's Hermetic interpretation of Plato's theology and consequently the emperor's decision to insert homoousios in the Creed of Nicaea."[707] Thus Gnostic, even Egyptian-pagan thinking was once again being redressed as orthodox Christianity; the moment was emblematic of the ongoing Christian practice of instituting pagan philosophy as the vehicle for biblical explication. It was also emblematic of the incredible influence the State would begin to assert over doctrinal matters within the Church.

Alexander, Athanasius, and their allies assented to Constantine's introduction of "homoousios." So did Bishop Hosius and Eusebius of Caesarea, who were forced to draft a new creed around the word. However, there is evidence that the emperor's imposition of this Gnostic term did not sit well with either party. After Constantine's death, at the Council of Sardica in 343 CE, Hosius drew a new creed which *removed* the word. Anti-Arians even complained that they had been "reduced to silence under the pretense of preserving peace."[708] As Beatrice reveals, "none of them was really interested in the addition of this new word... 'homoousios' was in fact a foreign body or stumbling block for all the people attending the council, without distinction, Arians and anti-Arians, and for this very reason it soon disappeared in the following debates."[709] Indeed, Athanasius himself, who championed the term for Constantine at Nicaea, would not even touch the word for fifteen years after the council ended.

Why then did the council agree to resurrect this condemned term which made both the Athanasians and the Arians uncomfortable? In addition to the obvious pressure from Constantine, there was the overwhelming desire to defeat Arius politically. Arius had personally rejected the term "homoousios" in his own writings, having explicitly connected the word with the teachings of the Gnostic Mani and Valentinus.[710] The implementation of that word in the official creed was bound to force his exile, and historians both ancient and modern have

---

[707] Ibid.

[708] Ibid. See Theodoret, *Church History*, 1, 8.

[709] Beatrice, "Homoousios." Like Constantine, Lactantius taught that "Plato spoke about the first God and the second god, not as a philosopher, but as a prophet" (Ibid.).

[710] See Hans-Georg Opitz, "Urkunden zur Geschichte des arianischen Streites 318-328," *Athanasius Werke*, Vol. 3, Pt. 1 (Berlin and Leipzing: W. de Gruyter, 1934-35), 21.

concluded that its acceptance was a deliberate attempt to publicly emphasize his rejection.[711]   In other words, the consensus was achieved for reasons just as political as theological.   Of course, the power of Constantine was not a thing to be ignored—this term was his chosen rallying point.   As one historian recognizes, "It was unlikely that the bishops, dependent as they were now on the patronage and support of Constantine, would have been able to resist him.   The result was an enormous majority for the new creed."[712]

Of course, the use of "homoousios" in the creed was met with the expected serious protest from Arius' sympathizers.   They quickly pointed out that the word had already been banned by the respected Council of Antioch in 268 CE. Athanasius himself was apparently quite flustered by this argument; he did not wish to appear to criticize the people who had condemned Paul of Samosata at Antioch, but he could not deny that they had damned the term which Constantine now endeavored to use.[713]   Athanasius' only recourse was then to argue that the anathematized Paul of Samosata and the supporters of the new Nicene Creed must be using the term "homoousios" in a different sense.   Yet, as Hanson notes, "the almost insoluble difficulty is to determine in what sense Paul used homoousios."[714]   The issue persisted: the proto-orthodox condemned Paul of Samosata as a heretic, yet here they were using the same language which contributed to his defamation.   This ultimately caused "considerable embarrassment to those theologians who wanted to defend its inclusion in an official doctrinal statement in the next history."[715]   Nevertheless, despite all protest, the term was enshrined as the hallmark of the Nicene code, being ultimately agreed upon, though under constraint, by the majority of the assembly.   The official statement read:

> We believe in one Lord, Jesus Christ,
> the only son of God,
> eternally begotten of the Father,
> God from God, Light from Light,
> true God from true God,

---

[711] Freeman, *Closing of the Western Mind*, p. 168.   Orthodox historian Photios, in his *Bibliotheca*, cites Philostorgius, *Church History*, Book 1, 7 for notice of the political alliance against Arius formed just prior to the council.

[712] Freeman, *Closing of the Western Mind.*, p. 169.

[713] Hanson, p. 192.

[714] Ibid.

[715] Ibid.

begotten, not made,

of one substance *(homoousios)* with the Father.[716]

Ultimately, Constantine's reason for implementing the above creed was two-fold: he had not only sought theological consensus and stability, he had sought to interpret Christianity through his inherited pagan background. His creed was meant to play mediator between not only the Christian factions, but between the Christian religion, Hermeticism, and the cult of Sol Invictus. Needless to say, this was a major turning point. Christian belief was now prescribed by a secular power, and it was officially delineated and warranted by the language of pagan, Gnostic speculation external to the biblical writings. Indeed, "the use of this term [homoousios] in a Creed meant that, from 325 on, Nicenes could and did proclaim other dogmas that have no basis in Scripture."[717] This unprecedented determination immediately rendered Arius and his fellows heretics, and they were promptly stripped of their posts and exiled. Though there were seventeen bishops in attendance who sided with Arius, only six suffered to be exiled with him, while the other eleven agreed to "subscribe with hand only, not heart" to the Nicene statement.[718] Rubenstein writes:

> That there was pressure brought to bear by Constantine is undeniable. The sentences of exile passed on the hard-line Arians demonstrated the consequences of opposing him. Clearly, to the extent that the bishops felt they had signed the [Nicene] creed under duress, they felt justified later on in qualifying and "explaining" (some might say, explaining away) their signatures.[719]

---

[716] Nicene Creed, 325 CE, emphasis added. Other English translations, instead of "eternally begotten," have read "begotten by the Father before all worlds."

[717] Ben H. Swett, *State Church of the Roman Empire.* 7 May 1998. Web. 15 December 2014. <http://bswett.com/1998-05Church300.html>.

[718] Philip R. Amidon, *The Church History of Rufinus of Aquileia, 10, 11* (London: OUP, 1997), p. 13.

[719] Rubenstein, p. 83. Eusebius of Caesarea's letter to his confused constituents regarding why he and other Arian-sympathizers eventually signed the creed explained that they were able to creatively interpret its strictures in a way that did not impugn their faith. For example, he felt he could comply with the council's condemnation of the statement "The Son did not exist before he was begotten," because, he says, that they all agreed that the Son did not exist until he was begotten according to the flesh. See Theodoret, *Church History*, 1, 12. See also Gelasius, *Church History,* 2, 35.

Regardless of the bishops' true personal beliefs, challenge to the homoousian would not be suffered in the Roman Empire (for now). The emperor himself issued an official edict proclaiming:

> If any writing composed by Arius should be found, it should be handed over to the flames, so that not only will the wickedness of this teaching be obliterated, but nothing will be left even to remind anyone of him. And I hereby make a public order, that if someone should be discovered to have hidden a writing composed by Arius, and not to have immediately brought it forward and destroyed it by fire, his penalty shall be death. As soon as he is discovered in this offense, he shall be submitted for capital punishment.[720]

Thus the writings of Arius would be destroyed and anyone not found adhering to the council's rule of faith would be harshly persecuted. This was a watershed moment: for the first time, the state got behind a doctrine. The result, as expected, was nothing less than an age of oppression and chaos. Ironically, Constantine's own 313 CE decree of religious tolerance, made only twelve years prior, had read:

> Our purpose is to grant both to the Christians and to all others full authority to follow whatever worship each person has desired... no person whatever should be refused complete toleration, who has given up his mind either to the cult of the Christians or to the religion which he personally feels best suited to himself... Christians may from this moment freely and unconditionally proceed to observe the same without any annoyance or disquiet.[721]

The wisdom of this edict was disastrously set aside after Nicaea. Not only were the Arians persecuted, but so were all other Christians who did not rally behind the new theology. Constantine confiscated their land, closed their churches and outlawed their meetings; specifically, between 325 and 326 he banned the Valentinians, the Marcionites, the Paulianists (unitarians), and the Montanists (Tertullian's group).[722] Thus the proto-orthodox faction's long-time

---

[720] Athanasius, *De Decretis*, 39; Socrates, *Church History*, 1, 9, 30; Gelasius, *Church History*, 2, 36, 1.
[721] "Edict of Milan," in R. H. Bainton, *Early Christianity* (Princeton: S.V.N. Co., 1960), p. 160.
[722] Lenski, p. 80.

rivals were systematically weakened by the state. These group's alternative interpretations of the Bible, far from being invalidated through episcopal persuasion, were simply legislated into submission. However, Constantine's stranglehold on theology did not last. For orthodoxy, Nicaea was only the beginning of the birth pains.

The Nicene Heresy

Though for Constantine "homoousios" had a specific, Hermetic meaning, the Church was now forced to try to interpret it in a non-Gnostic sense. Despite Constantine's forcing of a political consensus around the creed, the major underlying problem with the new standard was the fact that there was yet no true *theological* consensus on how to understand it. Thus the Nicene supporters, though claiming to lay out the proper theological requirements of orthodoxy, unintentionally opened a doorway to the acceptance of the hated Sabellian heresy, and perhaps even a doorway to their own condemnation by later orthodox councils.

At the end of the original version of the Nicene Creed there was affixed a series of anathemas, or damnatory clauses against heretical views. Condemned obviously was Arius' view of the Son created in time, but curiously there was also a condemnation of any "that say that he existed out of any other *hypostasis* or *ousia* than the Father."[723] Modern versions of the creed have since deleted this portion, and one can understand why: the purpose of the Nicene Creed, according to this anathema, had been to connect the Father and the Son to the same "ousia" *and* the same "hypostasis." This immediately seems to pose a problem for orthodoxy's doctrinal continuity narrative, since after the Council of Constantinople (381 CE) it was declared that the Father and the Son are explicitly *not* the same "hypostasis." And the Athanasian Creed (c. 500 CE) would likewise proclaim that "there is one hypostasis of the Father, and *another* of the Son, and *another* of the Holy Ghost" and that if anyone said that there was only one hypostasis, they were to perish everlastingly. Thus, strictly according to the language involved, the Nicene Creed appears to exhibit a "Sabellian" view (that God is one substance and one hypostasis in multiple modes), and

---

[723] The original three anathemas read: "But they who say, 'there was a time when the Son was not,' and that 'he did not exist before he was begotten'; or that say 'he was begotten out of nothing'; or that say 'he existed out of any other hypostasis or ousia than the Father'; or was created or liable to imitation or change—the Holy Catholic Church anathematizes" (Nicene Creed cited by Robert Clayton, *Bishop Clayton on the Nicene and Athanasian Creeds* (Dublin: Hodges, Foster & Col., 1876), pp. 25-26).

contradicts and condemns the Athanasian Creed and vice versa. As one vicar writes:

> I cannot help but say it is something odd to have these two Creeds established in the same Church, in one of which those are declared to be *accursed* who deny the Son to be of "the same ousia or hypostasis of the Father," and in the other it is declared that "they cannot be saved who do not assert that there is one hypostasis of the Father, and another of the Son, and another of the Holy Ghost."[724]

How do modern-day defenders of Nicaea explain this discrepancy? It is usually suggested that the word "hypostasis" did not mean "person" as it would later mean at Constantinople in 381 CE.[725] Indeed, we have already seen in chapter three how in the first few centuries Christians used "hypostasis" as a synonym for "ousia" (substance). In saying that the Father and the Son were of the same "hypostasis," the bishops were probably reemphasizing the point that the Father and the Son were of the same "ousia." Indeed, it seems obvious that at the time of Nicaea, "hypostasis" had not yet taken up that Gnostic meaning of "*person.*"

Athanasius obviously interpreted the creedal language in a way that did not demand Sabellianism, as his own writings demonstrate that he used "hypostasis" synonymously with "ousia."[726] But what is also certain is that there were some affirming members at Nicaea who *did* understand the language in a Sabellian way. There was indeed a Sabellian presence among the bishops who had no problem signing the statement of faith.[727] But if a Sabellian theology is not at all what the creed meant to Athanasius and the other bishops, we are compelled to wonder if the Nicene Creed was not ratified on the basis of a major misunderstanding among its supporters. Were Alexander and Athanasius so intent on installing the homoousian to oust their enemy Arius that they turned a blind eye to any

---

[724] Ibid., p. 26. (Thanks to Carlos Xavier at http://thehumanjesus.org for this source.)

[725] For the opposite view, see Philip Schaff's recollection of George Bull's argument that the word "hypostasis" and "ousia" were not the same thing at Nicaea (Philip Scaff, *Nicene and Post Nicene Fathers* (Oxford: Parker & Co., 1892), pp. 77-79). The evidence seems overwhelming, however, that the two words were synonymous.

[726] See Hanson, *The Search for the Christian Doctrine of God*, p. 445.

[727] For example, "[the bishops] knew that Marcellus of Ancyra must have accepted the words [homoousios] in a Sabellian sense at the Council, and he was still advocating his doctrines" (R. V. Sellers, *Eustathius of Antioch and His Place in Early Christian Doctrine* (Cambridge: CUP, 1928), p. 31).

misunderstanding of the creed so as long as it received the necessary votes for approval? After the bewildering council concluded:

> the majority of the Bishops in the East... came to see that they had signed something which, when they went to Nicaea, they had not the slightest intention of signing... it became apparent that the word [homoousios] still left open the door to the opposite error of Sabellianism.[728]

Athanasius himself, the very champion of Nicaea, demonstrated his own wariness of his recent achievement by avoiding even using the words "hypostasis" and "homoousios" for decades.[729] Was he all too aware of how precarious their situation really was? Does his reluctance reveal that "he had not yet come to a strong position" himself?[730] It was obvious that his newly minted brand of orthodoxy teetered dangerously on a fulcrum: on one side it hovered over the dreaded heresy of Sabellianism, and on the other side, Arianism, or even worse, polytheism. It was a balancing act Athanasius sustained as long as he could. But for now, in the immediate aftermath of Nicaea, all that mattered was that Jesus Christ had been enshrined as "God" (whatever that meant), and Arius and his allies had been defeated.

Ultimately then, Nicaea accomplished nothing for Christian theology. At worst, it produced a statement of faith which would later be considered heretical. At best, it produced a statement of faith which meant nothing at all. The Father and the Son were "homoousios" with no hope of qualification. For all intents and purposes, the very council intended to draw a clear line between orthodoxy and heresy made that line more ambiguous than ever. As Rubenstein so aptly concludes: "Achieving consensus was exactly what Constantine thought he had done at Nicaea, but the apparent unity manifested there proved illusory."[731]

---

[728] Ibid., p. 31.

[729] Athanasius' first defense of "homoousios" does not arrive until his *De Decretis* around 353 CE. He likewise avoids "hypostasis" as long as he can, and until he penned his *Tomus ad Antichenos* in 362 CE, Athanasius did view "hypostasis" as a synonym of "ousia." See Lewis Ayres, "Athanasius' Initial Defense of the Term homoousios: Rereading the De Decretis," *Journal of Early Christian Studies*, Vol. 12, No. 3 (John Hopkins University Press, 2004), pp. 337-359.

[730] Griggs, p. 172.

[731] Rubenstein, p. 181.

6

CREEDS AND CHAOS:
POST-NICENE CHRISTIANITY
STRUGGLES TOWARD THE TRINITY

"Persecution is not an original feature in any
religion; but it is always the strongly marked
feature of all religions established by law."
— Thomas Paine

O NE OF THE BISHOPS WHO HAD REFUSED to sign the Nicene Creed had called out to Eusebius of Nicomedia, "Eusebius, you subscribed to avoid exile! As God is my witness, you will have to suffer banishment on my account!" As predicted, three months after the council, Eusebius and several of his associates repented of having subscribed to the creed at all, and went to the emperor to make their confession. They admitted to Constantine, "We acted impiously, your majesty, in subscribing to the heresy from fear of you."[732] Enraged, Constantine swiftly banished them to Gaul (modern France).

---

[732] Nicetas Choniates, *Treasury of Orthodoxy*, 5, 7-9. See also Photios' epitome of Philostorgius' *Church History*, 2, 7-7b.

However, after three full years had passed, Constantine decreed that Eusebius and the exiled Arians should be permitted to return. They did so with a vengeance. Upon returning, they summoned a council of 250 bishops at Nicomedia (the same number who had attended Nicaea) and incredibly, in a major shift, the proceedings concluded with the successful deposition and excommunication of Bishop Alexander, and everyone else who had professed the homoousian doctrine at the previous Council of Nicaea![733] This was a dramatic shift to say the least: the very "Arians" whom Nicaea had supposedly stamped out once again found themselves in power. As Saint Jerome would so famously recall, it was at this time that "the whole world groaned and was astonished to find itself Arian."[734] But how was such a reversal possible if the Nicene Creed merely encapsulated what Christianity had already believed? Could it be that Nicaea was the real innovation?

Nicaea Overturned

By the middle of the fourth century, the majority of the Nicene supporters had been deposed, and the council's most poignant pronouncements were being loudly and repeatedly condemned by other major councils of the Church. As Freeman notes, "Traditionally, this [reversal] has been seen as the retaliation of frustrated Arians, but this is much too simplistic a judgment." Obviously, a great many Christians, despite the imperial force of Nicaea, "felt uneasy about the defeat of Subordinationism."[735]

During this era, even councils which were not particularly friendly to Arius himself decided in favor of many of his beliefs and ruled against the Nicene formula. For example, the council at Antioch in 341 CE, which was attended by about one hundred bishops as well as Emperor Constantius II, presented several creeds as replacements for the Nicene theology, all rejecting the "homoousios" language. The bishops furthermore defended the antiquity of their Subordinationist views against the claims of their opponents on a national stage. Athanasius had personally taken to derogatorily labeling his opponents "Arians" in hopes of not only painting their Subordinationist belief as a recent innovation, but also insulting them. But the new statement produced at the Council of Antioch would read:

---

[733] Ibid.
[734] Jerome, *Adversus Luciferianos*, 19.
[735] Freeman, *Closing of the Western Mind*, p. 170.

We have neither been followers of Arius (because how should we who are bishops follow a presbyter?), nor have we accepted any other form of faith than that which was set out at the beginning.[736]

The creeds from Antioch, in addition to omitting the "homoousian," worked to revise the rest of the troublesome language of Nicaea, which had stated that Jesus was "true God from true God," into a more ambiguous "God from God."[737] The Subordinationists had no problem with this language. After all, the preceding Subordinationist Christians such as Justin Martyr and Irenaeus had certainly called Jesus "god" in their own writings, though in a secondary or derived sense.

One of the most significant councils in the years after Nicaea, the Council of Rimini-Seleucia in 359 CE, would strike a serious blow to the efforts of the Nicene supporters. The *Catholic Encyclopedia* states that "the council was a sudden defeat of orthodoxy,"[738] as the bishops produced yet another creed that deliberately rejected the "homoousios" definition on the grounds that it was both confusing and unscriptural.[739] Today, Christians may be surprised at this repeated rejection of Nicaea, but in reality, "Few signers of Nicaea were fully satisfied with the creed, especially its use of the term homoousios, which had been rejected earlier at synods in Antioch (264, 268)... [That definition had not] preserved the New Testament distinction between Father and Son."[740]

Rimini-Seleucia convened with over *five hundred* bishops in attendance, dwarfing the Nicene attendance of around two-hundred and fifty. Unbeknownst to many:

> Only a handful of Western churchmen came to Nicaea... The Council of Nicaea, then, was not universal. Nevertheless, it is everywhere considered the first ecumenical (or universal) council of the Catholic Church. Several later gatherings would be more representative of the entire Church; one of them, the joint council of Rimini-Seleucia (359), was attended by more than five hundred bishops from both the East and the West.

---

[736] First Creed of Antioch, 341 CE, quoted in Hanson, p. 285.

[737] Hanson, p. 284.

[738] Umberto Benigni, "Council of Rimini," *Catholic Encyclopedia*. 2009. Web. 18 November. 2013.

[739] Gwynn, p. 94.

[740] J. Warren Smith, "The Fourth Century Fathers," *Oxford Handbook of the Trinity* (Oxford: OUP, 2011), p. 111.

If any meeting deserves the title "ecumenical," that one seems to qualify, but its result—the adoption of an Arian creed was later repudiated by the Church. Councils whose products were later deemed unorthodox not only lost the "ecumenical" label but virtually disappeared from official Church history. That Nicaea did not disappear is largely the result of the council's adoption of the Nicene Creed, an amended version of which is recited today by Christians around the globe.[741]

One thing that Rimini-Seleucia demonstrates is the bias of today's popular history. How many Christians today are even aware that there were far more than seven (or nine depending on tradition) councils of the Catholic Church? As it is said, "History is written by the conquerors,"[742] and Church history has proven no exception. Despite today's mainstream apologists loudly declaring that "The Council of Nicaea settle[d] the major heretical challenge to the Christian Faith posed [by] the heretic Arius,"[743] the new compulsory profession authored there would be successfully challenged and defeated by many Christian assemblies uncomfortable with its implications. Indeed, in another council in Constantinople in the year 360 CE, the term "homoousios" was once more resoundingly condemned as unscriptural.[744] Of course, this council of Constantinople in 360 is hardly mentioned today. The next council in held in that city, in 381, which famously solidified the Trinitarian doctrine, is now usually labeled "The *First* Council of Constantinople," perhaps in an effort to cover the existence of the first.

But even a cursory examination of the progressive evolution of the doctrine through the councils reveals that at Nicaea very little was actually done to finalize the foundational truths of the faith. As even Trinitarian Basil Studer recognizes,

---

[741] Rubenstein, p .75.

[742] Often attributed to Winston Churchill, but of disputed origin.

[743] "A Timeline of Church History," Self-Ruled Antiochian Orthodox Christian Archdiocese of North America. 2013. Web. 18 November 2013. <http://www.antiochian.org/orthodox-church-history>.

[744] The new creed said: "But since the term ousia [substance or essence]… not being understood by the people, has been a cause of offense, we have thought proper to reject it, as it is not contained even in the sacred writings; and that no mention of it should be made in future, inasmuch as the holy Scriptures have nowhere mentioned the substance of the Father and of the Son. Nor ought the "subsistence" of the Father, and of the Son, and of the Holy Spirit to be even named" (Zenos' Translation of Scholasticus, *Church History*, 2, 41).

"the Nicene synod had not yet answered the decisive questions."[745] Instead of uniting Christendom, Nicaea had actually ignited a firestorm of division that manifested in an age-long power struggle. In hindsight, Constantine's great solution had actually "struck a great blow to the unity of the Church."[746] The string of councils in the centuries that followed also never seemed to truly settle things, but only produced more doubt, questions, and segregation.

One particular issue which made these disputes nearly impossible to resolve was the use of identical terms in different senses by the disputing parties. Language suddenly shifted in meaning from council to council, and the different connotations of words in the Latin-speaking West and the Greek-speaking East only compounded the problem; one day's blasphemers were the next day's guardians of truth.[747] Should such proceedings really be known to us as the "Arian controversy," as if it were any novel ideas of Arius which were responsible for the chaotic sorting-out (or redefining) of the Christian doctrine of God? Or perhaps, as Hanson opined, the era might be better viewed as "a search in a fog, a situation when ignorant armies clash by night"?[748] Of course, the school which eventually prevailed would systematically paint a different picture for posterity. Supporters of Nicaea both past and present have sought to re-color history to the effect that this "orthodoxy" has always existed, and that the contest under review was but a stalwart defense of that established faith against new and egregious error. But it should be plain by now that this cannot have been the case. If the answers to the questions posed by the increasingly Trinitarian faith were clear from the start, then why did the debate over the fundamentals last more than sixty years? Why did the controversy require the involvement of several Roman emperors? As Hanson also noted, "The defense

---

[745] Basil Studer, *Trinity and Incarnation: The Faith of the Early Church* (Minnesota: T&T Clark Ltd, 1993), p. 107.

[746] Durant, *Caesar and Christ,* p. 660.

[747] "The key terms—such as *ousia, homoousios, hypostasis* and *logos*—had all been developed in non-Christian contexts (and even in them had unstable meanings). They could not easily be reformulated to deal with specific Christian issues such as the precise nature of Jesus and his relationship with God the Father. Formulating these concepts in two languages, Latin and Greek, when there was no strict equivalence between them further complicated the situation. Latin theologians translated the Greek ousia as substantia but the Greeks translate substantia as hypostasis, 'personality.' So when the Latins talked of *una substantia,* in the sense of one divine substance (within which might be found the distinct personalities of the Trinity), it appeared in Greek as if they were affirming that there was only one *hypostasis* for the three persons of the Trinity, in effect preaching what was to become [the Sabellian/Modalist] heresy" (Freeman, *Closing of the Western Mind,* pp. 179-180).

[748] Hanson, *Search for the Christian Doctrine,* p. xviii.

of well-established and well-known orthodoxy could not possibly account for such widespread and long-lasting disturbances."[749]

The Subordinationist Empire

In the years immediately following Nicaea we do not find a unified religion resting from a victorious defense of truth, but a tense spectacle of partisan jockeying. One moment the Arians were exiled, and the next they were being reinstated by personal letters from Emperor Constantine himself![750] Evidently, when the official pronouncements did not bring the unity Constantine had expected in his empire, he began to exhibit a sudden change of attitude towards the Arians. The very emperor who had ordered the erasure of all Arian memory in his lands on pain of death was now ready to recall whatever was necessary, or to broaden the scope of what was acceptable in terms of creedal adherence, in order to move towards accomplishing his purposes of unification. The impious employment of bans, exiles, and book-burning that occurred in this circus of political maneuvering by both the emperor and the bishops makes little sense from a purely theological perspective, but makes more sense if determining Christian truth was not the only goal of these proceedings. It soon became clear, in the raucous political aftermath, that Nicaea was indeed nothing more than an artifice manufactured by the bishops in their desire to please the emperor and restore the unity of the faith.[751]

Arius himself, though declared a heretic in 325, was later absolved in 335 at the First Synod of Tyre.[752] Incredibly, the deacon who had worked so tirelessly to ban Arius, the fiery Athanasius, was himself banned by the same First Synod of Tyre. The hot-headed Athanasius was charged with mistreatment of Arians and Meletians, another group ostracized by Nicaea's decrees. After being inundated by the news of other questionable charges, such as interfering with the supply of grain from Egypt meant for peasants, Constantine himself, though a personal supporter of Athanasius who we presume would have done anything he could to avoid it, was compelled to order Athanasius into exile.[753] Later, Athanasius would be reinstated, but only to undergo four more bans by massive

---

[749] Ibid., p. xix.

[750] Al Vasiliev, "The Empire from Constantine the Great to Justinian," History of the Byzantine Empire. 1928. Web. May 2012. <http://www.ellopos.net/elpenor/vasilief/arianism-council-nicaea.asp>.

[751] Rubenstein, pp. 103-104.

[752] Socrates, *Church History,* Book 1, Ch. 33.

[753] Timothy D. Barnes, *Athanasius and Constantius: Theology and Politics in the Constantinian Empire,* (Cambridge: Harvard University Press, 1993), p. 37.

Church councils for being both a heretic and an unscrupulous character. Councils which condemned him included the famous Milan (300 bishops) and Arminium (550 bishops, the largest council gathering ever).

After absolving Arius of heresy in 335, the Church moved to restore the man to communion in 336. But while Arius was on his way to this reunion, he suddenly became suspiciously and violently ill on the road. He perished, it is recorded by his detractors, in horrible agony in a bout of hemorrhaging of the bowels. Arius' enemies happily declared it a divine act of God for Arius' heresy, that God had miraculously prevented him from rejoining the Church.[754] However, Arius' friends and some historians believe that he was likely poisoned by his enemies.[755] Though Emperor Constantine had reversed his opinion on Arius before he died, Arius was posthumously re-pronounced a heretic nearly half a century later at the First Council of Constantinople in 381.

Despite the untimely death of Arius in 336, Arianism would return to the empire with a vengeance to close out the Constantinian era. For all the disputation that Constantine had fostered over Arianism, the emperor would choose to conclude his own life in a rather curious fashion. As he neared death, he was baptized by an Arian bishop, Eusebius of Nicomedia.[756] As we have seen, Eusebius had vigorously defended Arius at Nicaea and had himself been exiled shortly after the council. But after his return from exile in 329, Eusebius had ousted most of his Nicene opponents in a stunning reversal and had earned great influence with Constantine's family, including tremendous favor with Constantine's son who succeeded him and ruled as an openly Arian emperor. In a strange turn of events, in 337 Eusebius found himself baptizing the very man who had outlawed his faith. Upon this baptism, as Freeman notes, "the Nicene Creed appeared to be dead—even, in terms of what Constantine had hoped to achieve, a failure. If the issues had not been revived in the 350s, the council might have occupied no more than a footnote in history."[757]

In the era that followed, control over the post-Nicene Roman Empire was raucously passed back and forth between the Arian and Athanasian camps for decades at a time. Even the Roman Emperors Constantius II (337-361) and Valens (364-378) were Arians, and both held Arian councils and passed various

---

[754] Socrates, "The Death of Arius." *Church History.* Web. 2 May 2012. <http://www.ccel.org/ccel/schaff/npnf202.ii.iv.xxxviii.html>.

[755] S. M. Hopkins, "The Death of Arius," *The Biblical Repository* (London: John Wiley, 1850), p. 66ff; William Smith, *A Dictionary of Greek and Roman Biography and Mythology* (London: John Murray, 1880), p. 347; Gibbon, *Decline and Fall* (New York: Fed DeFau & Co, 1906), p. 366.

[756] Hans A. Pohlsander, *Emperor Constantine* (London: Routledge, 2004), p. 104.

[757] Freeman, *Closing of the Western Mind,* p. 171.

Subordinationist decrees against those authorities who had claimed that the Father and the Son were consubstantial at Nicaea.[758] But this era of mostly Arian dominance would not last forever.

The Faith of the Jewish Christians Perseveres

As mentioned previously, we find that the sect of Jewish Christians known as the Nazarenes, and the related Ebionites, actually persisted into the fourth century.[759] While the most prominent and well-documented Arian theologians had noticeably maintained a semblance of the belief of the old Jewish Christians, namely the distinction and subordination of Christ to God the Father, most of them had also entertained an important relationship with Greek philosophy. The personal pre-existence of the Son as an angelic being, and his human incarnation, was the most perceptible break between the Arians and the old Jerusalem tradition. However, we find that the Christology of the early Nazarenes was still maintained by some of the Gentile Fathers, even through the harrowing trauma of the post-Nicene disputes.

According to Eusebius, the orthodox Crypto-Gnostic Clement of Alexandria wrote against "Judaizing" among the Christians, which "proves that Jewish Christianity was still a threat at the beginning of the third century."[760] Of course, we do not know how widespread the Christology of the Jewish Christians actually was during this era. History, especially ancient history, has a remarkable tendency to lump objects together. One of the problems the modern historian encounters is the lasting effect of the persecutions enacted upon the heresiarchs and their literature; the beliefs of these maligned theologians must now be pieced together through the biased and damning summaries of their enemies. Nevertheless, there has been preserved, against all odds, a decent record of some who demonstrate the persistence of the unitarian Christianity of Jerusalem in the Gentile era.

We probably find in Paul of Samosata, bishop of Antioch from 260-272 CE, evidence of such faith. Today scholars still debate the particulars of his teaching, especially his own usage of the controversial word "homoousios" to describe the logos.[761] But it is clear Paul taught that the logos was not another Person, but

---

[758] Jean Guitton, *Great Heresies and Church Councils* (New York: Harper & Row, 1965), p. 86.

[759] Epiphanius, *Panarion*, 29, 5:4 and 5:6.

[760] Segal, "Jewish Christianity," p. 338.

[761] Paul nevertheless appears encumbered by Platonic and Gnostic terminology. He argued that while the logos is not a distinct person whom inhabited Jesus, it was somehow a principle "consubstantial" with God. Therefore, it could be said that for Paul, the Father, and the indwelt

only an impersonal divine virtue that inhabited the man Jesus.[762] Regardless of his immediate opponents' understanding or misunderstanding of him, it is now generally agreed that Paul maintained Jesus as the Messiah, the truly human Son of God, and God himself as only one Person.[763] Despite being accused by his ancient critics of degrading Christ into a "mere man,"[764] Paul professed that Jesus was uniquely born of a virgin, and that by remaining free from sin and conquering sin, was at his baptism specially indwelt with the logos (or God's reason or power), and was afterwards elevated to the highest dignity at the right hand of God. He furthermore taught that the same logos of God had indwelled Moses and the other prophets, but that it energized Jesus more fully than any other man before him;[765] the unison between logos and Christ being an intimate unity of will only.

In the motion to have Paul of Samosata excommunicated, only sixteen bishops signed the condemnation. When his opponents could not oust him from his office themselves, they called in the power of the state. Thus, it was actually in the third century that a secular government arrived to settle an affair of the Church for the first time. The Roman emperor Aurelian, in an effort to quell the discord in his empire, assisted the poor efforts of Paul's opponents and gave the order that he should be banished from his post.[766] Paul's followers, sometimes called the Paulianists, evidently continued into the fourth century, as

---

Jesus, could be described as having in some sense "the same substance." As we have seen, this "homoousios" term was banned as heretical in 269 CE, but was made orthodox at Nicaea.

[762] Paul is said to have "separated the one from the other, the Father and Son, far too much... he regarded the Logos as an impersonal virtue of God.... In Jesus he saw only a man penetrated by the Logos, who, although miraculously born of a virgin, was yet only a man, and not the God-man. The Logos had dwelt in the man Jesus not in person, but in quality as virtue or power.... Paul of Samosata further taught, that as the Logos is not a person, so also the Holy Spirit is only a divine virtue, impersonal, belonging to the Father..." (Charles Joseph Hefele, *A History of the Christian Councils From the Original Documents* (Edinburgh: T & T Clark, 1894), Book II, Ch. 2, 9).

[763] Henry Chadwick, *The Early Church* (New York: Penguin Books, 1967), p. 114; Kelly, *Early Christian Doctrines*, pp. 117-119; Schaff, *History of the Christian Church,* Vol. 2, p. 575.

[764] Mark M. Mattison, "Biblical Unitarianism from the Early Church Through the Middle Ages," *A Journal from the Radical Reformation*, Vol. 1, No. 2 (Atlanta, 1992), p. 9.

[765] Surely Christ's own explanation regarding the unique qualification of his ministry in John 3:34 is to be employed in this argument: *"For he whom God has sent speaks the words of God; for He gives the Spirit without measure"* or *"without limit"* (NIV). Though others like Moses (according to Paul's argument), had been indwelt by God, the degree to which Jesus was indwelt was unique. We might also reference Col 2:9 for further support of this: *"For in him dwelleth all the fullness of the Godhead bodily"* (KJV). It should also be noted that the Apostles remark that *"of his fullness we have all received"* (Jn 1:16), and even urge all disciples to *"become partakers in the divine nature"* (2 Pet 1:4). It seems reasonable then, in defense of Paul, that this indwelling of the Godhead, of the divine nature in Christ, is not necessarily a divine, personal Incarnation.

[766] Priestley, *Works*, p. 506.

a faith which historian Philip Schaff even describes as being "like the Socinians"[767] (modern-day Biblical Unitarians). The members of this group were forced to be re-baptized by the Canons of the Council of Nicaea in 325 CE.[768] But other groups in the empire continued to espouse the same theology.

The recollection of another unitarian Christian active during the Arian controversy, Photinus the Galatian, is noteworthy in this regard. Photinus, who died in 376 CE, was the bishop of the important city of Sirmium, one of the "four capitals" of the Roman empire.[769] What the daring and successful ministry of Photinus proves is that the Human Christology and unitarian monotheism practiced by the Nazarene Christians in the first century somehow, through the gloomy turmoil of post-Nicene history, not only endured but enjoyed a popular surge. The unitarian Photinus was elected as bishop by the Synod of Serdica in 343 CE, *eighteen years* after the pronouncements of Nicaea.[770] Thus even several decades before the massive Council of Rimini-Seleucia had so ecumenically reversed the homoousian, we find a tenacious "grass roots" movement in one of the largest cities in the empire recalling the precise faith of the Jewish Christians. The famous Church historian Jerome even explicitly calls Photinus an "Ebionite," an opinion which directly links him back to the Jewish Christians who succeeded the tradition of the Apostles in the holy city.[771] Like them, Phontius was most famous for preaching the unity of God and denying the pre-existence, incarnation, and deity of Jesus. One ancient historian writes that Photinus "acknowledged that there was one God Almighty, by whose own word all things were created, but would not admit that the generation and existence of the Son was before all ages; on the contrary, he alleged that Christ derived his existence from Mary."[772] While none of Photinus' own writings have survived, his teachings are mentioned by all of the famous Church historians including Hilary of Poitier, Socrates Scholasticus, Ambrosiaster, Ambrose of Milan, Augustine of Hippo, John Cassian, Jerome, Sulpicius Severus, and Vigilus of Thapsus. This fact may add to the noteworthiness of the Photinian movement's

---

[767] Ibid.

[768] Schaff, Roberts, Donaldson, Coxe, *Nicene and Post-Nicene Fathers, Series II*, Vol. IV, Discourse II (Grand Rapids: Eerdmans, 1885), pp. 42-43.

[769] Sirmium was located in the province of Pannonia, and with 100,000 citizens, was one of the largest cities in the empire. The site of an imperial palace, it was called "the glorious mother of cities" by ancient historians. This is the city of Sremska Mitrovica in modern Serbia today.

[770] Ibid.

[771] Henry Palmer Chapman, "Photinus," *Catholic Encyclopedia*, Vol. 12. 1913. Web. 14 November 2014.

[772] Sozomen, *Church History*, 4, 6.

accomplishment. It is recorded by these historians that Photinus held the logos to be simply God's wisdom, a personal attribute of a single monotheistic Father, not a literal, pre-existent Person. Like the Nazarenes, Photinus believed in the virgin birth.[773] While Jesus was certainly appointed in the mind and plan of God before creation, the biblical writings, such as Daniel, were viewed as speaking of the Messiah "prophetically, not as of the Son [already] existing."[774] Of course, some of Photinus' contemporaries who maintained the Nicene standard reproached him, claiming that he dishonored Christ by denying any pre-existence or inherent divinity. In response to his critics, Photinus repeatedly appealed to Scripture to demonstrate that Jesus was no "mere" man, but a supernaturally conceived, divinely inspired human mediator elevated to the right hand of God because of his ultimate commitment to God's divine intention (*logos*). Hanson recalls Photinus' consistent appeal to biblical testimony:

> Everybody in the ancient world accuses Photinus of reducing Christ to a mere man adopted by God, i.e. the union between Logos and man was one of inspiration and moral agreement only. Ambrose tells us that two favourite texts of Photinus were 1 Timothy 2:5 ("*There is one God and one mediator between God and man, the man Jesus Christ*"), and John 8:40 ("*You seek to kill me, a man who has spoken the truth to you that I heard from God*"), and one can see why. There is evidenced here a consistent determination to avoid recognizing any distinctions in the being of God.[775]

Synods held by supporters of Nicaea in 345 and 347 CE attempted to excommunicate Photinus. However, Photinus remained in office due to a dramatic outbreak of support from the populace.[776] It would not be until a subsequent synod in 351 that he would be successfully overthrown by the Nicene supporters and exiled, where he wrote many theological books which are now lost.[777] Photinus eventually returned to his bishopric, only to be exiled again by Emperor Valentinian I. By the time he finally resettled in his native Galatia, the popularity of his view had caused anyone in the empire who believed

---

[773] Schaff, "Photinus", *Nicene and Post-Nicene Christianity*, CCEL, Calvin College. Web. 02 February 2015.

[774] Ibid.

[775] Hanson, pp. 318-381, parentheticals added.

[776] Chapman, "Photinus," *Catholic Encyclopedia*, Vol. 12.

[777] Socrates Scholasticus, *Church History*, 2, 29.

that Christ was simply an elevated man and not God to be called "Photinians." It should be noted that sixth-century historian Vigilus, in his *Dialogue Against Arians, Sabellians and Photinians* records not only evidence of a sizeable theological movement, but a clear distinction between the Arians, whose Christ pre-existed and became incarnate, and the Photinians whose Christ "[took] his beginnings from Mary"[778] after the Holy Ghost descended.

We find in the understanding of the Photinians, as well as the Jewish Nazarenes who preceded them, a Christ immediately accessible to the human mind. No strenuous reconciliation needed to be manufactured between opposite human and divine natures, no unhappy balance between oneness and three-ness, no dangerously Gnostic incarnation, and no threat of violating the unique monotheism of the Jews which Jesus himself so unwaveringly secured in Scripture (Mark 12:28ff). God's supreme otherness and Jesus' perfect human relatability do not seem to require an education in Platonic metaphysics. Surely this system's rational viability contributed to its perpetuation against all odds. If we adopt the interventionist perspective of some Christians, perhaps even some degree of *Providence* reached down from heaven to stoke embers of this view in the smoldering heap of Christendom from time to time. Fanciful conjecture aside, this perspective would not end with Photinus.

We find that the unitarian faith and Human Christology of the Nazarenes and the Photinians inexorably continued even through the turmoil of the Middle Ages. After the collapse of the western half of the Roman Empire, the eastern half endured as the Byzantine Empire. In Byzantium, as well as several other eastern countries, remnants of this theology continued under the name of Paulicianism for centuries. While this name was doubtless awarded due to the movement's Christological similarity to the doctrine of Paul of Samosata, he was not himself the founder, as his direct followers had all but dissolved by 325 CE. This Byzantine movement however, continued the long tradition of vigorous rejection of Roman authority. They were especially characterized by an intense dependence on the Scriptures, the practice of adult baptism, rejection of Catholic icons in worship, and of course the profession that Jesus Christ was a man.[779]

Outside Byzantium, we find that the Christian profession of a unitarian Godhead and human Christ likewise survived. The Bonosians in Spain and

---

[778] Hanson, pp. 3118-381.

[779] Mattison, p. 11. Most of Paulicians appear to have adopted a semi-Gnostic dualist view of Creation, among other Gnostic ideas. Ebionite unitarian views are nevertheless thought to have persisted amongst some of them for another one thousand years. See Malcom Lambert, *Medieval Heresy: Popular Movements from Bogomil to Hus* (New York: Homes & Meier Publishers, 1977), p. 11.

Southern Gaul (modern France) were active from sometime before 431 CE all the way through the seventh century.[780] We furthermore detect this thought in Bishop Felix of Urgell (d. 818) leader of the Frankish church, the Ebionites who flourished in Spain, and the unitarian Szekelys in Hungary.[781] It has been postulated that this spirit "persisted in some of the sects until the time of the Reformation"[782] and that even the great martyr of the Reformation, the Spaniard Michael Servetus, may have been influenced by these groups.[783]

Though a precise continuity may be impossible to chart, the tradition of the Photinians, the Nazarenes, and others exhibited a tenacity that would, in spite of persecution, ultimately live on through the riotous confusion of Roman dogmatism. We see this Christology and monotheism eventually come roaring out from a humble hibernation to take Europe by storm during the era of the Socinians of the Radical Reformation,[784] and it is this tradition which enthusiastically persists today in the modern Biblical Unitarian movement. But what was the cause of the "hibernation" in the first place? As we will now observe, the history of Trinitarianism's victory in the late fourth century is really the history of the death of religious freedom and of the narrowing of the Christian mind by the point of the sword.

The Rise of Orthodox Trinitarianism

The painful fallout of Nicaea bred new Christian sects. Many who had reacted strongly to the introduction of the homoousian of the Nicene Creed,

---

[780] In 431 CE, Marius Mercator writes of Bonosus and his followers. They are characterized both as Ebionites and as Photinians by their critics. See Samuel Macauley Jackson (ed.), "Bonosus and the Bonosians," *The New Schaff-Herzog Encyclopedia of Religious Knowledge* (New York: Funk and Wagnalls Co., 1914), pp. 231-232.

[781] See Ferenc Frank Ehrenthal, *Szekely Origins and Radical Faith: From Mongolia to Transylvania, the Birth of Unitarianism* (North Charleston: CreateSpace, 2014).

[782] Albert Henry Newman, *A Manual of Church History*, Vol. 1 (Philadelphia: ABPS, 1942), p. 357.

[783] Mattison, pp. 12-13.

[784] A prolific Reformation tradition thriving during the 16th and 17th centuries. They advocated the pure humanity of Jesus and rejected any physical pre-existence outside of the divine plan, arguing Christ's beginning in the womb. Schaff writes, "The Socinian Christology [differs from] Arianism (which admitted the pre-existence and the incarnation of the Logos), and resembles the Christology of the dynamic Unitarians in the third century (Theodotus, Artemon, Paul of Samosata), who saw in Christ a mere man, though supernaturally conceived, and filled with divine power operating in him from the beginning... The Socinian Christology was anticipated by some Antitrinitarian Baptists (Denk, Heizer, etc.) who [were called] 'new Samosatenes' " (Philip Schaff, *Christ and Christianity* (New York: Scribner's Sons, 1885), p. 95). Between the 16th and 18th centuries, this belief was held by various groups in Europe and North America, and became especially popular in the United States. This theological tradition has remained unbroken into the 21st century through the "Biblical Unitarian" movement, a term which first arose in the 1880s.

such as the Anomoean Church, emphasized the sharp distinction between the uncreated substance of the Father and the created substance of the Son.[785] But there also emerged a great many Christians who found themselves evolving into a new camp which seemed to straddle the extremes. These "Semi-Arians" believed that the Son was of "like" or "similar" substance to the Father, still in opposition to the Nicene supporters who believed the Son was of the "same" substance. There was furious debate over the terms for "same substance" (homoousios) versus "similar substance" (homo*i*ousios), terms distinguished by only an "i," (iota). According to Gibbon, it is from this conflict that we gained the phrase *"it makes not an 'iota' of difference."*[786]

Ancient Church historians recall an interesting episode which may provide a view into the state of Christian theology in the mid to late fourth century. In 358 CE, Leontius (an Arian) had become Bishop of Antioch. Another bishop named Flavian (a supporter of Nicaea) gathered a crowd of monks outside Leontius' church and began loudly singing a new kind of proto-Trinitarian song. One ancient record recalls that:

> Flavian of Antioch... was the first to cry, "Glory be to the Father and to the Son and to the Holy Spirit!" For some of those before him had said, "Glory be to the Father, through the Son in the Holy Spirit," this being the more popular acclamation, while still others had said, "Glory be to the Father and to the Son in the Holy Spirit."[787]

We discover here a summary of three theologies. Flavian and his troop of monks were singing a "new" song which apparently awarded equal worship to the Father, Son, and Spirit. But the preceding model, and the one described as

---

[785] The Anomoeans (also known as the Heterousians, Aetians, or Eunomians), famously countered Trinitarian claims using not only arguments from Scripture, but also by dexterously meeting them on the battlefield of philosophy. Founded by Aetius of Antioch (d. 397 CE), these Christians focused their efforts on the homoousian and the contradiction of the Son's eternal begetting. The Nicene supporters had argued that somehow, despite being eternal, Christ was indeed "begotten," being "generated" out of the essence of God. However, the Anomoeans argued that for God, the eternal Unbegotten being, an act of generation would implicate a conflict within his essence. If the Son (the Begotten) is essentially God, the doctrine is self-contradictory, since the quality of unbegottenness is essential to the nature of God. They therefore held that Jesus was of a completely different substance from the Father. Their history is vibrant and substantial; records of their Church are preserved in the works of Anomoean Church historian Philostorgius, which we have largely recalled in an epitome by the historian Photios.

[786] See Gibbon, *Decline and Fall*, Ch. 21.

[787] Philostorgius, *Church History*, 3, 13; See also Theodoret, *Hist. Eccl.* 2, 24, 3, and Sozomen, 3, 20, 8.

still the most popular, was the Subordinationist view; the Son is a means to the Father, but not the same being. Lastly, some "others" were praising the Father and the Son, but not the Spirit. This may represent the Semi-Arian view (those who accepted a form of Nicaea's definition but had not moved into Trinitarian territory), but this certainly represents the widespread disagreement on the Spirit at that time.

Indeed, Nicaea had not attempted to settle anything on this point. Even Nicene Christians were still asking: is the Spirit another Person? Is this Person also consubstantial with God and Christ? Is he co-equal or subordinate? The creed of 325 had offered only a fleeting reference to the Spirit's status: "*We believe in the Holy Spirit,*" and nothing more. At that time, the lack of further speculation had seemed to satisfy and encompass the bishops' diversity. One theologian of the era reports that mid-to-late fourth century Christianity was indeed still greatly divided on this point:

> Of the wise among us, some hold the Holy Spirit to be a power, others a creature, others for God, and still others are unwilling to decide, out of reverence (or so they say) for the Scriptures, which do not speak plainly on the matter.[788]

Though the Nicene ambiguity had previously satisfied, the argument eventually began to boil. Around 340 CE, with the election of the brutal Macedonius to the bishopric of Constantinople, the Pneumatomachian controversy rose to the forefront: many Christians, even among those who had accepted the Nicene "homoousios," were beginning to loudly reject the advancing divinity of the Holy Spirit, being wary of officially introducing yet a *third* individual into the Godhead.[789] Contrary to popular belief, the co-equal deity of the Holy Spirit was not a fundamental characteristic of the earliest Christian theology. The very first creed to even contain any extended statement about the Spirit was the Dedication Creed of 341, and it was only in the 350's that significant debate over the Spirit's nature began.[790] In 357 we find the

---

[788] Gregory of Nazianzus, quoted by Philip Schaff, Samuel Macauley (ed.), "Macedonius," *The New Schaff-Herzog Encyclopedia of Religious Knowledge* (Grand Rapids: Baker House, 1963), p. 112.

[789] Pneumatomachi means "Fighters against the Spirit." The leader of this movement against the co-equal deity of the Spirit was ostensibly Macedonius I, the bishop of Constantinople, who ruled for roughly six years until his death around 360 CE. Socrates Scholasticus characterized the exploits of Macedonius on behalf of the faith as consisting of "murders, battles, incarcerations, and civil wars" (Socrates, *Church History*, 2, 38.) We find the movement dying out after the Council of Constantinople in 381 finally solidified the Trinity.

[790] Gwynn, p. 90.

earliest systematic defense of the position of the Holy Spirit within the Trinity, written by no other than Athanasius himself.[791] It was in seclusion, and during his third exile, that Athanasius was contacted by his friend Serapion regarding the widespread resistance to the equal deity of the Spirit. Thus Athanasius was compelled to pen his *Letter on the Holy Spirit*, which provides us now with a window to the progress of Trinitarian dogma in the mid-fourth century. By this we can confirm that there was still no formulated orthodox Trinitarian dogma; Athanasius not only has difficulty expressing how the three members are each God without falling into polytheism, he even reprimands anyone who would investigate the matter too closely:

> If one were to enquire… how is it really a Trinity if the three are depicted as one? … Let such an enquirer begin by separating the radiance from the light, or wisdom from the one who is wise, or else let him say himself how these things can be. But if this cannot be done, then how much more is it the presumption of insane people to enquire into these things with respect to God?[792]

Indeed, Athanasius' underdeveloped theory lacked the requisite language to avoid abrogating monotheism. As ever, he was stuck between a rock and a hard place. On the one hand, emphasizing the distinction of the Father, Son, and Spirit pulled the faith towards Arianism; on the other hand, emphasizing the unity of God pulled it towards Sabellianism. Athanasius disagreed with Sabellianism, or wanted to, since it was obvious that the Father, Son, and Spirit were distinct in some sense, and because Sabellianism had already been declared heresy by previous councils. Even one of Athanasius' contemporaries, Marcellus of Ancyra (the same Marcellus who had loudly protested the use of the Valentinian Gnostic models), had been recently deposed from his bishopric for Sabellianism in 336 CE. Interestingly, Marcellus had claimed that if the Father and Son were of the same substance *and* the same hypostasis, just as the anathemas of Nicaea had said, then there was no division in God at all—the Father and Son were one and the same.[793] But the post-Nicene faith was now so

---

[791] Ibid. See also Freeman, *Closing of the Western Mind*, p. 190. Roughly four years later Hilary of Poitier would write the first full defense of the Father, Son, and Spirit as a single Godhead in Latin.

[792] Athanasius, *Letter on the Holy Spirit*, 1, 20.

[793] "The language of Nicaea speaks of God simply as one hypostasis" (Thomas Marsh, *The Triune God* (Eugene: Wipf & Stock, 1994), p. 120). Accordingly, we find Marcellus of Ancyra in agreement with that standard: "Marcellus adamantly denied that one could speak about two (or

confused about the Greek philosophical terms foisted upon it that not even citing the very strictures of Nicaea could guarantee one's safety. No, Athanasius could not also afford to stress the unity of God over God's diversity—the solution likely lay somewhere in the middle, in a *compromise*. But this was ultimately a problem beyond Athanasius to solve. This precarious conundrum would require the efforts of the Cappadocian Fathers.

The Cappadocian Fathers, three theologians from eastern Asia minor, began to hammer out a new philosophy which would ultimately give definitive shape to the doctrine of the Trinity.[794] Basil the Great (330-379 CE), Gregory of Nazianzus (329-389 CE), and Gregory of Nyssa (332-395 CE) labored to address some of the most critical problems with the system of Athanasius: first, Athanasius, being an Origenist, had interchangeably employed the terms "ousia" and "hypostasis." Again, for both Origen and Athanasius, a "hypostasis" was an individual being. This had provided no difficulty for Origen, who had believed Christ to be of a different substance and different hypostasis than the Father; he gladly acknowledged the three members of the triad as different beings. But for Athanasius, who *did* believe Christ to be of the same substance (homoousios) as the Father, making a distinction between the two in order to avoid Sabellianism was impossible so long as the traditional definitions of the terms remained. This reworking of terms became the grand project of the Cappadocians.

According to the Cappadocians, using "hypostasis" as a synonym for "ousia" was a grave error. Instead, they postulated that the Father, Son, and Holy Spirit were in fact three distinct hypostases *within* a single ousia. To them, "hypostasis" did not mean being, but *"person."* The three were *personal entities* dwelling in or sharing in the one divine substance of God. One recent study notes that "the degree to which the Cappadocian Fathers innovated in moving hypostasis from an initial alignment along the ousia ("essence" or "substance") axis of meaning to the prosopon ("person") axis… is a question still debated by scholarship."[795] But in our own study, have we not already observed a Gnostic precedent? Indeed, Plotinus had not reasoned this way, nor had Origen. As Hanson confirms, Neoplatonism appears to have had "little effect" here.[796] But the Gnostics had believed the "hypostases" within God's fullness to be

---

three) hypostases in God. Such talk would postulate two Gods, or alternatively, deny the full divinity of the Son" (Tarmo Toom, *Classical Trinitarian Theology: A Textbook* (New York: T & T Clark, 2007), p. 97).

[794] Ryrie, p. 65.

[795] Matthew W. Bates, *The Birth of the Trinity: Jesus, God, and Spirit in New Testament and Early Christian Interpretations of the Old Testament* (Oxford: OUP, 2015), p. xli, emphasis added.

[796] Hanson, p. 872.

consubstantial persons derived from distinctive characteristics of God.[797] The final formula introduced by the Cappadocians, *"three hypostases in one ousia,"* may very well represent a clever, orthodox reformatting of an already widely used model of the Gnostic world. Did the Cappadocians draw directly from Gnostic traditions? Or was this model simply the inevitable working out of the deity of Christ, a system which the Gnostic theologians, being unencumbered by a controlling monolithic orthodoxy, had already arrived at more than two hundred years earlier? More study is certainly needed in this area. What is certain, however, is that the Cappadocian model was incredibly controversial, and was not widely adopted without serious political and theological struggle. For example, according to the Latin-speaking doctors in the West, "hypostasis" still meant "substance" (*substantia*). When the Cappadocians said there were three hypostases, their careful distinction between "being" and "person" was mostly lost on the Western theologians; they saw only tri-theism—if there were three substances, there were *three gods*.

An important issue arises here: the necessary verbal rapports of orthodoxy have only grown foggier in our own time while the struggle over the dogma carries the same confusion and precariousness today as it did in the fourth century. An entire doctrine, and even one's very salvation, may rest upon a single word or a single letter which we can now barely distinguish from another. As a top Trinitarian theologian has admitted, "the ideas of 'substance,' 'person' (in the Trinitarian sense) and 'nature' played an absolutely decisive part in ancient theology, but for us they are scarcely intelligible, or, if used without commentary, lead to gross misunderstanding."[798] The non-biblical delineations of the Fathers, refusal of which assured damnation, could easily oscillate in meaning and apparently did, with the result that those who were one moment considered orthodox could suddenly find themselves in danger of excommunication.

But the Western theologians appear justified in their wariness of polytheism. The Gnostic Christians are to this day still often accused of polytheism in popular discussion. But if they are to be considered polytheists, then the same should be said of Cappadocian Trinitarianism; both represent philosophical monotheisms which distinguish between the being of God and subsistent personalities or hypostases. Athanasius himself was hesitant about the strange,

---

[797] "The Valentinian Aeons were regarded as so many distinct personalities, produced according to human analogy" (Smith, Wace (ed.), "Irenaeus," *A Dictionary of Christian Biography*, Vol. 3 (London: John Murray, 1882), p. 269).

[798] Brunner, p. 70.

pseudo-polytheistic bent his theology was taking under the direction of the younger Cappadocians.[799] Harnack notes:

> The Cappadocians, theologians who reconciled the faith of Athanasius with the current philosophy, and apprehended it abstractly, did not retain his teaching pure and simple. This is especially shown by their doubtful contention that the Christian idea of God was the true mean between the Jewish and Greek. They boldly characterized the plurality of Hypostases as a phase of truth preserved in Greek polytheism. Athanasius, therefore, did not take unmixed pleasure in their work.[800]

The Cappadocian vision of one ousia and three hypostases "was not a formula that Athanasius ever used or would have wished to use."[801] Nevertheless, despite any discomfort, Athanasius deserted the anathemas he had won at Nicaea and conformed to the Cappadocian language for the sake of unity against the Subordinationists. As Schaff notes, while formerly Athanasius indeed used "hypostasis" to mean "substance," he "*abandons* the latter usage in his middle and later writings."[802] One historian summarizes:

> Thus Greek philosophical terms, in themselves complex, were *adapted and adopted* to produce a solution that allowed the Nicene formula to be reasserted and the Holy Spirit integrated into the Trinity without reverting to Sabellianism (Modalism). The doctrine of the Trinity is embedded so deeply in the Christian tradition that it is easy to forget how precarious was its birth. To the Cappadocians, in fact, it seems to have been a *compromise* formula. Within Christianity they had to find a middle path between the condemned Arianism and Sabellianism. In a wider world, the doctrine of the Trinity stood between the Jewish conception of a monotheistic God, in whose worship Jesus and the Holy Spirit had no place, and Greek polytheism that had no difficulty in accepting Jesus and

---

[799] "Apparenly Athanasius thought that hypostasis in theological contexts always meant ousia, and that if any spoke of three hypostasis they must mean three ousiai, and probably different ousiai at that, and so must be well on the way to Arianism [or polytheism]" (Hanson, p. 445).

[800] Adolph Harnack, *History of Dogma*, Vol. 3 (Boston: Little, Brown and Co., 1907), pp. 142-143.

[801] David M. Gwynn, *Athanasius of Alexandria: Bishop, Theologian, Ascetic, Father* (Oxford: OUP, 2012), p. 98.

[802] Schaff, Wace, *Nicene and Post Nicene Fathers*, Vol. IV, p. 80, emphasis added.

the Spirit as lesser divinities. Gregory of Nyssa suggested: "It is as if the number of the Three were remedy in the case of those who are in error as to the One, and the assertion of the unity for those whose belief are dispersed among a number of divinities."[803]

That this Trinity formula was a compromise between not only the Sabellian and Arian positions, but also between monotheism and polytheism has been widely recognized. As Wolfson summarizes:

It's a solution by harmonization, an attempt to combine, as Gregory of Nyssa characterizes it, the monotheism of the Jews and the polytheism of the Greeks. The method of harmonization used by them was to *thin down* the Jewish monotheism as a concession to Greek philosophy.[804]

But the Trinitarians were not true innovators here. Modern Gnostics, like Gnostic scholar Stephen A. Hoeller, explain that "The Gnostic God concept... unites the recognitions of monotheism and polytheism."[805] Others, like the prolific Samael A. Weor, reveal the Gnostic theology as "the synthesis of polytheism and monotheism," and proclaim, "Diversity is unity."[806] This is, not surprisingly, the same hymn of Trinitarianism; the Cappadocians also declared a mystical "diversity-in-unity and unity-in-diversity."[807] Of course, as Professor Werner writes, "Judged by a rigorous [Jewish] monotheistic criterion, not only Gnosticism, but also the teaching of the Church's theologians was defective."[808]

Theodosius Turns the Tide

The emperor Valens had been an Arian who upheld the cause of Subordinationism in the East. However, Valens' sudden death in the disastrous battle of Adrianople in 378 CE would change the Christian world forever. Since

---

[803] Freeman, *Closing of the Western Mind*, p. 190, emphasis added.

[804] Harry Austryn Wolfson, *The Philosophy of the Church Fathers* (Cambridge: Harvard University Press, 1970), pp. 578-579, emphasis added.

[805] Stephen A. Hoeller. "The Gnostic Worldview." The Gnosis Archive. Web. 13 December 2015. Hoeller is a scholar and the Regionary Bishop in the Ecclesia Gnostica.

[806] Samael Aun Weor, *The Revolution of the Dialectic* (Glorian Publishing, 2010 [1983]), p. 3. Weor is the founder of the modern Universal Christian Gnostic movement.

[807] Gregory of Nyssa, "Unity in Diversity," quoted in *Gregory of Nyssa's Mystical Writings*, translated and edited by Herbert Mursillo (Crestwood, N.Y.: St. Vladimir's Seminary Press, 1979).

[808] Martin Werner, quoted in Buzzard, *Jesus Was Not A Trinitarian*, p. 320.

Valens had no heir, a political technicality led to the appointment of Theodosius I, a military commander, as emperor. Theodosius was a supporter of Nicaea. He was more importantly a rash tyrant driven by fanatical intolerance, and a man even prone to the lawless massacre of his own subjects.[809] If ever there was a single magistrate at whose feet we might lay the transformation of the Christian faith into an apparatus of totalitarian coercion, it was Theodosius; the harshest exiles and threats imposed by Constantine pale in comparison to his unabashed exertion of secular influence over the establishment of saving belief.

Riding on the waves of a glorious military defeat of the barbarians, Theodosius made a blitz towards the city of Constantinople. He himself approached the capital of the Roman world (and the capital of Arianism) riding at the head of his intimidating army. Entering the city, in what has been described as "a propaganda show,"[810] he approached the Arian bishop there, and demanded that he accept the Nicene Creed. When he refused, the bishop was banished. Despite the protest of the gathered crowds supporting the Arian clergy, Theodosius unilaterally ousted all of the Arian leadership from the city and installed his own choice administrators who adhered to the homoousian definition, and by the force of arms.[811] He then officially criminalized Arianism, and also specifically banished "the contamination of the Photinian pestilence."[812] Thus all Human Christologies and all unitarian views of God were now illegal and suddenly the blossoming *Trinitarian*, that is, Cappadocian, interpretation of the Nicene faith was to be accepted on pain of death. Largely unknown in Christian circles today is the fact that Theodosius had already declared belief in the Trinity law *before* the allegedly "ecumenical" council of Constantinople ever "voted" on the matter. In January of 380 CE, Theodosius issued the following edict to the people of Constantinople:

---

[809] In 390, a popular chariot racer was arrested for attempted rape. The people of Thessalonica demanded his release, but upon the magistrate's refusal, a revolt ensued in the city. Enraged, Theodosius sent his army and massacred thousands of his citizens. One historian writes: "The anger of the Emperor rose to the highest pitch, and he gratified his vindictive desire for vengeance by unsheathing the sword most unjustly and tyrannically against all, slaying the innocent and guilty alike. It is said seven thousand perished without any forms of law, and without even having judicial sentence passed upon them, but that, like ears of wheat in the time of harvest, they were alike cut down" (Theodoretus, *Church History*, 5, 17).

[810] Charles Freeman, *AD 381* (New York: The Overlook Press, 2009), p. 23.

[811] "The purge against Arianism was not an edifying affair, as even its supporters admitted... The Arian clergy were supported by popular demonstrations, and at Constantinople the new Nicene priests were installed in the churches only by armed force, though a number of Arian clergy converted and kept their posts" (Stephen Williams, Gerard Friell, *Theodosius: The Empire At Bay* (London: B T Batsford, 1994), p. 41).

[812] Ibid., p. 42.

We shall believe in the single deity of the Father, the Son and the Holy Ghost under the concept of equal majesty and of the Holy Trinity. We command that persons who follow this rule shall embrace the name of catholic Christians. The rest, however, whom We judge demented and insane, shall carry the infamy of heretical dogmas. Their meeting places shall not receive the name of churches, and they shall be smitten first by Divine Vengeance, and secondly by the retribution of hostility which We shall assume in accordance with Divine Judgment.[813]

The Arian leadership in Constantinople was powerless against Theodosius. As the Roman saying goes, *"Falsum etiam est verum quod constituit superior"* (False becomes true when the boss decides it is). Thus the progress of Christendom shifted once again towards an affirmation of the Nicene homoousian, yet this time not only between the Father and Son, but between the three hypostases of the Cappadocians. It was, unquestionably, a standard achieved not by the force of any truly ecumenical decree, but by the tyranny of a violent government.

To further enhance his own theological control over the city, Theodosius made a strategic appointment of the Cappadocian Father Gregory of Nazianzus to the bishopric of Constantinople. The emperor introduced Gregory to the city with great pomp and fanfare, but even so, "it required a stiff guard against the jeering crowds, and Gregory himself, a gentle man, related sadly that it was more like the entry of a hostile conqueror into a defeated city."[814]

Before Gregory had even settled, however, Theodosius was moving to solidify the faith once and for all in the wider empire, and on terms favorable to his views. The emperor summoned one hundred and fifty bishops to Constantinople in May of 381. However, as historians have noted, there was virtually no representation from the West, and in fact the bishops of the Balkans met in another council of their own to condemn it.[815] Nevertheless, among the attendees at Constantinople were thirty-six of the Pneumatomachians, who had resisted the idea of the equal deity of the Holy Spirit. Here Gregory of Nazianzus designed to defeat them by forcing a "vote" in favor of the consubstantiality of the Spirit, and the new formulae devised by him and his

---

[813] *The Theodosian Code*, 16, 1, 2, quoted in Freeman, *AD 381*, p. 25.
[814] Williams, Friell, *Theodosius,* p. 41.
[815] Freeman, *Closing of the Western Mind,* p. 302.

fellow Cappadocians which had already been proclaimed law in Constantinople. But the attendees did not receive Gregory's mandate without protest. Gregory himself recalls the scene at the council: "They screeched on every side, a flock of jackdaws all intent on one thing... men with whom not even a ruler with the authority of fear or age would think it proper to reason."[816] Few details of the proceedings have survived, but ultimately, the Pneumatomachian bishops abandoned the council. Frustrated, Gregory "berated the bishops for preferring to have a majority rather than simply accepting 'the Divine Word' of the Trinity on his authority."[817] In a strange turn of events, the embarrassed Gregory would ultimately be forced to resign his seat over Constantinople by his opponents on a political technicality. So far, Theodosius' council was a disaster.

To counter the fallout from his blatant attempt to impose the Trinity, Theodosius installed another man in Gregory's place, Nectarius, a politically benign figure, unskilled in theology, and at the time of his installment still not even baptized as a Christian. Under Nectarius, the council instituted a significant *update* to the original Nicene Creed's brief mention of the Spirit:

> And [we believe] in the Holy Ghost, the Lord and Giver of life, who proceedeth from the Father, who with the Father and the Son together is worshiped and glorified, who spake by the prophets.[818]

This creedal decision still proved, however, to represent a *defeat* of Theodosius and Gregory's desire to impose the Cappadocian Trinity formula: the revised Creed of 381 CE, though now emphasizing the personality of the Holy Spirit beyond the Nicene definition, still did not mention his co-equal Godhood or his being "homoousios" with the Father or the Son. As Freeman explains, this is evidence that "Gregory's formula had been rejected," because "the form in which the creed is now used does not contain any statement endorsing a Trinity of three consubstantial persons. There was certainly no consensus on the nature of the Holy Spirit."[819]

Nevertheless, Constantinople had, through a series of other complicated political decrees concerning the bishops' authority, actually managed to cement Emperor Theodosius' power over the Church.[820] Shortly after the conclusion of

---

[816] Gregory of Nazianzus, quoted in Freeman, *AD 381*, p. 96.
[817] Ibid.
[818] Niceno-Constantinopolean Creed of 381 CE.
[819] Freeman, *AD 381*, p. 98.
[820] Ibid., p. 99.

the council, Theodosius issued a new decree that defined orthodoxy throughout the empire. But it did not mention the revised creed recently agreed upon by the council. Instead, it *declared* that the Father, Son, and Holy Spirit were *three persons in one divinity*. The result was once again a widespread, chaotic, and ultimately futile resistance. In essence, Constantinople was a farce. The professors of the Cappadocian philosophy were a minority group whose ideas were suddenly and forcefully proclaimed to be the only Christian truth by a secular authority, and they quickly found themselves even more embattled after the council. Widespread rioting of Christians was reported in the East,[821] and Gregory of Nazianzus and his fellows could hardly walk the streets without being besieged by protest and debate.

Here Freeman reminds us that "Theodosius had no theological background of his own and that he put in place as dogma a formula containing intractable philosophical problems of which he would have been unaware. In effect, the emperor's laws had silenced the debate when it was still unresolved."[822] We can now only wonder what direction Christian theology might have taken had the unitarian leadership not been forcibly removed by the state, and if the Church had been allowed to consider the Cappadocian ideas more objectively. The ruling about the Holy Spirit in particular produced endless theological difficulties which continue to plague orthodoxy. A professor of Divinity at Cambridge summarizes the new dilemma fostered by Constantinople:

> It was in the fourth century that the orthodox doctrine of the deity of the Holy Spirit was finally worked out… it asserted the doctrine of a third "person" of the deity. Yet it soon proved impossible to distinguish the entity from the other two… This presented a theological problem. If the Spirit was neither made nor begotten he would be a second ingenerate principle: there would be two Fathers. If he was begotten, there would be two Sons.[823]

The difficulty of this situation should not be overlooked. The dogma of the Father and Son's equal divinity as two distinct Persons was said to avoid polytheism because one was eternally generated from the other. But what about this third Person? From whence did he come and how? How would the

---

[821] Freeman, *Closing of the Western Mind,* p. 309.
[822] Ibid., p. 103.
[823] G. W. H. Lampe, *Explorations in Theology,* Vol. 8 (London: SCM Press, 1981), p. 30.

existence of this other fully divine entity not contravene the established relationship of the other members or produce another uncreated God? These incredible difficulties were simply swept under the rug, despite the clamorous resistance of many Christians.

As we will see, one method used by the Cappadocians to soothe the dreadful reaction to their formula was first to declare that it was *impossible* to know God, and then to declare that thinking too much about him was not only futile but a dangerous blasphemy. Those who could not tolerate this situation were promptly anathematized or executed by the government of Theodosius. The doctrine of the Trinity was to stay, and all dissenting voices were to fade, quietly or not, into the background. In the final analysis of the Trinity's troubled journey to 381 CE, it is clear that "this doctrine had only become orthodox because it had been enforced by the state."[824] The aftermath of 381 represents:

> a pivotal moment in classical and, indeed, European history. Never before in the Greek or Roman world had there been such a sweeping imposition of a single religious belief alongside the active suppression of alternatives… Theodosius' decrees were especially startling… [Because] as late as the 360s, the principle of freedom of speech and thought was being proclaimed by the court orators as essential to a healthy society… [But now] the free discussion of spiritual matters was constrained in the Christian world for centuries to come… One has to wait until the seventeenth century before the principle of religious toleration, so deep-rooted a part of ancient society, was reasserted in Europe.[825]

Bondage to the Mystery

In the course of "saving" Christian dogma from unabashed polytheism, the Cappadocians had transformed it into an unintelligible, awe-inspiring mass of contradictory terms. Gregory of Nyssa, who, among the three, is held as the "undisputed founder of mystical theology"[826] wrote: "Do not be surprised that we should speak of the Godhead as being at the same time both unified and differentiated. Using riddles, as it were, we envisage a strange and paradoxical

---

[824] Freeman, *AD 381*, p. 164.
[825] Ibid., pp. 1-2.
[826] Martin Laird, *Gregory of Nyssa and the Grasp of Faith* (Oxford: OUP, 2004), p. 175.

diversity-in-unity and unity-in-diversity."[827] For them, the Christ was a "riddle" and a "paradox," not by virtue of circumstance, as if he were a secret merely awaiting disclosure, but by fact of nature. If the conclusions of dogma were to make Jesus a walking contradiction, then the orthodox Christian must embrace him as such. However, the modern student might yet extract some benefit from the New Testament in this regard, a source which regularly appears to assume only peripheral authority here. The Apostle Paul trumpeted a call for all Christians to:

> *be encouraged, having been knit together in love, and attaining to all the wealth that comes from the full assurance of understanding, resulting in a true knowledge of God's mystery, that is, Christ himself, in whom are hidden all the treasures of wisdom and knowledge. I say this so that no one will delude you with persuasive argument* (Colossians 2:2b-4).

May a full assurance of understanding and a true knowledge of Christ be attained by the Christian if he *begins* by affirming that Christ is incomprehensible? Indeed the Apostles seem only to echo Jesus' own prescription to acquire knowledge of both God and his Messiah (John 17:3), while the later Christians seem to insist on the ultimate vanity of such efforts. Truly, it is not fair to say that a vast amount of education is required to articulate the Trinitarian system while only the layman suffers in ignorance, for even the wildly brilliant Cappadocians came full circle to meet the same opacity. We see then that it is really not faith in the *answer* to God's mystery that is required here, but faith in *the riddle itself.*

To this we might affix the same warnings offered by many Christians throughout history who have perceived the requirements of orthodoxy as ushering the believer into a dutiful indifference to rational evidence. While some modern Trinitarians have been reluctant to acknowledge a wholesale abandonment of reason, other authorities such as Martin Luther have directly instructed believers towards this very procedure: "I have often told you that this, as well as every other article of faith, must not be based upon reason."[828] Luther, swelling with emotion, continues:

> Reason is the Devil's greatest whore; by nature and manner of
> being she is a noxious whore; she is a prostitute, the Devil's

---

[827] Gregory of Nyssa, "Unity in Diversity," quoted in *Gregory of Nyssa's Mystical Writings*, translated and edited by Herbert Mursillo (Crestwood, N.Y.: St. Vladimir's Seminary Press, 1979).

[828] Martin Luther, *Complete Sermons of Martin Luther*, Vol. 2 (Grand Rapids: Baker Books, 2000), pp. 406-407.

appointed whore; whore eaten by scab and leprosy who ought to be trodden under foot and destroyed, she and her wisdom... Throw dung in her face to make her ugly. She is and she ought to be drowned in baptism.[829]

Interestingly, however, the Cappadocian Fathers, being philosophers of the first degree, apparently felt more indisposed to such a course, and sought in vain to somehow guard sacred Reason even in light of their theological machinations. In defending his fellow Basil, Gregory curiously claims that despite their mystery-theology, they did not necessarily "want the natural thought to be suppressed, [in order to] welcome the paradoxical."[830] Yet in describing his own doctrine as "new and paradoxical," is not his position a paradox unto itself? If our consideration of the Trinitarian Jesus is bewildering to the point of frustration, we "should not be surprised," as Gregory says. The overwhelming nature of the triune mystery should, according to him, dominate the very life of a Christian. For "instead of presenting the Christian life as a transformative journey towards increasing luminosity, St. Gregory put forward a vision of a person's ascent towards God in terms of increasing impenetrable opacity... [and] darkness."[831]

During the course of their speculating, the Cappadocian Fathers worked to provide metaphysical solutions for other matters of widespread dissention, namely the "problem" of the Son's subordination to the Father so clearly demonstrated in Scripture. Their most conspicuous advancement in this regard involved the attribution of "causality" to the Person of the Father, *from* whom the Son was made to exist *through* the Spirit. Essentially, they were able to ascribe a preeminence to the Person of the Father while maintaining a co-equality with the other Persons in regard to essence:

> The Cappadocian Fathers for the first time in history introduced into the being of God the concept of cause (aition), in order to attach it significantly not to the one (God's nature) —but to a person, the Father. By distinguishing carefully and persistently between the nature of God and God as the Father,

---

[829] Martin Luther, *Works*, Vol. 16 (Erlangen, 1851), pp. 142-148.

[830] Gregory of Nyssa, *Against Eunomius*, Book I, 38.

[831] Philip Kariatlis, "Dazzling Darkness: The Mystical or Theophanic Theology of St Gregory of Nyssa," *Phronema*, Vol. 27, No. 2 (Redfern: St. Andrew's Greek Orthodox Theological College, 2012), p. 100.

they thought that what causes God to be is the Person of the Father, not the one divine substance.[832]

This progress in philosophy evidently proved enough to draw many into the Trinitarian fold. The Cappadocians had presented the "perfect fix" for the problems generated by Nicaea: one substance/essence (ousia) in three persons (hypostases), paired with the Father's enigmatic primacy-in-equality, all bundled in an impenetrable veil of faith in mystery. These efforts, backed by the will of the state, soon began to solidify the bonds between many of the camps, and greatly served to ease the turmoil of East vs. West politics. The power of the majority would ultimately lie with those who could agree on statements unfavorable to the traditional Subordinationist view, and as a result, the Arians and other unitarian groups would began fading into the minority.

Yet we must not think that Trinitarianism was even close to being settled. Specifically, the orthodox Jesus' simultaneous Godhood and manhood was still proving more than problematic. Further arguments and ecumenical councils were required to harness the persistently bothersome humanity of Jesus beneath the impenetrable God envisioned by the flowering Cappadocian formula.

The Insoluble Trinitarian Jesus

What is clear to us now is that despite the efforts of the Cappadocians, the host of unanswered questions spawned by Nicaea's original "same substance" mandate continuously threatened to crack open any semblance of doctrinal unity their ideas had achieved. Even at the close of the fourth century, the miserable wonder which the homoousian still inspired in the soul of every Christian overwhelmed even the most restrained of those episcopal characters. So lacking was Nicaea's administration of harmony and clarity that a seemingly unending horde of unhappy theologians instigated one controversy after another until both religion and empire trod weary, bloodied footprints on the threshold of collapse. We will now briefly survey several of those infamous arguments.

In 381 CE, at Constantinople, another matter was being dealt with: Apollinaris of Laodicea (d. 390 CE) had attracted a following of Christians who concluded that Christ could not have had a human mind, rather, his mind could only be the one mind of the divine Person of God. Surely, the Apollinarians

---

[832] John D. Zizioulas, "The Doctrine of the Holy Trinity: The Significance of the Cappadocian Contribution," *Trinitarian Theology Today: Essays on Divine Being and Act* (Edinburgh: T & T Clark, 2000 [1995]), pp. 44-60.

thought, there could not be *two different minds* operating in the one Person of Jesus? This was, ultimately, a reaction against the old Gnostic vision of "two persons" in the Savior. Apollinaris argued against those who "confess, not God incarnate, but a man conjoined with God." He protested a "distinction between 'two Sons', the Son of God and the son of Mary." As J. N. D. Kelly explains, "Such distinctions imply that Christ is 'two', whereas Scripture is emphatic that he is a unity; and in any case, Scripture apart, such a duality is inconceivable."[833]

Apollinaris' theory was this: the divine Person was "the sole life of the God-man, infusing vital energy and movements into Him even at the purely physical and biological levels."[834] This made the "humanity" of Christ fundamentally different from all other men; he bore a "divinized" humanity, even "divine flesh." In this teaching of a heavenly humanity, Apollinaris resembled earlier teaching from Valentinus, Origen, and even the Nicene theologian Hilary of Poitier.[835] Indeed, as Hanson reveals, even "orthodox" authorities like Hilary, "in order to defend Trinitarian theology, plunge[d] wildly into docetism."[836] Thus Apollinaris, in trying to rescue orthodoxy from the Valentinian two persons, was only giving in to the same pressure towards the opposite docetism that even the most respected Nicene supporters could not escape. Regarding this heavenly humanity of Jesus, Kelly explains: "If it is objected that [Apollinarianism] makes [Jesus] different from ordinary men, Apollinaris had no hesitation in agreeing. He found confirmation of the difference in the wording of such texts as 'Found *as* a man,' and, 'In the *likeness* of men.' "[837] To most people, this thinking indeed sent Jesus careening backwards towards Gnosticism. In fact, "Doctrines like these caused Apollinaris to be accused of teaching that the Lord's flesh was heavenly in origin and pre-existent."[838] This accusation represents the precise teaching of the Valentinian Gnostics, that Jesus' human body had descended from heaven and passed through Mary. The Gnostic controversy of the mid-second century still raged on in the fourth! But

---

[833] Kelly, *Early Christian Doctrines*, p. 290.

[834] Ibid., p. 292.

[835] Valentinus taught that the body of Jesus was heavenly, even constructed by the join efforts of the Aeons. Origen taught that the true nature of Christ's heavenly flesh shone through at the Transfiguration (*Against Celsus*, 6, 77). Hilary (d. 367 CE) taught that "Christ's body having been conceived by the Holy Spirit, it was not really earthly but heavenly (*corpus coeleste*), and was raised above human weakness... the Transfiguration and the walking on the sea were not strictly miraculous, but were natural to a body such as his... *there was a strain in Hilary's thought which veered close to Docetism*" (Kelly, p. 335).

[836] Hanson, p. xix.

[837] Kelly, p. 335.

[838] Ibid., p. 294.

Apollinaris reacted strongly to this charge: "It is plain from all we have written that we do *not* say that the Savior's flesh has come down from heaven."[839] Nevertheless, the elimination of a human mind and will, and the "divinization" of his human nature simply brought Apollinaris too close to docetism. For the orthodox, his Christology was still "virtually docetic, implying that the Savior was not a real man but only appeared as a man."[840] The Cappadocians especially saw in Apollinaris' model a quashing of Christ's real humanity. They decreed Apollinarianism a heresy, and maintained Christ as truly God and truly man; if that meant he had to have two minds, then so be it. As one of the orthodox authorities commented around this time, true Christians should "accept what is said in faith, not pry impetuously."[841] Of course, this did not put an end to the questions.[842] If the conciliar result of the Apollinarian controversy represented a swing back towards the old "two persons" Christology of the Gnostics, the result of the next major controversy would represent a swing in the other direction.

The Council of Ephesus convened in 431 to deal with rekindled Christological dispute: the "Nestorian controversy" saw Christians questioning how Jesus could simultaneously entertain two opposite natures within a single person. Many assumed that there must exist an essential disunion between the natures. Their argument was that if Christ died, then it must have been only his human nature that died since God is immortal by nature. If Christ was tempted, it was only his human nature that was tempted, since God cannot be tempted, and so on. Furthermore, they argued that "an authentically human experience would have been impossible if the Lord's humanity had been fused with, or dominated by, his divinity."[843] However, yet another influential Alexandrian theologian, Cyril (d. 444 CE), issued a host of anathemas denouncing Nestorianism, claiming that Nestorius was teaching two persons in Christ. This was not explicitly the case of course, but for Cyril the consequences of Nestorius' objections made such a conclusion inevitable.[844]

---

[839] Ibid., emphasis added.

[840] Ibid., p. 295.

[841] John Chrysostom (d. 407 CE), as quoted by Freeman in *Closing of the Western Mind*, p. 311. Chrysostom furthermore suggests that we must "Restrain our own reasoning, and empty our mind of secular learning, in order to provide a mind swept clear for the reception of divine words" (p. 316).

[842] Apollinaris' memory did not die out; his followers kept his teachings alive by preserving his writings and pretending they were actually writings passed down by his friend Athanasius.

[843] Kelly, pp. 312-313.

[844] "It is little wonder that contemporaries, approaching Christology from the oneness of the Person rather than the distinction of the natures, jumped to the conclusion that this was a doctrine of an ordinary man, the human Jesus, linked to the Word by harmony of will and by divine favour.

Cyril himself presented an odd problem, however: his assertion that the Nestorians were splitting Christ into two persons by saying only one nature could suffer caused Cyril to contend that though there were truly two distinct natures in Christ, they were somehow also essentially united. This came to be called the "hypostatic union": the two natures were united in the one hypostasis of the Son, and whatever happened to the one nature, happened to the other. Therefore it was not only the humanity of Jesus that was crucified, but the Logos—*God himself.* Cyril was quick to point out, however, that the Son "suffered impassibly."[845] In other words, he claimed that the divine Person *suffered without suffering.* In addition to this strenuous paradox, Cyril's system forced another question: if the divine Person could indeed suffer, then why did the Logos need to take on a human nature at all? In this way, Cyril himself came close to denying the humanity of Christ: it was an unnecessary façade.

The Nestorians were unconvinced. To them, this suffering without suffering was only an abuse of words. But Cyril was an incredibly vindictive character and was prepared to take whatever measures necessary to ensure his view's success. Cyril employed "shock troops" called the Parabalani in order to intimidate his opponents. They were evidently so terrifying that the emperor himself even asked that their strength be limited to no more than 500 men.[846] As Griggs notes, "in many ways the [violent] tactics of Athanasius were renewed during his episcopacy."[847] Frend characterizes Cyril as "utterly unscrupulous, overbearing, turbulent and greedy for power, ready to use the mob and the monks to do his bidding against his opponents."[848] Ultimately, Cyril was so troublesome that upon his death one of his contemporaries would write:

> His departure delights the survivors, but possibly disheartens
> the dead… they may send him back again to us… [We must]

This was a travesty of what Nestorius intended to teach, but the fault lay with his inability to provide a deeper analysis of the substantial unity of the Lord's person of which he was convinced" (Kelly, p. 317).

[845] "The Logos, Cyril is careful to stress, suffered and died 'impassibly.' This should not be taken as an implicit denial that the Logos 'really' suffered and died, but rather indicates the unique mode in which not only suffering and death, but anything creaturely and human, can belong to a divine person. The impassible suffering of the Logos in the flesh strains, to be sure, the limits of our understanding…" (James F. Keating, Thomas Joseph White, *Divine Impassibility and the Mystery of Human Suffering* (Grand Rapids: Eerdmans, 2009), p. 257).

[846] Freeman, *Closing of the Western Mind,* p. 268.

[847] W. H. C. Frend, quoted in Griggs, p. 190.

[848] Ibid.

place a very big and heavy stone on his grave to stop him from coming back here.[849]

Nevertheless, the Roman emperor overseeing Cyril's dispute with Nestorius had evidently learned at least one lesson from past councils: theological matters could never be "settled" when personal conflicts were involved, at least not without the generous intervention of the government. Once again, imperial control was quickly assumed to bring an end to the disruption. When Cyril realized that he could not assert his position over the Church on his own, he turned to bribery of the state. The sums with which he bribed both imperial officials and Church leaders were staggering.[850] Nestorius himself was compelled to preach publicly against Cyril and his shameful activity, but to no avail. The Council of Ephesus resulted in an imperial order that made disagreeing with Cyril a punishable offense. In the end, Cyril does seem to closely parallel Athanasius' career. As Frend concludes, both Athanasius and Cyril "needed all their prestige and then skill to win the acceptance of these theological assumptions based on the Nicene Creed which could be at variance with the literal doctrines of the Bible."[851]

Interestingly, the condemned "Nestorianism" has not died out in mainstream Christianity. We recall that Nestorius himself had taken particular issue with Mary being called "the Mother of God" (*Theotokos*). He asserted that she must be the mother of the human nature of Christ only. Against this the Catholic Church had sided with Cyril and confirmed that Mary was indeed the Mother of God. But here we find a matter with which many Protestants today, even those who claim adherence to the ecumenical councils, vigorously disagree. Indeed, the Nestorian "heresy" remains strong with many evangelicals who claim the deity of Christ in a Trinitarian sense, but nevertheless assert that only the man nature was born, suffered, died or was tempted.[852]

As disagreement over the burgeoning Trinitarian codes continued in the late Roman Empire, it became clear that what disputes the conciliar debates between

---

[849] Theodoret, quoted in Robert L. Wilken "Cyril of Alexandria," *The Limits of Ancient Christianity* (University of Michigan Press, 1999), p. 42.

[850] For a window into the incredible substance in which Cyril dealt, see his *Letter 96*, which contains a detailed "catalogue of things dispatched" as payment for certain political outcomes. His desired results include the cessation of opposition to his party, mediation, certain officials' persuasion of other officials, the severance of an officials' friendship with Cyril's enemies, etc.

[851] W. H. C. Frend, quoted in Griggs, p. 146.

[852] See R. C. Sproul, "Did God Die on the Cross?" Ligonier Ministries. 14 April 2014. Web. 27 October 2014.

the churches could not settle, the heavy hand of Rome would be ever poised to fix. In 438 CE, Emperor Theodosius II, himself a Trinitarian committed to the Nicene-Constantinopolitan faith, issued decrees which once again ordered the death penalty for anyone denying the Trinity.[853] Yet even within the Trinitarian party itself there was still no full agreement on the nature of Christ's divinity, and that discord remains in our own time. Of course, as we must continually remind ourselves, the frequent lapsing into Nestorianism within modern Christianity is really the natural pressure towards the dual entities of Valentinianism; it has remained the path of least resistance for the doctrine of the deity of Christ. Interestingly, Valentinus' name would continue to surface in the disputes following Nestorius' defeat. In 448 CE, a synod even condemned the popular theologian Eutyches as both an Apollinarian and "a follower of Valentinus."[854]

Turmoil over the dual natures again came to a head in 449 CE. The Second Council of Ephesus, originally intended as an "ecumenical" council, has now been disowned by orthodoxy due to its anti-orthodox conclusions. This council determined, in a stunning reversal, that Christ was *not* a union of distinct divine and man natures, but had only *one* nature in his single person. This produced what is known as the "monophysite schism" and ultimately yielded the separation of the Oriental Orthodox Church which has lasted to this day.

In 451 CE, yet another convention, the Council of Chalcedon, was hastily assembled to "fix" this sudden shift caused by those who were still finding inconsistencies with the dual-natured God-Christ. Chalcedon succeeded in turning the tide, to the end that Christ reverted to being one person with two natures. But the dual natures view remained obstinately ambiguous; no solution as to *how* Christ could exist as one person with two natures was presented at Chalcedon and no model has ever been universally agreed upon. For the orthodox, the great questions about Jesus remain.[855] What was solidified,

---

[853] Roland H. Bainton, *Christendom: A Short History of Christianity and Its Impact on Western Civilization*, Vol. 1 (New York: Harper & Row, 1964), p. 101.

[854] Kelly, p. 331. Since Eutyches taught that Jesus' divinity absorbed his humanity, this accusation of being a follower of Valentinus was probably levelled at what Eutyches' opponents felt was actually a partly-docetic tendency. The Western school of Valentinians, at least, would have preserved a full human person alongside the divine, not absorbed the humanity into a new nature. But this may well have been the tendency in the East. Regardless, it is the general Gnostic shadow following orthodox Christology that Eutyches' critics detected.

[855] Hick writes that "the task facing one who wishes to reaffirm a Chalcedonian Christology is not that of translating into contemporary terms a Hellenistic account of how the one person, Jesus could have two natures; for no such account is contained in the original formula. As a historian of the period says, 'Chalcedon has proved less a solution than the classic definition of a problem which constantly demands further elucidation' (Young). That problem does not lie in an

however, was orthodoxy's overstepping of the Apostolic preaching. As one Catholic scholar reminds us:

> The New Testament gives no inkling of the teaching of Chalcedon. That council not only reformulated in other language the New Testament data about Jesus' constitution, but also reconceptualized it in the light of current Greek philosophical thinking. And that reconceptualization and reformulation go well beyond the New Testament data.[856]

Another Catholic scholar even admits that the reformulation of the dual natures at Chalcedon actually succeeded in so altering Jesus' humanity that it became "a humanity unlike that of the rest of us." He confesses that:

> the Chalcedonian formula makes genuine humanity impossible. The conciliar definition says that Jesus is true man. But if there are two natures in him, it is clear which will dominate. And Jesus becomes immediately very different from us... He knows exactly what everyone is thinking and going to do. This is far from ordinary human experience. Jesus is tempted, but cannot sin because he is God. What kind of temptation is this? Can it be called temptation at all? ... Jesus [does] not have a human personal center... we cannot identify with this Jesus.[857]

Indeed the humanity of the Chalcedonian Christ is external, while inwardly he lacks everything that makes that humanity real: uncertainty, vulnerability, true reliance on a higher power—the necessary features of a genuine human life are inevitably drowned out by a simultaneous existence as Almighty God. Because of the dual natures of Chalcedon, as one scholar rightly confirms, "One may affirm the humanity as a formal fact and then proceed to so define or portray it as to deny its reality in any ordinarily accepted sense."[858]

We have again come full circle—back to the docetic Jesus. It should be easy to recognize a similar suppression of Christ's humanity here. The human

---

outmoded language and conceptuality but in the fact that the Council in effect merely asserted that Jesus was 'truly God and truly man' without attempting to say how such a paradox is possible... Merely to assert that two different natures coexisted in Jesus... is to utter a form of words which as yet has no specified meaning" John Hick, *The Metaphor of God Incarnate* (London: Westminster John Knox Press, 2005 [1993]), pp. 47-48.

[856] Joseph Fitzmyer, *A Christological Catechism* (Costa Mesa: Paulist Press, 1991), p. 102.

[857] Thomas N. Hart, *To Know and Follow Jesus* (New York: Paulist Press, 1984), pp. 46-47.

[858] John Knox, *The Humanity and Divinity of Christ* (New York: CUP, 1967), p. 62.

experience of Jesus was effectively diluted and the human nature itself was made void of personality—it was once again a Gnostic mirage, a timeless abstraction affixed to a divine person. As Harnack reveals, it was at this point that "every thought of the real and complete human personality of the Redeemer was in fact condemned as being intolerable in the Church. Its place was taken by 'the nature' [of Christ], which without 'the person' is simply a cipher [a *nothing*]."[859] And so the man of history liquefied into the distant God of Christian dogma.

Interestingly, it was in the years after the Council of Chalcedon, according to one historian, that an active process of reconciliation with Church history began. After 451 CE:

> much tidying up of Christianity's turbulent past needed to be done to give it ideological coherence. The doctrines of orthodox Christianity, it was now said, had been known throughout the ages. Even the patriarchs, who had lived before the time of Moses, "knew that one Almighty God is the Holy Trinity," though Gregory admitted that "they did not preach very much publicly about the Trinity whom they knew." [...] the Church Fathers' impassioned and bitter disagreements of the interpretation of contradictory passages could be expunged from the record; in fact, they were now said to have spoken with unanimity. What the scriptures taught, Gregory argued, had been upheld by the four councils that could be associated with orthodoxy—Nicaea, 325; Constantinople, 381; Ephesus, 431, Chalcedon, 451—and these were given status as ecumenical councils at which the genuine voice of the Church had been heard... The role of emperors in calling the councils and pressuring them into consensus was, perhaps understandably, passed over, as was the lack of significant western participation. As orthodox doctrine was not presented as though it had been settled and accepted from the beginning of time, heretics were consequently accused of "bringing forth as something new which is not contained in the old books of the ancient fathers." So, whatever inspection of the historical record might suggest, it became impossible to see Christian doctrine as the product

---

[859] Harnack, *History of Dogma*, Vol. II, 1961, p. 10.

of a process of evolution. A "heresy" could not have "matured" into "orthodoxy."[860]

Nevertheless, we find that despite the solidified status of the Trinity doctrine, major internal disagreements over the increasingly complicated dogma continued into the *sixth century*, even to the point that the death penalty had to once again be asserted for denial of the Trinity by the violent emperor Justinian circa 530 CE.[861] As noted in previous chapters, not only was the Trinity imposed by Justin here, but so was the dreadful banning of the *Shema*, the biblical statement of faith claimed by Jesus himself (Mark 12:28ff), recognized as a denial of the Trinity.[862] Jewish citizens in the empire were now considered lower than animals; "correct" profession of certain Christian ideas became a fundamental requirement for full participation in the benefits of society.[863] Thus the triune God was once again pressed more firmly into ecumenical acceptance "by the sword of civil government."[864]

Despite the efforts of both the bishops and the state to bridle Christianity with a solidified and agreed upon Trinitarian dogma, yet another council, the Second Council of Constantinople, was required in 553 CE to further condemn persistent Nestorian views about Christ's natures. It was hoped by Emperor Justinian that this council would rejoin the churches still separated over the new standards, but it only caused further schisms and generated even more heresies.

Still in 681 CE a lack of clarity continued to disrupt the faith, and the Third Council of Constantinople met to confront several new controversies. At this council, the orthodox members determined that Jesus not only had two natures, he also harbored *two distinct wills*. The council was therefore compelled to even posthumously condemn a Pope, Honorius I, who had exhibited "Monothelitist" (one will) views.[865] Many evangelicals today are often surprised to learn that

---

860 Freeman, *Closing of the Western Mind,* pp. 313-314.

861 Justinian's excellence in violence towards his own subjects certainly rivaled the preceding Theodosius I. During the Nika revolt of 532 CE, it is said that Justinian massacred between 30,000 and 50,000 Roman citizens.

862 Joseph Melusky, Keith Pesto, *The Death Penalty: Documents Decoded* (Santa Barbara: ABC-CLIO 2014), p. 4.

863 Freeman, *Closing of the Western Mind,* p. 253, 255.

864 Thomas Jefferson, *Letter to Theologian James Smith*, December 8, 1822.

865 "Monotheletism," which held that the person of Jesus had only one will, probably had its birth in Syria around 629 CE, and was increasingly articulated around 638 CE, until it was ultimately rejected as heretical in 681 CE. The bishops had discovered writings of Pope Honorius I written to Sergius that revealed an agreement or a sympathy for Sergius' view that Jesus had only

orthodoxy demands such a staggering belief about the historical Jesus. But modern Trinitarian scholars, like Thomas Morris, agree that there were indeed two wills in Jesus, one human and one divine, and that if the human will ever tried to make a decision that deviated from those of the divine will, the divine would overrule it.[866] This ultimately represents, as Trinitarians conclude, "two minds" in Jesus, which is essentially an affirmation of Constantinople's anathemas (381 CE).[867] As one Trinitarian professor confirms: "An incarnation involving two minds is complicated, but such is the historic teaching of the church."[868] Scholars have nevertheless pointed out the difficulties with such a model. John Hick, recognizing that Jesus never did anything wrong, naturally wondered if Jesus ever, in his human will, intended to do something wrong, but was prevented by the overpowering will of the divine Person? Indeed for the dual-natured Jesus:

> his outwardly perfect life might, for all that we can know, conceal many wrong inner impulses that were nipped in the bud before developing into overt actions... The human part might intend to sin, but the divine part, being unable to sin, would necessarily over-rule or circumvent the intention. Such a person could not be tempted as we are tempted, or become good by overcoming temptation, and accordingly could not embody our human moral ideal. Nor—in relation to the doctrine of atonement—could his death constitute the sacrifice of a life of perfect human obedience to God... Was Jesus free to commit sin [and] free to reject the Holy Spirit's guidance and enlightenment? If not, he was not genuinely human.[869]

Here we again witness the return to the Valentinian Jesus. According to the Valentinian system, though both human and divine minds existed in Jesus, "every motion, every propensity and desire [was] subject entirely to the dictates

---

will. Thus he was condemned with shouts of "To Honorius, the heretic, anathema!" (Third Council of Constantinople, 680 CE, 16th session).

[866] Thomas Morris, quoted in John Hick, *The Metaphor of God Incarnate* (London: Westminster John Knox Press, 2005 [1993]), p. 57.

[867] For an example of a thoroughly developed modern "two minds" view, see Thomas Morris, *The Logic of God Incarnate* (Eugene: Wipf & Stock, 2001).

[868] John McKinley, "The Incarnation and the Mind of Christ, Part Two," The Good Book Blog. 18 December 2013. Web. 23 November 2015.

[869] Hick, *The Metaphor of God Incarnate*, pp. 58-60.

of the celestial mind."[870]   Regardless of how it is accomplished, or at what stage, both the Gnostic and the orthodox propositions will involve some suppression of the human psychology, and therefore the humanity of Jesus. Hick lends even further insight into the problems we encounter with an affirmation of the two minds of orthodoxy:

> Here are two streams of consciousness, A and B, one including the other in the sense that A is aware of everything occurring in the B stream of consciousness whilst B is entirely unaware of the contents of the A consciousness. Thus God the Son could know all that was going on in the conscious, and also in the unconscious, mind of Jesus whilst Jesus was entirely unaware that the Son was thus monitoring him, or even unaware of the Son's existence… such asymmetrical cognitive accessing would not constitute divine incarnation in any religiously significant sense.[871]

Indeed, by attempting to preserve Jesus' humanity, the two wills concept of orthodoxy effectively destroys the very incarnational relationship between the human and divine that the orthodox had sought to establish. How was the Church to ever properly recognize Jesus as the person of God incarnate? Could one ever do so in a way that did not overemphasize the overbearing divine entity and impugn the humanity (in a docetic sense), or separate Christ into two different people (in a "Nestorian" or even Valentinian sense)? Despite these problems, in 680 CE they stubbornly attested that the two wills and two natures of Jesus somehow, beyond all imagination, did not represent two persons. Externally, this incredible persuasion remains to this day. But internally, far from being universally settled among Trinitarian scholars, the minds and wills of Jesus are still hotly contested. For example, one of the most respected and popular Trinitarian apologists, Dr. William Lane Craig, has even felt compelled to openly resurrect the very "Monotheletist" (one will) heresy that the council of 680 CE condemned. Upon reviewing the many problems generated by the confirmation of the two wills, Craig feels that "the Church did overstep its bounds." He confesses: "I cannot understand how Christ's human nature could have a will of its own, distinct from the will of the Second Person of the Trinity,

---

[870] J. L. Mosheim, *Historical Commentaries on the State of Christianity During the First Three Hundred and Twenty-Five Years,* Vol. 1 (New York: Converse, 1851), p. 467.

[871] Hick, *The Metaphor of God Incarnate,* p. 51.

and not be a person."[872] In denying a human will for Jesus, Craig also denies a human mind, and even harkens back to the Apollinarian heresy condemned at Constantinople in 381 CE by describing his own proposed view as "a neo-Apollinarian Christology."[873] Thus even Dr. Craig, arguably "the premiere defender of the evangelical faith today," still struggles against the strictures of Trinitarian orthodoxy—a struggle for which some of his fellows have charged him with heresy.[874] These accusations he seems willing to brave, however, as the alternative is evidently much worse. Fully aware of the dire and necessary implications of the orthodox Jesus, he confesses: "While I don't like contradicting the decrees of an ecumenical Council, [there is a] danger of falling into Nestorianism [making Jesus two people]."[875] In reality, it is not actually "Nestorianism" that Craig is reacting to (since Nestorius did not really teach two persons) but a latent Gnosticism within orthodoxy. Again, in the Valentinian Gnostic system, Christ was indeed composed of human and divine persons, though the celestial mind had become the central ego. Thus Craig, in observing orthodoxy's inevitable and dangerous presentation of fully divine and human persons in Jesus, is really encountering a subterranean Gnostic tendency which the Catholic Church never overcame.

In discussions of the early Christian controversies, Arianism and Sabellianism have often been characterized as "Scylla and Charybdis," the two deadly theological options orthodoxy was forced to navigate between.[876] But it is obvious now that there was yet another dangerous maneuver the Church was attempting at the same time: sailing between the Gnostic docetism and Valentinianism. On the one hand there was the docetism (one divine person attached to an abstract, spiritual, and timeless humanity), and this is the ultimate

---

[872] William Lane Craig, "Monotheletism," Reasonable Faith. 21 September 2008. Web. 20 July 2015.

[873] William Lane Craig, "The Very Latest From Reasonable Faith," Reasonable Faith. 03 March 2015. Web. 20 July 2015. Craig cites the Protestant principle "Sola Scriptura" (Scripture alone) as his justification for challenging ecumenical decrees. If it is possible that the Cappadocians were wrong in their assessment of Apollinarianism at the council in 381 CE, could they not have been wrong about the "three hypostases in one essence" they established at that same council?

[874] See Douglas Beaumont, "Is William Lane Craig a Heretic?" Douglas Beaumont: Theology, Philosophy, Apologetics. 15 November 2010. Web. 20 July 2015.

[875] Craig, "The Very Latest From Reasonable Faith."

[876] Scylla and Charybdis are sea monsters in Homer's *Odyssey*. In the story, Odysseus is forced to choose which of the two sea monsters he will sail past; avoiding one only draws him closer to the other. Ultimately, Odysseus chooses to sail by Scylla and lose only a handful of men instead of risking the entire ship by passing Charybdis' whirlpool. For such characterization, see Lamson, *The Church of the First Three Centuries*, p. 288.

pitfall of Craig's Apollinarianism.[877]   On the other hand was the Valentinian Christology (unified divine and human persons), and this is the pitfall of Cyril's orthodoxy.   In the end, Christianity was not able to teach the deity of Jesus and completely avoid both of these Gnostic Christs; it could only lacquer one or the other with a Catholic veneer.

Ultimately, and despite the persistent illusion of ecumenical unity, the Trinitarian Jesus remains a figure ever on the verge of implosion.[878] Professor Jenkins thus encapsulates the ongoing quandary of today's Trinitarianism in this regard:

> Either we might think of Christ purely as God, in which case
> he is no longer human, has no share in our human experience,
> and becomes a divinity in the sky like Zeus or Thor; or else, in
> contrast, we focus so much on his humanity that we underplay
> the divine element and deny the Incarnation.   We would

---

[877] In the final analysis, the humanity of Apollinaris' Jesus is a humanity unlike that of the rest of us.   It is, as we have seen, an abstraction subsumed by the divine Person of the Logos.   This contravenes with the biblical testimony that Christ was *like his brothers in every way* (Heb 2:17), and tips the scales closer to the humanity-impugning docetism; this Christ's "human" life is a life without human thoughts, an experience completely unrelatable to humanity and thus *inhuman*. Kelly recounts the orthodox argument against Apollinaris: "if it is assumed that Christ lacked the most characteristic element in man's make-up, a rational mind and will, His alleged manhood was not in the strict sense human, but must have been something monstrous; it is absurd to call Him a man at all... it was man's rational soul, with its power of choice, which was the seat of sin; and if the Word did not unite such a soul with Himself the salvation of mankind could not have been achieved.   In a famous phrase of Gregory Nazianzus, 'What has not been assumed cannot be restored; it is what is united with God that is saved' " (Kelly, p. 296).

[878] In contrast, unitarian minister William E. Channing writes that just as unitarian Christians believe in the unity of God, "we believe in the unity of Jesus Christ.   We believe that Jesus is one mind, one soul, one being, as truly one as we are, and equally distinct from the one God.   We complain of the doctrine of the Trinity, that, not satisfied with making God three beings, it makes Jesus Christ two beings, and thus introduces infinite confusion into our conceptions of his character.   This corruption of Christianity, alike repugnant to common sense and to the general strain of Scripture, is a remarkable proof of the power of a false philosophy... According to this doctrine, Jesus Christ... consists of two souls, two minds; the one divine, the other human; the one weak, the other omniscient.   Now we maintain that this is to make Christ two beings.   To denominate him one person, one being, and yet to suppose him made up of two minds, infinitely different from each other, is to abuse and confound language, and to throw darkness over all our conceptions of intelligent natures.   According to the common doctrine, each of these two minds in Christ has its own consciousness, its own will, and its own perceptions.   They have, in fact, no common properties.   The divine mind feels none of the wants and sorrows of the human, and the human is infinitely removed from the perfection and happiness of the divine.   Can you conceive of two beings in the universe more distinct? ... The doctrine [is], we think, an enormous tax on human credulity" (William E. Channing, "Discourse at the Ordination of the Rev. Jared Sparks, Baltimore, 1819," *Works* (Boston: American Unitarian Association, 1894), p. 373).

preach a Christ of two natures and two minds, literally a schizophrenic being.[879]

Not surprisingly, even after the Roman age, debates over this bewildering Jesus continued into the new millennium, as still more orthodox councils were needed to confront the persistent doctrinal dissatisfaction of Christians. Also not surprising is the fact that as early as 1100 CE, scattered Christian groups were once again beginning to openly revolt against Catholic claims to doctrinal authority.[880] It is probably impossible to determine with certainty what these early dissenting groups, such as the Vaudois (Waldenses), believed regarding the Trinity. As one historian explains, wherever non-Trinitarian Bible teaching existed, "it would have had to have been believed and practiced in total secrecy… The papal bondage was so total in those Dark Ages that the endeavors we now know that the Vaudois bravely made to cast off the Romish shackles are such as to merit our appreciation, indeed our admiration."[881]

By 1215, groups such as the Vaudois were being declared heretics and harshly persecuted. In that same year, the Fourth Lateran Council was convened by the orthodox and continued to sort out issues regarding the three Persons of the Trinity, the Incarnation, and the essence shared by the divine members.[882] But none of this made a lasting end of the debates. Eventually, another orthodox gathering, the Council of Florence, convened in 1438 and lasted for seven years, ultimately determining "that the Holy Ghost proceeds *also* from the Son"[883] as well as the Father, in an evident reversal of the creed of the Council of Constantinople (381) which stated that the Holy Spirit "proceedeth from *the Father*" (of course, this also appears to contradict the testimony of Christ that the Holy Spirit is "*from the Father*" in John 15:26).

However, during the Protestant Reformation of the sixteenth century, some sectors of Christianity would take a Scripturally-motivated and dramatically *anti-Trinitarian* turn.[884] The Council of Venice, a 1550 convention of Anabaptists

---

[879] Jenkins, *Jesus Wars*, p. 2.

[880] The poem "La Nobla Leyzcon" confirms the existence of the "Vaudois" (Waldenses) 1100 CE.

[881] Alan Eyre, *The Protestors* (Worcester: Billing & Sons Limited, 1985), p. 14.

[882] See the Constitutions of the Fourth Lateran Council (1215).

[883] Léon van der Essen, "The Council of Florence," *The Catholic Encyclopedia*, Vol. 6 (New York: Robert Appleton Company, 1909). Web. 29 Sept. 2014. See note on the "Filioque" on p. 113.

[884] A respected companion of Luther, Martin Cellarius (1499-1564 CE), and the Anabaptist Hans Denck (1500-1527) are examples of prominent, early challengers to the doctrine. Another

pronounced starkly anti-Trinitarian principles.[885] From this point, the Christian world would see the rise of the prolific Socinian movement which once again expressed the theology of the Photinians and the Jewish Nazarenes: that God was one, the Father, and that Christ was his human son who had his literal beginning in the womb of Mary.[886]

While modern Trinitarians from all walks and denominations claim, and truly believe, that they operate a doctrine that is wholly agreed upon by all legitimate Christians, we find evidence that disagreement and confusion have persisted. Cyril C. Richardson, former president of the American Society of Church History, offers an insightful commentary:

> I cannot but think that the doctrine of the Trinity, far from being established, is open to serious criticism, because of both the modern understanding of Scripture, and the inherent confusions in its expression. It is not a doctrine specifically to be found in the New Testament. It is a creation of the fourth-century Church.[887]

Political Accident vs. Providence

A portrait of the tragic desperation of the Church must amend itself to this portion of the narrative. In summarizing the dark spiritual quality of the ecclesiastical activity of the Roman era relative to Trinitarianism, we find no more apt words than the record of one of those most actively involved at Nicaea, bishop Hilary of Poitiers (c. 300-368 CE):

> It is a thing equally deplorable and dangerous, that there are as many creeds as opinions among men, as many doctrines as inclinations, and as many sources of blasphemy as there are

---

voice, Giorgio Blandrata (1515-1588 CE), an Italian unitarian who had frequent contact with John Calvin, had great influence in Poland.

[885] E. Comba, "Un sinodo anabattista a Venezia anno 1550," *Rivista Cristiana*, Vol. 13 (1885): pp. 21-24, 83-87.

[886] The Socinians, enjoying early success around 1579, and known by the latter half of the 17th century as "Unitarians" or "Polish Brethren," accepted Jesus as God's Son and a genuine man sans literal pre-existence. The Socinians also famously advocated for the separation of church and state, stressed the importance of human morality, and held that Christian doctrine should be both found in Scripture and rational. The unitarian theology so stalwartly defended by them would eventually enjoy wide dissemination throughout Europe and the United States and relish in such famous adherents as Sir Isaac Newton, John Locke, John Milton, President Thomas Jefferson, President John Adams, President John Quincy Adams, Susan B. Anthony, Paul Revere, Joseph Priestley, William Whiston, King John Sigismund of Hungary, and President William Taft.

[887] Richardson, p. 17.

faults among us; because we make creeds arbitrarily, and explain them as arbitrarily. The Homoousion [the sharing of substance between the Father and the Son] is rejected, and received, and explained away by successive synods. The partial or total resemblance of the Father and of the Son, is a subject of dispute for these unhappy times. Every year, nay ever moon, we make new creeds to describe invisible mysteries. We repent of what we have done, we defend those who repent, we anathematize those whom we defended. We condemn either the doctrine of others in ourselves, or our own in that of others; and reciprocally tearing one another to pieces, we have been the cause of each other's ruin.[888]

In this deeply tragic confession, we find that it is not any particular heresy which is to blame for the ravaging of the Church's dignity. Rather the fault lies in the secularly powered creedal-council system itself. Observing this vicious cycle of condemnation, one cannot help but wonder whether or not this was the prescribed operation of the divinely ordained Body of the New Testament Jesus. Of course, the world had seen previously, in an era less removed from Christ and his Apostles, a brilliant compassion among Christians that ignited the pagans into feverish camaraderie and selflessness. But now there could be no mistaking it; already by the close of the fourth century, that spirit had largely, if not completely, departed.

While the persistence of the mystery schools within Christianity may surely be awarded a great sum of responsibility for the raucous discord of the faith, there existed at the heart of the Catholic council-system another foundational weakness that practically ensured corrupted results: the fact that secular government politics and practical Christianity have never proven able to mix without a degree of compromise. In hoping to make sense of the deceitfulness and brutality (on all sides), we might remember that the early fourth-century bishops had recently appreciated a wild shift in their lifestyles, a sort of "culture-shock" that may have pressed many of them towards exploitation. Only a handful of years prior to Nicaea, the same bishops were running for their lives beneath harsh Roman persecution; now they held the fate of the empire in their hands. This sudden role adaptation may have torn them between the life and

---

[888] Hilary, *Ad Constantium I*, quoted by John William Draper, *History of the Conflict Between Religion and Science* (New York: D. Appleton and Co., 1898), p. 203.

values they'd always known and the corruption facilitated by instant influence with the emperor. Such a precarious situation was hardly conducive to Church business. As Rubenstein aptly explains:

> Christian bishops, while expected to be pure and peaceful men, were now among the most powerful political figures in the empire. The contradictions between the ideals of behavior represented by Jesus Christ's life and the requirements for holding office in the fourth-century Church were agonizing. The bishop's worldly duties and ambitions often involved them in political intrigue, financial chicanery, abuse of legal processes, and sheer thuggery against their opponents—all of which might generate charges to be used against them by political or doctrinal enemies.[889]

After observing the wholesale moral corruption and political underhandedness of Church leadership in the early centuries, would the modern Christian not consider it at least imprudent to blindly trust that the council-system ultimately "got it right" for posterity without any consideration for the possibility of serious error? What might produce more dire consequences for Christianity than the mixture of the Christian cause with human ambition? No more pernicious a desire might have affixed itself to the operation of the religion of Jesus than the craving of hierarchical advancement, save perhaps the desire for personal survival. That some of the most influential episcopal jousters were actively engaged in the pursuit of both of these prizes is easy to observe.

The emperor Constantine, in a letter to the Church in Alexandria, had claimed that "We have received from Divine Providence the supreme favor of being relieved from all error."[890] But why should the dutiful trust of many mainline believers that God absolutely "presided" over the determinations of the Catholic councils not be seriously questioned? As Jenkins appropriately recounts:

> Looking at history, the process of establishing orthodoxy involved a huge amount of what we might call political accident—depending on the outcome of dynastic succession, on victory or defeat in battle, on the theological tastes of key

---

[889] Rubenstein, p. 101.

[890] Eusebius, *Life of Constantine*, quoted in R. MacMullen, *Christianity and Paganism in the Fourth to Eighth Centuries* (New Haven: London, 1997), p. 130.

royal figures. Throughout, we are always tempted to say: if only this event had worked out differently, or this, or this. It is a story of ifs, and matters might very easily have gone another way. For later generations of Christians—and, by implication, for other religions—that conclusion is humbling… Also, from a Christian perspective—or for other faith traditions—chance is not a valid concept.[891]

Jenkins touches upon an important point: it is difficult for many Christians to confront the possibility that God did *not* direct the doctrinal productions of the councils because of the common Christian belief that God himself enjoys uninterrupted regulation of everything that happens on the earth. For many, the implications of God's lack of absolute intervention in the conclusions of the synodic era, namely that millions of succeeding faithful might have been misled through a hereditary failure of leadership, seems almost too much to bear. But the New Testament writers actually reveal a startling truth for the believer, that even now *"the whole world is under the control of the evil one"* (1 John 5:19). This should not be too hard for the Christian to digest. One look around at the planet's sad state of affairs, especially at the fragmented body of more than 41,000 Christian denominations,[892] should testify to the Christian that God's desire for both clarity and unity in the Church is often spoiled, either by humanity, the forces of evil in the world, or a combination of both.

Regardless of how this history is processed, the fact remains that once the state Church had determined once and for all what was true, Christian exegesis became largely a task of interpreting the Bible, creatively if necessary, in order to support those requirements. But what could possibly be more damaging to the spiritual lives of millions of Christians than the setting up of a creedal roadblock in front of the teachings of the historical Jesus? The orthodox formulas have been, from the moment of their conception, theological tollbooths that must be paid before advancing onward to Christ, and standards which, as we have seen, might have easily gone another way.

---

[891] Jenkins, pp. 268-269.

[892] "Global Christianity: A Report on the Size and Distribution of the World's Christian Population," *The Pew Forum on Religion & Public Life*, December 19, 2011. Appendix B: Methodology for Estimating Christian Movements.

7

CONSEQUENCES OF DOGMA

---

*"I do not feel obliged to believe that the same God who
has endowed us with sense, reason, and intellect has
intended us to forgo their use."*

— *Galileo Galilei*

N OW THAT WE HAVE CONSIDERED the evolutionary history
of the orthodox dogma about God, we will consider several
significant consequences for the religion of Jesus. In particular we
will cast light on the dogma's effect upon the Jews, their traditional
monotheism, the words of Christ, Reason, and Christianity's relationship with
her parent Judaism. What we must emphasize first is the *source* of the theological
torment that fueled the tempest of erratic politics in post-Nicene Christendom.
More than anything else, at the heart of the burgeoning Trinitarianism's growing
pains was a deep conflict with Jewish monotheism. The emerging dogma of the
Father and Son's mutual and equal deity was understandably difficult to reconcile
with Judaism, especially since there existed no biblical record that the knowledge
of a profound update to the Mosaic tradition had been propagated amongst the
earliest disciples of Christ. As one professor has noted, "the attempts of the
'orthodox' to demonstrate the agreement of their dogma of two divine persons
with monotheism remained seriously uncertain and contradictory... The most
potent cause of all the difficulties, dilemma and sophistry of this situation was

the deficiency of the scriptural evidence."[893] Without direct scriptural support to substantiate this radical change, the Gentiles had turned to the polytheistic models of Greek philosophy, and extracted from them the most convenient terms to modify for their purposes. As we have already noted, the Cappadocian doctrine was seen as a compromise doctrine between the Arian and Sabellian positions; it was also a philosophical "fix" for the polytheistic quandary in which Athanasius had marooned the faith after Nicaea. Thus in the aftermath of 381 CE, orthodoxy found itself neither monotheistic nor polytheistic—it was somewhere in between. The Cappadocians had unapologetically borrowed from both the Jewish Bible and from the Greek religions to create the Trinity, as Gregory of Nyssa himself admitted: *"From the Jewish doctrine, then, the unity of the Divine nature has been retained: from Hellenism the distinction into hypostases.'*[894] As Wolfson observes, the fathers' concept of the Trinity was "a combination of Jewish monotheism and pagan polytheism, except that to them this combination was a good combination."[895] But now that the useful elements had been extracted from each religion, both Jewish monotheism and Greek polytheism were to be rejected, as the Cappadocians recommend:

> The Christian who combats polytheism has need of care lest in contending against Hellenism he should fall unconsciously into Judaism… Thus the mystery of the faith avoids equally the absurdity of Jewish monotheism, and that of heathen polytheism.[896]

What was this "Jewish monotheism" that so contrasted with the Trinity doctrine? If the pagans were teaching multiple Gods, and the Trinitarians were teaching multiple Persons in one God, then "Jewish monotheism" obviously taught only one Person in one God. Gregory confirms that just as the Trinity doctrine avoids polytheism, "neither does the statement harmonize with the Jewish dogma."[897] Though modern Trinitarians can be found painting the Trinity doctrine as "compatible with Jewish monotheism,"[898] the founders of

---

[893] Martin Werner, *The Formation of Christian Dogma* (Harper: New York, 1957), pp. 241-242.

[894] Gregory of Nyssa, *The Great Catechism*, I, 3.

[895] Wolfson, p. 362.

[896] Gregory of Nyssa, *The Great Catechism*, I, 1.

[897] Ibid., I, 3.

[898] Trinitarian John C. Merkle argues that "our Trinitarian perspective is compatible with Jewish monotheism," and for this understanding he cites the views of "the fourth and fifth-century framers of Trinitarian doctrine" (John C. Merkle, "Faith Transformed by Study and Friendship,"

orthodox Trinitarianism called the Jewish concept of God "heresy," "error," and "a profane view." For them, "the Jewish dogma is *destroyed*" by Trinitarian theology.[899] But what would the Jewish Jesus or the members of the New Testament community have thought of Gregory's opinion that Jewish monotheism was *"absurd"* and that the God of Judaism was to be avoided to the same degree as the gods of the pagans? As one professor reminds us:

> According to the NT witnesses, in the teaching of Jesus and the Apostles relative to the monotheism of the Old Testament and Judaism, there had been no element of change whatsoever. Mark 12:29 recorded the confirmation of Jesus himself, without any reservation, of the supreme monotheistic confession of faith of the Israelite religion in its complete form.[900]

The Trinitarian system authored by the Cappadocians, and still celebrated by the majority of Christians in the world today, is founded precisely upon the premise that Jewish monotheism was in error. But if scholars have not recognized any break from that historical religion in the teachings of Christ, and instead have identified his own public affirmation of it (Mark 12:28ff), what has the Cappadocian doctrine achieved but an insulting censure of Jesus? That, and a novel theology, which even now precariously inhabits the negative space between monotheism and polytheism; an undoubtedly tense and dangerous region which to this day remains impossible to chart.

Consequences for the Words of Jesus

The most noteworthy phrases from the Nicene Creed of 325 CE such as "very God of very God, begotten not made, one substance with the Father, incarnate" are strikingly non-biblical. Historically speaking, what the ancient creeds demonstrate is less of a "New Testament" standard for the faith and more a representation of how effectively philosophy had progressively encroached upon the Christian mind in the early centuries. The shocking effect is that later statements such as the Athanasian Creed (c. 500 CE) even project ideas that not only challenge Jewish monotheism, but directly contradict the precise words of Jesus.

Faith Transformed: Christian Encounters with Jews and Judaism (Collegeville: The Liturgical Press, 2003), p. 194).

[899] Gregory of Nyssa, *The Great Catechism*, 1, 3, emphasis added.

[900] Werner, p. 241.

The Athanasian Creed, not written by Athanasius himself of course (who died in 373 CE) but named in honor of him,[901] is still accepted by the Roman Catholic Church, Anglicans, Lutherans, and most liturgical Protestant denominations. The creed says about its tenets:

> Whosoever will be saved, before all things it is necessary that he hold the Catholic Faith. Which Faith except everyone do keep whole and undefiled, without doubt he shall perish everlastingly… This (Creed) is the Catholic Faith, which except a man believe faithfully and firmly, he cannot be saved.[902]

One would expect that if these statements truly represented the faith communicated to the Church by Jesus (the founder of Christianity), there would be some congruity with the Gospel record, with Jesus' own unrestricted preaching and dialogue. In other words, if the modern circles which maintain the Athanasian Creed are merely following Christ's lead in expecting true disciples to publicly confess these ideas, then Jesus should likewise have publicly demonstrated that he too kept the creed "whole and undefiled." Yet even a brief comparison yields notably incompatible results:

Athanasian Creed:
"And in this Trinity, no one is before or after, greater or less than the other"
Jesus:
"The Father is greater than I" (John 14:28b)

Athanasian Creed:
"Almighty is the Son"
Jesus:
"By myself I can do nothing" (John 5:30)

Athanasian Creed:
"We worship one God in Trinity"
Jesus:
"The true worshipers shall worship the Father" (John 4:23)

---

[901] George Ommanney, *A Critical Dissertation on the Athanasian Creed* (London: OUP, 1897), p. 404. See also Thomas Hartwell Home, *A Concise History and Analysis of the Athanasian Creed* (London: T. Cadell, Strand, 1834), p. 7.

[902] The Athanasian Creed, c. 500 CE.

Athanasian Creed:
"The Son is God"

Jesus:
"Father... You [are] the only true God" (John 17:1a, 3a)

Not only are the propositions demanded by the creed absent from the Gospel record, they appear to radically overstep Jesus' own confessions. If Christianity is to be defined as "following Christ," then how is it that these divergent creedal statements are beheld by the churches as being so fundamentally "Christian" that even one's very salvation is judged by personal and public devotion to these phrases?[903] The incredible truth is that this is only possible because popular Christianity is acutely disinterested in the words of Jesus. Trinitarian sources have comfortably acknowledged the fact that, despite hailing him as the central figure and founder of the faith, developed Christianity "centers not in the teachings of Jesus"[904] but it other's words *about him*. The Christian religion stands alone in this strange practice:

> While Buddhism and Islam are based primarily on the *teaching* of the Buddha and Mohammed, respectively, Christianity is based primarily on the *person* of Christ. Christianity is *not* belief in the teachings of Jesus, but what is taught *about* him... The appeal... 'to believe as Jesus believed,' rather than to believe in

---

[903] On the creed's promised damnation, some Trinitarians have admitted: "salvation may be obtained without a knowledge of the Athanasian Creed. Thousands and millions of Christians have gone to their graves, who have either never heard of it, or not understood it..." (Edward Burton, *Theological Works*, Vol. I (S. Collingwood, 1837), p. 283). Others have likewise admitted: "I do not believe the damnatory clauses in the Athanasian Creed" (Thomas Arnold, "Letter 185," in *Life and Correspondence*, Vol. 1 (London: George Woodfall and Son, 1844), p. 321). And another says: "I am ready to acknowledge, that, in my judgement, notwithstanding the authority of former times, our church would have acted more wisely and more consistently with its general principles of mildness and toleration, if it had not adopted the damnatory clauses of the Athanasian Creed. Though I firmly believe that the doctrines themselves of this creed are all founded in Scripture, I cannot but conceive it to be both unnecessary and presumptuous to say, that, 'except every one do keep them whole and undefiled, without doubt he shall perish everlastingly' (George P. Tomline, *Elements of Christian Theology*, Vol. 2 (London: Luke Hansard & Sons, 1815), p. 222). However, private opinion has not kept the Athanasian Creed off of the books. Despite the uneasiness among some bishops, when a serious effort was made by a major Pan-Anglican council to disown the Athanasian Creed or at least its damnatory clauses, the council voted to maintain the creed, "thus insisting that every minister of the denomination should be required still to subscribe to them" (Jabez Thomas Sunderland, *A Ministry of Twenty Years in Ann Arbor* (Ann Arbor: The Register Pub. Co., 1893), p. 6).

[904] James Kennedy, "How I Know Jesus is God," *Truths that Transform*. James Kennedy Ministries, 11 November, 1998. Web. 15 December 2015.

Jesus, is a dramatic transformation of the fundamental nature of Christianity.[905]

As it has been repeatedly admitted, Christianity has been more concerned with what has been taught "about Jesus." Indeed, as respected Lutheran theologian Hans Schwarz observes: "It is significant that none of the creedal statements contains sayings of Jesus, but rather are about him. This means that they are not a continuation of the proclamation of Jesus but rather a response to him."[906]

Beneath the custody of the Catholic creeds the teachings of Christ drift dangerously towards mystery and abstraction: Jesus means not what he says, his methods are lacking and underdeveloped, his sayings are forced to lie in miserable wait for later philosophers to infuse them with their fullest sense. The consequences for Christ's beloved words are profound, but this is not, unfortunately, the only casualty of the orthodox system.

Consequences for Reason

Facts must be intelligible. Reason is defined as "the thing which makes some fact intelligible," and as "the power of the mind to form a conclusion by thinking logically."[907] Of course, reason is often the first thing jettisoned in discussions about the Trinity. As Luther recommended: "this [doctrine], as well as every other article of faith, must not be based upon reason."[908] Other Reformers like Philip Melanchthon have likewise suggested that Christians should *skip* the debate over God altogether, saying "it is better to adore the mysteries of the Deity than to investigate them."[909] Amongst the general population this advice seems widely taken. Something described as "Faith" has gained preference over something pejoratively labeled "human" reason.

This lauding of "faith" over reason is a tradition which Christian academics have long utilized as both a means of bridling the wandering curiosity of the masses, and justifying the neglect of personal study and conviction. Origen in the third century explained that the idea of "faith" was seen by the theologians as "useful for the multitude, and that we admittedly teach those who cannot

---

[905] Harold Brown, *Heresies* (Peabody, MA: Hendrickson, 1984), p. 13.

[906] Hans Schwarz, *The Christian Church: Biblical Origin, Historical Transformation, and Potential for the Future* (Minneapolis: Augsburg Publishing House, 1982), pp. 87-88.

[907] See "Reasoning," Merriam-Webster's Dictionary. 2015. Web. 12 November 2014.

[908] See Luther, *Complete Sermons of Martin Luther*, Vol. 2, pp. 406-407.

[909] Wilhelm Pauck, *Melanchthon and Bucer* (London: The Westminster Press, 1969), pp. 9-10.

abandon everything and pursue a study of rational arguments to believe without thinking out their reasons."[910] Thus Basil likewise prescribed, "Let us Christians prefer the simplicity of our faith to the demonstrations of human reason."[911]

Christian leadership has certainly made the misleading proposition of "just believing" the creedal statements more attractive for the layman. The acceptance of statements without question is transformed by them from something foolish into something morally praiseworthy. Indeed, Melanchthon even attributed such practice to the Apostles, applauding Paul, since he did not "philosophize about the mysteries of the Trinity [and] the mode of the Incarnation."[912] Of course, this praise assumes Paul actually believed in the Trinity. But is it not more reasonable to conclude that, given the historical context in which Paul preached, he did not mention much less philosophize about the Trinity and the Incarnation because he had simply never heard of them?

The biblical model for "faith" does not contradict reason. The beliefs of the Apostles were evidently arrived at, not by their subsuming of arguments which had not been thoroughly tested, but by *destroy[ing] arguments and every lofty opinion raised against the knowledge of God*" (2 Cor 10:5). The biblical word for "faith" (Greek: *pistis*) actually describes a "*conviction* of the truth of anything."[913] Bullinger defines it as "firm persuasion."[914] One cannot have such conviction of any proposition unless it be firmly believed, and of course no proposition can be firmly believed unless the proposition is actually understood.

At this the Trinitarian will often protest, "You're using *human* reason to approach the truth about God; the truth of the Trinity doctrine is far beyond our limited minds." Here, lest normal modes of thinking immediately tarnish the philosophy, it is loudly asserted that there exists a vast difference between human and divine capacities to come to a conclusion about what is true. But is man's reason not equipped by God himself? Is it not a tool by which God expects him to discover the truth in a world of lies, and so be saved? In Isaiah, God instructs his people, "*Come now, and let us reason together*" (Is 1:18a). Both God's and man's reason are presented as operating on the same playing field, working together towards the conviction of a reality common to both parties.

---

[910] Origen, *Against Celsus*, 1, 10.

[911] Basil of Caesarea, quoted in Freeman, *Closing of the Western Mind*, p. 316.

[912] Ibid.

[913] Joseph Henry Thayer, *The New Thayer's Greek-English Lexicon of the New Testament* (Lafayette: Associated Publishers and Authors, 1979), emphasis added.

[914] E. W. Bullinger, *A Critical Lexicon and Concordance to the English and Greek New Testament* (London: Samuel Bagster and Sons Ltd., 1971).

Indeed, truth is not relative for anyone. Thus we continue with our challenge: how may the truth (God's truth or man's truth—there is no difference) of any proposition be believed if the proposition itself is not even comprehensible?

Beloved American pastor A. W. Tozer reveals that any hope of understanding the developed Trinitarian propositions "must remain forever futile," and that Christian churches, "without pretending to understand" their profession, nevertheless perpetuate calls for its universal acceptance.[915]   The orthodox creeds have not then communicated any rational belief, but are only sets of obtuse language approved for recitation. We must then ask ourselves: Can we afford to continue teaching Christians empty language?   Lest the Christian faith be reduced to a belief in nothing, that language must be comprehended.

For example, if one were asked to firmly believe in the proposition: "*ab abusu ad usum non valet consequentia*," it would be impossible to assent to its truth unless one understood Latin. Even if a chimpanzee were to write out perfectly the practiced English sentence: "*Rights abused are still rights*," we could not say that he had any true belief in it. No, one cannot truly affirm trained phrases if those phrases have for him no intelligible meaning.

In response to the Trinitarian argument that the doctrine of the Trinity is to be believed, not because it is logically cogent, but because it is a "revelation" from God,[916] we are obliged to assert that all "revelation" must be intelligible. What is a thing disclosed and undisclosed simultaneously? If one were to relay a secret to a trusted companion, but in a letter written in a language the companion did not understand, could that really qualify as a "revelation"? It cannot, for just as the companion did not know the secret before he received the letter, neither did he know it afterwards. We must acknowledge that there are mysterious things about the God of the Bible, and the responsible Christian does not presume to understand everything about him. But with regard to the Trinity dogma, we are not dealing with everything about God; we are dealing with alleged "revelations" about him. We cannot ultimately say that the Trinitarian creeds fit the bill of real, much less divine, *disclosures* as they really yield no truly comprehensible propositions.

That the creedal proposals of orthodoxy are unintelligible and self-contradictory is readily demonstrated. In their book *Answers to Tough Questions*,

---

[915] A. W. Tozer, *The Knowledge of the Holy* (New York: HarperOne, 1961), pp. 17-18, 23.
[916] Erickson, *Christian Theology*, p. 367.

Trinitarians Josh McDowell and Don Stewart respond to skeptics about presumed contradictions in the Bible:

> What constitutes a contradiction? The law of non-contradiction, which is the basis of all logical thinking, states that a thing cannot be both A and non-A at the same time. In other words, it cannot be both raining and not raining at the same time. If one can demonstrate a violation of this principle from Scripture, then and only then can he prove a contradiction.

McDowell and Stewart are correct when they say that it is contradictory to claim that anything can be *something* and *not-something* at the same time and in the same way. But shouldn't this principle also apply to the historical Jesus? Is he somehow exempt from the strictures of reason? The creedal propositions about him are simply brimming with violations of the law of non-contradiction: The one person of Jesus is said to be both human in regard to nature, and non-human in regard to nature. He is both omniscient and non-omniscient, temptable and non-temptable, mortal and immortal. According to the law cited by McDowell and Stewart, these are contradictions, and a contradiction is, of course, a statement which is always false.

The infamous Athanasian Creed further encapsulates and exemplifies these problems. It staunchly advises (rather, commands) that all must "believe and confess" that Jesus "is God and man," and furthermore that the one God is "three persons, coeternal and coequal."[917] But is this proposition regarding the threeness of God inherently contradictory as well? Many, including the Cappadocian Fathers, have sought tirelessly to free the dogma from the contradiction of saying that *one thing is three things*. They have therefore posited that "God" is "one *substance* and three *hypostases*." Here there are not three X's in one X, but three X's in one Y. Modern evangelicals have framed this idea as "one What and three Who's." It is admitted that a claim of "one Who" and "three Who's" would be contradictory, but by transforming the one God into a "What," they believe they have circumvented violations of logic.[918] And so, to

---

[917] Athanasian Creed, c. 500 CE.

[918] Prominent Trinitarian apologist James R. White emphasizes his belief in the mysterious substantive nature of God's being which is apparently capable of supporting three distinct personalities: "Within the one Being that is God, there exists eternally three coequal and coeternal persons, namely, the Father, the Son, and the Holy Spirit... Note immediately we are not saying there are three Beings that are one being, or three persons that are one person. Such would be

preserve dogma, "God" is turned into an abstraction, a substance, an *it*. In this system, "God" is explicitly *not a person*; "God" is an essence shared by three different Persons. As C. S. Lewis writes, "We must remind ourselves that Christian theology *does not believe God to be a person*... it believes him to be something very different from a person."[919] But the Trinitarian Christians are saying nothing new; the Greek philosophers had long acknowledged a transcendent, abstract, and "Unknown God." Anglican bishop Christopher Wright warns us, however, of an "abstract" or "philosophical monotheism," and reveals the danger in defining "God" as an abstract "divinity" or "being":

> A philosophical monotheism that leaves the divine reality
> unnamed and characterless is alien (both unknown and
> hostile) to the OT faith... The 'theos' at the center thus
> becomes abstract, impersonal, and finally ineffable (*nothing
> at all* can be said about him/her/it).[920]

The 'theos' at the center of this formula "one God (theos) and three persons (hypostases)" is certainly an abstraction. Trinitarians will doubtless protest that they have not left the divine reality "nameless"; in fact, they might say, this God is still named "Yahweh," or they might say that this God actually has *three* names. But the problem for the Trinitarian lies in how the Scriptures expect us to understand not simply "God" but the unique "Yahweh" of the Bible. In the Hebrew Scriptures, Yahweh is one to one equal with the true God: *"Yahweh is God"* (Ps 118:27). Trinitarians may argue that the reality described by the word "God" indicates a substance or a What, but the same cannot be said for the word "Yahweh," because this is a personal name: *"I am Yahweh, that is my name"* (Is 42:8); *"This is my name forever, the name you shall call me from generation to generation"* (Ex 3:15). We are to both *"know that Yahweh is God"* (Ps 118:27), and that he is also *"our God,"* (Deut 6:4). However, if the name "Yahweh" is, as many Trinitarians assert, simply the name used for *all three* of

---

self-contradictory. I emphasize this because, most often, this is the misrepresentation of the doctrine that is commonly found in the literature of various religions that deny the Trinity." Paraphrasing the so-described "wonderfully simple and clear" teaching of evangelical Hank Hanegraaff, White agrees that, "When speaking of the Trinity, we need to realize that we are talking about one *what* and three *who's*. The one *what* is the Being or essence of God; the three *who's* are the Father, Son, and Spirit. We dare not mix up the *what's* and *who's* regarding the Trinity" (James R. White, *The Forgotten Trinity: Recovering the Heart of Christian Belief* (Minneapolis: Bethany House Publishers, 1998), pp. 26-27).

[919] C. S. Lewis, *Christian Reflections*, p. 79.

[920] Christopher J. H. Wright, *Deuteronomy* (Grand Rapids: Baker Books, 2012 [1996]), 9, emphasis added. Source credit: Carlos Xavier (http://thehumanjesus.org).

the persons of the Trinity together, then "Yahweh" is proven to be not the name of a person in Trinitarianism but the name of a collection, or an *it*. As Christopher Wright explains, however, "Yahweh is not the brand name of a cosmic corporation. He is one God, our God, and Yahweh is his personal name."[921]   The philosophical definition of "God" as not an individual personality but a "being" or a "What" contravenes sharply with the biblical teaching, which not only emphasizes the "dynamic *personhood* of 'Yahweh our God' " but makes confession of that personhood a requisite part of saving faith.[922]   The world's enlightenment to the matchless *personality* of the Jewish God was without doubt the aim of both Jesus and his Apostles. We must not forget that:

> Paul labored in Athens to move his Greek audience away from belief in God as a "What" to belief in the God of Abraham and Isaac and Jacob who is a "Who," a Person! Note the subtle approach of Paul: "*What* you worship but do not know, I am now proclaiming to you: The God *who* made the world and everything in it" (Acts 17:23, 24). It is a considerable irony that leading proponents of "orthodoxy" today betray the very same tendency which Paul strove to correct when they inform the Bible-searching public that "God is one What in three Who's." Such a definition of God is not from Scripture at all, but from the world of Middle Platonism. It is Greek philosophy which promotes God as a "What," and it is contemporary fundamentalism which (often heavy-handedly) requires church members to acknowledge the "one What" presented as what they call the "Triune God." That God was not known to Jesus or Paul.[923]

Indeed, the God of the Bible is not the untouchable principle of Platonism. Though C. S. Lewis denied that this God is a person, Trinitarian Walter Martin admits:

> This Almighty Person performs acts that only a personality is capable of: God hears (Exodus 2:24); God sees (Genesis 1:4); God creates (Genesis 1:1); God knows (2 Timothy 2:19;

---

[921] Ibid.

[922] Ibid., emphasis added.

[923] Anthony F. Buzzard, "Keys Which Unlock the Bible," *Focus on the Kingdom*, No. 3, Vol. 4 (McDonough: Restoration Fellowship, 2001), p. 3.

Jeremiah 29:11); God has a will (1 John 2:17); God is a cognizant reflectable ego, i.e., a personal being—"I am that I am" (Exodus 3:14; Genesis 17:1). This is the God of Christianity, an omnipotent, omniscient, and omnipresent Personality, who manifests every attribute of personality.[924]

As the great B. B. Warfield confirmed, the teaching of the Old Testament, the teaching which composed the solid theological foundation for the Jewish Jesus and his disciples, was not simply that there is one "God," but that "the God of all the earth is one person."[925]

Another question arises when considering this common evangelical formula: what if the "three Whos and one What" proposition was reversed? Could one "Who" also contain three "What's"? The Trinitarian must also believe this is the case; the one person of Jesus is said to contain both human and divine substances.[926] As Augustine affirmed, the second member of the Trinity performed "a perfect assumption of the human substance."[927] Thus in the current Trinitarian Godhead there is not really "one what and three who's," but actually "*two* what's and three who's" (two natures or substances and three Persons). Needless to say, the *personality* of the biblical God seems ever lost in the fray, even dissolved.

Here it will of course be protested that the doctrine of the Trinity is intended to be a *mystery,* that the statements about God being three and one are to be believed and confessed, not understood. But again, no proposition can be truly assented to unless it is understood. Propositions like the Athanasian Creed

---

[924] Walter Martin, quoted by Ron Rhodes, *The Challenge of the Cults and New Religions* (Grand Rapids: Zondervan, 2001), p. 125.

[925] B. B. Warfield, "The Spirit of God in the Old Testament," *The Works of Benjamin B. Warfield* (New York: OUP, 1932), p. 127. Some Trinitarian theologians have been uncomfortable with accepting "God" as an abstraction and have attempted to resist the evangelical formula exemplified by White, Hanegraaff, and others. Reformed theologian Cornelius Van Til was so bothered by this idea that he asserted that the divine essence itself must somehow be personal, that there must be a sense in which God is one Person. But regarding exactly how the three Persons can be one Person without falling into Modalism, Van Til predictably claims "this is a mystery beyond our comprehension" (John M. Frame, *Cornelius Van Til: An Analysis of His Thought* (Phillipsberg: P & R Publishing, 1995), pp. 67-69).

[926] "Christ is one in substance (homoousios) with the Father in regard to his divine nature, and one in substance with humanity in regard to his human nature" (Kenneth Samples, "Thinking About the Incarnation: The Divine Word Became Flesh," Reasons to Believe. 1 October 2000. Web. 10 September 2014. <http://www.reasons.org/articles/thinking-about-the-incarnation-the-divine-word-became-flesh>.

[927] Augustine, *Sermo.*, 187, 3.

are consistently inconsistent, breaking their own ideological rules without qualification so as to make real faith (a firm conviction of the truth) practically impossible. For example, the Creed states:

> The Father eternal, the Son eternal, and the Holy Spirit eternal... And yet they are not three eternals but one eternal.

> The Father is almighty, the Son is almighty, and the Holy Spirit almighty...And yet they are not three almighties, but one almighty.

> So the Father is God, the Son is God, and the Holy Spirit is God... And yet they are not three Gods, but one God.

> So likewise the Father is Lord, the Son Lord, and the Holy Spirit Lord... And yet they are not three Lords but one Lord.

> For like as we are compelled by the Christian verity to acknowledge every Person by himself [is] God and Lord.[928]

In these statements, while there is a regular distinction presented between the members of the Godhead, we are also to believe that there is a certain unity amongst them that prohibits tri-theism. The proposition being made here is that adding up their qualities (eternality, almightiness, etc.) ultimately produces not three of those things, but only one. Yet the creed dramatically breaks its own rules when it comes to personhood. This is inconsistent at best: if there are "three Persons," why is there not ultimately "one Person?" If we look closely at the last line of the excerpt, each member is said to be "God" and "Lord" in a personal sense. So if there are not three Gods, but one God, there should not be three Persons, *but one Person*. Of course, if the creed properly followed its own model, the Trinity would prove to be Sabellianism. If not Sabellianism, then tri-theism; the three who are God, if not the same Person, are in fact three Gods. But if the creed is to be understood as presenting neither tri-theism nor Sabellianism, then we must conclude that its supporters really have no idea what it means. A great theologian from Harvard once wrote:

---

[928] Athanasian Creed, c. 500 CE.

> In the history of other departments of science we find abundant errors and extravagances; but orthodox theology seems to have been the peculiar region of words without meaning; of doctrines confessedly false in their proper sense, and explained in no other; of the most portentous absurdities put forward as truths of the highest import; and of contradictory propositions thrown together without an attempt to reconcile them. A main error running through the whole system, as well as other systems of false philosophy, is that words... when they express to human reason only an absurdity, they may still be significant of high mystery or a hidden truth, and are to be believed without being understood.[929]

Rather than finding this problematic, however, Tozer ultimately concludes, "The fact that it cannot be satisfactorily explained, instead of being against it, is in its favor."[930] In other words, the doctrine is protected from too much critical attention by its ability to swiftly dash behind an esoteric veil of "mystery." Whenever rational objections are brought against it, they may be summarily dismissed without potentially costly confrontation. Of course, this evasion is accomplished by its supremely varnished status, not the virtue of its proofs.

Basil, the Cappadocian Father referred to by the Catholic Church as "the revealer of heavenly mysteries," urges us to simply have "faith" that his system is true. He argues that just because each of the Persons of the Trinity can be counted individually, that does not mean that "an ignorant arithmetic could carry us away to the idea of a plurality of gods. Count if you must, but you must not by counting do damage to the faith!"[931] The Persons of Basil's Trinity are numbered then, but their number is ultimately meaningless. We wonder what then, if anything, Basil can really be credited with "revealing"? The Cappadocians had, after all, declared God to be "unknowable" in order to protect the Trinity doctrine from prying minds. But can the idea that God is unable to be known exist alongside the idea that God *is* a "Trinity"? In other words, if God really is fundamentally unknowable, then how could the Cappadocians ever make the various positive statements about God that they

---

[929] Andrews Norton, *A Statement of Reasons for Not Believing the Doctrines of Trinitarians* (Boston: Hilliard, Gray, and Co., 1833), pp. 78-79.

[930] Tozer, *The Knowledge of the Holy*, pp. 17-18, 23.

[931] Basil of Caesarea, *The Book of St. Basil on the Spirit*, Ch. XVIII, 44.

did? While they had hoped that establishing God's complete ineffability would shield the Trinity, the claim actually nullified their authority to lay down doctrine at all. It furthermore damaged the testimony and usefulness of the Bible, in which God had so often revealed himself.[932]

The Christ of dogma has remained stubbornly obtuse. The regularly expanding and contracting interpretations of the ancient creedal statements has brought the faith no closer to ecumenical resolution. What is the modern Christian to do with these ancient phrases which have yet to prove themselves useful in the Christian life? As one Baptist scholar has wondered, "In the view of the difficulty of the subject and the great amount of effort expended to maintain this doctrine, we may well ask ourselves what might justify all this trouble?"[933] A Catholic scholar also presses the question:

> Can we simply repeat classical formulae? Jesus Christ, the one—divine—person in two natures? God himself—one nature in three persons? Even on the Catholic side this is now felt to be problematical, however much the Chalcedonian "fully God—fully Man" is accepted as a 'waymark' of any Christological thought.[934]

Without doubt, the matter of Christ remains largely unsettled. Dr. Hick recognized that none of the Christological debates we have considered "have succeeded in squaring the circle by making intelligible the claim that one who was genuinely and unambiguously a man was also genuinely and unambiguously God.[935] Many have outwardly consigned themselves to the incomprehensible, but as Trinitarian John Polkinghorne acknowledges, "Living with unresolved paradox is not a comfortable situation."[936] The question is, if it were possible to extract oneself from unnecessary conflict with the content of the Bible, would the mental and spiritual freedom provided be counted valuable enough to forsake the comfortable boundaries of religious tradition? How much does the common Christian really care about resolving irrationality within his beliefs?

---

[932] Contrary to the Cappadocian assertion that God is "unknowable," the New Testament claims that Jesus Christ "*has made him known*" (Jn 1:18 NIV, ESV), and the Apostles heartily affirm that they "*know that the Son of God has come and has given us understanding, so that we may know him who is true*" (1 Jn 5:20a).

[933] Erickson, *God in Three Persons*, p. 12.

[934] Kuschel, p. 32.

[935] N. F. Gier, *God, Reason, and the Evangelicals: Case Against Evangelical Rationalism* (Lanham: Rowman & Littlefield, 1986), p. 3.

[936] Ibid.

Of course, there have been those recent apologists who have passionately labored to explicate the creeds in a way that avoids contradiction.[937] But what if the creeds present no intelligible ideas to begin with? It seems better to admit, with the other Trinitarians, that the dogma is by nature *impossible*. Some Trinitarians have even reveled in that fact, even holding it as evidence of its divine origin. Sir Thomas Browne once wrote, "I can answer all the objections of Satan and my rebellious reason with that odd resolution I learned from Tertullian, '*Certum est quia impossibile est*' (it is certain because it is impossible)."[938] To this, the Archbishop Tilloston prudently responded: "I know not what some men may find in themselves; but I must freely acknowledge that I could never yet attain to that bold and hardy degree of faith as to believe anything for this reason, because it was impossible."[939] Still, some contemporary apologists seem hesitant to concede the doctrine's impossibility:

> At first, some may look at this teaching and be confused by it. How can God be three persons in one God? This is a good question because it is a bit difficult to grasp. But that is what we would expect, isn't it, when we encounter God? ... This is not unreasonable. However, we must not make the mistake of saying something as ridiculous as, "It doesn't make sense. Therefore it isn't true."[940]

But the matter is not simply "difficult to grasp," as if more study or practice could forge some easier way; the Catholic Church has already labored through a thousand years of blood-drenched cogitation and came no closer than we are today. The above apologist claims that something which obviously "doesn't make sense" can still be "true." But if we are unable to comprehend a proposition how can we assent to it? We do, of course, have a word for things that don't make any sense: *nonsense*. As noted earlier, it should not be enough for

---

[937] "Since the revival of analytic philosophy of religion in the 1960s, many Christian philosophers have pursued what is now called analytic theology, in which central religious doctrines are given formulations which are precise, and it is hoped self-consistent and otherwise defensible... these recent 'rational reconstructions' of the Trinity doctrine... centrally employ concepts from contemporary analytic metaphysics, logic, and epistemology" (Dale Tuggy, "Trinity," *Stanford Encyclopedia of Philosophy*, 2009). The efforts of contemporary thinkers to draw the Trinity out of the realm of mystery has yet to produce a methodology which has proven ecumenically satisfying.

[938] Thomas Browne, *Religio Medici*, Sect. 9, 10, 12; in *Works*, Vol. 2, p. 332.

[939] John Tilloston, *Ser.* 194, in *Works*, Vol. 10, 180.

[940] Matt Slick, "The Trinity Makes No Sense. It Isn't Logical," *Christian Apologetics and Research Ministry*. Web. 5 May 2013. <http://carm.org/trinity-makes-no-sense-it-isnt-logical>.

Christians to merely repeat nonsensical formulae, to prop up a beloved sophistry. Has the endless speculation of theologians really soothed the concerns of the laity so much that statements don't even need to be understood before they are defended to the death, before other devoted Christians are ostracized or worse for their curiosity about them?

Within established Trinitarianism, the idea of Jesus is perhaps apprehensible by trained theologians to some shallow degree, but must ultimately be considered unintelligible because the triune system to which he belongs is admittedly inconceivable.[941]   As prominent Trinitarian Millard Erickson summarizes: "In the final analysis, the Trinity is incomprehensible."[942] Other major evangelicals report the very same conclusion: "Even with all the discussion and delineation that we attempt in relation to the Trinity," says Professor Ryrie, "we must acknowledge that it is in the final analysis a mystery."[943] Interestingly, though evangelical Trinitarians trumpet a call for every man to enter into a "personal relationship" with God or Jesus, how successful can they expect the common Christian to be at intimately relating to an object which is fundamentally unrelatable?   As Trinitarian theologian Dr. John Hey recommends, it would tend to reason and honesty if Trinitarians "were industrious on all occasions to represent our own doctrine of the Trinity as wholly unintelligible."[944]

Despite the admission of inscrutability, the vast energy required by the cruel mental argument of the Trinity continues to be expended in the most educated circles, while the unqualified masses hardly hope to join them. Like the initiated Gnostic philosophers, today's Trinitarian theologians remain the clever custodians of the obscure operation of the divine, while the majority of laymen are left to wonder. Any serious contemplation of the complex nature of Jesus and the bewildering multiplied identity of God has been left to the ultra-sophisticated. As Freeman notes, orthodox Christianity really has "much in common with these cults, not in the least the idea that a priestly elite had privileged access to the cult's secrets and the absolute right to interpret them for

---

[941] "And so one who severely studies the depths of the mystery, receives secretly in his spirit, indeed, a moderate amount of apprehension of the doctrine of God's nature, yet he is unable to explain clearly in words the ineffable depth of this mystery" (Greogry of Nyssa, *The Great Catechisim*, 1, 3).

[942] Erickson, *Christian Theology,* p. 363.

[943] Ryrie, *Basic Theology*, p. 61.

[944] John Hey, *Lectures in Divinity Delivered in the University of Cambridge,* Vol. 2 (Los Angeles: HardPress, 2013), p. 235.

others."[945]   There has always been an incentive for religious authorities to emphasize "mystery." Harnack observed that the Trinitarian theology promoted by the orthodox party could only be reached by "those who had been trained in philosophical explanations," and ultimately realized that:

> The establishing of Logos Christology within the rule of faith was equivalent for the great mass of Christians to the setting up of a mystery... But as soon as religion expresses the loftiest contents of its creed in formulas which must remain mysterious and unintelligible to the great mass of its adherents, those adherents come under guardians... they are dependent on the theologians, who, as professors of the mysterious, alone understand and are capable of interpreting and practically applying the creed.   The necessary consequence of this development was that the mysterious creed, being no longer in a position practically to control life, was superseded by the authority of the Church... [the result of this system] tranquilized the minds of the devout...[946]

Despite theological authorities appearing to possess some coveted insight into the Trinity, when it comes to truly grasping the doctrine's propositions, we nevertheless encounter the same miserable rational frustration amongst even amongst the most educated. One Catholic scholar has humbly admitted his own difficulty with the doctrine handed down by the ancient saints, a system which he says may have "the *form* of a logical system" but also bears:

> an essential weakness [which] lies in the flimsiness of its foundation... The speculations of Saint Thomas [Aquinas] on the Trinity—the mystery of a God who united three persons in one essence... had upon me the effect of a huge logomachy [a fight about words].   Instead of enriching my mind, these speculations left, as it were, a void, and their total effect was only to add to my inner confusion and distress concerning the invisible object of faith.[947]

---

[945] Freeman, *Closing of the Western Mind,* p. 71.

[946] Adolf Harnack, *History of Dogma*, Vol. 3 (Boston: Little, Brown and Company, 1907), pp. 2-3.

[947] Francesco Turvasi, *The Condemnation of Alfred Loisy and the Historical Method* (Rome: Storia E Letteratura, 1979), p. 1, emphasis added.

Popular Trinitarian author and apologist Lee Strobel writes, "theologians can come up with explanations that seem to make sense, even though they might not be able to explain every nuance."[948] The problem is that these Trinitarian "explanations" only *seem* to make sense. Strobel confronts his doctrine's difficulty in reconciling a man who is "fully God" but who exhibits a lack of fully divine attributes in the Gospel accounts: "On the surface these issues seem to suggest that Jesus doesn't resemble the sketch of God. Nevertheless, I've learned over the years that initial impressions can be deceiving."[949] Yes, first impressions can be deceiving, but so can theological explanations which *seem* to make sense. Strobel continues, "Let's admit it: the Bible itself seems to argue against Jesus being God."[950] Of course for Strobel, enough is inferred in what the Bible does *not* say to overpower what it actually does say. But here we must continuously ask, "what might justify all this trouble?"[951] Is the biblical data about God and Jesus really so abstruse? Is there really no other way to approach the Savior and his God without falling headlong into ineffability?

Tragically, the Trinitarian movement of the fourth century had, in the end, not only eschewed reason as an exegetical tool; it had effectively brought about the eradication of Christian theology itself. No longer were Christians allowed to search out new and possibly better interpretations of the data, to discover the God of the Bible for themselves. That work had already been done for them. Thus the Bishop of Melitene confessed to Emperor Leo I, "We uphold the Nicene creed but avoid difficult questions beyond human grasp. Clever theologians soon become heretics."[952] But asking the difficult questions is a fundamental part of theology. In our own time, Christianity's hesitancy to question continues to create a barrier against other potentially sound interpretations of the Bible which might prove more satisfying. But modern scholarship has already severely chipped away at this wall. Indeed, all of the aforementioned difficulty will soon appear tragically unnecessary in light of the abundant biblical information and the Jewish worldview which produced it.

---

948 Lee Strobel, *The Case For Christ: A Journalist's Personal Investigation of the Evidence for Jesus* (Grand Rapids: Zondervan, 1998), p. 160.
949 Ibid., p. 156.
950 Ibid., p. 158.
951 Erickson, p. 12.
952 Bishop of Melitene, quoted by Henry Chadwick in *The Church in Ancient Society* (Oxford: OUP, 2001), p. 591.

Consequences for Judaism and the Jewish God

It is important here to take notice of the declining relationships between orthodox Christianity, Judaism, and Jewish-Christianity of the Roman era. Historically, the so-called "parting of the ways" between Christianity and Judaism has been draped in shadows. Scholars have long attempted to pinpoint exactly when "Judaism" and "Christianity" separated into completely different, antagonistic religions. The problem has been in explaining how a religious movement whose original founders were all committed Jews could ever come to view Jews as mortal enemies. At fault for the thick fog surrounding this question has been the pre-programmed assumption that "Christianity" is fundamentally associated with a belief in Christ as a spiritual being. Since the deity of Christ is so inherently contrary to Jewish monotheism, and so allegedly fundamental to Christianity, one automatically expects that their separation must have been more or less immediate. However, scholars now agree that the "parting of the ways" actually took much longer than previously thought.

We have seen how "Catholic" Christianity began to diverge from its roots in Jewish thought in the second century, or at the rise of the Logos Christology amongst the Gentiles. But for centuries afterward Judaism and Christianity were still inextricably linked: Jewish-Christians were still attending synagogues alongside their fellow Jews, and Gentile Christians were still being cautioned by their more segregationist leaders against synagogue attendance and participation in Jewish festivals, even into *the fourth century*.[953] As Dunn observes:

> This clearly indicates that through the first three to four centuries, what we might call "ordinary Christians" did not see Christianity and Judaism as two separate, far less opposed religions. Rather, the position was more like what is common in the days of denominational Christianity... it was the Christian leadership [the Church Fathers] which considered it necessary to press for a much clearer and sharper divide... An appropriate question, however, is whether it was the Christian leadership or the "ordinary Christians" who were being truer to the heritage of first-century Christianity.[954]

---

[953] See James Dunn, *Neither Jew Nor Greek: A Contested Identity* (Grand Rapids: Eerdmans, 2015), pp. 18-19.
[954] Ibid., pp. 19-20.

Christianity had indeed already thrived for more than three hundred years before the final act of separation occurred, that is, when Jesus became God. Before then Jesus might have been little more than another sectarian nuisance to rabbinical Judaism, a failed messiah whose followers might be ridiculed, even hated, but could still be called Jews. But once the homoousian finally settled into acceptance, it became clear that the Jewish world could have absolutely nothing to do with Jesus or his followers, as long as his followers made acknowledgment of his divine nature a requisite part of Christian fellowship and identity. Likewise the Jews were forced to narrow their own self-definition on this issue, and quickly redefined Judaism as "not Jesus." The Jewish-Christians, like the Nazarenes and Ebionites who had always accepted Jesus as Messiah, but could never accept the homoousian, were caught in the middle. As one New Testament scholar has noted:

> Jewish people who remained in the Jewish community could not hail Jesus as God because this would infringe monotheism... Jesus was now a figure so elevated that observant Jews such as Jesus of Nazareth and the first apostles could not believe in him. The consequences of this for Christian belief are more serious than they are usually taken to be.[955]

Truly, the deity of Christ closed the door firmly on the Jewish world of Jesus, and it would be paid less and less attention until even the earliest Palestinian Jesus communities were left to tragically dissolve in isolation. Nicaea's legacy had made it obvious that there was now nothing within the Jewish matrix useful for the Christian life. Indeed, as A. D. Crown confirms, "the work of the Council of Nicaea must be seen as the parting of the ways for Judaism and Christianity."[956]

It was at this time that conditions rapidly began to deteriorate for Jews living in the Roman Empire "because of Christian theological dogmas that fueled an antipathy towards Judaism and things Jewish."[957] The eventual passage of Church and State codified ordinances such as the Justinian Code would not only

---

[955] Maurice Casey, *From Jewish Prophet to Gentile God: The Origins and Development of New Testament Christology* (Louisville: Westminster John Knox Press, 1991), p. 158.

[956] A. D. Crown, "Judaism and Christianity: The Parting of the Ways", in A.J. Avery-Peck et al., eds., *When Judaism and Christianity Began* (Leiden: Brill, 2004), p. 561.

[957] W. D. Davies, Louis Finkelstein, *The Cambridge History of Judaism,* Vol. 4 (Cambridge: CUP, 1984), p. 32

prohibit Jewish worship like the recitation of Jesus' own *Shema* confession,[958] but would strip away even the most basic of civil rights.[959] It would be negligent to ignore the rampant and penetrating anti-Semitism of many of the Christian forerunners and the influence their prejudices may have had upon their theological preferences. The anti-Jewish predilections of key figures such as Constantine and Athanasius were emblematic of Gentile theologians of the Roman era. The proto-orthodox party took great pride in their presentation not of a natural extension of Judaism but of a "sharp break with the past."[960] Athanasius industriously "removed from Christology every trace of Judaism,"[961] and applied "Jewishness" to his opponents as a sort of villainous moniker to discredit their positions.[962] There was an active push to separate Christians from the unique God of the Jews. As one professor so aptly notes:

> the real thrust of the Cappadocian doctrine was to differentiate the Christian "Godhead," which now incorporated Jesus and the Holy Spirit, from the monolithic God worshiped by Jews, radical Arians, and, later on, by Muslims, Unitarians, Bahais, and others... Christians who accepted this triune God, distributed over three Persons, no longer shared Jehovah with their Jewish forebears or the Supreme Being with their pagan neighbors, nor could Jews or pagans claim to believe in the same God as that worshiped by the Christians. Doctrinally, this is the point at which Christianity breaks decisively with its parent faith and with other forms of monotheism.[963]

The passionate rejection of the Jewish God by the Church Fathers continued with the leaders of the Reformation in the 16th century. The explicit and wanton anti-Semitism that thrived in the Reformation is an often-neglected

---

[958] See Mark 12:29

[959] See *"Corpus Juris Civilus," The Civil Law.* English translation (from Latin editions earlier than that of Mommsen and Krueger) by S.P. Scott, 1932. <http://www.constitution.org/sps/sps.htm>.

[960] Rubenstein, p. 74.

[961] Richard Gottheil, Louis Ginzberg, "Athanasius," *Jewish Encyclopedia.* 1906. Web. 21 May 2014.

[962] Christine Shepardson, *Anti-Judaism and Christian Orthodoxy: Ephrem's Hymns in Fourth-century Syria* (Washington D.C.: The Catholic University of America Press, 2008), p. 119. Around 340 CE, Athanasius argued that "the 'Jewish' beliefs and behaviour of the Arians proves that they are, in fact, Jews" and he "elaborates on his frequent references to his 'Ariomaniac' opponents by calling them 'new Jews' " (Ibid). As Gregory of Nyssa also distances the orthodox Christian belief from "Jewish monotheism," the Arians, who hold a unitarian view of God, are found to be in line with the Jews on the nature of the Deity. Our attention is, of course, routinely drawn to the interaction of the historical Jesus with this Jewish, unitarian theology in Mark 12:28ff.

[963] Rubenstein, p. 209.

piece of Protestant history, but it is perhaps a key to unlocking the mystery of how certain staunchly Catholic doctrines could carry on through the flames of 16th-century skepticism. The Jews, as both an ethnic and religious group, were considered detestable by the most well-known Protestant leaders, and so was any theological insight the Jewish heritage had to offer. Undoubtedly, the perpetual rejection of the Jewish perspective on the identity of God during the Reformation maintained the exegetical darkness in which Christians had been groping for centuries. John Calvin reveals his attitude towards the Jews thus: "[The Jews'] rotten and unbending stiffneckedness deserves that they be oppressed unendingly and without measure or end and that they die in their misery without the pity of anyone."[964] And Martin Luther writes, "Such a desperate, thoroughly evil, poisonous, and devilish lot are these Jews, who for these fourteen hundred years have been and still are our plague, our pestilence, and our misfortune."[965] The beloved Luther even openly called for the harshest oppression of the Jews, presenting a shameful plan for "dealing" with those Jews who refused orthodox Christian theology:

> What then shall we Christians do with this damned, rejected race of Jews? … First, their synagogues should be set on fire, and whatever does not burn up should be covered or spread over with dirt so that no one may ever be able to see a cinder or stone of it. And this ought to be done for the honor of God and of Christianity in order that God may see that we are Christians, and that we have not wittingly tolerated or approved of such public lying, cursing, and blaspheming of His Son and His Christians. Second, their homes should likewise be broken down and destroyed. Thirdly, they should be deprived of their prayer-books and Talmuds in which such idolatry, lies, cursing, and blasphemy are taught. Fourthly, their rabbis must be forbidden under threat of death to teach any more.[966]

Many of today's western Christians will undoubtedly be shocked at the words of their denominational founders. Many Christians around the world

---

[964] John Calvin, "Ad Quaelstiones et Objecta Juaei Cuiusdam Responsio," quoted in *The Jew in Christian Theology* (London: Gerhard Falk, McFarland and Company, Inc., 1931).

[965] Martin Luther, "On the Jews and Their Lies," quoted in Martin H Bertram, *Luther's Works,* Vol. 47 (Philadelphia: Fortress Press, 1971).

[966] Luther, "On the Jews and Their Lies."

today feel, especially in light of the Holocaust, a special duty to support or protect the Jewish people. But Luther concludes his own terrible plan for the Jews by boldly declaring that they "ought not to be protected. You ought not, you cannot protect them, unless in the eyes of God you want to share all their abomination."[967]

It is not hard to see why Jewish-Christian relations immediately disintegrated after the doctrine of the Trinity assumed its place at the forefront of Christian thought. From this point we can easily perceive a sharp shift in how Jewish and Christian groups interacted with one another. Evidently, thousands of Jews were once eager to hear of the Christ preached by the Apostles in the first century, yet something caused the Christ of the later Christians to be wholly incompatible with Judaism. On the day of Pentecost, Peter had stood in front of the Jewish multitudes preaching, "*Jesus of Nazareth was a man, accredited by God through miracles which God did through him!*" (Acts 2:22), and through this message the first-century Jews had believed and were added to the number of the Church (v. 41, 47). However, when the Jews were confronted by the later Trinitarians with the ineffable Christ who demanded worship as God, there came a resounding groan. If Peter had stood up on Pentecost and preached an incarnate God-man who existed alongside two other God-Persons, do we think for a moment that the Jews would have lined up in droves to be baptized in his name without serious question or complaint? Again, where is the record of argument or Apostolic exposition that the Jew required to soothe his fears of polytheism?

After the introduction of the homoousian at Nicaea and the subsequent circus of councils it engendered, we find the historical conversation between Jew and Christian growing colder and colder until the virtual silence of our present day. A contemporary Jewish historian writes:

> One reason the Arian controversy interests me... is that because before it ended, Jews and Christians could talk to each other and argue among themselves about crucial issues like the divinity of Jesus, the meaning of salvation, basic ethical standards... everything. They disagreed strongly about many things, but there was still a closeness between them. They participated in the same moral culture. When the controversy ended—when Jesus became God—that closeness faded. To Christians God became a Trinity. Heresy became a crime. Judaism became a form of infidelity. And Jews living in

---

[967] Ibid.

Christian countries learned not to think very much about Jesus and his message.... the doctrine of the Holy Trinity... reflected and encapsulated these problems.[968]

At the center of the chasm between the modern Jewish and Christian faiths, standing as a mountainous road-block against any possible bridges, is the insurmountable Trinity dogma. The worship of Jesus, a man from Nazareth, as the Almighty God, along with two other co-equal characters, is plainly impossible for the faithful Jew, and quite plainly will never be possible. To make matters worse, the topic of Trinitarianism's compatibility with biblical monotheism has been largely eschewed in mainstream Christian conversation. James Dunn aptly recognizes these impassible difficulties:

> So long as Christian theology remains ambivalent on its monotheism, and so long as any tendency to christolatry remains strong in Christian worship, for so long will Jew and Christian be unable to comprehend the other in regard to the most fundamental root of their common religion. And for a Christianity three-quarters of whose scriptures are the scriptures of Israel, that is a most serious crack in its own foundations. Not least is an adequate appreciation of Christianity's monotheism vital for Christian understanding of the continuities between Jesus himself and what was claimed for him subsequently... And without such continuity [between the Judaism of Jesus and the Trinitarianism of the later Christians], demonstrable or at least plausible Christian apologetics on this crucial point have an almost impossible task.[969]

The consistent and consummate rejection of all things deemed "too Jewish" in antiquity has, for the Christian, effected a virtual abandonment of any truly Jewish perspectives on the Scriptures in the modern era. But such a strident separation from Jewish thought seems to have been unwarranted. The Apostle Paul, arguing in the first century against the idea that the primacy of the Jew's relationship with God could be circumvented, declares that it was the Jews to

---

[968] Rubenstein, pp. xiv-xv.

[969] James Dunn, *Christ and the Spirit: Collected Essays of James D.G. Dunn*, Vol. 1 (Grand Rapids: Eerdmans, 1998), p. xiii.

whom the oracles of God were committed (Rom 3:2). Therefore it was to the Hebrew mind that God first gave the revelation of himself and his Son; the Gentiles were later graciously "grafted in" to the life awarded by this revelation (Rom 11:17). Knowing that the New Testament writers presented the revealed truth of God as coming to *"the Jew first and then also to the non-Jew"* (Rom 1:16), a worthy question for the modern Christian is this: did the God of Israel ever successfully communicate anything worthwhile concerning his identity and the identity of his Messiah in his thousands of years of intimate fellowship with the Hebrew people?[970] We wonder then if it is wise to *begin* by assuming, as the Trinitarian must, that the Jews have been grossly misinterpreting their own beloved Scriptures in this central regard, and that they continue to fundamentally misunderstand God's identity as well as his prescriptions for worshipping him. Or is it more reasonable to conclude that the original Jewish followers of Christ maintained a Christology that was in perfect keeping with their theological heritage, which was only later compromised by the introduction of Gentile philosophy in the second, third, and fourth centuries?

Christianity Today

In 2006, Pope Benedict XVI gave a speech at the University of Regensburg in Germany where he had functioned previously as a professor of theology. In this speech, which was hailed as "among the most important papal statements on world affairs,"[971] Benedict denounced what he called the "dehellenization" of Christianity that is presently taking place. He openly praised pagan Greek philosophers, and even equated the ideas of Socrates to the revelation God gave Moses at the burning bush.[972] He rhapsodized:

> Biblical faith, in the Hellenistic period, encountered the best of
> Greek thought at a deep level, resulting in a mutual

---

[970] "The Old Testament tells us nothing explicitly or by necessary implication of a Triune God who is Father, Son and Holy Spirit... There is no evidence that any sacred writer even suspected the existence of a divine [Trinitarian relationship] within the Godhead... Even to see in the Old Testament suggestions or foreshadowings or 'veiled signs' of the Trinity of persons, is to go beyond the words and intent of the sacred writers" (Fortman, *The Triune God*, p. 8, 9).

[971] See James V. Schall, The Regensburg Lecture (South Bend: St. Augustine's Press, 2007).

[972] Pope Benedict XVI, "Faith, Reason and the University, Memories and Reflections," Meeting with the Representatives of Science, Lecture of the Holy Father at the University of Regensburg, Tuesday 12 September 2006.
<http://www.vatican.va/holy_father/benedict_xvi/speeches/2006/september/documents/hf_be n-xvi_spe_20060912_university-regensburg_en.html>.

enrichment... The encounter between the Biblical message and Greek thought did not happen by chance.[973]

What Benedict validates is that Christianity in the modern era stands as a belief system wholly indivisible from the Hellenistic influence that saturated it in the early centuries. An observant professor of Philosophy at Cornell likewise recognizes that:

> The philosophy in Christianity is both inert and active. The late Greek metaphysics around which Christian doctrine first developed is Christianity's inert philosophical skeleton. Even if the dehellenizers could succeed in their efforts to remove it, Christianity itself would be unrecognizable without it.[974]

Christianity indeed seems to have never fully recovered from the Neoplatonic and Gnostic encounters in the post-Apostolic era. In a most poignant summary of our previous survey, renowned historian Will Durant tragically concludes that:

> Christianity did not destroy paganism; it adopted it. The Greek mind, dying, came to a transmigrated life in the theology and liturgy of the Church; the Greek language, having reigned for centuries over philosophy, became the vehicle of Christian literature and ritual... Other pagan cultures contributed to the syncretist result. From Egypt came the ideas of a divine trinity... and the mystic theology that made Neoplatonism and Gnosticism, and obscured the Christian creed... Christianity was the last great creation of the ancient pagan world.[975]

In the twenty-first century we find a mainstream Christianity which trumpets publicly the requisite teachings of the Jewish Jesus as her favorite and foremost guide, all the while consulting, in the private vaults of ecclesiastical scholarship, the dim apparitions of Plato and Valentinus. We might argue here that the only thing more regrettable than a religious academia which doesn't care that its most characteristic philosophies are found nowhere in the mouth of

---

[973] Ibid.

[974] Norman Kretzmann, "Reason in Mystery," *Royal Institute of Philosophy Lecture Series*, Vol. 25. (1989), pp. 15-39.

[975] Will Durant, *The Story of Civilization, Vol. 3: Caesar and Christ* (New York: Simon and Schuster, 1944), p. 595, 599.

Jesus and routinely in the teachings of pagan mystics, is a devoted majority which does not know it at all. But what would the modern student give to know it, and to know it publicly? Perhaps everything? It may very well cost him that. As the overwhelming of Christian theology did not occur overnight, we cannot believe its resurgence will arrive without the passing of considerable time and pain. Those activities which require the most effort are, of course, the most valuable, and surely there is nothing more valuable to the world than the recovery of Jesus of Nazareth's teachings about God.

In retrospect, the philosophical efforts of the theologians of the first six hundred years of Christianity are astounding. Many talented and devoted persons did the best they could to reconcile the heart of Judaism with the fashionable presuppositions that dominated the high mind of their day. The greatest thinkers anxiously fought to contain the explosive idea of the deity of Jesus within a framework of an absolute monotheism which it threatened to shatter at any moment. But the resulting heap of conjecture and formulae yielded by the pain of centuries only lent the surviving faithful the shallowest glimpse into an idea of God which they knew must ultimately remain an unyielding and unattainable conundrum. Truly, the third-fourth-and-fifth century theologians toiled, fought, and died with an awe-inspiring fervor, and the Trinitarian doctrine is nothing short of a work of passion. Yet Arthur Weigall wisely reminds the student: "The idea of a co-equal Trinity... offers a reasonable means of expressing the inexpressible; but it must not be forgotten that Jesus Christ never mentioned such a phenomenon."[976] What then, did Jesus of Nazareth really teach about God? What did the earliest Jews who followed him believe? We are better poised now than at any time in history to recover this obscured data. One modern historian provides some encouragement here and prepares us for the journey:

> The past thirty years have been especially fruitful for the study
> of early Christianity. This is partly because the churches
> appear to be more relaxed about the uncertainties of research
> findings but also because the available sources, particularly the
> range of Jewish texts, preeminent among them the Dead Sea
> Scrolls [discovered in 1945], have expanded enormously. We
> are better able to set Jesus within a historical context than at
> any time since the first century. If we can sum up the rich
> diversity of modern scholarship, it is distinguished both by the

---

[976] Weigall, p. 182.

acceptance of the essential Jewishness of Jesus and by a fuller understanding of what it means to say that Jesus was Jewish in the first century of the Christian era. While traditional interpretations of Jesus have seen him as somehow apart from Judaism, his mission always focused on the outside world, it is now argued not only that he preached and taught within Judaism but even that he was advocating a return to traditional Jewish values.[977]

In the coming chapters, we will discover that the aforementioned dogmatic system, the inherited Trinity model so beloved by the present majority, is radically unnecessary. It is high time to take the Jesus of the Bible, and what theological information he offers, more seriously. Indeed, as one Anglican professor of religion has recommended, "Christianity should be much more tightly focused upon Jesus' words than it usually has been in the past... The real Jesus is a much more interesting and religiously relevant figure than the divine Christ of later faith and he has the advantage of having actually lived."[978]

While the post-Apostolic Church Fathers may have established a novel, restructured theology wholly foreign to the Jewish mind, Christ himself never appears interested in aiming religion's endgame in any new direction. Instead we find a preacher standing readily upon Moses as his foundation and consistently citing another (his God, the Father of all) as the enabler and authorizer of his mission. The New Testament Jesus is one wholly preoccupied with the fundamentals of a long-established religion which he aimed to reclaim and illuminate in the hearts and minds of his countrymen; a teacher with unique passion and mission, but whose authority he admittedly derived from another, grander source deserving of not only the Jews' absolute devotion, but his own. It is to this personal, unyielding faith that we now turn.

---

[977] Freeman, *Closing of the Western Mind,* p. 88.
[978] Don Cupitt, *The Debate About Christ* (London: SCM Press, 1979), p. 138.

PART II

THE RECOVERY

*On the Theology of Jesus of Nazareth
and His Earliest Disciples*

"For there is nothing lost, that may be found, if sought"
– Edmund Spenser

"When the solution is simple, God is answering"
– Albert Einstein

8

THE JEWISH CREATOR

"Entities must not be multiplied beyond necessity."

— "Occam's Razor"
(William of Ockham 1287-1347)

THE PHILOSOPHICAL FORMULAS fashioned by the early Christians, being adapted from the colorful religions of the world, invariably drew the faith further and further from the language and message of the Jewish Scriptures. Despite the stalwart efforts of the Latin and Greek Fathers to produce an operable harmony between the Bible and the systems of the world, their agreed upon creeds still proved rationally unsatisfying and incapable of relating the person of Christ and his God to the Christian world in a practical sense. Yet over the din of the theological maneuverings of the later synodic administrators, those august philosophers who spent their wearisome lives pirouetting upon the hypothesis of plurality within unity, the brilliant voice of Christ can still be heard appealing to reason, history, and the Hebrew Scriptures. It is to this religion, the faith of Jesus and the rest of the biblical Jews, which we now affix our undivided attention.

The Role of Judaism

As second-century Christianity experienced a dramatic shift out of the world of Judaism and into the world of Greek philosophy, the Church Fathers found themselves with the daunting task of converting the religious thought of one culture into another. One encyclopedia comments on the incredible transformation the original Jewish-Christian teachings underwent in the early centuries:

> Like all concepts the meaning of religious terms is changed with a changing experience and changing world view. Transplanted into the Greek world view, inevitably the Christian teaching was modified—indeed transformed. Questions which had never been asked came into the foreground and the Jewish pre-suppositions tended to disappear... As thus the background is changed from Jewish to Greek, so are the fundamental religious conceptions... We have thus a peculiar combination—the religious doctrines of the Bible run through the forms of an alien philosophy.[979]

If the Jewish Scriptures are now popularly interpreted through an "alien philosophy," is it not the solemn obligation of every student interested in the message of the Bible to work diligently to reacquire the original perspective? If the teaching was indeed "transformed" as the encyclopedia explains, what would the millions of faithful believers not give to reverse that transformation, that is, to reform it? Returning to the Jewishness of the biblical documents—indeed to the Jewishness of Jesus—should be the starting point.

One professor of theology opens our discussion of Jesus' Judaism with the following portrait of the man:

> Christ had not been educated in any philosophical school, whether Jewish or Greek. There is no evidence that he had any acquaintance with the metaphysical ideas which were floating in the intellectual atmosphere of his time... he was [not] affected by the various Greek philosophical schools that were beginning to break down the partition walls of Jewish isolation. Neither Palestinian Sadduceeism nor Alexandrian Philonism ever disturbed with their skeptical or mystical clouds the intellectual serenity of his Galilean soul... It is true that

---

[979] G. W. Knox, "Christianity," *Encyclopedia Britannica,* Vol. 6 (Cambridge: CUP, 1910), p. 284.

Christianity was afterwards developed into a philosophical creed, as is true of all religious ideas, but this historical process cannot be traced to its founder.[980]

In Jesus' famous dialogue with the Samaritan woman we find an example of his reinforcement of the primacy of historical Judaism in a diverse religious world. The Samaritans,[981] who lived alongside the Jews in first-century Israel, had circumvented the Jewish strictures their interaction with the Divine, keeping their own Torah and their own temple mount amongst other traditions in antagonism to the ways of their Jewish cousins.[982] But Jesus rejected the idea that the true worship leading unto salvation would come through any other religious heritage:

> *The woman said to him, "Sir, I perceive that you are a prophet. Our fathers worshiped in this mountain, and you people say that in Jerusalem is the place where men ought to worship." Jesus said to her, "Woman, believe me, an hour is coming when neither in this mountain nor in Jerusalem will you worship the Father. "You worship what you do not know; we worship what we know, for salvation is from the Jews. But an hour is coming, and now is, when the true worshipers will worship the Father in spirit and truth; for such people the Father seeks to be his worshipers. God is spirit, and those who worship him must worship in spirit and truth." The woman said to him, "I know that Messiah is coming (he who is called Christ); when that one comes, he will declare all things to us." Jesus said to her, "I who speak to you am he"*
> (John 4:19-26).

Jesus declares emphatically here that "*salvation is from the Jews.*" Quite profoundly, God's redemptive program is to be discovered exclusively in the Jewish heritage. Jesus Christ, the very salvation that the Jewish God offers to mankind, is essentially bound up with the Jewish world. It is not merely the "human nature" of Jesus that is Jewish; he is a personality living through and

---

[980] Paine, *The Ethnic Trinities*, pp. 202-203.

[981] The Samaritans are descended from the half-tribes of Ephraim and Manasseh, two of the biblical Joseph's sons. The Samaritans to this day hold that their religion is the true religion of the Israelites prior to Israel's exile in Babylon. They claim that worship of Yahweh should not be performed on the traditional site of Solomon's temple, Jerusalem's Temple Mount, but on Mount Gerizim outside Shechem.

[982] See Oded Lipschitz, Gary N. Knoppers, Rainer Albertz, *Judah and the Judeans in the Fourth Century B. C. E.* (Warsaw: Eisenbrauns, 2007), p. 157ff, 176.

dependent upon the religious mind of historical Judaism. His work among the Jews was not to present a monotheism previously unknown to them, but to sound the call for reform and return to the heart and soul of a religion they already had. The boundaries of Jewish thought both initiate and facilitate every moment of his ministry. Many scholars recognize that "Jesus had rooted his teaching within his own religious tradition," and that Jesus making himself the Jewish God, as is popularly claimed, "effectively separates him from the world of Judaism."[983] Even Trinitarians have admitted that Jesus "appears to have plainly insisted, in his own teachings, upon no doctrines but those which were generally admitted by his countrymen as resting on the authority of Moses and the prophets."[984] Certainly the Messianism advocated by Jesus was not to be interpreted as a sharp break with the past, though this is precisely what Athanasius and the Cappadocians proposed during the Arian controversy.[985] Rather, Jesus presented an old and true religion from which he was purging the clutter of erroneous social and moral traditions, and one that was having the shadows of its unfulfilled prophecies diffused.[986]

What then is the most critical and distinguishing feature of this historical religion to which Jesus so faithfully clung? The Jews have always held that there is only one true and supreme God, and that this individual is named Yahweh: *"Yahweh, the God of your fathers… This is my name forever, the name you shall call me from generation to generation"* (Ex 3:15); *"I am Yahweh; that is my name!"* (Is 42:8); *"You, whose name is Yahweh… alone are the Most High"* (Psalm 83:18); *"You alone are Yahweh"* (Neh 9:6). Even one Trinitarian source explains that:

> In the Old Testament, God is distinctly announced as the one living and true God… the unity of God is made especially prominent, and contrasted strongly and variously with the idolatrous notions prevalent among men. It is a pure system of Theism, allowing not the slightest departure from the strict idea of one God only… God is distinctly an individual, not an abstract power.[987]

The suggestion that any plurality of different Persons might somehow subsist within the single individual named "Yahweh" is an idea innately divergent

---

[983] Freeman, *Closing of the Western Mind,* p. 133, 129.

[984] Smith, p. 509.

[985] Rubenstein, p. 74.

[986] See Mark 7:3ff, Matthew 5:17ff.

[987] Seth Sweetser, *Bibliotheca Sacra,* Vol. XI (Dallas Theological Seminary, January, 1854), p. 88.

from the spirit of the Jewish monotheism.[988] Certainly Jewish objections to the Trinitarian concept of God have been heard from the very outset of the doctrine's formulation. From the Nazarene Christians of Jerusalem professing God's unitary oneness alongside the Messiahship of the human Jesus, to the rabbis of the third and fourth century who fiercely debated Christian teachers on the nature of God in the Scriptures[989]—the Jewish idea of God has clashed with Christian orthodoxy throughout history. Regarding attempts to locate the Trinity in the Jewish Bible, Jewish historians in the twentieth century reveal that the Jews have consistently "reject[ed] every proof brought forward by their opponents… the Jews have always regarded the doctrine of the Trinity as one irreconcilable with the spirit of the Jewish religion and with monotheism.[990] In the medieval era also, famous Jews like Maimonides (1135-1204 CE) are found still defending God's strict unity against the plurality of the Christian view:

> [God], the Cause of all, is one. This does not mean one as in one of a series, nor one like a species (which encompasses many individuals), nor one as in an object that is made up of many elements, nor as a single simple object that is infinitely divisible. Rather, God is a unity unlike any other possible unity. This is referred to in the Torah: "Hear Israel, the Lord is our God, the Lord is One."[991]

Many Christians today are quick to say that the Jews were simply not yet blessed with the revelation of the true God's nature as three different Persons before Jesus' arrival.[992] But Trinitarians have also admitted that Jesus did not preach the Trinity, or ever divulge that he was the Jews' Creator,[993] and that

---

[988] Again, many Trinitarians have admitted that the monotheism of the Jews was and is to this day *unitarian*, that is, they believe that God is a certain single self: "The Jews… to this day they could never make [the Trinity] an article of faith; but they still assert that God is only one in person, as well as nature" (Beveridge, p. 66). See also Warfield, p. 127.

[989] Some of these discourses can be found in the great corpus of rabbinical Judaism, *The Talmud.*

[990] Kaufmann Kohler, Samuel Krauss, "Trinity," *Jewish Encyclopedia.* 1906. Web. 05 May 2014.

[991] Maimonides, *Thirteen Principles of Faith*, Second Principle.

[992] "The mystery of the most holy Trinity was not yet [at the time of Christ] divulged, so that the Jews could expressly believe that he was by nature the Son of God, God of God, of one substance, power, and glory with God the Father. This doctrine Jesus reserved to himself to promulgate… though he did not at the beginning expressly teach it to his disciples, but led them to it by degrees. (Lucas Brugensis, "On John 1: 49," as quoted in Wilson, *Uni. Princip. Conf. by Trini. Testimonies,* 1888, p. 334).

[993] "[Jesus] never declared himself the creator of the world (an argument apparently in the Socinian's favor)" (J. F. Flatt, *Dissertation on the Deity of Christ, in Biblical Repertory*, Vol. 1 (New Jersey: Princeton, 1829), pp. 174-175).

neither were his Apostles aware of it at the end of his ministry.[994] So what did Jesus really teach them? Did he promote or inspire any restructured belief in the Deity? No, Jesus directly affirmed, in his conversation with the Samaritan woman, that the identity of the true God was already known to the Jews, and that both he and his countrymen indeed worshiped him correctly: *"we worship what we do know"* (Jn 4:22). This uniquely Jewish knowledge about God is the waypoint of religious truth to which the Messiah will direct the nations. As no scholar believes the Jews ever worshipped a Trinity, and if Jesus joins them in their worship, have we not great cause to doubt that Jesus worshipped a Trinity? He did, after all, *worship God* alongside them, didn't he (Jn 4:22, 20:17)? As a perfect, law-abiding Jew, how might he have gone about this? Acknowledging God as the Father as his fellow Jews did? This must be what we observe Jesus advocating in his dialogue with the Samaritan woman, and elsewhere: *"Father... You* [are] *the only true God"* (Jn 17:1a, 3). As so many academics have noted, within the biblical data "there is no reason to see Jesus as anything other than a pious monotheist."[995] This great tradition of Jesus became the undeniable heritage of the New Testament community.

The Language of the Biblical God

The Christian student should have no difficulty in joining the most respected Trinitarian scholars in recognizing that "if we compare the language of these [Trinitarian] dogmas with the language of the New Testament the difference is obvious. The terminology... is alien to the New Testament."[996] But if the Platonic jargon is absent, what sort of language do we find?

The New Testament contains over 1,300 passages in which the word "God" (Greek: *theos*) occurs. In none of these instances do we find a distinction within the Godhead. The Old Testament likewise presents us with thousands upon thousands of singular personal pronouns, singular verbs and adjectives used in conjunction with Adonai (Lord), "elohim" (God/god/gods), and YHWH (or Yahweh, the divine personal name). Overwhelmingly, God's presentation of himself is of an absolutely singular being. As has been observed, "The unity of

---

[994] "Nor understood they (our Savior's own disciples) the mystery of the Sacred Trinity as we do..." (John Evelyn, *The History of Religion,* Vol. 2 (London: Forgotten Books, 2013 [1859]), pp. 87-88); "It is true he also was God. This, however, they knew not: they did not regard him as God, but more as a man, like, though far superior in power and wisdom, to themselves" (Julius Charles Hare, *Mission of the Comforter,* Vol. 1 (Boston: Gould and Lincoln, 1877), pp. 9-10).

[995] Tom Holmen, Stanley E. Porter, *Handbook for the Study of the Historical Jesus* (Leiden: Brill, 2011), p. 1205.

[996] Brunner, Emil. *Dogmatics,* Vol. I. London: Lutterworth Press, 1949. p. 56.

the Godhead is a truth not barely founded on a few places of Scripture that expressly assert it, but it may be deduced from every part thereof."[997]   Plural verbs, pronouns, and adjectives are used in only a handful of instances when a plurality of God's majesty is being invoked by the writer, or when God is speaking to his royal heavenly court as we find in the Genesis creation account.[998]   It is infinitely easier to explain the few textual exceptions to the singular personal pronouns through an examination of context and a consideration for Hebraic idiom, than to override the overwhelming Scriptural burden of more than 7,000 references to God using singular personal pronouns.

Considering the whole of the Hebrew Scriptures, it is not difficult to grasp how and why the Jews have affirmed their God to be a singular personality.   He provided them every reason to:

The Hebrew Scriptures:

- "There is no one like YHWH our God" (Ex 8:10)
- "You shall have no other gods besides me" (Ex 20:1-3)
- "YHWH, he is God; there is no other besides him" (Deut 4:35)
- "YHWH, he is God in heaven above and on the earth below; there is no other" (Deut 4:39)
- "See now that I, I am he, and there is no god besides me" (Deut 32:39)
- "YHWH is our God, YHWH is one" (Deut 6:4)
- "For there is none like you, and there is no God besides you" (2 Sam 7:22)
- "YHWH is God; there is no one else" (1 Kings 8:60)
- "There is none like you, nor is there any God besides you" (1 Chron 17:20)
- "You alone are YHWH" (Neh 9:6)
- "You alone, Lord, are God" (Is 37:20)
- "Before me there was no God formed, and there will be none after me" (Is 43:10)
- "I am the first and I am the last, and there is no God besides me" (Is 44:6)
- "Is there any God besides me? Or is there any other Rock? I know of none" (Is 44:8)
- "I am YHWH, and there is no other; besides me there is no God" (Is 45:5)
- "I am YHWH, and there is none else" (Is 45:18)
- "Is it not I, YHWH? And there is no other God besides me, a righteous God

---

[997] Ridgley, Thomas. *Body of Divinity*, Vol. I. New York: R. Carter, 1855. p. 194.

[998] Jewish sources regularly reject Trinitarian claims that the employment of "us" by God in Genesis denotes plurality within God. Rather, they resolutely confirm the likelihood of God's conversation with his heavenly court of angels. See Gerald Sigal, "What is the meaning of God said: 'Let us make man in our image'?," Jews for Judaism. Web. Accessed 22 September 2014.

and a Savior; there is none except me" (Is 45:21)
- "I am God, and there is no other; I am God, and there is no one like me" (Is 46:9)
- "In that day YHWH will be the only one, and his name the only one" (Zech 14:9)
- "Do we not all have one Father? Has not one God created us?" (Mal 2:10)

The language regarding God's unity in the later New Testament writings is remarkably consistent with this spirit:

The New Testament:
- "The Lord our God is one Lord" (Mk 12:29)
- "You do not seek the glory that is from the one and only God" (Jn 5:44)
- "We have one Father, even God" (Jn 8:41)
- "That they might know you, the only true God" (Jn 17:3)
- "Since indeed God is one" (Rom 3:30)
- "To the only wise God, Amen" (Rom 16:27)
- "There is no God but one" (1 Cor 8:4)
- "For us there is but one God, the Father" (1 Cor 8:6)
- "God is only one" (Gal 3:20)
- "One God and Father of all" (Eph 4:4-6)
- "The King eternal, immortal, invisible, the only God" (1 Tim 1:17)
- "For there is one God and one mediator between God and men" (1 Tim 2:5)
- "You believe that God is one. You do well; the demons also believe, and shudder" (Jas 2:19)
- "The only God our Savior" (Jude 1:25)

One must ask why the Supreme Being, who created language and designed the human mind, would choose to employ language which he knew the world would think meant that he was only one individual, when in fact he was a unified collective of individuals, a *society?* Even in the language of the New Testament, the documents which allegedly publicize the Triune God, we find no indication that the fundamental perspective of the Jews had been updated; the language of Jesus and his Apostles in regard to God is the same language of Moses.

A. E. Harvey reveals that "there is no unambiguous evidence that the constraint of monotheism was effectively broken by any New Testament writer,"[999] and these authors certainly take the reader's understanding of Jewish monotheism for granted. For the ancient nation of Israel, this particular model

---

[999] A. E. Harvey, *Jesus and the Constraints of History* (London: Duckworth, 1980), p. 178.

had been critical to their survival; whenever they strayed from its practice, tragic consequences swiftly followed. But there is no evidence that anything the Apostles encountered in the person of Christ posed concern for this traditional theology. If the later Gentile converts in the Roman era worried during their councils over the possibility of abrogating the monotheism of the Bible, how much more would the intensely devoted Jewish community of the first century have risen up in fiery contest at the suggestion that rabbi Jesus was not only their God, but that Abraham and Moses had been unknowingly worshipping *three* different Persons all along? The deafening silence of the lack of Apostolic debate, combined with the perfect maintenance of Old Testament language to describe God in the New Testament, strongly suggests that such a dramatic expansion of the Godhead was not promulgated by the earliest Christians.

The theology of Jesus and his Apostles had indeed operated painlessly through the classic Old Testament language without need for amplification or clarification: God was always *"only one"* (Gal 3:20), or *"one Lord"* (Mark 12:29), or *"the Father"* (1 Cor 8:6) or *"[the] Father… the only true God"* (Jn 17:1a-3). The language conveyed a straightforward, intelligible idea: God was a solitary identity whom they called Father. This God was *a single self.* He says: *"I myself will search for my sheep"* (Ezek 34:11); *"I am Yahweh… by myself… all alone"* (Is 44:24). Even after the advent of Jesus, the New Testament Jews continued to portray the Old Testament God as a single self: *"For when God made the promise to Abraham, since he could swear by no one greater, he swore by himself"* (Heb 6:13-20). In Scripture, single persons are described as single souls: *"eight souls were saved through water"* (1 Pet 3:20 NET); *"that is, eight persons"* (NASB). Human persons say *"my soul"* (Ps 35:9), and are described as *"his soul"* (Matt 16:26), and God likewise says *"my soul"* (Matt 12:18), and is described as *"his soul"* (Ps 11:5). What good reason do we have to we assume that when the Jew said *"God is one"* (Gal 3:20; Deut 6:4), he did *not* mean it in the same sense that he meant *"Abraham is one"* (Is 51:2; Ezek 33:24)?

For most Trinitarians, God is a *substance* in which there are *three different selves;* God is a single "being," but not a single person. Of course, there are no biblical texts which teach a distinction between Being and Personhood. On the other hand, if the Bible intended to identify single beings as unipersonal, or as single selves, how would it do so? The biblical language describing single human beings (singular personal pronouns) is the same language used to describe God. But when it comes to God, Trinitarianism cannot afford to make the natural inference, that single beings are single persons. Instead Trinitarianism suddenly exchanges the normative use of language for a metaphysical and often ambiguous usage. But this is an unnecessary switch; the Bible does not support any such distinctions. Humans and God are presented in the same terms without qualification: they are described in the way that we ordinarily speak about single persons.

In contrast, the present Trinitarian faith requires constant, detailed qualification through the use of extra-biblical terminology to extract itself from the dangerous spiral of polytheism. Yet even these escape ropes have become frayed, the precise meanings of the abstract terms involved being now mostly foggy and elusive. As we read earlier from Emil Brunner, while these words play decisive parts in the inherited Trinitarian system, "for us they are scarcely intelligible, or, if used without commentary, lead to gross misunderstanding."[1000] But without the critical play of these Greek phrases, the worship of the Triune God swiftly falls apart into the worship of many gods, or perhaps worse, a metaphysical muddle. The great lecturer George Burnap exposed the problem:

> A man demands my assent to the proposition, "there are three Persons in one God"; I ask him what he means by "person"? I ask him if he means a separate independent intelligent Being? He answers, he does not. He says he does not use the word in the common sense, but in a sense peculiar to this case. I ask him what that sense is? He cannot tell. You demand of me then, I answer, to assent to a proposition which conveys to my mind no intelligible idea, and, it appears to be equally unintelligible to you. We both... assent to nothing but words, and if they convey to us no intelligible meaning, to us they are nothing, and we assent to nothing. Were these words in the Bible, then I might say that I believed they expressed truth, though I could not understand it. But not being in the Bible... I consider them the mere invention of fallible men. I cannot believe on their authority. As I cannot understand them myself, and no one can explain them to me, I think it fair to conclude that those who framed them had no clear ideas.[1001]

The average western Christian seems to be scarcely troubled or even aware that millions of Jews, Muslims, and non-Trinitarian Christians are seriously

---

[1000] Brunner, p.70

[1001] George Washington Burnap, *Lectures On The Doctrines of Christianity* (Wm. R. Lucas & R. N. Wright, 1835), pp. 18-19.

concerned by the identification of the existing orthodox system with monotheism. In most mainstream circles, the monotheism of orthodoxy seems taken for granted, while any private concerns are often swiftly dismissed or discouraged.[1002] Despite the lack of interest, however, these are very real problems. What if, during an evangelical service, several members began to exclaim: "*They* created us!" or "We worship *all of you!*" or "All praise to the *three* of them!" Would it produce serious questions? As one illuminating book recognizes:

> In American Church history, the Protestant majority has remained Trinitarian chiefly by practicing serial monotheism— focusing now on one, now on another member of the Holy Trinity. Apparently this is a practical accommodation to confusing Trinitarian terminology that can be avoided if one does not try to talk about all three persons in one breath.[1003]

Indeed the Trinitarian must not only believe in, but worship each of these persons equally as God while simultaneously balancing between monotheistic and polytheistic language. If, in prayer, the Trinitarian calls upon his one single God, employing the usual singular-personal language "You" and "Your," then the Trinity is practically dissolved from his worship. He worships three different persons only in his official statement of faith, while in his practice there is only one.[1004]

Of course we do not find any biblical disciple of Jesus assuaging any Jew of natural concerns about monotheism. The historical record of debate between Jews and Christians in later centuries is, however, riddled with such disputation. This seems immediately due to the later Christians' theology interacting very differently with Jewish monotheism than Jesus and his Apostle's theology did in the first century.

[1002] One modern Christian writes: "A common phrase I hear all too often about the doctrine of the Trinity is that 'it's a mystery' and that's all you really need to know. Followed by, 'Just make the Sign of the Cross and be on your way!' " (Marion De La Torre, "Is the Trinity Too Much of a Mystery to Understand?" Knowing Is Doing. 31 May 2015. Web. Accessed 10 August 2015. <http://www.knowingisdoing.org/2015/05/31/is-the-trinity-too-much-of-a-mystery-to-understand/>).

[1003] Mark H. Graeser, John A. Lynn, John W. Schoenheit, *One God & One Lord: Reconsidering the Cornerstone of the Christian Faith* (Indianapolis: Christian Educational Services, 2000), p. 544.

[1004] Didymus the Blind of Alexandria, a Trinitarian, moderately prescribes that the three Persons of the Trinity are to be heard, known, worshipped and glorified "as one Person" (*De Trinitate*, 2, 36). See also Thomas F. Torrance, *The Christian Doctrine of God: One Being Three Persons* (London: T&T Clark, 1996), p. 135.

"One" or "More Than One"?

Jesus' confirmation of the Jew's interpretation of the *Shema*, the "foremost" rule of the faith (Mk 12:28ff), can hardly be stressed enough. The creed's subsequent ban by the later Catholic authorities who detected within it an opposition to their Trinitarian dogma is equally eye-opening.[1005] We must keep in mind that no verse in the Hebrew Scriptures has been awarded more attention by the Jewish mind than Deuteronomy 6:4; it has remained the test for all doctrines and the firm rock upon which all chances of polytheism are dashed to pieces:

$$שְׁמַע יִשְׂרָאֵל יְהוָה אֱלֹהֵינוּ יְהוָה אֶחָד$$

Sh'ma Yisra'el YHWH Eloheinu YHWH Echad
"Hear O' Israel, Yahweh is our God, Yahweh is one"

What this faith statement meant to Christ's first-century Jewish audience, indeed what it still means to Jews today, can hardly be disputed. The Jewish scribe interpreted Christ's recitation thus: "*Right, teacher; you have truly stated that he is one, and there is no one else besides him*" (Mk 12:32). Upon the Jew's identification of the *Shema's* "one" as a singular "he" (one person), Jesus confirmed that the man "*had answered wisely*" or "*intelligently*" (v. 34). It is therefore not merely the *Shema* but the acutely Jewish, even Pharisaic interpretation of the *Shema* that Jesus affirms. The great Jewish historian Joseph Klausner of the Hebrew University in Jerusalem writes:

> How far, even to the last, Jesus remained a true Pharisaic Jew is to be seen from [Mark 12:29]. The scribe supports Jesus [vv. 32-34]. Jesus is thus still a Pharisee, and finds himself in agreement with a scribe... Like every Pharisaic Jew, he believed in the absolute unity of God.[1006]

In response to the argument that the unity in the *Shema* points to God's numerical singularity, Trinitarians often assert that the "oneness" must be only an indication of the Jewish God's *uniqueness*, or that this God is *alone,* set apart from other gods. However, Anglican scholar Christopher Wright explains:

[1005] Davies, Finkelstein, *The Cambridge History of Judaism*, Vol. 4, p. 17.
[1006] Klausner, *Jesus of Nazareth: His Life, Times, and Teachings*, p. 319, 377.

An exegetical understanding would be that the second two Hebrew words mean 'Yahweh is one,' rather than 'Yahweh alone'... the verbal forms that usually express the uniqueness and incomparability of Yahweh are quite different from the expression in [Deut. 6:4], which seems to suggest the oneness or singularity of Yahweh... [It is possible that] there is a polemical intent to define God as wholly different from the multitude of gods that surround Israel, perhaps especially from the multiple manifestations and forms of Baal in the Canaanite cults. *Yahweh is not the brand name of a cosmic corporation.* He is one God, our God, and Yahweh is his personal name. On this understanding, the emphasis lies on Yahweh's singularity... the sharp precision of the Shema cannot be evaporated into a philosophical abstraction or relegated to a penultimate level of truth. [It is a] majestic declaration of monotheism defined by the history-laden, character-rich, covenant-related dynamic personhood of 'Yahweh our God.'[1007]

Indeed, Jesus' citation of the Shema was, as even N. T. Wright has observed, thoroughly *"noncontroversial."*[1008] There was no question as to the creed's meaning for the Jews: "God is only one in person."[1009] As one scholar rightly states, "Mark 12:29 recorded the confirmation of Jesus himself, without any reservation, of the supreme monotheistic confession of faith of the Israelite religion *in its complete form.*"[1010] Of course, his disciples likewise maintained this precise standard.[1011] As J. N. D. Kelly explains, "The doctrine of one God, the Father and creator, formed the background and indisputable premise of the Church's faith. Inherited from Judaism, it was her bulwark against pagan

---

[1007] C. Wright, *Deuteronomy*, 9, emphasis added.

[1008] Wright, *Jesus and the Victory of God*, p. 305.

[1009] A notice from the Trinitarian Bishop Beveridge (See *Private Thoughts*, p. 66). Again we take note of the agreement of Trinitarian Leonard Hodgson: "the [Jewish] monotheism was then, as it still is, unitarian" (*Christian Faith and Practice*, p. 74).

[1010] Werner, pp. 241-242, emphasis added.

[1011] Note the *Black's New Testament Commentary on the Epistle of James*: "James cites what must be central tenet both for himself and his supposed objector: *'You believe that God is one, do you?'* ... *God is one.* The datum of faith thus appealed to is not specifically Christian. It is of course characteristic of Judaism (Deut. Vi. 4 makes the acceptance of it basic to Israel's behavior and this formed part of the twice-daily recitation of the *Shema* [...]) but it is equally [characteristic] of Christianity in its Jewish heritage (cf. 1 Cor viii. 4-6; Gal. iii. 20; Eph iv. 6; 1 Tim. Ii. 5; Hermas, Mand. i. and Didache i. 1), and it has a special place in this author's thought..." (Sophie Laws, *A Commentary on the Epistle of James* (London: A. And C. Black, 1980), p. 125).

polytheism, Gnostic emanationism and Marcionite dualism."[1012]   If Professor Kelly is correct, and the monotheism enshrined in the *Shema* of Jesus rejects the pluriform of personal hypostases of Gnosticism, what does that mean for Christian orthodoxy? Can the Christian continue to so easily assert the existence of multiple God-Persons in the Yahweh of the *Shema*, and to hold that conviction as fundamental to the religion of the historical Jesus?

Today, mainstream apologists can be heard explaining that one cannot even be a Christian, that is, be "saved," if one does not accept Christ's deity or that God is more than one Person. But if this were so, if the Jews' salvation really rested upon the acquisition of such an understanding, then why does Jesus not lift a finger to inform his people that the fundamental belief requirement (as it relates to God) had been restructured? If Christ, the great revealer of God (Jn 1:18), truly was a good teacher desiring the Jews' acceptance, he certainly neglects to relate the most pertinent and valuable information he has. Furthermore, if the man from Nazareth was indeed the God of Abraham, Isaac and Jacob, could he really blame their descendants for rejecting him and this new form of triune worship when he had also communicated that they *already* worshiped God with knowledge (Jn 4:22)? If God had previously warned them to reject and even to stone anyone teaching *"a different God that neither you nor your ancestors have known"* (Deut 13:6-11), how directly could we blame his Jewish enemies for rejecting an alleged God-man who gave them little, if any, assistance in acquiring this new information? One Trinitarian source even claims that "it was our blessed Lord's Divinity, which, we have seen, he studiously *concealed*, but wished all men to come to the knowledge of."[1013] If Jesus really was a just God seeking the Jews' acceptance, his failure to assist those gathered around him during his public debates in Jerusalem is abysmal and terrifying.

How then does the modern Trinitarian escape the implications of the *Shema*? Obviously the key Hebrew word in Deuteronomy 6:4 is "echad" (one). The word is defined as *"one, each, a certain, only, once."* The term means "one" in the simplest sense of the word; *only* one, and not two or more.[1014] But Trinitarian Christians have invoked a colorful *interpretation* of the word "one" as "a *compound* one." Needless to say, the Jews themselves have justifiably been up in arms over this assertion for centuries. The *Jewish Encyclopedia* of 1906 reads:

[1012] Kelly, p. 87.

[1013] Isaac Williams, "On Reserve in Communicating Religious Knowledge," *Tracts for the Times*, Vol. IV, No. 80 (London: J. G. F. & J. Rivington, 1837), p. 38, emphasis added.

[1014] "echad," *Brown-Driver Briggs Hebrew Lexicon*.

The boldness of the Christian exegetes, who converted even the "Shema," the solemn confession of the Divine Unity, into a proof of the Trinity... furnishes an explanation of the bitterness of the Jewish apologists... the Jews have always regarded the doctrine of the Trinity as one irreconcilable with the spirit of the Jewish religion and with monotheism.[1015]

Some Trinitarians have even argued that "echad" actually *demands* plurality, that "one" *must* mean "more than one within one." Indeed, some have not ceased their clamor for "the *inherently* plural word echad."[1016] This assertion often involves citation of Genesis 2:24: "*For this reason a man shall leave his father and his mother, and be joined to his wife; and they shall become one* (echad) *flesh.*" The Trinitarian will say this "echad" includes two persons, the man and his wife, and therefore it is implied that the "echad" in Deuteronomy 6:4 also contains two (or more) persons. This is a misuse of language, however. The word "echad" is a numerical adjective that modifies a noun. Any noun can be modified by "echad" but "echad" still means one and not two. In the case of Genesis 2:24, it is describing one "*flesh*" and not two "*fleshes.*" Trinitarians have also cited Numbers 13:23 which describes "*one* (echad) *cluster of grapes*" to support their argument. But again, "echad" is modifying only *one cluster.* It is the noun cluster that signals plurality, not the word "one."

In the 960 times that "echad" appears in the Hebrew Bible, in no instance does it denote a plurality within the one; rather it is simply identifying something as "one thing in number," and not two or three things. For example, Abraham is also said to be "echad" in Ezekiel 33:24: "*Abraham was one* (echad)." Abraham was one what? One person. Indeed this is how the most recent Baptist translation has rendered this language: "*Abraham was only one person*" (HCSB). But when the same language is used of Yahweh in Deuteronomy 6:4, of course the Trinitarian translators refrain from consistency. Nevertheless, Yahweh is described as "echad," not because there exists within him a plurality of Persons, but because he is simply *one individual in number.* Jewish apologists have long argued from Scripture that the word demands no Trinitarian plurality, and when applied to individuals (such as the God Yahweh) it simply and obviously implies unitary personhood:

[1015] Kohler, Krauss, "Trinity," *Jewish Encyclopedia*, 1906.

[1016] Woodrow Whidden, Jerry Moon and John Reeve, *The Trinity* (Hagerstown: Review and Herald Publishing, 2002), p. 76, emphasis added.

This is illustrated by such verses as 2 Samuel 13:30: "*Absalom has slain all the king's sons, and there is not <u>one</u> of them left*" 2 Samuel 17:12: "*And of all the men that are with him we will not leave so much as <u>one</u>*"; Exodus 9:7: "*There did not die of the cattle of Israel even <u>one</u>*"; 2 Samuel 17:22: "*There lacked not <u>one</u> of them that was not gone over the Jordan*"; Ecclesiastes 4:8: "*There is <u>one</u>* [that is alone], *and he has not a second; yea, he has neither son nor brother.*" Clearly, the word "one" used in these verses means an absolute one and is synonymous with the word yachid, "the only one," "alone." It is in this sense, with even greater refinement, that "echad" is used in Deuteronomy 6:4: "*Hear, O Israel, the Lord our God, the Lord is <u>One</u>.*" Here, "echad" is used as a single, absolute, unqualified one. There is no mention of a triune god.[1017]

None of this has silenced the Trinitarian, however. Unfortunately, Reformed theologian and former Chairman of the International Council on Biblical Inerrancy, J. M. Boice even goes so far as to assert that "the word is never used in the Hebrew Bible of a stark singular entity"![1018] We must, by all means, denounce this as categorically false and irresponsible at best. We might ask those dogmatists who advocate an implicit plurality within "echad" what they would do with examples such as Nehemiah 11:1: "*one (echad) out of ten,*" or Ecclesiastes 4:12: "*Where a lone (echad) man may be overcome, two together may resist.*" The exhausting verbal gymnastics executed on this simple word have unfortunately been enough to persuade those already willing to look beyond the plain meaning of words in the name of safeguarding sacrosanct belief or grasping at the abstruse. Yet the argument is, ultimately, an exercise in confusion and distraction. As N. T. Wright correctly noted, the *Shema* cited by Jesus in Mark 12:28ff was indeed "*noncontroversial,*"[1019] that is, the statement was simple and clear to everyone.

The Greek rendition of the *Shema* is also worth noting. Both the *Septuagint* (at Deut 6:4), and the New Testament (at Mark 12:29) read: "*The Lord our God is one Lord*" (Κύριος ὁ Θεὸς ἡμῶν Κύριος εἷς ἐστιν). The word for "one" here, the Greek "heis" (εἷς), is the term used for a singular person—never multiple

---

[1017] Gerald Sigal, "In What Sense Is 'Echad' [one] used in the Shema?" Jews for Judaism. Web. 20 October 2014, emphasis added.

[1018] James Montgomery Boice, *The Sovereign God* (Downer's Grove: IVP, 1978), p. 139.

[1019] Wright, *Jesus and the Victory of God*, p. 305.

Persons. Wuest writes: "The word 'one' is masculine in gender, and therefore is personal, referring to a person,"[1020] and Robertson likewise identifies "heis" as meaning "*one person*."[1021] This word provides great difficulty for the Trinitarian interpretation; in the over 90 times the word appears in the New Testament relating to people, never once is it used for more than one person. The same word which is used to describe human beings as single selves is used to describe God as "one God" (Matt 19:17, Mark 12:29, Luke 18:19, Gal 3:20, 1 Tim 2:5, etc.) and also as "one Father" (Matt 23:9, Jn 8:41, Heb 2:11, etc.). "One Father" obviously describes one person, and on this we can all agree. But what about "one God" or "one Lord"? The Greek usage of "one Lord" (*kurios eis*) by the Jews is clear. In the Old Greek (LXX) version of Daniel 3:17 we read: *"for there is a God who is in heaven, <u>our one Lord</u>, whom we fear."* Compare this with 1 Corinthians 8:6 or Ephesians 4:5, in which we read that Jesus (one person) is "one Lord." As the one person of Jesus is described as one Lord, so is the one person of God described as one Lord in Daniel 3:17, and, ultimately, in the *Shema* of Mark 12:29.

Nevertheless, some modern Trinitarians attempt to avoid the implications of the *Shema* by claiming that the specific way in which the Jewish God is "one" is not provided by the text. For them, an alleged ambiguity is an open door to speculation. There is no reason, however, in either Deuteronomy 6:4 or Mark 12:29, for readers to understand this "one" in any other sense than the sense which the rest of the Bible gives it. When the Bible says that Abraham is "one," are we so free to speculate? Furthermore, if it is true that the nature of God's "oneness" is not actually articulated, does that not immediately impugn the authority of the Trinitarian explanation? Why is the explanation that the "one" refers simply to one Person invalid, but a reference to three or more Persons is not? When it comes to the "one" of the *Shema*, this Trinitarian interpretation throws biblical language into a strange muddle: its meaning is indefinite and all interpretations are possible except the unitarian interpretation. Nevertheless, both biblical exegesis and historical analysis bring us inevitably to the conclusion that the *Shema* was not understood by either the ancient Israelites or the Jews in Jesus' time in the metaphysical way that Trinitarianism requires. Since the *Shema* was an integral part of the Sinai revelation to Israel, we should not begin by assuming that its meaning was not actually revealed. We need not conclude that

---

[1020] Ibid.

[1021] "one person (εἰς — heis masculine singular)..." See A. T. Robertson, "Commentary on John 17:1," *Robertson's Word Pictures of the New Testament* (Nashville: Broadman Press, 1932, 1933).

the Jews misunderstood God or that God had left room for variant interpretation of his "foremost commandment."

Let Us Make Man

Much has been made of the plural words employed in the opening pages of Genesis. It has been rather popular for Trinitarians to say that the Hebrew word for God, "elohim," which carries the plural ending *"im,"* denotes the existence of more than one Person in the Godhead. This argument is thought to be further enhanced by the Creator speaking to an "us" in the creation narrative: *"Then God (elohim) said, "Let us make man in our image, after our likeness"* (Gen 1:26a ESV).

But does the plural form of the word "elohim" (in English translated as God, god, or gods) really require a plurality of gods or that the Creator himself is made up of more than one personality? To make such an inference oversteps the bounds of Scripture. As one respected Trinitarian scholar affirms, "To conclude a plurality of persons from the name itself is dubious."[1022] While *"elohim"* is used many times by the Hebrew Scriptures to refer to multiple divine beings (Jer. 25:6), it also is used of divine beings that are singular in number. The Philistine god Dagon, who was not a trinity,[1023] is called "elohim": *"When the men of Ashdod saw that it was so, they said, 'The ark of the God of Israel must not remain with us, for His hand is severe on us and on Dagon our god* (elohim)' " (1 Sam 5:7).

"Elohim" is not the only noun in Hebrew that can appear in a plural form but carry a singular meaning. *Gesenius' Hebrew Grammar* presents several examples: "zequim" (old age - Gen 44:20), "panim" (face - Num 6:25), and "ne'urim" (youth - Ps 127:4). These words all have the plural ending *"im"* but carry singular meanings. Clearly the form of these words in no way dictates their sense, but we are provided the singular meaning of these rare plural forms by the singular adjectives and verbs which surround them. Speaking specifically about "elohim," Gesenius comments: "The language has entirely rejected the idea of numerical plurality in *'elohim'* (whenever it denotes *one* God).... [This] is proved especially by its being almost invariably joined with a singular attribute."[1024] The word "elohim" cannot be taken out of its context and be expected to retain the writer's intended meaning. The connected words "us" and "our" cannot surmount the context in which we find them; the lucid opinion of the rest of Genesis is that a single individual personality acted as Creator. The Jews

---

[1022] Ryrie, p. 58.

[1023] See Charles Souvay, "Dagon," *The Catholic Encyclopedia*, Vol. 4 (New York: Robert Appleton Company, 1908), Web. 12 August 2013.

[1024] E. Kautzsch (ed.), *Gesenius' Hebrew Grammar* (Oxford: Clarendon Press, 1910), pp. 398-399.

understood this very well. Charles Hunting and Anthony Buzzard, in their landmark book *The Doctrine of the Trinity*, write:

> We must respect the fact that the Jews' familiarity with their own language had never led them to conclude that a plurality of persons in the Godhead was remotely hinted at in this creation chapter of Genesis. In the event that we might feel the Jews missed something from their own Bible, we should note in the succeeding verses (vv. 27-31) that the singular pronoun is always used with the word of God: "*in His* [not Their] own *image, in the image of God He* [not They] *created them*" (v. 27). One would be hard-pressed to conclude from this verse, where the personal pronoun describing God (His) is singular, that a plurality of beings was intended. Note further: "*Look, I* [not We] *have given you every plant yielding seed… for food…and God saw all that He* [not They] *had made, and it was very good*" (vv. 29-31)[1025]

What then of the phrase "Let us make man" in Genesis? Despite the common Christian speculation about an inner metaphysical dialogue between multiple Persons, widely respected Trinitarian Old Testament scholar and commentator Gordon Wenham offers some confidence on the matter: "Christians have traditionally seen [Genesis 1:26] as adumbrating [foreshadowing] the Trinity. It is now universally admitted that this was not what the plural meant to the original author."[1026] Arguably, a much more direct and comprehensive interpretation may be found in the suggestion that God is speaking, not to some other aspect of himself, but to his *angels*:

> "Let us create man" should therefore be regarded as a divine announcement to the heavenly court, drawing the angelic host's attention to the master stroke of creation, man… And in fact the use of the singular verb "create" in 1:27 does, in fact, suggest that God worked alone in the creation of mankind.[1027]

[1025] Anthony F. Buzzard, Charles F. Hunting, *The Doctrine of the Trinity: Christianity's Self-Inflicted Wound* (Lanham: International Scholars Publications, 1998), p. 23, emphasis added.

[1026] Wenham, p. 27.

[1027] Ibid., p. 28.

Though Wenham, a Trinitarian, still believes that Christ was active in Creation with the Father, he admits that "such insights were certainly beyond the horizon of the editor of Genesis."[1028] As with the rest of the Old Testament, in regard to the doctrine of the Trinity, we find absolute silence. That the Genesis writer intends not to suggest Trinitarianism, but to simply present God as the sole Creator speaking to his holy council, is widely supported. The staunchly pro-Trinitarian *NIV Study Bible* even contains this note:

> "*Us... Our... Our.*" God speaks as the Creator-king, announcing His crowning work to the members of His heavenly court (see 3:22; 11:7; Isaiah 6:8; I Kings 22:19-23; Job 15:8; Jeremiah 23:18).[1029]

We learn elsewhere from the biblical documents that the angels were indeed present and interacting with God during the creation of our world: "*Where were you when I laid the foundation of the earth... When the morning stars sang together and all the sons of God shouted for joy?*" (Job 38:4a, 7).[1030] We must ask then if it is really the best course of action to insert other unmentioned personalities (such as Jesus) into the established Genesis scenario.

In several places in the Bible we find that God refers to himself with his angelic court in the plural, and directly confers with them over important matters:

> *In the year of King Uzziah's death I saw the Lord sitting on a throne, lofty and exalted... Seraphim stood above Him... Then I heard the voice of the Lord, saying, "Whom shall I send, and who will go for us?" Then I said, "Here am I. Send me!*
> (Isaiah 6:1-2, 8)

> *Micaiah said, "Therefore, hear the word of the LORD. I saw the LORD sitting on His throne, and all the host of heaven standing by Him on His right and on His left. The LORD said, 'Who will entice Ahab to go up and fall at Ramoth-gilead?' And one said this while another said that. Then a spirit came forward and stood before the LORD and said, 'I will entice him.' The LORD said to him, 'How?' And he said,*

[1028] Ibid.
[1029] *NIV Study Bible* (Grand Rapids: Zondervan, 1985), p. 7.
[1030] See Job 1:6, 2:1, Genesis 6:2

'I will go out and be a deceiving spirit in the mouth of all his prophets.'
Then He said, 'You are to entice him and also prevail. Go and do so.' "
(1 Kings 22:19-22)

That Genesis 1:26 displays God's declaration, not to himself or another aspect of himself, but to his angelic council, has also been the understanding of Jewish scribes throughout history. Philo, the Alexandrian Jew living before Christ, wrote in his commentary that in Genesis 1:26, "The Father of the universe discourses to his own hosts."[1031] The *Targum of Pseudo-Jonathan*, an Aramaic translation thought to be from the fourth century, says, "And the Lord said to the angels who ministered before him, who had been created in the second day of the creation of the world, let us make man in our image, in our likeness."[1032] A more recent rabbinical commentary states, "God took counsel with the ministering angels, and said unto them, let us make."[1033]

We should consider the simplicity of the above interpretation against the improbability of the standard Trinitarian view. Furthermore, when Trinitarians say that the plural language used by God in Genesis 1:26 indicates a plurality of Persons in God, then it only follows that God's use of singular personal pronouns elsewhere indicates only one Person. If "Us" means the three Persons in Genesis 1:26, then when God says *"I am Yahweh, and there is no other; apart from me there is no God"* (Is 45:5), then there is only one Person who is God. Surely the Trinitarian does not intend for us to draw this conclusion, but he cannot have it both ways: either the biblical use of pronouns is an effective way to discern how many Persons are in God or it is not. Ultimately, we should not make too much of Genesis 1:26. It is, in the final analysis, a rather unassuming passage.[1034]

[1031] Philo (i. 556, ed. Mangey)

[1032] Genesis 1:26, *Targum of Pseudo-Jonathan*.

[1033] Solomon Buber (ed.), *Pesikta de-Rav Kahana* (Lyck, 1868), 34a.

[1034] In addition to the angelic interpretation, there is yet another, albeit less popular (and less likely) interpretation of the Genesis phrasing which ably avoids any Trinitarian implications. Some scholars are of the persuasion that the employment of the plural pronouns "us" and "we" in Genesis are simply Hebraisms, turns of the Hebrew language which intend to emphasize the overflowing grandeur of the subject. For example, in Genesis 42:30, 33 Joseph is called "the lords of the land." This called a "Plural of Majesty"; the use of plural terms to describe a single subject. A similar concept within Western language might be the "Royal We." Popes, bishops, and Victorian-era royalty are all known to have used the royal "we" to refer to themselves in their official declarations. The Creation of Man in Genesis is certainly a holy, royal act and such language may be employed in its account. In support of this view, The *Liberty Annotated Study Bible*, edited by Trinitarian Baptist minister Jerry Falwell, contains a note on Genesis 1:26 which argues that, "The plural pronoun "Us" is most likely a majestic plural from the standpoint of Hebrew grammar and syntax" (Jerry Falwell (ed.), *Liberty Annotated Study Bible* (Lynchburg: Liberty

Jesus: The Genesis Creator?

We should not, of course, disregard the direct testimony of Jesus concerning the identity of the Creator: "*And he answered and said, 'Have you not read that he who created them from the beginning made them male and female'*" (Matt 19:4). Note that Jesus does not say "They" or "We" or "I" created them. Even the rare Trinitarian can be found admitting: "[Jesus] never declared himself the creator of the world, an argument apparently in the Socinian's [Biblical Unitarian's] favor."[1035] Indeed for Jesus, the Creator was none other than the God of Jews, a person whom he consistently identified as the Father: "*It is my Father... of whom you* [the Jews] *say, 'He is our God'*" (Jn 8:54).

Still, some have attempted to highlight Apostolic verses such as "*All things were made by him*" (Jn 1:3 KJV), and "*For by him all things were created*" (Col 1:16 NASB) as proof that Jesus was the one who personally performed the Genesis creation. But we encounter in these citations both the misappropriation of biblical figures of speech and translation bias. One scholar notes, "Neither Paul nor any other New Testament writer uses the preposition 'by,' in speaking of the agency of the Son or Logos in creation."[1036] The *King James Version* of the Bible indeed translates "by" what most modern versions have recognized should be "through." Virtually every major English translation has now corrected this error in the Gospel of John's introduction. One theologian and Bible publisher confirms that:

> The KJV misleads us on this matter. In the first chapter of John's account we read that "All things were made *by* him" (John 1:3), and again, "the world was made *by* him" (John 1:10). In both cases it should be *through*. The Logos, or Word, of God was the means of making all, not the efficient first Cause of all. Christ is never set forth as the absolute Source.[1037]

University, 1988), p. 8). While earlier theologians may have viewed Genesis 1:26 as indicative of the Trinity, modern analysts (both Trinitarian and otherwise) widely regard it as either a plurality of majesty (with some even affirming it as the only possible explanation; see Keil & Delitzsch, *Commentary on the Old Testament*, Vol. I (Peabody: Hendric., 1989), p. 62), or a declaration to God's angelic court. Regardless of which interpretation one favors, both avoid projecting philosophical and theological anachronisms onto the writer of Genesis.

[1035] Flatt, pp. 174-175.

[1036] Ezra Abbot, *The Authorship of the Fourth Gospel, and Other Critical Essays* (Boston: Geo. H. Ellis, 1888), p. 369.

[1037] Adolph Ernst Knoch, *Christ and Deity* (Birkenfeld: Concordant Publishing, 1958), p. 45.

Even Origen in the third century likewise concluded that when the Apostolic witness speaks of things being made "through" Christ, it is an argument that the Son himself was not the originator of the creative act:

> And the Apostle Paul says in his epistle to the Hebrews: "*At the end of the days He spoke to us in his Son, whom He made heir of all things, 'through whom' also He made the ages,*" showing us that God made the ages through His Son, the "through whom" belonging, when the ages were made to the Only-begotten. Thus if all things were made, as in this passage also, through the Logos, then they were not made by the Logos, but by a stronger and greater one than He. And who else could this be but the Father?[1038]

Without question, for the Jews, including Jesus, the creative source and prime cause of everything is the Father: "*For us there is but one God, the Father, from whom are all things…*" (1 Cor 8:6a). For the earliest Christians, Jesus was not the originator, but the conduit through whom God's activity and expression flows: "*…and there is but one lord, Jesus Christ, through whom all things came and through whom we live*" (1 Cor 8:6b).

Nevertheless, it is still routinely reported by many Christians that the Son was not only present during Creation, but the very one who spoke it into existence. John MacArthur writes that Jesus "spoke the world into being at creation,"[1039] and other apologists echo his assertion, claiming that "God the Father planned the world, Jesus (the Word) spoke it into existence."[1040] Of course, the Bible nowhere exhibits such a scene. Far from presenting the Son as *speaking* at any time before his birth, the New Testament offers a picture of a Son who has only recently come onto the scene:

> God, *after* he spoke long ago to the fathers in the prophets in many portions and many ways, *in these last days* has spoken to us in his Son, whom he appointed heir of all things, through whom also he made the world (Hebrews 1:1-2 NASB).

[1038] Origen, *Commentary on John. The Ante-Nicene Fathers,* Vol. 10, Book 2 (Grand Rapids: Eerdmans, 1969), p. 328.

[1039] John F. MacArthur, *The MacArthur Bible Commentary* (Nashville: Thomas Nelson, 2005), p. 1368.

[1040] James B. Hoffman, *Sin and Life in the Kingdom of God* (Indianapolis: Dog Ear Publishing, 2009), p. 320.

Here a period of time in which the Son was *not* active in the divine revelation is described, despite the various Christological theories regarding the pre-birth activity of Jesus. Recalling part one of this book, Justin Martyr and others believed "the angel of the LORD" who spoke to the Hebrews was actually Christ. Likewise some Christians today, especially in evangelical circles, can still be found postulating that the priest Melchizedek who spoke with Abraham was actually the pre-incarnate Son.[1041] Evangelical author Hank Hanegraaff writes, "Melchizedek is in fact a Christophany. He is in fact a preincarnate appearance of Jesus Christ."[1042] But God, according to Hebrews 1, explicitly did *not* speak to the fathers through his Son until *these last days*, that is, until the recent days of Christ's ministry and the founding of the Church. It should be impossible to say that it was actually the Son speaking to Abraham in Genesis 14. We should also have great difficulty saying that the Son is the one who spoke creation into existence.

God, by himself, is always the creative source: "*I, the LORD, am the maker of all things, stretching out the heavens by myself and spreading out the earth all alone*" (Isaiah 44:24). Indeed, God's language describing his own solidarity is emphatic:

> *I am the LORD, and there is no other; besides me there is no God. I will gird you, though you have not known me; that men may know from the rising to the setting of the sun that there is no one besides me. I am the LORD, and there is no other, the one forming light and creating darkness* (Isaiah 45:5-7a).

God does not say "there is no other besides *us*," or "no other besides *our substance*," but no other besides "*me*," that is, "me, *personally*." It is thus reasonably understood to be the Father only; it is this person who says that no one else is God besides him, and that no other spoke the universe into being but he: "*For he spoke, and it was done*" (Ps 33:9), and "*at his command they were created*" (Ps 148:5).

[1041] "In the tradition of the early Church, patristic reflection on the significance of Melchizedek stimulated Christological formulations especially of pre-incarnate Christ and his pre-existence. The comparison between Christ and Melchizedek provided Augustine with a basis for a profound theological thought that is the foundation of his Christology and Marian theology" (John M. Norris, "Augustine's Interpretation of Genesis in the City of God XI-XV," *Studia Patristica*, Vol. XLIII (Louvain: Peeters Publishers, 2006), p. 218).

[1042] Hank Hanegraaff, "Who Was Melchizedek?" Hank Hanegraaff Blogspot. 13 September 2010. Web. 22 December 2015. <http://hankhanegraaff.blogspot.com/2010/09/who-was-melchizedek.html>.

Jesus himself not only confirms with the Jews that another person was responsible for creation (Matt 19:4), but even explains that *"God created the world"* (Mk 13:19). By this he means, of course, the God of the Jews. Jesus identified the traditional God of the Jews as *"the Father"* (Jn 8:54). Indeed for the Jews, the Creator God had always been the Father: *"Do we not all have one Father? Has not one God created us?"* (Mal 2:10). Even in the Trinitarian system, the Father is explicitly *not* the Son; thus even Trinitarians agree that when Jesus speaks of "God" he means "the Father." It is this traditional God, the Father, who says he performed the Genesis creation *"all alone"* (Is 44:24), excluding the Son or anyone else.

We must be understand that the Jewish Creator is not a Platonic deity. Contrary to the opinions of the Greek fathers, God does not require an intermediary to do his "dirty work" for him. He uses no Demiurge (angel or eternal Son) to create—he accomplishes it himself: *"Has not my hand made all these things?"* (Is 66:2). The creative activity he performs is always direct and personal. The Hebrews concur: *"Your hands made me and formed me"* (Ps 119:73), and on this point Jesus likewise stands in full agreement: *"God [the Father] created"* (Mk 13:19).

Jesus and the Age to Come

The previously cited NASB translation of Hebrews 1:2, which reads: *"in his Son, through whom also he made the world,"* is emblematic of the Trinitarian effort to connect Jesus to the Genesis creation. The NIV even renders it, *"through whom he made the universe."* However, the word translated as "universe" and "world" here is actually the Greek "aionas," which literally means "ages."[1043] Though the NASB translates it "world," the *NAS Exhaustive Concordance* also defines it as "a space of time, an age." The writer of Hebrews might have employed other Greek terms to mean planet earth or the created universe, such as "oikoumene" or "kosmos," yet he was deliberately referring to the *ages*, and from the rest of Hebrews we can assume that this is the time of *"the world to come, about which we are speaking"* (Heb 2:5).

Yet what does it mean that the ages of the world to come are *made* through Christ? The Greek word translated "made" (poieo) has a wide range of meaning and is rendered dozens of different ways by the NASB.[1044] We might consider

---

[1043] See *Thayer's Greek Lexicon*. See also *Englishman's*, which defines "aion" as "forever, an unbroken age," and *Strong's* which defines it as "an age, a cycle of time, especially of the present age as contrasted with the future age, and of one of a series of ages stretching to infinity."

[1044] The NASB has translated "poieo" in the following ways: accomplished, acted, appointed, committed, establishing, execute, performed, composed, produced, worked, etc.

the translation *"established"* here. In Hebrews 1:1a, 2b we see that it was actually *"God... [who] established the ages."* The Son is not then the original creator of our planet, but the one through whom *God* has established the new age after Christ's resurrection, God's new world order, his new system of things. Indeed, when Christ was exalted by God, the power structure of the universe was dramatically rearranged. Hebrews says that *"when [Jesus] had made purification of sins,"* that is, after his death and resurrection, *"he sat down at the right hand of the Majesty on high, having become as much better than the angels"* (Heb 1:3b-4a). By God's command, the angels are now subject to Jesus. Paul writes that:

> *The God of our Lord Jesus Christ, the glorious Father... raised [Jesus] from the dead and seated him at his right hand in the heavenly places, far above all rule and authority and power and dominion, and every name that is named, not only in this age but also in the one to come.*
> (Ephesians 1:17a, 20-21)

Note Paul's emphasis above, that *the God of Jesus*, the Father, established a new power structure when he exalted Christ, a new organization that continues into "the age to come." And so the writer of Hebrews concurs that "the ages" have been established by God through Jesus; that is, the rearrangement of the heavens and the earth was initiated through the Father's elevation of Jesus to his right hand.

In this light, the popularly cited Colossians 1:15-16, which is still one of the most hotly debated passages in the New Testament, also becomes more clear. The text is usually rendered this way by Trinitarians:

> *He is the image of the invisible God, the firstborn of all creation. For by him all things were created, both in the heavens and on earth, visible and invisible, whether thrones or dominions or rulers or authorities—all things have been created through him and for him.*
> (Colossians 1:15-16 NASB)

First, we must note that Paul was writing this letter to the Colossians because they had become detached from Christ as the Head of the Body (Col 2:19). Paul is working here, first and foremost, to emphasize Christ's importance as the foundation of both the present Church and the coming Messianic Age.

Secondly, verse 15 in the above passage is actually one of the strongest evidences against the deity of Christ. To Paul, Jesus is not the invisible God himself; he is the invisible God's *image*. The Greek word for "image" here is "eikon," defined as "a likeness, (literally) a statue, profile, or (figuratively) representation, resemblance—image." We must emphasize that the image of something is not the thing itself, but only a depiction of the thing. In Luke 20:24 and Mark 12:16 Jesus asked the Jews whose "*image*" (eikon) was on the denarius, and they replied "*Caesar.*" Of course, Caesar himself was not on the coin; it was only a representation of Caesar, a depiction. In the same way, Jesus is not God himself, but a representation of him, even the "*exact representation*" (Heb 1:3) due to his perfect exhibition of God's qualities, words and works. To say that Jesus is "*the firstborn of all creation*" (v. 15b) furthermore places him squarely within the realm of created things.[1045] The designation "firstborn" means simply that he is preeminent within that group, that he has priority among the other subjects in that category.[1046] As the King James renders it, Jesus is the preeminent one "*of every creature*" (KJV). We must conclude that Jesus is designated the "firstborn" by Paul in the sense that he is the first in ascendency or rank, since several verses later Paul says that Jesus became the "*firstborn from the dead*" specifically "*so that he himself will come to have first place in everything*" (Col 1:18).

Now verse 16 is translated by the NASB and many other Trinitarian translations as "*For by him all things were created.*" This is not the best wording. Several other translations, such as the NIV, ERV, ASV, YLT, and the Douay-Rheims, better translate it "*For in him all things were created.*" The Greek phrase for "in him" is "en auto." The "en" here is causal and, as Buzzard notes, means "because of him, for his sake, with him in view, with him in intention."[1047] We must place our greatest attention however on the following phrase "*were created*"

[1045] Note also Revelation 3:14 which describes Jesus as "*the chief of the creation of God*" (YLT), or "*the beginning of the creation of God*" (NASB).

[1046] Many "Arians" have attempted to use this verse to demonstrate that a pre-existent Son was chronologically the first creation of God before he made the world. But "firstborn" is used in both the Old and New Testaments not only to indicate chronology but priority: "The firstborn was given priority or preeminence, as well as the best inheritance, by their parents. 'Firstborn' can also be used figuratively to denote the most or best of something. For example, the expression 'firstborn of the poor,' (Isa. 14:30, NRSV) means one who is supremely poor, or the poorest of the poor. *Protokos*, the Greek word for "firstborn," is used eight times in the New Testament, usually with reference to Jesus. He is called Mary's firstborn son (Luke 2:7), the firstborn of all creation (Col. 1:15), the firstborn of the dead (Col. 1:18; Rev. 1:5), the firstborn of God's family (Rom. 8:29), and simply the "firstborn" (Heb. 1:6; 12:23). The intent of all of these references is to show Jesus' priority and preeminence in the church as the firstborn from the dead and firstborn of all God's family" (Eugene E. Carpenter, Philip W. Comfort, *Holman Treasury of Key Bible Words* (Nashville: Broadman & Holman Publishers, 2000), p. 281).

[1047] Anthony F. Buzzard, *The One God, the Father, One Man Messiah Translation* (McDonough: Restoration Fellowship, 2015), p. 497. Buzzard cites several sources here regarding the causal nature of "en": *Expositor's Greek Testament*, Vol. 3, p. 504; Turner, *A Grammar of NT Greek*, Vol. 3, p. 253; Dunn, *Christology in the Making*, p. 190.

in 11:16b. This is the aorist form of "create" and a verbal construct known as "the divine passive."[1048]

When actions are placed in the passive, *God is the obvious agent*.[1049] For example, "*to those who have, more will be given*" (Mark 4:25) means "to those who have, *God* will give more." The divine passive occurs in at least ninety-six separate instances in the Synoptics,[1050] and may have even been a way for the pious Jew, who wished to avoid disrespecting God, to speak of him without uttering his name.[1051] There are over fifty instances in the New Testament in which God, the Father, is designated as the Creator.[1052] When Paul says "in him all things were created" in Colossians, he does not intend to celebrate the man from Nazareth as Creator, but means "because of Jesus all things were created by God, the Father."

What was it that God created here in Colossians 1:16ff? Was it the Genesis creation or the new Messianic power structure? Even Trinitarians such as Thomas C. Oden have admitted that "the 'all things' in Colossians 1:16 could be taken as a reference to the entire cosmos *or* to the new creation in Christ."[1053] Many are convinced that Paul has this new creation, not the original construction of our world, in mind.[1054] One reason is that the context of the passage does not appear to refer to the Genesis creation, in which the luminaries, plants, and animals were created. Instead Colossians speaks about thrones, dominions, and authorities—as if a new government had been established. If that is the case, we have already seen how it was the God of Jesus, the Father, who established both a new heavenly hierarchy and a new age to come through his exaltation of Christ (Heb 1:1, 3-4, 2:5, Eph 1:17a, 20-21).[1055]

[1048] A. T. Robertson writes that "created" here is "the connotative aorist passive indicative of 'ekisthe'... Have been created (ektistai). Perfect passive indicative of kitzo, 'stand created,' 'remain created.' ... [Christ is] the intermediate and sustaining agent" (A. T. Robertson, *Word Pictures in the New Testament*, Vol. IV (Grand Rapids: Baker Book House, 1933), p. 478). Garland also writes that this expresses "a divine passive, 'in him [not by him] all things were created' " (David E. Garland, *The NIV Application Commentary: Colossians, Philemon* (Grand Rapids: Zondervan, 1998), p. 44).

[1049] Daniel B. Wallace, *Greek Grammar: Beyond the Basics* (Grand Rapids: Zondervan, 1996), p. 437.

[1050] Robert H. Stein, *The Method and Message of Jesus' Teaching* (London: Westminster John Knox Press, 1994), p. 64.

[1051] J. Jeremias, *New Testament Theology* (New York: Scribner's, 1971), pp. 9-14.

[1052] Buzzard, *The One God*, p. 188.

[1053] Thomas C. Oden, Peter Gorday, *Colossians, 1-2 Thessalonians, 1-2 Timothy, Titus, Philemon* (New York: Fitzroy Dearborn Publishers, 2000), p. xxvii, emphasis added.

[1054] See for example Grotius' interpretation as cited by Barnes' *Notes on the New Testament* on Colossians 1:16.

[1055] Many scholars have suggested that Paul understood the new creation to have begun in Christ's death and resurrection. See T. Jackson, *New Creation in Paul's Letters* (Tubingen: Mohr Siebeck, 2010), p. 95.

Nevertheless, even if Paul intends to refer to the Genesis creation here, it ultimately does not necessitate a "Jesus is God" interpretation. It is still God the Father enacting the creation in either case. But what might Paul mean by saying that the Father created "through" Jesus?

Here Paul likely alludes to the "Wisdom" tradition, prevalent in the Psalms, Proverbs and other Jewish literature, in which God is said to have constructed the world *through his wisdom*. In the Jewish tradition, God's wisdom, God's word, and even God's Torah are used interchangeably.[1056] More on God's creation through his word (Hebrew: "davar," Greek: "logos") will be covered in a later chapter of this book. But for now, we will focus briefly on God's employment of *wisdom* and its identification with Jesus by Paul.

In the Old Testament, God's wisdom was a principle through which God created the universe. In the *Septuagint* version of Psalm 103:24 we read: "*How great are thy works, O Lord! In wisdom hast thou wrought them all.*" Through this same principle of wisdom, "*kings reign and rulers decree what is just*" (Prov 8:15). Solomon needed wisdom to execute proper order over the nation (1 Kings 3:1-15); God needed it to order creation. For Paul, Jesus is seen as a representation of God's wisdom. Indeed Jesus bears the Messianic "spirit of wisdom" (Is 11:3-5), and himself "increased in wisdom" (Lk 2:40), and ultimately represents God's wisdom to his disciples. Paul expresses that Christ himself "*has become for us wisdom from God*" (1 Cor 1:30). "Wisdom" is not then a pre-existent person who later became the human Jesus; it is a principle that the man Jesus had come to represent. As it has been noted, Jesus is "not simply the fulfillment of the Mosaic Torah but also *the embodiment of the wisdom of God seen in the revelation of the created order itself.*"[1057] If for Paul the person of Jesus is an embodiment or a representation of the wisdom that God used when he structured the world, then Paul's statement that God made all things "through Jesus" should be seen as an encapsulation of that idea.[1058] As Dunn notes:

[1056] Wisdom is equated with God's word in the Jewish work *Wisdom of Solomon* (Wisdom 9:2). In *Sirach*, wisdom is equated with God's Torah (Sirach 24:23). Philo says that Moses was the embodiment of Torah (thus God's wisdom, God's word) in *On Moses* 1, 162. And the Apostle John says that Jesus is the embodiment of God's word (thus God's wisdom, God's Torah) in John 1:1-1:14.

[1057] Daniel L. Aikin, *A Theology for the Church* (Nashville: B & H Publishing Group, 2007), p. 109, emphasis added.

[1058] "Paul—and other early Christians—borrow from Jewish wisdom traditions which spoke of God's wisdom as the means though which God created the world (Proverbs 8; Wisdom 7). By assigning to Jesus the role previously assigned to God's Wisdom, equated in some places with God's Torah or Law (e.g., Sirach 24:23), Paul has attributed to Jesus Christ the place in God's

[Paul] presented the Lordship of Christ within the context of Jewish monotheism and Christ as one whom Christians now see to embody and mediate that power of God which created and sustains the world... he sees Jesus not as a pre-existent divine being, but as a man, a Jew, whose God is the one God, and yet who so embodied God's creative power and saving wisdom... that he can be identified as "the power of God and the wisdom of God."[1059]

As for the last half of Colossians 1:16, we find another helpful parallel in Ephesians, where Paul says that God's original purpose was *"that in the dispensation of the fullness of time he might gather together in one all things in Christ, both which are in heaven, and which are on earth"* (1:10 KJV). Thus in Colossians Paul reaffirms that "all things" were created for him by God (1:16); God has made the exalted Jesus *"head over all things to the church"* (Eph 1:22).

In summary, we see that God placed Jesus, via his resurrection, over every *"authority, power, and dominion, and every name that is invoked"* in Ephesians 1:21, and these are the same *"thrones, dominions, rulers, and authorities"* that God makes in Christ in Colossians 1:16. In the former passage, it is clearly *"the God and Father of our Lord Jesus Christ"* (v. 1) who performs the rearrangement, and this activity establishes a new order that exists now and will exist in the age to come (v. 21b). Jesus himself, the culmination of God's works, is now to be seen as a representation of the wisdom that God used to structure both the original creation *and* this new creation.

There is not then, of necessity, a presentation of Jesus as the Jewish Creator. As it has been observed:

In the early stages [Paul's era] it would be inaccurate to say that Christ was understood as a pre-existent being become incarnate, or that Christ himself was thought to have been present and active in creation... in the Pauline letters and probably the introduction to Hebrews also the thought is primarily of Christ as the eschatological embodiment of the

---

purposes elsewhere delegated to Wisdom or the Law" (Marianne Meye Thompson, *Colossians and Philemon* (Grand Rapids: Eerdmans, 2005), p. 30).

[1059] Dunn, *Christology in the Making,* p. 211.

wisdom of God, as the one through whom the creator God...
[brings] creation's renewal.[1060]

The Jewish writings of the New Testament will not prove an able defender
of the idea that Christ was himself the Creator, the primordial Hebrew God. As
Emil Brunner admitted: "God alone is the Creator... the Son is called simply and
solely the mediator of the Creation. In the New Testament the Son, or Jesus
Christ, is never called the Creator. The title is given to the Father alone."[1061] We
have already observed that the language of the Jews describing God remained
the same even after the advent of the Messiah. God was ever the Father, the
Almighty Creator, a single monolithic personality whose strict unity was stressed
above all doctrines. This unmistakable ancestral deity was, even after the advent
of Jesus, constantly juxtaposed with his anointed servant:

> *"The God of Abraham, the God of Isaac, and the God of Jacob, the God
> of our Fathers, glorified his servant Jesus"* (Acts 3:13).

> *"The God of our ancestors raised Jesus from the dead after you killed him
> by hanging him on a cross"* (Acts 5:30).

> *"The God of this people Israel... raised [Jesus] from the dead"*
> (Acts 13:17, 30).

How would a first-century Jew have understood this language? Would they
have gathered from these sermons that this Jewish man whom the Jewish God
raised from the dead somehow *was* the Jewish God? Modern Jews have
unambiguously explained: "Judaism has always been rigorously unitarian,"[1062]
and many Christian scholars have confirmed that belief in "a second being in
God involves departure from the Jewish community."[1063] Even well-respected
Trinitarians have agreed: "Judaism [is] unitarian,"[1064] and "the monotheism was
then, as it still is, unitarian,"[1065] and that just as Old Testament Jews had been
taught by God himself that God is "one person,"[1066] so Jews to this day "still

---

[1060] Ibid.
[1061] Brunner, *Dogmatics*, Vol. I, p. 232.
[1062] "Deism," *The Jewish Encyclopedia*, 1906.
[1063] Casey, *From Jewish Prophet to Gentile God*, p. 176.
[1064] Brunner, p. 205.
[1065] Hodgson, p. 74.
[1066] Warfield, p. 127.

assert that God is only one in person."[1067] This harmony is important since, as noted previously, "in the teaching of Jesus and the Apostles relative to the monotheism of the Old Testament and Judaism, there had been no element of change whatsoever."[1068]

We must always take care not to fall into the disrespect of some Trinitarian theologians, who portray the Jewish idea of God as underdeveloped or unrealized, treating the Jews like theological children unable to master the requisite metaphysics in which the later Gentiles thrived.[1069] The monotheism of Israel, and those who affirmed it (like Jesus), must not be underestimated. Since he was a faithful Jew, even the ultimate Jew, we should not expect to find in Jesus' sayings about his God's identity a recondite meaning. His profession, as we shall next discover, was always the simple, yet fully formed doctrine of the Jew, a confession of a single personal Father. His confessions about himself involved only a claim to be that one God's specially chosen and faithful servant—God's Messiah.

[1067] Beveridge, p. 66.

[1068] Werner, p. 241.

[1069] "But that the [Jewish] people at large were entirely without the notion of a Trinity, is evident enough; and, in the scheme of the divine nature delivered to them, they were not cautioned against confounding the persons in the Godhead, lest, from the natural tendency of weak minds, they should fall into the opposite extreme of dividing the substance, which, according to their moral and intellectual state at the time, would have proved to them the far more dangerous delusion" (John Browne, *Sermons Preached at the Lecture founded by John Bampton* (Oxford: OUP, 1809), p. 88); The idea of the Trinity "had never at any time penetrated the mind... That article was not laid down in the Old Testament as an object of belief, because the people as yet were incapable of receiving it" (Salmeron; *Comm.*, tom. i. pp. 201-2; Prolog. Xi. Can. XXV, quoted in Wilson, *Uni. Princip.*, p. 334).

9

GOD AND HIS MESSIAH

"If a prophet or a dreamer of dreams arises among you…
saying, 'Let us go after other gods (whom you have not
known) and let us serve them,' you shall not listen to the
words of that prophet or that dreamer of dreams; for
Yahweh your God is testing you to find out if you love
Yahweh your God with all your heart and with all your
soul. You shall follow Yahweh your God and fear him;
and you shall keep his commandments, listen to his voice,
serve him, and cling to him."

— Deuteronomy 13:1-4

D URING THE COURSE OF JESUS' THREE-YEAR MINISTRY,
as recorded by the Gospels, the Nazarene offered many profound
statements about himself and his relationship to God. Some of these
sayings were misinterpreted by his enemies (often to be reprimanded
or corrected), but his direct teachings about who God is are unmistakable. As
some of the most daring academics have noted, when one refrains from applying
the framework of developed Trinitarianism to the Jesus narrative, the rhetorical
fire of an erudite, reflective, and sternly monotheistic rabbi leaps off the pages to
illuminate an upsetting incongruity with modern Christianity. Contemporary
academics, both liberal and conservative, can be found acknowledging a stark
difference between the modes of developed orthodoxy and Christ:

It is indeed an extraordinary and thought-provoking fact that these traditional Christian doctrines play no part at all in Jesus' own summary of his message to mankind. Indeed it would certainly seem, on a straightforward reading of the Synoptic Gospels, that Jesus thought of God in purely monotheistic and unitarian terms.[1070]

We must keep in mind the fact that "no responsible NT scholar would claim that the doctrine of the Trinity was taught by Jesus."[1071] Therefore all of Christ's modern acolytes should join together happily, not in the seeking out of fuel for a stilted sophistry, but in the celebration of the primal center of the genuinely Jewish faith which propelled the life and operating spirit of the most celebrated teacher in human history. In essence, Christ's students must stop clinging to their own inference of the Trinity and open their arms to whatever information he readily and unequivocally presents. That Jesus directly advocates a spirit of what today we would define as "unitarianism," or the belief that God is a single self, is surely the most critical unsung communiqué of the New Testament.

Father of Jesus, God of the Jews

For all Jews, including Jesus, "God" and "the Father" are always one and the same. To the Samaritan woman Jesus made the identity of God quite clear, and the requisite appreciation of him quite practical: *"The true worshipers will worship the Father in spirit and truth... God is spirit, and those who worship him must worship in spirit and truth"* (Jn 4:23b-24). Many times the New Testament portrays the purpose of Christ as one of disclosure concerning the person of God (Jn 1:18, 17:25). Did he fail in his revelatory mission when he taught that to worship "the Father" was to worship "God"?

Armed with a respectful consideration of the historical God of Judaism, all of Rabbi Jesus' instructions and demands for those around him regarding their perception of and devotion to God should be carefully examined. The Apostles, carrying on Christ's tradition, can likewise hardly be approached outside this context. Both the Greek and Hebrew Scriptures are emphatically clear on the issue, loudly confirming that to both the ancient Israelites and the Jews of the early Church, "God" was unequivocally the "*Father*":

[1070] John Hick, *The Concept of Monotheism in Islam and Christianity, A Recent Development within Christian Monotheism* (Austria: Typostudio & Druckkunst Wie, 1982), p.63

[1071] Hanson, p. 87.

"Do you thus repay the LORD, O foolish and unwise people? Is not He your Father who has bought you? He has made you and established you" (Deuteronomy 32:6 NASB).

"Call me 'Father' and [do] not turn away from following me... declares the LORD" (Jeremiah 3:19b-20 NIV).

"He shall cry to Me, 'You are my Father, My God, and the rock of my salvation" (Psalm 89:26 NKJV).

"Do we not all have one Father? Has not one God created us?" (Malachi 2:10 NASB).

"Yet for us there is but one God, the Father" (1 Corinthians 8:6 NASB).

"Grace and peace to you from God our Father and from the Lord Jesus Christ" (Romans 1:7 NIV).

"One God and Father of all who is over all and through all and in all" (Ephesians 4:6 NASB).

Jesus, in his conversation with the Samaritan woman, taught that one *must* worship God "in truth," that is, to worship God for who he truly is and in the way that he requires (Jn 4:24). Who Jesus believes this God is, is not easily missed. His presentation of Yahweh as the Father of all, the one true God, is in firm agreement with the Jewish legacy:

"But Yahweh is the true God" (Jeremiah 10:10a).

"For you are our Father... You, O Yahweh, are our Father" (Isaiah 63:16).

"Father... you [are] the only true God" (John 17:1a, 3b).

Considering the above verse, *"Father... This is eternal life, that they may know You, the only true God, and Jesus Christ whom You have sent"* (Jn 17:1a-3), we find that according to Christ, the very essence of life in the age to come is to be found in an express knowledge of two characters, one who is described as the only individual who is genuinely God, and the other who is someone else external to that exclusive class. Christ's unabashed distinction between the one God and himself is clear and consistent: *"Let not your heart be troubled. Believe in God, believe also in me"* (Jn 14:1). Of course, we do wonder where the alleged *third* person of Trinitarianism is in this instruction.

For the Trinitarian, a unique problem arises when considering John 17:3. That "the Father" is the true God is not disputed by anyone. What is debatable is whether or not "the Son," who according to Trinitarian dogma is explicitly *not* the Father (as he is a completely distinct Person), is *also* the "true God." But Jesus did not simply call the Father "God," thus leaving room for himself and yet another to also bear this description, but he called the Father "the only true God." In other words, Jesus made two arguments: first, that the Father is the true God (a sentiment with which Trinitarians would agree), and second that the Father is the only one who is true God (a sentiment which Trinitarians reject).

In John 17:3, the investigator finds theologians both ancient and modern dashing themselves on the rock of Christ's declaration with an astonishing and disquieting contempt for the Scripture. Augustine (d. 430 CE), the former Gnostic and revered forerunner of Calvinistic theology, certainly provides an example of this. When he came to John 17:3, he exposed at once an inability to resolve his dogma of the Son's true deity with the precise language of Christ, and an outrageous willingness to even alter said expression for the sake of backwards conformity. Augustine writes:

> "And this," He adds, "is eternal life, that they may know Thee, the only true God, and Jesus Christ whom Thou hast sent." The *proper* order of the words is, "That they may know Thee *and* Jesus Christ, whom Thou hast sent, as the only true God."[1072]

The audacity of Augustine, as he blatantly alters the words of Jesus in hopes of dogmatic preservation without even a hint of qualification, should rattle the teeth of every Bible student. Despite the inexcusable efforts of such doctors as

---

[1072] Augustine, *Homilies on the Gospel of John*, Ch. XVII, 1-5, Tractate CV, 3, emphasis added.

Augustine, the Christian still finds relief in Christ as he reminds the world: *"Heaven and earth will pass away, but my words will never pass away"* (Matt 24:35).

Throughout his recorded ministry, Jesus emphasized that the one he called "Father," not himself, is the traditional God of Judaism: *"It is my Father who glorifies me, of whom you say, 'He is our God' "* (Jn 8:54b). Though much confusion has been propagated over the centuries regarding the Jewish God's identity, a major part of the mission of the long-awaited Christ was to openly promote the identity of God among his countrymen. Indeed the Messiah comes saying, *"I will declare your name to my brethren...' "* (Heb 2:12), and according to Jesus, he was successful in that mission: *"O righteous Father... I have made your name known to them, and will make it known"* (Jn 17:25a-26a). Glorification of the Father as Jesus' ultimate purpose should always be kept in view (Matt 5:16; Jn 12:28; Jn 17:1). God himself has likewise been concerned with his proper honor as "Father." As he admonished Israel, *"A son honors his father, and a servant his master. Then if I am a father, where is my honor? And if I am a master, where is my respect?"* (Malachi 1:6).

The Messiah, the Associate of the One God

Just as we can immediately derive from Scripture that God is one in number, we find that Jesus is also numerically distinct from him. Christ demonstrates this himself: *"In your own Law it is written that the testimony of two witnesses is true. I am one who testifies for myself; my other witness is the Father, who sent me"* (Jn 8:18). The Law had presented this oft-cited principle, that the testimony of *two* is valid (Num 35:30), and Jesus affirms, *"If I alone bear witness about myself, my testimony is not deemed true"* (Jn 5:31). Christ quite obviously considers himself *only* one witness, but he needs the testimony of at least *two completely distinct individuals* in order to be credible in the eyes of the people. In John 8:18 Jesus explains that his Father is the second witness, making two total. But if Jesus is actually one-and-the-same with the Father in *any* sense, Christ has actually invalidated his testimony by claiming this Torah principle. The Trinitarian can often be heard, in defense of his questionable monotheism, declaring his agreement that God is only one. But if true, how does a single being occupy the position of two distinct witnesses? Would the Trinitarian be willing to admit a separation of the divine Persons just as thoroughly as one man must be separate from another in order to facilitate the testimony of two? Here we might also say that if Jesus is God, then as thoroughly as the Son and the Father are two distinct witnesses, so are the Son and the Father two distinct Gods. We may conclude that Jesus believes that he and the Father are completely separate; God being *one* and Jesus being another *one* making *two* different witnesses total.

We never encounter Jesus claiming to be the one God of Israel, rather we find him habitually asserting a lofty second place alongside the Deity, a divinely authorized man closely associated with God. This status and arrangement we find clearly and routinely prophesied in the Hebrew Scriptures. Of the Christ, God says: *"Awake, O sword, against My Shepherd, and against the man, My Associate"* (Zechariah 13:7a NASB), or *"the man who stands next to me"* (ESV) or *"the man who is my partner"* (NLT). In Matthew 26:31 Jesus explains that this prophecy applies to himself, and therefore so does its explicit description of the God-to-Messiah relationship.

Always in these Old Testament prophecies, Yahweh plays the solitary role of God for Israel, while God's "anointed one" plays the role of lord and king, a man foretold to be *"from among you, from your countrymen"* (Deut 18:15), and particularly *"coming up from the stump of Jesse"* (Is 11:1). The prophets had long described the Christ's origin: *"the House of Judah... from them will come the cornerstone"* (Zech 10:3b-4a), and even more precisely: *"But as for you, Bethlehem Ephrata... from you one will go forth for me to be ruler in Israel"* (Micah 5:2a). We see in Micah how the awaited Messiah was an individual chosen by God to rule *in God's stead* as his divinely appointed representative. If the Messiah were God himself, could he truly be said to be ruling instead of God? We might benefit from an appeal to the consensus of the Old Testament which places Yahweh in the exclusive role of the one God, and the Messiah in the secondary role of the one Davidic King:

> Then I will set over them one shepherd, My servant David, and he will feed
> them; he will feed them himself and be their shepherd. And I, Yahweh, will be
> their God, and my servant David will be prince among them; I Yahweh have
> spoken (Ezekiel 34:23-24).

The Hebrew prophecies about the Messiah and his relationship to God must comprise the foundation of the Christian understanding of Jesus' identity and role; these were in fact the same authoritative sources quoted by him and his disciples as proof of their message. Yet except perhaps for a few misappropriated passages from Isaiah, how often does the Christian run to the Old Testament prophecies to prove that Jesus was God in the flesh? On the other hand, the Hebrew Scriptures are simply brimming with indications that the prophesied Messiah would be an individual close to, distinct from, and in subjection to *his* God. Indeed the indisputable fact that the Messiah is said to *have a God* should be enough to give anyone pause:

> "*He shall stand, and shepherd them in the strength of Yahweh, in the majestic name of Yahweh his God*" (Micah 5:4a HCSB).

> "*You have loved righteousness and hated wickedness. Therefore God, your God, has anointed you with the oil of gladness beyond your companions*" (Psalm 45:7 ESV, Heb 1:9).

In Isaiah 11:2 we read: "*And the spirit of the LORD shall rest upon him, the spirit of wisdom and understanding, the spirit of counsel and might, the spirit of knowledge and of the fear of the LORD*" (Isaiah 11:2 KJV). Here the spirit of God is put on the Messiah. We would overly complicate this otherwise simple idea if we demand the interpretation that God (the Father) is anointing himself (the Son) with himself (the Holy Spirit). One wonders, if all three persons really are co-equal and all-powerful, what the purpose is in such a bizarre, circular exchange of anointing. One might also wonder if this is the best, most forthright reading of the text. Furthermore, the suggestion that the "spirit of knowledge" is being given to the all-knowing "God" here also seems rather obtuse. Likewise "the fear of Yahweh" which abides in this Messiah, a genuinely praiseworthy quality if he is a creature and a true subject, is turned into nonsense if the Messiah just *is* Yahweh. Did God and the prophet he spoke through intend the world to understand that God in any way fears himself? That the Messiah truly inhabits a subjected position in which a sincere fear of God is actually possible and morally praiseworthy, is surely what is being communicated in the prophetic record of the Hebrew people. The nature of this role is further elucidated as the Messiah is consistently portrayed, not as God, but as the *servant* of God. A servant, of course, is not equal to his master:

> "*Behold, my servant, whom I uphold; my chosen one in whom my soul delights. I have put my spirit upon him; he will bring forth justice to the nations*" (Is 42:1; Matt 12:18).

The New Testament continues:

> "*The God of Abraham, Isaac and Jacob, the God of our fathers, has glorified his servant Jesus… God raised up his servant.*"
> (Acts 3:13, 26)

> "[God spoke] *through the mouth of our father David, your servant…*
> *For truly in this city there were gathered together against your holy servant*
> *Jesus, whom you anointed, both Herod and Pontius Pilate, along with the*
> *Gentiles and the peoples of Israel… And now, Lord, look upon their*
> *threats and grant to your servants to continue to speak your word with all*
> *boldness, while you stretch out your hand to heal, and signs and wonders*
> *are performed through the name of your holy servant Jesus."*
> (Acts 4:25b, 27, 29-30 ESV)

The above passage is particularly interesting in that David, Jesus, Peter and the other disciples are each described as God's "servant." We might posit that just as thoroughly as the persons of David and Peter are subjected in absolute service to God, the person of Jesus is to be viewed in the same way. Indeed, by the very fact that Christ is explicitly identified as the "servant" of God, his inferiority is clearly communicated. Jesus himself delivers the principle: *"A disciple is not above his teacher, nor a servant above his master"* (Matt 10:24), and again, *"Remember what I told you: 'A servant is not greater than his master'"* (Jn 15:20), and again, *"Truly, truly, I say to you, a servant is not greater than his master, nor is a messenger greater than the one who sent him"* (Jn 13:16). This becomes all the more clear as Jesus explains: *"God sent me"* (Jn 8:42).

The Apostle Paul reveals that even after all things are subjected beneath Christ's feet through his glorification, he remains God's inferior:

> For *"God has put all things in subjection under his feet."* But when it says, *"all things are put in subjection,"* it is plain that he is excepted who put all things in subjection under him. When all things are subjected to him, then the Son himself will also be subjected to him who put all things in subjection under him, that God may be all in all.
> (1 Corinthians 15:27-28 ESV)

Here we see that all things are beneath Christ, except one thing: God. Paul even assumes that *"it is plain"* or *"it is obvious"* (HCSB) to everyone that when we speak of Christ's exalted status over everything, *"this does not include God himself, who put everything under Christ"* (NIV).[1073] Many Trinitarians will be quick to explain these verses by citing their belief that the second Person of the Trinity

---

[1073] "No words, one would think, could more clearly discriminate Christ from God, and declare his dependency and inferiority; and, of necessity, his infinite inferiority; because an inferior and dependent being must be a finite being, and finite and infinite do not admit of comparison" (Norton, p. 29).

engaged in some sort of self-deprivation at the Incarnation, temporarily divesting himself of his co-equal status with the Father while he was on the earth. Though we will better explore this contention in the coming sections of this chapter, we can immediately note that 1 Corinthians 15:27-28 says that even after the risen Messiah's dramatic exaltation, he remains God's inferior subject. Again, the Bible nowhere speaks of a metaphysical hierarchy of one member of a triune God having some inexplicable priority over a co-equal second Person, temporarily or not. The language of the Bible is clear. Paul furthermore demonstrates the unequivocal inferiority of Jesus to "God" in chapter 11:

> But I want you to understand that Christ is the head of every man, and
> the man is the head of a woman, and God is the head of Christ.
> (1 Corinthians 11:3 NASB)

1 Corinthians 11:3 is perhaps one of the most pointed and inescapable New Testament examples of Christ's inferiority and total subjugation to God. Here we have an equation of relationship: just as completely as every man is subject to the risen Christ, the risen Christ is subject to God. Similarly, in 3:23 we read that *"you belong to Christ; and Christ belongs to God."*

While it is asserted that the Father and Son are co-equal, Trinitarian theologian James Hastings, in his renowned *Hastings' Dictionary of the Bible,* reveals uncertainty here:

> It may be that St. Paul nowhere names Christ "God"... Still
> more explicit is 1 Corinthians 11:3: the head of the woman is
> the man, and the head of Christ is God; and in 1 Corinthians
> 15:28 Christ is portrayed as delivering up the Kingdom to
> God, and as finally submitting even Himself to a higher, 'that
> God may be all in all.' St. Paul does not give us much help,
> perhaps in solving this antinomy [inconsistency with
> Trinitarianism].[1074]

It is not only the Apostolic writings which bear witness to this arrangement; Jesus himself proudly demonstrates his inferiority to the Deity, saying, *"the Father is greater than I am"* (Jn 14:28b) and furthermore, *"My Father... is greater than all"* (Jn 10:29). Paul agrees on this point; after mentioning both Jesus and the Holy Spirit, he then declares that there is still *"one God and Father of all, who is over all,*

[1074] James Hastings, *Hasting's Dictionary of the Bible* (Grand Rapids: Baker Books, 1994), pp. 707-708.

and through all in all" (Eph 4:6). Of course the opinions of Paul and Jesus stand in sharp contrast to orthodoxy which demands that: "in this Trinity, no one is before or after, greater or less than the other; but all three persons are in themselves, coeternal and coequal."[1075]   But Jesus also provides us with a startlingly clear explanation of his association to the Deity:

> *Jesus said to her, "Stop clinging to me, for I have not yet ascended to the*
> *Father; but go to my brethren and say to them, 'I ascend to <u>my Father</u>*
> *<u>and your Father, and my God and your God</u>'"* (John 20:17).

What we have here is another equation of relationship. The association to God that Mary and the disciples enjoy is the same association that Jesus does. The God and Father of the Jews is the God and Father of Jesus. Interestingly, Christ echoes the sentiments of his family ancestors in this regard: *"your God [is] my God"* (Ruth 1:16). Indeed the Davidic Messiah was always prophesied to exhibit this express relationship to the Divine:

> *I have found David My servant; I have anointed him with My sacred*
> *oil… He will call out to me, <u>You are my Father, my God</u>, the rock of*
> *my salvation.*
> (Psalm 89:20, 26 HCSB)

Jesus himself expresses plainly that he *has* a God:

> *And about the ninth hour Jesus cried out with a loud voice, saying, "Eli,*
> *Eli, lama sabachthani?" that is, "<u>my God, my God</u>, why have you*
> *forsaken me?"*
> (Matthew 27:46 ESV)

> *Wake up, and strengthen the things that remain, which were about to die;*
> *for I have not found your deeds completed <u>in the sight of my God</u>.*
> (Revelation 3:2 NASB)

> *I will make him a pillar in the temple of <u>my God</u>… and I will write on*
> *him the name of <u>my God</u>, and the name of the city of <u>my God</u>, the new*
> *Jerusalem, which comes down out of heaven from <u>my God</u>.*
> (Revelation 3:12 NASB)

[1075] The Athanasian Creed, c. 500 CE.

The question now is obvious: how can Jesus be the one God and have a God, if there is only one God? If we are going to attribute a higher level meaning to plain words, we must have extremely good and consistent reasons for doing so. Our inferences about what Jesus *really means* when he claims to have a God should be reinforced by the Bible itself. Do the Apostlic writings support Jesus' claim to simply "have a God," as surely as they themselves do, without qualification?

> *Blessed be the God and Father of our Lord Jesus Christ, the Father of mercies and God of all comfort.*
> (2 Corinthians 1:3)

> *That the God of our Lord Jesus Christ, the Father of glory, may give to you a spirit of wisdom and of revelation in the knowledge of Him.*
> (Ephesians 1:17)

> *Praise be to the God and Father of our Lord Jesus Christ! In his great mercy he has given us new birth into a living hope through the resurrection of Jesus Christ from the dead.*
> (1 Peter 1:3)

That the apostles were convinced that even the risen Christ worshiped the same God they did is undeniable, though we cannot say the same for Trinitarians who seem to have difficulty with what should be a straightforward proposition. When asked if Jesus has a God, Trinitarian apologists can be found saying, "The answer to this question is yes and no."[1076] In their argument, it is only because Jesus (God) took on a man-nature that he "had someone he would *call* his God."[1077] Quite plainly, this Trinitarian proposition does not actually provide a true God for Jesus in any practical sense. The Trinitarian Jesus does not cry out to God in the same way that every other man does, from a place of inferiority and need; rather he somehow, inexplicably, calls out to God from a place of co-equality, perhaps in some perfunctory or metaphysical sense. Here Jesus is, paradoxically, both the dependent and the dependable. Of course this idea is nowhere presented in Scripture, and should be recognized as rendering Christ's

---

[1076] Matt Slick, "Does Jesus Have a God?" Christian Apologetics and Research Ministry. Web. 24 October 2014. <http://carm.org/does-jesus-have-a-god>.
[1077] Ibid, emphasis added.

calling out to his God in desperation on the cross ("*My God, my God...*") a strange outward demonstration void of any reliance on a higher power.

To those evangelical defenders who say that Jesus calls out to God "from his human nature only," and thus it is a genuine calling, we might point out that he is still not calling out from the totality of his Person. No, an abstract human nature cannot have a God; only a person can, and as Trinitarians have said, the personhood of Christ is "the personhood of the eternal second person of the Trinity. The fully divine Son is the person."[1078] Therefore, if it is confessed that his dependence on God was only in his man nature, we must point out that a break has likely been made with orthodoxy.

Recalling the Nestorian controversy which took center stage at the orthodox Council of Ephesus in 431 CE, the idea that the human and divine natures of Christ were separated within his person was pronounced heretical. Nestorius was anathematized because he was uncomfortable with calling Mary the "Mother of God" and instead called her the "Mother of Christ" only, meaning she was the mother of the human nature only, not of the God nature. But the orthodox party argued that since the two natures of Christ were necessarily united, Mary was the mother of both natures as both natures simultaneously experienced the birth. The later Council of Chalcedon in 451 CE solidified for orthodoxy the notion that "the one person Jesus Christ [has] two natures... and that these two natures are organically and indissolubly united."[1079] What orthodox Trinitarianism actually professes here is that the human and divine natures are united in such a way that one side cannot undergo an experience while the other side is completely segregated and unaffected; this would, as the synods argued, create two different persons within Christ. Therefore, the *one person* of Jesus cannot have a God in only one nature but not in the other. If Mary is the true mother of the God nature, then the one called the Father is the true God of the God nature. In the orthodox model, God, inexplicably, *has a God*. Furthermore, God was also born, tempted, became tired, matured, grew in wisdom, and suffered. Despite the unpopularity of these notions among many modern evangelicals, these are the implications of orthodoxy.

Many of the very same mainstream Christian theologians who have decried other Christians as "heretical" because they do not adhere to council decisions, have proven equally unorthodox by espousing Nestorian or semi-Nestorian

---

[1078] David Mathis, "Enhypostasis: What Kind of Flesh Did the Word Become?" Desiring God. 25 December 2010. Web. Accessed 27 July 2015.
<http://www.desiringgod.org/articles/enhypostasis-what-kind-of-flesh-did-the-word-become>.
[1079] Augustus H. Strong, *Systematic Theology* (Philadelphia: Judson Press, 1985), p. 673.

views on the dual natures. As we saw in earlier chapters, evangelicals like R. C. Sproul teach that "atonement was made by the human nature of Christ... death is something that is experienced only by the human nature."[1080] But is this not the "heresy" of Nestorius who claimed that "the human aspect of Christ died on the cross, but not the divine"?[1081] Incredibly, while Sproul elsewhere denounces Nestorius as heretical and praises the triumph of the council which declared him so, we wonder if Sproul is able to recognize his own thoughts in the heresiarch.[1082] As Saint Hilary so pointedly remarked, "We condemn either the doctrine of others in ourselves, or our own in that of others."[1083] Such has been, it would seem, the standard practice for Trinitarian doctors who, despite their public profession of a great ecumenical unity, to this day cannot entertain a comprehensive harmony between themselves and the difficult demands of orthodoxy.[1084] In contrast to the idea that only the human nature perished on the cross, the New Testament tells us that "*we were reconciled to God through the death of his Son*" (Rom 5:10). It is not a "nature" then, but "the Son" himself who dies. A "human nature" cannot atone for the sins of the people, only the *human person* of the Son who is qualified to perform the saving work (Heb 2:17).

Ultimately, the subordination of Christ to God proves to be well-substantiated in the New Testament. The ancient Subordinationist Christians—the Nazarenes, the Theodotians, the Artemonites, the Paulianists, the Photinians, and others—were right in claiming to hold to the teaching of the earliest Jesus community on this point. But what about these historical groups' insistence on Jesus as an exalted *human* figure? Do they harmonize with the New Testament witness on this point as well?

[1080] R. C. Sproul, "Did God Die on the Cross?" Ligonier Ministries. Web. 27 October 2014. <http://www.ligonier.org/blog/it-accurate-say-god-died-cross>.

[1081] "Nestorian Christianity," *New World Encyclopedia*. Web. 27 October 14.

[1082] R. C. Sproul, "None Dare Call It Heresy," Ligonier Ministries. Web. 27 October 2014. <http://www.ligonier.org/learn/articles/none-dare-call-it-heresy>.

[1083] Hilary, *Ad Constantium*, I.

[1084] It is important to note that, traditionally speaking, Roman Catholicism, Protestant Christianity, Greek Orthodoxy, Oriental Orthodoxy, Eastern Catholicism, etc., all claim to believe in the doctrine of the Trinity, but differ severely on the definitions, principles, and dogmas which compose it. Their scholars usually view each other as heretical in many of their doctrines about Christ's nature, nevertheless, today their populations can be found generally accepting one another as more-or-less legitimate Christians, whereas those other Christians which deny the Trinity dogma altogether are marginalized or worse. It will behoove us to constantly illuminate the facade of perfect Christian unity on "orthodox Trinitarianism," an illusion which has only been manufactured and perpetuated by taboo and ignorance.

The Man, the Mediator

Since the disaster in the Garden, mankind has required a mediator to bridge the gap fostered by his sin against a holy God. Job lamented his separation from him: *"If only there was someone to mediate between us, someone to bring us together"* (Job 9:33 NIV). The required mediation between God and man was a major theme of the Apostle Paul, and he writes in Galatians: *"Now a mediator is not for one party only; whereas God is only one"* (Gal 3:20). As noted earlier, the modern *Amplified Bible*, a Trinitarian translation which aims to convey the full meaning of the original text, actually translates Galatians 3:20 as *"God is only one Person"* (a statement with which Trinitarian theology vehemently disagrees). At any rate, the two parties requiring mediation in this passage are the one God and mankind. Our question is, to which party does the mediator Jesus Christ belong? Is he God representing the party of God? Or man representing the party of man? Perhaps he is somehow both?

Paul, in his first letter to Timothy, makes a succinct and stirring announcement: *"For there is one God, and one mediator between God and men, the man Christ Jesus"* (1 Timothy 2:5). Here Paul defines Jesus as *the man* who stands between the two parties, not as a hybrid God-man, but explicitly as a representative of *mankind.* The majority of churches today diverge from Paul in this regard. The Southern Baptist Convention boldly *enhances* Paul's statement, saying that there "is the One Mediator, *fully God*, fully man."[1085] They evidently find Paul's words inadequate, as if he neglected or was unaware of some other fundamental data. Indeed, how often do we hear from Trinitarian apologists that Jesus *must* have been *both* God and man to qualify as mediator?[1086] But this is not the plain requirement of Paul. The only New Testament stipulation for the Messiah, in order to qualify as intercessor, is that he be fully *man:*

> *"Therefore, he had to be made like his brethren in all things, so that he might become a merciful and faithful high priest in things pertaining to God, to make propitiation for the sins of the people"* (Hebrews 2:17).

[1085] "The Baptist Faith & Message," SBC, Official Website of the Southern Baptist Convention. Web. 5 May 2013. <http://www.sbc.net/bfm/bfm2000.asp#I>, emphasis added.

[1086] Trinitarian Warren Wiersbe's comments are emblematic: "As the God-man, Jesus Christ is the perfect Mediator between the holy God and his failing children... No other person can qualify. Jesus Christ is both God and man..." (Warren Wiersbe, *Ephesians Through Revelation*, Vol. 2 (David C. Cook, 2003), p. 216). Observe also the stunning eisegesis of one Austrian professor, "Paul's reference to Him as the 'man Christ Jesus' expresses His unique quality of being both human and divine" (Martin Probstle, *Where God and I Meet: the Sanctuary* (Hagerston: Review and Herlad Publishing, 2013). No such divine nature is stated by Paul, however.

When God made the Messiah he had to be human *"in every respect"* (ESV), and *"fully human in every way"* (NIV). If the Messiah were really an angel, or a God-man hybrid housing a human and a divine nature, two minds and two wills, being the very Almighty God himself, he would seem to be disqualified. No, it appears if anyone would mediate on behalf of mankind to God, that is, to be a priest to God, he must be exclusively from the pool of humanity. The New Testament confirms our assessment. Concerning Jesus as high priest we read:

> *"For we do not have a high priest who cannot sympathize with our weakness, but one who has been tempted in all things as we are, yet without sin... For every high priest taken from among men is appointed on behalf of men in things pertaining to God"* (Heb 4:16, 5:1).

The Weymouth translation reads, *"For every high priest is chosen from among men, and is appointed to act on behalf of men in matters relating to God."* The NLT reduces this to, *"Every high priest is a man chosen to represent other people in their dealings with God"* (NLT). The sphere of humanity, and nowhere else, is the category from which *"every high priest is selected"* (NIV). A proper understanding of Paul's mediatorial scheme in 1 Timothy 2:5 is foundational to understanding not only Christ's relationship to God, but man's relationship to God through Christ. We must take care not to abrogate his precise words, not to interject our own thoughts or chronologically inconsistent dogmas back into his formula. Catholic priest and professor Raymond Collins offers an insightful commentary into Paul's polemical language in 1 Timothy 2:5:

> Echoing the Jewish Shema (Deut 6:4) and Paul's hymnic confession (1 Cor 8:6) [*For there is one God, the Father... and one Lord, Jesus Christ*], the Pastor affirms the uniqueness of God... then affirms that there is only one mediator between God and human beings. The Pastor uses the noun *anthropos*, "human," "a person," to designate human beings. His usage follows the practice of other New Testament authors who regularly use this generic term to designate human beings as distinct from God. Throughout the New Testament, "human" (*anthropos*) stands always in explicit or implicit contrast with "God" (*theos*)... By affirming the humanity of the mediator before he identifies the mediator demonstrates his apologetic intent. The

mediator is not a divinized emperor [*a god-man*][1087]; the mediator is a human being. Then, and only then, does the Pastor identify the mediator as Christ Jesus... the humanity of Christ Jesus is a very important factor in the Pastor's theological scheme. This is due to the subtle polemicizing against the divinization of emperors and *his radically Jewish view of God*—unique, dynamic, and transcendent... It also underscores Christ Jesus' solidarity with all humanity insofar as he is a human, an Anthropos, one among and in relationship with other human beings.[1088]

Collins' reference to Paul's argument against *divinized emperors*[1089] recalls our earlier study in part one regarding the Egyptian kings being recognized as divine incarnations, as mediating god-men. One encyclopedia reveals that:

the imperial cult [of Rome] can be traced to ancient Egypt, where for millennia the pharaoh was thought to be a god incarnate. After Alexander the Great created his Macedonian-Greek empire, he conquered Egypt, where an oracle proclaimed him to be a god. The ruler cult was disseminated throughout the kingdoms... [The Roman emperor Augustus'] achievements were proof that a deity was present in their emperor [and] the Senate decreed that Augustus was a god after his death (14 CE)... The cult played an important role in spreading Roman civilization, fostering civic pride and

---

[1087] "Roman emperors, like the pagan Babylonian, Egyptian, and Greek kings before them, were looked upon by many as the living embodiment of their gods, or the god-men" (Steve Urick, *Major Cults and False World Religions* (Bloomington: Authorhouse, 2014 [2011]), p. 222).

[1088] Raymond F. Collins, *First and Second Timothy and Titus: A Commentary* (Louisville: Westminster John Knox Press, 2002), pp. 60-61, emphasis added.

[1089] "Alexander was the first Greek to claim that he had actually been born the son of a god. He failed to convince the Greeks, but in Egypt the Ptolemies were more successful in assuming divinity. They made use of the tradition that the pharaoh was the son of the god Amun..." (Freeman, *Closing of the Western Mind,* p. 40); "The first Roman emperor, Octavian was instrumental in creating the imperial cult, which associated living emperors with the gods... he was adopted as the son of Julius Caesar, who claimed descent from Venus and the kings of Rome... Caesar was acknowledged as a god, thus making Octavian a *divi filius* (son of a god)" (Michael Bland Simmons, *Holy People of the World: A Cross-cultural Encyclopedia,* Vol. 1 (Oxford: ABC-CLIO, 2004), p. 83). Gaius Caligula, Nero and Domitian are perhaps the best examples of Roman emperors purported to be gods; one is also reminded of the Emperor Vespasian's remark upon his death-bed: '*Vae, puto deus fio!*' or 'Woe, I think I'm turning into a god!' (M. F. Wiles, *Studia Patristica,* Vol. 34 (Oxford, 1999), p. 204).

allegiance to Roman rule, assimilating traditional polytheism, and *competing* with the claims of [orthodox] Christianity that Jesus Christ was God incarnate.[1090]

The god-man Augustus was the same emperor mentioned at the time of Christ's birth in Judea (Luke 2:1); the tradition of the god-man was thus rich by the time of Paul's writing,[1091] and, as Collins has observed, it is precisely such a mediating being, both divine and human, which Paul likely argues against in 1 Timothy 2:5. Paul's Christianity does not *compete* for attention with the god-man of the pagans; for Paul it is the *man*, and only the man Jesus, who offers service on behalf of his brothers to the great and transcendent God. Nevertheless, as historians have noted, "Jesus as intermediary between man and God was *eclipsed* by the later doctrine of the Trinity, stating that he was an intrinsic part of the Godhead."[1092]

The Law of Agency

A critical concept for understanding the Jesus of the New Testament is a Jewish principle known as "the law of agency."[1093] The concept has been regularly summed up in this way: *a man's agent is equivalent to himself.* When God imparts his authority to his agent, that agent may himself be called "God" and may speak and act as God on his behalf. This ancient principle was frequently cited and in common use by Jews in the Second Temple period. It was being used in social situations, in which a man may send another on his behalf to conduct business, as well as in biblical commentary.[1094] As McGrath observes:

[1090] Simmons, p. 83, emphasis added.

[1091] Coins declaring Octavian's divine status emerge around 38 BCE, and the "divi filius" title begins to be used of him by 40 BCE. After his death in 14 CE, he became "inter deos relates" (enrolled among the gods). Paul's earliest writings are thought to have been composed around 52 and the latest around 64 CE. On the dating of the Pauline epistles, see Raymond E. Brown, *An Introduction to the New Testament* (New York: Doubleday, 1997), p. 424.

[1092] Freeman, *Closing of the Western Mind,* p. 117.

[1093] The *Jewish Encyclopedia* defines the Hebraic law of agency, also known as "shaliah," in this way: "The Law of Agency deals with the status of a person (known as the agent) acting by direction of another (the principal), and thereby legally binding the principal in his connection with a third person. The person who binds a principal in this manner is his agent, known in Jewish law as *sheluah* or *sheliah* (one that is sent): the relation of the former to the latter is known as agency (*shelihut*). The general principle is enunciated thus: A man's agent is like himself (Kid. 41*b*)" (Lewis N. Dembitz, "Law of Agency," *Jewish Encyclopedia*, 1906, p. 232).

[1094] See the various rabbinical sources for application (b. Nazir 12b; m. Ber. 5:5; b. B. Mes. 96a; b. Qidd. 42b, 43a; b. Menah. 93b, etc). See also the *Oxford Dictionary of the Jewish Religion* (New York: OUP, 2011), p. 24.

Agency was an important part of everyday life in the ancient world. Individuals such as prophets and angels mentioned in the Jewish Scriptures were thought of as "agents" of God. And the key idea regarding agency in the ancient world appears to be summarized in the phrase from rabbinic literature so often quoted in these contexts: "The one sent is like the one who sent him." The result is that the agent can not only carry out divine functions but also be depicted in divine language, sit on God's throne or alongside God, and even bear the Divine name.[1095]

Examples of this principle in action in the Old Testament include Moses: "*Then Yahweh said to Moses, 'See I have made you GOD to Pharaoh, and Aaron your brother shall be your prophet*'" (Ex 7:1); the human rulers and judges of Israel: "*I said, 'You are GODS,' you are all sons of the Most High*" (Ps 82:6; Jn 10:34). These individuals, endowed with God's authority, were to be addressed as God himself by the parties to whom they were sent.[1096]

Throughout both the Old and New Testaments, the principal and his agent are so closely identified that they become nearly confused in the text. For example, in Exodus 7:17 Yahweh says, "*Behold, I will strike the water that is in the Nile with the staff that is in my hand.*" But in verse 19, we read that it is Aaron who actually takes his staff and strikes the Nile. Verse 25 concludes that "*Yahweh had struck the Nile.*" In the Gospel of Matthew, we read that a Roman Centurion had come to speak with Jesus (Matt 8:5). But in Luke 7:3 we read that the Centurion had sent Jewish elders to speak with Jesus on his behalf. Matthew views the agents (the elders) as if they were the principal (the Centurion); the messengers were treated as if they were the Centurion himself.

We encounter this principle of agency several times in the New Testament teachings of Jesus.[1097] Understanding this important system will clarify some of the Gospel narrative's otherwise potentially puzzling features. Christ's incredible miracles, his pronouncements of judgment and forgiveness—all were accomplished explicitly because Jesus came "in the name of" (or in the authority

---

[1095] James F. McGrath, *The Only True God: Early Christian Monotheism in its Jewish Context* (Urbana and Chicago: The University of Illinois Press, 2009), p. 14.

[1096] See Exodus 4:16; 7:1, 21:6, 22:8-9, Psalm 45:6, 58:1, 82:6, John 10:34.

[1097] See Matt 10:40, Mark 9:37, Luke 9:48, 10:16, John 13:20.

of) the one God.[1098] While John's Gospel is commonly cited as proving Jesus' deity or his identification as God, scholars have noted that the fourth Gospel in particular is supremely concerned, not with making Jesus God himself, but with distinguishing him as God's *agent*. Jesus performs God's will (4:34), speaks God's words (8:28), and obeys God's commandments (14:31). As Marianne Meye Thompson affirms:

> Jesus is presented in the Gospel [of John] against the backdrop of the Jewish concept of agency and, furthermore, against the understanding that there is one chief agent through whom God acts [the Messiah]... Because Jesus is the chief agent of God, when one confronts him, one confronts God.[1099]

Indeed, the Johannine Jesus is regularly emphatic on this point: *"The one who looks at me is seeing the one who sent me"* (Jn 12:45 NIV); *"He who has seen me has seen the Father"* (Jn 14:9 ESV). This "law of agency" will continue to play an important role throughout the rest of our investigation and will ultimately prove the best method for interpreting the Jesus narrative in its native Jewish, monotheistic context.

Messiah ben Joseph: Understanding Christ's Submission and Role

There exists a useful biblical illustration for further understanding Jesus' submissive relationship to and *functional* equality with God as his agent: the Old Testament narrative about Joseph.

In one rabbinic tradition, scribes investigating the Messianic prophecies of Scripture actually perceived what they assumed to be more than one Messiah due to their radically different roles. Two of these eschatological figures were called "Messiah ben David" and "Messiah ben Joseph."[1100] These hypothetical characters were so named due to the prophetic typography which surrounded the biblical David and Joseph. For example, "Messiah ben David" was

---

[1098] Jesus is explicitly identified, both by himself and the crowds who loved him, as a king who had been sent in the authority of Yahweh: *"For I tell you, you will not see me again until you say, 'Blessed is he who comes in the name of the Lord'"* (Matt 23:29); *"Blessed is the king who comes in the name of the Lord!"* (Luke 19:38).

[1099] Marianne Meye Thompson, *Dictionary of Jesus and the Gospels* (Downer's Grove: IVP, 1992), p. 377. Understanding this principle, that "seeing the agent is the same as seeing the one that sent him," will be helpful when we consider the words of Thomas in John 20:28 in Chapter 12 of this book.

[1100] See John Parsons, "Mashiach ben Yosef: Joseph as a Type of Messiah," Hebrew for Christians. Web. 29 October 2014.

recognized as "the conquering king of Israel," while "Messiah ben Joseph" was "the suffering servant." Those who accept Jesus of Nazareth as the Messiah will quickly recognize both of these typographic figures in him. However, most Jews awaiting the Messiah seem to have had only the "conquering king" in mind. This may be why so many were and still are shocked that the Messiah, who to them should have immediately conquered the Romans, would be put to death on a Roman cross. However, even in this rabbinic tradition, "Messiah ben Joseph" was expected to arrive on the scene first, only to actually be put to death before "Messiah ben David" came to inaugurate the Kingdom of God on the earth.[1101] Again, the Christian recognizes these things as obvious in the person of Jesus, but they are nevertheless difficult for many Jews.

In the recognition of the biblical Joseph as an archetypal Messiah, we discover a rich parallel with our investigation. Joseph, after being unjustly condemned to suffering alongside two criminals in the land of Egypt (Gen 40:2-3), was raised up from the pit and given fine linen (Gen. 41:42), just as Jesus was crucified between two criminals, was raised up from the grave and clothed with immortality (Matt 28:6). Likewise, after the "resurrection" of Joseph, Pharaoh crowned him with honor and power and made him second-in-command of Egypt (Gen 41:39-45). As Psalm 105:21 recalls, Pharaoh made Joseph "lord" and "ruler over all his possessions." Likewise, God made Jesus "lord" and "Messiah" (Acts 2:36) and gave him "all authority" (Matt 28:18). In the Joseph narrative we readily discover the same power relationship between the exalted Jesus and his God:

> *"You will oversee my household, and all my people will submit to your commands. Only I, the king, will be greater than you. See here," Pharaoh said to Joseph, "I place you in authority over all the land of Egypt." Then Pharaoh took his signet ring from his own hand and put it on Joseph's. He clothed him with fine linen clothes and put a gold chain around his neck. Pharaoh had him ride in the chariot used by his second-in-command, and they cried out before him, "Kneel down!" So he placed him over all the land of Egypt. Pharaoh also said to Joseph, "I am Pharaoh, but without your permission no one will move his hand or his foot in all the land of Egypt." Pharaoh gave Joseph the name Zaphenath-Paneah.*

[1101] See Gerald J. Blidstein, "Messiah in Rabbinic Thought," Jewish Virtual Library and Encyclopedia Judaica. The Gale Group. 2008. Web. 2 December 2012. See also Markus Bockmuehl, James Carleton Paget (ed.), *Redemption and Resistance: The Messianic Hopes of Jews and Christians in Antiquity* (Continuum, 2009), p. 269.

> *He also gave him Asenath daughter of Potiphera, priest of On, to be his*
> *wife. So Joseph took charge of all the land of Egypt.*
> (Genesis 41:40-45 NET)

Joseph was elevated to a place of the highest honor and power, and was even awarded functional equality with Pharaoh. Though Joseph was given Pharaoh's power over every man in Egypt, Pharaoh nevertheless remained greater; Joseph was "lord" and "second-in-command," while the king alone was "Pharaoh." Likewise we see that Jesus was elevated to a position of great honor, given God's authority over all men, and made second only to God himself (1 Cor 15:27-28). The Father retained, however, his sole identification and honor as the one true God: *"I, Yahweh, will be their God, and My servant David will be a prince among them"* (Ezek 34:24); *"They will serve Yahweh their God and David their king, whom I will raise up for them"* (Jer 30:9).

Certainly some of Christ's enemies, overwhelmed by misunderstanding and hatred of the young rabbi, asserted that he claimed to be equal with God, or to put himself in God's own place in some sense.[1102] In John we read that Jesus' enemies were enraged because *"He was even calling God his own father, making himself equal with God"* (Jn 5:18b). But what sort of equality is being asserted here? One need not go further than Christ's own words in John 14:28, *"the Father is greater than I,"* to quickly dismiss any suspicion. As McGrath observes:

> For John, Jesus *functions*, in practical terms, as *equivalent* to God,
> in accordance with the basic principle of agency that "the one
> sent is like the one who sent him"... The issue central to the
> conflict is whether Jesus *"makes himself* equal to God," rather
> than being God's appointed agent. The Johannine Jesus avidly
> denies that he is making himself anything; rather, he does the
> will of him who sent him.[1103]

[1102] Misunderstanding is a major theme of the Gospel narratives, particularly in John. Both Christ's disciples and his opponents consistently misinterpret his sayings. While his enemies were not enlightened as to the true meaning of many of his statements, the disciples who loved him were permitted. Interestingly enough, many today still fail to grasp the real meaning Christ's sayings and may find themselves echoing the very misapprehensions and complaints of his enemies. See John 2:19-22, 3:13-13, 4:31-34, 6:51-61, 71, 7:33-36, 7:37-39, 8:18-19, 21-22, 27, 33-34, 38-44, 51-52, 56-58, 9:39-41, 10:1-6, 26-36, 11:11-14, 11:23-25, 12:16, 32-34, 40, 13:6-12, 27-29, 33-37, 14:2-5, 7-11, 16:16-18, 16:25-29, 20:9, 15, 21:4, 21:22-23, Matthew 13:10-17, 13:34-36, 15:11-20, 16: 5-12, 22:29, 27:46-47, Mark 4:10-13, 33-34, Luke 2:50, 9:45, 18:34. See also Proverbs 28:5, Isaiah 6:9.

[1103] James F. McGrath, Jerry Truex, "Two Powers and Early Jewish and Christian Monotheism," *Journal of Biblical Studies*, Vol. 4, No. 1 (2004), pp. 50-51, emphasis added.

Indeed, John records that Jesus believed the Father was "greater" than himself, and even *"greater than all"* (Jn 10:29). Christ's authority, though it was God's authority, was by his own admission wholly derived. By calling God his own Father he naturally asserts a second place to God, a position of the most intimate relationship which would ultimately yield the authority of a son over his father's house. But it is not Jesus who has usurped power for himself; it is something conferred on him by his Father. The question in John's narrative was over Jesus' authority and how he obtained it: was it really given to him by God or not? Was Jesus' claim to sonship valid, or had he presumed to make himself God's son and take charge of God's house on his own? That Jesus could not be accused of claiming to personally be God himself is obvious. Indeed, at this fateful trial, the worst his accusers could say was that he claimed to be God's *son* (Luke 22:70).[1104]

Recognizing the patriarchal culture of the Jews, we may note here that authority over the family and its possessions was customarily awarded to first-born sons by their father's decree.[1105] Jesus consistently testified that this was

---

[1104] Dustin R. Smith writes: "[in the Gospel of John] Jesus could have been understood as a *rebellious* son taking prerogatives which are not rightfully his… within first century Judaism, a claim to sonship implied obedience and dependence, not equality (Deut 21:18; Sir 3:6-16; Philo, *Conf.* 63; *Dec.* 118). In other words, for a son to claim equality with one's father in a manner which laid claim to the father's unique prerogatives (thus dishonoring the father) would make the son into a rebellious son [See McGrath, *John's Apologetic Christology*, p. 87]. If the Johannine 'Jews' understood Jesus as a rebellious son, who illegitimately claimed the right to break the Sabbath and give life, then they would have interpreted Jesus' claim to messiahship as a false claim. In their eyes, Jesus was a false Messiah. In order to counter this claim, Jesus stated, '*the son can do nothing of himself, unless it is something he sees the Father doing*' (John 5:19, 30). In other words, Jesus responded to this misunderstanding (a prevalent motif in the Fourth Gospel) by claiming to be an obedient son rather than a rebellious son" (Smith, Irons, Dixon, *The Son of God*, p. 39).

[1105] That the son, particularly the "firstborn son" of the family is given great rank and entitlement by his father is a well-known aspect of the Jew's familial system. The right was invested in him by the Father specifically, his endowment being a derivation of the Father's own right to the property and management of the family. Jewish sources recognize that *"the first son born to the father occupied a prominent place in the Hebrew family… The first-born son took rank before his brothers and sisters. Usually the father bequeathed to him the greater part of the inheritance…"* (Morris Jastrow, B. Eerdmans, Marcus Jastrow, Louis Ginzberg, "Birthright," *Jewish Encyclopedia*, 1906). Rabbinical sources comment: *"The prerogatives of the first-born, as the real head of the family after the father's death, were… deeply rooted in the domestic life of the Jews"* (Bek. VIII, 1; compare "Maggid Mishnah" in Maimonides, "Yad," Nahalot, II. 12). Most useful for understanding Christ's sonship is the fact that: *"The father's identification of the first-born was most important… only he was the first-born whom the father recognized as such, even should it be contrary to the general presumption"* (B. B. 127b; Sifre, Deut. 216). Note God's official recognition of Jesus as the beloved Son whom he has chosen: *"This is my son, my chosen one"* (Lk 9:35), and *"You are my beloved son, in you I am well-pleased"* (Mk 1:11), and *"Behold, my servant whom I have chosen; my beloved"* (Mt 12:18), and *" You are my son, today I have begotten you… I will*

the case, saying, "*All authority has been given to me*" (Matt 28:18), and "*The Father loves the Son and has given all things into His hands*" (Jn 3:35). Jesus then did not have the authority inherently, nor had he any equality with God by nature, for all things were indeed provided him by another. By God's permission only, the Son *became* authoritative where he had not been on his own. Trinitarian A. W. Tozer rightly states: "For God to become anything that He has not been is unthinkable."[1106] Yet we have in view a great transformation for Jesus: he was *given* rights and power, and *made* both Lord and Christ by divine fiat (Acts 2:32). The Old Testament prophets foresaw this great transference, that the Messiah would be "*given authority, glory and sovereign power*" (Dan 7:14).[1107] However, we must not make the mistake of concluding that because God awarded functional equality to his son that his son must be of one substance with him.

When Jesus exercised God's authority there were those who misunderstood or deliberately mischaracterized him, as well as those who properly apprehended and rejoiced in Christ's empowered *humanity*. Today's audience still seems to fall into those same categories. The Son's received authority evidently enabled him to even forgive sins, a deed which his first-century opponents (and many modern Trinitarians) argued could be accomplished only by God: "*Why does this man speak that way? He is blaspheming; who can forgive sins but God alone?*" (Mark 2:7). Yet upon this charge, rather than asserting his right to forgive due to his own deity, he demonstrates, to the crowd's great appreciation, that he indeed enjoyed this God-given right as a man:[1108]

---

be a Father to him and he shall be a son to me.' And when he again brings the firstborn into the world..." (Heb 1:5-6a). Note also 2 Pet 1:7: "*He received honor and glory from God the Father when the voice came to him from the Majestic Glory, saying, 'This is my son, whom I love; with him I am well pleased'* " (2 Pet 1:17).

[1106] Tozer, p. 22.

[1107] Jesus, along with other Jews of his day, interpreted the "son of man" figure in Daniel 7:13 messianically. Jesus' citation of the figure in John 12:34, in response to the Jews' accusations that he claimed to be the Messiah, allows us this inference. Scholars have noted that "For much of Jewish and Christian history, this figure [in Dan 7:13] was interpreted as the messiah" (John Collins, *The Scepter and the Star: The Messiahs of the Dead Sea Scrolls and Other Ancient Literature* (New York: Doubleday, 1995), p. 36); "The messianic view is the eldest and, in past Jewish and Christian exegesis, the prevailing opinion" (Stephen Miller, *The New American Commentary: Daniel* (Broadman & Holman Pub., 1994), p. 209). Jesus' linkage in John 12:34 of the (Davidic) Messiah and the Danielic Son of Man image reinforces the notion "that Jewish tradition also developed a co-regency between God and this Son of Man to reign in the Kingdom" (Douglas Welker Kennard, *Messiah Jesus: Christology in His Day and Ours* (Oxford: Peter Lang, 2008), p. 388).

[1108] Another perspective: When Christ forgives sins, he does not say "I forgive you," as if he were God himself, the one recently offended. Instead he simply states that "your sins are forgiven," indicating that God has forgiven the sins. This same right, to pronounce that God had forgiven sins, was reserved also for the high priests of Israel who made sacrifices at the temple. Who is to say that Jesus has not claimed this precise right of priesthood, and not the right of the

> *"But so that you may know that the Son of Man has authority on earth to forgive sins"*—then he said to the paralytic, *"Get up, pick up your bed and go home." And he got up and went home. But when the crowds saw this, they were awestruck, and glorified God, who had given such authority to men"* (Matthew 9:6-8).

J. R. Daniel Kirk of Fuller Theological Seminary confirms in his recent study that despite popular "divine" Jesus interpretations of the Mark 2/Matthew 9 story:

> an authoritative, *human* representative is a better reading of the passage's Christology. One problem with the divine Christ interpretive is that the scribes, as opponents of Jesus in the narrative, are not trustworthy interpreters of Jesus' identity. Another point of caution [is the fact that] the crowds celebrate God giving such authority "to" or "among" people (Matt 9:8)… It is unlikely to the point of near impossibility that the readers of Mark are to assume that Jesus is himself the "God alone" who can forgive sins.[1109]

Just as the man Jesus received the right of forgiveness from God, he likewise transferred this same authority to other men, saying to his Apostles: *"If you forgive the sins of any, their sins have been forgiven them; if you retain the sins of any, they have been retained"* (Jn 20:23). If the ability to forgive sins indicates intrinsic deity in the New Testament, then we have a strange situation here with the Apostles.

In this we again detect our parallel with Joseph. Though remaining subservient to Pharaoh, Joseph performed all of Pharaoh's duties. Thus people recognized his equality, in a functional sense, with the king. For example, Judah recognized, *"You are equal to Pharaoh himself"* (Gen 44:18). Other translations are useful in understanding the exact sense of their equality: *"You are as powerful as Pharaoh"* (NLT); *"For you are like Pharaoh himself"* (ESV); *"For thou art even as*

---

offended God? Jesus is certainly made a priest (Heb 4:14-16), and makes others priests as well: *"He has made us to be a kingdom, priests to his God and Father"* (Rev 1:6). Some scholars, such as R. T. France (*The Gospel of Mark* (Grand Rapids: Wm. B. Eerd. Pub. Co., 2002), pp. 125-126) and Sherman E. Johnson, (*Gospel Acc. to Mark* (Black, 1960), p. 56), have identified Christ's passive expression (*afientai sou hai hmartiai* "your sins are forgiven") as a "divine passive" in that they refer to the person of God in action. Thus, the meaning is "God forgives your sins." Of course, Christ's opponents do not seem to take it this way.

[1109] J. R. Daniel Kirk, "Mark's Son of Man and Paul's Second Adam," *Horizons in Biblical Theology*, Vol. 37 (Leiden: Brill, 2015), pp. 175-176, emphasis added.

Pharaoh" (KJV); *"For thou art as Pharaoh"* (YLT). Judah then pleads with his brother because he recognizes that Joseph has the right to do whatever Pharaoh does. Indeed Pharaoh had decreed: *"without your permission no one shall raise his hand or foot in all the land of Egypt"* (Gen 41:41, 44). An appeal to Joseph was as good as an appeal to Pharaoh due only to Pharaoh's imparted authority. Here we naturally recall Thompson's earlier observation: "Because Jesus is the chief agent of God, when one confronts him, one confronts God."[1110] It is this precise position, the same relationship which Joseph had to Pharaoh, which Jesus claims. Some in Jesus' audience were obviously angered that this "mere man" might put himself in God's place in these matters. They said to him: *"Who do you make yourself out to be?"* (Jn 8:53b), to which he replied, denying any natural right or status beyond what had been unilaterally provided by another, *"If I glorify myself, my glory is nothing; it is my Father who glorifies me, of whom you say, 'He is our God'"* (Jn 8:54).

New Testament Adam Christology

Throughout the New Testament, Jesus is presented as the ideal human being. The Synoptic portrait of this human Jesus is encapsulated by his own frequent use of the expression "son of man" for himself.[1111] In the Gospels this phrase is used only in descriptions of Jesus and only by Jesus. In the Old Testament book of Ezekiel, the prophet is described and addressed as "son of man" ninety-three times, and the phrase was used as a reference to human beings in general. But Jesus' consistent self-designation as "the son of man" was, as scholars have recognized, likely intended to draw out two different associations: *1)* the apocalyptic figure of the Book of Daniel, and *2)* Adam, the first man.[1112]

First, it is Jesus himself who links his use of "son of man" to the "one like a son of man" character of Daniel 7:13, who is to receive authority and a kingdom from the Ancient of Days. Jesus furthermore links this Danielic figure to the

---

[1110] Thompson, *Dictionary of Jesus and the Gospels*, p. 377.

[1111] The "son of man" is used as a self-reference by Jesus more than eighty times in the Greek Gospels. In the Hebrew Scriptures, "son of man" occurs over one hundred times, where it is used as an expression for *man* in general in contrast to God or angels (Num 23:19, Ezek 2:1). See Geoffrey W. Bromiley, *The International Standard Bible Encyclopedia*, Vol. IV (Grand Rapids: Eerdmans, 1995), p. 574. In the Jewish work *1 Enoch*, which was certainly read in the NT community (see Jude 1:14), "the Son of Man" becomes a title for the messianic figure who will judge God's world.

[1112] See Joel Marcus, "Son of Man as Son of Adam" *Revue Biblique*, Vol. 110 (Paris, 2003), pp. 38-61.

Davidic Messiah by making an allusion to the second lord (adoni) of Psalm 110:1 and his exaltation to the right hand of God in Matthew 26:64.[1113] Jesus thus identifies himself as a human lord who receives from God the right to rule over not only Israel, but the nations.

Second, scholars have also connected Jesus' usage of "son of man" to what has been called an "Adam Christology" in the writings of Paul.[1114] In 1 Corinthians, Jesus is designated *"the second Adam"* (15:45) and is portrayed as an eschatological redeemer who fulfills Adam's primordial commission to rule over all the earth (1 Cor 15:21-28; cf. Gen 1:26-28). As God had always intended that a human being would "subdue" the world (Ps 8:6), so are all things to be *"subjected under [Jesus'] feet"* (1 Cor 15:27). Paul also alludes to the Davidic Messiah, who will have his enemies subjected as *"a footstool under [his] feet"* (1 Cor 15:25; cf. Ps 110:1). Paul's quotation of Psalm 8:6 explicitly recalls the primeval, royal destiny of *mankind*, and in tying the fulfillment of this destiny to Jesus as the Messiah, Paul recognizes Jesus as the second Adam, *a human being*.

We see that each of these Old Testament figures—Adam, the Davidic Messiah, and Daniel's Son of Man—receive rulership from God. In the New Testament, both Jesus and Paul link these figures together and identify them as being fulfilled in the person of Christ. Thus, as Kirk concludes, "Jesus' authority is located in his filling the role of idealized human figure: an Adamic and/or Davidic claim mediated through the imagery of Daniel 7's one like a human being."[1115]

The restoration of man's rulership over the earth is, in fact, the central theme played out across the whole of biblical literature. Adam had once been given authority to reign as God's vice-regent, only to lose it to a commandeering Satanic power, leaving the world to suffer under catastrophic mismanagement. The Jews eagerly looked forward to a future when Adam (that is, mankind) would reassert his place over the nations (the wild beasts), and fulfill his destiny of glory and world-wide dominion (Ps 8:5-6).[1116] The coming "one like a son of

---

[1113] In Chapter 12 we will perform and in-depth analysis of Psalm 110:1 and Jesus' self-identification as the Psalm's second lord, David's "adoni"—a Hebrew term used of non-deity superiors 195 times in the Scriptures.

[1114] Kirk, pp. 170-195.

[1115] Ibid., p. 177.

[1116] The first century Jewish document *the Testament of Abraham* portrays Adam as taking up a golden throne from where he oversees the souls of all mankind and is *"adorned with glory"* (11:1ff); compare with Ps 8:5, in which mankind is intended to be *"crowned with glory."* In another first century Jewish work, *the Life of Adam and Eve*, the angels are ordered to worship Adam as the image of God; Satan refuses to bow down to Adam because he believes Adam is an inferior creature, and instead seeks worship for himself. Satan is expelled, and in retaliation he devises the deception

man" in Daniel would be God's agent in accomplishing this restoration for the human race, and the one to whom God would give the nations (7:14). This dramatic narrative is the presupposed backdrop of the New Testament. It is also the central focus of Jesus' own preaching.[1117] The tale of *human* fall and the expected *human* reinstatement is the essential frame story through which the Jesus of the Gospels and the Jesus of Paul must be viewed.

The Suffering Adam

Paul draws an explicit parallel between Adam, the one man who lost mankind's dominion through sin, and *"the one man Jesus Christ"* whose obedience to God ultimately reclaimed that reign for *"all men"* (Rom 5:17-18). Obedience is the turn-key for the second Adam's victory, and the catalyst for that obedience is suffering. Consider the following: the first Adam was born as God's son (Luke 3:38), and God's image, and was given God's world as his possession—he was effectively put in God's functional role over the earth. Being God's representative, Adam was able to do as he pleased in the world, though he was ultimately required to submit in obedience to God's will. But seeking to transcend his position, he fell into disobedience and went beyond the strictures of his rule. But about Jesus we read that *"Although he was a son, he learned obedience from the things which he suffered"* (Heb 5:8). While Jesus was likewise God's son and God's image, and therefore the rightful ruler of the earth, he embraced the fact that dominion over all was only to be gained by suffering in obedience. After confirming with his disciples that he was *"the Christ,"* he taught them that *"the Son*

---

which caused the de-glorification of Adam and his wife. See *Life of Adam and Eve* 12:1-17:3. The Apostle Paul also likely references *the Life of Adam and Eve* 9:1 at 2 Corinthians 11:14, evidencing a familiarity with Adamic worship within the NT community. The story of Satan's rejection of the worship of Adam is also retold in the Qur'an (2:34, 7:11-13, 17:61-62).

[1117] Jesus defines his gospel as a message about the coming restoration of God's rule on the earth (Mark 1:14-15). He explains: "*I must preach the kingdom of God... because that is why I was sent*" (Luke 4:43). Paul, as a disciple of Jesus, centers his own gospel teaching in the things of the kingdom (Acts 20:25, 28:23, 31). Though preaching "the gospel about the kingdom" was Jesus' solemn charge to his followers (Matt 24:14), in mainstream Christianity "the gospel" has widely been diluted to involve only a message about Jesus' sacrificial atonement. But Jesus, who never spoke of dying for sins, and did not even mention his own death until late in his ministry, is said by the Synoptics to have gone everywhere "*preaching the gospel*" (Matt 4:23), that is, announcing "the kingdom" and its impending restoration. In contrast to the limited presentation of evangelicalism, the NT community paired the information about Jesus *with* the kingdom message as gospel: "*they believed Philip as he preached the gospel about the kingdom of God and the name of Jesus Christ*" (Acts 8:12). Modern Christianity has yet to grasp the significance of this, and has largely traded Christ's apocalyptic vision of an impending real-world theocracy for a hope in a Gnostic escape to heaven. For more on this topic see Anthony Buzzard, *Our Fathers Who Aren't in Heaven* (McDonough: Restoration Fellowship, 1999).

of man must suffer many things… and after three days rise again" (Mark 8:29b, 31). His study of Scripture had made this clear to him. Jesus said, *"This is what is written: the Messiah will suffer"* (Luke 24:46), and he obediently welcomed that fate, saying, *"The Son of man will go just as it is written about him"* (Matt 26:24). After God resurrected him, Jesus pointed his worried disciples back to *"all that the prophets had spoken"* and confirmed that *"it [was] necessary for the Messiah to suffer and then to enter his glory"* (Luke 24:25b-26).

Few texts better exhibit Paul's own "Suffering Adam Christology" than Philippians 2:6-8. However, this passage has long been one of the key and most famous texts used by Trinitarians in attempts to substantiate the doctrine of the Incarnation. The passage reads:

> *who, although he existed in the form of God, did not regard equality with God a thing to be grasped, but emptied himself, taking the form of a bond-servant, and being made in the likeness of men. Being found in appearance as a man, he humbled himself by becoming obedient to the point of death, even death on a cross* (Philippians 2:6-8 NASB).

Trinitarians assert that this means Jesus literally pre-existed as God in heaven, but temporarily "set aside" his rights as deity and took on a human nature. Trinitarians, like the translators of the NIV, are so convinced of this, that they have even rendered the phrase "existing in the form of God" (Phil 2:6) as *"being in very nature God."* But is this really what the passage says? Dr. Jason BeDuhn, in his seminal investigation into bias in mainstream translations, reveals that the Greek word for "form" here does not mean "nature" or "essence," and therefore the members of the NIV translating committee:

> do not translate the Greek, but substitute interpretations of their own that are not based in Paul's language at all. Therefore they are inaccurate; and their bias is evident in what they try to import into the passage. [They] have tried to introduce a "two-nature" Christology (first worked out by Christians at the Council of Chalcedon over three hundred years after the New Testament was written)… We do not gain much confidence in their interpretation of the passage when we see how they tamper with the text to support it.[1118]

[1118] BeDuhn, p. 53.

So what does this portion of Philippians 2:6 really intend? The Greek for "form" here is "*morphe.*" *Thayer's* explains that the term denotes "the form by which a person or thing strikes the vision; the *external appearance*: children are said to reflect [the morphe] of their parents." Thayer also cites 4 Maccabees 15:4 which explains that the "form" of a parent is impressed upon his children. Compare this to: "*Adam… became the father of a son in his own likeness, according to his image, and named him Seth*" (Gen 5:3), and "*God created man in his own image.*" (Gen 1:27). The word in Genesis here for "image" is the Hebrew "*tselem,*" defined as: "form, image, images, likenesses, phantom." The Hebrew "tselem" is then analogous to the Greek "morphe," and both are translated "image." We know that "tselem" must refer to the *external appearance* of a thing due to its use in 1 Samuel 6:5 to describe "*images of tumors and mice*" that were made of gold, and Ezekiel 16:17 which likewise describes idols made in the "*male image.*" In the *Septuagint* we find the Greek word "morphe" used in this same sense: "[the idolater] *shapes it in the form* ('morphe') *of a man*" (Isaiah 44:13 LXX). These instances of "tselem" and "morphe" are obviously not concerned with the *inner nature* of a subject but the outward appearance.[1119] But does the "morphe" of Philippians 2:6 carry this same usual meaning? One more look at the New Testament use of the Greek "morphe" (form) should round out the argument: Mark 16:12 says that the risen Jesus appeared on the road to Emmaus "*in a different form* (morphe)," so that two of his disciples did not recognize him. Obviously Christ's inner nature was not different, it was only his "representation" or "image" that was different, so that what struck the disciples' eyes they did not perceive as their Master. We should therefore not break with the biblical usage and suddenly understand "morphe" in Philippians as a reference to "inner nature," as the NIV would have us believe. Rather, we should recognize that essentially "morphe" is a synonym for "image" or "representation."

Many scholars agree that "being in the form of God" is synonymous with "being in the image of God," and that "the 'image' terminology points to Christ

---

[1119] Another similar Hebrew word may assist us—"likeness": "*When God created man, he made him in the likeness of God*" (Genesis 5:1). This Hebrew word for "likeness" is "*demuth,*" which is translated several times in the NASB as "form" (Ezekiel 1:5, 10, 16, 10:21). *Thayer's Lexicon* expounds upon "demuth" as meaning "…of external appearance." It should begin to be clear at this point that the Greek "morphe" in Philippians 2:6 is akin to the Hebrew "teselem" and "demuth" in that they all relate to the outward "representation" of a thing, not the inner nature of a thing.

in Adamic terms."[1120] We must keep in mind that for Paul, Genesis 1-3 provides the historical framework for his Christology (Rom 5:12-21, 1 Cor 15:21ff, 45-47). Modern scholarship therefore concludes that the Philippians hymn is a reflection of Jesus against the life of Adam.[1121] In this light, Jesus' *"being made in the likeness of men"* (v. 7) is not a retelling of an Incarnation story, but a reference to his divesting himself of his Adamic rulership as Messiah and living in submission "as every other man does." Even Trinitarian commentators have recognized that:

> the key to the text lies in the intended parallel between the first Adam and the second Adam... this is the generally prevailing modern view... The former senselessly sought to grasp at equality with God, and through pride and disobedience lost the glorious image of his maker; the latter chose to tread the pathway of lowly obedience in order to be exalted by God.[1122]

There are essentially two ways to interpret the controversial language used by Paul in verse 6. Some scholars have suggested that Jesus' refusal to grasp at *"equality with God"* (v. 6) is to be contrasted with Adam's ill-fated desire to be *"like God"* in Genesis 3:35. In this view, Jesus has refused to pursue something that did not belong to him. In support of this view, Dr. BeDuhn says, "there is not a single word derived from harpazo [grasped] that is used to suggest holding on to something already possessed."[1123] One Protestant theologian agrees that "the old contention about harpagmos is over: equality with God is not a *res rapta*... a position which the pre-existent Christ had and gave up, but it is a *res rapienda*, a possibility of advancement which he declined."[1124] However, the Greek used by Paul in this passage has made an incontrovertible interpretation difficult.[1125]

[1120] David Steenburg, "The Worship of Adam and Christ as the Image of God," *Journal for the Study of the New Testament*, Vol. 39 (New York: Sage, 1990), p. 99.

[1121] See Dunn, *Christology in the Making*, p. 115; Kirk, "Mark's Son of Man and Paul's Second Adam," *Horizons*, p. 192; O'Connor, "Christological Anthropology," *R.B.*, pp. 37-42. Steenburg, "Adam and Christ as the Image of God," *JNST*, pp. 95-109; Martin, *Carmen Christi: Philippians 2.5-11*, p. 108.

[1122] Ralph P. Martin, *Epistle of Paul to the Philippians: An Introduction and Commentary, Tyndale New Testament Commentaries* (Grand Rapids: Eerdmans, 1987), p. 102.

[1123] BeDuhn, p. 55.

[1124] Ethelbert Stauffer, *New Testament Theology* (London: SCM Press, 1955), p. 284.

[1125] Wallace argues that the purpose of the article preceding "einai" is to identify "einai isa theo" as the direct object in the statement. See Daniel Wallace, *Greek Grammar: Beyond the Basics* (Grand Rapids: Zondervan, 1996), p. 186. On the other hand, Blass argues that the article here is anaphoric and signals that the term it modifies points to an object already mentioned in the statement. See Friedrich Blass, A Greek Grammar of the New Testament and Other Early Literature (Chicago: University of Chicago Press, 1961), sect. 205. Since we are not able to prove

Other scholars have challenged the aforementioned view, arguing that the "equality with God" here is to be thought of as something that Jesus already had, but did not exploit or use to his own advantage. There does appear to be considerable (though perhaps not indisputable) linguistic evidence to support that the two objects mentioned here, "the form of God" and "equality with God" are to be thought of as basically synonymous.[1126] On both linguistic and historical grounds, this does seem to be the stronger position. However, there remains no necessary implication of a Trinitarian view.

If being in the "form of God" is synonymous with being in "the image of God," and if this language draws an Adamic parallel,[1127] we should have little difficulty in understanding what Paul means when he says "equality with God." The first Adam, *"the son of God"* (Lk 3:38), represented God as his image. Being in God's delegated role as ruler of the earth and its creatures, Adam enjoyed a functional, not an ontological equality with God. As far as the world was concerned, Adam was *equivalent* to God; he acted in God's stead, commanding God's authority. Likewise Jesus, the second *"son of God"* (Lk 1:35), was also in the image of God, and the rightful king—he was God's ruler, *equivalent* to God. According to Paul, Jesus having "equality with God" does not then mean that Jesus was *in very nature* God himself, but means that Jesus functioned *as* God as his representative. Paul's Greek endorses this interpretation. Several Catholic scholars have confirmed that the phrase "equality with God," (Greek: "isa theou"):

> may not simply be translated with terms like "equality to God" … That would require the form "isos theos." What we have in the text is the adverb "isa," and that merely means "as God," "like God." So there is no statement about Christ *being* equal to God, and this in turn tells against an interpretation in terms of pre-existence. So on both traditio-historical linguistic grounds, according to the Catholic exegete and Jerusalem Dominican Jerome Murphy-O'Connor, there is "no

---

indisputably that the article is anaphoric, we are not able to produce an indisputable interpretation on this one point.

[1126] For examples of support for this view see: Robert H. Gundry, "Style and Substance in 'The Myth of God Incarnate' according to Philippians 2:6-11," in *Crossing the Boundaries* (Leiden: Brill, 1994), pp. 283-284; H. A. W. Meyer, *Critical and Exegetical Handbook to the Epistles to the Philippians and the Colossians* (Edinburgh: T & T Clark, 1875), p. 88; N. T. Wright, "Harpagmos and the Meaning of Philippians 2:5-11," *Journal of Theological Studies*, Vol. 37 (Oxford: OUP, 1986), p. 344.

[1127] Steenburg, p. 99.

justification for interpreting the phrase of the hymn in terms of *being* of Christ."[1128]

For Paul, Jesus was not God himself, but was *"as God,"* that is, he functioned as God because he was God's representative, or earthly equivalent. Recalling our typological parallel with Joseph will again prove useful. In Genesis 44:18, Joseph's brothers had recognized that Joseph was *"as Pharaoh"* (KJV, YLT), or *"as powerful as Pharaoh"* (NLT), or *"equal to Pharaoh himself"* (NASB). Via the principle of agency, he was, as Pharaoh's representative, equivalent to Pharaoh. Moses, himself a type of Christ, was also said to be made *"as God"* to Pharaoh (Ex 4:16, Ex 7:1). The same is thus said of Jesus by Paul after identifying him as God's image or representation.

But in Paul's eyes, Jesus did not attempt to lord his great status over his brethren but was made, or found to be *"in the appearance of* [all other] *men."* He had not lived as the king that he was, but washed the feet of his own disciples (Jn 13:12), and made it known to them: *"I am among you as one who serves"* (Lk 22:27). As Kuschel notes, the first Adam's punishment had been to "live a kind of slave's existence."[1129] It is the second Adam's voluntary assumption of this sort of undeserved life that makes Jesus morally praiseworthy. He did not exploit his kingly right, but consistently submitted himself in suffering, even to the point of death (Phil 2:8). Murphy-O'Connor expertly summarizes the passage thus:

> As the Righteous Man par excellence Christ was the perfect image *(eikon)* of God. He was totally what God intended man to be. His sinless condition gave him the right to be treated as if he were God, that is, to enjoy the incorruptibility in which Adam was created. This right, however, he did not use to his own advantage, but he gave himself over to the consequences of a mode of existence that was not his by accepting the condition of a slave which involved suffering and death.[1130]

The first Adam had exploited his status and dispensed with the boundaries that God had prescribed; he had pursued his own desires in opposition to God. Jesus, however, denied his own desire to escape the cross, and submitted to God's will (Lk 22:42). Paul elsewhere explains that the weight of *"one man's*

[1128] Kuschel, p. 251, emphasis added.
[1129] Ibid.
[1130] Jerome Murphy-O'Connor, "Christological Anthropology in Phil 2.6-11," *Revue Biblique*, Vol. 93 (Paris, 1976), p. 49f, emphasis added.

disobedience" (Adam's non-compliance) was surmounted by *"one man's obedience"* (Jesus' submission, Rom 5:19), and it is for this reason that Christ is now to be awarded great honor.

But what about verses 7-8 of Philippians 2? Doesn't this just imply an incarnational event? We read that Jesus *"emptied himself, taking the form of a bond-servant, and being made in the likeness of men"* (Phil 2:7 NASB). The question is this: what exactly did Jesus empty himself of? The Trinitarian argument is that Philippians 2:6-8 is concerned with inner nature, but there are several major problems with this view. The Trinitarian NIV reads: *"Who, being in very nature God, did not consider equality with God something to be grasped, but made himself nothing, taking the very nature of a servant, being made in human likeness."* But if it is true that the verse is concerned with inner nature (as God), then when Christ "empties himself" and takes on the "nature" of a servant (man), has he not dispensed with his divine nature, assuming only the human? The word for "empties" here is *"kenoo"* (κενόω), and is defined as: "to empty, deprive of content, make unreal," and is elsewhere translated in the NASB as "made void," and "made empty." *Thayer's* understands it in the sense that one makes something "hollow" or "false." Interestingly, Romans 4:14 employs the word in this way: *"For if they which are of the law be heirs, faith is made void* (kenoo)*, and the promise made of none effect"* (KJV), or *"faith is empty* (kenoo) *and the promise is nullified"* (NET). If Philippians 2:7 really is speaking of making Christ's divine nature "kenoo," then it has been made void, hollow, useless, false, null, and of no effect. The Trinitarians seem to have suggested themselves that the earthly Jesus was void of a God nature and was only human.[1131] Of course, this passage is not speaking of Jesus giving up his deity or "hiding" his God-nature at all. We know this because it says that in exchange for what he emptied, he *"took the form of a bondservant"* (v. 7b). Deity is a nature. But servanthood is a *role*.

So what exactly is Paul telling us? We must keep in mind that the context of Philippians 2 is humility amongst brethren.[1132] In this light, a more appropriate

---

[1131] Some Trinitarian scholars have suggested a "kenosis theory" in which the Son divested himself of his divine attributes in the Incarnation. According to this theory, this "emptying" accounts for Jesus' lack of omniscience in Mark 13:32 and other inconsistences produced by the doctrine of the dual natures. Of course, the question remains about his alleged divine nature. If Jesus has divested himself of God's qualities, how can he be fully God? Most have disowned such theories as unorthodox and dangerous. For more on this topic see C. Stephen Evans (ed.), *Exploring Kenotic Christology: The Self-Emptying of God* (Oxford, 2006); Oliver Crisp, *Divinity and Humanity: The Incarnation Reconsidered* (Cambrdige, 2007), esp. pp. 118-153.

[1132] Paul admonishes the reader to *"Do nothing out of selfish ambition or vain conceit. Rather, in humility value others above yourselves, not looking to your own interests but each of you to the interests of the others"* (Phil 2:3-4).

interpretation would be that Jesus set aside his *role* as God's rightful ruler, and took up the *role* of a servant. Though the divinely appointed representative of God, who might have lorded it over his brothers, he instead became as one of them, lowly and submissive. So committed was he in his adopted role of servitude to both God and his fellow man, that he went to his death without exerting the rights of the Son of God, which he could have easily done: *"Or do you think that I cannot appeal to my Father, and he will at once put at my disposal more than twelve legions of angels?"* (Matt 26:53). But instead of exerting this right, he *"humbled himself by becoming obedient to the point of death, even death on a cross"* (Phil 2:8). Christ was obedient to *God* in the abandonment of his princely capacity and suffered the fate of a common criminal.

In Philippians 2:7, when Paul says that Jesus "emptied himself," Paul is likely drawing on the "Suffering Servant" imagery of Isaiah 53:12 where the Messiah is said to *"pour out himself to death."* In this light, Christ empties himself of his own life as the earthly Messianic ruler, not a pre-existent divine nature. In Isaiah, because of the Messiah's willingness to submit to death, God declares: *"Behold, my servant... will be high and lifted up and greatly exalted"* (Is 52:13). In this, Paul's portrait of Christ is complete: Jesus is the second Adam who, by setting aside his rights and taking on the role of a suffering servant, obeyed unto death. Though as God's representative he should have been treated as if he were God himself, he accepted spite and shame willingly. This is the act that glorified the Father, and so permitted his own glorification:

> *Therefore God has highly exalted him and bestowed on him the name that is above every name, so that at the name of Jesus every knee should bow...* *and every tongue confess that Jesus Christ is Lord, to the glory of God the Father* (Philippians 2:9-11 ESV).

The keyword is *"therefore,"* meaning "for this very reason." It is precisely because Jesus submitted himself and obeyed that he is worthy of exaltation above not only the earthly domain, which was his by right, but now over even the angels and all heavenly powers, everything except God (1 Pet 3:22, Eph 1:20-22, 1 Cor 15:45). This super-exaltation had, after all, always been the destiny that God had designed for humanity. Jesus was now the first to receive it; he became the forerunner, the *"pioneer of our salvation"* (Heb 2:10). As we read in Hebrews:

> [Jesus] *became as much superior to the angels as the name he has inherited is superior to theirs...* [God] *did not subject to angels the world to come, concerning which we are speaking. But one has testified* [in

Psalm 8:4-6] *saying, 'What is man, that you remember him? Or the son of man, that you are concerned about him? You have made him for a little while lower than the angels; you have crowned him glory and honor, and have appointed him over the works of your hands; you have put all things in subjection under his feet.' For in subjecting all things to him* [mankind], *he left nothing that is not subject to him. But now we do not yet see all things subjected to* [mankind]. *But we do see him who was made for a little while lower than the angels, namely, Jesus, because of the suffering of death crowned with glory and honor, so that by the grace of God he might taste death for everyone.* (Hebrews 1:4, 2:5-9)

The above passage from Hebrews is nearly a summary of Paul's "Suffering Adam Christology" in Philippians 2:6-11: God's dream had been for human beings to rule over the earth, and, eventually, over the heavens and the angels. But the global fulfillment of this grand vision has not yet come to pass. It has only recently been achieved for one member of that browbeaten race, the man Jesus, and he accomplished it only by way of suffering in obedience to the point of death. Because of this, he was given a name above every name, even the angels. This event opened the door for the future installment of the rest of mankind in authority over not only the earthly but the heavenly powers. Jesus' becoming superior to the angels was but the first step in a larger program of Adamic reinstatement, the first shots fired in God's human revolution. For Paul, the brothers of Jesus are destined be *"co-heirs with Christ"* (Rom 8:17), partakers in whatever birthright Jesus himself has. As Paul reminds us, *"Do you not know that we will judge angels?"* (1 Cor 6:3).

Ultimately, in Philippians 2, it is because of Jesus' participation in God's work that he is awarded his status, not because he bears an inherent divine nature. All honor that is now rightfully paid to Jesus for what he has done also glorifies God the Father (v. 11). We should not miss the fact that the endgame of Jesus' acknowledgment as "lord" is not the glorification of Jesus *as God*, but a glorification of the great God who exalted him: *"Every tongue [that] acknowledge[s] that Jesus Christ is Lord [does so] to the glory of God the Father"* (Phil 2:11). In this light, James Dunn clearly explicates Paul's Adam parallel:

> In short, the case for hearing a deliberate allusion to and contrast with Adam in Phil. 2:6-11 remains strong… the Adam-Christ, by his own choice, freely embraced the outcome which Adam's grasping and disobedience brought humankind.

He freely embraced the lot of humankind as slave to sin and death, which was the consequence of Adam's grasping. And he freely accepted the death which was the consequence of Adam's disobedience. In consequence, he was super-exalted... to the status and role originally intended for Adam (Ps. 8:6)... To argue that the exaltation or hyper-exaltation of 2:9 was a resumption of the divine mode of existence already enjoyed in 2:6 ignores not only the Adam motif, but also the consistent emphasis that *kyrios* (lord) was bestowed on Jesus *at exaltation.*[1133]

Dr. Kuschel also recognizes the significance of Paul's Adam-Christ contrast. He writes:

Jewish heritage *rather than Hellenistic syncretism* may be the key to understanding the Philippians hymn... Indeed an increasing number of present-day New Testament scholars with good reason question the premises of exegesis hitherto and cannot see pre-existence, let alone incarnation, in the Philippians hymn... in this text Christ is not celebrated as a pre-existent heavenly being, but in good Jewish fashion as a human counterpart to Adam... Christ is the great contrasting figure to Adam:

Adam the audacious man—

Christ the man who humbled himself;

Adam the one who was humbled forcibly by God—

Christ the man who voluntarily humbled himself before God;

Adam the rebellious man—

Christ the man who was utterly obedient;

Adam the one who was ultimately cursed—

Christ the one who was ultimately exalted;

Adam who wanted to be like God, and in the end became dust;

Christ, who was in the dust and indeed went to the cross, and is in the end the Lord over the cosmos.[1134]

[1133] James Dunn, *The Theology of Paul the Apostle* (Grand Rapids: Eerdmans, 1998), p. 287, emphasis added.

[1134] Kuschel, pp. 250-252, emphasis added.

As Murphy-O'Connor concludes: "the original hymn represents an attempt to define the uniqueness of Christ considered precisely as man. *This is what one would expect at the beginning of Christian theology.*"[1135]

Did the Messiah Teach a Triune God?

Continuing our investigation of the biblical distinction between God and his Messiah, we will consider one more frequently cited New Testament passage: *"Go therefore and make disciples of all the nations, baptizing them in the name of the Father and the Son and the Holy Spirit"* (Matthew 28:19 NASB). In their apologetic book *The Trinity*, the Trinitarian authors state that "probably the strongest clue to such a divine triunity occurs in the famous gospel commission that Jesus gave the church in its baptismal formula."[1136] But note that the authors concede that it is only a "clue" to the existence of the Trinity, not an actual presentation of the concept.

While this passage may mention the Father, the Son, and the Holy Spirit, it does not, however, teach that these are divisions within the Godhead. We find no declaration in this verse that the Father is true God, the Holy Spirit is true God, and the Son is true God, and that all three exist as co-eternal, co-equal members of the same being. If Matthew 28:19 is left as it is, what we have is the instruction of Jesus to baptize in the *authority* of God, Jesus, and the Holy Spirit.

The Jewish crowds in Jerusalem had recognized that Jesus was the king of Israel who came *"in the name of Yahweh"* (Matt 21:9), that is, that he was coming to them with God's authority. Similarly, about the angel who wielded God's authority in Exodus 23:21, God said *"my name is in him."* The phrase "in the name of" actually appears several times in Matthew as a reference to a given subject's authority: *"Many will say to me on that day, Lord, Lord, did we not prophesy in your name, and in Your name cast out demons, and in Your name perform many miracles?"* (Matt 7:22). The authority into which one is baptized need not be God; Paul states that the Israelites *"were all baptized into Moses"* (1 Cor 10:2), or, by the authority that Moses' name carries. Jesus' prescription to baptize in the authority of both the Father and the Son, and also in the authority carried by the Holy Spirit, is similar to a police officer commanding someone to stop "in the name of the Law," or by the authority that the Law carries. There is no clear and necessary Trinity here.

[1135] Murphy-O'Connor, p. 49, emphasis added.

[1136] Woodrow W. Whidden, Jerry Moon, John W. Reeve, *The Trinity: Understanding God's Love, His Plan of Salvation, and Christian Relationships* (Review and Herald Publishing Association, 2002), p. 32.

That being said, many New Testament scholars have actually suggested that the original text of Matthew 28:19 may not have been preserved in extant manuscripts. The form of the passage existing in our modern editions, with references to the Father, Son, and Holy Spirit, does appear to bear an inconsistency with the practice of the disciples in the New Testament. If the present version is correct, Christ's specific "formula" (if it really is a formula) seems to be ignored in favor of baptism only *"in the name of Jesus"* (Acts 2:38; 8:16; 10:48; 19:5; Gal 3:27; Rom 6:3). Throughout the record of the New Testament community, Christ's disciples are always baptizing (Acts 2:38), speaking (Acts 4:17-18), teaching (Acts 5:28), commanding (Acts 16:18), and healing (Acts 4:7-10) all *"in the name of Jesus."* Does the trine formula's absence evidence an Apostolic failure to follow Christ's instructions or have we encountered what may actually be a textual corruption in Matthew? Eusebius (d. 340 CE), may provide a glimpse at an earlier version of Matthew 28:19 when he quotes it in his *Oration* as: *"Go, and make disciples of all nations in my name."*[1137] Again, in his *Church History*, he quotes his manuscript as reading *"in my name."*[1138] This does seem more in alignment with the historical practice of the figures of the New Testament Church. This discrepancy has been noted by many scholars who point to the possibility of later ecclesiastical interpolation.[1139]

Nevertheless, the existing form of the verse in extant manuscripts still does not describe Trinitarian doctrine. It is by no means a Trinitarian proof-text. If Matthew 28:19 is the best example of the Trinity in the New Testament, we may confidently agree with the Trinitarian scholars who admit that "there are *no* proof-texts,"[1140] and that "the doctrine of the Trinity was not preached by Jesus."[1141]

Ultimately, we find that in both the Old and New Testaments, the Messiah is always a man worthy of honor as the exalted prince of mankind, but in no way a

---

[1137] Eusebius of Caesarea, *Oration of Emperor Constantine*, 16, 8.

[1138] Eusebius of Caesarea, *Church History*, 5, 2.

[1139] "It is often affirmed that the words in the name of the Father, and of the Son, and of the Holy Ghost are not the ipsissima verba [exact words] of Jesus, but... a later liturgical addition" (*Tyndale New Testament Commentaries*, I, p. 275); "The formal authenticity of Matt. 28:19 must be disputed" (*Schaff-Herzog Encyclopedia of Religious Knowledge*, p. 435); "The historical riddle is not solved by Matthew 28:19, since, according to a wide scholarly consensus, it is not an authentic saying of Jesus, not even an elaboration of a Jesus-saying on baptism" (*The Anchor Bible Dictionary*, Vol. 1, 1992, p. 585); "On every point the evidence of Acts is convincing proof that the tradition embodied in Matthew 28:19 is late and unhistorical" (F.J. Foakes Jackson & Kirsopp Lake, *The Jewish Gentile and Christian Backgrounds*, pp. 335-337).

[1140] Ryrie, *Basic Theology*, p. 89.

[1141] Hanson, *The Image of the Invisible God*, p. 87.

figure usurping the credit and position of the one God (Ezek 34:23-24). Jesus himself explained that he worships the one God (Lk 4:8, Jn 4:22), a God who is neither himself, nor a triune committee of different Persons, but a God whom he instead describes as *"one Lord"* (Mk 12:29), and as the traditional deity of Judaism (Jn 8:54). There is no difference then between the God portrayed by Moses and the other Old Testament prophets, and the portrait painted by Jesus. One Professor of Church history confirms:

> The Old Testament is strictly monotheistic. God is a single personal being. The idea that a trinity is to be found there... is utterly without foundation... On this point *there is no break between the Old Testament and the New.* The monotheistic tradition is continued. Jesus was a Jew, trained by Jewish parents in the Old Testament scriptures. His teaching was Jewish to the core... not a new theology... And he accepted as his own belief the great text of Jewish monotheism: "Hear, O Israel, the Lord our God is one God."[1142]

Might the modern student be moved by the Messiah's stirring testimony that this one entity is always greater than he is (Jn 14:28), that he is *"my God and your God"* (Jn 20:17), that he is specifically *"the Father"* (Jn 4:23-24), and that this Father alone is *"the only true God"* (Mk 12:32, 34, Jn 17:1-3)? These straightforward claims, however, seem to have largely fallen on deaf ears in favor of extrapolations of subtlety which invariably lead, not into any practical revelation, but headlong into confusion.

[1142] L. L. Paine, *A Critical History of the Evolution of Trinitarianism* (Boston: Houghton, Mifflin & Co., 1900), p. 4, emphasis added.

10

BEFORE THE WORLD BEGAN?

"The most useful piece of learning for the
uses of life is to unlearn what is untrue."
— Antisthenes (444 - 371 BCE)

T HROUGH OUR PREVIOUS SURVEY of the metaphysical models
of the Platonists and the Gnostics, we have already observed how
fundamental that framework was to Trinitarian principles, and how
directly it was introduced to the historical Christian faith. The Platonic
and Gnostic notions of real pre-existence, the transmigration of the soul, the
true unison of human and divine natures—the ancient Catholics had lovingly
gathered these models and propped Christ uncomfortably upon them, fostering
an infatuation with a "pre-human" Jesus still found energizing popular
Christianity today. Not exclusive to Trinitarian circles, the notion that Christ
somehow literally and personally existed prior to his conception in Mary is also
found driving the modern "Arians" (Jehovah's Witnesses), Mormons, Binitarians
(Armstrongism), and Sabellians (Oneness Pentecostals), though they differ on
exactly who Christ was before his birth. Trinitarians maintain that Christ pre-
existed as the eternally begotten second Person of the Trinity. Arians hold that
Christ pre-existed as a high spiritual being, or an angel, the chronologically first
creation of God. Mormons say that he was the first and greatest of the spirit-
sons of God, with Lucifer as his brother. Sabellians (Modalists) say he was first

God the Father before he became the Son. Despite the wide variety of theories regarding his pre-human identity, we will presently encounter evidence of a great disparity between these popular views and the defined opinion of the Gospels. It is the biblical data which presses us to wonder whether the argument over who Jesus was before his birth is really the right debate. Perhaps we should instead wonder if he really pre-dated his own birth at all?

There exists a modest collection of Jesus' Gospel sayings which are commonly said to support the notion of his own personal existence in some remote sphere before the Genesis creation. Due to the ambiguity of these passages, however, they are doggedly employed by a variety of divergent Christologies. None of these sayings can be seen as exclusively Trinitarian. Indeed pre-existence is one thing; pre-existence as the second member of a Triune God is another. These sayings of Christ we shall soon investigate, but only after making some acquaintance with some of the problems of the literal pre-existence tradition, as well as the exegetical methodology and worldview which a proper interpretation of Christ's teachings demands.

Platonic Pre-existence vs. Classical Jewish Pre-existence

It is of foremost importance to determine exactly what one means by "pre-existence." The concept varies immensely between the people-groups and religions of antiquity, yet for the purposes of this investigation we will demarcate these views into two types: Greek and Jewish. It is fair to say that the Jews believed in the pre-existence of all things, as did the Greeks.[1143] Yet their conceptions of pre-existence are as divergent as the cultures and religions which propagated them. The general views can be summarized in this way: Greek pre-existence is literal and actualized, while Jewish pre-existence is ideal and conceptualized.[1144]

As explored in part one, in the Greek or Platonic worldview, all humans were believed to harbor immortal souls which previously dwelt in a higher,

---

[1143] Some Hellenizing elements of Second Temple Judaism, being profoundly influenced by Platonic philosophy, had adopted a literal view of the pre-existence of every human being. History evidences however that this was not the opinion of the dominant Judaism of the first century, nor of the most ancient Hebrews, who conceived of an ideal or contemplated pre-existence for everything within the mind, plan, or Wisdom of God. This Hebrew "Wisdom" of God would be perceived as directly corresponding to the Greek "logos" of God by the later Jewish synthesizers like Philo of Alexandria.

[1144] The *Dictionary of the Later New Testament* confirms this distinction: "the pre-existent state may be described as ideal (existence in the mind or plan of God) or actual (existence alongside and distinct from God)" (David Capes, "Preexistence," *Dictionary of the Later New Testament* (Downer's Grove: IVP, 1997), p. 956).

heavenly plane of existence before their birth into our terrestrial sphere. Before the soul's incarnation as a human being, it existed in a perfect, unchanging world where it knew everything. At the moment of conception, the pre-existing identity was inserted into the baby's form and his knowledge was suppressed so that he must learn everything all over again. Generally speaking, the literal pre-existence of all humans has been rejected as unbiblical by both Jews and Christians. Citations of Zechariah 12:1 are often found in the classical arguments: *"The Lord… formed the spirit of man within him."* Rather than human life pre-existing and only awaiting insertion into a body from the outside, it has been argued by historical Christianity that God either creates each human soul ex-nihilo at the moment of conception,[1145] or that each soul is generated off of the parents.[1146] In fact, belief in the literal pre-existence of humans was ruled heretical in 553 CE by the Second Council of Constantinople. Even modern defenders of the literal pre-existence of Christ affirm that the pre-existence of human souls "was not the product of biblical but Platonic thinking."[1147] Not surprisingly, however, the man Jesus Christ is excused from this ruling. Jesus' conscious life is purported to have actually preceded his birth by billions of years, even eternity. The Trinitarian therefore esteems the Gospel birth narratives as relaying that a supernatural non-human being entered the young girl's womb *from the outside.* Indeed, to them, the Son was *"put* into the Virgin Mary's womb,"[1148] where he united with an abstract human nature. Of course, the narrative of history has already demonstrated that this metaphysical thinking arrived in Christianity only by the intense intermingling of Greek philosophy with the faith after the Apostles died. As one scholar reminds us, "the habits of thought which the Gentiles brought into the church are sufficient to explain the corruptions of apostolic doctrine which began in the post-apostolic age."[1149] Nevertheless, Douglas McCready, in his popular book defending the pre-existence of Jesus, asserts that "[Literal] Pre-existence remains the best

---

[1145] This concept is known as "Creationism."

[1146] Known as "Traducianism" or "Generationism."

[1147] Douglas McCready, *He Came Down From Heaven: The Preexistence of Christ and the Christian Faith* (Downer's Grove: IVP Academic, 2005), p. 220.

[1148] "When Did Jesus Know He Was the Son of God?" The Bible Study Site. Barnabas Ministries. Web. 16 December 2014. <http://www.biblestudy.org/question/when-did-jesus-know-he-was-god.html>.

[1149] G. T. Purves, *The Testimony of Justin Martyr to Early Christianity* (New York: Randolph and Co., 1889), p. 167.

explanation of the evidence."[1150] We will soon discover whether or not this is really the case.

What we will call the classical Jewish view of pre-existence is much different. The oldest Hebrew conception was not in the literal and ontological sense of the Greeks; rather it was an existence only in the "foreknowledge" or "foreordination" of God. In this sense, important figures, objects, and symbols first "existed" in heaven with God before being made a reality at their appointed times. All of these things did not literally and physically dwell in some far removed dimension, but were only personally envisioned by God in his eternal plan for the universe. One scholar explains:

> When the Jew said something was "predestined," he thought of it as already "existing" in a higher sphere of life. The world's history is thus predestined because it is already, in a sense, preexisting and consequently fixed. This typically Jewish conception of predestination *may be distinguished from the Greek idea of preexistence* by the predominance of the thought of "preexistence" *in the Divine purpose.*[1151]

In the coming sections we will examine this Hebraic understanding and how it relates to the sayings and theology of Jesus in the New Testament. But first we must recognize that several difficulties immediately arise when the model of literal "Greek" pre-existence is applied to the Jesus texts by Trinitarians. In this chapter we will address only a few of the problems with the literal system before considering the alternative view in the next chapter.

Problems with Literal Pre-existence:
The Mind of Christ

Trinitarians have said that Christ, though man, is also fully God and therefore exhibits the full characteristics of God. God must exist in such a way that his own identifying traits (omnipotence, unbegotten nature (aseity), omniscience, etc.) are inhibited. One line of questioning highlights a wealth of problems: *What happened to Jesus' memories and knowledge as omniscient God when he allegedly transformed himself into a human baby? Did Jesus know, as a crying infant, that he was the Creator of all things? How is it that a being, who is claimed to have never experienced*

[1150] McCready, p. 316.

[1151] E. C. Dewick, *Primitive Christian Eschatology* (Cambridge: CUP, 1912), pp. 253, 254, emphasis added.

a moment when he was not fully God, fails to exhibit the precise qualities that make him so? Was there a time when Jesus did not know that he was God?

As we will see, in the Gospel narratives there is presented what appears to be a striking dissolution of Christ's pre-existent omniscience. But this has not prevented Trinitarian apologists from claiming that: "During His days in the flesh, Jesus *remained* omniscient God."[1152] Other Trinitarian ministers have affirmed: "To be omniscient is to have all knowledge, unlike normal men. The Bible declares that Jesus was indeed omniscient."[1153] Of course it is easy to say that "the Bible declares" this opinion, but it is another thing to demonstrate it consistently.

Despite these claims, we discover in the Gospels that the young Jesus, not having all things before him from eternity, worked towards the achievement of insight: "*And Jesus grew in wisdom and stature, and in favor with God and man*" (Luke 2:52). Here Christ is said to have progressively attained to a higher level of *wisdom* (Greek: "sophia"), defined as "insight, skill, knowledge, or intelligence."[1154] Jesus, evidently, is the God who had all knowledge but forgot exactly how to apply it. But is this really the most straightforward reading of the text?

Consider this quote from an apologist's article: "Not one Bible passage can be produced saying Jesus acquired information from man."[1155] This statement, though impetuous, is honestly what one would expect if the Bible really did advocate an omniscient God-Christ. However, there are several passages which contradict this claim: "*Now when Jesus heard that John had been taken into custody, he withdrew into Galilee*" (Matt 4:12), and "*Jesus heard that they had thrown him* [the blind

---

[1152] Tim Haile, "How Did Jesus 'Grow in Wisdom'?" The Bible Banner. Web. 15 December 2014. <http://www.biblebanner.com/ga_art/lk_2_52.htm>, emphasis added.

[1153] James L. Melton, "The Deity of Jesus Christ: Scriptural Proof That Jesus Christ is God," Bible Baptist Publications. Web. 15 December 2014. Apologists sometimes argue that because several verses say that Jesus knew what was in people's hearts or minds, the Bible is portraying him as omniscient God. But "knowing all men" or "knowing what was in man" (Jn 2:24-25) hardly requires a God-like omniscience; it requires only knowing what human beings are like. Matthew 9:4 does depict Jesus as "knowing their thoughts" and knowing what people were "thinking" in their hearts; while we can argue that his conclusions could have been drawn by natural means, even if he literally knew what was going on in their minds, this would not require deity. Other men in the Bible were empowered to "read minds" by the holy spirit. For example, Peter knew that Ananias had lied to him about the sale of his property (Acts 5:3), similar to John 1:48 in which Jesus says that he knew Nathanael had been sitting under a fig tree before Philip called him. Likewise in the Old Testament, the prophet Elisha said that he knew his lying servant had met with a man on a chariot before meeting Elisha (2 Kings 5:26). Having this kind of knowledge does not require being "fully God."

[1154] "Sophia," *Thayer's Greek Lexicon.*

[1155] Haile, "How Did Jesus 'Grow in Wisdom'?"

man] *out, and when he found him, he said, 'Do you believe in the Son of Man?'* " (Jn 9:35). The word in these passages for "heard" is the Greek "ekousen" which *Thayer's* defines as "to get by hearing, to learn, to understand, etc." Jesus was evidently involved in some activity, was introduced to information by men, and reacted to this information by changing course.

In so readily demonstrating Jesus' acquisition of information from a source outside himself, we wonder what the Trinitarian response might be. That Jesus acquired information in his human nature only, but not in his God nature? If that is the case, have we split the natures into two separate persons like the "heretical" Nestorian or Valentinian Christologies do? Though the average Trinitarian may still be uncomfortable with the idea, conciliar orthodoxy will push them to affirm that a dual-minded Jesus received knowledge *into one of his minds, but not the other.* But what is an abstract *mind* without a real person behind it? Regardless of which mind or nature is said to have facilitated the reception of this knowledge, is it not the *one Person* of Christ who has taken it in?[1156]

The most apt demonstration of Christ's lack of omniscience comes to us towards the end of Matthew's Gospel. When asked about the time of the Christ's Second Coming, Jesus admits: *"But about that day or hour no one knows, not even the angels in heaven, nor the Son, but only the Father"* (Matt 24:36). In this famous passage we encounter yet again some significant information that is unknown to Jesus. This is knowledge that belongs exclusively to the Father, the one whom Jesus publicly recognized as the one and only true God of the Jews (Jn 8:54; 17:3). Is it therefore not reasonable and scriptural to conclude that the reason why the Father is the only owner of God's omniscience is that the Father is the sole owner of true Godhood? Is this not precisely what Jesus said in John 17:3? How it is possible for a supposed co-equal and co-essential participant in God's very existence to not be privy to what God knows has been the subject of endless musing. Yet the plainest reading hardly requires such antics. The Jesus of the New Testament constantly ascribes certain prerogatives to the Father only, such as the right to assign places of honor in God's Kingdom: *"to sit at my right or left is not mine to give, but it is for those for whom it has been prepared by my Father"* (Matt 20:23). How God cannot delegate rights in God's Kingdom escapes the reader as much as a God who always knows everything except for when he doesn't. But there is another matter to consider here: Jesus' exclusion of not only himself from certain prerogatives of God, but his exclusion of the supposed third Person of the Holy Spirit. We must not forget that in Trinitarian theology,

---

[1156] For further analysis of the two minds, see Hick, *The Metaphor of God Incarnate*, p. 51ff.

the Father, the Son, and the Holy Spirit are not the same Person; they are completely different Persons. If it is claimed by the Trinitarian that Jesus did not "know the day nor the hour" only because he had set aside his godly prerogatives through the Incarnation, and thus his adopted human nature was the foundation of his ignorance, what about the Person of the Holy Spirit? Why does this distinct Person, like the Son, also not know what only *the Father* knows? In light of Matthew 24:36, the common interpretation seems troubled at every turn.

While many apologists appear unwilling to accept the implications of Christ's confident admission of the Father's exclusive knowledge, some, like Trinitarian philosopher Brian Leftow, have admitted that Jesus did not have "full access" to his knowledge about his relationship to the Father.[1157] One popular Trinitarian ministry likewise demonstrates this strain of Trinitarianism which confesses Christ's *diminished awareness* of his own deity during his life, which is, we must agree, the most forward (however unpalatable) conclusion. They write, in response to the question "When did Jesus know that he was God?":

> The Bible does not clearly state that there was a point at which He knew that He was the second Person of the Trinity. At some point, Jesus fully realized who He was from eternity past... We can conclude that although the preincarnate Jesus knew from eternity past who He was... the incarnate Jesus came to that realization at some point in His earthly life.[1158]

This scarcely seems helpful in understanding the recorded ministry of the historical Jesus. Even towards the end of his life, in the *twenty-fourth* chapter of Matthew, we see that he still has not fully regained his omniscient mind as God. How then are we to interpret his many statements before and after this? Indeed, they conclude that while this realization that he was the Creator of all things occurred at some point, "just what that point was, we cannot know for sure."[1159] N. T. Wright agrees, in light of the Gospel portrait of Jesus, that Jesus must not have really known who he was, at least not "in the same way that one knows one is male or female, hungry or thirsty... [Jesus' knowledge of himself was] of a more risky, but perhaps more significant sort: like knowing one is loved."[1160]

[1157] Brian Leftow, *God and Necessity* (Oxford: OUP, 2012), p. 322.

[1158] "When Did Jesus Know That He Was God?" Got Questions Ministries. Web. 16 December 2014.

[1159] Ibid.

[1160] Wright, *Jesus and the Victory of God*, pp. 652-653.

Jesus' self-awareness, it would seem, was a thing of faith or trust. The degree of surety with which one knows one is hungry or thirsty was supposedly lacking in Christ.

The implications are unfortunate: if the one Person of the Son is Almighty God, integral and vital to God, then there was a time when Almighty God didn't really know who he was. Therefore Jesus is, according to this systematized identity crisis, the God who deliberately forgot what he knew, then had to re-learn it all over again. This entire system smacks of the Platonic model of pre-existence which holds that the soul first exists in heaven where it knows everything, but its knowledge is diminished at birth so that it must be re-learned. Regardless of the system's true origins, modern Christians seem to have no way of comprehending, in any practical or edifying way, how God could forget that he is God and not know that he is God until he somehow reminds himself.

Here we might append that great wisdom from J. W. Bowman, who asserts that "the Church cannot indefinitely continue to believe about Jesus what he did not know to be true about himself."[1161] Far be it from the devoted Christian, endeavoring only to faithfully follow the teachings and life of his master, to prop up a misinformed, ignorant, or, God forbid, virtually schizophrenic Christ. Orthodoxy surely does not want the Christian professing or convincing others of such a thing. But with two natures, two wills, and two minds (which hold different understandings and degrees of self-awareness), it seems that the Christian is doomed to be just as uncertain about the Trinitarian Jesus as the Trinitarian Jesus was about himself.

Problems with Literal Pre-existence:
Incarnation of the God-Fetus

These problems reflect only a small sampling of the massive complications one produces for the faith by saying that the God of the Bible turned himself into "a little baby."[1162] Yet this is the increasing practice of popular Christian voices. Trinitarian Max Lucado, named "America's Pastor" by *Christianity Today* and "The Best Preacher in America" by *Reader's Digest*,[1163] writes:

> He who was larger than the universe became an embryo. And
> he who sustains the world with a word chose to be dependent

---

[1161] Bowman, *The Intention of Jesus*, p. 108.

[1162] Michael Najim, "Why God Became a Baby," Catholic News Agency. Web. 23 December 2014. <http://www.catholicnewsagency.com/cw/post.php?id=65>.

[1163] Tiffany Taylor, "Reader's Digest honors alumnus: Max Lucado named Best Preacher in America in magazine," *The Optimist* (Abilene Christian University, 2005).

upon the nourishment of a young girl. God as a fetus. Holiness sleeping in a womb. The creator of life being created. God was given eyebrows, elbows, two kidneys, and a spleen. He stretched against the walls and floated in the amniotic fluids of his mother... Angels watched as Mary changed God's diaper. The universe watched with wonder as The Almighty learned to walk.[1164]

This attitude provides biblically and rationally troubling conclusions, namely that "the creator of life was created." Could there be anything more antagonistic to the spirit of Judaism, the religion of Jesus? The New Testament represents the Apostolic (Jewish) view on the subject:

> *For even though they knew God, they did honor him as God or give thanks, but they became futile in their speculations, and their foolish heart was darkened. Professing to be wise, they became fools, and exchanged the glory of the incorruptible God for an image in the form of corruptible man... For they exchanged the truth of God for a lie, and worshiped and served the creature rather than the Creator, who is blessed forever. Amen.*
> (Romans 1:21-23a, 25)

God is fundamentally and inexorably different from his creatures. He is the supreme *Other* whom no creature is like (Isaiah 46:9). Paul explains that there have been those who indeed knew about God, but who tragically confused the fixed boundary between creature and Creator. On the surface, these devotees proclaimed wisdom, but to the Apostle, the idea that the unique and immortal God could ever himself be an image in the form of a man was only foolishness. Recalling that the Bible calls Jesus *"the image of God"* (2 Cor 4:4), even *"the image of the invisible God"* (Col 1:15), we wonder at the implications of what Paul is saying. It seems that within mainstream Christianity, an image, indeed a representation of God in the form of a man (Jesus), has been viewed as the unique, incorruptible Creator himself. One is led to believe that mainstream Christianity has not yet grasped the significance of the matter. While Christians today marvel at a God who became a human being, for Paul, blurring the lines between Creator and creature is a tremendous error leading ultimately to a *"depraved mind"* (Rom 1:24). One biblical scholar recognizes that:

[1164] Max Lucado, "It Began in a Manger (Christmas)," Max Lucado. Web. 23 December 2014. <https://maxlucado.com/read/topical/it-began-in-a-manger-christmas>.

The Greeks might identify God and man, but to an Israelite there was no distinction so deep and impassable of the Creator from all His creatures, even the highest. Nor was it at all within the compass of contemporary Jewish imagination that God should manifest himself in human form.[1165]

Paul, as a good Jew, always preserves God in the exclusive realm of the Creator, while he places Jesus squarely in the world of creation, even calling him *"the firstborn of all creation"* (Col 1:15). We easily understand the meaning here: Christ belongs to creation; he is the chief member of all created things. The Trinitarian publishers of the *New International Version* of the Bible also must have recognized this, which is possibly why they felt compelled to diverge from other major translations and render the verse: *"the firstborn over all creation."* This is, of course, an unabashed attempt at distancing Christ from creation.

Beyond the Incarnation's contest with the New Testament, the rational problems are equally extensive. One Trinitarian professor of philosophy writes:

God the Fetus, God the Embryo, and God the Holy Zygote. This is the God I worship... the God who saw the dark inside Mary's womb, the God of the Dark. How can God have seen these things? How can God's head and shoulders have cramped small enough to pass through Mary's vagina?[1166]

Trinitarians seem just as perplexed over the suggestion as anyone. But that is easily covered over by placing faith in the infallible principle of mystery; that which is impossible to comprehend is ultimately impossible to disprove—a "God of the Dark" indeed. In many cases, we find the sheer wonder of the whole idea even being pitched as part of the attraction of this lovingly described "Deity in Diapers."[1167] Nevertheless, the nagging problems abound. Max Lucado even writes that Mary may have felt awkward teaching God how he created the world, and when she prayed to the God sleeping under her roof, she may have accidently called her son "Father." He speculates that God may have woken up afraid from a bad dream, had questions for his parents about Scripture, and had drawn distant looks on his childish face as he silently listened

---

[1165] Charles Gore, *Belief in Christ* (New York: Charles Scribner's Sons, 1922), p. 11.

[1166] Mark S. McLeod-Harrison, *Apologizing For God: The Importance of Living in History* (Eugene: Cascade Books, 2011), p. 138.

[1167] Greg Laurie, "Was Jesus God?" Cross Map. Web. 26 December 2014. <http://www.crossmap.com/blogs/greg-laurie-was-jesus-god-3907>.

to people's prayers. Lucado is emphatic: "Jesus may have had pimples. He may have been tone-deaf. Perhaps a girl down the street had a crush on him or vice versa… One thing's for sure: He was, while completely divine, completely human."[1168] When we join Trinitarians in saying that Jesus was genuinely human but somehow, beyond all intelligible means, he was also God Almighty, we head down a slippery slope. Ultimately we may end up like Lucado, claiming that it is possible that God was romantically interested in a young girl.

This dogma is likely to be damaging, not only to Christians' personal concept of the Creator, but to the reputation of Christianity in the world. Inevitable speculations like Lucado's are bound to be welcomed by the mainstream Christian community as tender sentiments of beauty that demonstrate the loving willingness of God to identify with his creatures. However, they are only offensive and disturbing to adherents of the classic monotheism of the Bible like the Jews.

Modern Jews, like Meir Y. Soloveichick, explain that Judaism has historically rejected "Neoplatonic ideas" which seek to bring the divine into communion with us through "finite means," that is, through the real joining of infinite God with finite man.[1169] At Sinai, the God of the Bible had forbidden his depiction as a graven image; the person of God was not to be thought of as coming down to be contained in the material realm. He was not to be experienced with the natural senses. God's method of communion was to express himself through his word or commandments, or through agents to whom he had given his word. As Jewish scholar Jacob Neusner explains: "Judaism knows God through God's own self-manifestation in the Torah of Sinai, oral and written. God makes himself known through what he does, through his relationships, the rules to which those actions and transactions conform."[1170] A literally incarnate God, as Neusner confirms, is thus "utterly incompatible with [the God] of Judaism—any kind of Judaism."[1171] The biblical God is to be communed with, not by sight, touch, and smell, but by engaging with God's mind through his word, his Torah. Soloveichick reveals that Judaism has long been focused on the word of God as the embodiment of God's will. Christianity on the other hand has been focused on an embodied God. Indeed, as respected evangelical teachers confirm,

---

1168 Lucado, "It Began in a Manger (Christmas)"

1169 Meir Y. Soloveichick, "Torah and Incarnation: Torah Learning Bridges the Gap Between Man and God," First Things. 01 October 2010. Web. 14 June 2015.

1170 Jacob Neusner, *The Incarnation of God: The Character of Divinity in Formative Judaism* (Binghamton: Global Academic Publishing, 2001 [1998]), p. xiii.

1171 Ibid., p. 6.

mainstream Christianity is a belief, not in the express teachings of Jesus, but in Jesus as the person of God incarnate.[1172] In this way, for Christians, "the gap between finite man and infinite God is bridged; for Jews, Christians are succumbing to the temptation that Deuteronomy warns against: seeking to bridge the gap between man and God through finite means."[1173] Throughout Jewish history, God's word has remained the vehicle by which heaven comes to earth. As we will discover in later chapters of this book, in Second Temple Jewish circles, God's word or Torah was even said to be "embodied" in Jewish teachers. This may ultimately prove helpful in understanding controversial Jewish texts from that era, such as the prologue of John's Gospel, in which God's word is said to have "become flesh" in the person of Jesus Christ.

But for now we will focus on the incongruity between the real Incarnation of Christian orthodoxy with the long-standing worldview of the Jews. We must ultimately conclude that the only reason the notion of the crying, urinating God is not as shocking to the Christians as it is to the Jews, is that the Christians, through all the exercise of culture and Church tradition, are simply used to it. For the Jewish writers of the Bible, however, such an idea would have been at best an intolerable blasphemy.

Furthermore, we are forced by the weight of the New Testament to object to any theology of Incarnation as a wholesale misunderstanding of the intentions of God in the mission of Jesus Christ. God's grand endeavor was to reveal himself *through* a human being, not *as* a human being. The Apostolic testimony, even after Jesus' ministry, was that *"no one has ever seen God"* (1 Jn 4:12). Indeed, God himself cannot be seen because he is *"invisible"* (Col 1:15). It was clearly necessary for God to reveal himself through *another* individual who could be seen. Thus God elected the man Jesus, whom he declared *"my servant, the one whom I have chosen"* (Matt 12:18), for this very purpose. The vibrant testimony of John is useful here: *"No one has seen God at any time; the only begotten Son, who is in the bosom of the Father, he has revealed him"* (Jn 1:18). The mission of Christ therefore was not to *be* God, but to demonstrate God to the world. The uniqueness of Jesus' unparalleled ministry lies squarely in its heavenly origin, in the supernatural power of its operation, not in the initiative of the man himself. While Jesus was truly the uniquely begotten Son of God, he did not profess to gather any power from himself, but directed men always towards his Father's divine prerogative. Jesus' deeds and the ability to do them came from someone outside of himself:

<hr />

[1172] See James Kennedy, "How I Know Jesus is God"; Harold O. J. Brown, *Heresies*, p. 13.
[1173] Soloveichick, "Torah and Incarnation."

"*I can do nothing on my own initiative*" (Jn 5:30); "*I can of mine own self do nothing*" (KJV). Even his own teaching he did not personally develop but received from another source: "*If anyone is willing to do His will, he will know of the teaching, whether it is of God or whether I speak from myself*" (Jn 7:17). Simply put, it was another, his own God and Father, who had authorized every moment of his ministry. It is this exclusive and powerful partnership with God that was Christ's emphasis, not that he was identical to him. That God was proven, by all manner of signs and testimonies, to be "with" Christ and "in" Christ is undoubtedly the express intention of the New Testament. On this point there should be no mistake: "*God was in Christ*" (2 Cor 5:19), not "God *was* Christ." In Acts we find the Apostolic Church preaching this message consistently to the Gentiles: "*You know of Jesus of Nazareth, how God anointed him with the Holy Spirit and with power, and how he went about doing good and healing all who were oppressed by the devil, because God was with him*" (Acts 10:38). The Church preached the same message about God's partnership with the man Jesus to the Jews who had previously persecuted him: "*Jesus of Nazareth was a man... God did [signs] through him*" (Acts 2:22). The testimony of Nicodemus agreed: "*Rabbi, we know that you are a teacher who has come from God. For no one can do these signs that you do unless God is with him*" (Jn 3:2). Note once again that the Christ performs all of these things not because "he *is* God," but because God is "*with*" him; another more powerful entity had partnered with Jesus to both sanction and accomplish the effort. Christ's audience therefore did not rejoice at the sight of his miracles because they understood them as proof that God himself was standing in their midst, but instead "*When the crowd saw this, they were filled with awe; and they praised God, who had given such authority to men*" (Matt 9:8). This human Jesus, it was evident, was not alone; something powerful was operating behind the scenes. Indeed, Christ affirms: "*I am not alone, for my Father is with me*" (Jn 16:32), and "*I do not speak on my own authority. Rather, it is the Father, living in me, who is doing his work*" (Jn 14:10). It is this vivid and continuous testimony of Jesus which caused the Apostles, the Jews at Pentecost, and later the Gentiles to believe that Jesus was a man whom the great and invisible God operated through (Acts 2:22), not that a man somehow *was* God. As one historian observes, the idea that the Nazarene was God himself "was completely alien to any orthodox Jewish belief," and instead, Jesus was seen by the earliest Jewish-Christian community as "one through whom God worked (as with the earlier Jewish prophets) and who had been exalted by God through his death. Peter [explains this in] Acts 2:22-24."[1174]

[1174] Freeman, *Closing of the Western Mind,* p. 104.

If the pre-existent God had truly become a human being, we find countless opportunities for the biblical authors to expound on the matter. But, as scholars have reported, "Incarnation, in its full and proper sense, is not something directly presented in Scripture."[1175] Especially in the Apostolic ministry to the Gentiles we find a host of missed opportunities to explain the alleged Incarnation. In fact, the pagans at the time of Christ already held divine incarnation as an important religious concept. As we saw in part one of this book, the story of a deity joining in the human experience existed in the pagan mythos of many world religions long before Christianity arrived on the scene.[1176] The God-man of orthodoxy was therefore nothing new, as the founding father of modern anthropology, Sir James George Frazer, reports: "the notion of a man-god... belongs essentially to that earlier period of religious history" and members of those societies were well acquainted with "the idea of a god incarnate in human form."[1177] Christianity, it would seem, has perpetuated the concept into the world of modern religion:

> Incarnation... the assumption of human form by a god is an idea common in religion... India and Egypt were especially rich in forms of incarnation in men as well as in beasts. Incarnation is found in various phases of Greek religion, in which the human body of a god was a disguise or a temporary means of communication. Among western cultures the most widely accepted belief in incarnation is in that of Jesus, held by Christians to be God in the flesh.[1178]

But could such a transmigration of religious thought have really taken place, so that such critical Christian dogmas as the Incarnation were facilitated by the inoculation of paganism into Christianity? Even respected scholars such as James Dunn do not preclude such a transmission and candidly admit that, "There is of course always the possibility that 'poplar pagan superstition' became popular Christian superstition, by a gradual assimilation and spread of belief."[1179] The historical *Greek* concept of the incarnation is important to this conversation

---

[1175] M. Wiles quoted in Dunn, *Christology in the Making*, p. 4.

[1176] See Sir James George Frazer, *The Golden Bough: A Study in Magic and Religion* (New York: The Macmillan Company, 1922), Part VII, p. 2.

[1177] Ibid.

[1178] "God incarnate," *Collins Discovery Encyclopedia*, 1st Ed. HarperCollins Publishers. 2005. Web. 23 December 2014.

[1179] Dunn, *Christology in the Making*, p. 211, 251.

as it is this belief system which runs up against the religion of the Jewish Jesus and the first-century Apostles in the post-Easter period. As Freeman observes:

> In the Greco-Roman world, unlike the world of Judaism, human beings could appear to cross the boundary between human and divine. While Peter and Paul had implied that Jesus became someone "exalted" by God only on his death, [after the transition of Christianity into the world of the Greeks], it was now possible in this very different spiritual setting, to assume that he might have always been divine. The interplay between the [Apostolic] memories of Jesus and the spiritually fertile culture of the Greek world was to be an immensely creative one, and its legacy survives in interpretations of Jesus still held today.[1180]

The meeting of these vastly different religious worldviews is preserved for us in the New Testament record of the early Church. The missionaries Paul and Barnabas, during their visit to the Greeks, healed a man, and *"When the crowds saw what Paul had done, they raised their voice, saying in the Lycaonian language, 'The gods have become like men and have come down to us' "* (Acts 14:11). Here would have been a most fitting moment for the disciples of Jesus, teachers whom Trinitarians so often insist believed in Jesus as the incarnate God, to correct the error of the pagans and direct them to the real Christian Incarnation. "No," they might easily have said, "But there *is* a God, the highest God, who has done this very thing... he is Jesus Christ, both God and man!" Of course, this opportunity to explain what the early Christians supposedly held as the core of their faith was spectacularly missed, like every other chance the great figures of the New Testament had to expound on basic Trinitarian principles:

> But when the apostles Barnabas and Paul heard of it, they tore their robes and rushed out into the crowd, crying out and saying, "Men, why are you doing these things? We are also men of the same nature as you, and preach the gospel to you that you should turn from these vain things to a living God, who made the heavens and the earth and the sea and all that is in them (Acts 14:14-15).

The Apostles, rather than explaining that there was a man who was in nature both human and divine, one who had come down from heaven just as they had

---

[1180] Freeman, *Closing of the Western Mind,* p. 128.

said, instead adjure them to *"turn from these vain things."* They immediately point them to *"the living God"*[1181] of their fathers (Deut 5:26, Josh 3:10, Ps 42:2, Jer 10:10, Dan 6:20), the sole Creator of all things. Paul refers to their deity as "El Chai," one of the traditional names of the Hebrew God. As *The Jewish Encyclopedia* remarks, Yahweh's name means "He who lives"; he is presented as "the living God, as contrasted with the lifeless gods of the heathen."[1182] This ancient and unique God of the Israelites, without any concern for the Greeks' incarnational ideas, is the solemn recommendation of Paul. Throughout his ministry, as one historian notes, "Paul was true to his Jewish inheritance… he was challenging the deep-rooted spiritual tradition of the Greco-Roman world, which allowed the gods to be shown in human form."[1183]

Considering all of this information, the Incarnation already seems lacking in support. Yet there is one more matter relating to the Greek style of pre-existence, as expressed through orthodox Trinitarianism, which should be analyzed before considering the alternative view.

Problems with Literal Pre-existence:
Eternally Begotten or Begotten Within Mary?

While reason may prevent us from wholesale trust in the incarnation of a literally pre-existent Jesus, the Bible has continuously proven the most stalwart and able of the dogma's opponents. One of the most famous and essential features of the orthodox tradition which we will test against the New Testament is the idea that Jesus is, being God, *eternal*. This is to say that the Son of God has "no beginning."

As we saw in part one of this book, the first of the proto-orthodox theologians to develop this idea of a "beginningless" Christ was the Alexandrian philosopher Origen (185-254 CE), who "drew upon pagan philosophy in an effort to elucidate the Christian faith in a manner acceptable to intellectuals."[1184] Origen's Platonism necessitated that there was never a time in which God was not creating; thus he placed God into an "eternal now" in which the Son was

---

[1181] See Jeremiah 10:10: *"But Yahweh is the true God; he is the living God and the everlasting King…"* Compare with Christ in John 17:3, *"You* (Father), [are] *the only true God."* Likewise in Matthew 16:16, Jesus affirms Peter's testimony, not that Jesus is that one living God himself, but that he is *"God's anointed one, the Son of the living God."*

[1182] J. F. McLaughlin, Judah David Eisenstein, "Names of God," *The Jewish Encyclopedia.* 1906. Web. 23 December 2014.

[1183] Freeman, *Closing of the Western Mind,* p. 120.

[1184] Edward Moore, "Origen of Alexandria (185-254 C.E.)," *Internet Encyclopedia of Philosophy.* Web. 30 December 2014.

being continuously generated. All of this had profound influence on the later Alexander and Athanasius, who proceeded one step further, asserting the real and unique co-eternality of the Son at the Council of Nicaea.[1185]

However, they did not arrive at this position without considerable, even insurmountable difficulty. The Gospel accounts of Christ proved most problematic, namely their constant description of Jesus as God's *"begotten son"* (Jn 3:16).[1186] This term "begotten" is found throughout the New Testament: *"Abraham begat Isaac; and Isaac begat Jacob; and Jacob begat Judah and his brothers"* (Matt 1:2). The root here is "gennao," defined as "to beget, bring forth, give birth to," and it is also translated in this way by the NASB: "become the father of, produce," and so on. We should understand this language without difficulty: to "beget" is to father a child, to procreate at a point in time.[1187] *Merriam-Webster's* likewise defines "beget" as "to cause something to exist, to become the father of."[1188] If words mean anything, when Jesus was begotten, he was caused to exist by a father. Biblically speaking, it is God who is the cause of the begetting, the beginning of a new person. As one theologian observes, "It is easy to see why this little word could cause so much trouble for those who believe Jesus has always existed."[1189]

If God "begat" Jesus, that is, if he *became* the father of Jesus, then it was an episode *in time*, not outside time in eternity. Indeed, a father and his son cannot both arrive simultaneously. The many prophetic declarations of God to the coming Messiah in the Old Testament affirm this point: *"You are my Son, today I have begotten you!"* or in some translations, *"today I have become your father!"* (Acts

---

[1185] Rowan Williams, *Arius: Heresy and Tradition* (London: Darton, Longman and Todd, 1987), p. 175.

[1186] Toom, *Classical Trinitarian Theology: A Textbook*, pp. 66-68.

[1187] See also Liddell and Scott's authoritative lexicon which even provides the meaning "create" for "gennao" (Henry Liddle, Robert Scott, *Greek-English Lexicon* (New York: Harper & Brothers Pub., 1870). Bruce Metzger likewise provides this meaning (Bruce Metzger, *A Textual Commentary on the Greek New Testament* (London: United Bible Societies, 1971), p. 8).

[1188] "beget," Merriam-Webster Dictionary. Web. 30 December 2014.

[1189] Sean Finnegan, "Jesus Has A Beginning," Christian Monotheism. Web. 30 December 2014. <http://www.christianmonotheism.com/media/text/Jesus_Has_A_Beginning_issue_62.pdf>. Finnegan also includes this insightful footnote: "This is probably why most modern translations have changed the phrase "only begotten" to "one and only" (See NIV/HCSB/NLT/NRSV/BBE on John 3:16)." For the translators to so drastically alter the wording of the Bible because the original seems to impugn a traditional doctrine should be considered reprehensible by all parties. It is not the responsibility of Bible translators to protect dogma, but to accurately and responsibly deliver an unprejudiced transmission of God's message. For more on how theological bias has influenced our modern Bible translations, see the landmark book from Dr. Jason BeDuhn, *Truth in Translation: Accuracy and Bias in English Translations of the New Testament*, University Press of America, 2003.

13:33; Heb 1:5; 5:5; Ps 2:7). *Today* is, of course, a specific moment in time, not a timeless, foggy eternity. Indeed, the Messianic prophecies drive the argument: *"I will be his Father and he will be my Son"* (Heb 1:5; 2 Sam 7:14). Interestingly, in the proximate Second Temple community that produced the Dead Sea Scrolls, we find one document which likewise envisions a future time *"When God begets the Messiah..."* (1QSa 11-12). It was clear to them that God had projected a *future* date for the institution of his fatherhood of the Messiah, not that it had literally already happened before all time. This was the messianic expectation of the Jewish world, including the New Testament community, who identified this expectation as satisfied in the Jesus event.

All of this data later provided a major hurdle for the proto-Trinitarian theologians at the Council of Nicaea. To them, Jesus *must* be God; but what to do with all of this begetting language? The conflict between Christ's "begotteness" and his supposed "eternality" was impossible to ignore. Without doubt, the philosophers had recognized that if Jesus was simply "begotten," or "generated," he could not be "eternally God" in the sense the Athanasians were suggesting. After all, God is God because he is uniquely ungenerated or unbegotten, completely self-sufficient and requiring no initiation of his being.[1190] As the Scriptures explain that the Deity is from *"everlasting to everlasting"* (Psalm 90:2), we might agree that *unbegotteness* is an essential quality of the God of the Bible; he lives thanks to no other source. However, we find Jesus gladly announcing his own life's dependence on another, declaring: *"I live because of the Father"* (Jn 6:57), and *"For just as the Father has life in himself, even so he gave* [or 'granted'] *the Son to have life in himself"* (Jn 5:26).[1191] Throughout both the biblical documents and Second Temple Jewish literature, *begotteness* is an undeniable quality of the Messiah.[1192]

[1190] This concept is often encapsulated in the word "aseity," which comes from the Latin *"a"* meaning "from" and *"se"* meaning "self." It describes a property which allows a being to exist in and of itself, or to exist as so-and-such of and from itself. (See George Sauvage, "Aseity," *Catholic Encyclopedia*, 1907.) Though the word's usage originates in the Middle Ages (Thomas Aquinas, d. 1274 CE, for example), the concept was widely circulated by Augustine (d. 430 CE) and can also be traced back to Plato (d. 347 BC).

[1191] The precise wording here indicates that "life" was a possession first of the Father—no mention is made of any other source for his life. But the "life" that was in the Son only arrived after another permitted it to enter him. Thus the Son has no life *"a-se"* or from himself. Having an absence of life before it was "granted" by another, the Son was thus not in existence until the Father said so, and was not eternal.

[1192] Again, the DSS document 1QSa envisioned a point in time *"when God begets the Messiah"* (2:11), which certainly reflects the view of the OT Psalms in which the Davidic king says: *"I will surely tell of the decree of Yahweh: He said to me, 'You are my son, today I have begotten you' "* (Ps 2:7). This

Again, *what was the Nicene theologian to do with all of this?* There was only one solution: the biblical description of Christ's generation must be changed. What else could the dogmatists do to salvage their view but obscure the very meaning of the word "begotten"? Thus they elected to introduce one of the most serious conundrums into the community of faith: the idea that the Son was *"eternally begotten."*

This incredible dogma is at once tragically self-contradictory. To argue that the Son was "eternally begotten" is really to say that he was "eternally coming into being" or that he had a "beginningless beginning." This thinking immediately sends our entire Christology into a world of unintelligible muddle. Recalling the lexical definitions of "gennao," we are being asked to believe that God *eternally became* the father of Jesus. Yet one cannot eternally *become* anything. To become something demands that there was a time when this was not so. Nevertheless, this was the bitter conclusion of the Catholic Church. The creed authorized by Constantine at Nicaea read thus:

> We believe in one Lord, Jesus Christ,
> the only son of God,
> *eternally begotten* of the Father,
> God from God, Light from Light,
> true God from true God,
> *begotten, not made,*
> of one being with the Father.[1193]

The statements "eternally begotten," and "begotten, not made" seem to consciously hijack the actual meaning of the words. So evident is the spurious redefinition of the terms involved that a polemical clarification is even employed in the wording: they want Christians to be aware that they are not using "begotten" in the usual, straightforward sense, but in some remote, metaphysical sense that is somehow different from "made." But is such a distinction even intelligible? Recalling the NASB's definition of begotten as "produced," are we really prepared to argue for a distinction between "produced" and "made"? What right do Trinitarians have to employ the biblical term "begotten," but deliberately *not* use it in the biblical sense, that is, in the sense that *"Abraham begat*

Psalm is interpreted messianically by the NT community and applied to Jesus at Heb 1:5 and Acts 2:34-36.

[1193] The original Nicene Creed, 325 CE, emphasis added.

Isaac"?[1194]   As we observed in part one, this idea is actually representative of a *Gnostic* emanationism being adapted into orthodoxy, a generation distinguished from creation or formation (being made).[1195]

Ultimately, we must say that anyone campaigning for this "beginningless beginning" is suggesting square triangles, cold heat, and bright darkness. Nevertheless, to deny this meaningless definition of Christ's origin immediately yields anathemas by the orthodox.   Catholics and Protestants must publicly confess these incongruous creedal statements or face swift rejection.   This harassment of rational integrity has been in vogue since the fourth century, when the Arians, who could not accept this point in good conscience, were treated most harshly. The Arians wrote:

> We cannot assent to these expressions, "always Father, always Son;" "at the same time Father and Son;" that "the Son always co-exists with the Father;"... But this we think and teach, that the Son is not unbegotten, nor a part of the unbegotten by any means... But we are persecuted because we say that the Son has a beginning, and that God has no beginning.[1196]

The modern Christian finds himself in the same predicament. He is being required to faithfully assent to the same abstract theories of an archaic, unfathomable philosophy.   One daring Catholic scholar asks, "Do not statements about an existence of Jesus Christ before the world, his eternal divine Sonship, require of modern men and women a complete *sacrificium intellectus*, a sacrificing of their understanding to a church doctrine which is alien to them?"[1197]   Naturally, our next question is whether or not these requirements are really posed by the New Testament, Christ himself, or only by the churches which bear his name. In hindsight, while fourth-century Christians may have been hoping to intellectualize the faith and extract it from the mystical, paradoxical liturgy of the Gnostics, they nevertheless fell headlong into the same

---

[1194] Nicaea commandeered both the New Testament's "begetting" language and its "Son of God" title. Though in the Jewish world "begotten" had once referred to both the creation of a son by a father (Matt 1:2), and to the adoption of a son (Ps 2:7), after Nicaea "Jesus was now the begotten one, and everything else was *made*—and made now meant 'created,' not 'adopted' " (Michael Peppard, *The Son of God in the Roman World: Divine Sonship in Its Social and Political Context* (Oxford: OUP, 2011), p. 5).

[1195] See pp. 121-122; Grillmeier, "Christ in Christian Tradition," p. 109; "Emanation," IEP.

[1196] Epiphanius, *Haeres.*, 69, 6.

[1197] Kuschel, p. 58.

dark cloud of incomprehensibility by binding themselves to this obtuse definition of Christ's origin.[1198] Those modern apologists wishing to maintain Nicene Christology at all costs are the ones who must deal with these pervasive issues; they are not the problems of the New Testament.

Despite the tiresome confusion propagated by fourth-century disputation over the origin of Jesus, the New Testament provides extensive clarification on the matter. Contrary to the eternally begotten divine character of Trinitarianism, the New Testament Jesus, like all human beings, is shown to have had a genuine beginning. But this beginning did not take place before the creation of the world as the Arians believed. Again, the Arians said that Christ was chronologically the first of all God's creatures, a high spiritual being employed by God in the act of creation. This Arian understanding was, like the Trinitarian view, also acquired through a misinterpretation of biblical language and thought, as well as the influence of Plato's doctrine of the literal pre-existence of the soul. In contrast, the New Testament explicitly portrays the Son of God as beginning *on the earth*, not in a heavenly timelessness, nor before the creation of the world. Rather, the Son of God's beginning occurs, according to the Gospels, *within the womb of Mary*.[1199]

Matthew begins his record of the life of Jesus with a detailed account of his ancestry. Here one immediately wonders how it is possible to precede one's own ancestors? For the Messiah to be "*a descendant of David*" (Rom 1:3), as the official record says and as he is often described by those around him (Mark 10:47), he must come *after* David (2 Sam 7:12). Absent any metaphysical musing, the Gospel of Matthew puts forth a simple model for the real origin of Christ:

> *This is how the birth of Jesus the Messiah came about: His mother Mary was pledged to be married to Joseph, but before they came together, she was found to be pregnant through the Holy Spirit* (Matthew 1:18 NIV).

[1198] See again Rudolph's observation that the early Christian fathers strove hard to find "intelligible" and "non-Gnostic" ways of affirming a spiritual, pre-existent, and divine Jesus who was also human. He writes: "Strictly speaking, they did not succeed... Even the later councils of the Church which discussed the Christological problems in complicated, and nowadays hardly intelligible, definitions did not manage to do this; the unity of the Church foundered precisely on this [problem]" (Rudolph, p. 372).

[1199] *For clarity:*

Trinitarianism: "*the Son of God is 'eternally begotten' before all time, had no beginning.*"

Arianism: "*the Son of God had a beginning, was created before the world.*"

Socinianism (Biblical Unitarianism): "*the Son of God had a beginning, was begotten in the womb of Mary.*"

Let us examine the text in detail:

Tou	de	Iesou	Christou he	genesis	houtos en	mnesteutheises	tes	metros
now		of Jesus Christ	the origin	thus came about	having been betrothed	the	mother

The word translated "birth" in the NIV is "genesis," which means "origin."[1200] Anyone even rudimentarily familiar with the Bible knows that the first book is named Genesis for its famous introduction: *"In the beginning..."* (Gen 1:1). Simply put, "genesis" means "beginning." The beginning of Jesus Christ therefore, the beginning which he supposedly does not have according to orthodoxy, is being explained here by Matthew.[1201] Further clarity on the word "genesis" is provided by its root word "ginomai," defined by *Strong's* as "to come into being." *The NAS Exhaustive Concordance* and *Thayer's Lexicon* agree that the essential meaning of the word is "to come into existence."

This information should be shocking to those who have been taught that there was never a time when the Son of God came into existence. Yet Matthew describes the event plainly for every reader: "this is how *the coming into existence* of Jesus the Messiah happened... Mary became pregnant through the Holy Spirit." There is no suggestion here that Jesus already existed, then stepped into time to take on a human nature. Rather, Christ's "beginning" (genesis) came about at a clearly specified period: during Mary's betrothal, but before she'd had relations. The *English Standard Version* displays this wonderfully:

> Now the birth [beginning, coming into existence] *of Jesus Christ took place in this way.* <u>When</u> *his mother Mary had been betrothed to Joseph,* <u>before</u> *they came together she was found to be with child from the Holy Spirit* (Matthew 1:18 ESV).

In contrast to the metaphysical and contradictory speculation of orthodoxy, the Gospels communicate that Jesus experienced his "coming into existence

---

[1200] The earliest Greek manuscripts have "genesis" (birth or origin) at Matt 1:18. Some later manuscripts have a similar word "ge<u>nn</u>esis" (birth) which may evidence an attempt by later copyists unhappy with the notion that the "origin" of Jesus was when God made Mary pregnant. Nevertheless, critics have confirmed that "genesis" is the most original reading. Metzger confirms that "genesis" also means *"creation"* (Bruce Metzger, *A Textual Commentary on the Greek New Testament* (London: United Bible Societies, 1971), p. 8).

[1201] Matthew has, in fact, already used this same word to preface his Gospel: *"This is the genealogy (genesis) of Jesus the Messiah the son of David, the son of Abraham..."* (Matt 1:1 NIV). He is explaining here, the precise origin of Christ; a necessary understanding for his readers if they are to think of Jesus as the inheritor to the rights of David as his lineal descendant.

moment" during Mary's betrothal when God caused her to be pregnant. Geographically speaking, it is claimed by Trinitarians (and Arians) that Christ was begotten in the eternal heavens. But there is absolutely no suggestion that the Son actually entered Mary's womb from the outside. On the contrary, the Gospels not only tell us *when* Christ came into existence, but also *where*:

> *But as he considered these things, behold, an angel of the Lord appeared to him in a dream, saying, "Joseph, son of David, do not fear to take Mary as your wife, for that which is <u>begotten in her</u> is from the Holy Spirit* (Matthew 1:20).

en	**aute**	**gennethen**	**ek**	**Pneumatos**	**estin**	**Hagiou**
in	her	having been begotten	from	[the] Spirit	is	Holy

The word "gennethen" here is a derivative of "gennao," which means "to beget, to bring forth, cause to arise." It is important to note that of the 96 times the Greek word "gennao" appears in the New Testament, this is the only instance in which it is deliberately translated "conceived" by the Trinitarian translators of the NASB.[1202] This should inform us that "conceived" is not the most appropriate rendering. Rather, we should stick to the literal meaning: *begotten*. Notice also the words "*in her*" connected to this word. According to Matthew, Jesus was literally begotten by God, geographically speaking, *within Mary*, not in the heavens.

A controversial portion of Psalm 110, the chief Messianic text of the New Testament, is worth noting here. In the most widespread Hebrew manuscripts, verse 3 contains the word "yaldutheka" ("your youth"), and is often translated in English as *"from the womb of the dawn, your youth are to you as the dew"* (NASB). However, many commentators believe the original Hebrew may have intended that the king himself, not the king's youth, is to be brought forth from the womb. Many of the Masoretic manuscripts actually read "yelidtika" ("I have begotten you"), and by rearranging the vowel-pointing we read: *"In sacred splendor, from the womb, from dawn, you have the dew wherewith I have begotten you."*[1203] This corresponds with the *Septuagint* reading: *"I have begotten thee from the womb before the*

[1202] Most Trinitarian translations obscure the "begotten" here; See the NASB, ESV, KJV, HCSB. In the margin of the great Revised Version of 1881 however, we find a note revealing that the Greek literally says "begotten." Other versions like the DBY and YLT likewise appropriately read "begotten in her" at Matt 1:20.

[1203] See Collins, *King and Messiah as Son of God*, pp. 16-17. See also Aubrey R. Johnson, *Sacral Kingship in Ancient Israel* (Cardiff: University of Wales Press, 1955), p. 95.

morning" (Brenton's LXX 109:3). This is the preferred reading of many experts.[1204] Thus, in the Jewish world of the New Testament, the Davidic Messiah is not only to be begotten by God, as reflected in DSS 1QSa, but is even begotten "from the womb," as reflected in the LXX.

Still more evidence for Jesus' lack of pre-existent eternality is demonstrated by the birth narrative in the Gospel of Luke:

> *And the angel answered her, "The Holy Spirit will come upon you, and the power of the Most High will overshadow you; therefore the child being begotten will be called holy—the Son of God."* (Luke 1:35).

dio	*kai*	*to*	*gennomenon*	*hagion*
therefore	also	the [one]	being begotten	Holy One

Again "gennomenon," another derivative of "gennao," means "to beget, to bring forth, cause to arise." Luke is literally calling Jesus "the one *being begotten.*" Of course, this is a temporal phrase. The Son's begetting occurs inside time, not outside.

We must take a moment to carefully consider another aspect of Luke 1:35; in this text we find one of the key witnesses against the Trinitarian notion of a Jesus who is eternally the Son of God. The angel Gabriel declares: "*The Holy Spirit will come upon you, and the power of the Most High will overshadow you; and for that reason the holy child shall be called the Son of God*" (Luke 1:35). We see that Christ is not "the Son of God" due to his eternal pre-existence as God the Son, nor due to any "eternal begetting." No, he is not here *eternally* God's Son; he is only the Son of God after a particular moment in time: his conception within Mary by way of miracle.

Even further assistance is provided to us by Luke in the fact that there is another person called "the Son of God" within this Gospel: Adam, the first man. In Luke's third chapter, a genealogy which climbs backwards through Christ's ancestors culminates in "*Seth, the son of Adam, the son of God*" (Luke 3:38). Clearly, the reason why Adam is called God's son is that he was brought about by no human agency; in other words, God was Adam's father. This is likewise why Jesus is called "*the second Adam*" by Paul in 1 Corinthians 15:45: after Adam, Jesus was the second human being directly fathered or "brought into existence" by God. The angel Gabriel thus explained that it is precisely because of the manner in which Jesus' existence came about in Mary, with no human father, that Jesus is

---

[1204] See Collins, *King and Messiah as Son of God*, p. 17.

named *"the Son of God."* James Dunn agrees here that: "In Matthew and Luke, Jesus' divine sonship is traced back specifically to his birth or conception... he was Son of God because his conception was an act of creative power by the Holy Spirit."[1205]

As mentioned earlier, the New Testament community was not the only Jewish body holding the belief that God would father the Davidic Messiah. The divine sonship of the king of Israel envisioned in Psalm 2 and 2 Samuel 7 is echoed in the Dead Sea Scrolls document 4QFlor, which portrays the Messiah as both "son of David" and "son of God." In another document known as 4Q246 we also read:

> *"Son of God he shall be called, and they will name him 'Son of the Most High'... His (or its) kingdom is an everlasting kingdom... The great God will be his strength."*[1206]

The reflection of this Jewish expectation is obvious in Luke's Gospel, as the angel says of Jesus:

> *"He will be great and will be called the Son of the Most High; and the Lord God will give him the throne of his father David, and he will reign over the house of Jacob forever, and his kingdom will have no end"*
> (Luke 1:32).

God's fatherhood of the Messiah, David's successor, is not then a particularly "Christian" concept; that is, it is not an inherently Trinitarian idea. "Son of God" does not mean "God the Son." As one Catholic professor at Yale reveals: "Both Matthew (1:20) and Luke (1:35) portray Jesus as begotten by God in the sense that he was conceived by the power of God and had no human father. In neither case, however, is this idea combined with the notions of preexistence and incarnation."[1207] More on Jesus' identification as "the Son of God" in the context of first-century Judaism will be covered in the coming chapters, but for now we may conclude that the *eternal* Sonship of Jesus is not grounded in the Gospel birth narratives.

[1205] Dunn, *Christology in the Making,* p. 61.

[1206] 4Q246 translation quoted in Collins, *King and Messiah as Son of God,* p. 67. Some scholars have speculated that this is actually a reference to a wicked figure, such as a Seleucid or Syrian king, but there seems to be little evidence for this. Regardless, the uncanny parallel with the text of Luke 1:32-33 demonstrates that the NT community saw this figure as not only positive, but as messianic.

[1207] Collins, *King and Messiah as Son of God,* p. 209.

The renowned Methodist scholar Adam Clarke, upon reviewing Luke's account, writes: "Here, I trust, I may be permitted to say, with all due respect for those who differ from me, that the doctrine of the eternal Sonship of Christ is, in my opinion, anti-scriptural and highly dangerous."[1208] Clarke perceived that the Bible had made *at least* this component of conventional Christology clearly unsalvageable:

> Son implies a father; and father implies, in reference to son, precedency in time, if not in nature too. Father and son imply the idea of generation; and generation implies a time in which it was effected, and time also antecedent to such generation...
> To say that he was begotten from all eternity, is, in my opinion, absurd; and the phrase eternal Son is a positive self-contradiction.[1209]

Ultimately, the sum of evidence leads us to agree with German theologian Wolfhart Pannenberg, that "Jesus' virgin birth stands in an irreconcilable contradiction to the Christology of the Incarnation of the preexistent Son of God."[1210] Rightly then did the Scottish Reformer John Knox admit: "We can have the humanity without the pre-existence and we can have the pre-existence without the humanity. There is absolutely no way of having both."[1211]

Though by now we fear belaboring the point, the student cannot afford to continue to be misled that the idea that Jesus was somehow the Son of God before he was fathered in Mary is the opinion of the Bible. A last, insightful commentary from Anthony Buzzard will conclude this chapter. He writes:

> I do not think that churchgoers have pondered these amazing accounts of the beginning and creation of the Son of God. Do they see the marvel that God wrought when He decided to repeat His activity in creating Adam—the second time producing His own Son, not from the dust, but within the human biological chain and in the family of David? Many have not sat down to think what a confusing contradiction is forced on Scripture when the "later" theology of an uncreated Son of God with no beginning was substituted for the historically

---

[1208] Adam Clarke, "Commentary on Luke 1:35," The Adam Clarke Commentary. Web. 07 December 2015.

[1209] Ibid.

[1210] Wolfhart Pannenberg, *Jesus: God and Man* (Westminster John Knox, 1977), p. 120, 142, 143.

[1211] John Knox, *The Humanity and Divinity of Christ* (Cambridge, CUP, 1967), p. 106.

created Son of God. It would seem that this "later" Jesus was radically different from the one presented by Gabriel, the one whom Mary recognized as her son and the Son of God. The "later" Jesus was Son of God in eternity, consciously active in Old Testament times and then decided one day to reduce himself to a fetus and pass into the world through Mary[1212] instead of originating in and from Mary by divine creation.[1213]

If Christ's origin was really in Mary, then what is the truly biblical model of pre-existence? How might we understand the several sayings of Jesus in the Gospel of John which seem to suggest an existence of the Messiah before the foundation of the world? We will find our answers in the next chapter.

[1212] As we observed in part one, the Valentinian Gnostics attested: "This Christ passed through Mary just as water flows through a tube" (Irenaeus, *Against Heresies*, 1, 7, 2).

[1213] Anthony F. Buzzard, "Imagine Meeting a Man Whose Father is God," *Focus on the Kingdom,* Vol. 5, No. 10 (McDonough: Restoration Fellowship, 2003).

11

BIBLICAL PRE-EXISTENCE AND THE CHRISTOLOGY OF CHRIST

---

*"Before I formed you in the womb I knew you, before
you were born I set you apart; I appointed you as a
prophet to the nations... everywhere I send you, you
shall go, and all that I command you, you shall speak."*
— Jeremiah 1:5, 7

*"[I am] one whom the Father set apart as his very own
and sent into the world...," "For the one whom God has
sent speaks the words of God..."*
— John 10:36, 3:34

THE STATE-CODIFIED JESUS OF NICENE CHRISTOLOGY immediately threatened to engulf both the person and the religion of the man of history. Jesus' worldview, his philosophy, his personal concept of the divine—all were summarily dissolved into the dogma of the Church. The historical language of the Jews was likewise progressively subjugated to the philosophical models of the Hellenizing doctors. These philosophers, scrambling the distinction and subordination which so characterized the original faith, pressed the Messiah into the mold of the eternally pre-existent God of Heaven. Yet we find that in the oldest realms of traditional Hebraic thought, Messianic pre-existence operated in a form radically different from the persuasion of later Christianity.

For the Hebrew, scriptural suggestions of the Messiah's existence in heaven were relegated to the divine intentions of the Almighty and his design for history; hardly intended was the popular portrait of a ontologically realized divine being, much less a second Person within God. Yet within the rapidly amalgamating Christianity of the late Roman Empire, the concepts and phraseology of classical Judaism assumed new and elevated interpretations via the dominant philosophy of the age. That later Christianity deliberately worked to distance itself from "the old religion" is certain.[1214] What is also clear is that the Messiah of Judaism underwent a swift and dizzying transformation in the early centuries of Gentile control. Martin Werner, Professor of Theology at the University of Bern, located the precise agitation:

> The cause of the Trinitarian-Christological problem, which so perplexed post-Apostolic Christianity, lay in the transition from the apocalyptic Messiah-Son of Man concept of the primitive Christian eschatological faith, with its sense of imminence, to the new dogma of the divinity of Jesus. [1215]

The Platonic model of the pre-existence and transmigration of the soul, already accepted by the Gentile converts of the first century, was deftly adapted here, and, as Werner explains, a dramatic and unqualified *switch* transpired, a replacement of:

> the original concept of the Messiah for a Hellenistic analogy such as that of a redeeming divine being. The analogy... was wholly invalid. It was a myth, behind which the historical Jesus completely disappeared, because there was nothing in common between them.[1216]

While in most churches the theological opinions of the historical Jesus have largely and tragically fallen into obscurity, one scholar nevertheless recognizes that today "the question about the Jesus of history is increasingly regaining its theological importance."[1217] Our present Christological disputes will be greatly served if they are couched in questions about history. If Christ indeed claimed

---

[1214] Rubenstein, p.74

[1215] Werner, p. 298.

[1216] Ibid.

[1217] Ernst Kasemann, "The Problem of the Historical Jesus," *Essays on New Testament Themes* (London, 1964), pp. 15-47:17.

to be pre-existent, we cannot hope to understand his claim before we understand the contrasting models of pre-existence found in his own time.

Judaism vs. Mystical Hellenistic Judaism

As mentioned in part one of this book, Palestine had already, as a whole, undergone a cultural Hellenization by the first century CE.[1218] But it is obvious that this protracted shift had not completely engulfed the religious mind of most Jews in that era, a majority which produced the Jewish Apostles of the New Testament. Paul, a self-confessed specimen of Pharisaic Judaism who studied under the leading Pharisee Gamaliel, could quote Greek poets, even contextualize his gospel in Greek categories, and still distinguish and oppose the world's "philosophy" (1 Cor 1:18-31; Col 2:8; Acts 17:18). We know that the Pharisees to whom Paul belonged were the largest and most widely respected of the three major Jewish sects.[1219] Their bitter rivals, the Sadducees, were an elitist, overtly Hellenized minority who controlled the Temple in Jerusalem. It was the Sadducees' openness to Hellenization, their cooperation with the Romans, and their haughtiness towards the common Jew that caused them to be severely disliked by the populace. The third major sect of that era, the Essenes, considered the Temple and those who controlled it to be so hopelessly corrupt that they retreated to desert monastic communities to await God's final judgment on the apostates. Sufficient to say, there were still Jews distinguished by the mainstream of Palestinian Judaism as having compromised with the outside world to an irreparable degree.[1220] This continuous struggle over cultural

---

[1218] For a detailed investigation into the Hellenization of Judea, see Martin Hengel's detailed analysis, *Judaism and Hellenism: Studies in their Encounter in Palestine During the Early Hellenistic Period* (Eugene: Wipf & Stock, 2003 [1974]). Many scholars have concluded that Jewish society was influenced by both the Hellenistic empire and its Hellenizing Roman successor "to some extent" (Anthony J. Saldarini, *Pharisees, Scribes and Sadducees in Palestinian Society* (Grand Rapids: Eerdmans, 2001 [1988]), p. 302), and that "by the first century Hellenism itself had been Hebraized and Judaism itself Hellenized" (W. D. Davies, *Christian Engagements with Judaism* (Harrisburg: Trinity Press International, 1999), p. 10). There nevertheless remained an observable distinction among the Jews, particularly regarding religious syncretism.

[1219] "Pharisees were generally farmers and artisans drawn from the middle and lower class... thus, they tended to be less Hellenized... In contrast... Sadducees were generally upper-class, Hellenized Jerusalemites. They rejected the oral tradition of the Pharisees. Instead, they interpreted the Torah in their own way" (Howard N. Lupovitch, *Jews and Judaism in World History* (London: Routledge, 2010), p. 32).

[1220] "Throughout all their history the Jews of the dispersion had shown themselves more friendly toward new ideas... The Jews of Palestine, on the other hand, were, as a rule, self-satisfied and inclined to look down upon other members of their race, whom they regarded as contaminated by contact with the heathen and by long residence in foreign lands. They also viewed askance their more tolerant attitude toward Greek culture and life and the customs of the

and religious syncretism also characterized the first Christian community, and that rift is still easily detectable within the New Testament.[1221] Peter and James were certainly not part of a syncretistic fringe, but were traditionalists who appealed to the old prophets over the paganized elite and maintained their Jewish background in spite of the encroaching Greek philosophy and life. Paul, though born into the Hellenized world, likewise did not "deviate from the genuine Jewish creed" and maintained a view of the Messiah which scholars have described as "*Jewish Messianism* such as it was determined by the apocalyptic Book of Daniel."[1222] On the other hand, Paul's contemporary Philo, the greatest of the Hellenizing Jews, had his syncretistic blend of Platonism and Judaism (characterized by literal pre-existence, the transmigration of the soul, etc.) rejected by mainstream Judaism.[1223] This is all to say that in the first century CE there was indeed a segment of Hellenizing Jews who had appropriated Greek notions of literal pre-existence and applied them to biblical stories, and there is no doubt that this was not the common Judaism of first-century Judea. Rather, it was viewed as explicitly Hellenistic, the habit of the elites, highly speculative, and in some cases worthy of outright rejection.

---

outside world. It was probably this inherited and inbred attitude that led the Palestinian Jewish Christians to neglect the needy members of the Hellenistic group" (Charles Foster Kent, *The Work and Teachings of the Apostles* (New York: Scribner's, 1916), pp. 50-51). In the book of Acts we find that the Hellenistic Jews were indeed being neglected by the Palestinian Jews regarding the serving of food, and seven elders were appointed to make sure the food was being properly distributed: "The Greek names of the seven, as well as the narrative, indicate that they were probably all Hellenistic Jews by birth... they appear to be a committee appointed to represent the Hellenistic group in the Christian community in very much the same way as the apostles represented the Palestinian group... Their appointment is a convincing proof that the rift between the Palestinian and the Hellenistic Jews, even within the Christian community, was practically inevitable, and that it was recognized long before Paul entered upon his campaign to liberate Gentile Christians from Jewish bonds" (Ibid., p. 51).

[1221] Acts 6:1ff describes both "Hellenistai" and "Hebrews." Elsewhere, when the writer wishes to identify Gentiles, he uses the term "Hellenes," but in Acts 6 we encounter a dispute between the "Hellenistai" and the "Hebrews," both of which, according to the context, are groups of Jews living in Jerusalem. For notice of Stephen's dispute with Hellenized Jews, see Paton James Gloag, *A Critical and Exegetical Commentary on the Acts of the Apostles*, Vol. 1 (Edinburgh: T & T Clark, 1870), p. 214. For notice of Paul's dispute with them, see G. Campbell Morgan, *The Acts of the Apostles* (Eugene: Wipf & Stock, 2011 [1934]), pp. 242-243.

[1222] Daniel R. Langton citing Leo Baeck, *The Apostle Paul in the Jewish Imagination* (Cambridge: CUP, 2010), p. 85, emphasis added. Baeck continues: "Paul's approach to the Hellenistic world was the same as that of some Palestinian teachers. Tarsus, in which Paul had grown up was a place of 'Hellenism, with all its philosophies, beliefs, annunciations, and cults' and yet 'Paul was a Jew of Tarsus, not a Syrian or Persian or Egyptian of Tarsus... His background was that of the Jewish people' " (Ibid).

[1223] For more on the Jewish rejection of Philo's syncretistic Judaism, see C. H. Toy, C. Siegfried, J. Z. Lauterbach, "Philo Judaeus," *Jewish Encyclopedia*, 1906.

Scholars have thus identified the emergence of a "Hellenistic Jewish mystery religion" during the first to the third centuries CE.[1224] The mythological work known as *The Prayer of Joseph*, which famously features a pre-existent angel incarnating as the patriarch Jacob, provides a "prime example" of this acutely Hellenistic development within Judaism.[1225] Though debate still surrounds the precise origin of this text, scholar J. Z. Smith confirmed the myth as a first or second-century CE product of this "mystical Hellenistic Judaism."[1226] Philo's notion of the angelic Logos certainly provides a striking parallel to the angel in *Prayer of Joseph*. However, dating *Prayer* is difficult, making it impossible to determine with certainty whether Philo or *Prayer* relied upon one another. It is more likely that the two "result from mutual dependence upon common traditions."[1227] That common tradition was an acutely Platonized Judaism. Professor Broek confirms that "before the arrival of Christianity at Alexandria, Jewish and Platonic speculations already had merged into a special brand of Judaism that was able to satisfy the religious and intellectual needs of widely Hellenized Jews and was also attractive to interested pagans."[1228] Thus, as John J. Collins explains, "The conceptions of *the Prayer of Joseph* are remarkable but have enough in common with those of Philo and other documents from the turn of the era to support Smith's thesis that the work is indeed a product of Hellenistic Judaism."[1229] As scholars have confirmed, these interpretations of the Bible "were undreamt of by the average Jew."[1230]

In regard to pre-existence, the prevailing Judaism of the first-century maintained that the scriptural portrait of the Messiah described not an ontological pre-birth reality, but a foreknowledge of the Messiah in God's mind.

[1224] See J. Z. Smith, "The Prayer of Joseph," *Religions in Antiquity: Essays in Memory of E. R. Goodenough* (Leiden, 1968), pp. 253-294.

[1225] Michael Tuval, *From Jerusalem Priest to Roman Jew* (Tubingen: Mohr Siebeck, 2013), pp. 45-46. The intent of the myth was probably to inspire Jews of the Diaspora to realize their own identity within that milieu; they each share in the heavenly glory of an angelic ancestor. J. Z. Smith explains that "the myth may be ritually appropriated by its believers, that the 'objective' narrative has a 'subjective' correlative. That which is accomplished by the paradigmatic figure of the Patriarch Jacob-Israel may, presumably, also be achieved by the 'sons of Jacob' " (Smith, "The Prayer of Joseph," p. 288).

[1226] James Charlesworth citing J. Z. Smith, *Pseudepigrapha and Modern Research* (Scholar's Press, 1981 [1657]), pp. 141-142.

[1227] See Darrell D. Hannah, *Michael and Christ: Michael Traditions and Angel Christology* (Tubingen: Mohr Siebeck, 1999), pp. 89-90.

[1228] Broek, p. 117.

[1229] John J. Collins, *Between Athens and Jerusalem: Jewish Identity in the Hellenistic Diaspora* (Grand Rapids: Eerdmans, 2000), p. 240.

[1230] M. Smith, "Goodenough's Jewish Symbols in Retrospect," *Journal of Biblical Literature*, 86 (1967), 61, as cited in Tuval, p. 72.

This model of Jewish pre-existence was antecedent to the literal, Platonic system of the Hellenizers. As Harnack reveals, this "old Jewish model of pre-existence... [is] the earliest view."[1231]

The Alternative:
Classic Jewish Pre-existence in God's Plan

In the Jewish system, all things were considered truly "with" God from eternity, but only in the sense that they existed within his eternal purpose. The life of these expected things, we might say, was conceptual, ideal, and temporarily unrealized. As noted previously:

> When the Jew said something was "predestined," he thought of it as already "existing" in a higher sphere of life. The world's history is thus predestined because it is already, *in a sense,* preexisting and consequently fixed. This typically Jewish conception of predestination *may be distinguished from the Greek idea* of preexistence by the predominance of the thought of *"preexistence" in the Divine purpose.*[1232]

For the Jewish mind, it was God's inexorable power to shape history which solidified his every thought and intention, making the persons and events which composed his grand design virtually tangible. This celebration of the inevitability of God's intentions consequently bolstered the apocalyptic hopes of the Jewish people. Their punishments, their sufferings, their consecutive mistreatments at the hands of the nations—all were made bearable by a palpable Messianic future in the presence of God. Anglican theologian and scholar Gordon Selwyn rightly identified the linguistic custom of the Hebrews in relation to God's predetermination: "When the Jew wished to designate something as predestined, *he spoke of it as already 'existing' in heaven.*"[1233] Likewise Protestant scholar Emil Schurer recognizes that "In Jewish thinking, everything truly valuable preexisted in heaven."[1234] While the Jew might identify all things as first being with God, he especially asserted that persons and things integral to God's great plan of redemption were "stored up" in the heavenly realm, awaiting realization on earth

---

[1231] Harnack, *History of Dogma*, Vol. 1, p. 47.

[1232] E. C. Dewick, *Primitive Christian Eschatology, The Hulsean Prize Essay for 1908* (Cambridge: CUP, 1912), pp. 253-254, emphasis added.

[1233] E. G. Selwyn, *First Epistle Of St. Peter* (Grand Rapids: Baker, 1983), p. 124, emphasis added.

[1234] Emil Schurer, *The History of the Jewish People in the Age of Jesus Christ*, Vol. 2 (Edinburgh: T & T Clark, 1979), p. 522.

at their proper times. Even Tertullian in the third century wrote that all things "had been planned and disposed, yea, and already made, so far forth as (they were) in the mind and intelligence of God."[1235]

Certainly the Messiah, the ultimate servant of God who would finally manifest the patriarchal promises, was thought to be *with* God from the beginning. Yet his presence with God did not differ from the kind enjoyed by Moses or John the Baptist or any of the great figures of God's history. As one scholar writes: "Judaism has never known anything of a pre-existence peculiar to the Messiah antecedent to his birth as a human being."[1236] Charles Gore, one of the most influential theologians of the 19th century, challenges the assumption of Christendom that the incarnation of a pre-existent Messiah finds any compatibility with the historical religion of Jesus: "The dominance of the idea in any Jewish circle whatever cannot seriously be upheld. Judaism knew nothing of the [literally] pre-existent ideal man."[1237] A Catholic professor also observes that "in the synagogue a particular kind of pre-existence was always associated with the Messiah, but it did not set him apart from other men. This is pre-existence in God's thought, the *ideal* pre-existence of the Messiah."[1238]

A wealth of scholarship has correctly recognized that the concept of pre-existence employed by Jesus and the New Testament writers reflects not the literal model of Plato and the Alexandrian philosophers, but the older Hebraic tradition which was the accepted view in the prevailing Second Temple Judaism of Christ's day.[1239] As one specialist in the field confirms, "*a virtual consensus* exists today among scholars that the most fundamental background for the idea of preexistence in the New Testament is the Jewish tradition (rather than the Platonic)."[1240] To its great detriment, most of Christendom is quite unaware of this information. It is education that is in order here, a restitution of the proper meanings of the phrases and thought-forms of the first-century Church. Reverend Maurice Wiles, Professor of Divinity at Oxford, comments:

> Within the Christian tradition, the New Testament has long been read through the prism of the later conciliar creeds... Speaking of

---

[1235] Tertullian, *Against Praxeas*, 6.

[1236] G. Dalman, *Words of Jesus* (Edinburgh: T & T Clark, 1902), pp. 128-32, 248, 252.

[1237] Charles Gore, *Belief in Christ* (New York: Charles Scribner's Sons, 1922), p. 31.

[1238] Kuschel, p. 218, emphasis added.

[1239] See Willibald Beyschlag (1823-1900), *Life of Jesus*. H. H. Wendt, *The Teaching of Jesus* (1892). George H. Gilbert, "An Important Unnoticed Argument in John Chapter Seventeen" (1899). Gustaf Dalman *Words of Jesus* (1930). E. G. Selwyn, *First Epistle of Peter* (1983). Maurice Wiles, *The Remaking of Christian Doctrine* (1973). E. C. Dewick, *Primitive Christian Eschatology* (1908).

[1240] Smith, *The Son of God: Three Views*, p. 40, emphasis added.

Jesus as the Son of God had *a very different connotation* in the first century from that which it has had ever since the Council of Nicaea (325 CE). Talk of his pre-existence ought probably in most, perhaps in all, cases to be understood on the analogy of the pre-existence of the Torah, to indicate the *eternal divine purpose* being achieved through him, *rather than pre-existence of a fully personal kind.*[1241]

Jewish texts from a variety of eras provide observable examples of this model in Second Temple Jewish thought. The *Genesis Rabba*, a homiletical commentary from Judaism's classical period, states that:

> *Six things preceded the creation of the world; some of them were actually created, while the creation of the others was already contemplated. The Torah and the throne of glory were created... The creation of the Patriarchs was contemplated...* [The creation of] *Israel was contemplated...* [The creation of] *the temple was contemplated... The name of Messiah was contemplated.* (Genesis Rabba 1.4)

Here we see that it was the *name* of the Messiah which was conceived of in the mind of God. This is a very different thing from the literal pre-existence of a divine person. As A. E. Harvey observes, the Jews thought that the Messiah's name, among other important things, "was there at the beginning. But no one thought of the Messiah as 'divine.' "[1242] The Talmud reiterates:

> *Seven things were created before the world was made, and these are they: Torah, repentance, the Garden of Eden, Gehenna, the throne of glory, and house of the sanctuary, and the name of the Messiah.*
> (Babylonian Talmud, Peshaim 54a)

The Parables section of the famous *Book of Enoch*, often dated during or just prior to the first century,[1243] likewise explains that the Messiah was:

[1241] Maurice Wiles, *The Remaking of Christian Doctrine, The Hulsean Lectures* (London: SCM Press, 1974), emphasis added.

[1242] A. E. Harvey, *Jesus and the Constraints of History* (London: Duckworth, 1980), p. 178.

[1243] See Gabriele Boccacini, *Enoch and the Messiah Son of Man: Revisiting the Book of Parables* (Grand Rapids: Eerdmans, 2007). See also R. H. Charles. *The Book of Enoch, or, 1 Enoch* (Oxford at Clarendon Press, 1912).

> *named in the presence of the Lord of Spirits, even before the creation of the*
> *sun and the moon, before the creation of the stars... he was chosen by God*
> *and hidden with God before the world was created.*
> (I Enoch 48:3, 6)

Rather than revealing the existence of a physically pre-existent being, this selection of the chosen one was seen by the Jews simply as his primordial calling to service.[1244] While in the above quotation Enoch attests that the Messiah was "named" or elected within the sphere of God's knowledge, nothing is said of his active existence as a conscious and spiritual being, much less as God himself. What pre-existed was only the commission of the Son of Man.

Sigmund Mowinckel, one of the world's premiere authorities on the Psalms, expands on the pervasiveness of this Jewish view in his sweeping work *He That Cometh: The Messiah Concept in the Old Testament and Later Judaism:*

> Attribution of preexistence indicates religious importance of
> the highest order. Rabbinic theology speaks of the Law, of
> God's throne of glory, of Israel... as things which were already
> present with [God] before the creation of the world. The same
> is also true of the Messiah... in *Pesikta Rabbati* 152b it is said
> that *"from the beginning of the creation of the world the King Messiah*
> *was born, for he came up in the thought of God before the world was*
> *created."* This means that from all eternity it was the will of
> God that the Messiah should come into existence, and should
> do his work in the world to fulfill God's eternal saving
> purpose.[1245]

As Mowinckel emphasizes, "coming up in the thought of God" is practically synonymous to actual life to the Jew, though we see that the Messiah's true existence was still a thing yet future. We must emphasize here that it is not some segment of mystical Judaism which operated through this model of pre-existence, but the whole of the national faith. The Hebrew Bible, in perfect congruence with this thought, demonstrates the principle that all things (such as the Messiah) are *named* (or foreknown) by God before they actually come into existence:

[1244] Gottfried Schimanowski, *Wisdom and Messiah* (Tubingen: Mohr Siebeck: 1985), p. 170.
[1245] Sigmund Mowinckel, *He That Cometh* (Grand Rapids: Eerdmans, 2005 [1956]), p. 334.

> *Whatever exists has already been named.*
> (Ecclesiastes 6:10 NASB)
> *Whatever comes to be has already been named.*
> (ESV)

The inexorable Jewish God's foreknowledge permitted the yet unrealized world to be described in concrete terms. The Jewish world of Christ was certainly historically accustomed to this attitude. Their Scriptures had spoken of future persons, as well as their future accomplishments, as having long been completed before their actual arrival. God said:

> *Have you not heard? Long ago I did it. From ancient times I planned it.*
> *Now I have brought it to pass, that you should turn fortified cities into*
> *heaps of ruin* (2 Kings 19:25).

While it was truly only planned by God in ancient times, it was, for all intents and purposes, as good as done. *"Long ago I did it,"* claims God, while in reality it has only *"now"* been brought to pass.[1246]

Perhaps the best example of this idea is God's prophetic address to the future King Cyrus in the book of Isaiah. At the time of Isaiah's writing, Cyrus' birth was still 150 years in the future, yet God speaks to him as if he already exists, using the past tense:

> *Thus says the LORD to Cyrus his anointed* [his messiah], *whom I*
> *have taken by the right hand, to subdue nations before him… I have also*
> *called you by your name; I have given you a title of honor though you have*
> *not known me* (Isaiah 45:1a, 4).

The New Testament demonstrates the perpetuation of this concept into Apostolic Christianity. Revelation 4:11 says, *"Worthy are you, our Lord and our God… for you created all things, and because of your will they existed, and were created."* Here we again encounter the Jewish two-stage creation model: all things first came to exist in God's heavenly will, *"and* [then] *were created."* Even in early Gentile Christian thought this idea remained prevalent. The mid-second century patriarch of Antioch, Theophilus (d. 183 CE), writes that God "willed to make man to whom he might be made known; for him, therefore, he prepared the

---

[1246] This figure of speech is known as "prolepsis," a term of Greek origin (from "prolambanein," meaning "to take beforehand"), and a word which *Merriam-Webster's* defines as: "the representation or assumption of a future act or development as if presently existing or accomplished."

world in advance."[1247] Because God had first prepared the world in heaven, it could be said that he had already created it; both God and the Jews could speak of his future activity as already accomplished. The Apostle Paul similarly expounds on the surety of God's prophecy concerning Abraham:

> As it is written, "I have made you a father of many nations." This is in the presence of him whom he believed: God, who gives life to the dead, and calls the things that are not, as though they were.
> (Romans 4:17 WEB)

While Abraham and his wife were yet barren, God had already designated him the father of many in his pre-existing plan. Biblically speaking, God, and those who put their faith in his promises for the future, have always been permitted to speak not only with confidence concerning the things to come, but as if God's vision for the future had already arrived. We will find this method useful for understanding the New Testament portrayal of Jesus as the long-foretold Messiah.

Jewish Pre-Existence and the New Testament Christ

Within the world of Judaism it was often said that God had prepared all persons, their works, and their rewards "from the foundation of the world." An example of this locution is encountered in the Jewish text *The Assumption of Moses*, dated to the early first century and so contemporary with the teachings and customs of Jesus and his Apostles. Here Moses says:

> "But He did design and devise me, and He prepared me from the beginning of the world to be mediator of His covenant."
> (Assumption of Moses 1:14)

Of course we would be hard-pressed to locate arguments for Moses' own literal pre-existence because of this language. Yet we find this langauge in the New Testament describing the person of Jesus:

> "... the Lamb who was slain from the creation of the world."
> (Revelation 13:8 NIV)

The consequences should be obvious here. Of course Jesus was not literally slain before the world began, but he *was* slain in God's eternal plan and foreknowledge. The Apostle Peter explains as much:

[1247] Theophilus, *Apology to Autolycus,* 2, 10.

"This man, delivered over by the predetermined plan and foreknowledge of God, you nailed to a cross by the hands of godless men and put him to death" (Acts 2:23).

Paul agrees that it was God's *purpose* regarding Christ that pre-existed eternally: *"This was in accordance with the eternal purpose which he carried out in Christ Jesus our Lord"* (Eph 3:11). In this light, even the most contested "pre-existence sayings" of Christ begin to shed their difficulty. For example, John 17:5 is often employed by those wishing to demonstrate Jesus' literal pre-existence:

"And now, Father, glorify me in your presence with the glory I had with you before the world began" (John 17:5).

The exaltation of the Christ into God's presence, to his right hand, was explicitly foretold from ancient times (Ps 110:1; Is 52:13). This reward was *stored up* with God and awaited only the fulfillment of his vision. Here in John 17, after consigning himself to death and to the fulfillment of God's vision, Jesus prays for his predetermined and rightly-expected glorification upon the completion of his mission. As the ruin of the cities was "as good as done" in 2 Kings 19:25, so was Christ's reception of his reward. Yet just as Jesus was not literally *"slain from the foundation of the world"* (Rev 13:8), neither had he literally already enjoyed glory in God's presence. A professor at Chicago Theological Seminary observes that in John 17:5:

> This glory seems to be regarded as a reward for the work which Jesus has now accomplished… This order of thought suggests that he looked at the *anticipated* glory as his proper reward… The inference from this in regard to the pre-existence of the Messiah is obvious. Rewards are bestowed after the work is done, and only then can be appreciated as rewards. Jesus possessed this glory before the foundation of the world in the sense that it was divinely purposed for him. He knew that the glorious outcome of his Messianic work had been fixed, and that the reward was kept in store for him. Thus in the very shadow of the cross, when to human view the work of Jesus seemed to be a complete and shameful failure, he calmly and confidently asks for the glory which he had with the Father before the world was. This is surely the utterance

of one who was conscious of being the Messiah sent from God, but the pre-existence which is involved is ideal.[1248]

We remember that King Cyrus was given glory by God 150 years before he was born. God had told him, "I *have given* you a title of honor" (Is 41:1-4). When Cyrus finally became king, he received the glory God had stored up for him. In the same way, Jesus was given glory by God before he was born, and at his exaltation he received the title of honor God had prepared (Acts 2:36).

Concerning the particular kind of glory awarded to Christ, which modern dogmatists assert must be the exclusive glory of deity, Jesus elucidates several verses later:

> "*The glory which you have given me I have given to them, that they may be one, just as we are one*" (John 17:22 NASB).

If the glory enjoyed by Christ was indeed glory as God, then he has evidently given the same glory of deity to his disciples. Surely this is not the case. We know that the particular kind of glory which Jesus bears is the glory of *sonship*, not glory as God. The opening chapter of John's Gospel explains: "*and we saw his glory, glory as of the only begotten from the Father*" (Jn 1:14b NASB), "*glory as of the only Son from the Father*" (ESV). The glory of Sonship is clearly appreciated by the man Jesus, and it is perfectly acceptable that such a thing would be distributed amongst his followers: "*But as many as received him, to them he gave the power to become the sons of God*" (Jn 1:12).

Of course, the unique glory of God is not shared with any, but is reserved by Yahweh for himself: "*My glory I will not give to another*" (Is 48:11). Yet we see that God *does* in fact distribute some degree of glory to others: "*Yahweh gives grace and glory; he does not withhold the good from those who live with integrity*" (Ps 84:11b). It is evidently a different glory, not his own glory as God, which he dispenses amongst his children. The New Testament vigorously attests that the glory offered by God to those who please him is, in fact, the same glory had by Jesus Christ: "*We are the children of God: and if children, then heirs: heirs of God, and joint-heirs with Christ; if so be that we suffer with him, that we may also be glorified together*" (Rom 8:16-17). We furthermore read that the endgame of God's glorification of Jesus was to subsequently facilitate his "*bringing many sons to glory*" (Heb 2:10). Paul agrees that God's entire program concerning Christ was a plan "*destined for our*

[1248] George H. Gilbert, "An Important Unnoticed Argument in John Chapter 17," *The Biblical World*, Vol. 13, No. 5 (Chicago: University of Chicago Press, 1899), p. 308, 311, emphasis added.

glory before the world began" (1 Cor 2:7). Paul additionally reveals that our future glorious bodies (the same reward which the resurrected Jesus received) have also been stored up with God in heaven: "*For we know that if the earthly tent which is our house* [body] *is torn down, we have a building from God, a house not made with hands, eternal in the heavens*" (2 Cor 5:1). Note that "*we have*" this reward presently with God in heaven, though it has not yet been made manifest, just as in John 17:5 Christ claimed that his reward had already been in his possession before creation. Evidently, every disciple of Jesus might utter prayers to the same effect as Christ's in John 17, as all Christians likewise "had glory with God before the world was." Indeed, Paul further affirms that every disciple of Jesus was already *given* grace "*before the beginning of time*" (2 Tim 1:9). Of course, this indicates only that these persons were known by God beforehand.

Biblically speaking, all of God's holy agents were *foreknown* by him in advance of their true existence: "*Before I formed you in the womb I knew you, and before you were born I consecrated you; I have appointed you a prophet to the nations*" (Jer 1:5). The New Testament ultimately explains that God's people have not only been foreknown, but also pre-destined for the glory of sonship with Jesus: "*For those whom he foreknew, he also predestined to become conformed to the image of his son, so that he would be the firstborn among many brethren*" (Rom 8:29). However, we do not believe that any of this language demonstrates the true existence of every Christian with God before creation. There is no question that the writers of the New Testament mean that believers have merely been present in God's mind. This is, of course, the same language used to describe Christ: "*For he was foreknown before the foundation of the world*" (1 Peter 1:20).

If the Apostolic writers hold that they themselves were known by God and had rewards with him before the world began, and Christian posterity neither hypothesizes nor demands a belief in their literal pre-existence, why do the same locutions necessitate such for the man Jesus? One Anglican theologian recognizes that:

> We are not entitled to say that Peter was familiar with the idea of Christ's pre-existence with the Father before the incarnation. For this idea is not necessarily implied in his description of Christ as "foreknown before the foundation of the world," since Christians are also the objects of God's foreknowledge. All that we can say is that the phrase *pro kataboles kosmou* (before the foundation of the world) affirms

for Christ's office and work a supramundane range and importance.[1249]

We observe in this inconsistency of interpretation the dramatic sway of dogma as it selectively isolates and redefines linguistic models to suit its purposes, namely the unrestricted defense of the doctrine of the deity of Jesus. Passages concerning the Christ are suddenly excused from the normal, historical modes of interpretation as a means to an end; the rules simply do not apply in the realm of orthodox Christology when dogma is at stake. Nevertheless, the modern Bible student must insist on exegetical consistency in this regard. One unitarian lecturer put it this way:

> Orthodox commentators are aware that the idiom of the New Testament frequently uses the tense grammatically past, to signify events which are actually future. I ask those critics what they usually urge against Roman Catholic controversialists, who, in proving the doctrine of Transubstantiation, quote the text, "This is my body *which is broken* for you"? What says the Protestant opponent? "Oh, it is a mere idiomatic expression, by which an event is represented as complete, which is yet to be accomplished." In a like manner, and with a like interpretation, we hear the Orthodox use the phrase, *"The lamb slain from the foundation of the world."* They have in this case no scruple to speak of that as actually existing, which was merely contemplated in eternal foreknowledge. If it be said that all events are present to the mind of God, so, we answer, are all persons, and so was Christ. This view of the subject has satisfied many reflective, and, whatever our opponents may think, many able and honest minds.[1250]

What John 17:5 therefore contains is not a celebration of Christ's reclamation of a previously divested, pre-creation majesty as God—indeed he does not say "give me *back*," but "give me *now*"—rather it is a faith-filled affirmation of the promised exaltation which had awaited the fulfillment of his suffering. Evidently, knowledge of the Messiah's linear progression from

---

[1249] E. G. Selwyn, *First Epistle of St. Peter* (Grand Rapids: Baker Book House, 1983), p. 248, 250.

[1250] Henry Giles, *There is One God, and One Mediator between God and Men, the Man Christ Jesus: a Lecture, delivered in Paradise-Street Chapel, Liverpool, March 5, 1839* (Liverpool: Willmer & Smith, 1839), p. 16, emphasis added.

inglorious suffering to glory (*not* glory, to suffering, and back to glory again) was to be duly grasped by Jesus' students. Christ himself, lecturing his bereaved and disappointed disciples on the road to Emmaus, pointedly reminded them: *"Did not the Messiah have to suffer these things and <u>then</u> enter his glory?"* (Luke 24:26 NIV). Accordingly, this was also the proper expectation of those who likewise suffered and received him.

Coming "From Heaven"

There are several Gospel sayings concerning "heaven" which are commonly encountered in arguments for literal pre-existence. We will presently discover that these sayings of Christ are, in fact, Hebrew idioms which have not been fairly considered in their native context.

The preponderance of evidence draws us to conclude that when Jesus says, *"I have come down from heaven, not to do my own will, but the will of him who sent me"* (Jn 6:38), he does not mean that he has literally traveled from the heavenly realm. Rather, he intends only to comment on the heavenly origin of his mission, on his personal charge from the very throne room of God.

At this explanation, we might expect the accusation that we have abandoned straightforward interpretations of the Bible and have unduly consigned the text to abstraction. To this we would respond with a question about rigidly literal interpretations of any historical dialogue. Imagine if some future anthropologist unearthed this book many ages from now, and upon reading that "today it rained cats and dogs," began to demand absolutely literal interpretations from his colleagues with no respect for culture and idiom. In this light, should we not think twice about passages such as: *"I am the bread that came down from heaven"* (Jn 6:41)? One classic publication illuminates the issues surrounding overly literal analyses of these sayings:

> Now, on such verses as these, let us just put a question to the Trinitarian… Is the language of Jesus to be construed literally or figuratively? We do not insist on his adopting the alternative we adopt—let him take his choice. If it be said, 'Christ is to be understood literally, as speaking of an actual personal descent from heaven,' then let us apply this mode of interpretation to the other parts of the passage and surrounding context. If Christ came down personally from heaven as the true bread, then he tells us, this very *"bread that he will give is his flesh"* [Jn 6:51]; *"my flesh is meat indeed, and my blood is*

drink indeed" [Jn 6:55]; and that it is necessary to eat the one, and drink the other, in order to secure the possession of eternal life, verse 58. *"This,"* he concludes, *"is that bread which came down from heaven; not as your fathers did eat manna, and are dead. He that eateth of this bread* (Christ's flesh and blood) *shall live forever."* Now if we interpret Christ's statements here literally, it is thus proved, not only that he came down from heaven, as Trinitarians believe, but that he came down in real flesh and blood, in human nature, not in a Divine nature, for that is not stated. Now will [Trinitarians] pursue the literal interpretation of Christ's language to this, its legitimate conclusion?[1251]

Recalling that "when the Jew wished to designate something as predestined, he spoke of it as already 'existing' in heaven,"[1252] the meaning of the "came from heaven" idiom found in John 6:41-42 and elsewhere becomes clear. Christ means not to explain that he has literally traveled through the dimensions to earth, nor that the Almighty God has performed an "incarnation" of himself to become one of his creations. Christ recognizes that a thing which has been stored up with God, which has its foundation in God, has now been made manifest. Helpful passages for assisting our interpretation of the idiom come from the Epistle of James:

> *Every good and perfect gift is from above, coming down from the Father of lights, with whom there is no variation or shifting shadow.*
> (James 1:17)

> *This wisdom is not that which comes down from above, but is earthly, natural, demonic... But the wisdom from above is first pure...*
> (James 3:15, 17a)

Of course, in James 1:17 we are not meant to believe that every good gift (like Jesus) physically comes down from the heavenly realm. Rather, we should understand that God is the source and author of all that is good. When we consider our children, we recognize that they are precisely what Psalm 127:3 explains: *"Children are a gift from the LORD."* God is certainly the source of the

---

[1251] George Harris (ed.), "The Christian Pioneer, No. 160, Vol. XIII," *The Christian Pioneer, January 1839-December 1839* (London: Simpkin, Marshall & Co, 1839), pp. 451-452.

[1252] Selwyn, *First Epistle Of St. Peter*, p. 124.

blessings that come to us through our children's lives, but we know that they do not physically come from God out of heaven. We can also observe the clearly metaphorical use of the idiom as God challenges his people:

> *"Bring the whole tithe into the storehouse, that there may be food in my house. Test me in this," says the LORD Almighty, "and see if I will not throw open the floodgates of heaven and pour out so much blessing that there will not be room enough to store it"* (Malachi 3:10).

The people hearing this understood that God was simply promising blessings which had their derivation in heaven to those who trusted him.

The heavenly plan for the Messiah was personally designed and instituted by the Father, and it was he himself who begat Jesus in the womb of his mother (Ps 2:7; Matt 1:20; Lk 1:31-35; Heb 5:5; 1 Jn 5:18). Jesus' personal claims therefore have everything to do with his assignment as God's appointed agent and nothing to do with his physical, geographic origin. Famed theologian Robert Bultmann acknowledges that from a historical perspective, Christ's language in the Gospels was not intended to describe a physical traversal through time and space. He urges that in the text:

> Jesus is not presented in literal seriousness as a pre-existent divine being who came in human form to earth to reveal unprecedented secrets. Rather the mythological terminology is intended to express the absolute and decisive significance of his word.[1253]

Other exegetes have likewise admitted that the New Testament writers "do not think of Jesus as the incarnation of the Spirit, nor of Jesus as already Spirit prior to his existence on earth."[1254] So what then did they think? Simply that this Jesus was a man uniquely commissioned by God? This is, we recognize, the loudly trumpeted message of the Church on the Day of Pentecost: *"Jesus of Nazareth was a man accredited by God"* (Acts 2:22). Incredibly, the divine Incarnation, the most critical mechanism of Trinitarian thought, is recognized by many scholars as "Christological thinking which cannot be traced back to Jesus himself. We cannot claim that Jesus believed himself to be the *incarnate* Son of God."[1255] Indeed the whole weight of Jewish thought and history would have

---

[1253] Bultmann, Rudolph. *Theology of the New Testament*, Vol. 2 (Waco: Baylor University Press, 2007 [1951]), p. 62.

[1254] Dunn, *Christology in the Making*, p. 61.

[1255] Ibid., p. 254, emphasis added.

precluded him from doing so. Since Jesus advocates no such philosophy, it is a wonder that so many later Christians have been led to believe so dogmatically on this point and encourage, often by the force of anathema, a total subjection to doctrines wholly foreign to the recorded teaching of Christ.

Does "Sent from God" Mean Literal Pre-existence?

Jesus frequently claimed to be *"sent"* by God (Jn 12:44; 17:3) and even *"sent into the world"* (Jn 3:17). Common understanding interprets this language to mean that while Christ had always been God in heaven, he recently became incarnate as a human being in order to accomplish the redemptive mission. In other words, to the Trinitarian, Jesus' being *"sent from God"* or *"sent into the world"* means that he physically traveled from another realm to planet earth.[1256] However, in the New Testament, Christ is not the only human figure so described. John the Baptist furnishes a prime example: *"There came a man sent from God, whose name was John"* (Jn 1:6). Jesus' cousin was directly commissioned by God for his baptismal ministry (Jn 1:33), and Christ even argues that John's baptism came directly *"from heaven"* (Matt 21:25). Linguistically speaking, Moses (Ex 3:12), Jeremiah (Jer 43:1), Paul (2 Cor 2:17), and the angel Gabriel (Luke 1:26) also experienced God's dynamic "sending" without necessitating the incarnation of preceding identities. Nevertheless, the dogmatists assert that the man Jesus being *"sent into the world"* implies such activity. Yet we find Christ himself explaining, in prayer to God concerning his own disciples, that *"Just as you sent me into the world, so I sent them into the world"* (Jn 17:18). The words "just as" should not escape us here; in the same way that Jesus was sent, so his disciples were also sent. This is certainly through commission, not through incarnation. The idiom "coming into the world" seems to have carried then a surprisingly similar meaning to our own modern sense, as even now a parent may remind their child that they "brought them into the world." The disciples themselves also said that *"we have brought nothing into the world"* (1 Tim 6:7), and Jesus furthermore says that all mothers, upon giving birth, experience *"joy that a human being has been born into the world"* (Jn 16:21). We should recognize that much of the biblical language bears no more metaphysical connotation than it does today. If we ever want to truly understand Jesus and his contemporaries, they simply must be allowed to use figures of speech.

[1256] See Louis Rushmore, "Come Meet Jesus Christ as Pre-Incarnate God," *Gospel Gazette*, Vol. 8, No. 6. 2006. Web. 23 September 2015.

On a related note, because God had appointed Jesus for his heavenly task (Acts 17:31), Jesus could rightly be called *"the man from heaven"* (1 Cor 15:47), and even *"not of this world"* (Jn 17:14). Because God's Messiah subsequently appointed his own disciples, they could also be described in this way. Yet while some have claimed that Christ being styled "not of this world" means that he is actually a being from another plane, Jesus explains: *"I have given them Your word; and the world has hated them, because they are not of the world, just as I am not of the world"* (John 17:14). The disciples were made "not of this world" by their commission from heaven through Jesus Christ, that is, by their entrusting with God's word or Gospel message. Clearly, these other-worldly descriptions, mutually enjoyed by both Christ and his followers, do not demand a tangible pre-existence, much less deity. Indeed, we find that just as Jesus says he is *"from God"* (Jn 8:42), the Apostle John confidently says the same about himself:

> They are from the world and therefore they speak as from the world, and
> the world listens to them. <u>We are from God</u>, and whoever knows God
> listens to us (1 John 4:5-6a).

This returns us to the idea presented by Jesus about John's baptism when he claimed that it *came from heaven* (Luke 20:4). We observe that within the Jewish worldview, messengers were seen as being either "from heaven" or "from the world." In 1 John 4:5-6, John demonstrates the use of this metaphorical distinction in a contrast between teachers who were either authorized or unauthorized by God. Jesus echoes this distinction in John 8:23: *"And he was saying to them* [his interrogators at the Temple], *'You are from below, I am from above; you are of this world, I am not of this world.' "* In this case, there were certain persons who were sanctioned by heaven, and certain men who were not, and the ministries operating by earthly authority paled in comparison to ministries with heaven's sanction: *"They were amazed at his teaching; for he was teaching them as one having authority, and not as the scribes"* (Mark 1:22). Therefore both Christ and his disciples, being similarly imbued with God's right to preach, were both recognized as operating through an other-worldly prerogative; the same heavenly language was employed to portray not simply the foundation of their power, but the resulting quality of their persons.

If words are allowed to retain their meaning, we must furthermore argue that Christ's claim to be *sent* by God should imply that he is not that sending God himself. In describing himself as *a prophet* (Luke 4:24), Jesus recognizes that he does not act on his own behalf, but on behalf of another: his God and Father.

Indeed he consistently finds none of his activity's authorship in himself, but in another, grander source, and labors to make this obvious: *"For I did not speak on my own, but the Father who sent me commanded me to say all that I have spoken"* (Jn 12:49); *"My teaching is not mine, but his who sent me"* (Jn 7:16); *"The words I say to you I do not speak on my own authority"* (Jn 14:10); *"I do nothing on my own"* (Jn 8:28); *"By myself I can do nothing"* (Jn 5:30); *"the Son can do nothing by himself"* (Jn 5:19), and so on. Christ presents himself as being both unwilling and incapable of any action which has its origin in his own determination or devices, a hard proposition for anyone who must be fully God, and a proposition which seems intolerable in light of his repeated presentation of another outside himself as the originator of his authority and mission. As Christ faithfully reports, *"I have not come on my own. God sent me"* (Jn 8:42). We naturally wonder how Christ can be the same one God who sent and empowered him, and how being that God, he can then declare his own powerlessness and inherent lack of authority to his audience with any honesty. If Jesus wants everyone to believe that he truly is God himself, could he expect their successful education with this sort of preaching? The more palatable conclusion is that Christ simply means what he says. When he says *"God sent me,"* he intends not that the Jews would believe that he somehow *is* that same eternally existent being, now miraculously come into their presence as one of them, but simply that he is a divinely-appointed messenger invested with authority by their ancestral God.

We must recognize that the widespread, dogmatic demand for universal acceptance of Christ's statements as clear claims to personal pre-existence, especially pre-existence as God himself, is a post-Apostolic development. Jesus himself, it would seem, would not have expected such a thing from his earliest followers. Instead:

> Jesus saw himself as spokesman for God and emissary of divine Wisdom, as in Mark 9:37 and Luke 7:31-35. Even if Jesus occasionally spoke of himself as "the son (of God)" or God's "beloved son" (Matt. 11:27; Mark 13:32), though the point is disputed, there would have been no implication in the category itself of any claim to pre-existence, since divine and intimate sonship was already attributed to a messianic king and the righteous person within Israel (Ps. 2:7; Isa. 42:1; Wis. 2:16-18). And Jesus' talk of himself as "the son of man," even where an allusion to Dan. 7:13 is given, would not be understood as a claim to preexistence, since Dan. 7:13 was

evidently not yet interpreted as speaking of a divine individual.[1257]

Jesus, along with the first Christians, readily promoted the Messiah's spiritual *inspiration* by God, but stopped well short of a physical *incarnation*. That Jesus was also, in some sense, the representational manifestation of God's wisdom, or God's word or divine reason, was also celebrated in the post-Easter community (Jn 1:1-14). But the later Christian transformation of Jesus from the culmination and embodiment of God's word and wisdom, into a second Divine Person who later transformed himself into a human being, certainly did not occur within the Apostolic church. As Dunn concludes, despite the opinion of later eras, there is no real weight behind the claim that Jesus believed in and openly taught the Christian dogma of the Incarnation:

> Within the earlier strata of the Jesus tradition there is substantive evidence that Jesus laid claim to speak with divine inspiration and authorization as in some sense the representative of God. But there is nothing of consequence to support the thesis that Jesus saw himself in some sense as God, as the incarnation of the deity… It is unlikely, therefore, that the thought of incarnation was part of earliest Christian faith.[1258]

Before Abraham

During an argument with his enemies over the primacy and salvific efficacy of the Jews' blood-ties to Abraham, Christ says to them, "*I assure you: Before Abraham was born, I am*" (Jn 8:58). Trinitarians often explain that Christ's being "before" Abraham here proves that he literally and consciously preceded Abraham's birth by billions of years, being Abraham's own Creator. Yet the dogmatic clamor for a presentation of literal pre-existence here should likewise subside in light of our investigation. Indeed, Christ is shown here to pre-exist Abraham, yet in what sense? Physically, as a realized, conscious person? Or within God's mind, in his plan for human redemption?

In the context of John 8, the evidence points to an affirmation of pre-eminence over Abraham in the grand scheme of God's history, not of a

---

[1257] James Dunn, *Christ and the Spirit: Collected Essays of James D.G. Dunn,* Vol. 1 (Grand Rapids: Eerdmans, 1998), p. 37.
[1258] Dunn, *Christ and the Spirit,* Vol. 1, p. 38, 40.

primordial, sentient reality. Two verses prior, Jesus says: "*Your father Abraham rejoiced to see my day: and he saw it, and was glad*" (Jn 8:56 KJV). Christ's statement was then understood by his enemies, as it is still misread by many today, to mean that Jesus was personally older than Abraham: "*You are not yet fifty years old,*" they said to him, "*and you have seen Abraham?*" (Jn 8:57). This is, of course, an example of the "misunderstanding motif" prevalent in John. Jesus did not say that he himself had seen Abraham, rather that Abraham had seen "*his day.*" What was this day of Christ that Abraham bore witness to? Was Jesus literally alive before their mutual ancestor?

The New Testament tells us that "*the Gospel was preached beforehand to Abraham*" (Gal 3:8), and through faith Abraham "*looked forward*" (Heb 11:10) to the day when the Messiah would fulfill God's promises by setting up the Kingdom of God (Rom 4:13). We may therefore understand that the context in John 8 is God's plan regarding *the Gospel*, and in this sense Christ was certainly preeminent.

It is reasonable to conclude that Christ's preceding existence here was only in God's plan; after all, Abraham was said to have been "*made the father of many nations*" while he and Sarah were yet barren (Rom 4:17). Likewise King Cyrus was even spoken to by God while he only existed in God's unrealized purpose (Is 45:1-13), and the prophets David and Isaiah spoke of Christ as if they personally beheld his future sufferings. Furthermore Jesus' own disciples, well-versed in the prophecies of the Old Testament, continuously portrayed the Messiah as being foreknown and foreordained before the foundation of the world (1 Pet 1:17-21), and even spoke of themselves as each having received grace through Christ's sacrifice before the world began (2 Tim 1:9). It is therefore not unreasonable to assert that the Messiah's existence before Abraham in John 8 is in the future intentions of God. Many commentators, both Trinitarian and otherwise, and from all eras of scholarship, have come to this conclusion. Even the famed Trinitarian theologian Hugo Grotius viewed the passage in this way, explaining that the language of Christ means simply "That Jesus was before Abraham in the divine decree."[1259] One scholar gathers that Grotius' interpretation:

> harmonizes with what goes before; Abraham rejoiced or
> desired to see my day, and he saw—foresaw it; and was glad:
> for before Abraham was, I was—I was in the divine purpose; it

---

[1259] Samuel Bache, Charles Clarke, *Examination of Objections Made to Unitarianism by the Rev. J.C. Miller* (London: Whitfield, Strand, 1854), p. 29.

was arranged that the Messiah should come. It was God's plan
or purpose, before Abraham's time, to introduce the messiah
into the world.[1260]

The great Reformer and Trinitarian Theodore Beza likewise follows in this
interpretation, saying, "I do not think that Christ here simply speaks of himself
as God, but as he was seen by Abraham with the eye of faith… otherwise he
would not have spoken to the purpose."[1261]

Indeed we find in the surrounding context that Jesus had instructed the
hostile Jews to look to his teachings for salvation, to which they responded that
they needed no assistance from him due to their ancestral ties to Abraham (Jn
8:31-40). Jesus thus answers their contest with a claim to precedence over even
their father Abraham in God's salvific purposes for the nation. The intentions of
Christ here are absolutely to emphasize his priority as the long pre-destined
Messiah, the catalyst of God's saving work.

Upon saying that even Abraham looked forward to him, Jesus somberly
added, *"Before Abraham was, I am"* (v. 58). Trinitarians have been prone to
arguing that the Jews immediately sought to stone him for these remarks because
Christ was claiming not only to literally pre-exist their ancestor, but to be God
himself. The Trinitarian hopes to prove this by citing Christ's lack of visible
rejection of their understanding. "They took up stones to stone him," says the
Trinitarian, "and he did not for one instant correct their impression."[1262] In
essence, because Jesus does not correct them, he is thought to endorse their
view. First of all, this argument is assuming that they meant to stone him for
claiming to be God. Why could they not have stoned him for claiming to be the
Messiah? They did have a certain law among them prescribing death for such a
claim (Jn 19:7, Matt 26:63). Could he not also have so enraged them by claiming
precedence over their great ancestor? By claiming that they must turn to him for
freedom from sin? It is in no way clear that they hoped to murder him for a
claim to deity. Secondly, apart from being an argument from silence, this
thinking also neglects the fact that Jesus repeatedly leaves his audience, especially
his most antagonistic critics, to founder in their ignorance. For example, when
Jesus said that the Jews must eat his flesh and drink his blood, his hearers were
perplexed, even outraged:

[1260] Joseph Barker, *Authentic Report of the Public Discussion Between Joseph Barker and William Cooke*
(London: J. Barker, 1845), p. 443.
[1261] Bache, Clarke, p. 29.
[1262] J. C. Miller (Trinitarian) quoted in Bache, Clarke, p. 29.

> *Then the Jews began to argue sharply among themselves, "How can this man give us his flesh to eat? Jesus said to them, "Very truly I tell you, unless you eat the flesh of the Son of Man and drink his blood, you have no life in you... For my flesh is real food and my blood is real drink." ... On hearing it, many of his disciples said, "This is a hard teaching. Who can accept it?" But Jesus, conscious that his disciples grumbled at this, said to them, "Does this cause you to stumble?"* (John 6:51ff).

The Jews took him literally and were not corrected. Even his own disciples were left to wonder at his sayings. The motif of constant misunderstanding by Christ's audience throughout the Gospel of John, and his frequent refusal to directly and immediately counter that misunderstanding, must be considered here. What should not be considered an object of any real weight or consequence, is a manufactured admission of Deity from the sealed lips of Jesus. Yet one further portion of this episode in John must now be analyzed.

The "I Am" Sayings

The argument for Jesus' literal pre-existence "before Abraham" in John 8 is commonly thought to be enhanced by Christ's use of the phrase "*I am,*" (Greek: *ego eimi*) which Trinitarians claim is the "divine name" of the God of Israel in Exodus 3:14. Most translations render Exodus 3:14 in this way: "*God said to Moses, 'I am who I am. This is what you are to say to the Israelites: "I am has sent me to you" ' "* (NIV). On the surface, this link between the two texts seems plausible, yet we will presently discover both the inadequacy and the exploitative bent of this argument.

Under closer scrutiny, Christ's use of "I am" (ego eimi) does not constitute a daring and shocking claim to be the God of Israel. The "I am" statements of Jesus, in their context, merely indicate that Jesus is the Messiah in question. This Greek phrase "ego eimi" is, in reality, only the usual way many persons identify themselves as the subject of conversation throughout the New Testament. Jesus' use of "I am" does not necessarily refer to the divine name of God. In fact, the traditional translation of the Hebrew in Exodus 3:14 as "I am who I am" is not really the best rendering. The Hebrew literally means "to become" or "to be," and would be better rendered "I will be what I will be."[1263] Therefore the precise

---

[1263] The Hebrew reads "ehyeh asher ehyeh." This phrase is related to the Hebrew name of God, YHWH, which is derived from the verb HAYAH, *to be.* While the traditional rendering is often

wording does not match Christ's "I am" language in the Gospel of John. Even Trinitarian scholar and staunch opponent of unitarianism Dr. John Pye Smith writes:

> Some suppose, that, in using the expression "I am," our Lord intended a reference to the divine appellation announced to Moses, "I am that which I am." But it is to be remarked, that the words of that passage are in the future tense, "I will be that which I will be," Exod. 3:14; and most probably it was not intended as a name, but as a declaration of the certain fulfillment of all the promises of God, especially those which related to the deliverance of the Israelites. There does not appear, therefore, sufficient ground to sustain the idea of an allusion to this.[1264]

Nevertheless, modern Trinitarians often claim that those in Christ's audience simply knew that to use the words "ego eimi" was to refer to Exodus 3:14 and thus constituted an open claim to be the God of Exodus. But if this is true, then we have encountered a serious theological problem in the New Testament, as many others use the same phrase to describe themselves:

- Judas Iscariot: "ego eimi" ἐγώ εἰμι (Matthew 26:25)
- The blind man: "ego eimi" ἐγώ εἰμι (John 9:9)
- Paul of Tarsus: "ego eimi" ἐγώ εἰμι (1 Timothy 1:15)
- John the Baptist: "ego eimi" ἐγώ εἰμι (John 1:27)

Though this is the same statement of Christ, no one argues that these men were quoting Exodus, much less claiming to be God. The truth is that "ego eimi" is not any sort of "divine name"; it is simply the Greek for "I am he," or "I am the man," or "I am the one you are speaking about/in question." Indeed in the structure found in John 8:58, the Greek pronoun "autos" (he), though not stated, is implied. For example, in John 9:9, the people were looking for the blind man whom Jesus had healed, and when they found him some said, *"This is he; others said, he is like him; but he said, I am he"* (KJV), or *"I am the man"* (NIV).

---

preferred, many modern English language editions, such as the ESV and AMP provide the proper translation *"I will be what I will be"* in their footnote for Exodus 3:14.

[1264] John Pye Smith, *Scripture Testimony to the Messiah*, Vol. II (Edinburgh: London: Hamilton & Co. Jackson & Walford, 1759), p. 161.

Neither the words "he" or "the man" are actually in the text, but the translators understand that they are implied by his use of the simple phrase "ego eimi" (I am). Trinitarian translators have even followed this model with Jesus' other sayings, such as John 8:24, *"for if ye believe not that I am he, ye shall die in your sins"* (KJV), and *"I am he"* (NIV). But when the same language appears in John 8:58, their practice shifts to: *"I am"* (KJV); *"I am!"* (NIV). The usually inserted "he" is suddenly dropped, obviously in hopes of creating a connection with the inadequate, traditional translation of Exodus 3:14.

John, early in his Gospel, actually demonstrates what Jesus' use of "ego eimi" means. In John 4:25, the Samaritan woman says to Jesus: *"I know that the Messiah is coming (he who is called Christ). When he comes, he will tell us everything."* Jesus answers her: *"I who speak to you am he."* The Greek in Jesus' answer is "ego eimi"—it means "I am the Messiah you are speaking about." This first occurrence of the phrase helps us understand what he means by it in the subsequent passages. We must keep in mind that Jesus' identification as the Messiah, not as the one God, is John's stated purpose in writing his Gospel (Jn 20:31).

Furthermore, if we assert that Christ's use of "ego eimi" really does imply "I am almighty God," we threaten to toss the entire text into an odd confusion bordering on the absurd. Jesus says, *"When you lift up the Son of Man, then you will know that I am he* [ego eimi], *and I do nothing on my own initiative but I speak these things as the Father taught me"* (Jn 8:28). One biblical scholar writes, "It is intolerable that Jesus should be made to say, 'I am God, the Supreme God of the OT, and being God I do as I'm told.' "[1265]

What's more, if Christ truly desired to quote Exodus 3:14, he would have likely said: "ego eimi *ho on.*" This is because "ego eimi *ho on*" is the Greek rendering for the verse, as evidenced by the *Septuagint*, the Greek Old Testament available in Christ's day from which he quotes repeatedly.[1266] The *Septuagint* renders the phrase: "ἐγώ εἰμι ὁ ὤν" (ego eimi *ho on*) meaning "I am *the Self-Existing One,*" or "I am *He Who Is,*" or "I am *The One Being.*"[1267] The *Septuagint* reads:

[1265] C. K. Barrett, *Essays on John* (Philadelphia: Westminster, 1982), p. 9; cf. p. 32.

[1266] There is no doubt that the *Septuagint* (LXX) was the Bible of Jesus' day. Protestant scholars Archer and Chirichigno list 340 places where the New Testament cites the *Septuagint,* as opposed to only 33 citations from Hebrew texts (G. Archer, G. C. Chirichigno, *Old Testament Quotations in the New Testament: A Complete Survey* (Chicago: Moody Press, 1983), pp. 25-32).

[1267] L. Perkins, *A New English Translation of the Septuagint,* Electronic Edition, available online at: http://ccat.sas.upenn.edu/nets/edition/. The Greek *ho on* has also been translated as "The

> *And God said to Moses, I am the one being* [ἐγώ εἰμι ὁ ὤν]. *And he said, Thus shall you say to the sons of Israel, The one being* [ὁ ὤν] *has sent me to you"* (Exodus 3:14 LXX).

Here, God is clearly not calling himself "I am," but "the Existing Being." Brenton's *Septuagint in English* is also helpful in this regard:

> *And God said unto Moses, "I am HE WHO IS* [ho ōn]: *and he said, Thus shalt thou say unto the children of Israel, HE WHO IS* [ho ōn] *hath sent me unto you"* (Exodus 3:24, LXX, Brenton).

Notice what has been rendered in capitals here. What could be called God's "name" is the "ho on" segment, since the "ego eimi" is simply the predicating identifier. A man named Thomas would be expected to say, "ego eimi Thomas," and no one would think "ego eimi" was any sort of name in itself.

Furthermore, in the works of other Greek-speaking Jews living around the time of Jesus, we find the same form when they quote Exodus 3:14; they obviously demonstrate an understanding that God's name or title is not the "ego eimi" portion, but the "ho on." Observe how the Jew Philo (d. 50 CE) renders the "title," and even calls God by different variations of "ho on":

- ho Ōn, "He who is" (Philo, *Life of Moses I*, 75)
- to Ōn, "the Being who is" (Philo, *Life of Moses II*, 67)
- tou Ontos, "of Him that is" (*Life of Moses II*, 99)
- tou Ontos, "of the Self-Existent" (*Life of Moses II*, 132)
- to Ōn, "the Self-Existent" (*Life of Moses II*, 161)

The great F. F. Bruce writes: "If a direct reference had been intended to Ex. 3:14 in the present passage [Jn 8:58], one might have expected *ho on* rather than *ego eimi*."[1268] It is wrong to demand an interpretation of "ego eimi" as a quotation of Exodus 3:14 or as an open claim to deity. If Jesus sought to refer to himself as the God of Exodus, then he could have done so easily: "I am GOD." Far from professing to be the "self-existent one," however, Jesus is content to portray himself as one whose existence relies completely on another source: "*I*

Being", for which see: The *Septuagint Version of the Old Testament, with an English Translation*, (London: Samuel Bagster and Sons, 1879), p. 73ff.

[1268] F. F. Bruce, *The Gospel of John* (Grand Rapids: Eerdmans, 1983), p. 193.

live because of the Father" (Jn 6:57). Ultimately, the far-reaching argument over "ego eimi" reveals a deep desire to find Jesus claiming literal pre-existence and deity in the New Testament. This is so dearly sought that apologists seem to have grasped at and abused Christ's sayings in a radical way. The simple message of the New Testament, that Jesus is the Messiah, God's *Son*, is also radically compromised by this popular but problematic interpretation.

In summary, we will appeal to more reasonable analysis from James Dunn, who admits to discovering no biblical evidence for the assertion that either Christ or his Apostles promoted the doctrines of Jesus' pre-existence or Incarnation:

> There is no thought in any of the passages we have studied of Jesus existing prior to his birth whether as an angel or archangel, a spirit or the Spirit. There is no thought whatsoever of Jesus on earth as the incarnation of an angel or archangel, spirit or Spirit.[1269]

Here we must again emphasize that all Jews, from ancient times till now, have awaited the coming of an anointed *human being*, not an angel, much less God himself in human form. The Messiah's origins as a man from Israel were clearly prophesied: "*The LORD your God will raise up for you a prophet like me from among you, from your countrymen, you shall listen to him*" (Deut 18:15). There is nowhere in the New Testament the explicit and copious evidence that would be required to dislodge this vivid image from the Jewish mind. We will therefore allow Dunn to end this chapter with a stirring and conclusive observation along these lines:

> In the early stages of this development *(the first century)* it would be inaccurate to say that Christ was understood as a pre-existent being become incarnate, or that Christ himself was thought to have been present and active in creation... There is no indication that Jesus thought or spoke of himself as having pre-existed with God prior to his birth or appearance on earth.[1270]

[1269] Dunn, *Christology in the Making*, p. 159.
[1270] Ibid., p. 211, 254, emphasis added.

12

THE SON OF GOD

"I said, 'I am the Son of God' "
— Jesus (John 10:36)

"He said, 'I am the Son of God' "
— the Jews (Matthew 27:43)

THANASIUS AND HIS PARTY vigorously employed John 10:30 during the Nicene strife to prove their homoousian dogma. In this passage, during an argument with the Jews, Jesus says: *"The Father and I are one."* This text is still often quoted by Christians wishing to demonstrate that Jesus shares *one essence*, or the *same substance* with the Father. Yet this meaning is not demanded here, and, when viewed in the light of Christ's claims of inferiority and subjection to God, proves increasingly problematic.

As we have seen previously, despite the long employment of John 10:30 in the arguments of Trinitarians, some modern Trinitarian commentators admit that this passage reflects simply *a unity of purpose* between Jesus and the Father, not of essence, substance, or being.[1271] This interpretation aligns with the

---

[1271] R. V. G. Tasker, *Tyndale NT Commentaries: John* (Grand Rapids: Eerdmans, 1975), p. 136; J. N. Sanders, B. A. Mastin, *The Gospel According to John*, (London: Randomhouse Publishers, 1968), p. 258; J. H. Bernard, *A Critical and Exegetical Commentary on the Gospel According to St. John* (Edinburgh: T & T Clark, 1928), pp. 365-366; Karl Josef Kuschel, *Born Before All Time*, p. 170.

consistent Gospel demonstration of the Son's unity of will and function with the Father. We are reminded by commentators that:

> A unity of fellowship, of will, and of purpose between the Father and the Son is a frequent theme in the Fourth Gospel (cf. 5:18,19; 14:9,23 and 17:11,22), and it is tersely and powerfully expressed here; but to press the words so as to make them indicate identity of "ousia" or "essence," is to introduce thoughts which were not present to the theologians of the first century.[1272]

While the esoteric application of the patristic commentators is still favored by many in popular apologetics, no longing for the obscure should confuse Christ's intentions. In verses 28-30, we see that Jesus had spoken of his disciples as sheep who had been placed under his supervision by God: *"No one will snatch them out of my hand. My Father, who gave them to me, is greater than all; and none is able to pluck them out of my Father's hand. I and my Father are one."* Both Christ and his Father are shown here to be responsible for protecting the sheep; they are perfectly united in this common purpose.[1273]

Elsewhere Jesus uses the same language to describe the relationship of the Church to himself and to God, praying that *"they may all be one, just as you, Father, are in me, and I in you, that they also may be in us, so that the world may believe that you have sent me"* (Jn 17:21). Christ also asks for his disciples to *"be one just as we are one"* (v. 22), and furthermore that they would also be *"one"* with Jesus and his Father (v. 23). The common purpose is, of course, the spreading of the Church's message, or, *"so that the world may believe that you have sent me"* (v. 21). The same language is also used by Paul to describe the relationship between himself as the founder of a certain church, and Apollos as the nurturer of that church: *"He who plants and he who waters are one"* (1 Cor 3:8). There is no indication therefore that this same language in John 10:30 implies a unity of substance or being, a thoroughly Greek metaphysical notion far from the minds of Jesus, his Jewish audience, and his immediate Jewish historians.

Experts from various backgrounds and periods are in agreement on this point, despite any apologetic clamor, ancient or modern. The wording used by

---

[1272] Bernard, pp. 365-366.

[1273] Even the Reformer John Calvin recognized that "The ancients made a wrong use of [John 10:30] to prove that Christ is...of the same essence with the Father. For Christ does not argue about the unity of substance, but about the agreement that he has with the Father" (John Calvin, *Commentary on John*, John 10:30).

Christ to describe his relationship to the Father is, in a Christological sense, benign:

> *"One"* translates the Greek neuter *"hen."* This verse was much quoted in the Arian controversy by the orthodox in support of the doctrine that Christ was of one substance with the Father. The expression seems however mainly to imply that the Father and the Son are united in will and purpose. Jesus prays in [John 17:11] that His followers may all be one (*hen*), i.e. united in purpose, as He and His Father are united.[1274]

> That the Son and the Father are one (HEN, neuter, literally *one thing*), is not offered as a proposition in metaphysics, but simply as the explanation why an attack on the Son is also an attack on the Father, and so bound to fail.[1275]

Trinitarians have historically, in fear of Sabellianism, been quick to point out that the Greek word here for "one" is *not* "heis," which would mean that the Father and the Son are "one person." Interestingly, this *is* the word Jesus uses to describe God in Mark 12:29: God is "heis" (masculine singular), one person.

Locating Trinitarian theology within Christ's philosophically unassuming statement in John 10:30 should be precluded, in light of the linguistic and contextual evidence, as mere speculation. We must, as students, be careful to always cultivate a healthy respect for context, and even more careful to refrain from summoning anachronistic controversy into the midst Jesus' sayings.

"Son of God" or "God the Son"?

Just as many today still misunderstand or misappropriate Christ's words, many in his antagonistic Jewish audience, blind with intolerance, likewise severely missed his intentions. After his declaration of unity with God in John 10:30, we read in verse 33 that some of the Jews sought to stone Jesus *"because you, being a man, make yourself out to be God."* Here we find one of the most oft-cited passages used to prove Jesus' claim to deity. But the argument is founded upon the testimony of Christ's enemies, a less than trustworthy source, and

---

[1274] Tasker, *John, 1960,* p. 136.
[1275] Sanders, Mastin, *Black's New Testament Commentaries: The Gospel According to Saint John,* p. 258

persons whom Christ had already recognized "*do not understand my speech*" (Jn 8:43).

As mentioned in previous chapters, misunderstanding Jesus is a major theme of the Gospel of John, as episodes involving his audience's misinterpretation of him occur in at least fifteen out of the twenty-one chapters.[1276] Both Christ's disciples and his opponents constantly mistake his sayings, and while Jesus often corrects those mistakes, he deliberately keeps many of his most unsavory critics un-enlightened as to the real sense of his statements. The disciples who loved him, however, were often permitted to understand: "*Because the knowledge of the secrets of the kingdom of heaven have been given to you, but not to them*" (Matt 13:11). Interestingly enough, many of Christ's hearers today not only perpetuate this failure to grasp the real meaning of his sayings, many even echo the very complaints of his historical adversaries. Some of Jesus' opponents perceived that he was claiming to be God (in some sense) in John 10:30-33, or at least putting himself in God's place of authority, and mainstream Christian dogma has loudly echoed this allegation.   Yet knowing how often the Pharisees misinterpreted him, we must ask ourselves if these witnesses are truly the best and most reliable sources for the appropriate interpretation of the man's teachings. Again, the very crowd who perceived a claim to deity or to literal existence before Abraham was said by Christ to misunderstand him because they were willfully hard of hearing: "*Why do you not understand what I say? It is because you cannot bear to hear my word... the reason why you do not hear them is that you are not of God*" (Jn 8:43a, 47b). Accordingly, the Pharisees were not in error because they simply could not accept some purportedly clear declaration that "Jesus is God", rather they were missing the very meaning of his words. Had the Jews in John 10:33 been correct in their assessment that "*you, being a man, make yourself out to be God*," Jesus might have easily welcomed the charge and admitted it, or summoned some biblical passage to corroborate the assertion as was his custom. However, instead of affirming any claim to be God, Jesus actually corrected them with his usual sublime reasoning and command of the Scriptures:

> *Jesus answered them, "Has it not been written in your Law, 'I said you are gods'? If he called them gods, to whom the word of God came (and the Scripture cannot be broken), do you say of him, whom the Father*

[1276] See John 2:19-22, 3:4-13, 4:31-34, 6:51-61, 71, 7:33-36, 8:18-19, 21-22, 27, 33-34, 38-44, 51-52, 56-58, 9:39-41, 10:1-6, 26-36, 11:11-14, 11:23-25, 12:16, 32-34, 40, 13:6-12, 27-29, 33-37, 14:2-5, 7-11, 16:16-18, 16:25-29, 20:9, 21:22-23. See also Matthew 13:10-17, 13:34-36, 15:11-20, 16: 5-12, 27:46-47. Mark 4:10-13, 33-34, Luke 2:50, 9:45, 18:34. See also Proverbs 28:5, Isaiah 6:9.

*sanctified and sent into the world, 'You are blaspheming,' because I said 'I
am the Son of God'?"*
(John 10:34-36)

The brilliance of Jesus reveals itself in this restrained but powerful rebuttal.
Christ expertly demonstrates that in their own Scriptures the human prophets
and judges of Israel, like Moses (Ex 7:1), were permitted even to be designated
"God" due to their reception of the Deity's authoritative inspiration. If such
high appellations were appropriate for them, then surely Jesus, who was set apart
by God as the Messiah and was thus even greater than Moses, should be
permitted to enjoy the designation "*son* of God," which implied his own
dependence. Though he could have assumed for himself the demonstrably
appropriate title of "God," Jesus wisely dismantled their accusation by
deliberately forgoing that great title for himself and instead emphasizing his
consistent claim to be God's beloved *son*.

It must be noted that while the Gospel of John records a variety of episodes
featuring the misunderstanding of Christ's enemies, and perhaps a few involving
their perception of a claim to deity or at least to being on the same level as the
Deity, by the end of the narrative the world appears to have finally grasped his
intentions. When the Jesus incident came to a head in Jerusalem, the final charge
was brought forth against him at his fateful trial: "*Art thou the Christ, the Son of the
Blessed?*" (Mark 14:61b KJV). Matthew records it thus: "*And the high priest said
unto him, 'I adjure you by the living God, that you tell us whether you are the Christ, the Son
of God'*" (26:63). Clearly he was not charged with claiming to be Yahweh, the
living and Blessed God himself, but with making himself that living God's *son*.
When accused of claiming to be God previously, Jesus had not embraced the
perception but corrected them (Jn 10:36). Yet now, being accused of claiming to
be their ancestral God's *son*, Jesus answers *immediately* in the affirmative: "*I am,
and you shall see the Son of man sitting at the right hand of power*" (Mark 14:62a). At this
verification, "*the high priest tore his garments, saying, 'He has spoken blasphemy: what
further need have we of witnesses?'*" (Matt 36:65). It was certainly not for the
blasphemy of claiming to be identical to the one God that he was condemned, as
is made clear during his sentencing before Pilate. The Roman had found no guilt
in him, but "*the Jewish leaders replied, 'We have a law, and according to our law he ought to
die, because he claimed to be the Son of God'*" (Jn 19:7). Evidently, any perceived
claim of Jesus to be Yahweh had vanished from the consensus of his enemies;
the shift was made to accusations of a claim to *sonship*, a relationship of the most

intimate and highest order with the Creator. Indeed, had not Jesus himself previously corrected them publicly: "*I said, 'I am God's son'*" (Jn 10:36 NIV)? Even as his dreadful sentence was being carried out, the precise claim for which he was crucified was again made known by his enemies: "*He trusts in God; let God deliver him now if he wants him! For he said, 'I am the Son of God'*" (Matt 27:43). It was not suggested then, even by the Jews who urged his execution, that he had claimed to be identical to God, rather that he had believed himself to be a man in closest possible relationship to the divine. As the ground shook upon his dramatic expiration, this incredible sign testified that what Jesus had so often said was really the truth: "*Truly this man was the Son of God!*" (Mark 15:39).

If this indeed was Jesus' precise claim, then what does "Son of God" really mean? Does it just mean "God" as some modern voices have urged? What did it mean to the Jews? Jesus' frequent use of this title within his first-century Jewish environment must now be considered. As scholars have urged, "It is obvious the messianic terms used by Jesus are to be found in the Old Testament and in later Jewish literature, and there they have, as a matter of course, to be analyzed in their context."[1277]

Today's Trinitarians are intent on representing "Son of God" as necessarily describing the eternally pre-existent God-the-Son figure of post-Nicene Christianity. Indeed, the exercise of Church tradition seems to have effectively trained many students' eyes so that when they fall upon Christ's confession: "*I am the Son of God*" (Jn 10:36), they instinctively read "I am *God*" or "*I am God-the-Son.*" As one Trinitarian apologetics source vigorously argues: "Jesus being called the Son of God means that Jesus is God... the term Son of God means that Jesus is God in the flesh."[1278] But is this accurate? In this apologist's argument we discern no cautious regard for history. A more judicious Anglican scholar correctly recognizes that "the New Testament never suggests that the phrase 'Son of God' just means 'God.' "[1279] While many in the mainstream traditions have unfairly promoted the title "Son of God" as a clear denotation of Jesus' deity, respected voices within Christian apologetics nevertheless confess that "neither the Judaism nor the paganism of Jesus' day understood the title in

---

[1277] H. Riesenfeld, "The Mythological Background of New Testament Christology," *The Background of the New Testament and Its Eschatology* (Cambridge: CUP, 1956), p. 91.

[1278] Matthew Slick, "What is Meant When It Says Jesus is the Son of God?" Christian Apologetics and Research Ministry. Web. 30 December 2014. <http://carm.org/jesus-son-of-god>.

[1279] Don Cupitt, *The Debate About Christ* (London: SCM Press, 1979), p. vii, 4.

this way. Neither did the early church."[1280] If this is true, then why has an ill-timed definition of the first-century "Son of God" metaphor remained with us to this day? A Catholic expert on this issue has recently argued that:

> Scholarship on divine sonship in the New Testament has relied anachronistically on the philosophical and theological categories of fourth-century Christianity, especially the key [Nicene] distinction, "begotten not made." In the Roman world before Nicaea, begetting and making sons was not primarily a philosophical distinction... the [orthodox] approach to biblical texts... is often an unconscious combination of fourth-century Christological categories with first-century texts.[1281]

As we have seen, those fourth-century categories were as thoroughly Platonic as they were separated from the Jewish world. Thus Nicaea only requisitioned the New Testament language about sonship, and, as Peppard notes:

> with the predominance of philosophical categories among Christian leaders, the terms "begotten" and "made" changed in meaning: they ceased functioning as metaphors linked to human practices. They became increasingly abstract concepts, until the watershed debates of the Nicene era established them finally as the property of theologians alone.[1282]

What then did the earliest Jesus community mean when it identified Jesus as "the Son of God"? What did Jesus himself mean by it? We should expect the Jews of the New Testament to have interpreted the phrase according to its historical usage within their own Scriptures, that is, as a title frequently applied to mighty human characters who enjoyed special endowments and relationships to God. The Old Testament, particularly the Psalms, had portrayed the Davidic kings who preceded and typified the Messiah in this way: *"I will be his father and he shall be My son; and I will not take My lovingkindness away from him, as I took it from him who was before you"* (1 Chron 17:13). One evangelical scholar has determined that "In the Old Testament, kings (especially David), righteous individuals and even

---

[1280] McCready, p. 56

[1281] Michael Peppard, *The Son of God in the Roman World: Divine Sonship in Its Social and Political Context* (Oxford: OUP, 2011), p. 4.

[1282] Ibid., p. 5.

Israel are called sons of God."[1283] Specifically we find Solomon (1 Chron 17:13), angels (Job 38:7), and especially Adam (Luke 3:38) so described. Another scholar postulates that "Jesus may well have been called Son of God in the earliest [Christian] community on the basis of Psalm 2, in which the Israelite king is designated Son of God by the use of the ancient oriental formula of adoption."[1284] In this way, says German scholar Martin Noth, "the Davidic king in Jerusalem was not god incarnate, was not of divine origin, but is designated 'son' by gracious assent of his God."[1285] This application of "son of God" for a normal human being stands in sharp contrast to its usage in the system of incarnational, dual-nature kingship ascribed to the Pharaohs of ancient Egypt observed in part one of this book. As Noth concludes, the usage among the Hebrews is "an indication of a *rejection* of real divine king ideology."[1286] Indeed, scholars draw a strident distinction between the Egyptian god-man kingship and the Judean notion. One scholar concludes that in Israel the "son of God" language was "primarily a way of marking the king off as superior to other human beings, although not on par with the Most High."[1287] Another concludes that "in spite of all the mythological metaphors about the birth of a king, we never find in Israel any expression of a 'metaphysical' conception of the king's divinity and his relation to Yahweh."[1288]

The Israelite custom was evidently to award this title to figures who, though obviously mundane in nature, were transcendent in designated office or relationship—special persons elected by God into an inimitable affiliation for their unique virtue or prominence in his grand design or government. The Judean distribution of the title was certainly accomplished without any hypothesis regarding a real divine nature. A simple survey of the phrases' wide biblical application should therefore silence the clamor for implicit deity.

Adam's description as God's son is particularly interesting as we observe that he is called "*the son of God*" in Luke's genealogy precisely because God was

---

[1283] McCready, p. 56.

[1284] Kuschel, p. 141. See also Peppard in his investigation into the Synoptic use of "Son of God" in its first-century Roman context: "the resonance of 'son of God' changed over time. Many authors of the first and second centuries, when describing the divine sonship of Christ and Christians, mixed the begotten and adoptive metaphors. But by the fourth century, adoption was no longer a crucial, visible component of imperial ideology and thus lost some (but not all) of its appeal as a metaphor of power and exaltation" (Peppard, p. 5).

[1285] Martin Noth, "God, King and Nation," in *The Laws in the Pentateuch and Other Studies* (Philadelphia: Fortress, 1966), pp. 172-173.

[1286] Ibid.

[1287] Collins, *King and Messiah as Son of God*, p. 204.

[1288] Mowinckel, *He That Cometh*, p. 78.

his father (Luke 3:38). In this instance we find a most direct and appropriate parallel with Christ's own sonship: Adam's declared status reflects an exceptional association to the Father, not a simultaneous sharing of his essence. A Professor at Edinburgh admits that biblically speaking, "divine sonship did not function to connote divinity, but it certainly indicated a special status and relationship with God."[1289] Certainly Jesus claimed such a unique affiliation throughout his ministry, and the Gospel writers too are happy to recognize and promote it in their accounts of the Nativity. The explication of Christ and the Father's relationship is found plainly in the record of the man's significant birth, in which he is *designated* God's son: *"The angel answered and said to her, 'The Holy Spirit will come upon you, and the power of the Most High will overshadow you; and for that reason the holy Child shall be called the Son of God'"* (Luke 1:35 NASB). His direct creation by God in Mary is explicitly what has afforded him the immediate recognition of an exceptional, personal rapport with the Creator. All other men after Adam had obviously experienced sonship through a human father, but Christ's existence, being accomplished in Mary by no agency but God's, unquestionably provided him this designation. Ultimately, we should say that Jesus is called the Son of God not because he somehow is God himself, but on the grounds that God is his father, because of their close relationship.[1290]

It is for this familial relationship, a relationship of transcendent love, that the Son is allotted his far-reaching rights and privileges, even the very prerogatives of God: *"The Father loves the Son and has given all things into his hand"* (Jn 3:35). Respected Lutheran theologian Oscar Cullman is correct when he recognizes that "Son" and other titles which are often claimed to express an inherent deity, actually explain a *functional* rather than an ontological harmony: "the titles 'Logos' and 'Son of God'... do not indicate unity in essence or nature between God and Christ, but rather a unity in the work of revelation."[1291] A wealth of Christian scholarship likewise affirms that "son" not only fails to promote a unity of essence, but actually endorses a sharp distinction between God and the one so-called. Professor Colin Brown of Fuller Theological Seminary explains that this title actually works to disprove any identification of Jesus as the God of the Bible:

> The title "Son of God" is not in itself a designation of personal
> deity or an expression of metaphysical distinctions within the

---

[1289] Larry W. Hurtado, *Lord Jesus Christ* (Grand Rapids: Eerdmans, 2003), p. 103.

[1290] See Collins, *King and Messiah as Son of God*, p. 209.

[1291] Oscar Cullmann, *The Christology of the New Testament* (Philadelphia: Westminister Press, 1963), p. 247.

Godhead. Indeed to be a "Son of God" one has to be a being who is not God.[1292]

Old Testament scholar Herbert Haag also informs us that "In the Old Testament and early Judaism 'son of God' signifies creatureliness, election and intimacy... far less is it intended to signify divinity."[1293] The renowned Rudolph Bultmann agrees: "It is clear that neither in Judaism nor in the Christian church could this title have had the mythological meaning it had in later Hellenistic Christianity; that is, it did not designate the Messiah as a supernatural being begotten by God, but was simply a royal title."[1294] In the New Testament era it was indeed, as modern scholarship has resoundingly confirmed, a royal title—one which referred specifically to the Messiah who was to emerge from the family of King David. As noted earlier, both Second Temple Judaism and the New Testament Christian community interpreted key passages, such as Psalm 2:7, 89:26-27, and 2 Samuel 7:14, as Messianic prophecies.[1295] In the case of 2 Samuel 7:14, the future son of David (Solomon) would also be identified as the son of God, and 4QFlor recasts the prophecy messianically. In other words, the title "Son of God," in its first-century Messianic context, was virtually synonymous with both "Son of David," and "King of Israel."[1296] Note that Luke 1:35 explicitly identifies Jesus as simultaneously the "Son of the Most High" and a descendant of King David.[1297] Note also the synonymous

---

[1292] Colin Brown, "Trinity and Incarnation," *Ex Auditu*, Vol. 7 (Eugene: Wipf & Stock, 1991), p. 90.

[1293] Herbert Haag, 'Son of God', *Concilium* (Norwich: SCM Press, 1996), p. 36.

[1294] Bultmann, *Theology of the New Testament*, Vol. I, p. 50.

[1295] See Hebrews 1:5: "*For to which of the angels did [God] ever say, "You are my son, today I have begotten you"? And again, "I will be a Father to him and he shall be a son to me"*"? (NASB). Jews outside of the Christian community had certainly interpreted these passages as messianic—the Qumran writing known as 4QFlorilegium (4Q174) identifies the "Branch" of David figure from Jeremiah and Zechariah with 2 Sam 7:12-14 and Amos 9:11: "*... he shall be a son to me. He is the Branch of David who will arise with the interpreter of the Law... in Zion in the last days according as it is written, 'I will raise up the tent of David that has fallen,' who will arise to save Israel.*" Also worth noting is the document 1QSa which awaited the day "*when God begets the Messiah*" (2:11), and the LXX rendering of Psalm 110:3 "*I have begotten thee from the womb.*" The Davidic Messiah was to be "begotten" or brought into existence, not by a human father, but by God.

[1296] At his trial, when Jesus is questioned by the Jews about his identity, they ask: "*If you are the Messiah, tell us*" (Luke 22:67). Jesus then identifies himself as "*the Son of Man*" (v. 69). In their follow-up question, they press him: "*You are then the Son of God?*" (v. 70). Their first and second questions are therefore interdependent and "Messiah," "Son of David," "Son of Man," "Son of God," and "King of Israel" are consequently all to be viewed in the Gospel context as Messianic titles.

[1297] "As in Mark, 'son of God' and 'son of Man' are equivalent in Matthew... In Luke, as in Mark and Matthew, it is clear that 'son of God' (or 'son of the Most High') is equivalent to

parallelism in the exclamation of Nathanael upon meeting Jesus: *"Nathanael answered Him, 'Rabbi, you are the Son of God; you are the King of Israel' "* (Jn 1:49). In light of the evidence, "We must stress," as N. T. Wright admits, "that in the first century the regular Jewish meaning of this title [Son of God] had nothing to do with an incipient Trinitarianism; it referred to the king as Israel's representative."[1298]

The post-Apostolic Gentile Church, however, with its wholesale consignment to the operating spirit of the Greeks, regrettably pressed this title through the framework of their mythical worldview and recognized the phrase as virtual proof of Christ's essential and natural deity. The epithet formerly enjoyed by Jewish kings had become the exclusive brand of a demi-god, a Hercules or a Dionysus, a supernatural figure come down from the celestial realm to execute divine privilege among humanity. It is clear, unfortunately, that much of modern Christianity has perpetuated this mistake. Nevertheless, modern New Testament scholars have suggested that the New Testament perspective on "Son of God" does not deviate from the historical interpretation of the ancient Israelites. Dr. Kuschel's valuable commentary should not be neglected:

> In keeping with its Jewish origin, the title "Son of God" was never associated with a heavenly existence before time or with divinity... the basic foundation of post-Easter talk of Jesus as Son of God does not lie in Jesus' "divine nature," in a pre-existent divine Sonship, but in the praxis and preaching of the earthly Jesus himself: in his unique relationship to God, whom in an unprecedentedly familiar way he was accustomed to address as "Abba"... in Israel the title of son of God referred for the most part to the unique dignity and power of the supreme political ruler.[1299]

Thus Jesus is called "son of God" because God brought him into existence in his Mother, and because he is the heir to David's throne over Israel. But if "son of God" actually indicates deity, then the New Testament immediately unravels.

'messiah'... 'son of God' and 'messiah' are equivalent in John, just as they are in the Synoptics" (Collins, *King and Messiah as Son of God*, pp. 209-210). See also the precedent DSS 4Q246 which identifies a figure as "Son of God... Son of the Most High," which "should be identified as the Davidic Messiah, as also in Luke 1:32, 35" (Ibid., p. 206).

[1298] Wright, *Jesus and the Victory of God*, pp. 485-486.

[1299] Kuschel, p. 238.

John writes: "*Dear friends, now we are the sons of God*" (1 Jn 3:2), and Paul tells us, "*We are the sons of God,*" with the added assurance that "*if we are sons, then heirs: heirs of God, and joint-heirs with Christ*" (Rom 8:16-17). In light of God's work to bring "*many sons to glory*" (Heb 2:10), and in conjunction with John's prologue which reveals that to many "*he gave the right to become sons of God*" (Jn 1:12), we cannot accept the dogmatist's interpretation of the language. While the Son of Trinitarianism stands alone in his peculiar pseudo-relationship with the Father, the Jesus of the New Testament opens wide the door to a shared sonship for all. The sonship which Christ offers is not, however, a poor imitation of the mysterious, ineffable Father-Son relationship between the hypostases of the Trinity—rather it is the same relationship status of Christ which he gladly shares; a bond not of substance, but of love.

The Gospel of John is often said by Trinitarians to be the most avid supporter of the idea that "Jesus *is* God in the flesh." Trinitarian Bible publishers even claim that relaying this doctrinal message was the explicit intention of John's work; that is, his mission was to fill in critical information concerning Christ's deity which Matthew, Mark, and Luke's accounts supposedly inadequately relayed.[1300] Yet John makes his own intentions quite clear, summarizing his message in his final chapters thus: "*these have been written so that you may believe that Jesus is the Christ, the Son of God; and that believing you may have life in his name*" (Jn 20:31).

Jesus as "god"

Christian usage of the word "God" in our day is usually reserved for a reference to the one God of the Bible. Yet in the times of the biblical authors, the term was used much more freely, even to describe human beings or angels. There are only two instances in which the word "god" (Greek: "theos") is used of Jesus for certain in the New Testament.[1301] It is often said by Trinitarians that

---

[1300] The preface to the Gospel of John in Harvest House Publisher's *New Inductive Study Bible* reads: "God in the flesh. The incarnation would be hard for some to believe, but their belief or unbelief would be a matter of life or death. Three other Gospels had been written, and years had passed. One more Gospel was needed, one which would answer these questions and more, one which would illumine the shadows of doubt. So the apostle John answered God's call to write a fourth and final Gospel..." (*The New Inductive Study Bible* (Eugene: Harvest House Publishers, 2000), p. 1711).

[1301] There are seven other highly disputable texts (John 1:18, Rom 9:5, Titus 2:13, 2 Pet 1:1, 1 Jn 5:20, Acts 20:28, 2 Thess 1:12). These have been widely doubted as identifying Jesus as "God" by textual analysts for a variety of reasons. Trinitarian Christopher Kaiser notes that "explicit references to Jesus as 'God' in the New Testament are very few, and even those few are generally plagued with uncertainties of either text or interpretation" (Christopher Kaiser, *The Doctrine of God*

these instances qualify as the best proof that the biblical writers believed the man was nothing less than the one and almighty God, and that this is the central, most overwhelming revelation of the New Testament. Our suspicions are raised however, when, in the over 1,327 occurrences of the word "god," only two of them refer to Christ. The lack of evidence for consistent application of the word God to Jesus is widely considered, even by Trinitarians, to be problematic. One scholar writes:

> For example, Jesus never used the term "God" when referring to Himself, none of the synoptic gospels (Matthew, Mark, or Luke) ever explicitly gives the title "God" to Jesus, no sermon in the Book of Acts attributes the title "God" to Jesus, no existing Christian confession(s) of Jesus as "God" exist earlier than the late 50s and, although there are seventeen texts that are considered to be possible "Jesus-God" passages, only four of them appear in the approximately fifty Greek New Testament manuscripts that predate the fourth century. Also, and perhaps the biggest obstacle in ascribing the title "God" to Jesus, the existing New Testament manuscripts differ in *all* potential passages that explicitly call Jesus "God."[1302]

Furthermore, "god" is found to be used just as many times of other persons in the New Testament, once of Herod (Acts 12:22), and another time of Satan (2 Cor 4:4). The standard lexicons provide these usages of the Greek word "theos": "a god or goddess, a general name of deities or divinities, whatever can in any respect be likened unto God or resemble him in any way, God's representative or vice-regent, magistrates and judges."[1303] Looking back to the Old Testament, we find that the Hebrew for "god" (el or elohim) is used in this same way for other men or angels (Ps 45:6; Ps 82:1-6; Ex 7:1). In Psalm 8:5, the Hebrew text refers to "elohim" (god), but when the passage is quoted in the New Testament, the Greek says "angels" (ἄγγελος). Similarly, in the *Septuagint*

(London: Marshall Morgan & Scott, 1982), p. 29). Trinitarian William Barclay agrees: "On almost every occasion in the New Testament on which Jesus is to be called God there is a problem either of textual criticism or of translation" (William Barclay, *Jesus as They Saw Him* (Grand Rapids: Eerdmans, 1978), p 21). We will thus focus only on the less disputable "theos" texts. For more on the textual issues surrounding the other passages, see Bart D. Ehrman's *The Orthodox Corruption of Scripture* (Oxford: OUP, 1993).

[1302] Brian J. Wright, "Jesus As God," *Christian Research Journal*, Vol. 31, No. 4 (CRI, 2008), emphasis added.

[1303] "theos," *Strong's*.

version of Job 20:15, the Hebrew word "God" (el) was even replaced with the Greek "angel" (ἄγγελος) by the Jewish scribes. Because the title "god" is often found in the biblical documents describing kingly persons with god-like authority, such as human judges of Israel (Jn 10:34) or angels (Ps 8:5), many popular English editions of the Bible even translate "god" as "judge" or "ruler."[1304]

Identifying other beings who were not Yahweh as "god" did not pose a "theological problem" for either the ancient Hebrews or the New Testament Jews. As mentioned previously, the biblical principle usually at work here is known as "the law of agency."[1305] When God imparts his authority to his agent, that agent may himself be called "God," and may speak and act as God on his behalf. Again, Moses and the judges of Israel were addressed as God: "*Then Yahweh said to Moses, 'See I have made you GOD to Pharaoh, and Aaron your brother shall be your prophet'*" (Ex 7:1); "*I said, 'You are GODS, you are all sons of the Most High'*" (Ps 82:6). Exodus 22:8 also speaks of the human rulers of Israel in this way; the Hebrew refers to these persons as "God" or "the gods," but the *Amplified Bible* translation makes it clear: "*the house owner shall appear before God, the judges as His agents, to find whether he stole his neighbor's goods.*"

There are in fact many "gods" mentioned in the Scriptures, though for the nation of Israel there is clearly only one *true* God; the others are evidently gods in a representational, derived, or secondary sense. The Apostle Paul even defines *which* god is the true god of the New Testament community: "*There are many Gods, but for us there is but one God, the Father*" (1 Cor 8:6). Indeed, as Christ agreed, "*the Father*" is "*the only true God*" (Jn 17:1a, 3). It is this great God who designates certain other persons, those whom he has directly authorized or inspired, as "God." Christ himself explains the principle:

> Jesus answered them, "*Has it not been written in your Law, 'I said you are gods'? If he called them gods, to whom the word of God came (and the Scripture cannot be broken), do you say of him, whom the Father sanctified and sent into the world, 'You are blaspheming,' because I said 'I am the Son of God'?*" (John 10:34-36).

[1304] At Exodus 22:8-9, 28 the word "judges" is used, for example, in the KJV, NIV, NASB, HCSB, ISV, and NET translations, while "God" is used in the ASV, ESV, JPS, ERV, and WEB.

[1305] Again, the *Jewish Encyclopedia* defines the Hebraic Law of Agency, also known as "sheliah," in this way: "The Law of Agency deals with the status of a person (known as the agent) acting by direction of another (the principal)... The general principle is enunciated thus: A man's agent is like himself (Ḳid. 41*b*)" (Lewis N. Dembitz, "Law of Agency," *Jewish Encyclopedia* (1906), p. 232).

Jesus being called "the Son of God" or even "god," does not mean that he is to be identified himself as Yahweh. Certainly Christ is the supreme agent of God, but he is no more Yahweh than Moses is, according strictly to the language involved. Nevertheless, the claim persists that the New Testament clearly identifies Jesus as the one God due to the use of "theos" to describe him.

Hebrews 1:8, which applies the classic Psalm 45:6 to Jesus, is a prime citation in this popular argument: *"But of the Son He says, 'Your throne, O God, is forever and ever, and the righteous scepter is the scepter of his kingdom' "* (Heb 1:8). Certainly the writer identifies Jesus as "God" in this passage. However, the original Psalm the writer is quoting was evidently addressing the *human* king of Israel at that time:[1306]

> *I address my verses to the king... Grace is poured upon your lips,*
> *therefore God has blessed you forever... Your throne, O God, is forever...*
> *you have loved righteousness, therefore God, your God, has anointed you*
> *with the oil of joy above your fellows... King's daughters are among your*
> *noble ladies; at your right hand stands the queen...* (Psalm 45).

As the king of Israel, this man was representationally "god"; he sat on God's seat of authority over the nation (see 1 Chron 29:23). Of course, this pattern applies directly to Jesus as the Messiah, the ultimate king of Israel (Jn 1:49). It is also important to note that the very next verse applied to the Son in Hebrews says that the Son, like the human king to whom the hymn was originally addressed, actually *has a God* himself: *"Therefore God, your God, has anointed you with the oil of joy above your fellows"* (Heb 1:9). This reference to the king's own God serves as a helpful mechanism for achieving a better view on his exalted status. Jesus, as king of Israel, may be recognized as "divine," but that "divinity" is diffused through a Subordinationist prism and ultimately reflected back onto his God as a representational divinity.

The writer of Hebrews furthermore argues here that because Jesus had *"loved righteousness,"* his God had now highly exalted him, making him even superior to the holy angels (Heb 1:4). In the next chapter of the epistle, it is even argued that Jesus has now been deemed worthy of even more glory and honor than Moses (Heb 3:3). This of course is an entirely pointless argument if both the writer and the other Christians at that time believed Jesus was Yahweh. It would

---

[1306] See Nancy L. DeClaisse-Walford, "Psalm 45," *Psalms for Preaching and Worship: A Lectionary Commentary* (Grand Rapids: Eerdmans, 2009), p. 156. See also Graham Cole, *The God Who Became Human: A Biblical Theology of Incarnation* (Downer's Grove: IVP, 2013), p. 84.

have gone without saying that God was greater than Moses. Certainly the writer's intentions are not to identify the man Jesus as "god" in the exact same sense that Yahweh is God. Nevertheless, we will here perform an in-depth examination of the surrounding context in Hebrews to prove our point.

Before verse 8 we read that the Son:

- was not speaking to the fathers in ages past (1:1-2)
- had to become superior to angels, meaning he previously was not (1:4)
- gained an inheritance he didn't previously have (1:4)
- would be considered a son to God *(not God himself)* (1:5)
- was "begotten" by God (1:5)
- is a representation of God *(not God himself)* (1:3)

Now, *after* verse 8 we read that the Son:

- has a God (1:9)
- has been anointed above his fellows (1:9) *(God has no fellows and no need for anyone to anoint him)*
- was made lower than the angels (2:9)
- is *now* crowned with glory and honor because he died (2:9) *(he wasn't crowned beforehand)*
- is the pioneer of man's salvation (2:10) (i.e. *the first to receive salvation*)
- calls men his brothers (2:11) *(God does not have brothers)*
- says that he will put his trust in God (2:13)
- was made like his brothers in every single way (2:17)
- was tempted (2:18) *(God cannot be tempted)*
- is now counted worthy of more glory than Moses (3:3) *(if he is Yahweh, this should go without saying)*

In light of the immediate context, how pressed are we to deduce that the writer is not describing an exalted human being, but the Almighty Yahweh, the monolithic Creator of all things? Of course, Jesus is never explicitly called Yahweh by the writer of Hebrews or by any other biblical author, but he is described as *"a man"* (Acts 2:22; 1 Tim 2:5; Jn 8:40) who has been invested with divine authority (Matt 28:18). Jesus is thus certainly "god" in the sense that he is a chief dignitary, a holy prince, and a powerful ruler who represents God. The

Father himself had *given* Jesus this lordly status (Acts 2:36; Phil 2:9), and the writer of Hebrews clarifies that it is precisely because of his great service to God that he has "*now been crowned with glory and honor*" (Heb 2:9). Jesus has thus been made "a god" in the most biblical sense of the term.

Ultimately, the "law of agency" interpretation remains the best choice for making sense of the New Testament community's view of Jesus while avoiding conflicts with Jewish monotheism.

Seeing God in Jesus

The other instance in which the word "theos" is used in relation to Christ is in the exclamation of Thomas in John 20:28: "*Thomas answered and said to him, 'My Lord and my God!'*" Trinitarians have taught that this verse demonstrates Thomas' belief that Jesus was actually the one true God, and on the surface, the statement may seem fairly black-and-white to the English reader. However, lifting a passage out of its environment can easily obscure an intended meaning.

First let us consider what both the Old and New Testaments say about "seeing God." Yahweh says to Moses: "*You cannot see my face, no man shall see me and live*" (Exodus 33:20). John's Gospel begins by saying: "*No one has ever seen God*" (Jn 1:18a). Even after Christ's very visible ministry and ascension into heaven, John still maintains the declaration verbatim in his subsequent letters: "*No one has ever seen God*" (1 Jn 4:12). Paul certainly agrees with John on this point, describing God as one "*who lives in unapproachable light, whom no one has seen or can see*" (1 Tim 6:16). If God is truly "invisible" (Col 1:15), then how is it that Jesus could say, "*If you have seen me, you have seen the Father*" (Jn 14:9)? Again, the law of agency plays a role here.

Since God cannot be seen, and because God heard the request of the Israelites at Horeb that he should speak to them only through representatives (Ex 20:19), God instituted the office of the Israelite prophet. When he put his words into that prophet's mouth, it made that man "God" to the party to which he was sent (Ex 7:1). This is the explanatory framework surrounding the presentation of Jesus in the Gospel of John: Christ is portrayed as God's supreme representative who performs God's own will (Jn 4:34), speaks God's own words (Jn 8:28), and more. As Marianne Meye Thompson affirmed for us previously:

> Jesus is presented in the Gospel [of John] against the backdrop
> of the Jewish concept of agency and, furthermore, against the
> understanding that there is one chief agent through whom

God acts [the Messiah]... Because Jesus is the chief agent of
God, when one confronts him, one confronts God.[1307]

One of the Gospel's major themes, therefore, is the idea that when one
looks at or encounters Jesus, one "sees" God: *"Then Jesus cried out, 'Whoever believes
in me does not believe in me only, but in the one who sent me. The one who looks at me is seeing
the one who sent me'* " (Jn 12:44 NIV). Turning to Jesus' conversation with Thomas
in John 14, we find Jesus prescribing a belief in two distinct individuals:

> *Do not let your heart be troubled; believe in God, believe also in Me...*
> *Thomas said to Him, "Lord, we do not know where you are going, how*
> *do we know the way?" Jesus said to him, "I am the way, the truth, and*
> *the life; no one comes to the Father but through me. If you had known me,*
> *you would have known my Father also; from now on you know him, and*
> *have seen him"* (John 14:5-7).

To see and know Jesus was to see and know the Father. Seeing with the eyes
here is an easy metaphor for perceiving or recognizing with the mind. But after
Jesus' instruction to Thomas, we find that Philip, apparently not satisfied that
they could now "see" the Father, leaps into the conversation:

> *Phillip said to him, "Lord, show us the Father, and it is enough for us."*
> *Jesus said to him, "Have I been so long with you, and you have not come*
> *to know me, Philip? He who has seen me has seen the Father; how can*
> *you say, 'Show us the Father'?"* (John 14:6-9)

Jesus explains once again:

> *Do you not believe that I am in the Father, and the Father is in me? The*
> *words that I say to you I do not speak on my own initiative, but the*
> *Father abiding in me does his works. Believe me that I am in the Father*
> *and the Father is in me; at least believe because of the works themselves*
> (John 14:10-11).

Jesus' desire for his disciples to recognize God in him is clear. Jesus'
evidence for this is his words and works. There is no need to see God with
physical eyes—if the disciples wanted to know what God was like, they had no
further to look than Jesus. Now, in John 20:25, after Christ's burial and

---

[1307] Thompson, *Dictionary of Jesus and the Gospels*, p. 377.

resurrection, the disciples run to Thomas and claim, *"We have <u>seen</u> the Lord!"* But Thomas says, *"Unless I <u>see</u>... I will not believe."* Then Jesus appears to Thomas:

> *Then he said to Thomas, "Reach here with your finger, and see my hands; and reach here your hand and put it into my side; and do not be unbelieving, but believing." Thomas answered and said to him, "My Lord and my God!"* (John 20:27-28).

This is not the first time that Jesus had asked Thomas to believe. Jesus had taught him earlier: *"Whoever believes in me does not believe in me only, but in the one who sent me. The one who looks at me is seeing the one who sent me"* (John 12:44 NIV). Through the powerful testimony of the resurrection, Thomas was now able to "see" what he had missed previously—both his Lord Jesus, and his God.

John 20:28, far from being a master Trinitarian text, is simply the resolution of Christ's earlier teaching in John 14. Thomas meant "my Lord" to apply to the Jesus standing before him, and "my God" to apply to the Father who was at work in him. Trinitarian opinion can be found to waver on Thomas' statement, and to even confirm our interpretation of it:

> In giving this interpretation, I do not affirm that Thomas passed all at once from the extreme of doubt to the highest degree of faith, and acknowledged Christ to be the true God. This appears to me too much for the then existing knowledge of the disciples; and we have no intimation that they recognized the divine nature of Christ, before the outpouring of the Holy Spirit. I am therefore inclined to understand this expression, which broke out from Thomas in the height of his astonishment, in a figurative sense, denoting only, "Whom I shall ever reverence in the highest degree." If he only recollected what he had heard from the mouth of Jesus ten days before (Chapter 14: 9-10), that recollection might have given occasion to an expression which probably Thomas himself could not have perfectly explained; as is often the case with such words as escape us when we are under the most overpowering surprise. *But yet the expression might be equivalent to saying, "He! My Lord! With whom God is most intimately united, and is in him!—in whom I behold God as it were present before me!"* Or a person raised from the dead might be regarded as a divinity;

for the word "God" is not always used in the strict doctrinal sense.[1308]

Christ, the Lord

Jesus is many times addressed as "Lord" in the New Testament. In the minds of many modern Christians, the word *Lord* has become a sort of proper name for the God of the Bible. The thinking that often results is that if the same honorific is used to describe both God and Jesus, then it points to them being actually one and the same being. Nevertheless, *Lord* is strictly a title, similar to "King," "Master," or "Captain." As scholars have noted, this is a title which the New Testament says was awarded to Jesus for his great merit. Peter explains: "*Therefore let all Israel be assured of this: God has made this Jesus, whom you crucified, both Lord and Messiah*" (Acts 2:36). And according to Paul, Christ received this status specifically because "*he humbled himself and became obedient to the point of death—even death on a cross. Therefore God also highly exalted him and gave him the name that is above every name*" (Phil 2:8-9).

Interestingly, we do find the New Testament referring to both God and Christ by this title: "*turning the grace of our God into lasciviousness, and denying the only Lord God, and our Lord Jesus Christ*" (Jude 1:4). Obviously, "Lord" is not anyone's name, but only an honorific. While we have *two* "lords" in view here in Jude 1:4, we should remember that Jesus succinctly explained in Mark 12:29 that "*Yahweh our God is one Lord.*" Thus if we believe Jesus that Yahweh is only *one* Lord, then when we encounter *two* Lords in a particular text, should we not agree that only one of them can be Yahweh?

Nevertheless, many readers still confuse the "Lord" God and the "Lord" Messiah. This is, unfortunately, often made difficult by many mainstream translation committees' perpetuation of the curious Jewish tradition of obscuring God's personal name "Yahweh" (sometimes translated "Jehovah"), in print. Since about the second century CE, Jews have refrained from saying, and often even from writing, the Tetragrammaton (the letters "YHWH") out of fear of taking God's sacred name in vain. To this day, the Jew will recite Scripture substituting the word "Lord" (Adonai) for Yahweh, and many English editions of the Christian Bible continue to follow in this method and replace God's name in the text with the all-capitalized "LORD."[1309] This common practice has likely

---

[1308] J. D. Michaelis, note on John 20:28; as quoted by J. P. Smith in *Script. Test.*, Vol. 2. pp. 68-39.
[1309] David, Moses, and other biblical writers seem to have had no qualms about the writing and utterance of God's personal name. After all, it seems to be a name strongly promoted by God to

contributed to the perpetuation of the notion that due to Christ's designation as "Lord" in the New Testament, he is to be identified as the "LORD" of the Old Testament. The issue is further compounded by the fact that in the Jewish translations of the Old Testament into Greek, they adhered to their tradition of pronunciation and substituted the Greek "kurios" or "lord" for each instance of the Tetragrammaton.[1310] The Greek texts of the New Testament would follow suit. What this means is that in the New Testament, it can sometimes be difficult to know definitively whether an occurrence of "lord" (kurios) signifies a replacement of God's name, or if it is simply being employed in the typical sense as an honorific for a respectable person. Best-selling Trinitarian author Don Stewart, while personally believing that the application of "lord" (kurios) to Jesus in the New Testament is likely a reference to deity, admits that its usage does not *demand* an indication of deity, but that the term was indeed a commonly used epithet for individuals who were *not* God:

> The fact that Jesus is addressed as Lord does not necessarily mean that people acknowledged his Deity. The Greek word for Lord, *kurios*, can be used for God's name—Jehovah or Yahweh. However *kurios* can also be merely a polite way of addressing someone. For example, there are people apart from Jesus who are addressed as *kurios* in the New Testament... At times [kurios] is a polite form of address. However at other times it is a translation of the divine name for God... The context must determine which is so.[1311]

---

be used of him: *"God also said to Moses, 'Say to the Israelites, "Yahweh, the God of your fathers, the God of Abraham, the God of Isaac and the God of Jacob, has sent me to you." This is my name forever, the name you shall call me from generation to generation' "* (Exodus 3:15). Many Christian translations have reversed the obscuration practice and now print some form of the name within the text of the Old Testament, for example the Holman (2002), the Emphatic Diaglott (1864), the ERV (1885), the NEB (1961), the NWT (1984), the Darby (1890), the WEB (2000), and others.

[1310] Evidence points to the earliest versions of the LXX retaining the divine name. Later manuscripts, which we have in our possession, took up the practice of obscuration. One dictionary reveals that: "Recent textual discoveries cast doubt on the idea that the compilers of the LXX translated the Tetragrammaton YHWH by kurios. The oldest LXX MSS (fragments) now available to us have the Tetragrammaton written in Heb[rew] characters in the G[ree]k text. This custom was retained by later Jewish translators of the OT in the first centuries AD" (*The New International Dictionary of New Testament Theology*, Vol. 2, (1984), p. 512).

[1311] Don Stewart, "Why Was Jesus Called Lord?" The Blue Letter Bible. Web. 5 May 2013. <http://www.blueletterbible.org/faq/don_stewart/stewart.cfm?ID=787>.

We wonder then which sort of "Lord" the Bible truly designates Jesus as: a human superior, or God himself? When Jesus readily received the recognition, just what did he himself take it to mean?

There is an Old Testament verse, referenced repeatedly in the New Testament, which serves to reveal the precise nature of this title as applied to Christ: Psalm 110:1. This passage is, in fact, the most frequently cited Old Testament verse in the New, being either quoted or alluded to at least twenty-three times by both Jesus and his disciples. In Psalm 110, King David has assumed the role of prophet and witnesses an interaction between God and the future Messiah:

> *The LORD said to my lord: "Sit at my right hand until I*
> *make your enemies a footstool for your feet."*
> (Psalm 110:1, quoted by Jesus in Mark 12:37)

Here David considers the Messiah his "lord," but in what sense?[1312] Some Trinitarians have actually attempted to turn this verse into a proof of the Trinity, claiming that we can see two "LORDs" here, and thus two who are Yahweh. Essentially what is being claimed is that the text reads "Adonai said to Adonai" or "Yahweh said to Yahweh." But is this really the case? Does the verse truly indicate that there are *two* who are Yahweh?

A simple investigation will prove immediately that the two Lords in Psalm 110:1 are not the same. The second lord here, the one Jesus claims to be in Mark 12:37, is not the Hebrew word "Adonai," the common stand-in for God's name, rather it is "*adoni*." The different ending *(-nai* versus *-ni)* is significant; *195 times* in the Hebrew Bible, adoni is used to describe a non-deity superior, such as David, Abraham, the angels, and so on—it is never used of God.[1313] As Popular

---

[1312] Though the Messiah would be David's descendent, and in the patriarchal Hebrew society would not be considered greater than his father, Jesus turns to David's vision as proof that he was to afford a greater respect and authority than even his most illustrious forebear: *"Now while the Pharisees were gathered together, Jesus asked them a question: 'What do you think about the Christ, whose son is he?' They said to him, 'The son of David.' He said to them, 'Then how does David in the Spirit call him "lord," saying, "The LORD said to my lord, 'Sit at my right hand, until I put your enemies beneath your feet.'" If David then calls him "lord," how is he his son?'* No one was able to answer him a word, nor did anyone dare from that day on to ask him another question"* (Matt 22:41-46, also reported in Mark 12:37, Luke 20:44). See also n. 1309 on p. 425.

[1313] Anthony F. Buzzard, *The One God, the Father, One Man Messiah Translation* (McDonough: Restoration Fellowship, 2015), p. 145. "Lord in the Old Testament is used to translate Adonai when applied to the Divine Being. The [Hebrew] word... has a suffix [with vowel pointing] presumably for the sake of distinction... between divine and human appellative ("Lord," *Hastings Dictionary of the Bible*, Vol. 3, p. 137).

English translations performed by Trinitarians have deliberately misrepresented the word *adoni* (lord) in Psalm 110:1 by rendering it with a capital "L" in an attempt to make it appear as if God is speaking to God. However, it should be rendered as the lowercase "lord," as we see the word displayed in every other instance in English translations. Indeed, many non-deity individuals were addressed as "adoni," and the translations represent the word accurately:

> Sarah calls Abraham her lord:
> *Sarah laughed to herself, saying, "After I have become old, shall*
> *I have pleasure, my lord [adoni] being old also?"*
> (Genesis 18:12)

> Eliezer also calls Abraham his lord (twice):
> *He said, "O YHWH, the God of my master [adoni]*
> *Abraham, please grant me success today, and show*
> *lovingkindness to my master [adoni] Abraham."*
> (Genesis 24:12)

> Abigail calls David her lord and worships at his feet:
> *She fell at his feet and said, "On me alone, my lord [adoni], be*
> *the blame. And please let your maidservant speak to you, and*
> *listen to the words of your maidservant?"* (1 Samuel 25:24)

> Joshua calls Moses his lord:
> *"Then Joshua the son of Nun, the attendant of Moses from his*
> *youth, said, "Moses, my lord [adoni], restrain them." "*
> (Numbers 11:28)

Again, for clarity's sake: the root word is *adon*; the ending Adon*ai* is applied when used of God, and the ending adon*i* is applied when used of men or sometimes angelic authorities.[1314] Frederick Bruner, though a committed Trinitarian, recognizes:

[1314] The Hebrew Lexicon by BDB makes the clear distinction, that *adoni* consistently refers to lords who are not Almighty God: "a reference to men: *my lord, my master:* (adoni) (a) *master:* Ex. 21:5 (Covenant code) Gen. 24:12+, 44:5 (J, 20t.), 1 Sam. 30:13 and 15; 2 Kings 5:3, 20 and 22; 6:15; (b) *husband:* Gen. 18:12 (J); (c) *prophet:* 1 Kings 18:7 and 13; 2 Kings 2:19; 4:16 and 28; 6:5; 8:5; d) *prince:* Gen. 42:10 (E), Gen. 23:6,11 and 15 (P), Gen 43:20; 44:18+ ; 47:18, + (J, 12t.); Judges 4:18; (e) *king:* 1 Sam. 22:12+ (S&K 75t.); (f) *father:* Gen. 31:5 (E); (g) *Moses:* Ex. 32:22; Num. 11:28; 12:11;

"The Lord said to my Lord" meant "God said to my king." ... In Hebrew the phrase says, "Yahweh said to adoni"... Adoni means "my master" or "my lord." The devout Jew would read this phrase by covering "YHWH" (Yahweh), saying instead, "Adonai said to Adoni." Adonai (in distinction from adoni) means Yahweh, the God revealed to Israel. The Greek translation of the Hebrew text wrote simply here, "The kyrios said to my kyrios," using the same word for both Hebrew terms... [But] the second, apparently human "lord" in the Psalm's second noun is distinguished from the deity of the first "LORD," as strict exegesis suggests.[1315]

Should we not be supremely concerned with "strict exegesis"? If the textual data designates the second lord as non-deity, and Jesus himself claims to personally occupy that space, would not any other interpretation be *eisegetic*? In light of this reading, even John Calvin raised the question: "Might not God have raised up someone of the *human race* as Redeemer to be David's Lord and Son at the same time?"[1316] We must, under Scriptural pressure, answer emphatically *yes*. Of course Calvin and other exegetes who are so "hopelessly committed"[1317] to

---

32:26 and 27 (J); Num. 36:2 (2x) (P); (h) *priest*: 1 Sam. 1:15 and 26 (2x); (i) *theophanic angel* [an angel representing God]: Josh. 5:14; Judges 6:13; (j) *captain*: 2 Sam. 11:11; (k) *general recognition of superiority*: Gen. 24:18; 32:5+; 33:8+; 44:7+ (J 13t.), Ruth 2:13; 1 Sam. 25:24+ (15t.)"

[1315] Frederick Dale Bruner, *The Churchbook: Matthew 13-28* (Grand Rapids: Eerdmans, 1990), p. 423.

[1316] Calvin, 3:43, as quoted by Bruner. In Matt 22:42ff, Jesus' question *"What do you think about the Messiah? Whose son is he?"* seems to be a rephrasing of his earlier question to his disciples: *"Who do you say that the Son of Man is?"* (Matt 16:13ff). In Matt 22:42, Jesus is concerned with his primacy as God's chosen agent. He is establishing that God has raised up a man to be both David's son and lord simultaneously. He is clarifying that the Davidic Messiah was not simply another prince in a long line of royalty—otherwise his progenitor David would have been considered greater than him. The Messiah was also to be the Adamic master of the earth, the Son of God (See Luke 3:38, Gen 3:15, Ps 8:6, Rom 4:13). Jesus' tactic was to connect the Davidic Messiah of Psalm 110:1 to the eschatological Adamic ruler (son of man/adam) of Daniel 7, as seen in Matt 26:64. In Matt 22:42ff he appears to be engaging in a similar polemic: he makes himself 'son of David' and the inheritor of David's throne over Israel, as well as 'son of God' and the inheritor of Adam's throne over the earth. Thus, the Messiah is David's son, but he is also David's superior. That Jesus does not mean with this question to imply that he is somehow the one true God is obvious. In the Markan parallel, Jesus establishes that *"Yahweh our God"* is only *"one Lord"* (Mk 12:29), then immediately cites Psalm 110:1 in which there are two Lords, before asking his questions about the Messiah's identity. If God is only one Lord, then what about the other lord in Ps 110:1? It is a human figure (adoni) exalted by God even over his own father, the great king David.

[1317] "We are hopelessly committed to the Chalcedonian formulation" (Geivett, Phillips, Okholm, McGrath, Pinnock, Hick, Phillips, *Four Views on Salvation in a Pluralistic World*, p. 74).

the interpretive framework of Chalcedon, provide the usual orthodox answer. "No," they protest, "he *must* have been more than that, even God himself, though the text does not say it expressly." Truly, the repercussions of the biblical data are serious for the traditional doctrine. Anthony Buzzard, recognizing the significance of an accurate reading of Psalm 110:1, describes the passage in this way:

> [Psalm 110:1 is] the Bible's supreme proof text for telling the difference between the One God and the Messiah who is not God... If the Messiah were called Adonai this would introduce "two Gods" into the Bible and would be polytheism. Psalm 110:1 should guard us all against supposing that there are two who are God. In fact the Messiah is the supreme human being and agent of the One God. Psalm 110:1 is the Bible's master text for defining the Son of God in relation to the One God, his Father.[1318]

In light of this threatening evidence, some Trinitarians have attempted to evade the implications of Psalm 110:1 by resorting to the groundless speculation that the original Hebrew texts may have been altered by the Masoretes in the seventh century, as they adorned the consonant-only text of the Hebrew with the nikkud, or vowel-pointing, in order to preserve pronunciation. The speculators have claimed that the Jews must have deliberately forced the text to indicate that the Messiah was an "adoni," a non-deity superior, in order to combat Christian claims about the deity of Christ. The Trinitarian argument is essentially that because the two "lords" appear the same without the vowel-pointing, the original pronunciation of Psalm 110:1 was "Yahweh says to my Yahweh" or "Yahweh says to Adonai" before it was corrupted. But we must reject this suggestion as nothing more than a conspiracy theory. The assertion of scribal intrigue would never exist if the verse were not so destabilizing. As we will soon discover, there is no evidence that a mischievous shift has taken place.

The *Septuagint* (LXX), the Old Testament Scriptures translated into Greek by Jewish sages around 250 BCE (long before the Masoretic texts were developed), maintains a distinction between the first and second lords of Psalm 110:1 by translating the first LORD as "ho kurios" (the Lord) and the second as "to kurio mou" (to my lord). The latter is the standard form address for non-deity

---

[1318] Anthony F. Buzzard, "Adonai and Adoni," Focus on the Kingdom. Web. 10 September 2014. <http://www.focusonthekingdom.org/articles/adonai.htm>.

superiors in the LXX.[1319] If the second lord was actually supposed to be Yahweh before the Masoretes allegedly corrupted it, we would then be left with the textually anomalous phrase *"to my Yahweh."* In the Hebrew, there is no instance of the divine name being prefaced by the *lamed* prefix ("to my"). As scholars have revealed:

> The form "to my lord" is never used elsewhere in the Old Testament as a divine reference… [This observation] lend[s] further credence to the generally accepted fact that the Masoretic pointing distinguishes divine references (adonai) from human references (adoni).[1320]

Likewise in the Greek, the form "to kurio mou" is never used of God. This form always indicates a human superior. Note the stunning parallel between Psalm 110:1 and 1 Samuel 25:30, which reads: *"when Yahweh [kurios] does to my lord [to kurio mou/l'adoni] according to all the good that he has spoken concerning you…"* This second lord is the human lord David. Thus in Psalm 110:1, scholars conclude that "the phrase 'to my lord' apparently indicates that David was directing this oracle from Yahweh to a human lord."[1321]

[1319] In LXX, the Hebrew "adoni" is translated as the Greek "kurio mou" at Gen 24:14, 36, 39, 44, 32:5, 19; 1 Sam 24:7, 25: 26, 30; 2 Sam 18:28, 19:29; 1 Kings 18:13; 2 Kings 18:23; 1 Chron 21:3; Isa 36:8, and more. There are three rare exceptions where "kurio mou" (my Lord) is used to refer to God in the LXX. However, in these examples there is only one person being addressed with double titles. In the Greek translation of Exodus 34:9, both "kurios" and "kurios mou" are used to describe the same subject; it is a way of framing a second, superfluous reference to the same Lord. In Psalm 16:2, "kurios mou" is used as a secondary title for "Yahweh," and in Psalm 35:23, "kurios mou" is also used as a secondary title—he is "my God" and "my Lord" (kurios mou). In each of these unusual cases, there is no second, contrasting lord. We should not compare apples to oranges: these exceptions involve only one subject, while Psalm 110:1 involves God speaking to another lord. In the Hebrew Bible, when Yahweh is presented alongside another lord, the second lord is always the non-deity "adoni" (see 1 Sam 25:30; 2 Sam 4:8; Gen 24:27). Thus in the LXX, "kurios mou" is used for every other lord appearing in relationship to God. It is true that Greek has only one word for both Lord and lord: "kurios," but this does not change the fact that the particular form in Psalm 110:1, "to kurios mou" (to my lord), is never used as a reference to God in the LXX, nor the fact that in the 6,828 instances of Yahweh in the Greek, none of them are translated "kurios mou." This phrase is never a substitution for the divine name. Furthermore, Yahweh is never once called "adoni" in the Hebrew Bible, and "l'adoni" (to my lord) is never used as a divine reference. See also Hermann Cremer, *Biblico-Theological Lexicon of New Testament Greek* (Edinburgh: T & T Clark, 1878), pp. 382-384.

[1320] Herbert W. Bateman, "Psalm 110:1 and the New Testament," *Bibliotheca Sacra*, Vol. 149 (Dallas: DTS, 1992), p. 448; See also G. V. Wigram, *The Englishman's Hebrew and Chaldee Concordance of the Old Testament*, 5th ed. (Grand Rapids: Zondervan, 1970), p. 22; See also O. Eissfeldt, "adhon; adhonai," *The Theological Dictionary of the Old Testament*, Vol. 1 (Grand Rapids: Eerdmans, 1974), p. 62.

[1321] Bateman, p. 448.

All of this forces Trinitarians to push the theory that the Masoretes changed the meaning of the text in the 7th century. But history works against this speculation. There is no question that the Hebrew text did not yet have the vowel-pointing in the first century CE, but we must remember that the pointing was only introduced as a way of preserving a long-standing tradition of pronunciation. Psalm 110:1 had been read aloud in Hebrew communities for centuries. In Jewish writings pre-dating the Masoretic texts, the understanding of those Hebrew communities has been preserved: the second lord of Psalm 110:1 was not considered God, but a non-deity human lord.

By the end of the first century, rabbinical teachings were being collected in fear that Jewish traditions might be lost to war and persecution. One collection, the Mishnah (compiled around 200 CE), recalls Scriptural interpretations from the Second Temple period (536 BCE – 70 CE), and clearly identifies the second lord as *Abraham*. The Babylonian Talmud (c. 300 CE) follows suit.[1322] The third century Rabbi Zechariah speaks on behalf of the first century Rabbi Ishmael (90-135 CE) and also identifies the second lord as Abraham.[1323] The great Rabbi Akiva (40-137 CE) likewise makes this conclusion.[1324] Akiva is noteworthy in that he was a close friend and devotee of Gamaliel (d. 63 CE), who was also the tutor of the Apostle Paul (Acts 22:3). This places the Abrahamic (human) reading of the second lord squarely in the world of the earliest Jesus community. Another later work recalling these earlier interpretations confirms that "Our Rabbis interpreted it as referring to Abraham our father." This commentary even connects the "lord" in Psalm 110:1 to the "adoni" used of Abraham in Genesis 23:6.[1325] Scholars conclude that this "gives a good summary of the *early* rabbinic interpretation of this psalm."[1326] Moving to the middle of the second century, we find Trypho the Jew interpreting Psalm 110:1 as a reference to King

---

[1322] See Francis A. Sullivan, Robert Faricy, *Ignation Exercises: Charismatic Renewal* (Eugene: Wipf & Stock, 1977), p. 34.

[1323] Talmud, b. Ned. 32b. The rabbis explained that the priesthood had been taken from Melchizedek (identified as Noah's son Shem) and was given to Abraham. See M. McNamara, "Melchizedek: Gen 14, 17-20 in the Targums, in Rabbinic and Early Literature," *Biblica*, Vol. 81 (Rome: Pontifical Biblical Institute, 2000), pp. 1-31. See also Gard Granerod, *Abraham and Melchizedek: Scribal Activity of Second Temple Times in Genesis 14 and Psalm 110* (Berlin: Walter de Gruyter, 2010), pp. 217-219.

[1324] See Genesis Rabbah 46:5, Cf. 55:6, 7; Leviticus Rabbah 25:6.

[1325] The Midrash Schocher Tov (Tehillim), Psalm 110. See Maye Irwin Gruber, *Rashi's Commentary on Psalms* (Leiden: E.J. Brill, 2004), p. 645.

[1326] Gard Granerod, *Abraham and Melchizedek: Scribal Activity of the Second Temple Times* (New York: Walter de Gruyter, 2010), p. 218. See also Gerhard Bodendorfer, "Abraham at God's Right: Psalm 110 in the Rabbinic Tradition," *Evangelische Theologie*, Vol. 59 (1999), pp. 252-266.

Hezekiah,[1327] and others as a reference to King Saul.[1328] Though it is clear that "the Second Temple period reader took David to be the speaker of Psalm 110,"[1329] still other later interpretations argued that the second lord was actually David himself.[1330] All of this is significant because the Jewish sages could not have arrived at the conclusion that the second lord was non-deity if the original text had always read "Yahweh" or "Adonai" as the conspiracy theory suggests.

It is clear that one of the most widespread views in the pre-Masoretic world was that Psalm 110:1 was a reference to Abraham. But how did the Jews arrive at this? One scholar explains that an "observation of Second Temple period readers" led them to this interpretation: Abraham was frequently called *"adoni"* in Genesis.[1331] Thus it is obvious that even in the centuries before the Masoretic texts, Psalm 110:1 had read "adoni."

The frantic argument that the Masoretes deliberately and erroneously changed the standard pronunciation is disproven by the fact that the earlier Targums support a non-deity second lord, and the earlier rabbis interpreted the second lord as Abraham or David; the Masoretes were simply preserving an inherited tradition. There is no proof of any Second Temple Jewish interpretation of Psalm 110:1 that identified the second lord as Yahweh himself, and no evidence that the later Masoretic reading differed in any way from the reading in the New Testament community. Indeed, when Jesus cites Psalm 110:1 in Mark 14:62, and when Stephen cites it in Acts 7:56, they both reference *"the son of man,"* not God, at the right hand of God. "Son of man" simply means a human being.[1332] The reading among the earliest Christians must have been "adoni," not "Yahweh" or "Adonai," since God is nowhere designated "son of man" in the Hebrew Bible, and is explicitly *not* "a man... nor the son of man"

[1327] Justin Martyr, *Dialogue with Trypho*, Ch. 32-33, 83.

[1328] Granerod, p. 224.

[1329] Ibid.

[1330] Midrash, Psalm 110; Targum, Psalm 110. See Granerod, p. 218, fn. 14. See also David M. Stec, *The Targum of Psalms: Translated, with a Critical Introduction, Apparatus, and Notes* (London: T & T Clark, 2004), pp. 202-203.

[1331] Granerod notes that Abraham is called "adoni" in "Gen. 18 (v. 12 by Sarah) and 24 (several times by his servant). In Gen 24:65 Isaac is called "adoni" (by Abraham's servant). Moreover, in the Joseph novella, Joseph is called lord several times: Gen 42:10, 30, 33; 43:20; 44:8, 16, 18, 19, 20, 22, 24, 33 (by his brothers); Gen 44:5 (by his steward); Gen. 45:8, 9 (by himself/Yahweh?); Gen. 47:18, 25 (by the Egyptians)" (Granerod, p. 224, fn. 2). Rashi's commentary on Psalm 110, recalling earlier rabbinical tradition, reads: "The word of the Lord to Abraham, whom the world called 'my master,' as it is written (Gen. 23:6): *'Hearken to us, my master'* (adoni)."

[1332] "The designation 'son of man' simply means 'human being' [or] 'man' " (W. S. Lasor, D. A. Hubbard, F. W. Bush, *Old Testament Survey: The Message, Form, and Background of the Old Testament* (Grand Rapids: Eerdmans, 1996 [1982]), p. 581).

(Num 23:19). It is obvious that in the first century Psalm 110:1 was not believed to portray God speaking to God, which would have been the case if the text had always pronounced "Adonai" before an alleged Masoretic conspiracy. The metaphysical Trinitarian reading of Psalm 110:1 is an anachronism and the vacant theory about a Jewish plot is a needless distraction.

Ultimately, the Trinitarian should not hope for the original text to have read "Yahweh said to my Yahweh," that is, for a presentation of *two Yahwehs*, as such is not in accord even with Trinitarian belief. If it said "Yahweh said to my Adonai," we would still have two Gods, one speaking to another. The idea of two Yahwehs or two Adonai's is antagonistic to the religion of both the ancient Israelites and the first-century Jews (see Neh 9:6; Deut 4:35; 6:4; Mk 12:32). Psalm 110:1 remains a brilliant standard of clarity on the person of the human Messiah and his relationship to God, and continues to deal a staggering blow to the orthodox doctrine of the Trinity. Furthermore, Hebrews 1:3-4, 13 confirms that it is not an angel who sits at the right hand of God, thus making an angelic "Arian" view as impossible as the Trinitarian hypothesis.[1333]

One God and One Lord

Recalling the previously mentioned Jude 1:4, "*the only <u>Lord God</u>, and our <u>Lord Jesus Christ</u>*," we have certainly observed proof that Christ's designation as "Lord" does not mean he is "the only Lord God," and in fact he is noticeably distinct. We must also note that when Jesus is described as "lord" it is often in conjunction with a description of the Father as "God." A clear distinction is routinely made not only between the individuals but between the natures of the titles. This difference is emphasized by Paul:

> "*For even if there are "gods" in heaven and on earth (as indeed there are many so-called "gods" and "lords"), yet for us there is only one God, the Father, from whom everything came into being and for whom we live. And there is only one lord, Jesus the Messiah, through whom everything came into being and through whom we live.*" (1 Corinthians 8:6)

This is an enlightening declaration. Paul has identified two categories here: "God" and "lord." He has also defined exactly who belongs in these exclusive categories, and further explained their role and function: the one God of the

---

[1333] *"When he had made purification of sins, he sat down at the right hand of the majesty on high, having become as much better than the angels... But to which of the angels has he ever said, 'Sit at my right hand until I make your enemies a footstool for your feet'?"* (Heb 1:3b-4a, 13).

Christians is only "the Father," *from* whom are all things. The Father's role is that of Creator—while the Lord Jesus Christ is the one *through* whom are all things, that is, his role is that of an intermediary between God and the world. This echoes Paul's teaching in 1 Timothy 2:5: *"For there is one God, and one mediator also between God and men, the man Christ Jesus."* While the Lord Jesus' role is the critical focal point of creation, all things find their *source* only in the "one God, the Father." One Catholic scholar even writes:

> For these early Christians, then, the title "Lord" did not identify Jesus with God. It did two things at the same time—it associated the risen Jesus as closely as possible with the God whose honor he shared, and it distinguished him from the god who raised his dead humanity to life. Because of the role to which God had appointed Jesus by raising him from the dead, that is, by God's gift, the risen Jesus is entitled to the honor due to God. This is a long way from the developed Christian creeds of the fourth and fifth centuries.[1334]

Nevertheless, many evangelical scholars claim that in 1 Corinthians 8:6, Paul actually *"splits* the Shema" in order to include Jesus in the one God of Judaism.[1335] But such activity seems unthinkable for a Pharisaic monotheist like Paul. Jesus of course does not engage in such a revocation and affirms the *Shema,* as it still stands to this day within Judaism, as the "foremost commandment" (Mk 12:29). But if Paul really did intend to "split" the creed of Israel to include Jesus within it, we might have expected him to say: "For there is one God, the Father and the Son." Instead, Paul succinctly encapsulates the *Shema* confession: "There is one God," and in addition to this statement, he affixes another confession: "and there is one Lord." This information about Jesus is brought *alongside* the creed of Israel, it does not break it apart. Scholar James F. McGrath writes:

> The "many gods" are best understood as a reference to the gods which are thought to exist in the heavens, and the "many

---

[1334] Jerome Crowe, *From Jerusalem to Antioch: The Gospel Across Cultures* (Collegeville: The Liturgical Press, 1997), pp. 114-115.

[1335] See Andrew Y. Lau, *Manifest in Flesh: The Epiphany Christology of the Pastoral Epistles* (Tubingen: Mohr Siebeck, 1996), pp. 73-74; Richard Bauckham, *God Crucified: Monotheism and Christology in the New Testament* (Grand Rapids: Eerdmans, 1999), p. 31, 37; James Dunn, *The Theology of Paul the Apostle* (Grand Rapids: Wm. B. Eerdmans Pub. Co., 1998), pp. 267-268; Richard N. Longenecker, *The Road from Damascus: The Impact of Paul's Conversion on His Life, Thought, and Ministry* (Grand Rapids: Eerdmans, 1997), pp. 127-128.

lords" are then the rulers or lords on the earth, who represented the authority of the gods in the sphere of human existence. Paul's statement in 1 Corinthians 8:6 is best interpreted over against this aspect of contemporary Greco-Roman belief. For Christians, says Paul, there is only one God in heaven, and there is only one Lord, one agent and mediator, who rules on his behalf over all creation... Paul has already affirmed that there is "no God but one," and verse 6 expands and comments on this affirmation of monotheistic faith by adding that there is also one figure appointed by God as ruler over all things.[1336]

We return to the parallel confession in 1 Timothy 2:5. Here we find another Pauline statement which confirms the "one God" of the *Shema* while adding "one mediator" alongside of it. No update to the traditional monotheism of the Jews is inferred or necessary here. Likewise, in 1 Corinthians 8:6, as McGrath concludes, "by appending something additional to the Shema one need not 'split' it nor be understood to be incorporating the additional person or thing mentioned into the divine identity."[1337] Pauline Christology does represent a development within Judaism, but it is the addition of Jesus as an exalted mediator between God and man. As scholars have recognized, this was a development "within the bounds of Jewish monotheism, not beyond them."[1338] Paul's update was concerned with *who* the mediator between God and man is, not who their ancestral God is now understood to be. If this were not the case, one should discover evidence of controversy over monotheism in the Pauline letters. As we have seen, Judaism and the earliest Christianity were inextricably linked; Jews and Christians attended synagogue together where the *Shema* was read publicly. How could the Jew have recited the traditional *Shema* while his neighbor proclaimed a newly "split" *Shema* beside him? As it is, we have no reason to infer that Paul has done anything to the *Shema* of Judaism but affirm it completely.

What this evangelical theory about 1 Corinthians 8:6 ultimately neglects is the fact that when Paul begins to speak about the "one Lord, Jesus," he has already moved on from speaking about the "one God." Indeed, when we read

---

[1336] McGrath, *The Only True God*, p. 41.

[1337] Ibid., p. 42.

[1338] Maurice Casey, "Monotheism, Worship and Christological Developments in Pauline Churches," *The Jewish Roots of Christological Monotheism* (Leiden: Brill, 1999), p. 231.

the passage through the lens of Trinitarian claims, Paul's statement quickly falls apart. If we are to define "Lord" as "Yahweh," we force Paul to say: "For there is one God, the Father, and one Yahweh, Jesus Messiah." This is like saying: "For us there is one emperor, Constantine, and one Theodosius, Bishop Ambrose." Surely Paul did not intend to make such a fragmented, confused declaration. Instead, Paul uses "Lord" of Jesus not to identify him as Yahweh, but only as a title, in the same way that he has used "God" as a designation for the Father. The Father is, of course, also "Lord" of the universe, but he is not "Lord" in the sense that he was made that way by another. Because the New Testament states explicitly that God *made* Jesus Lord (Acts 2:36), Jesus is only to be thought of as Lord in this particular sense: it is a title or rank conferred on him by God.

"Divine Identity"?

We must take a moment to examine another Trinitarian argument involving Christ's identification as "Lord" in the New Testament. Trinitarian scholar Richard Bauckham has proposed a now-popular theory known as "Divine Identity Christology" which identifies certain traits as belonging only to God, and concludes that if Jesus also has these traits, then Christ must be "included in the divine identity."[1339] For example, God's name, God's privileges, God's honors—if Jesus is found to participate in these unique identifiers, then he must be identical to God. But making these identity statements is not as easy as it seems.

One obvious problem for Bauckham's proposition is that in order for any two things to be identical, they cannot be different in any way. This simple and obvious principle is sometimes called the indiscernibility of identicals.[1340] Indeed, it is impossible for anything to differ with itself; if one person is found to differ from another in even the smallest way, they cannot share the same identity.[1341] Of course "God" and "Jesus" differ in many ways. Even for the Trinitarian, "God" is a tri-personal essence, but "Jesus" is not a tri-personal essence. "God" sent his only begotten son, "Jesus" did not send his only

---

[1339] See Bauckham, *Jesus and the God of Israel*, pp. 24-25, 130.

[1340] Philosophers have framed the principle in this way: if two objects are in fact one and the same, they have all the same properties. In other words, if x = y, then x has all the properties y has (and vice versa). The identity symbol "=" in this equation represents "numerical identity," or, being the very same thing and not just being similar. Two widgets manufactured by the same plant may be exactly similar but they are not numerically identical.

[1341] See Dale Tuggy, "On Bauckham's Bargain," *Theology Today*, 70:2 (Los Angeles: Sage, 2013), pp. 128-143.

begotten son, and so on.[1342]   One pair of evangelicals who subscribe to Bauckham's thesis admit:

> The New Testament makes a distinction between [Jesus and God the Father]… sometimes as God and the Son of God. Although it's hard to understand, the New Testament both distinguishes Jesus from God and identifies him as God— sometimes in the same breath.[1343]

But does the data really force the conclusion that the New Testament positively identifies Jesus as "God" and "not God" at the same time? Is this conclusion only "hard to understand" as these apologists claim, or is it impossible? Dr. Dale Tuggy, in response to these scholars, writes:

> As these authors read the New Testament, it is riddled with self-contradictions on the subjects of God and Jesus, saying or clearly implying both that they're numerically the same, and that they are not. But this, they urge, is not a problem—either for the New Testament, or for their interpretations of it—for they urge that God is "incomprehensible" and thus we should "expect paradoxes or mysteries, all down the line, with respect to [God's] attributes." As they claim to base their beliefs about Jesus firmly on the New Testament, one would expect them, based on this reading, to affirm both that Jesus is God, and that Jesus is *not* God. But in fact, they strenuously assert only that he is. At the climax of their book, they claim to have proven "beyond a reasonable doubt that Jesus Christ is God." [This is] a patently incoherent reading… [They] choose to say loudly only the positive side of the contradiction.[1344]

Ultimately, this theory does not hold much water, and other top New Testament scholars have likewise found it problematic.[1345] Nevertheless, the system continues to prove popular among evangelicals who are looking for a way to reframe Trinitarianism that does not rely on the creedal language of the fourth

---

[1342] Ibid.

[1343] Robert M. Bowman, J. Ed Komoszewski, *Putting Jesus in His Place* (Grand Rapids: Kregal Publications, 2007), p. 1. Credit and thanks to Dr. Dale Tuggy for this citation.

[1344] Tuggy, "On Bauckham's Bargain," *Theology Today,* pp. 11-12. (*emphasis his*)

[1345] See James Dunn, *Did the First Christians Worship Jesus?* (Louisville: Westminster John Knox Press, 2010), p. 144.

century Catholics.[1346]   We will now continue to deconstruct this "Divine Identity" view while simultaneously reconstructing the identity of the New Testament Jesus through both the biblical data and the worldview of extra-biblical Jewish sources.

According to the "Divine Identity" view, when God's name is given to a person in the biblical documents, that person is to be "included in the divine identity."[1347] As Trinitarian Charles Lee Irons asserts, "God does not share his name with creatures."[1348] If Jesus is found to share in the name of Yahweh, it is argued that he must be, in some sense, Yahweh himself. One of the main texts used to demonstrate that Jesus bears the divine name is Romans 10:13, which says, *"Everyone who calls on the name of the Lord will be saved."* In context, the "Lord" is the Lord Jesus. But Paul is quoting Joel 2:32 which states, *"Everyone who calls on the name of the LORD* [Yahweh] *shall be saved."* This has led some to say that the Lord Jesus bears God's name, and is thus "included in the identity" of Yahweh. Passages like this, which previously applied only to Yahweh in the Old Testament, when applied to Jesus in the New Testament, are thought to demonstrate their identification.[1349]

This sort of theory might be compelling if not for two glaring facts: first, in both the Hebrew Bible and in first-century Jewish literature, God does give his name to other figures. Second, the Jews of the first century (including the Apostles) exhibit a tradition of *reapplying* various Old Testament passages (including Yahweh texts) rather freely. The "Divine Identity" argument is ultimately built upon a false premise; God sharing his name with a creature was not seen by the Jews as an infringement upon monotheism, and there is nothing acutely "Christian" (i.e. Trinitarian) about it.

Let us first examine the sharing of God's name with creatures in the Hebrew Bible. In Exodus 23:20-21, God commands Israel to submit to his angel: *"Do not*

[1346] Modern Trinitarian scholars have sometimes shied away from relying on the language of the extra-biblical creeds to frame their theology. Nevertheless, their systems are almost always reduced to the proposition that the name "Yahweh" identifies each member of the Trinity, so that the Father is Yahweh, the Son is Yahweh, and the Holy Spirit is Yahweh, but there are not three Yahwehs, only one Yahweh. This proposition cannot help but mirror the Athanasian Creed which says "the Father is Lord, the Son is Lord, and the Holy Spirit is Lord. And yet there are not three Lords, but one Lord." Trinitarianism invariably fails to uproot itself from the philosophical fourth-and-fifth century soil in which it was grown.

[1347] See Bauckham, *Jesus and the God of Israel*, pp. 24-25, 130.

[1348] Smith, Irons, Dixon, *The Son of God*, p. 19.

[1349] See N. T. Wright: "The context makes it clear both that [Rom 10:9-13] refers to Jesus himself, the one who is confessed as kyrios [Lord], and that Paul intends the full meaning of kyrios/YHWH to resonate across from Joel's statement to his own" (N. T. Wright, *Paul and the Faithfulness of God* (Minneapolis: Fortress Press, 2013), p. 703).

rebel against him; he will not forgive your rebellion, since my Name is in him." Here we encounter yet another example of the Hebrew "law of agency." The angel is imbued with God's authority, God's right to judge and forgive, and even God's name. We must ask: does the angel then also share in Yahweh's divine identity as the Trinitarian "rule" stipulates? Is he God?

A late first-century CE (possibly second-century) Jewish work provides another example. In the *Apocalypse of Abraham*, God commands the angel Yahoel to *"Go... through the mediation of my ineffable name"* (10:3). McGrath notes:

> The name Yahoel is clearly made up of the two divine names, Yah(weh) and El. Yet the reason the angel bears his name is not because he has been confused with or absorbed into God but because the angel has been given the divine name by God.[1350]

God's name is certainly borne by Jesus as well: *"Holy Father, keep them in your name, the name which you have given me"* (Jn 17:11b). However, we see that Jesus, like the angel Yahoel, was actually *given* this name by God. Before God gave it to them, they did not have it, nor would their reception of it cause first century Jews to immediately and necessarily ascribe real deity to them. The monotheistic (unitarian) matrix of Judaism is then able to be preserved despite the existence of exalted secondary figures sharing in the attributes of God.

Richard Bauckham, despite being one of the prime exponents of the "Divine Identity" theory, actually admits that in the *Apocalypse of Abraham*, the angel Yahoel truly "bears the divine name and employs its authority."[1351] But if Bauckham and others demand Jesus' inclusion in "the identity of Yahweh" on these grounds, will they not afford the same for the creature Yahoel, or the angel of Exodus 23:20-21? What about for the exalted Christians in John's Apocalypse? Christ himself promised that for the disciple who overcomes, *"I will write on him the name of my God... and my new name"* (Rev 3:12). No, the bearing of God's name, according to both the Bible and Jewish literature, does not and cannot necessitate their deity in the worldview of the earliest Christian Jews.

But what about the Old Testament "Yahweh texts" being applied to Christ in the New? Doesn't that practice clearly identify Jesus as the God whom those original texts describe?

[1350] McGrath, *The Only True God*, p. 49.
[1351] Bauckham, *Jesus and the God of Israel*, pp. 226-227.

We must begin by recognizing the liberality with which the first disciples of Jesus handled the Hebrew Scriptures. Longenecker identifies no less than four types of Old Testament exegesis employed during the era of the early Church: literal interpretation, midrash, pesher, and allegory.[1352]   In the "midrash" and "pesher" methods, Old Testament passages could be reapplied to current events without destroying the original intentions of the passage.   Midrash looks to go beyond the "plain meaning" of a text and provide an additional meaning without completely replacing the original; a pesher interpretation is a particularly eschatological one which assumes the meaning of a Scripture is being fulfilled in the presently living community.[1353]   As scholar Tim McLay explains, "the element of *reapplication* is key to the identification of pesher."[1354]   Scholars reveal that "midrashic" interpretations "often read OT words or phrases in new contexts drawn from other portions of divine revelation."[1355]   In other words, terms and phrases found in Old Testament passages, which previously meant one thing, could be taken out of that context and reapplied to new subjects, and be given new and *additional* meanings.   The Jewish writers of the New Testament are found to have freely used these techniques, especially when making Christological use of the Old Testament.

One example of midrashic interpretation in the New Testament is Matthew's treatment of Hosea 11:1: "*When Israel was a child I loved him, and out of Egypt I called my son.*"   Though this passage was originally about the Exodus of the Israelites from the land of Egypt, Matthew finds a new meaning fulfilled in Jesus: "*[Jesus' family] remained there until the death of Herod. This was to fulfill what the Lord had spoken by the prophet, 'Out of Egypt I called my son'* " (Matt 2:15).

We find this practice of reapplication also employed by Paul.   In Isaiah 42:6 and 49:6, God prophetically appointed his servant, the Messiah, to be "*a light for the Gentiles,*" to "*open blind eyes,*" to "*set the captives free*" and to bring "*salvation to the end of the earth.*"   But in Acts 13 we find that:

> "*Paul and Barnabas spoke out boldly and said... 'For so the Lord has commanded us, "I have placed you as a light for the Gentiles, that you may bring salvation to the end of the earth" ' "* (v. 46a, 47).

[1352] R. Longenecker, *Biblical Exegesis in the Apostolic Period* (Grand Rapids: Eerdmans, 1975).

[1353] Tim McLay, *The Use of the Septuagint in New Testament Research* (Grand Rapids: Eerdmans, 2003), p. 34. It is interesting to note that American evangelical Christianity can be found still using this sort of interpretation in its popular apocalyptic literature which portrays the United States or other present-day powers fulfilling endtimes prophecy.

[1354] McLay, p. 34.

[1355] Martin Pickup, "New Testament Interpretation of the Old Testament: The Theological Rationale of Midrashic Exegesis," *JETS,* Vol. 51, No. 2 (June 2008), p. 355.

Paul and Barnabas have actually applied these famous "suffering servant" passages not to Jesus but to themselves. Does this mean that Paul is to be viewed as the Messiah? No, but Paul and Jesus do serve the same function and participate in the same Messianic mission. As one scholar recognizes:

> the Isaiah 49 servant could apply to [Paul] without distorting the way in which [Paul] thought it may have been intended originally. Furthermore, in that he was continuing the mission of Jesus, the Servant, he could easily apply this Servant prophecy to himself.[1356]

Another example of Old Testament reapplication can be found in the writer of Hebrews' application of Psalm 102:25-27 to Jesus:

> *And, "You, Lord, in the beginning laid the foundation of the earth, and the heavens are the works of your hands; they will perish, but you remain; and they all will become old like a garment. And like a mantle you will roll them up; like a garment they will also be changed. But you are the same, and your years will not come to an end"* (Hebrews 1:10-13).

The original Psalm indeed referred to Yahweh and his primordial creation of the world. However, the passage is now being reapplied to Jesus, the founder and ruler of the new creation (Rev 3:14).[1357] That the writer is certainly *not* speaking of Christ's participation in the Genesis creation here is made plain only a few verses later:

> *"It is not to angels that he has subjected <u>the world to come, about which we are speaking</u>."* (2:5)

Indeed, at the end of the age, the Messiah will lead the exchange of this present creation for a new one, founding a *"new heavens and a new earth"* (Is 51:16;

[1356] G. K. Beale, "The Old Testament Background of Reconciliation in 2 Corinthians 5–7," in *The Right Doctrines from the Wrong Texts* (Grand Rapids: Baker, 1994), pp. 230-231.

[1357] The writer of Hebrews quotes from the *Septuagint*, not the Hebrew text. In the Hebrew version, the word 'lord' is missing. In the LXX, we find that Ps 102:23-25 has taken on a different meaning and has, through a shift in the vowel-pointing, introduced a second lord who is being addressed by the one God. Evidently, this Psalm had come to enjoy an apocalyptic messianic meaning; God now speaks to another 'lord' about a 'shortness of days' until God's work would be completed, that is, until the arrival of the messianic Kingdom. This reading appears to have informed the opinions in Mark 13:20 and Matt 24:22, and the author of Hebrews is drawing upon this eschatological interpretation to emphasize Jesus' role in founding *"the world to come, about which we are speaking"* (2:5).

Rev 21:1).[1358] Hebrews is looking forward to *"the good things to come"* which are *"not of this creation"* (Heb 9:11), not looking backward to the original Genesis creation. The writer's application of functional Yahweh passages to Christ, even playing off the Hebrew stand-in term "LORD" (Adonai) and the more ambiguous Greek "Lord" (kurios), does not prove indisputably that they were to be viewed as one and the same being. There is much reason to believe this was expressly not the case.

To reinforce the historical usage of Old Testament reapplication techniques, we can look outside the Christian world of the first century to discover that Jews from other communities were also readily employing these interpretive devices. The Dead Sea Scrolls furnish perhaps the best example. The Qumran community reapplied various "Yahweh" texts from the Old Testament (such as Ps 7:7-8; Ps 82:1; Is 61:1-3) to a historical figure: Melchizedek, the priest of Salem encountered by Abraham in Genesis.[1359] Scholars have noted that several names are applied to Melchizedek that are usually names for God, such as the Hebrew "el" and "elohim," and in the author's citation of Isaiah 61:2, Melchizedek's name is even directly *substituted* for God's name, Yahweh. Scholars have debated whether Melchizedek is depicted as an angel or as an exalted human being in the Dead Sea Scrolls.[1360] Regardless, we have discovered

---

[1358] Buzzard notes that "Isaiah 51:16 confirms this explanation. It speaks of an agent of God in whom God puts his words and whom he uses to 'plant the heavens and the earth.' The *Word Biblical Commentary* says: 'That makes no sense if it refers to the original [Genesis] creation... In the other instances God acts alone, using no agent. Here the one he has hidden in the shadow of his hand is his agent. Heavens and land here must refer metaphorically to the totality of order in Palestine, heavens meaning the broader overarching structure of the Empire, while land is the political order in Palestine itself' (*WBC: Is 34-66* (Word Books, 1984), p. 212). Thus both in Psalm 102 (LXX) and in Isaiah the Messiah is the agent whom God will use to establish the new political order of the age to come" (Anthony F. Buzzard, *Jesus Was Not a Trinitarian*. McDonough: Restoration Fellowship, 2012), p. 423).

[1359] See *11QMelch, 4QAmram,* and *Songs of the Sabbath Sacrifice.*

[1360] See Michael Wise, Martin Abegg Jr., Edward Cook (ed.), *Dead Sea Scrolls: A New Translation* (San Francisco: Harper, 1996), p. 455. While analysts like Geza Vermes have suggested that the Melchizedek of the Dead Sea Scrolls should be identified with the archangel Michael, (Geza Vermes, *The Dead Sea Scrolls in English* (Sheffield: JSOT Press, 1987), p. 300), many scholars feel that the weight of the evidence lies in his identification as an exalted human being. David C. Mitchell explains that the way in which the Qumran writers present Melchizedek alongside other human messiahs clearly "indicates that their Melchizedek is a human priestly figure" (David C. Mitchell, *The Review of Rabbinic Judaism: Ancient, Medieval, and Modern*, Vol. VIII (Leiden: Brill, 2005), p. 87). Of course, the widespread rabbinic tradition that posited that Melchizedek was actually Shem, the son of Noah (See B. Ned. 32b, Lev. Rabbah 25:6), a theory which even Martin Luther subscribed to in the sixteenth century, requires a human being (See Martin Luther, *Lectures on Genesis*, 14.18).

first century Jewish sources reapplying Old Testament passages about Yahweh to a creature (either human or angelic) in a new and spiritual sense.

What then of Romans 10:13 and its application of "calling upon the name of the Lord" to Jesus? We now know that Paul, like the other New Testament writers, often read Old Testament passages in new contexts, and even applied Messianic prophecies to himself on the basis of his performing the same functions as the Messiah. It should therefore be quite easy to understand Paul's application of Romans 10:13 to Jesus: in the days of the Old Testament, people were to call upon the name of Yahweh for salvation (per Joel 2:32); after Christ's exaltation, however, people can now call on the name of the Lord Jesus for salvation. There is not intended here an identification of persons or being, but a transference or a sharing of duty or function from Yahweh to the exalted Messiah.[1361] As in other midrashic exercises, the original meaning of Joel 2:32 is not replaced by its reapplication in Romans 10:13.

The "divine identity" argument of Bauckham and others ultimately quashes the most important aspect of Paul's OT reapplication: the Messianic story behind it. To simply say that Paul is identifying Jesus *as* Yahweh, because he does the things that Yahweh does, skips over the fact that the Messiah was *exalted* and *given* all authority by God. Paul, in Romans 10:13, does not intend to say that "Jesus is Yahweh"—that would run contrary to his Pharisaic Judaism—but simply presupposes the New Testament narrative in which the one God exalted the man Jesus and transferred all authority to him.

Consider the weakness of this Trinitarian argument: In Joel 2:28, "God" says *"I will pour out of my spirit on all flesh."* But later Peter says that "Jesus" poured out the holy spirit in Acts 2:32-33. Thus the Trinitarian concludes that Jesus must be the God who spoke in the Old Testament.[1362] Again, this sort of reasoning represses both the biblical narrative and the essential mediatorial framework of Judaism through which that narrative runs. We cannot ignore the fact that the monotheism of the Bible is built on a long-standing system of mediation in which God interacts with agents who carry out his functions, and both the Old and New Testaments assume our familiarity with this structure. For example, in Ezekiel we read that "Yahweh" gave the commandments to Israel (Ezk 20:11). But in Joshua we read that it was "Moses" who gave the commandments to

---

[1361] One Catholic scholar writes that Psalm 110:1, which calls the Messiah to the right hand of God, and which is proclaimed fulfilled in Jesus on the Day of Pentecost (Acts 2:34), indicates that after the resurrection, "the exalted Jesus will in the future fulfill functions which are really functions of God himself" (Kuschel, p. 269).

[1362] See Bowman, *Putting Jesus in His Place*, pp. 219-221.

Israel (Josh 22:5). According to the Trinitarian argument, we should include Moses in the identity of Yahweh. Similarly, Paul says that the commandments were actually given by angels (Gal 3:19; Acts 7:53). Shouldn't the angels be identified as Yahweh as well? Of course, no one will argue for these shallow interpretations. It is understood that God gave the law to mediators who then gave it to the people of Israel. In the same way, God gave the spirit to the mediator Jesus (Jn 3:34; Matt 12:18), and Jesus then gave it to the people (Acts 2:32-33).

But let us imagine for a moment that the greatest, most stunning revelation awarded to the Apostles was that this *man* Jesus actually *was* the great Yahweh himself. One would hope that Paul might be clearer, or affix some helpful commentary to such a jaw-dropping assertion. Would Paul's readers gather from the unassisted application of this Yahweh passage in Romans 10:13 to a recently crucified man, that he was suddenly arguing that this Nazarene was the Jews' ancestral, immortal God? Especially if Paul provided every opinion to the contrary elsewhere? As some Trinitarian scholars have repeatedly admitted, "Paul habitually differentiates Christ from God,"[1363] and "Paul never equates Jesus with God."[1364] In light of this fair assessment, should we conclude that Paul suddenly *is* doing this very thing in Romans 10:13?

For the Trinitarians who argue that "Lord" (kurios) in the New Testament equals the "Yahweh" of the Old Testament, there might be other serious and probably unintended consequences. First, we find the Apostles expounding on Jesus' assumption of the status of "Lord" at the inauguration of the Church:

> *This Jesus God raised up again... Therefore let all the house of Israel know for certain that God has made him both Lord and Christ—this Jesus whom you crucified* (Acts 2:32a, 36).

According to the Apostles, God *made* Jesus "Lord." If "Lord" means "Yahweh," does this mean that Yahweh made Jesus Yahweh? Which seems more correct: Jesus was given lordship by God (in the sense that he was established as the master and superior of all things), or Jesus was given Yahwehship by God (he was made Yahweh himself in some sense)?

Some Trinitarians have suggested that Christ actually divested himself of his Yahwehship at the Incarnation, and at his exaltation was simply taking it back again, so in this sense he was *re-made* Yahweh. But the Apostles do not say that

---

[1363] C. J. Cadoux, *A Pilgrim's Further Progress* (London: Religious Book Club, 1945), p. 40, 42.
[1364] W. R. Matthews, *The Problem of Christ in the 20th Century* (Oxford: OUP, 1949), p. 22.

Jesus was taking lordship *back,* simply that God made him into something he was not. Second, how could someone who is Yahweh set aside his Yahwehship without ceasing to be Yahweh? That is not orthodox doctrine; the Son is supposed to have remained fully God even when uniting with a human nature. Thus others have claimed that it must have been his co-equality that he divested himself of, submitting to God the Father on earth, and it was his co-equality that he was resuming when he was made Lord. But this seems both impossible and contrary to orthodoxy. The three Persons are supposedly by nature co-eternal, co-essential, and co-equal; if the second Person of the Trinity was made fundamentally unequal to the others, then the three Persons are not, by necessity of nature, co-equal; they are only co-equal by agreement. Furthermore, how could the one God make any aspect of himself unequal with himself? Are we not speaking about one being? Surely the Jewish Apostles lacked both the means and the need to inform the churches of such grasping abstraction.

We should not think that Paul meant to say that the crucified Jesus *became* Yahweh in any sense. As Hastings writes, "We must avoid every kind of language which suggests that to St. Paul the ascension of Christ was deification. To the Jew the idea that a man might come to be God would have been an intolerable blasphemy... It may be that St. Paul *nowhere* names Christ 'God.' "[1365] It seems obvious then that Paul would not identify him as *Yahweh*, either. But if Paul does not mean by his application of this Old Testament passage that Jesus was transformed or remade into Yahweh in any sense, then what does he mean?

We should not forget that it was *after* Christ's resurrection that he was made "Lord" by God (Acts 2:32, 36).[1366] The reason for this exaltation was explicitly the selfless service he rendered to God (Phil 2:8-9). The ultimate aim of Jesus now being confessed as "Lord" is not merely the glorification of Jesus, but of the God who exalted him: "*Every tongue [that] acknowledge[s] that Jesus Christ is Lord [does so] to the glory of God the Father*" (Phil 2:11-12).

Upon reception of his great office, all authority was bestowed upon him; all matters in the universe were placed under his purview, though he remained

---

[1365] Hastings, pp. 707-708, emphasis added.

[1366] The use of the title "Lord" for the pre-resurrection Jesus in the Gospel narrative may be understood as an identification of his kingly status as God's son, but may also demonstrate the writer's post-resurrection perspective. Dunn writes: " 'Prime Minister Wilson studied economics at Oxford.' No one misunderstands the phrase to mean that Harold Wilson was already Prime Minister when he was at Oxford (though it is the "natural" meaning of the sentence). Each one who reads it consciously or unconsciously interprets it as saying (in more precise language): 'Harold Wilson, who later became Prime Minister, studied economics at Oxford' " (Dunn, *Christology*, p. 334, n. 121).

subject to only God (1 Cor 1:27). As one scholar writes, "Jesus is not God but God's representative, and, as such, so completely acts on God's behalf that he stands in God's stead before the world."[1367] Another scholar explains Paul's application of Lord in this context: "When [the Apostles] assigned Jesus such honorific titles as Christ, Son of Man, Son of God and Lord, these were ways of saying not that he was God but that he did God's work."[1368] Therefore, God's role as the source of salvation was transferred to Jesus, when he had not enjoyed it previously. This is not speculation, but the straightforward witness of the New Testament:

> *And having been made perfect, he <u>became</u> to all those who obey him the source of eternal salvation* (Hebrews 5:9).

Here we see that Jesus has undergone some great change, a perfection, an exaltation; only after this process was complete did he become the one to whom people may look for salvation. Of course, people have always been able to call on Yahweh for salvation, and whoever went to him received it. But now, in the new scheme of things, salvation is to be found in the man Jesus Christ. Recalling the exemplary relationship between Joseph and the Pharaoh who made him "lord" over Egypt (Gen 41:40, Ps 105:21), we find that people had previously gone to Pharaoh for their needs, but upon Joseph's installment as viceroy, Pharaoh told them, *"Go to Joseph"* (Gen 41:55). In Romans 10:13, Paul is saying precisely this: everyone who goes to Jesus will be saved. Yet another scholar confirms Paul's view: "The Pauline Christ who accomplishes the work of salvation is a personality who is both human and superhuman, not God, but the Son of God."[1369]

Ultimately, we should not conclude that the application of God's names or titles to Jesus, even in a citation of the Old Testament, means they are one and the same being. Biblically speaking, if two individuals are given the same honorific, even a high and lordly title, they are not to be viewed as one identity. On Jesus' robe and on his thigh he has a name written, *"King of kings, and lord of lords"* (Rev 19:16), and God himself is given the title *"King of kings"* in 1 Timothy 6:15. But this cannot prove that they are the same, since King Artaxerxes is also called *"the King of kings"* (Ezra 26:7), and Daniel calls King Nebuchadnezzar by this same title in Daniel 2:37. The New Testament's use of princely titles for the

---

[1367] Jacob Jervell, *Jesus in the Gospels* (Minneapolis: Augsburg Publishing House, 1984), p. 21.

[1368] G. H. Boobyer, "Jesus as Theos in the New Testament," *Bulletin of the John Rylands Library 1967-1968*, Vol. 50 (Manchester University Press, 1968), p. 250.

[1369] See Maurice Goguel, *Jesus and the Origins of Christianity* (New York: Harper, 1960), p. 109.

exalted Christ, and even the application of Yahweh texts to him, is easily explained by the midrashic interpretation of Scripture used by the Apostles, their understanding of the Hebrew "law of agency" (in which a representative figure bears the authority and name of his commissioner), and by the fact that God explicitly *made* Jesus "Lord." Because the New Testament already explains that God's power, name, and authority were *given* to Jesus by his God, there is no need to seek out another explanation. We do not have to assume that Jesus must somehow be Yahweh himself. In light of 1 Corinthians 15:27-28, Jesus is to be viewed as God's exalted, but subordinate, agent. As McGrath notes: "Monotheism is preserved not because Jesus is absorbed into God or included in the divine identity but because even though Jesus reigns over absolutely everything else on God's behalf, God himself is not subjected to Christ, but Christ is subjected to God."[1370]

In conclusion, we will continue emphasize, as many scholars have already admitted, that, "When the New Testament writers speak of Jesus Christ, they do not speak of him nor do they think of him as God."[1371] This includes, of course, the aforementioned titular applications. Another Oxford professor judiciously reinforces the fact that throughout the New Testament, "We are not to suppose that the apostles identified Christ with Jehovah; there were passages which made this impossible, for instance, Psalm 110:1."[1372] There is ultimately an impenetrable barrier preventing the Apostles from identifying even the glorified Messiah as their ancestral God, and too little reason for us to think they must have viewed him as anything other than the great flesh and bone man who walked and talked with them in Galilee, the man whom they touched and shared meals with even after his resurrection. To close this chapter regarding Christ's alleged deity, we will append the observation of one Professor of Biblical Studies which encapsulates our findings:

> The truth is that Jewish sources never thought of Messiah as divine or pre-existent—in mainstream Judaism he is the descendant of David's covenant in 2 Samuel 7... If Jesus thought of himself as Messiah it is this human figure that he had in mind, with the traditional terms "the Son of God," "the Son of Man," "Lord"—all used of human Jewish kings in the Psalter (2:7; 80:18; 110:1, etc.)... Being a monotheist, Jesus

---

[1370] McGrath, *The Only True God*, p. 50.

[1371] J. M. Creed, *The Divinity of Jesus Christ* (London: Fontana, 1964), pp. 122-123.

[1372] Charles Bigg, *International Critical Commentary on Peter and Jude* (Edinburgh: T & T Clark, 1910), p. 99.

cannot have thought of himself sanely as being Yahweh; and in the more primitive traditions he always speaks of himself in the human, messianic categories… [He did not think] he was God, but that he was God's viceroy… It is the bias of orthodoxy constantly to overlook middle terms. The earliest church [did not view him] as God the Son, but as the man whom God raised up and [assigned] the Holy Spirit to pour out upon the church (Acts 2:33).[1373]

[1373] Micahel Goulder, *Incarnation and Myth: the Debate Continued* (Grand Rapids: Eerdmans, 1979), p. 143.

13

THE WORSHIP OF THE LORD

"When I use a word," Humpty Dumpty said in a rather scornful tone, "it means just what I choose it to mean—neither more nor less."
> — *Lewis Carroll*

T HE WORSHIP OF JESUS IN THE NEW TESTAMENT is often presented as the greatest proof of his deity. Many modern Trinitarians, especially in evangelical circles, have reasoned this way: *Premise 1*: "Only God can be worshipped"; *Premise 2*: "Jesus was worshipped"; *Conclusion*: "Jesus is identical to God." Of course, if both premise 1 and 2 are correct, then this conclusion would also be correct. But if either premise is incorrect, then we need another solution. We will begin by acknowledging the validity of premise 2. It is absolutely true that Jesus is worshipped in the New Testament, both by various persons during his earthly ministry, and later, as the exalted Christ, by the whole world in Revelation. Our question will be, *in what sense* was Jesus worshipped? Was it *as God*, or as something else? If Jesus is a creature, then how did his worship fit with the established monotheism?

Trinitarians often wrongly define monotheism as not only the belief that there is only one God, but also as the belief that only one entity can be worshipped. The reason Trinitarians define monotheism in this way is simply because they hope to use the veneration of Jesus as proof of his deity. However, as Andrew Perry explains, the Jewish monotheism of the Bible is not defined by veneration practices, but simply by belief about *what there is* with regard to gods: *"there is only one God, the Father"* (1 Cor 8:6); *"I am Yahweh, and there is no other; Besides me there is no God"* (Is 45:5).[1374] As one scholar puts it, monotheism is simply "the theory, doctrine, or belief that there is but one God."[1375] This doctrine is clearly maintained by the Jews in the New Testament community, while at the same time "devotional practices for Christians have been enlarged to include *confession* about Christ."[1376] The earliest Christian confession about Jesus was not, as we have seen, confession that he is Yahweh, rather that he is the Davidic lord and Messiah of God. Thus our proposition in this chapter will be that the worship of Jesus in the New Testament does not represent any violation or update to Jewish monotheism. Jesus is not worshipped *as God*, but receives worship in a secondary sense as God's *son* and *agent* whom God has exalted. There is no worship of the man Jesus *in neglect* of God, but a worship of Jesus in *obedience* to God who commanded it (Heb 1:6).

Worship According to the Biblical Worldview

As for premise 1, that "Only God can be worshipped," the Bible itself immediately proves this statement false. The worship of various individuals who are obviously not the one true God can be easily found throughout the Scriptures. These non-deity persons receive worship without refusal or correction, and some are even worshipped *alongside* God. For example, in the Old Testament, Daniel was worshiped by the king of Babylon:

> *Then King Nebuchadnezzar fell on his face, and worshipped Daniel, and commanded that they should offer an oblation and sweet odours unto him. The king answered unto Daniel, and said, Of a truth it is, that your God is a God of gods, and a Lord of kings, and a revealer of secrets, seeing thou couldest reveal this secret* (Daniel 2:46-47 KJV).

Daniel did not correct their worship of him, nor did he refuse their offerings. Was Daniel then committing blasphemy? Was he wrongly receiving what God reserves only for himself? Elsewhere in the Old Testament we find that David, the King of Israel, was even worshipped *together* with God:

[1374] Andrew Perry, "Jewish Monotheism in the First Century," *One God, the Father* (East Bolden: Willow, 2013), pp. 40-55. Thanks to Brian Wright for this notice.

[1375] G. F. Moore, quoted Ibid.

[1376] Ibid., p. 55, emphasis his.

*And all the congregation blessed the LORD God of their fathers, and
bowed down their heads, and worshipped the LORD, and the king.*
(1 Chronicles 29:20 KJV)[1377]

Though here we find both God and David being "worshipped" by the
people, surely we do not think that they are being worshipped in the same way.
We also find that the people of Israel themselves are to be "worshipped" and
even "prayed to" by their enemies (Isaiah 45:14). Abraham also "worships" the
heathen people of the land (Gen 23:7). Are these being recognized as deity?
When Israel worships King David, has it forgotten God's commandment, *"you
shall worship no other gods before me"* (Ex 34:14)? Surely not. Worship is obviously
able to be given to authoritative figures who are not the one God while avoiding
a betrayal of monotheism.

What then does "worship" really mean? In Hebrew it is represented by the
word *"shachah,"* a verb which literally means to "do homage by prostration"[1378]
or to "bow down" or "fall down."[1379] The same Hebrew word is used to
describe the activity paid both to God (Gen 24:48), and to non-deities (Gen
23:7). The New Testament follows suit: the Greek word is "proskuneo," a verb
which literally means "by kneeling or prostration to do homage"[1380] or to "bow
down, bow before."[1381] Again, the same word is used to describe the activity
paid to both God (Rev 16:12), and to non-deities (Matt 18:26).

"Worship" therefore, in the biblical sense, is not something able to be given
only to the one God. While the bodily position may look the same (prostrated),
the attitude of the heart, the inner motive, must be different. We may
understand this easily when we consider that while we stand in honor when
either a county judge or the President of the United States enters the room, we
are standing and honoring them for different reasons. Therefore, if Jesus were
really a man, the exalted King of Israel, and not God, it would still be acceptable
for a Jew to "worship" him, say, in a similar way to King David. Of course,
worshipping any man *as the one true God* would be unacceptable per Exodus
34:14. According to that specific commandment, it seems not that God forbade

---

[1377] The *Septuagint* translates the "worship" of 1 Chron 29:20 as the Greek "προσεκύνησαν," or
"proskeynesan"; there is no doubt that the same act received by Jesus in Revelation is received by
David in the Old Testament.

[1378] *Brown-Driver-Briggs Hebrew and English Lexicon*, 2002.

[1379] *NAS Exhaustive Concordance of the Bible with Hebrew-Aramaic and Greek Dictionaries*, 1981. The
Lockman Foundation.

[1380] *Thayer's Greek Lexicon, Strong's* NT 4352.

[1381] *NAS Exhaustive Concordance*, 1981.

the "worship" of anyone besides him, but that he forbade the "worship" of anyone else *as their God*, in preference to him. Of course, according to Jesus, the specific worship *as God* should be given, by the true worshippers, to *"the Father"* (Jn 4:21ff).

Nevertheless, it is routinely claimed by Trinitarians that persons in the New Testament worshipped Jesus explicitly as deity. It is postulated that because we have no record that he publicly corrected anyone who worshipped him, then he would be guilty of stealing God's own glory for himself were he not God. But did Jesus himself believe the various persons in the Gospels were giving him the specific honor due only to God, against his own regular instructions to *"worship the Father"* as God (Jn 4:23)? What he privately thought about their activity towards him is not stated, though he certainly appears complicit in receiving whatever they were offering. Yet as many Trinitarians have admitted, the doctrine of the Trinity, or even the deity of Christ, were not things known to the Jews at this time. Thus it already seems unreasonable to conclude that the Jews meant to pay Jesus the specific honor due only to Almighty God, or that he himself regarded these instances of worship as anything beyond the proper adoration paid to persons of great office. His audience always spoke of him as a man among them, and while many of them believed him to be the prophesied Messiah, even Trinitarians admit that none of the Jews believed or expected the Messiah to be God.[1382]

We wonder then if *translation bias* could have anything to do with the common perception that Jesus was worshipped as God in the New Testament. Indeed, what real evidence is there, in the biblical data alone, which unequivocally demonstrates that his worship by the Jews was the kind reserved only for a deity, and *not* the sort offered to other human or angelic superiors? Is there any?

[1382] The worship of Christ in the Gospels is actually theologically benign, neither proving nor disproving anything about a hypothetical "inner divine nature." Many scholars have affirmed that "Such worship affords no proof that Jesus was a divine being. His character must be determined by other evidence" (Lucius Robinson Paige, *A Commentary on the New Testament,* Vol. 1 (Boston: Benjamin B. Mussey, 1849), p. 92). One Anglican priest writes, "The Jews paid civil adoration, both to kings and prophets, either by bending of the knee, or by prostration, or falling down before them... Whence I conclude, that the adorations given to our blessed Saviour, by those Jews and Gentiles who knew nothing of his Divinity, could be no argument of his divine nature, but rather were paid to him as the Messiah, or as a prophet sent from God, or as the King of Israel" (Daniel Whitby, "Annotations on [Matthew] Chap. VIII," *A Critical Commentary and Paraphrase on the Old and New Testaments,* Vol. 5 (London: Richard Preistly, 1822), p. 103).

Translations Forcing the Worship of Deity

It is perhaps here more than any other area of Christological investigation that we encounter one of the staunchest companions of orthodox interpretation in the battle for hearts and minds: *translation bias*. When translation committees, particularly those interested in defending the post-Nicene portrait of Jesus, become so narrowly focused on a single interpretation of a word, and exclude other tenable meanings except where theologically expedient, much trouble is made for the Bible student. Those Christians interested in education have come eagerly to the experts, to the professional exegetes; they have entrusted their understanding to the committee's dedication to lexical accuracy and expect the surest possible interpretation of languages beyond their own reach. Yet in many instances the communication of the Bible is frustrated by a severe inclination towards translation choices which serve more to justify certain doctrinal investments than to offer the full breadth of understanding behind culturally-empowered historical terms. Few cases better illustrate this issue than the Greek word "proskuneo," the word sometimes translated as "worship" in English versions of the New Testament.

Above all, we must allow the Bible to breathe. The writers operated not in a vacuum but in a living culture which must be consulted beyond the rigid fiat of orthodox interpretation. When we visit the ancient world of the Bible we are at once confronted by a system of public demonstrations of hierarchy, that is, body language which visibly communicated superiority and inferiority between members in that environment. Kissing another's feet, falling to one's knees, or bowing low with one's face to the ground immediately indicated awe, respect, or deference to another person of higher rank, and in Jesus' day such expressions were commonplace. The prime Greek vehicle of this sentiment in the New Testament is the aforementioned Greek word "proskuneo," which *Thayer's* defines as: "to do reverence," "to do obeisance," "to kiss," and of course, "to worship." Again, this worship-gesture, or family of gestures, was not reserved only for God, but was offered between all varieties of hierarchical parties. Debtors kissed the feet of their lenders, servants bowed before their masters, subdued nations paid homage in the dust before their conquerors—it was simply a full-bodied indication of one's reverence.

While the modern English word "*worship*" once carried a much broader meaning, a meaning more aligned with the breadth of the Greek "proskuneo," it has since taken on a much more constricted role. Today when a Christian uses the word "worship," he is almost always indicating a religious veneration which he feels should be reserved only for God. While it was not wrong for older English translations such as the *King James Version* to translate the Greek word "proskuneo" as the English word "worship" in 1611 CE, a time when human kings and lords were commonly referred to as *"your worship,"* to continue to use the now much-restricted "worship" for all instances of "proskuneo," or even worse to use it selectively of certain subjects when one wishes to cast them in a certain religious light, is imprudent at best. If a certain term, like the English "worship," has taken on a different meaning in our time, such a shift should be accounted for in translation. Should we not expect modern translations to use modern language? We would, unless there was something to gain by the retention of antiquated linguistic forms which now suggest something more theologically profound than they once did.

Our complaint in this regard is that many modern translators, due to Christological bias, deliberately translate "proskuneo" as *"bow down,"* or *"pay homage"* when the action is directed to other men, but translate it as *"worship"* when directed towards Jesus. Though the word only indicates an act of submission, the term is suddenly transformed, via an advantageous reversion to the KJV's "worship," into a public recognition of deity. We find an apt example of this bias in popular English versions of the story of the rich man in Matthew 18:26. Observe here how popular mainstream translations *do not* use the *King James Version's* rendering of the word; they rightly avoid the antiquated "worship" due to the word's modern shift in meaning:

KJV: *The servant therefore fell down, and <u>worshipped him</u>, saying, Lord, have patience with me, and I will pay thee all.*

NIV: *At this the servant <u>fell on his knees</u> before him. "Be patient with me," he begged, "and I will pay back everything."*

NASB: *So the slave fell to the ground and <u>prostrated himself</u> before him, saying, "Have patience with me and I will repay you everything."*

The translators do not want anyone to make the mistake that the servant is offering the rich man religious veneration as God, thus the *King James* tradition is neglected.

We find another example of this reasonable practice in Revelation 3:9: Here the risen Jesus, speaking through an angel, says that he will make wicked persons "proskuneo" at the feet of Christians at the end of the age. Of course, no one argues that Jesus intends the wicked to worship Christians in a way that should be meant only for God; therefore the translators once again correctly refrain from the KJV's rendering:

KJV: *I will make them to come and <u>worship before thy feet</u>, and to know that I have loved thee.*

NIV: *I will make them come and <u>fall down at your feet</u> and acknowledge that I have loved you.*

NASB: *I will make them come and <u>bow down at your feet</u>, and make them know that I have loved you.*

These translation choices all seem appropriate thus far. But observe how this same word "proskuneo" is suddenly handled by these same translators when used of Jesus:

KJV: *And as they went to tell his disciples, behold, Jesus met them, saying, All hail. And they came and held him by the feet, and <u>worshipped him</u>.*

NIV: *Suddenly Jesus met them. "Greetings," he said. They came to him, clasped his feet and <u>worshiped him</u>.*

NASB: *And behold, Jesus met them and greeted them. And they came up and took hold of His feet and <u>worshiped Him</u>.*

Why do the translators feel the need to suddenly revert to the KJV tradition here? Though the word is used fifty-eight times in the New Testament, why do only the instances in which it is used of Jesus or God receive a translation that suggests a certain religious devotion? Dr. BeDuhn explains:

> It is always *possible* that the *interpretation* of the significance of the gesture may be correct (that the people are worshipping Jesus as God). But the simple translation "prostrate," or "do homage," or "do obeisance" is *certainly* correct. So the question is raised, why depart from a certain, accurate translation to a questionable, possibly inaccurate one? The answer is that,

when this occurs, the translators seem to feel the need to add to the New Testament support for the idea that Jesus was recognized to be God. But the presence of such an idea cannot be supported by selectively translating a word one way when it refers to Jesus and another way when it refers to someone else. Since such "acts of worship" are made to others beside Jesus in the New Testament, and Jesus even tells a story in which such a gesture is made to an ordinary person, we can rule out the idea that "prostration" means "worship" in the modern sense of the English word. When we observe how these same translators choose "worship" when the gesture is made to Jesus by certain persons, and choose other English words to translate the very same Greek term when the gesture is directed to someone other than Jesus, or is directed to Jesus by someone whom they regard as not qualifying as a true believer, their inconsistency reveals their bias. They might argue that the context of belief surrounding Jesus implies that the gesture is more than "obeisance" or "homage." It's not a very good argument, because in most of the passages the people who make the gesture know next to nothing about Jesus, other than that it is obvious or rumored that he has power to help them.[1383]

BeDuhn's note is worth observing, that Trinitarian translators deliberately translate the word differently if they perceive the worshippers as not having what they believe is proper theology. Observe in Mark 15:17-19 the Roman soldiers mistreating Jesus:

KJV: *And they clothed him with purple, and platted a crown of thorns, and put it about his head, And began to salute him, Hail, King of the Jews! And they smote him on the head with a reed, and did spit upon him, and bowing their knees <u>worshipped him</u>.*

NIV: *They kept beating His head with a reed, and spitting on Him, and kneeling and <u>bowing before him</u>.*

[1383] BeDuhn, pp. 47-48, emphasis added.

NASB: *Again and again they struck him on the head with a staff and spit on him. Falling on their knees, they paid homage to him.*

The Trinitarian translators believe that the Romans do not view this man in a Trinitarian sense; that is, they do not properly believe that this man also has a divine nature, or that he *is* God. So their "worship" is branded in the translation as the kind paid to non-deity. But to the translators, those who loved Jesus *must* have viewed him in a Trinitarian sense; thus their "worship" is presented as something reserved only for God. Of course, this is *not* translation. This is not an unadorned presentation of raw biblical data with the intention of letting believers read and draw their own conclusions. This is top-down speculative theologizing of the worst kind. Dr. BeDuhn makes a tragic and pointed observation in this regard:

> The Reformation fought for the access of all believers to the Bible and the right of the individual to directly encounter and interpret the text. Modern translators undermine that cause when they publish interpretations rather than translations, still trying to direct readers to the understanding acceptable to the beliefs and biases of the translators themselves.[1384]

One further Gospel episode should put to rest the argument that "proskuneo," when used of Jesus, must indicate religious or faith-induced "worship" as God:

> But the eleven disciples proceeded to Galilee, to the mountain which Jesus had designated. When they saw him, *they worshiped him; but some were doubtful* (Matthew 28:16-17 NASB).

If it is true, as Trinitarians claim, that the disciples' "proskuneo" designates a modern sense of worship, a confession or acknowledgment of deity, then we must ask how they could both "worship" and doubt simultaneously. Obviously this is impossible; they were either both cognitively and faithfully acknowledging Jesus as their God or they were doubting that he was their God. In another context we might say that one could not both publicly confess and truly believe that John Doe is the only true President of the United States, and simultaneously doubt that he is the only true President of the United States. It should therefore be obvious that the word "proskuneo," even when used towards Jesus as it is

---

[1384] Ibid.

here, indicates only a visible act of submission and reverence and does not necessarily say anything about the prostrator's attitude towards the object's potential deity.

Ultimately, in the biblical model, even if Jesus were not God, public gestures of adoration towards him during his earthly ministry would have been culturally acceptable and would not have interfered with the Jews' acknowledgment of Yahweh as their only God. But what about the worship of the *glorified* Jesus? Does the Book of Revelation, which paints Jesus as being highly exalted, sitting on a throne of glory, and judging the world, demonstrate that the earliest Christians paid the *heavenly* Jesus worship as God?

Exaltation in Second Temple Judaism

Late Second Temple Jews, including Jesus and his Apostles, were rather flexible in distributing praise and honor to creatures. We can easily observe that even the heavenly exaltation of figures outside the Godhead was not viewed as blasphemous during this phase of Judaism. For example, in the first-century CE Jewish work *The Testament of Abraham*, the first human being Adam is exalted and seated on a golden throne, oversees the souls of men, and is *"adorned with glory"* (11:1ff). Similarly, in the second-century BCE Jewish drama *The Exagoge*, Moses is put upon a throne and made the judge of the world by God. Moses says, *"I had a vision of a great throne... a noble man was sitting on it... He gave me the scepter and instructed me to sit on the great throne. Then he gave me the royal crown and got up from the throne... A multitude of stars fell before my knees"* (v. 70-60). Another character explains the vision's meaning: *"You will establish a great throne, and become a judge and leader of men"* (v. 85). In the Dead Sea Scrolls document 11Q13 we of course have the Melchizedek figure (either a human priest or an angel) who is set above the world as *"your God"* and designated as a great judge, even *"judging the holy ones of God."* And in yet another work, the 1st-3rd-century BCE *Book of Enoch*, which the Apostles were demonstrably familiar with (and even quote),[1385] we find a similarly exalted figure. An individual named the Son of Man sits on the *"throne*

[1385] *1 Enoch* (either 1:9 or 2:1 depending on edition) is directly quoted in Jude 1:14-15. Griggs writes that "this work, accepted as inspired and canonical in many Jewish and Christian circles from the second century BCE, was quoted as scripture in Jude and, according to Charles, 'has had more influence on the New Testament than has any other apocryphal or pseudepigraphic work' " (Griggs, p. 7). After the publication of the DSS, it became obvious that Enoch influenced the NT. For example, consider 1 En 5:7 *"the elect... shall inherit the earth"*, and Matt 5:5 *"the meek... shall inherit the earth"*; 1 En 69:27 *"judgement was assigned to him, the Son of Man"* and Jn 5:22 *"the Father... has assigned all judgment unto the Son"*; 1 En 100:3-4 *"the horses will wade through the blood... it will come up to their chest"* and Rev 14:20 *"Blood came out of the winepress and came up to the horses' bridles."*

of glory" (51:3; 55:4; 61:8, etc.), judges mankind (51:2-3), and is worshipped—"*all who dwell on earth shall fall down and worship before him*" (48:5). It is important to note, however, that here "it is not implied that the Son of Man is worshipped as the supreme God, but rather that people perform *proskynesis* before him in recognition of his authority."[1386] This is all said to be done for him "*because the Lord of Spirits has given them to him and has glorified him*" (51:3). Richard Bauckham's popular "Divine Identity Christology" view seems to falter here as well, as even Bauckham admits that *Enoch's* Son of Man figure "is the exception that [tests] the rule" that only God is able to be worshipped.[1387]

There is another important Second Temple source which features the worship of beings who are not God, while demonstrating no infringement of Jewish monotheism: the first-century *Life of Adam and Eve*. In previous chapters we reviewed Paul and other New Testament writers' "Adam Christology." Hebrews 2:6, citing Psalm 8:4, had described Jesus as the "son of man/adam," drawing on Jesus' own self-identification as the eschatological "one like a son of man" of Daniel 7:13.[1388] The Apostle Paul, even more explicitly, designated Jesus as "*the second Adam*" (1 Cor 15:45), and furthermore identified the first Adam as "*a type of him who was to come*" (Rom 5:14). Paul clearly saw God's enthronement of Jesus as a fulfillment of God's original delegation of rulership over the earth to Adam. To Paul, Adam was one made "in the image of God" who failed to live up to his potential, while Jesus was the "image of God" who succeeded. In the *Life of Adam and Eve* we find material that Paul was evidently familiar with, which sheds further light on the worship of Jesus, the second Adam, as "the image of God" in the New Testament. In *Life* we read of a conversation between Satan and Adam, in which Satan explains that he was disgraced because he refused God's command to worship Adam.[1389] Satan says:

> *When you were formed... God then said: "Behold, Adam, I have made you in our image and likeness." Having gone forth Michael called all the angels saying: "Worship the image of the Lord God, just as the Lord God has commanded." Michael himself worshipped first then he called me and said: "Worship the image of God Yahweh." I answered: "I do not have it within me to worship Adam." When Michael compelled me to worship, I said to him: "Why do you compel me? I will not worship him who is*

[1386] Collins, *King and Messiah as Son of God*, p. 206.

[1387] Bauckham, p. 171.

[1388] See Marcus, "Son of Man as Son of Adam" *Revue Biblique*, Vol. 110, pp. 38-61.

[1389] This story of Satan's rejection of the worship of Adam is also retold in the Qur'an, evidencing the widespread popularity of the ideas expressed. See Qur'an 2:34, 7:11-13, 17:61-62.

lower and posterior to me. I am prior to that creature. Before he was made, I had already been made. He ought to worship me." Hearing this, other angels who were under me were unwilling to worship him. Michael said: "Worship the image of God. If you do not worship, the Lord God will grow angry with you." I said: "If he grows angry with me, I will place my seat above the stars of heaven and I will be like the Most High." Then the Lord God grew angry with me and sent me forth with my angels from our glory. On account of you we were expelled from our dwelling... By a trick I cheated your wife and caused you to be expelled through her... just as I had been expelled from my glory (13:2-16:3).

Adam was to be worshipped, or paid homage, because he bore the *"image of God"* (Gen 1:27). For Paul, all of mankind was indeed created to be *"the image and glory of God"* (1 Cor 11:7). But the first Adam, for Paul, was an example of a disobedient humanity which failed to live up to its potential. Jesus, on the other hand, was also *"the image of God"* (Col 1:15, 2 Cor 4:4), but one who represented a successful and obedient humanity who properly exhibited God's glory. Just as Adam was to be honored as God's image before he disobeyed, Jesus was now likewise to be paid homage, according to Paul, precisely because of his obedience, because of his maintenance of God's image (Phil 2:6-11).

It is possible that the imagery of the *Life of Adam and Eve* influenced Paul's presentation of his Adam Christology. Paul does appear familiar with this work; in 2 Corinthians 11:14 Paul says that Satan *"disguises himself as an angel of light"*—an apparent allusion to the *Life of Adam and Eve* which says that Satan *"transfigured himself into the brilliance of an angel"* (9:1). The New Testament community may have thus been familiar with the book's Adamic worship as God's image. Scholars have postulated that if Paul was not directly referencing the text, then Paul and the author of *Life of Adam* were near contemporaries who "moved in the same circle of ideas."[1390] In this circle, the worship of Adam, a man, was not thought to infringe Jewish monotheism, but was obedience to God's command.

As Perry concludes, "The exaltation of Jesus to a position next to God is shocking if you have a low estimate of humanity. The purpose of man was to be an image of God and to exercise dominion (Gen 1:26-27). The exaltation of Jesus is a fulfillment of this divine intention."[1391] Indeed, many Christians who

---

[1390] Wells, *APOT*, Vol. 2, p. 130 as cited by James H. Charlesworth, *The Old Testament Pseudepigrapha*, Vol. 2 (Peabody: Hendrickson Publishers, 1983), p. 255.
[1391] Perry, p. 52.

claim to hold a "High Christology" often hold a low anthropology. But as Perry recommends:

> we should have a high anthropology in terms of the intended destiny of man. The conviction that Jesus was exalted to heaven, or that Jews believed figures such as Enoch had been so exalted, does not give us ground for defining monotheism to include whoever has been exalted; such individuals were men and the visions that describe them distinguish them from God.[1392]

Is Worshipping Jesus Idolatry?

We have already determined that Jesus was, in some sense, worshipped in the New Testament. Therefore premise 2 from our aforementioned argument, that "Jesus was worshipped," still stands. However, premise 1, that in the biblical worldview "Only God can be worshipped," already seems, in light of a survey of both the Bible and other Jewish literature, ready to fall. Nevertheless, many will doubtlessly continue to assert it, citing various references from Revelation and Exodus to prove that if Jesus is not God, Jesus cannot be worshipped in a biblical sense.

It is true that Exodus clearly says, *"for you shall not worship any other god"* (Ex 34:14), and the pre-exaltation Jesus, being a good Jew, strongly agrees: *"For it is written, 'You shall worship the Lord your God, and serve him only' "* (Matt 4:10). But we should understand that both references here are to deity-worship. A closer examination of the language in Matthew 4:10 is useful: the "worship" in this passage is the usual "proskuneo/proskynein," but the word "serve," which is what Jesus actually describes as belonging to God only, is the Greek "latreuein." This word is also usually translated "worship" in English editions, but it refers to a particular kind of "cultic" worship that is awarded to deities. In the Bible, this word only refers to the special worship of God, and is never used to describe the honors paid to Jesus (Jn 16:2; Rom 9:4; Heb 9:1, 6). Dunn explains:

> ["Latreuein"] basically means "to serve." In biblical literature, however, the reference is always to religious service, the carrying out of religious duties, "to render cultic service." So it is not surprising that it appears in conjunction with proskynein in (once again) Jesus' reply to the temptation to worship other than God: "(You shall) worship the Lord your God and (shall)

[1392] Ibid.

serve (latreuseis) only him" (Matt. 4:10/Luke 4:8). And in several passages latreuein is translated "worship" in English translations. It is noticeable that in each case the object of the verb, the one who is (to be) served/worshipped, is God. Apart from one or two references to false worship, the reference is always to the cultic service/worship of God. In no case in the New Testament is there talk of offering cultic worship (latreuein) to Jesus.[1393]

This fact weakens the proposition of those who continue to claim that the same "cultic" worship of Yahweh was given to Jesus by the earliest Christians. We will soon investigate this claims further, but we should first recognize that both the Old Testament and the New Testament agree that only one entity should be worshipped *as God*. The God of Moses and of Jesus certainly demands the specific religious service awarded to deities and reserves it for himself; "worship" is still permitted of other beings, however, as evidenced by the fact that in both the *Septuagint* version of the Old Testament and in the New Testament many persons other than God receive worship ("proskynesis").

It may also be interesting to note that even though it was permitted for him, we actually never find the Jesus of the Gospels personally seeking "worship" from his audience. In fact, he explicitly states that receiving glory from mankind was not his intention: "*I do not accept glory from human beings*" (Jn 5:41 NIV), or "*I do not accept human praise*" (ISV); a seemingly strange thing to say for the God who always requires praise from men. Instead, Jesus attests, "*I am not seeking glory for myself, but there is one who seeks it, and he is the judge*" (Jn 8:50). Jesus only anticipates the fulfillment of God's desire to glorify him, specifically, an exaltation foretold of the Messiah from ancient times (Ps 110:1; Mk 12:36). Nevertheless, Jesus, in his earthly life, often received the honor or worship given to him by other men, and, according to the narrative, refrained from correcting them. We have already seen it is highly improbable that he was being worshipped as God by the Jews, and we know at least, by his own admission, that receiving glory from men was neither his expectation nor his goal, but he believed he would receive in the future a glory that was promised to him by God upon the fulfillment of his work, that is, after the resurrection.

Upon Christ's exaltation to heaven, things changed. Evidently, God now *commanded* the worship of Jesus. The Apostles indeed declared that an incredible

---

[1393] James Dunn, *Did the First Christians Worship Jesus?*, p. 13.

change had taken place in the heavens: previously this Jesus had not been exalted, but now *"this man, after he had offered one sacrifice for sins for ever, sat down at the right hand of God"* (Heb 10:12 KJV), and *"God placed all things under his feet and appointed him to be head over everything for the church"* (Eph 1:22). It is at the awarding of this status that God commands: *"Let all the angels of God worship him!"* (Heb 1:6). Apparently, they had not been expected or required to worship him before his exaltation, for looking more closely at Hebrews 1:6, it says *"And <u>when he again brings the firstborn into the world</u>, he says, 'And let all the angels of God worship him'"* (NASB). The time when God *again* brings him into the world, is likely a reference to God's resurrection of Jesus from the dead.[1394] Paul writes that God *"raised Christ from the dead and seated him at his right hand in the heavenly realms"* (Eph 1:20). Peter writes: *"through the resurrection of Jesus Christ, who is at the right hand of God, having gone into heaven, after angels and authorities and powers had been subjected to him"* (1 Pet 3:22). It should be quite obvious that it was after Jesus had been exalted that subjection to and worship of Christ was demanded by God; this was something new. The same God who had commanded, *"you shall not worship any other gods"* (Ex 34:14), was now commanding worship of Jesus. But did God mean that the man Jesus should be worshipped *as the one true God?*

Revelation paints a glorious picture of the exalted Jesus receiving worship alongside God. Beginning first with the worship of the one God, we read:

> *Immediately I was in the spirit; and behold, a throne was standing in heaven, and one sitting on the throne. And he who was sitting was like a jasper and a sardius in appearance… the twenty-four elders will fall down before him who sits on the throne, and will worship him who lives forever and ever, and will cast their crowns before the throne, saying, "Worthy are you, our Lord and our God, to receive glory and honor and power; for you created all things, and because of your will they existed, and were created* (Revelation 4:2, 3a-10b-11).

This one is obviously Yahweh, the one whom Jesus calls Father, and is the same ancient figure who was seen sitting on this same heavenly throne in the visions of Isaiah, Micaiah, Daniel and others.[1395] But now we find someone *new* introduced into the picture:

[1394] See Col 1:18: *"He is also the head of the body, the church; and he is the beginning, <u>the firstborn from the dead</u>, so that he himself will come to have first place in everything"* (NASB); *"Jesus Christ… <u>the firstborn of the dead</u>"* (Rev 1:5 NASB).

[1395] *"In the year of King Uzziah's death I saw the Lord sitting on a throne, lofty and exalted, with the train of hi robe filling the temple"* (Is 6:1); *"I saw the LORD sitting on his throne ith all the multitudes of heaven standing*

Behold, the lion that is from the tribe of Judah, the root of David, has overcome so as to open the book and its seven seals." And I saw between the throne... a Lamb standing, as if slain... And he came and took the book out of the right hand of him who sat on the throne. When he had taken the book, the four living creatures and twenty-four elders fell down before the Lamb... And they sang a __new__ song, saying, "Worthy are you to take the book and to break tis seals; for you were slain, and purchased for God with your blood men from every tribe and tongue and people and nation... Worthy is the Lamb that was slain to receive power and riches and wisdom and might and honor and glory and blessing." And every created thing which is in heaven and on the earth and under the earth and on the sea, and all things in them, I heard saying, "To him who sits on the throne, __and__ to the Lamb, be blessing and honor and glory and dominion forever and ever." And the four living creatures kept saying, "Amen." And the elders fell down and worshipped
(Revelation 5:5b-6-9, 12-14).

There are plainly two distinct recipients of worship here: the Lamb, and the one who sits on the throne, who is the Lord God Almighty. Because of this text, historian Larry Hurtado postulates that the earliest Jewish Christians were worshipping both Jesus and the Father in a full and equal sense. This worship, he argues, was not the kind given to other agents of God.[1396] He writes:

> these two distinguishable yet closely related figures are referred to and treated as the rightful and sole recipients of the sorts of devotional actions that early Christians characteristically refused to offer to other figures, whether humans (e.g., the Roman Emperor), heavenly beings such as angels, or, most emphatically, other putative deities... early Christian circles exhibited their derivation from, and continuing faithfulness to, the strong Jewish religious scruple against undue reverence of anything or anyone other than the one God, a scruple that the

---

around him on his right and on his left" (1 Kings 22:19); *"I kept looking until thrones were set up, and the Ancient of Days took his seat..."* (Dan 7:9).

[1396] Hurtado, *Lord Jesus Christ*, p. 592.

The Worship of the Lord

Christian movement inherited from its Jewish religious matrix.[1397]

This is what Hurtado calls a "binitarian" view among the earliest Jesus community, perhaps an evolution of the original Jewish monotheism which came to include Jesus in the full reverence of Yahweh.[1398] But there are several fundamental problems with Hurtado's binitarian-worship thesis. As we will soon discover, this "inherited Jewish religious matrix" exhibits the very characteristics Hurtado claims it excludes.

First, Hurtado contends that the earliest Christianity prohibited offering the devotional acts that Jesus receives in Revelation to human beings. But in that book, the prime devotional act is the world's "proskynesis," or prostration before Christ. It cannot be asserted that this devotion was clearly the kind paid only to the one God and not to other agents, since the Christians themselves are found to also receive "proskynesis" from the world, and by Christ's own command (Rev 3:9). Again, "proskynesis" is awarded to many others apart from God, while "latreuein" (cultic/religious service) is given only to God and never to Jesus. While both God and Jesus are "worshipped," Jesus has not been paid the particular "full and equal" religious devotion due only to God; the New Testament writers, and Jesus, reserve that sort of service for the Father only. Furthermore, Hurtado has missed the significance of the *reason* which Revelation provides for the world's recognition of both God and Jesus.

One of these figures is worshipped explicitly as *"our God"* (4:11) and as the Creator. The other is worshipped as *"the Lamb,"* and is worshipped precisely because of the *great service* that he has rendered to "our God." Here Jesus receives glory because of his obedience to another, the Creator, not because he is somehow identical to the Creator himself. Throughout the New Testament, the reason Jesus is afforded such honor is specifically because:

> *he humbled himself by becoming obedient to the point of death—even to death on a cross. <u>For this reason</u> God highly exalted him and gave him the name that is above every name, so that at the name of Jesus every knee will bow… and every tongue should confess that Jesus Christ is Lord, to the glory of God the Father* (Philippians 2:8-10a, 11).

[1397] Larry Hurtado, "The Binitarian Pattern of Earliest Christian Devotion and Early Doctrinal Development," *The Place of Christ in Liturgical Prayer* (Collegeville: Liturgical Press, 2008), p. 30.

[1398] See Hurtado, *Lord Jesus Christ*, pp. 29-53, see also p. 592.

It is noteworthy here that any worship that is paid to Christ is ultimately to the credit of God the Father, not simply to Jesus himself. Nevertheless, many Trinitarians have echoed Hurtado's argument about the worship of Jesus in Revelation to definitively prove his deity, again, under the pretense of premise 1: *Only God can be worshipped.* This argument is thought to be reinforced by the fact that not only does Jesus receive worship in Revelation, but the angel who presents Jesus' vision to the Apostle John actually rejects worship himself when John offers it to him, and instructs him: *"Worship God"* (Rev 22:8b-9). And so the common argument goes: "Jesus received worship and did not correct anyone. But when the angel received worship, he corrected John and said to worship God only." One problem with this is that the angel simply says, *"worship God"*—he does not say worship God *only*, which would have been inconsistent if in this same book the world worships not only "God" and another distinct figure called "the Lamb," but also the many exalted Christians (Rev 3:9). Of course John should worship God. The angel's decision to direct glory away from himself and onto God has nothing to do with our question of whether or not the worship of the man Jesus is permitted within the inherited Jewish matrix of the first Christians. As Hurtado noted, "undue reverence" was certainly to be avoided, but great reverence, even prostration must be seen as permissible for anyone to whom God has granted the right to be worshipped. This angel either did not have that right or chose not to exercise it. Ultimately, the angel's decision to direct honor away from himself does not suddenly create a rule that only God can be worshipped within the monotheistic world of the Jews. As we have already seen in the Old Testament and in other Jewish literature, non-deity figures enjoyed worship, even corporate worship alongside God in a religious setting (1 Chron 29:20). Furthermore, as we will presently discover, even other *angels* received worship from men and *did not refuse it.*

Let us consider a few examples to make our point. In the Old Testament, when Joshua encountered the angel at Gilgal, we read that *"Joshua fell on his face to the earth and did worship, and said unto him, What saith my lord unto his servant?"* (Joshua 5:14). The Hebrew word for "worship" here is the same word used in Genesis 24:26, when Eliezer *"bowed down his head and worshiped Yahweh."* The *Septuagint*, the Bible of the New Testament community, describes this act paid to the angel as the Greek "proskuneo," the same act of devotion paid to Christ and the Christians in Revelation. This angel who Joshua reverenced, who identified himself as "the captain of Yahweh's host," did not reject this worship, but even instructed Joshua: *"Remove your sandals from your feet, for the place where you are standing is holy*" (5:15). This is, of course, the same language that the angel in the burning bush used when he was approached by Moses (Ex 3:5).[1399] Furthermore, in Genesis 19:1, we observe that Lot also venerated the two angels who visited him at the gate of Sodom and *"bowed himself with his face to the earth."*[1400] Hurtado's contention that in the Jewish monotheistic world the reverential activity received by Jesus in Revelation was strictly forbidden for anyone but the one God, and was specifically prohibited for human beings or angels, appears to falter.

Another work of Jewish literature lends further insight: *Joseph and Aseneth*. Dating this work has been difficult, but some scholars have concluded that it originates from between the first century BCE to the second century CE, and some have even recognized it as an early Christian work from around the time of the composition of John's Revelation.[1401] The story centers on Aseneth, the wife that Pharaoh gave to Joseph in Genesis 41:45, and her journey from polytheism and idolatry to monotheism. Being a pagan princess, she had worshipped many gods before Yahweh sent an angel to enlighten her. Interestingly, after Aseneth is converted and embraces Jewish monotheistic worship, Aseneth actually worships the angel, and the angel does not refuse it. In a Jewish text that is concerned about the neglect of Yahweh in favor of other gods, one would expect that the worship of the angel would be prohibited if it were really the case that only God can be worshiped in Jewish monotheism. Some scholars such as Hurtado and Bauckham have attempted to downplay the significance of this,

---

[1399] Moses was instructed: *"remove your sandals from your feet, for the place on which you are standing is holy ground"* (Exodus 3:5). This angel in the burning bush spoke as Yahweh and was addressed as God; he was treated with the same reverence as if he were God himself. But we should conclude that it was, in fact, an angel, since Exodus 3:2 tells us explicitly that it was *"the angel of Yahweh"* who appeared to him in flames of fire, and Stephen in Acts 7:30 confirms that *"an angel appeared to Moses in the flames."* The text in Exodus actually oscillates back and forth between an identification of "the angel" and "God"—so closely was God's agent identified with him that the two nearly became confused.

[1400] These angels appear to be the same two angels with whom Abraham was conversing at his tent. These angels even distinguish themselves from Yahweh (Gen 19:13).

[1401] "H. F. D. Sparks and James H. Charlesworth... think it originated in early or even pre-Christian times... Pierre Batiffol... dated it to the 1st century C. E.... Christoph Burchard... contended that the writing originated either in the 1st century B. C. E. or the 1st century C. E... Giddeon Bohak placed the origin of the work even earlier than all others, dating it to the time of Maccabean revolt in the 2nd century B. C. E.... all the scholars are clear that *Joseph and Aseneth* represents a very ancient text, the origins of which go well beyond the 6th-century Syriac manuscript in our possession. But how far back is a question open to debate. Many think the 1st century C. E. is likely—that is, during early Christian times, perhaps dating to Jesus' lifetime, or some time right after his crucifixion" (Simcha Jacobovici, Barrie Wilson, *The Lost Gospel*, New York: Pegasus Books, 2014), p. 33). One possible indication that the text is an early Christian work written after the crucifixion is the fact that the angel, in a peculiar ritual cleansing, makes the sign of a cross on a honeycomb.

even claiming that the angel did not receive Aseneth's worship. However, as Andrew Chester confirms:

> It is misleading of Hurtado (and Bauckham) to imply that the angel thus refuses to be worshipped. In fact, in *Joseph and Aseneth* 14-15, Aseneth has already fallen down and worshipped the angel twice. Hence if the angel was really concerned to prevent improper worship and protect and explain "the scruples of Jewish monotheism," he should have acted very differently. That is, he should have said very clearly that he was not to be worshipped, and explained to Aseneth the terrible mistake she was making; in fact he does neither... [in Aseneth's] full acceptance of Judaism, worship of an angel is represented as apparently unproblematic.[1402]

The argument that the angel's redirection of John's worship in Revelation proves that only God could be venerated in the worldview of the biblical Jews is unfounded. In the late Second Temple Judaism inherited by the writers of the New Testament, the "worship" of Adam, angels, and other human lords in no way compromised their monotheistic acknowledgment of Yahweh as the only true God. Thus the earliest Jewish-Christian community's veneration of Jesus Christ does not imply that they viewed him as Yahweh, or that his arrival on the scene necessitated a "binitarian" update to their traditional view. "There is no indication," concludes Hurtado, "that among the problems [Paul] had to deal with he was ever anxious about devotion to Jesus as a possible neglect of God or threat to God's centrality."[1403] This is true, but our question is *why* Paul was unconcerned by this? Is it because the earliest Christians somehow recognized the man Jesus as Yahweh as Trinitarians assert? Or was it simply because in their worldview the worship of exalted human or angelic agents posed no threat to their monotheism?

Honor and Glory

On the heels of these popular arguments from Revelation comes a citation of Christ at John 5:23: "*That all men should honor the Son, even as they honor the Father.*" It is said by Trinitarians, who seek to establish the co-equality of the

---

[1402] Andrew Chester, *Messiah and Exaltation: Jewish Messianic and Visionary Traditions and New Testament Christology* (Tubingen: Mohr Siebeck, 2007), pp. 112-113.

[1403] Larry Hurtado, "The Binitarian Shape of Early Christian Worship," *The Jewish Roots of Christological Monotheism* (Leiden: Brill, 1999), p. 208.

Father and the Son (and the Holy Spirit, lest we forget), that Christ intends for himself to be worshipped equally with the Father. Yet there is no permit from this verse to ascribe ontological co-equality to them, for neither nature nor religious worship is the subject of Christ's discourse here. The honor which Jesus refers to in this passage is not religious veneration, but acceptance of a heavenly message. It is the desire of God, Jesus explains, that all should accept him in the function of God's messenger, to receive him as a divine emissary to the same degree that they would receive God himself. In context, Jesus says:

> *For not even the Father judges anyone, but he has given all judgement to the Son, so that all will honor the Son even as they honor the Father. He who does not honor the Son does not honor the Father who sent him* (John 5:22-24).

Certainly Christ's concern is his acceptance as God's agent. Jesus demonstrates this same principle of agency elsewhere, telling his disciples, "*Whoever listens to you listens to me; whoever rejects you rejects me; but whoever rejects me rejects him who sent me*" (Luke 10:16). The Apostle John echoes this in his other writings: "*No one who denies the Son has the Father; whoever <u>acknowledges</u> the Son has the Father also*" (1 Jn 2:23). One cannot be had without the other; if Christ is not honored, then God is not honored. This is surely Jesus' intention in John 5:22ff, that he be received as if he were the Father, not that he actually be thought of as the Father or the same God as the Father.

Yet many have persisted in arguing that worshipping Jesus is *idolatry* if he is not God. Some have even cited Romans 1:25, in which Paul admonishes those who have "*worshipped and served the creature rather than the Creator, who is blessed forever*" (NASB). If Jesus is indeed a creature,[1404] they argue, then he should not be worshipped at all. But what is really being said by Paul here? The KJV at Romans 1:25 reads that they "*worshipped and served the creature <u>more than</u> the Creator who is blessed forever*," and the Darby also reads, "*and honored and served the creature <u>more than</u> him who had created it.*" The actual Greek here is rendered by the *Greek Testament Critical Exegetical Commentary* as "beyond," and it explains that the worship referred to here "would amount to the exclusion of the Creator."[1405] Another commentary says that the admonition here is that certain people "honored the creature and *not* the Creator, whom they ought to have

---

[1404] Jesus, according to the NT, belongs to the sphere of creation. He is "*the faithful and true witness, the beginning <u>of the creation</u> of God*" (Rev 3:14), and "*the firstborn <u>of every creature</u>*" (Col 1:15 KJV).

[1405] Henry Alford, "Commentary on Romans 1:25," *The New Testament for English Readers,* Vol. 2 (London: Gilbert and Rivington, 1865), p. 13.

honored."[1406] Another says it is worship "to the neglect of" God.[1407] A further reads that it is worship "to the disregard or contempt of the Creator."[1408] Indeed many respected commentaries present Romans 1:25 as a criticism of those who honored creatures "more than"[1409] the one who created them. We might then define idolatry, in light of Romans 1:25, as worship or honor of anything in disobedience to God, or to the neglect or substitution of God.[1410]

In reality, early Christian worship of the man Jesus is neither in disobedience to God nor to the neglect of God; it is, in fact, treatment that is only given after God commands it. There is no preference of Jesus to the neglect of the Father, it is worshipping the Father *through* worshipping a creature whom God has specifically designated as a worthy and proper vehicle of that honor. God is always the ultimate object of any worship given to the Son. As Paul said, the world will bow before Christ *"to the glory of God the Father"* (Phil 2:11). Rather than worshipping something in opposition to the Father, or instead of the Father, the honor of Christ is an action made *towards* the Father through an intermediary of his own choosing.

Still, it is difficult for many to think that Jesus, full of glory, is not viewed in the New Testament as deity. But biblically speaking, we have little reason to view the glory that Jesus received from people bowing down to him as glory as Yahweh. In light of the earlier chapter on pre-existence, we should remember that the kind of glory Jesus enjoys is explicitly *"glory as of the only begotten of the Father"* (Jn 1:14), that is, the glory of sonship. Christians, in fact, will receive this same glory: *"you will also appear with him in glory"* (Col 3:4). This is accomplished by Christ himself: *"The glory which you have given me I have given to them"* (Jn 17:22). Christ even insists that men are to seek glory from God: *"you [should] seek the glory that is from the one and only God"* (Jn 5:44; cp. Rom 2:7). This is the same glory which Jesus expected to receive from God: *"I do not seek my own glory, there is one who seeks it"* (Jn 8:50). Christ enjoys not the glory of God, but the glory of the Son of God. It is in this capacity that he is rightly worshipped.

[1406] Heinrich Meyer, "Commentary on Romans 1:25," *Heinrich Meyer's Critical and Exegetical Commentary on the New Testament* (Edinburgh: T & T Clark, 1832), emphasis added.

[1407] "Commentary on Romans 1:25," *Cambridge Greek Testament for Schools and Colleges* (London: Cambridge Warehouse, 1896).

[1408] W. Robertson Nicol, "Commentary on Romans 1:25," *The Expositor's Greek Testament.* 1897-1910. Web. 02 December 2015.

[1409] E. W. Bullinger, "Commentary on Romans 1:25," *E. W. Bullinger's Companion Bible Notes.* 1909-1922. Web. 02 December 2015.

[1410] "The first commandment is to have no gods before God (Ex 20:3, Deut 5;7) ... idolatry substituted another for God..." (Walter A. Elwell, "Idol, Idolatry," *Evangelical Dictionary of Theology* (Baker Pub. Group, 1996), p. 3).

Still, we find that many Christians believe that Jesus must be identical to God on the grounds that the Lamb receives "*honor and glory and praise*" (Rev 5:12). However, *all* steadfast disciples, according to the New Testament, are set to receive the same:

> *Your genuine faith will result in praise, glory and honor for you when Jesus Christ is revealed* (1 Peter 1:7 CEB).

> *To those who by persistence in doing good seek glory, honor and immortality, he will give eternal life. There will be... glory and honor and peace to every one who does good* (Romans 2:7, 9a, 10 NIV).

If we are to conclude that the New Testament presents Jesus as the only true God because Jesus sits down with God, either on his throne or at its right hand (Rev 5:12-14, Ps 110:1), then what about Solomon? 1 Chronicles 29:23 says that "*Solomon sat on the throne of the LORD (Yahweh) as king.*" Jesus' own disciples are also invited to sit in that same place: "*He who overcomes, I will grant to him to sit down with me on my throne, as I also overcame and sat down with my Father on his throne*' " (Rev 3:21). Furthermore, if Jesus is the one God because the people of the world come and worship at his feet in Revelation 5, then what about the other exalted servants of God who are worshipped in the same book? As God commands the world to bow before the Christ, so Christ commands the same for other human beings (Rev 3:9). We cannot think that the worship of the glorified, empowered Christians here impugns the worship awarded to God. Likewise, the adoration of the man Jesus does not assail the honor of the one God; it is not worship of Christ in opposition to God, but in deference to God's decree.

None of the surveyed information regarding Christ's exaltation and worship is evidence that the New Testament presents Jesus as identical to God, or as having the same substance as the Father. As Perry concludes:

> The reverence of Jesus, the acknowledgment and honor ascribed to him, and the obeisance, the calling upon him, and the remembrance of him—all these actions are part of Christian devotion and reflect Jesus' exaltation as 'lord' and Davidic king. [This] is entirely compatible with the Jewish monotheism of the time, because it is the Father who is said to be the one God by the Jews and the earliest Christians alike.[1411]

[1411] Perry, p. 55.

14

IN THE BEGINNING WAS THE WORD

"When the writers of the New Testament speak of God they mean the God and Father of our Lord Jesus Christ. When they speak of Jesus Christ, they do not speak of him, nor do they think of him as God. He is God's Christ, God's Son, God's Wisdom, God's Word. Even the Prologue to St. John, which comes nearest to the Nicene Doctrine, must be read in the light of the pronounced subordinationism of the Gospel as a whole; and the Prologue is less explicit in Greek with the anarthrous 'theos' than it appears to be in English."
— John Martin Creed

IN CONTINUING OUR INQUIRY INTO THE DOCTRINES of Christ's pre-existence and deity, it is necessary to dedicate a chapter to the famous and controversial preamble to John's Gospel: *"In the beginning was the Word, and the Word was with God, and the Word was God. The same was in the beginning with God. All things were made by him; and without him was not anything made that was made"* (Jn 1:1-3 KJV). Without doubt, this one text has served as the single greatest source of exegetical dispute in the history of Holy Writ; it is also the passage which seems to most easily bend to the Platonic interpretation of the New Testament. Though surrounded by great controversy even today, the passage becomes clearer in light of the Jewish concept of pre-existence, creation, and a commitment to strict exegesis. One professor at Fuller Theological Seminary even postulates that:

> the thorny questions of later ages might have been avoided if the church fathers had not embarked upon the language of the "eternal generation of the Son." How things might have been different if the fathers had kept strictly to the language of John's prologue as their paradigm.[1412]

Let us first consider the traditional translation of John 1:1-3. In the aforementioned *King James* rendering of the passage, the translators have translated the Greek term "logos" as "Word." This is not necessarily an incorrect translation,[1413] but notice that the translators have chosen to capitalize the *W*. Obviously the capitalization of "Word" is a not-so-subtle attempt at presenting the word/logos as the proper name of a *person*. This is evidenced by the fact that the term "logos" occurs over three hundred times in the New Testament, but in translations like the NIV and KJV it is only capitalized seven times. Not only that, but they disagree with one another on exactly when it should be capitalized.[1414] This reveals that the impetus to capitalize or not (therefore when to represent "logos" as a Person or not) is generated not necessarily by the text but by the translators' personal interpretation.

Truly, the "word" (logos) should not be thought of as a unique Person. The term has a broad scope, but is essentially represented by two general meanings in the Bible: "logic" (or reason), and "speech" (or word). The great *Bauer Lexicon* provides these examples of the term's wide application:

- *speaking; words you say* (Rom 15:18, "what I have *said* and done").
- *a statement you make* (Luke 20:20 *NASB*), "they might catch him in some *statement*).
- *a question* (Matt 21:24, "I will also ask you one *question*").
- *preaching* (1 Tim 5:17, "especially those whose work is *preaching* and teaching").
- *command* (Gal 5:14, "the entire law is summed up in a single *command*").

[1412] Brown, "Trinity and Incarnation," *Ex Auditu*, Vol. 7, p. 90.

[1413] The traditional King James rendering of "word" or "Word" does, however, appear to owe more to the Latin translation of "logos" as "verbum" from the Vulgate, than to a direct translation which considers the whole scope of the term's meaning. See BeDuhn, p. 114.

[1414] See "John 1:1 – But What About John 1:1?" *Biblical Unitarian*. Spirit and Truth Fellowship International. 2013. Web. 25 November 2015.

- *proverb; saying* (John 4:37, "thus the *saying*, 'One sows, and another reaps'").
- *message; instruction; proclamation* (Luke 4:32, "his *message* had authority").
- *assertion; declaration; teaching* (John 6:60, "this is a hard *teaching*").
- *the subject under discussion; matter* (Acts 8:21, "you have no part or share in this *ministry*." Acts 15:6, "And the apostles… came together to look into this *matter*").
- *revelation from God* (Matt 15:6, "you nullify the *word of God* ").
- *God's revelation spoken by His servants* (Heb 13:7, "leaders who spoke the *word of God*").
- *a reckoning, an account* (Matt 12:36, "men will have to give *account*" on the day of judgment).
- *an account or "matter" in a financial sense* (Matt 18:23, A king who wanted to settle "*accounts*" with his servants. Phil 4:15, "the *matter* of giving and receiving").
- *a reason; motive* (Acts 10:29, "I ask *for what reason* you have sent for me").[1415]

Though it is translated thirty-seven different ways by the NASB (including "account, answer, exhortation, message, news, matter, report, teaching, story, and reason"), one guide effectively sums up the meaning of "logos" as "*reasoning expressed by words*."[1416] Here the emphasis is not on the words themselves but on the *reasoning* or the *ideas* behind them. Likewise, *Strong's* defines it as "a word *(as embodying an idea)*."

It must be noted that no lexicon defines "logos" as "a person," yet this is what Trinitarians demand the word means in John. Nevertheless, even orthodox scholars have recognized the widespread misreading, with one Catholic scholar pointedly wondering: "Why do we instinctively read: 'In the beginning was the Son and the Son was with God'?"[1417] Dr. Brown of Fuller Seminary reminds us of course that "To read John 1:1 as if it said, 'In the beginning was the Son' is patently wrong."[1418]

[1415] William F. Arndt and F. Wilbur Gingrich, *A Greek-English Lexicon of the New Testament and Other Early Christian Literature (The Bauer Lexicon)* (Chicago: University of Chicago Press, 1957), p. 480.

[1416] "#3056 (logos)," *Helps Word-studies*. Helps Ministries. 2011. Web. 01 November 2015.

[1417] Kuschel, p. 381.

[1418] Brown, *Ex Auditu*, Vol. 7, p. 89.

Possible Influence

In previous chapters we observed how, in the early Christian centuries, the Greek notion of the logos took on various meanings within the circles of synthesizing Platonists. To Philo of Alexandria the logos was a sort of intermediary, angelic being; to Justin Martyr this angelic figure was the pre-incarnate Jesus. These conceptions drew their power from Platonism's metaphysical doctrines of pre-existence, the migrating soul, and the Demiurge.[1419] But where does the Jewish John's concept of the logos come from? Could his own Jewish environment have employed a logos concept that owed little to the Hellenists? One theologian comments on this question:

> The [Platonic] philosophers conceived the idea of two or three divine beings, and, becoming acquainted with the Jews, found them using the phrase, Logos of the Lord, and without inquiring into the Jewish use, were led into the erroneous belief that the Jewish *logos* and their *nous*[1420] mean the same thing—a divine person.[1421]

One error committed by much of Christian scholarship on this point is the presentation of a faulty either-or paradigm. Many hastily presume that John either received his concept of the logos from the parallel Platonic tradition, or that his logos was completely original. Of course, Trinitarian apologists often gravitate towards the second option, that John's notion of the logos as a real divine person was not influenced by pagan sources. Indeed Trinitarian scholars have claimed that "there is no proof that John got his Logos from Philo... in his use of the term Logos, he followed not the Gnostic nor the Alexandrian nor the

---

[1419] As we discovered in Part I, Philo of Alexandria had subsumed the concept of the logos from the preceding Platonists, to them the established blueprint or mind of the universe, and was ostensibly the first to make it into some sort of a person, both created and uncreated (Lamson, Abbot, p. 68.). For Philo, the logos was both God's divine reason and an angel which he had used to make the world. The later second century Christian Platonist Justin Martyr then postulated that the logos-angel was none other than the pre-incarnate Jesus Christ. Justin too had read the New Testament using the same interpretive methods by which Philo had read the Old; where Philo had read the *Septuagint* translation of the Hebrew "davar" (word) and found Plato's "logos," Justin had read the Greek New Testament and found Philo's logos in John's prologue.

[1420] In Neoplatonic thought, that is, in Plotinus (204-270 CE), the *Nous* is an image of God, or the Demiurge, distinct from God (or "the One"). The *Nous* is seen as an "emanation" from the One. This relationship of emanation is certainly paralleled in the Trinitarian "begetting" of the God-the-Son from the God the Father, and the "proceeding" of the God-the-Holy-Spirit from the Father (or in Western Churches from both the Father and the Son).

[1421] Charles Upham, quoted in *The Baptist Quarterly*, Vol. 10 (Philadelphia: American Baptist Publication Society, 1876), p. 131.

Neo-Platonic nor any other meaning *save his own and that of Jesus Christ*, the Founder of Christianity."[1422] There is a concerted effort to portray the "Logos-Christology" which John allegedly exhibits in his prologue as a brand new Trinitarian revelation. However, this assertion is often made under the pretense that Philo's logos is not a real person, but John's logos *is*. Indeed, assessments like, "Philo's Logos is not really personal; St. John's certainly is"[1423] have been provided regularly. Of course, there is still much debate about how to properly frame Philo's logos, and many do believe it *was* a person. Perhaps some of those who argue this way about John exhibit a wariness of drawing too close to the thought-forms of the synthesizers, an eagerness to portray the whole Trinitarian concept as an exclusively Christian teaching, not based on Platonic thought. And why shouldn't we desire to swiftly and publicly distance John's Christology from any preceding pagan influence? After all, John was not a Greek philosopher. However, by immediately asserting that John's logos is certainly a "person," and by this they mean a pre-incarnate, eternally generated *hypostasis*, Trinitarians have nevertheless lapsed backwards into Platonic thinking.

Is John's logos either only the product of Platonism, *or* a brand new Trinitarian revelation? What prevented John from gaining his logos concept from his inherited Judaism, the only religious source we can all agree he was intimately connected with? Indeed, scholars are now convinced that the Gospel of John should be interpreted through a fundamentally Jewish framework.[1424] James McGrath affirms that:

> we are correct, with the majority of scholars, to set the Fourth Gospel in the context of Judaism… it is in no way implausible to suggest that John's Gospel is correctly classed as *Jewish Christian*, and, [does not] demonstrate distance from Judaism… the burden of proof rests on those who seek to deny a *Jewish/Jewish-Christian* setting for the Fourth Evangelist's community and Gospel.[1425]

By "Jewish Christian" we of course mean the historical Nazarene and Ebionite groups who did not believe in the literal pre-existence of the Son. It is within *this* framework that we are pressed to reexamine John's Gospel, and thus the logos concept in his prologue. Could the very Jewish John have entertained

---

[1422] Heuser, p. 229, emphasis added.
[1423] Hastings, *Dictionary of the Bible*, p. 550.
[1424] See Severino Pancaro, *The Law in the Fourth Gospel* (Leiden: E.J. Brill, 1975), p. 530
[1425] McGrath, "Johannine Christianity," pp. 14-15, emphasis added.

a far less personal concept of the logos than has been previously assumed? Was it a concept derived not from the Hellenizers of his day, nor from a new Trinitarian revelation, but from the old Hebrew Bible itself? One scholar makes a worthwhile suggestion: "What we *do* know is that John was steeped in the Old Testament Scriptures. If we wish to understand the historical ancestry of John's Logos concept as he himself understood it, we have to go back to those Scriptures."[1426]

John's Hebrew Logos

George Ladd, the famous Baptist professor of theology, observed that "Scholars have often attempted to find the source of John's concept of the Logos in Hellenistic thought."[1427] Our question is *why?* By all accounts, John, like Jesus, was a committed Jew. As recognized in our earlier chapter regarding the intrusion of Gnosticism, John himself wrote ardently to protect the faith from encroaching Hellenistic influences which threatened to destroy the legacy of the human Messiah. So why begin by giving preference to the idea that John was influenced by, say, the Platonists, over an inherited mainstream Judaism? One Presbyterian scholar locates John's logos in a more obvious source: "It is, I think, indisputable that the roots of the doctrine are in the Old Testament and that its main stem is the [word of] Yahweh, the creative and revealing Word of God, by which the heavens and earth were made and the prophets inspired."[1428]

Indeed, the "word of God" was already an important article of John's Judaism. In the Jewish Scriptures, all of creation came into being through God's *spoken word*. God "*said*," and the universe was made (Gen 1:3); all things came to be by his *speech*. Note the famous Psalm: "*By the <u>word</u> of the LORD the heavens were made, their starry host by the breath of his mouth*" (Psalm 33:6). Here the *Septuagint* translation actually renders this "*By the <u>logos</u> of the LORD the heavens were made*" (LXX). Thus the Hebrew "word" (davar) and the Greek "logos" are synonymous for the Jew—they indicate God's expressed ideas. As Dunn reveals, "nowhere either in the Bible or in the extra-canonical literature of the Jews is the word of God a personal agent or on the way to become such."[1429]

[1426] C. J. Wright, "Jesus the Revelation of God," in *The Mission and Message of Jesus: An Exposition of the Gospels in the Light of Modern Research* (New York: E.P. Dutton and Co., 1953), p. 677, emphasis added.

[1427] George Eldon Ladd, *A Theology of the New Testament* (Grand Rapids: Eerdmans, 1974), p. 274.

[1428] Thomas Walter Manson, *Studies in the Gospels and Epistles* (Manchester: University Press, 1962), p. 118.

[1429] Dunn, *Christology in the Making*, p. 219.

Indeed throughout the Bible we read that it was God's own expression or command, not a distinct person from God, which facilitated his creation:

> *By faith we understand that the universe was formed by God's <u>command</u>,*
> *so that what is seen was not made out of what was visible*
> (Hebrews 11:3).

> *And God <u>said</u>, "Let there be light," and there was light*
> (Genesis 1:3).

> *Let them praise the name of the LORD, for at his <u>command</u> they were*
> *created* (Psalm 148:5).

> *For he <u>spoke</u>, and it came into being; he <u>commanded</u>, and it came into*
> *existence* (Psalm 33:9).

As we observed in the earlier chapter on the Jewish concept of pre-existence, everything had first existed in God's mind or plan; it was stored up with him before creation. When God finally spoke, his word made all these things manifest. Every creeping and crawling thing was conceived of in his mind before being made, and his spoken word was the vehicle which carried those ideas out into the universe. John follows in this vein: he writes that everything was made through the word, and apart from the word nothing was made (Jn 1:3). Far from being a novel revelation, however, this same locution was already common among the Jews, that is, among a people who did not believe in a Trinity theory. Examples of this widespread usage include the *Book of Jubilees*, dating between 200-150 BCE, which reads that God "*created everything by his word*" (Jubilees 12:4). The Greek language *Wisdom of Solomon*, from the first century before Christ, reads, "*O God... who have made all things by your word* [logos], *and by your wisdom have formed humankind*" (Wisdom 9:1-2a). One of the Dead Sea Scrolls contains the lines: "*By [God's] knowledge everything came to be, and everything which is happening—He establishes it by his design and without him [nothing] is done*" (DSS 1QS XI: 11), and "*By the wisdom of thy knowledge thou didst establish their destiny ere they came into being, according to [thy will] everything came to be, and without thee [nothing] is done*" (DSS 1QH 1:19-20). Here God's word is identified with his "knowledge," his "wisdom," and his "design."

The Old Testament Book of Proverbs follows the aforementioned sources in presenting God's creative word as virtually synonymous with his wisdom. While in Proverbs 1-9 the writer even describes God's wisdom as a woman, giving her long speeches about her importance and her involvement as a co-worker in God's formation of the world, it is appropriate for us to view this only as the literary technique of personification.[1430] Of course the Hellenizing Jews, like Philo, had speculated freely on the nature of this wisdom. In Philo's view, the logos was a hypostatization (individualization) of God's wisdom, a mediating angel, the firstborn Son of God.[1431] Still, "within Judaism, including Hellenistic Judaism, there is no evidence that such talk of God's (pre-existent) wisdom ever transgressed Jewish monotheism."[1432] Indeed, "Philo is religiously a true Jew, and still holds to one personal God."[1433] And as Dunn notes, "No worship is offered to Wisdom; Wisdom has no priests in Israel."[1434] Ultimately, "Wisdom never really became more than a convenient way of speaking about God acting in creation, revelation and salvation; Wisdom never became more than a personification of God's own activity."[1435] Certainly in the tradition of the average Jew, God's "word" or "wisdom" was viewed as something belonging to God and "certainly not as a personal being or hypostasis."[1436]

All of this suggests that in order for John to accomplish his prologue, he did not need to diverge from the long established ideas of his religious background; he did not need to assign God's word a real personhood. Not one of the 1,400 uses of "davar" (word) in the Hebrew Bible means a person. But Trinitarians and Arians contend that John was indeed a great innovator on this point who suddenly and dramatically deviated from the historical, Jewish usage of the word.

[1430] Lady Wisdom is widely regarded, not as a real person, but as God's wisdom *personified*: "That this woman is not a real person is evident" (Robert Kappelle, *Wisdom Revealed: The message of Biblical Wisdom Literature, Then and Now* (Eugene: Wipf & Stock, 2014), p. 43); "It is agreeable... not to understand by wisdom a real person, but an attribute, or property clothed with a personal character, or a feigned personage introduced" (Nathaniel Lardner, *Works*, Vol. 5 (London: T. Bensley, 1815), p. 90); "No actual woman, Hausmann asserts, could fit the extravagant description" (Michael V. Fox, *Proverbs 10-31*, Vol. 2 (New York: Yale University Press, 2009), p. 908).

[1431] Philo uses the words "wisdom" and "logos" interchangeably. See Sherwood Eddy, *Man Discovers God* (New York: Books for Libraries Press, 1968), p. 27.

[1432] Dunn, *Christology*. p. 210.

[1433] Paine, *The Ethnic Trinities*, p. 132.

[1434] Dunn, *Christology*. p. 170.

[1435] Ibid., p. 210.

[1436] Bruce Chilton, *Do Jews, Christians, and Muslims Worship the Same God?* (Nashville: Abingdon Press, 2012), p. 57.

But isn't it much more plausible that John was simply drawing on his own religious background? Christopher Wright explains:

> When John presents the eternal Word he was not thinking of a Being in any way separate from God, or some "Hypostasis." The later dogmatic Trinitarian distinctions should not be read into John's mind... in light of a philosophy which was not his... We must not read John in the light of the dogmatic history of the three centuries subsequent to the Evangelist's writing...
>
> John's language is not the language of philosophical definition. John has a "concrete" and "pictorial" mind. The failure to understand John [in his prologue] has led many to the conclusion that he is "father of metaphysical Christology," and therefore responsible for the later ecclesiastical obscuration of the ethical and spiritual emphasis of Jesus... The evangelist did not think in terms of the category of "substance"—a category which was so congenial to the Greek mind. [1437]

Yet, we might wonder why John would use a Greek term such as "logos" which had already performed so long in the philosophical arena? Scholars explain that "John deliberately seized upon a term widely known in both the Hellenistic and the Jewish worlds in the interests of setting forth the significance of Christ."[1438] In that Hellenistic world, the idea of the logos is traced back to the philosopher Heraclitus (fl. 500 BCE), and was first seen as the underlying principle of order in the world. But how might John have employed "logos" as a Jew? Wright explains:

> An author's language will confuse us, unless we have some rapport with his mind... The evangelist John takes a well-

---

[1437] C. J. Wright, "Jesus the Revelation of God," p. 707, 711.

[1438] George Eldon Ladd, Donald Alfred Hagner, *A Theology of the New Testament* (Grand Rapids: Eerdmans, 1993), pp. 275-276. Similarly, Dunn writes that in Corinthians "Paul took up the language of wisdom and drawing on the wisdom tradition of Hellenistic Judaism and on Stoic terminology he framed a Christology which met the needs of the Corinthian situation... He presented the Lordship of Christ within the context of Jewish monotheism and Christ as one whom Christians now see to embody and mediate that power of God which created and sustains the world... he sees Jesus not as a pre-existent divine being, but as a man, a Jew, whose God is the one God, and yet who so embodied God's creative power and saving wisdom... that he can be identified as 'the power of God and the wisdom of God' " (Dunn, *Christology*, p. 211).

known term *logos,* does not define it, but unfolds what he himself means by it. The idea belonged to the Old Testament, and is involved in the whole religious belief and experience of the Hebrew Scriptures. It is the most fitting term to express his message. For a man's "word" is the expression of his "mind"; and his mind is his essential personality. Every mind must express itself, for activity is the very nature of mind.[1439]

The foundational text of Genesis 1:1-3 provides a stunning parallel to John 1:1-3. In Genesis 1:1 we find that *"In the beginning"* God creates by way of his word: *"And God said, 'Let there be light,' and there was light"* (Gen 1:3). Through God's word, the light of creation, the light of life and wisdom dawned and gave birth to the world. John 1:4 accordingly reads, *"The Word gave life to everything that was created, and his life brought light to everyone"* (NLT), and in other versions, *"In him* [or "it," the logos] *was life, and the life was the light of men."* The renowned evangelical scholar F. F. Bruce writes that John 1:3 aptly:

> sums up the teaching of Genesis 1, where the record of each creative day is introduced by the clause, *"And God said."* In Ps. 33:6 this is interpreted as meaning that *"by the word of the LORD"* the heavens (and everything else) came into being; in the Wisdom literature it is similarly interpreted to mean that all things exist by his wisdom (cf. Prov. 3:19; 8:30; also Ps. 104:24).[1440]

In other words, John 1:1-3 does not present new information beyond what was already long appreciated by the Jews in Genesis 1. John's Gospel usage of logos (word) therefore correlates precisely with the word which God spoke to create the universe. There is no secondary divine Person or a distinction within God evidenced or necessitated thus far. John is simply speaking out of his Old Testament worldview while recruiting a commonplace and analogous term from the culture of his day.

But did not John say that the word *"became flesh and dwelt among us"* as Jesus Christ (1:14)? How can we assert that John's logos is not the divine and pre-existent Son who became incarnate in human form? Having established the

---

[1439] C. J. Wright, p. 707.

[1440] F. F. Bruce, *The Gospel of John, Introduction, Exposition and Notes* (Grand Rapids: Eerdmans Publishing, 1983), p. 32.

origin of John's logos concept not in the world of the Platonists but in the world of traditional Judaism, we are ready to consider information which will help us understand how John's word or wisdom could "become flesh."

In Jewish wisdom literature, God's logos (word), God's wisdom, and God's Torah are used virtually interchangeably. While in Proverbs we read that *"The Lord by wisdom founded the earth; by understanding he established the heavens"* (3:19), in rabbinical sources we read that *"God consulted the Torah and created the world"* (Genesis Rabba 1:1). In the 1st-2nd century BCE book *Wisdom of Sirach*, a work ostensibly alluded to by Jesus and his disciples,[1441] God's wisdom is equated with the Torah, the law handed down to Moses at Sinai:

> Sirach 24 is the most familiar place where wisdom and Torah are identified. The first 22 verses parallel the long hymn in Proverbs 8 as well as Proverbs 1:20-33; Job 28 and Wisdom 6-10... The second major section (verses 23-29), identifies wisdom with "the book of the covenant of the Most High God, the law that Moses commanded us..." (v. 23).[1442]

In verse 8 of Sirach 24 we read: *"Then the Creator of all gave me [Torah] his command, and my Creator chose the spot for my tent. He said, 'In Jacob make your dwelling, in Israel your inheritance.' "* The idea of God's wisdom or Torah coming down and making a tent among Israel should seem familiar. In John 1:14 we read that God's word *"became flesh and dwelt among us,"* or literally: *"pitched a tent among us."* With the equation of God's word, God's wisdom, and God's Torah, along with the idea that it can be spoken of as coming down and dwelling among us, we have laid a non-metaphysical foundation for John's logos. This picture is further realized by the fact that Jewish circles in the centuries preceding and following Jesus' ministry even spoke of this word as "becoming flesh" or being personified in a living rabbi. In Sirach 50:1-21, the historical Jew Simon ben Onias is treated as an embodiment of wisdom, *without* literal pre-existence.[1443] Could the historical Jew Jesus also be seen as embodying wisdom without literal pre-existence? Jacob Neusner reveals how the *Jerusalem Talmud*, a reflection on

---

[1441] Compare Matt 6:19-20 with Sirach 29:11; Matt 7:16, 20 with Sirach 27:6; Matt 11:28 with Sirach 51:27; James 1:19 with Sirach 5:11; Matt 7:16-20 with Sirach 27:6; Matt 6:12 with Sirach 28:2.

[1442] Ryan O'Dowd, *The Wisdom of Torah: Epistemology in Deuteronomy and the Wisdom Literature* (Gottingen: Vandenhoeck & Ruprecht, 2009), p. 177.

[1443] Simon J. Gathercole, *The Preexistent Son: Recovering the Christologies of Matthew, Mark, and Luke* (Grand Rapids: Eerdmans, 2006), p. 197.

second century rabbinical thought, portrayed Jewish teachers as the "incarnation" of God's word or Torah:

> The reason that the Torah was made flesh was that the Torah
> was the source of salvation. When the sage was transformed
> into a salvific figure through his mastery of the Torah, it was
> an easy step to regard the sage as the living Torah.[1444]

Philo himself appears to exhibit very similar thinking: in his *Life of Moses I*, Philo says that Moses was the *embodiment* or *personification* of Torah. Since "Moses was also destined to be the lawgiver of his nation, he was himself... a living and reasonable law" (*Life of Moses I* 28:162). Regarding Moses as king, Philo again writes that "the king is a living law" (*Life of Moses II*, 4). Because Moses had been designated as the conduit through which God's word, wisdom, and Torah would be delivered (See Ex 4:12; 15, Deut 18:18), Moses was himself a seen as an embodiment of that divine word, wisdom, and Torah. He was called "the law-giving Word" because he himself received "divine communication."[1445]

How might all of this be helpful for understanding John 1:1? At the beginning of part two, we reviewed how Paul, John's contemporary, understood that Jesus had come to represent God's wisdom to the disciples: *"Christ Jesus... has become to us the wisdom of God"* (1 Cor 1:30). God's wisdom, Torah, or word is not, then, a pre-existing divine person who later took on an abstract human nature. It is the man Jesus who became God's wisdom. He was a living personification of that principle. Indeed, God's wisdom/word dwelled in Jesus; he was the conduit through which God's own word would be delivered (Jn 3:34; 8:28). As we read from Dunn previously:

> [Paul] presented the Lordship of Christ within the context of
> Jewish monotheism and Christ as one whom Christians now
> see to embody and mediate that power of God which created
> and sustains the world... he sees Jesus not as a pre-existent
> divine being, but as a man, a Jew, whose God is the one God,
> and yet who so embodied God's creative power and saving

[1444] Jacob Neusner, *The Incarnation of God: The Character of Divinity in Formative Judaism* (Binghamton: Global Academic Publishing, 2001 [1998]), p. 202. The incarnation of Torah as a sage, says Neusner, "is represented by the claim that a sage himself was equivalent to a scroll of Torah—a material, legal comparison, not merely a symbolic metaphor. Here are expressions of that conception in the Talmud of the Land of Israel: 'He who sees a disciple of a sage who has died is as if he sees a scroll of the Torah that has been burned' " (Ibid., p. 203).

[1445] O. W. Holmes, "Competing Concepts of the Cosmos in the Sixteenth and Seventeenth Centuries," *Phenomenology and the Human Positioning in the Cosmos* (London: Springer, 2012), p. 57.

wisdom... that he can be identified as "the power of God and the wisdom of God."[1446]

Indeed, for the early Christians, Jesus was "not simply the fulfillment of the Mosaic Torah but also *the embodiment of the wisdom of God seen in the revelation of the created order itself.*"[1447] And so Paul says that Jesus is himself *"the wisdom of God"* (1 Cor 1:24). And likewise, John says in his prologue that God's word (or wisdom) *"became flesh"*—was embodied or personified—in the living man Jesus Christ (1:14).

We will presently discover, through a textual examination of the prologue, that to John, Jesus is not an eternally existent divine being called the logos. Rather, he is simply what God's logos later *became.* There is a careful sequence set forth by John in his introduction, one that consciously avoids placing another literal, Gnostic entity in heaven, and one that does not identify God's impersonal logos as becoming a person until later in verse 14.[1448] As one scholar writes, "The common notion that the logos is to be identified *immediately* with Jesus in the prologue is to some extent based upon a reading of the text in Greek which does not attend adequately to its obviously deliberate sequence."[1449]

"In the beginning was the Word..."

We will begin our analysis by first examining a few popular translations of John 1:1-3:

KJV: *"In the beginning was the Word, and the Word was with God, and the Word was God. The same was in the beginning with God. All things were made by him; and without him was not anything made that was made."*

[1446] Dunn, *Christology in the Making*, p. 211.

[1447] Daniel L. Akin, *A Theology for the Church* (Nashville: B & H Publishing Group, 2007), p. 109, emphasis added.

[1448] "The heresy of Docetism was always present to the mind of John (while it is most plainly in view in his First Epistle); the idea of Christ as a mere phantasm, without human flesh and blood, was destructive of the Gospel... the explicit declaration that 'the Word became flesh' was necessary to exclude Docetic teaching. A characteristic feature of the Fourth Gospel is its frequent insistence on the true humanity of Jesus" (John Henry Bernard, *International Critical Commentary: St. John,* Vol. 1 (Edinburgh: T & T Clark, 1999), p. 20).

[1449] Chilton, p. 58, emphasis added.

NASB: *"In the beginning was the Word, and the Word was with God, and the Word was God. He was in the beginning with God. All things came into being through Him, and apart from Him nothing came into being that has come into being."*

The beginning referenced here is usually thought to be the beginning of Creation, or sometime before. Many Trinitarians, desiring to find here the eternality of the Son, have insisted on a more profound interpretation of "beginning" as "eternity." But the famous Reformation-era unitarian Socinus challenged that:

> Those who in this place wish to have the word "beginning" designate the eternity of Christ stand convicted of the most egregious error from the mere fact that their opinion is supported by no authority whether in the New Testament or the Old. As a matter of fact you will not find "beginning" used for eternity anywhere in the Scriptures.[1450]

Indeed "beginning" implies a point *in time*, not outside it. Some, like Socinus, have even believed this beginning to be the "beginning of the Gospel" as referenced in the parallel Mark 1:1: *"The beginning of the Gospel about Jesus Christ."*[1451] But the opinion of this book, as mentioned previously, is that the beginning referenced in John 1:1 is indeed sometime before the Genesis creation.

Another parallel New Testament introduction of note is Acts 1:1: *"The first account I composed, Theophilus, about all that Jesus began to do and teach..."* This word which the NASB renders "account" is actually "logos." And so the "logos" is again shown to be an expressed set of ideas. Yet another introduction, that of Titus, reveals a similar view. Paul writes that the hope of eternal life was *"promised [by God] long ages ago, but at the proper time [it was] manifested, even his word [logos], in the proclamation with which I was entrusted"* (Titus 1:2b-3a). God's "logos,"

[1450] Paul C. H. Lim, *Mystery Unveiled: The Crisis of the Trinity in Early Modern England* (London: OUP, 2012), pp. 296-297.

[1451] The unitarian Laelius Socinus (1525-1562) "utilized the hermeneutical principle of *analogia fidei*: since the Gospels of Mark and Luke and also Acts all begin with some reference to the beginning, namely, 'the beginning of the gospel of Jesus Christ, the Son of God' (Mark 1:1); 'which from the beginning were eyewitnesses' (Luke 1:2); and 'the former treatise... of all that Jesus began both to do and teach' (Acts 1:1), the beginning referred to in the Gospel of John also had to mean the same" (Lim, p. 299). Socinus writes: "On this account, we maintain that the word 'beginning' in this passage refers not to eternity, but to the order of the thing which John is writing about Jesus Christ as the beloved son of God, in this matter imitating Moses who, writing his history, made this word 'beginning' also the very opening of Genesis 1:1" (Socinus, quoted in Lim, p. 297).

an expressed idea which contained a plan for eternal life, was made manifest in the message, or account that Paul was entrusted with. Might God's "logos" in John 1:1 also be an expressed, wise intention for the world?

As we observed in the previous chapters concerning the Jewish conception of pre-existence, God's plan encompassed everything relating to God's purposes, including the future works of Christ and the glorification of humanity. His word was the encapsulation of his master plan for the universe, his own unique and intimate design. While the Jewish "logos" is not a distinct person, it certainly contains the *personal ideas* of God. This helps us understand the second portion of John's introduction: *"and the word was with God."*

"...And the Word was with God..."

The phrase translated "with God" (*pros ton theon*) is often claimed by Trinitarians to prove the unique personality of the logos, in that it demonstrates a relationship between God and the word as one person *with* another person. Upon review, however, we find John's habit was to employ the preposition "para," not "pros" to describe one person alongside another person (Jn 1:39; 4:40; 14:17, 23, 25; 19:25).[1452] Several verses later, when John certainly does want to indicate that there is one person beside another, he writes, *"the only one who is from beside God* [para tou theou]" (Jn 1:14). Trinitarians have been surprised at John's use of "pros" in John 1:1-3, calling it "a remarkable proposition, since we would normally expect *para* and the dative."[1453] Of course, they only *expect* John to use certain language because they have certain theological expectations of him, expectations which he does not readily fulfill. So how can we better understand John's "pros"?

Elsewhere in the New Testament the same "pros" used by John is used in the sense of a principle or an idea within one's mind. In John's other writings we read about *"the eternal life, which was with the Father* (pros ton Patera) *and was manifested to us"* (1 John 1:2). Paul writes, *"so that the truth of the gospel would remain with* [pros] *you"* (Gal 2:5). Here the gospel is obviously not an entity alongside the disciples, but is "with" them in the sense that it abides within their consciousness.

Elsewhere we see that in the Hebrew mind, God's word, by no means an actual person, may be said to be "with" a person: *"But if they are prophets, and if the*

[1452] Colin Brown, *The New International Dictionary of New Testament Theology*, Vol. 3 (Regency Reference Library, 1979), p. 1205.

[1453] Jean Borella, *Secret of the Christian Way* (New York: Suny Press, 2001), p. 137.

word of the LORD is with them, let them entreat the LORD of hosts" (Jer 27:18). In Job, decrees concerning future events are stored up with God: *"For he performs what is appointed for me, and many such decrees are with him"* (Job 23:14). Here a decree, speech, or command regarding God's wise plan for Job is "with" God. Might this be the sense in which John means that the word (decree) was *with* God?[1454]

In his prologue, John's phrase "with God" (*pros ton theon*), is actually found in two other places in the New Testament. Both of these instances are regularly translated as follows:

> *For every high priest taken from among men is appointed on behalf of men in things <u>pertaining to God</u>* [pros ton theon], *in order to offer both gifts and sacrifices* (Hebrews 5:1 NASB).

> *Therefore in Christ Jesus I have found reason for boasting in things <u>pertaining to God</u>* [pros ton theon] (Romans 15:17 NASB).

In both of these examples, we see that the exact phrase translated "with God" in John 1:1 by the Trinitarians is translated "pertaining to God" by the same committee. They have indicated that the "things" in Hebrews 5:1 and Romans 15:17 are not "with" God as conscious entities alongside him, but are simply ideas which are related to, or have something to do with God.[1455] This is a more consistent and appropriate understanding of what John is telling us in his prologue: God's word, or his spoken idea, is something that pertains to God, something that is inherently related to his person. If we then recognize that the

---

[1454] Sirach 1:1 similarly says: *"All wisdom is from the Lord and remains <u>with him</u> forever."* If we understand God's "logos" as his reason, plans, or wisdom, other passages begin to closely align. Proverbs 8 says that God created the world through his wisdom, and that wisdom was *"from the beginning"* (v. 30). The Greek *Septuagint* even reads that God's wisdom was *"with him."* Though the Hebrew poets often used the literary method of personification, no Jewish reader would have concluded that God's wisdom was actually a real person. (*Note:* Trinitarian commentators have agreed that the "Lady Wisdom" motif in Proverbs is not describing an actual person, much less an active, pre-incarnate Jesus. See Max Anders, *Holman Old Testament Commentary: Proverbs* (Nashville: B&H Publishing Group, 2005). See also: "Why is wisdom referred to as a She in Proverbs?" Got Questions Ministries. Web. 24 July 2015).

[1455] The translation *"towards God,"* is the best *literal* translation of the phrase. John Wycliffe's first English language Bible of 1370 renders the "pros ton theon" of John 1:1-2 as "at God." In this way, it is seen as something actively reflecting some service in God's direction, aligning with the Heb 5:1 presentation of a priest's holy service regarding things "pertaining to God." The *Alfred Marshall Diaglott* of 1968 translates "pros ton theon" as "in regard to God." Flavius Josephus, the first century historian in his *Antiquities* (9:236) also uses the Greek "pros ton theon," to instruct King Jotham to be holy "in things pertaining to God" (Steven Mason (trans.), *Flavius Josephus on the Pharisees* (Leiden: Brill Academic Publishers, 2001), p. 87).

ideas spoken of here include God's creative intentions for the world, much becomes clear.

God's entire physical creation bears the beautiful impression of her wise Creator (Ps 19:1-4). Again, while God's wisdom is not a distinct Person, it reflects God's very own personal attributes. These attributes can be observed in the execution of his plan, in the creative manifestation of his private designs. Paul explains: *"For his invisible attributes, namely, his eternal power and divine nature, have been clearly perceived, ever since the creation of the world, in the things that have been made. So they are without excuse"* (Romans 1:20 ESV). As Paul says that God himself is reflected in all of "the things that have been made," this same phrase is presented by John in the third verse of his preamble: *"all things were made"* through God's logos, and apart from this logos, *"nothing was made"* (Jn 1:3). We turn our attention to the common Trinitarian translation of this verse:

NASB: *All things came into being through Him, and apart from Him nothing came into being that has come into being.*

Notice the use of the capitalized "Him" for the logos. Of course this pronoun does not actually have to be translated "him" and may legitimately be rendered "it." True, the masculine Greek pronoun "autou" (him) is used here, but only because it refers to a masculine noun, "logos." While "logos" is grammatically masculine, this does not mean that the logos is actually male, or a person in any sense. We must remember that "logos" is never once defined as a person by the lexicons, but only as (impersonal) speech or reason. Consider this example from the Gospel of Matthew: *" 'Put your sword back in its place,' Jesus said to him, 'for all who draw the sword will die by the sword' "* (Matthew 26:52). The word for "its" is actually the feminine pronoun "her" (auten). But in English we do not translate it as if it were a person because the subject (the sword) is not a person. The word "sword" in Greek, in hundreds of instances, is never a person, thus it is not accompanied by personal pronouns in the English translation. Likewise, no lexicon defines "logos" as a person in its hundreds of instances. So why must the translators use personal pronouns to describe it in English? Grammatical gender is common in languages other than English. For example, the word for "book" in Spanish is masculine, and a proper English translation takes this into consideration. Even though it is masculine, we would never call the book a "him" in English; the book is obviously not a person, therefore we translate the Spanish as "it." Likewise, just as "the sword" (feminine Greek noun) is not regarded as a person in English, neither should "the logos" (masculine Greek noun) be awarded personhood and described by the personal pronouns "he" and "him." Again, the definition of the subject at hand, not necessarily the grammatical gender of the word, should assist our interpretation of the text. At this, we must question the wisdom in building such a substantial and critical dogma as the true personhood of the logos on an anomalous English translation. Again, just because the Greek masculine noun demands a Greek masculine pronoun, this does not mean that "logos" should be given a masculine pronoun in English translations: *grammatical gender must never be confused with sexual gender.* Ultimately, the pronoun in John 1:2-3 could (and arguably should) be translated "it," since no lexicon defines logos as a person. From this vantage point, there seem to be more theological rather than textual reasons for calling the "logos" a "He" in John.

The text of the prologue would better read, in opposition to the KJV, NASB and others, *"All things were made by it; and without it was not anything made that was made."* In fact, before the King James Version of 1611, this was how the verse was routinely translated in English:[1456]

> *All things were made by it and with out it was made nothinge that was made.*
> (The Tyndale New Testament, 1534)

> *All thynges were made by it: and without it, was made nothing that was made.*
> (The Bishop's New Testament, 1595)

> *All things were made by it, and without it was made nothing that was made.*
> (The Geneva Bible, 1599)

"...And the Word was God"

The common assertion is that here we see a second Person who is God. This argument is, of course, still assuming that the Word is necessarily a divine person, and that the Word and Jesus are synonymous. When the logos is considered an expression of God, however, namely his own creative word, then

---

[1456] See The Tyndale Bible (1535), Matthew (1535), Taverner (1539), Cranmer's (1539), Whittingham (1557), Geneva (1560) and the Bishop's Bible (1568).

the passage quickly becomes far less problematic. Elsewhere John makes use of the "to be" verb to portray attributes of God. He writes "*God is spirit*" (Jn 4:24), "*God is love*" (1 Jn 4:8, 16), and "*God is light*" (1 Jn 1:15). Of course God is not completely equal to "light" or "love," but such language serves to emphasize the qualities of one in the other. Identifying love *as* God in 1 John 4:8 should not make us think that "love" is an entity which shares the identity of God. It goes without saying that "God is love" is merely metaphorical language expressing that something essential about God's character can be identified in the principle of love. In this vein, "*the word was God*" means that the word was perfectly expressive of God's character; just as one may not separate God from his love, one may not separate God from his word. We find similar ideas in common English today when we say that a person is "a man of his word," or that "a man is his word," or "a man, without his word, is nothing." The man's word articulates something integral about him, so much so that it can be figuratively said to constitute his whole personality. Thus, as A. T. Robertson writes, "God and Love are not convertible terms any more than God and Logos."[1457] Robertson's revelation that God and logos are not interchangeable is quite telling. Just as a man's word, despite its identification with him, is not actually him, neither is God's word, though a reflection of his character, actually a unique and divine personality. Interestingly, this understanding is reflected in the Greek itself.

In nearly all of its over 1,300 occurrences, the word "God" designates the personal God of the Bible. It very often appears with the article "*ho* theos." However, in the third clause in John 1:1, "*the word was God*" actually reads just "theos en ho logos"; there is no article "ho" (the) in front of "theos." F. F. Bruce comments: "Had theos as well as logos been preceded by the article the meaning would have been that the Word was completely identical with God."[1458] *The Expositor's Greek Testament* agrees that the Word is *not* "identical with all that can be called God, for then the article would have been inserted."[1459] So what does this mean? Essentially we might take "ho theos" as a kind of proper name for God. The article-less "theos," however, is qualitative, describing the character of God. Famous commentator William Barclay writes:

[1457] A. T. Robertson, *A Grammar of the Greek New Testament in the Light of Historical Research* (Nashville: Broadman Press, 1934), pp. 767-768.

[1458] F. F. Bruce, *The Gospel of John* (Grand Rapids: Eerdmans, 1983), p. 31.

[1459] Nicoll Roberston (ed.), *The Expositor's Greek Testament*, Vol. 1 (Grand Rapids: Eerdmans, 1983), p. 684.

When Greek speaks about God it does not simply say "theos"; it says "ho theos." Now, when Greek does not use the definite article with a noun that noun becomes much more like an adjective; it describes the character, the quality of the person. John did not say that the Word was "ho theos"; that would have been to say that the Word was identical with God; he says that the Word was "theos"—without the definite article—which means that the Word was, as we might say, of the very same character and quality and essence and being as God.[1460]

Robertson observes, "The absence of the article here is on purpose and essential to the true idea."[1461] The idea is that the logos and God are not identical, but are qualitatively related. Now, the Trinitarian will say, yes, they are distinct, but they are also in some sense the same, hence the Trinitarian view. But all of this immediately falls away when we realize that John's logos, at this stage, *is not a second person.*

God's Word Finally Becomes a Person

There is certainly a calculated progression of John's logos from God's impersonal word into a truly personal being: Initially, there is the word of God. Then, within it, "life" is said to dwell: "*In* [the logos] *was life, and the life was the light of men*" (v. 4). It is the light that "*shines in the darkness*" (v.5). Of critical note is the fact that "the light" (Greek: *to phos*) is here represented as *neuter.* But *later* in verse 10, it will suddenly begin to be represented as masculine. However, this transition occurs after verse 10, which is describing Jesus *in his later earthly ministry.* In other words, it is only even possible to view it as a person, grammatically speaking, *sometime after Jesus' birth.* Before verse 10, John the Baptist is described as witnessing about "the light," and only after this point do the pronouns describing that light show a striking change from neuter to masculine:

> *There was the true light which, coming into the world, enlightens every man. It was in the world, and the world was made through <u>him</u>,* [Greek: *autou*] *and the world did not know <u>him</u>. He came to his own, and those who were his own did not receive him* (vv. 9-11).

[1460] William Barclay, *The Gospel of John*, Vol. 1 (Glasgow: Saint Andrews Press), p. 39. Barclay is right that it certainly communicates something about God's character and quality, but there is no metaphysical connotation of "essence" or "being" demanded by this text.

[1461] Robertson, p. 68.

It is only during the time of Jesus' ministry that the language shifts to present "the light" as in any way personal, and to drive home that fact, John then writes, *"And the word was made flesh, and dwelt among us, (and we beheld his glory, the glory as of an only begotten of the Father) full of grace and truth* (v. 14)."

Of course Justin Martyr, Irenaeus, Athanasius and other Christians would later view this as a reference to an incarnation of a pre-existent divine *person* called the logos. But again, as Chilton affirms, "all such readings and construals are possible only on the assumption that the logos and Jesus are interchangeable... The problem with such an exegesis of the Johannine text is the care with which Jesus is not directly identified as the logos in verses 1-13."[1462] So what is verse 14 saying? Obviously the person Jesus is presented as the embodiment of God's word. We have no reason to understand Christ's embodiment of God's word in a strictly literal sense, that a pre-existent and bodiless personality named "word" decided to literally be united to flesh and blood, since John has not presented the logos itself as anything but God's own creative word. It is more appropriate that we understand Jesus as the manifestation of God's word concerning the light; God's program of truth was now to be seen in the man and his works. Indeed, Jesus would speak God's own words to the world (Jn 14:10), and in this sense Jesus embodies God's logos. In Deuteronomy 18:18, God prophesied about the future Messiah saying, *"I will put my words in his mouth, and he shall speak to them all that I shall command him."* In the Greek *Septuagint*, God's word here is the term "rhema." Scholars recognize that "the Septuagint treats logos and rhema as synonyms,"[1463] thus we can say it is God's *logos* in Deuteronomy 18:18 that he puts into the Messiah's mouth. When the Messiah speaks, it is God's logos, his own word that is manifested. This is the precise claim of Jesus: *"For I did not speak on my own initiative, but the Father himself who sent me has given me a commandment as to what to say and what to speak"* (Jn 12:29). Again, it is God's "command" that is described as having made the universe in Hebrews 11:3. Furthermore, God's "command," synonymous with his "word," is what the Scriptures say God *sends* from heaven: *"He sends forth his command to the earth; his word runs very swiftly"* (Ps 147:15). The Hebrew word for

---

[1462] Ibid.

[1463] Gerharrd Kittel, *Theological Dictionary of the New Testament: Abridged in One Volume* (Grand Rapids: Eerdmans, 1985), p. 508. See also Dwight Moody Smith, *Abingdon New Testament Commentaries, John* (Abingdon Press, 1999), p. 50; *Bangalore Theological Forum*, Vol. 25-26 (United Theological College, 1993), p. 50; *The Lutheran Quarterly*, Vol. 5 (1953), p. 214.

"command" here is translated as "logos" in the *Septuagint*. Thus we encounter surprisingly Johannine language in the Old Testament: "God sends forth his logos to the earth," and we are able to make perfect sense of its meaning for the Jew: God sending his logos to our world is equivalent to transmitting to us his commandment, his wise word, the expression of his will or ideas.

Jesus Christ describes himself, not as an incarnation of a divine being, but as the one who is transmitting this command or word or logos of God to his fellow man. He calls himself *"a man who has told you the truth that I heard from God"* (Jn 8:40). Indeed, it was God's eternal wisdom and truth that was coming to them in the form of Jesus. Verse 17 of the prologue lends to this conclusion: *"grace and truth came through Jesus Christ"* (ESV). The light of God's divine logos did come down to earth, but it was not truly *as* Jesus Christ, but *through* Jesus Christ. John himself reinforces that it was not actually God who had been literally made visible by the arrival of Christ, as he closes his prologue saying, *"No man has seen God at any time; the only begotten Son, which is in the bosom of the Father, he hath declared him"* (v. 18), or *"He has explained him"* (NASB). Even after Jesus was born, still no one had ever seen God; but because the light in God's logos had been made to shine through the man Jesus, God could be known. Of course, the Trinitarian approach, that the logos is identical to Jesus, and that the logos is identical to God, makes a serious mess of the whole passage in light of verse 18. How could Jesus be the visibly manifested logos, if the logos just is God, and if no one has ever seen God at any time, which includes during and after the ministry of Christ?

To put all of this information into perspective, we might say that in the beginning there was the logos, God's creative reason and his expressed decree concerning his personal grand design for the world. Nothing has ever come into existence that was not expressed by God's wise command (*"Then God said, 'Let the earth bring forth living creatures'"* Gen 1:24a). Of course these creatures were not literally pre-existent, but only came into being once the word went out. One of the things abiding in God's wise plan until the proper time was a principle which John calls *"the light,"* which is to be thought of as synonymous with *"the truth."* It was this light of truth, God's own wisdom, which was perfectly representative of the character of God, and which eventually became manifested in the word and works of Jesus Christ. That Jesus is the "light" and the "life" and the "truth" from John's prologue, he himself makes known many times: *"I am the light of the world"* (Jn 9:5), *"I am... the truth and the life"* (Jn 14:6). In further connection with John's prologue, which portrays "the light that comes into the world" eventually being embodied as a "he" (Jesus), the Christ himself proves that this light, the light he now manifested, was not a pre-existent person—it was indeed a principle. Jesus says:

> *light has come into the world, and men loved the darkness rather than the light, for their deeds were evil. For everyone who does evil hates the light, and does not come to the light for fear that his deeds will be exposed. But he who practices the truth comes to the light, so that his deeds may be manifested as having been wrought in God* (John 3:19-21).

He obviously speaks of himself as the light, as John did of him, but also shows the light to be a principle; it is the antithesis of darkness and evil, it is God's wisdom. Those who "come to Jesus" are in effect "coming to the light of truth" which he represents. It should therefore not be thought that this light of truth, God's wisdom, was a pre-existent being, much less that it was the second Person of a divine Trinity. No, the Son metaphorically embodies the principle of truth. As John said "*truth came through Jesus Christ*" (Jn 1:17), that is, through his word and works.

Alternative Translations

In light of the preceding information, the traditional translation of "*and the Word was God*" may be easier to understand. However, because "theos" in the third clause does not include the article, several alternative translations have been suggested by scholars. We will investigate those options and determine which bests suits the ideas presented by John.

1)   "The Word was a god"

This translation of the article-less "theos" as "*a god*" is found most famously in the New World Translation[1464] produced by the Jehovah's Witnesses (modern-day Arians). It is also found in the translations of Becker,[1465] Wilson,[1466] Young,[1467] and Jannaris.[1468]   Of course, Trinitarian critics have

---

[1464] Frederick Franz (ed.), *New World Translation of the Christian and Greek Scriptures Rendered from the Original Language by the New World Translation Committee* (Brooklyn: Watchtower Bible & Tract Society, 1950).

[1465] Johannes Becker, *Das Evangelium nach Johannes* (Gütersloh/Würzburg, 1979).

[1466] Benjamin Wilson, *The Emphatic Diaglot* (New York: Fowler Wells & Co., 1865).

[1467] Robert Young, *Concise Commentary on the Holy Bible* (Grand Rapids: Baker, 1885), p. 54.

[1468] A. N. Jannaris, *Zeitschrift fur die Neutestamentliche Wissenschaft* (London: Macmillan, 1897), p. 20-21.

shunned this translation as it so easily lends support to the Arian view, that Christ first pre-existed as another divine being, or an angel, before becoming incarnate. Their criticism comes mainly in the form of accusing supporters of "adding" the word *"a"* in front of theos to make "a god." But Dr. BeDuhn explains their justification:

> Greek only has a definite article, like our *the*; it does not have an indefinite article, like our *a* or *an*... We are not "adding a word" when we translate Greek nouns that do not have the definite article as English nouns with the indefinite article. We are simply obeying the rules of English grammar that tell us that we cannot say "Snoopy is dog," but must say "Snoopy is a dog."[1469]

There are good grammatical reasons to consider this translation. In light of other plausible translations, however, this one seems to be given preference by Arians under the assumption that the logos is a person. If it is not a person, there seems little reason to render it this way over the others.

2) "The Word was divine"

This translation, presented by Moffat,[1470] Schonfield,[1471] Goodspeed,[1472] Temple,[1473] and many others, appears to emphasize the qualitative nature of the logos. Brun and Pfafflin render it "the Word was of divine kind."[1474] Here the Word is of the same character or nature as the one God. This translation would fit with our previous assessment of God's word as something fully expressive or reflective of him, and provides a balanced middle ground. As Murray J. Harris notes:

> On the matter of word usage, there can be no doubt that in English the word divine has a much wider range of applications and a more attenuated meaning than does the term God. In modern parlance, for instance, "divine" may describe a meal that is "supremely good" or "fit for a god" or

---

[1469] BeDuhn. p. 114.

[1470] James Moffatt, *Jesus Christ the Same* (Abingdon-Cokesbury, 1945), p. 61.

[1471] Hugh J. Schonfield, *The Original New Testament* (Rockport: Element Books Ltd, 1985).

[1472] Edgar Goodspeed, John M. P. Smith, *The Bible, An American Translation* (Chicago, 1935).

[1473] William Temple, *Readings in St. John's Gospel* (London: Macmillan, 1933).

[1474] Friederch Pfafflin, *Die Briefe des Neuen Testaments in der Sprache von heute* (Heilbronn: Salzer, 1993).

may be used of human patience that is "God-like" or "of a sublime character."[1475]

BeDuhn writes, "Greek has a particular way of expressing the nature or character of something that employs predicate nouns before the verb and without the article, just as in John 1:1. The nature or character of ho logos ('the Word') is theos ('divine')."[1476] It is only if the word "divine" is construed as meaning that the subject has a personal "divine nature" identical to God that the phrase takes an orthodox meaning, and again, only on the assumption that the logos itself is a person. All in all, this is a good translation which seems to appropriately grasp John's intention to present the logos as something distinct from God, but qualitatively the same.

3) "What God was, the Word was"

This translation is found in the NEB[1477] and the REB,[1478] and is the one proposed by Dodd,[1479] Fuller,[1480] J. A. T. Robinson,[1481] and others. In this vein we find several related renderings:

> TEV: "What God was, the Word also was"[1482]
> Barclay: "the nature of the Word was the same as the nature of God"[1483]
> Scholar's Version: "it was what God was."[1484]

Here the logos is represented as "what" God was, not "who" God was. Like the previous translation, this seems to properly convey John's intent to present a qualitative relation between God and his logos. Other translations

---

[1475] Murray J. Harris, *Jesus as God: The New Testament Use of Theos in Reference to Jesus* (Eugene: Wipf & Stock Publishers, 1992), p. 68.

[1476] BeDuhn, pp. 120-121.

[1477] *The New English Bible* (OUP, 1961).

[1478] *The Revised English Bible* (CUP, 1989).

[1479] C. H. Dodd, "New Testament Translation Problems II," *The Bible Translator*, Vol. 28, No. 1 (1977), pp. 103-104.

[1480] R. H. Fuller, "Pre-existence Christology: Can We Dispense with It?" *Word and World 2* (St. Paul: Luther Seminary, 1982), p. 33.

[1481] J. A. T. Robinson, *The Human Face of God* (Philadelphia: Westminster Press, 1873).

[1482] *The Good News Translation (Today's English Version)* (American Bible Society, 1966).

[1483] William Barclay, *The Gospel of John*, Vol. 1 (Edinburgh: Saint Andrews Press, 1956), p. 38ff.

[1484] Robert W. Funk, *The Five Gospels (Scholar's Version)* (New York: Macmillian, 1993).

have also attempted to render the logos itself as something more indicative of the creative word:

> Heinfetter: "As a god the Command was."[1485]
> Faircloth: "and what God was, the declared purpose was."[1486]

"Command" or "declared purpose" do seem to take the wider scope of the Greek term "logos" into account.

Either the second or third alternative translation seems preferable to the first, mostly on the grounds that the logos is not represented by John as a person before the birth of Jesus, but as a principle, God's own word. Again, it is not that the traditional translation "and the word was God" is incorrect, but either "the word was divine" or "what God was, the word was" seems to better relay the adjectival use of John's "theos."

Ultimately, we do not find in John's prologue a purported Trinitarian master-text; we do not find anything which would impugn the unitarian monotheism ardently practiced in John's Jewish environment. John's logos concept is not extracted from Platonic or Gnostic sources, but from the inherently Jewish, Old Testament notion of God's creative word and wisdom. In this scheme, the Jewish concept of pre-existence plays a foundational role; nothing has come into being which did not exist first in God's mind, including Jesus. As the Protestant exegete Paul Billerbeck reminds us, "The doctrine of the ideal pre-existence of the Messiah in the world of God's thought makes the Messiah an essential ingredient of the eternal and therefore unchangeable plans of God for the world."[1487] We therefore find in John no newly restructured theology to account for a literally pre-existent and eternally begotten divine being, but simply a poetic and deeply Jewish hymn recalling the light and truth dwelling in the primordial purpose of the eternal Father, now made manifest in the person and work of the man Jesus Christ.

[1485] Hermann Heinfetter (Frederick Parker), *A Literal Translation of the New Testament of our Lord and Saviour Jesus Christ* (London: Evan Evans, 1863).

[1486] Raymond C. Faircloth, *The Kingdom of God Version* (Lexington: CreateSpace, 2013).

[1487] Paul Billerbeck, quoted in Kuschel, p. 218.

15

CHRIST AND THE SPIRIT OF GOD

*"We cannot deny that our proofs
for the independent Divinity of the
Holy Spirit are very weak."*
– C. T. Bretschneider
(Bibliotheca Sacra, October, 1852; vol. IX)

LAST BUT NOT LEAST IN THIS INVESTIGATION, we turn our attention to the matter of the Holy Spirit. It is quite fitting that the alleged "Third Person of the Trinity" should be nearly an after-thought; he has received the very same treatment by orthodoxy. Recalling our earlier survey of mainstream Christianity, while most evangelicals say they affirm the Trinity, more than half (51%) actually said that the Holy Spirit is a force, not a personal being. Seven percent weren't sure.[1488] This means that half of all evangelicals are by definition not Trinitarians. Such confusion or disagreement represents a theological crisis of epic proportions.

[1488] Kevin P. Emmert, "New Poll Finds Evangelical's Favorite Heresies," *Christianity Today*. 28 October 2014. Web.14 November 2014.

Indeed, the nature of the Spirit has proven a cause for vexation across all Christian eras. In the early periods of speculation, the Spirit appears to have languished in uncertainty for decades, being virtually by-passed as the Gentile Christians struggled so visibly to define the natures of Jesus and the Father. Indeed the famous Nicene Creed of 325 CE nearly neglected the matter of the Spirit completely, save for a vague reference. Evidently, even the episcopal jousters at Nicaea avoided speaking dogmatically about the Spirit due to a perceived biblical ambiguity on the topic. If this is true, we wonder how the orthodox party could reasonably force acceptance of the three-person dogma on pain of anathema and even death? One of the most famous Church Fathers and prominent developer of Trinitarian doctrine, the Cappadocian Gregory of Nazianzus admitted in 381 CE:

> Of the wise among us, some hold the Holy Spirit to be a power, others a creature, others for God, and still others are unwilling to decide, out of reverence (or so they say) for the Scriptures, which do not speak plainly on the matter.[1489]

We must point out that if the orthodox doctrine of the Trinity, even the general idea of the Trinity, had existed in thorough acceptance by the Church from the times of the Apostles, this prominent Church doctor seems painfully unaware. We find that it was not until the year 381 CE, "at the Council of Constantinople, that the divinity of the Spirit was affirmed."[1490] It is interesting that Gregory's comment about the confusion and disagreement on the Spirit was made in the same year in which the "ecumenical" council, backed by the spears of the violent emperor Theodosius I, decided for all Christians that the Holy Spirit was unquestionably a third co-equal Person. What about those who had always followed in the tradition that the spirit was God's power or even a lesser creature? Though the force of the civil government ensured the Third Person's acceptance, the theological difficulties were unabated. In fact, they only intensified.

The co-eternal personhood of the Spirit presented then, and still presents to this day, a serious problem. If the Person of the Holy Spirit was eternal God, he was, therefore, uncreated. Yet he could not be considered "begotten" by God; that unique existence belonged to the "only begotten" Son. But if the Person of

---

[1489] F. A. Loofs, "Macedonius," *The New Schaff-Herzog Encyclopedia of Religious Knowledge* (Grand Rapids: Baker House, 1963), p. 112.

[1490] Howard Marshall, Alan Millard, J.I. Packer, "Trinity," *New Bible Dictionary* (Downers Grove: IVP, 1996).

the Holy Spirit was neither created nor begotten, yet was still eternal God, this would make him a second "ingenerate principle." In other words, there would be two Fathers. But if he was indeed generated by the Father, then there would be two Sons.[1491]

Many modern Christians, even those in the Trinitarian camp, evidently still struggle with the matter. We carry on this tradition of uncertainty, and question whether the Bible supports the constrained interpretation of orthodoxy, that "the spirit of God" is another self of God. Could the biblical view of the Spirit be much more broad and complex? Could grasping it also pave the way for a more rational theology in line with the express teachings of Jesus?

Our premise is this: that the "spirit of God," or "the Holy Spirit," is not a deity or a person distinct from the Father or Jesus at all. Rather, in most cases, it is simply the personal power and influence of God, *"the spirit of your Father"* (Matt 10:20). The spirit is God's personal operation in the world, which enables the accomplishment of his work. After Christ's exaltation to the right hand of God, the Holy Spirit can now also be described as the personal influence of the glorified Lord Jesus, the Christians' *"one advocate with the Father"* (1 Jn 2:1), who baptizes believers with God's power (1 Cor 15:45; Jn 14:18; Matt 3:11). Both God and his Son now work together through this spiritual power on behalf of the believer.

An Admitted Deficiency of Support

There exists substantial evidence that the Holy Spirit is not, in fact, another co-equal Person distinct from God the Father. One Trinitarian scholar admits:

> It cannot be proved, out of the whole number of passages in the Old Testament in which the Holy Spirit is mentioned, that this is a person in the Godhead; and it is now the almost universally received opinion of learned commentators, that, in the language of the Jews, the "Holy Spirit" means nothing more than divine inspiration, without any reference to a person.[1492]

The New Testament likewise supports this visible lack of a "third Person." For example, "the Holy Spirit" is not addressed in worship or prayer, and neither

---

[1491] See G. W. H. Lampe, *Explorations in Theology*, Vol. 8 (SCM Press, 1981), p. 30.

[1492] J. D. Michaelis, Note on John XVI, 13-15, as quoted in John Wilson, *Uni. Princ.*, (Boston: American Unitarian Association, 1888), p. 477.

Jesus nor his Apostles prescribes any necessary acknowledgement of any person outside the Father and the Son. Despite the arguments of many apologists that the Spirit is presented clearly in the New Testament as a unique individual, some scholars in the Trinitarian camp reveal a more tempered observation, such as one Professor of Theology from the University of Halle:

> Writers have thought too much of a number of texts, and have collected indiscriminately many which have only an apparent relation to the subject... It is doubtful, in many of these texts in which the predicate "God" is used, whether the Holy Spirit as a person is intended. Many of them, at least, may be explained without necessarily supposing a personal subject... Some have endeavored to prove the Divinity of the Holy Spirit from a comparison of different texts; but, in doing this, they have often resorted to forced and unnatural interpretations.[1493]

Even some classical Trinitarian scholars have recognized that the Spirit as a third Person is a thing "totally foreign from the train of reasoning pursued by the apostle[s], nor could [they] have introduced it there without doing violence to the law of thought and association."[1494] We must presently investigate the matter for ourselves.

The Neglected Third Person

Even today we find the grave deficit of biblical communication regarding the identity and operation of this nameless God-Person presenting one of the most enduring challenges for the entire Trinitarian conundrum. Some modern Trinitarians have even humorously taken to calling him "the shy member of the Trinity."[1495] But there should be nothing humorous about the very real possibility of a manufactured God.

The Trinity doctrine teaches that the Holy Spirit is fully God, equal in status and glory with the Father and the Son, and worthy of worship along with them.[1496] If this is truly the case, why do we not encounter specific teaching

---

[1493] G. C. Knapp, *Lectures on Christian Theology* (London: Thomas Ward and Co., 1831), p. 128.

[1494] J. D. Knowles, Barnas Sears, *Christian Review for June*, Vol. 2 (Boston: Gould, Kendall and Lincoln & Utica, 1837), p. 212.

[1495] See "Thankful for the Shy Member of the Trinity," Straight Thinking. Reasons to Believe. Web. 02 November 2015. <http://www.reasons.org/podcasts/straight-thinking/thankful-for-the-shy-member-of-the-trinity>.

[1496] See The Constantinopolitan Creed, 381 CE: "We believe in the Holy Spirit, the Lord, the giver of life... who with the Father and the Son is worshiped and glorified."

from Jesus or his Apostles about any necessary devotion to this unique individual, an identity of which the Jews knew nothing and surely would have required intense education? Indeed, what could be more critical than the revelation concerning the accurate worship of the third Person of the uncanny triune God?

What we do encounter in the writings of the Apostles is a theological worldview virtually absent any acknowledgment of such a supposedly crucial personality. John writes: *"our fellowship is with the Father and with his Son, Jesus Christ"* (1 Jn 1:3). Also, *"No one who denies the Son has the Father; whoever acknowledges the Son has the Father also. If what you heard from the beginning abides in you, you will also abide in the Son and in the Father"* (1 Jn 2:24). But what about the other co-equal person? If only real persons can have relationships, is it John's lack of understanding of the Holy Spirit as unique person which enables his omission?

The greetings in almost all of the New Testament epistles furnish perhaps the best and most sweeping example of the consistent Apostolic omission. While all of the authors recognize "God the Father" and "the Lord Jesus Christ," they seem to be ever missing the essential third member of the group:

> *"Grace to you and peace from God our Father and the Lord Jesus Christ"* (2 Corinthians 1:2).

> *"Paul, an apostle… through Jesus Christ and God the Father, who raised him from the dead"* (Galatians 1:1).

> *"Grace to you and peace from God our Father and the Lord Jesus Christ"* (Ephesians 1:2).

> *"Grace to you and peace from God our Father and the Lord Jesus Christ"* (Philippians 1:2).

> *"Paul, an apostle of Jesus Christ… Grace to you and peace from God our Father"* (Colossians 1:1).

> *"Paul, Silas and Timothy, to the church of the Thessalonians in God the Father and the Lord Jesus Christ: Grace and peace to you"* (1 Thessalonians 1:1).

"To the church of the Thessalonians in God our Father and the Lord Jesus Christ" (2 Thessalonians 1:1).

"Grace, mercy and peace from God the Father and Christ Jesus our Lord" (2 Timothy 1:2).

"Grace to you and peace from God our Father and the Lord Jesus Christ" (Philemon 1:3).

"To those who have been called, who are loved in God the Father and kept for Jesus Christ" (Jude 1:1).

We must wonder why only the Father and the Son greet the churches. Again, could this be because only real persons send personal greetings, and the Apostles had no understanding of "the Holy Spirit" as such? If they did not, and if the true nature of the Trinity was only being progressively revealed to the Church, would this not make them poor Apostles, inadequately entrusted with only half-truths? If they did understand it, why the exclusion? Critics of these questions may protest an argument from silence, but it is the wide scope and necessary implication of the Apostolic silence on this issue that should be more troubling—or is it not fair to wonder at the consistent oversight of the indispensable third Person, the very one who makes the Christian God "triune," in early Christian teaching and history? We would agree, however, that arguments about omission alone should not build our foundation, but neither should they be neglected in this case. After all, the Apostles *should* be eager to elucidate the newest, most exciting information in Jewish religious history: that the one God was actually *three* different Persons all along. If their objective was to act as the appointed ambassadors of these three unique entities to the world, as evidenced by the communication of greetings from the heavenly parties, they artfully miss every opportunity to openly demonstrate what should be the core and unique revelation of their Christian faith.

Trinitarian translators have not failed to notice that the only individuals the Apostles identify as objects of necessary fellowship are the Father and the Son. They therefore have sometimes felt the need to impose requisite fellowship with the missing third Person onto the text. In the Trinitarian *New International Version*, Philippians 2:1-2 is deliberately translated to read that we are to have *"fellowship __with__ the Spirit."* Other more appropriate translations, such as the KJV,

NASB and others, read "*fellowship of the Spirit.*" The NIV committee has attempted to portray "the Spirit" as an individual with whom Christians should have personal communion. This does, of course, appear to contradict the explicit Apostolic prescription elsewhere that "*our fellowship is with the Father and with his Son, Jesus Christ*" (1 Jn 1:3). Nevertheless, we see that even the NIV reading of "*fellowship with the Spirit*" has undergone a serious revision in the 2011 NIV update so that it now reads: "*common sharing in the Spirit.*" Regardless of the reason for the NIV's drastic change, this new rendering does seem to better convey the Apostolic instruction here: the disciples of Christ should enjoy a common "spirit" with one another, that is, they should operate in harmony (see also 2 Cor 13:14—the commonality between the disciples is to be a fellowship "of" the spirit, not "with" the Spirit).

It is not only in the epistles, however, that we encounter the stunning neglect of the hypothetical third Person; the visions of John's Apocalypse paint a similar picture. Throughout the narrative, a distinction between Jesus and God is repeatedly recognized (Rev 7:10; 5:13; 11:15; 12:10; 20:6; 21:22), and they are each awarded a throne in Revelation 22:1. But where is the throne of the co-equal Holy Spirit? As Revelation depicts the dramatic conclusion of the Age and the ultimate resting place of God and his Christ in total victory, we wonder why the third member of the Trinity is not likewise awarded his rightful honors, or even made mention of, in these glorious closing scenes.

While we might be ready to conclude that this consistent omission of any third Person confirms the equally consistent and simple teaching that there are only two individuals Christians are required to recognize and enter into communion with: "*the Father… the only true God, and Jesus Christ*" (Jn 17:3), there is still more argument to be constructed.

Biblical Usage of "Spirit"

Far from simply meaning "a person," the biblical application of the word "spirit" (both the Hebrew "ruach" and the Greek "pneuma") is broad. It refers to: *wind* (Dan 7:2), *breath* (2 Thess 2:8), *vitality* (Gen 2:7), *rational discernment* (Job 32:8), *the mind* (Mark 2:8), *attitude* (Deut 2:30), *disposition* (Luke 1:17), *an individual under divine inspiration* (1 John 4:1-6), *an incorporeal entity* (Luke 24:39), *a demon* (Matt 8:16), *power* (Ps 33:6-9), *divine knowledge* (Num 11:29), *instruction* (Neh 9:20), *supernatural impulse* (Acts 16:6), and more.

From this selection we may observe several general categories of application: a) *wind or breath*, b) *life or intelligence*, c) *attitude or mind*, and d) *power or influence*.

Professor Dunn likewise observes the broad meaning of the word and concludes that the Jews never viewed "the spirit of God" or "the Holy Spirit" as a unique person apart from God the Father:

> There can be little doubt that from the earliest stages of pre-Christian Judaism, "spirit" (*ruach*) denoted power—the awful, mysterious force of the wind (*ruach*), of the breath (*ruach*) of life, of ecstatic inspiration (induced by divine *ruach*)... In other words, on this understanding, Spirit of God is in no sense distinct from God, but is simply the power of God, God himself acting powerfully in nature and upon men.[1497]

The Spirit as Breath, Life or Attitude

First, the word "spirit" itself derives from a Hebrew verb meaning "to breathe out," and thus describes the literal breath of a person or animal. As breath serves to produce and sustain a being's existence, "spirit" naturally functions to relate the concept of the life of a soul. When God breathed into Adam the "breath" of life, it was only then that he became a rational being: *"Then the LORD God formed a man from the dust of the ground and breathed into his nostrils the breath of life, and the man became a living soul"* (Gen 2:7). One dictionary explains:

> When used of living beings, *ruach* refers to the essence of the life and vitality in both human beings and animals that is manifested through movement and breathing (Genesis 2:7; 6:17; 7:15; Numbers 16:22; Ezekiel 10:17). Just as "spirit" was considered the essence of human life, so analogously the term "spirit" was used of the presence, activity, and power of God, that is, characteristics that demonstrate that God is truly a "living God" (Deuteronomy 5:26; Joshua 3:10; 1 Samuel 7:26; Isaiah 37:4; Daniel 6:20; Matthew 16:16; Revelation 7:2).[1498]

The imparted spirit is therefore the intellect or understanding of a being: *"But there is a spirit in man, the inspiration of the Almighty giveth them understanding"* (Job 32:8). In this way "spirit" denotes the mind or reason of a particular person, not

---

[1497] Dunn, *Christology in the Making*, p. 133.
[1498] Jacob Neusner, William Scott Green (ed.), *Dictionary of Judaism in the Biblical Period* (Peabody: Hendrickson Publishers, 1996), p. 298.

another person distinct from him. That the word may refer to the rational principle of a conscious being is certain:

> *For who among men knows the thoughts of a man except the spirit of the man which is in him? Even so the thoughts of God no one knows except the spirit of God* (1 Corinthians 2:11).

The spirit of a man is akin to the spirit of God. These are not distinct intelligences in their own right, but simply the mind of both the man and God.

We may furthermore relate one's "spirit" to one's own heart or will. Observe the parallelism in the following verses:

> *Yahweh your God hardened <u>his spirit</u>, and made <u>his heart</u> obstinate* (Deuteronomy 2:30).

> *The sacrifices of God are a <u>broken spirit</u>; <u>a broken and contrite heart</u>, O God, You will not despise* (Psalm 51:17).

God's "spirit" is connected to his heart, the seat of the will and the attitude, as is man's. Again, the word is describing only an individual's personal operating force: "*So the LORD stirred up the spirit of Zerubbabel... and the spirit of the whole remnant of the people*" (Hag 1:14); "*So the God of Israel stirred up the spirit of Pul, king of Assyria, even the spirit of Tilgath-pilneser king of Assyria*" (1 Chron 5:26). The spirit of man has the same relationship to the man as the spirit of God does to God; it is something which belongs to him, not another person.

The Spirit as Power and Influence

In Scripture, "the spirit" is most often a divine influence or energy. In the Old Testament, the spirit of God is portrayed as his own power or initiative at work. In many cases it is his creative power: "*By the word of the LORD the heavens were made, their starry host by the spirit of his mouth*" (Ps 33:6). In the New Testament the angel equates "*the Holy Spirit*" with "*the power of the Most High*" which was to "*come upon*" and "*overshadow*" Mary in order to create Jesus within her womb (Luke 1:35). Yet neither the command nor the power of God should be seen as a separate divine person.

Biblically speaking, beyond a creative power or energy, "spirit" can also refer to any influence over a person. For example, one may act under the influence of "*the spirit of truth*" (Jn 14:17), or "*the spirit of error*" (1 Jn 4:6). Obviously these are not unique persons, but forces affecting the thinking and conduct of individuals.

To therefore think of the "the spirit of God" or "the Holy Spirit" primarily as God's personal influence or presence is helpful. While God is described as occupying a throne in heaven (Dan 7:9), we read that the heavens cannot contain him (1 Kings 8:27). Though his dwelling place is in another realm, God is able to be elsewhere via his spirit, or his presence, which fills the universe and also indwells his servants. This influence is characterized in various ways in the Scriptures. It is described as God's "*hand*" (Ezek 3:14), or even God's own "*breath*" (Ps 104:29, Jn 3:38). In Zechariah 7:12 we read about "*the words which the LORD of hosts had sent through his spirit.*" It is through this extension of spiritual energy that God reaches out and affects the world from his throne room.

Myriad biblical episodes portray God's own spirit coming upon various individuals to perform work he has appointed for them. When this influence arrives, it urges activity to be conducted on behalf of, or in the same manner as, the influencer. Prophets speak the words of God: "*and the spirit of God rushed upon him, and he prophesied among them*" (1 Sam 10:10); kings carry out the wrath of God: "*When Saul heard their words, the Spirit of God came powerfully upon him, and he burned with anger*" (1 Sam 11:6); and artisans fulfill the designs of God: "*I have filled him with the Spirit of God in wisdom, in understanding, in knowledge, and in all kinds of craftsmanship, to make artistic designs… and in the hearts of all who are skillful I have put skill, that they may make all that I have commanded you.*" (Ex 31:3, 6b). Ultimately, as Jesus explains, the function of the spirit is to enable God's work in the recipient: "*You will receive power when the Holy Spirit has come upon you; and you will be witnesses in Jerusalem, and in all Judea and Samaria, and to the ends of the earth*" (Acts 1:8).

In the Gospels we read that Jesus himself was empowered to perform incredible wonders "*by the spirit of God*" (Matt 12:28). In the parallel Gospel of Luke, this reads: "*by the finger of God*" (Luke 11:20). God's "*spirit*" and God's "*finger*" are therefore synonymous, and simply describe God's outstretched power. Indeed, the NLT, ISV and others even render it "*by the power of God.*" It should be obvious that the spirit is only a personal attribute of God; we need not assign personhood and deity to "God's finger."

The Spirit as the Mind of God

As the New Testament says that the "*spirit of God… knows the thoughts of God*" (1 Cor 2:11), we might wonder, in light of Trinitarianism, if this spirit is another person distinct from God the Father? In opposition to this idea, Jesus explains that the Holy Spirit is actually *"the spirit of your Father"* (Matt 10:20). This is no more a different person from the Father than *"the spirit of Elijah"* is a distinct person from Elijah. The Old Testament reports that *"the spirit of Elijah rests on Elisha"* (2 Kings 2:15), and in the New Testament, John the Baptist is also said to operate *"in the spirit and power of Elijah"* (Luke 1:17). It is meant of course that Elisha and John both came with the same mind, passion, or influence as Elijah. When Jesus tells his followers, *"For it is not you who speak, but it is the spirit of your Father who speaks in you"* (Matt 10:20), he means not that some other person, someone who is *not* the Father according to Trinitarian doctrine, would lend his operational mind to them, but simply that the Father himself would supply the ability. The same "spirit" in God's mouth (Ps 33:6) would now occupy their own mouths; in other words, to a certain degree the very mentality of God would become intimately available.

The Spirit as the Mind of Christ

In the same way, when the disciples are said to have a mind that is set on good things, a mind that rejects evil and is subservient to God's law, they are said to *"have the spirit of Christ"* (Rom 8:5-9). Possessing Jesus' spirit means not that Jesus, or some other literal person sits within their bodies; rather that they are participating in the same mindset, the same spiritual mode of action as Jesus himself. Paul charges believers to *"Let this mind be in you, which was also in Christ Jesus"* (Phil 2:5), and indeed the Apostles affirm, *"But we have the mind of Christ"* (1 Cor 2:16). In the same way that harboring the spirit of Elijah was to act in Elijah's characteristic spiritual and rational manner, so having the spirit of Jesus is likewise to operate by his same mind and ability.

In the post-ascension Christian community, the Holy Spirit is recognized as both "the spirit of Christ" and "the spirit of God," in that it is both the spiritual mindset of Jesus, and the same power and ability through which Jesus himself operated, that is, the power of God. *"Now we have received,"* says Paul, *"not the spirit of the world, but the spirit which is of God; that we might know the things that are freely given to us of God"* (1 Cor 2:12). The spirit which is of God is the same spirit by which Jesus operated, and that spirit is now distributed so that participation in the things of God is open to everyone: *"The person without the spirit does not accept the things that come from the spirit of God but considers them foolishness, and cannot understand them because they are discerned only through the spirit"* (1 Cor 2:14).

The Spirit as the Gift of God

In the Bible, the spirit of God is presented as a thing to be *distributed*. God says, *"I will take some of the spirit that is upon you, and put it on them"* (Num 11:17 ESV). The ISV reads, *"some of the spirit… and apportion it among them."* The NET reads, *"part of the spirit."* Of course, in an attempt to preserve the orthodox view, some Trinitarian translations like the NASB present the rendering: *"and I will take of the Spirit <u>who</u> is upon you, and will put <u>Him</u> upon them."* This is problematic in that "a person" cannot be taken, divided, or distributed. Despite the activism of the NASB, others like the ESV, ISV, KJV, and ASV properly represent the nature of this spirit, in alignment with other passages such as Joel 2:8, quoted by Peter in Acts 2:17: *"ekcheo apo tou Pneumatos"* (the sense is: I will apportion *out of* the Spirit). It makes little sense to say that a person, a unique individual in the same category as Jesus, could be "apportioned," but it makes much more sense to acknowledge the spirit as the power of God; it is God's own energy that dwells in his people. No one is to be inhabited (or "possessed") by a *person*. 1 John 4:13 is clear: *"By this we know that we abide in him and he in us, because he has given us <u>of his Spirit</u>"* (ESV).

Making a Mess of the Spirit

When we take passages regarding the spirit of God and replace the terms with their Trinitarian interpretation, we immediately force a muddle of virtually every text dealing with the Spirit. Substituting "God the Holy Spirit," or "the third Person of the Trinity," should produce clarity if the interpretation were true, but we are instead left only with confusion.

In the Gospels, Jesus claims that he casts out demons *"by the Spirit of God"* (Matt 12:28). The Trinitarian should understand this to mean, *"by the third Person of the Trinity."* However, Jesus routinely clarifies that it is *"the Father"* who does the works (Jn 14:10). Similarly, the angel told Mary that *"the Holy Spirit"* would overshadow her and produce Jesus within her womb (Luke 1:35), and it was later confirmed with Joseph: *"the child who has been begotten in her is of the Holy Spirit"* (Matt 1:20). If we perform the Trinitarian reading, we are left to wonder who Jesus' real father is? Again, according to the Trinity doctrine, the Father and the Holy Spirit are two *completely different Persons*. If the third Person is the one who came upon Mary, why do we call another, who did not come upon Mary, his father? Of course, for the non-Trinitarian who understands that the Holy Spirit is primarily the spirit (power and influence) of God, the Father of Jesus, the matter is easily settled. Buzzard and Hunting report that:

If one combs through standard Bible dictionaries, it is obvious that ninety-eight percent of the biblical data is satisfied if we define the Spirit as God in effective action, God in communication, His power and personality extending his influence to touch the creation in a variety of ways... Is the Spirit really anything other than God's energy, inspiring human beings to perform extraordinary feats of valor, endowing them with special artistic skill or miraculous powers, and especially communicating divine truth?[1499]

Personification of the Spirit

In the New Testament, because the Holy Spirit is a personal influence, the literary technique of personification is sometimes employed in its description. The spirit speaks (Jn 16:13), teaches (Jn 14:26), can be outraged (Heb 10:29), can be blasphemed against (Matt 12:32),[1500] can be lied to (Acts 5:4),[1501] and intercedes (Rom 8:26). But Trinitarian apologists have chosen these

---

[1499] Buzzard, Hunting, *The Doctrine of the Trinity*, p. 226. A further note: if we hold that "God's spirit" in the Bible is indeed the unique Person of post-Constantinopolitan theology, we may create problems in the Old Testament. Zechariah 6:5 features *"the four spirits of heaven,"* and Revelation 1:4 mentions *"the seven spirits of God."* Revelation 1:4 seems to correlate with Isaiah 11:2 which features, *"the spirit of the Lord, the spirit of wisdom, the spirit of understanding, the spirit of counsel, the spirit of might, the spirit of knowledge and the spirit of the fear of the Lord."* Is this a reference to multiple personalities, or simply seven powers and influences?

[1500] Finnegan's note is useful here: "Occasionally, people claim that denying the personality of the holy spirit is the unforgivable sin of blaspheming the spirit. In order to get to the bottom of the matter, we must remember the context of Jesus' remarks about blaspheming the holy spirit. A demonized man was healed by Christ, and the Pharisees accused Jesus of casting out demons by Beelzebub, the ruler of demons. Christ pointed out the absurdity of *'Satan casting out Satan'* and then confessed that it was by God's spirit that he cast out demons. Then he made the statement, *'Whoever speaks a word against the Son of Man, it shall be forgiven him; but whoever speaks against the holy spirit, it shall not be forgiven him, either in this age or in the age to come'* (Matthew 12:32). Blasphemy against the holy spirit is observing God in action through His human Messiah and declaring that the source of his power was demonic rather than divine. In essence, they were calling God the prince of demons. This sort of unrepentant, hardhearted, intentional blasphemy against God at work in His Messiah is unforgivable" (Finnegan, p. 5).

[1501] One Trinitarian scholar admits: "The term 'God' is never [in Scripture] expressly attributed to the Holy Spirit, though it is usual to infer it from Acts 5:4, where Peter, who in the third verse had asked Ananias, 'Why hath Satan filled thy heart to lie to the Holy Spirit?' says, 'Thou has not lied unto men, but unto God.' But, in our opinion, this deduction is not valid; for by the 'Holy Spirit' are to be understood the gifts of the Holy Spirit, with which the apostles were furnished, and spoke in the name of God. Persons, therefore, who lie to the apostles speaking by the Holy Spirit of God, are rightly said to lie to the Holy Spirit; as those who despise the apostles are said to despise the Lord, and those who despise the Lord Jesus despise Him that sent him" (Philip Limborch, *Theol. Christiana*, lib. II. Cap. 17 & 23, quoted in Wilson, *Uni. Princ.*, p. 477).

personifications as their prime battlefield, and most of the arguments follow this line of reasoning:

> *"And do not grieve the Holy Spirit"* is Paul's instruction to the Ephesian believers (Ephesians 4:30). If the Holy Spirit were simply a power or a force, and not a person, he could not be grieved.[1502]

What they are really arguing is that because the Holy Spirit is presented as a thing both distinct from God and Jesus, and sometimes in personal terms, it must be a separate person who is not the Father or Jesus. But the truth is that other persons' spirits are described in the Bible using the literary technique of personification, and no distinct person is implied. For example, in the Old Testament we read:

> But he would not <u>grieve the spirit of Amnon</u> his son, for he loved him, because he was his first born (2 Samuel 13:21).[1503]

Is Amnon's spirit another person? No, this kind of language is simply Hebrew idiom. We find it also in first-century Jewish writings such as the *Gospel of the Hebrews*. The Catholic translator Jerome (347-420 CE) recalls a quote from the document:

> In the Gospel According to the Hebrews, which the Nazarenes are wont to read, there is counted among the most grievous offenses: "He that has <u>grieved the spirit of his brother.</u>"[1504]

The Jews seem ever unaware of the Trinitarian rule that person's spirits cannot be "grieved" or participate metaphorically in any number of personal activities unless they are distinct persons themselves. Again, at 2 Samuel 13:39 we read that "*<u>the spirit of the king longed</u> to go out to Absalom*" (2 Samuel 13:39). Grieving, longing, etc.—these are the same examples provided by Trinitarians as absolute proof that God's spirit must be a distinct person. But the spirit of

---

[1502] "How Can We Grieve the Holy Spirit?" Bible Answers. Ranelagh Christian Church. 2015. Web. 27 December 2015. <http://www.bibleanswers.ie/short-bible-studies/62-the-holy-spirit/102-how-can-we-grieve>, emphasis added.

[1503] See Adam Clarke's Commentary: " Και ουκ ελυπησε το πνευμα Αμνων του υἱου αυτου, ὁτι ηγαπα αυτον, ὁτι πρωτοτοκος αυτου ην ; *But he would not grieve the soul of Amnon his son, for he loved him, because he was his first-born.*' The same addition is found in the Vulgate and in Josephus, and it is possible that this once made a part of the Hebrew text" (Adam Clarke, "Commentary on 2 Samuel 13:2," The Adam Clarke Commentary. 1832. Web. 27 December 2015).

[1504] Jerome, *Commentary on Ezekiel*, 6 (on Ezekiel 18:7).

Elijah is not a separate person from Elijah. Neither is the spirit of the Father. It is simply not a biblical argument that stands up under scrutiny.

The Exalted Jesus: Baptizing with the Spirit

An interesting passage in the Gospel of John reads: *"But this he spoke of the spirit, which those who believed in him were to receive; for the spirit was not yet given, because Jesus was not yet glorified"* (Jn 7:39). Of course we know that the spirit of God had already come upon countless persons in the Old Testament, and even Jesus himself was given the spirit at his baptism (Jn 1:32-33); evidently there was to be something extraordinary about this future outpouring of power.

In John 13 through 17, Jesus explains that this approaching manifestation of the spirit would now be intimately connected with the glorified Lord Jesus. According to Jesus, this spirit would actively teach the disciples, and specifically, it would call into remembrance all of the things that Jesus had said (Jn 14:26). Christ even explains this new arrangement would be better for them than if Christ were physically still with them (Jn 16:7) and that this spirit would reveal Christ to his disciples (Jn 16:14-15). This is hitherto unprecedented activity for the spirit of God; whereas formerly the spirit communicated only the influence of the Father (as the pre-ascension Jesus describes it in Matthew 10:20), it would now also transmit the influence of Jesus.

In John 7, John predicates the arrival of this new spirit on the future exaltation of Christ; it was unable to be given precisely because Jesus was still among them. Christ's transference to heaven, however, would enable its distribution. This is because the "spirit" that was to come to them was in a sense the heavenly Jesus himself.

When the disciples mourned his imminent departure, he assured them, *"I will not leave you as orphans; I will come to you"* (Jn 14:18). The "helper" is, in effect, Jesus present with them; the spirit influences Christ's students and guides them exactly as Jesus would if he were physically present. The post-Easter spirit is Jesus himself, still at work in the world for the mission and glory of God, coming to each of his disciples by way of God's great power.

In the same way that God is able to dwell in the heavens and yet be omnipresent via the spirit,[1505] the exalted Jesus, seated at the right hand of God, is the one who *"baptizes with the holy spirit"* (Mark 1:8; Acts 11:16); it is he who

---

[1505] God *"sits in the heavens"* (Ps 2:4), but his spirit allows him to be everywhere: *"Where can I go from your spirit? Or where can I flee from your presence? If I ascend to heaven, you are there; if I make my bed in Sheol, behold, you are there. If I take the wings of the dawn, if I dwell in the remotest part of the sea, even there your hand will lead me, and your right hand will lay hold of me"* (Ps 139:7-11).

sends the believer God's power from heaven. Just as God in ancient times had reached down and empowered people through this spirit, so too may the risen Lord Jesus *"come to the aid of those who are tempted"* (Heb 2:18) while still remaining seated at the right hand of the Majesty in the heavens.

When Jesus says that he will ask the Father to send *"another helper"* (Jn 14:16), the Greek for "another" (allos) actually refers to "another of the same kind of thing." It is another version of Jesus, or, as F. F. Bruce writes, "his alter ego."[1506] A biblical dictionary assists us further:

> The Spirit is now definitely the Spirit of Christ, the other Counselor who has taken over Jesus' role on the earth. This means that Jesus is now present to the believer only in and through the Spirit, and that the mark of the Spirit is both the recognition of Jesus' present status and the reproduction of the character of his sonship and resurrection life in the believer.[1507]

We see in the rest of the New Testament that the "spirit of Christ" is still frequently referred to as "the spirit of God" by the Church. This is simply because it is the same spirit, mutually enjoyed and operated by both of them. As stated previously, it is now to be recognized as both "the spirit of Christ" and "the spirit of God" in that it is equal parts the spiritual mindset of Jesus and the same power and ability through which Jesus himself operated, that is, the power of God. As one theologian so succinctly puts it, "The spirit which inspired Jesus during his ministry on earth would now enable him to be present within his disciples in a new advantageous way."[1508] He continues:

> The spirit of God, the spirit of Christ, and Christ himself are all equivalent ways of communicating the same essential truth. Paul does not focus on ontological and metaphysical distinctions; rather, he sees the spirit primarily in functional terms within the experience of the Christian. From this perspective the spirit is Jesus.[1509]

In the first chapter of Acts, Jesus instructs his followers *"to wait for what the Father had promised, 'which,' he said, 'you heard of from me; for John baptized with water,*

[1506] Bruce, *The Gospel & Epistles of John*, p. 302.

[1507] D. G. Douglas, *New Bible Dictionary* (Tyndale House Publishers, 1962), pp. 1140-1141.

[1508] Sean Finnegan, "A Unitarian View of the Holy Spirit," 21st Century Reformation. 2006. Web. 28 December 2015. p. 3.

[1509] Ibid., p. 3.

but you will be baptized with the holy spirit not many days from now' " (Acts 1:4-5). On the day of Pentecost, the new spirit indeed descended upon the Church. The disciples explained that it was precisely because Jesus, *"having been exalted to the right hand of God, and having received from the Father the promise of the holy spirit, he has poured forth this which you both see and hear"* (Acts 2:32-33). Because Jesus is the owner of the spirit (having received it from God), and the distributer of the spirit (the "baptizer"), the spirit may be personally attributed to him and rightly called "the spirit of Jesus." Jesus explains that it is both he and the Father who are working on behalf of the believer through the power of the spirit: *"If a man love me, he will keep my words: and my Father will love him, and we will come unto him, and make our abode with him"* (Jn 14:23). Does the hypothetical third Person not abide with the disciple? Again, the spirit can be considered an influence belonging to both the Father and the Son. An adequate analogy might be provided if we imagine a father who allows his son to take his car out in public. Everyone who sees it will refer to it as the son's car, because he has possession of it, but it is still ultimately the father's car. Anyone who knows where the car came from will still call it the father's car, but would not be wrong in describing it as belonging to the son. It is the same with God's power which has been entrusted to Jesus to distribute as he will.

Some Trinitarians argue against the idea that an agent of God could ever give God's spirit to others on the grounds that such activity was "unprecedented," and on the grounds that it would be impossible for God to delegate the sending of God "himself."[1510] However, a lack of precedent for the Son's level of delegated authority is a non-issue; he is clearly portrayed by the New Testament as the first man to achieve his status (see Heb 1-2). Regarding God's delegation of "himself," we must first recognize that God's "spirit" is not always synonymous with the whole "person" of God. Again, "some" of God's spirit was said to have been taken and "apportioned" among the elders of Israel (Num 11:17). The spirit need not be exclusively identified as the very "person" of God, since it is divided like a substance or property, distributed, and received in various measures by different parties. Regarding an agent's ability to perform this distribution, we may observe the very channeling of God's spirit which these apologists say is impossible for human agents in the book of Acts. In Acts 8:16ff, we find that some Christians did not receive the holy spirit until the Apostles came and laid their hands on them: *"Simon saw that the spirit was given through the laying on of the Apostles' hands"* (v. 18). Upon witnessing their ability to

---

[1510] See Bowman, *Putting Jesus in his Place*, pp. 219-221.

delegate the spirit, Simon requested that he too would be given this power, saying: *"Give this authority to me as well, so that everyone on who I lay my hands may receive the holy spirit"* (v. 19). But the Apostles described their authority as "the gift of God" and as their "ministry," a vocation which Simon could not participate in because he was not approved (vv. 20-21). Paul explains that the "gift of God" is *"in you through the laying on of my hands"* (2 Tim 1:6), and Acts 8:18 explicitly says that it was only *at* the laying on of the Apostles' hands that the spirit was "given" to these men. This word for "given" in Greek ("didomi") is the same word used in John 3:34 by Jesus to describe how God himself "gives" the spirit. This word is also translated by the NASB as "bestowed," "commanded," "granted," and even "poured." It is not then impossible for a human agent to act as a conduit for God's spirit. The model presented by the New Testament is simple and ably avoids the pitfalls of Trinitarian identity theories: God gave his agent Jesus the right to give or pour out the spirit, and in turn Jesus gave that right to his own agents, the Apostles.

Confounding the Bible

An interesting problem arises here for the Trinitarian when we consider the Spirit's new intimate relation with the glorified Jesus: the confusion of the God-the-Holy Spirit with God-the-Son. The doctrine of the Trinity stipulates that there are three distinct Persons, each with his own distinct role and function. This is correct in the sense that the Father and the Son are certainly not the same person, and play distinct roles—the Father is the "begetter" and the Son is the "mediator" to the Father, for example. But Trinitarians insist that the three Persons of the Trinity are distinct not only in their identity but also in their functional role within that Trinity. Popular theologian Charles Stanley writes that the Father, the Son, and the Spirit are:

> all equally omniscient, omnipotent, omnipresent, eternal, and unchanging, but each one has unique functions. Scripture shows how each member of the Trinity fulfills His specific role... The Father, Son, and Spirit are equal in their divine attributes. Yet each relates to mankind in a different way because He has a specific role. It's very important to understand this distinction.[1511]

[1511] Charles Stanley, "The Truth About the Trinity," In Touch with Dr. Charles Stanley. InTouch Ministries. 16 February 2010. Web. July 21, 2015.

But the Bible ignores a distinction between the roles and functions of the Spirit and the risen Jesus. The Holy Spirit is called *"the Advocate"* ["parakleton"] in John 14:26, and is described as the go-between, interceding on our behalf with God (Rom 8:26-27). But John writes that *"we have an Advocate* ["parakleton"] *with the Father, Jesus Christ the righteous"* (1 Jn 2:1). So which Person is the one Advocate between us and the Father, the third Person or the Second Person? Is it both? No, there is only one go-between mediating between mankind and God and it is specifically *the man* Jesus, not a non-human third Person who is distinctively *not* Jesus: *"For there is one God, and one mediator between God and men, the man Christ Jesus"* (1 Tim 2:5). In post-ascension Christian thought, the spirit is obviously used interchangeably with Jesus (Rom 8:9-11). But this is often by-passed by orthodox interpreters. In order to maintain the distinction of the Persons of the Trinity, Augustine was forced to write: "The Son is not the Holy Spirit."[1512] But the Apostle Paul wrote that *"the Lord [Jesus] is the Spirit"* (2 Cor 3:17)! Paul does not speculate about the metaphysical distinction of Persons; he does not believe that the Spirit is a different Person than Jesus—to him the Spirit is the Lord Jesus working through God's power.

The lack of proof of the Apostles' consistent separation of the persons and their functions reveals an underlying discrepancy between the Bible and orthodox interpretation. But if the Trinitarians says that this only proves they are all "the same God," we wonder what might constitute any uniqueness over, say, its rival Modalism, a theology which stipulates that the Father, Son, and Spirit are merely three modes of the same Person. This is precisely *not* what orthodoxy teaches; it demands a true distinction between the Persons—three completely different Persons with different roles who share a divine essence. To practically abandon the Trinity's foremost characteristic and to dangle over the flame of "heresy" by blurring the lines between the Persons when the doctrine seems lost on the text, seems an imprudent route for the orthodox believer. Indeed, the Athanasian Creed threatens certain damnation for anyone who would confound or confuse the Persons.[1513] But the Bible itself seems to be ever "confounding" the hypothetical God-Persons. The third Person is the one who begets when it should be the first Person (Lk 1:35), the third Person advocates when it should be the second Person (Jn 14:26), the third Person does the works when it should be the first Person (Jn 14:10), etc. Is it not much more practical

---

[1512] Augustine, *On Christian Doctrine*, 1, 5, 5.

[1513] "Neither confounding the persons nor dividing the substance. For there is one person of the Father, another of the Son, and another of the Holy Spirit... except a man believe faithfully he cannot be saved" (Athanasian Creed, c. 500 CE).

to say that the spirit is only the influence of both the Father and the Son in their different capacities, and avoid the muddle?

In summary, we have witnessed the active prejudice of many present-day Bible translators and their haphazard obscuration of the nature of the spirit. While literary personification of the spirit is provided as the uncontestable proof of the spirit's unique personhood, the personification of other person's spirits in biblical literature is ignored. Regardless of any translator's piety or intentions, a serious theological emergency is revealed by even this cursory investigation into the alleged third Person. At the very least, the orthodox idea of God is discovered to teeter precariously upon the neglect (abuse) of biblical language. A radical reconsideration of the theology of the New Testament, of the God of Jesus, is desperately needed. As already more than half of all evangelicals fail to recognize the third Person,[1514] the doctrine of the deity of the Holy Spirit presents itself as the weakest link in the scheme, and seems ever ready to collapse the entire Trinity theory.

[1514] Kevin P. Emmert, "New Poll Finds Evangelical's Favorite Heresies," *Christianity Today*. 28 October 2014. Web. 14 November 2014.

DENOUEMENT

"Too often we hold fast to the clichés of our forebears. We subject all facts to a prefabricated set of interpretations. We enjoy the comfort of opinion without the discomfort of thought."
— John F. Kennedy
(Commencement at Yale, June 11, 1962)

IN THE COURSE OF THIS INVESTIGATION we have sought to answer whether or not Trinitarian dogma really provides the best explanation of the historical Jesus' theology, or whether there exists a more viable alternative. We have examined the essential features of Trinitarian dogma: the three-in-one paradox, the pre-existence and dual natures of Christ, the personal deity of the Holy Spirit—and we have located the essential metaphysics which enable these views not in the sayings of the biblical authors but in the various philosophies of history.

It is clear that the problem of Christian dogma lies in the subversive Hellenistic syncretism which took place in the early centuries, and in how that syncretism affected Christian readings of the Bible. As Buzzard surmises: "the early Church Fathers, influenced by Gnosticism, misunderstood the book of John, neglected the evidence of the rest of the New Testament and Old Testament, relied on a handful of difficult Pauline verses and presented a Jesus who was literally pre-existent. But this is not the Jesus of the Bible."[1515]

The Fathers struggled for centuries to maintain the dual natures of this pre-existent Jesus in a non-Gnostic sense; they worked tirelessly to express the tri-personal God in a way that mutually protected Greek philosophy and monotheism, and they endeavored to accomplish these feats without doing great

---

[1515] Buzzard, *Jesus Was Not a Trinitarian*, p. 336.

violence to both Scripture and reason. Nevertheless, the mighty crash of their abject failure at each of these points still reverberates in our own time.

Truly, the discord of the earliest Christian centuries has never gone away; it has only been internalized and muted. Many faithful believers still perpetuate the great controversies quite unaware, while those who reject the conciliar standards are rejected themselves, despite their judges holding equally condemnable views. In mainstream Christianity we find that a heavy hand continues to prod the faithful to speak of Christ in language unknown to his Apostles, and to view the biblical God through a religious framework not communicated by him. The Bible is thus found to be paid a glorious lip service; its publicly celebrated teachings are truly inadequate: they ever require the skill of the later philosopher to make them useful for proper, saving belief.

Looking back, the Platonists and the Gnostics who cleaved to the faith in the earliest centuries were never completely detached. Their philosophies endured, transmigrated, and united with the heart and soul of the Catholic administration. Thus were the great mystics of old transformed: they became our leaders, our heroes, our trusted doctors serving theological remedies for ailments the biblical faith never had. Their ghosts still lecture in our universities; they stand nodding behind the pews in our churches; their hands guide the writing of our formal statements of faith. Yet in every Christian age, their guidance has proven unhelpful, even bewildering. A Protestant professor of church history writes:

> My conclusion, then, about the doctrine of the Trinity is that it is an artificial construct... It produces confusion rather than clarification; and while the problems with which it deals are real ones, the solutions it offers are not illuminating. It has posed for many Christians dark and mysterious statements, which are ultimately meaningless.[1516]

The Trinity doctrine is indeed a construct, but are the problems it addresses real? Is there truly some great fissure between the Old and New Testaments that only the Trinity can mend? Is the language of the biblical Jesus so divergent from his contemporary Judaism that we are forced to embrace him as Almighty God, and his doctrine as a new and incompatible religion?

[1516] Richardson, *The Doctrine of the Trinity*, pp. 148-149.

The Athanasian Creed, still so widely repeated today, says of belief in the doctrine of the Trinity, "we are compelled by the Christian verity,"[1517] and by the Christian verity we suppose it includes the Scriptures. But does the Bible really *compel* us to acknowledge Christ and the Spirit as co-equal God with the Father, as if there were no other sound alternative? No, as we have seen there exists another satisfactory approach to the biblical evidence which takes into account language and reason in equal measure; one that consults directly with the Christ of history over the Christ of the creeds.

What we have thus surveyed here as the epic story of orthodox theology is truly but one page in the troubled history of man's religion. The modern Trinitarianism is merely a single current flowing out into a vast ocean of religious interchange, an ocean where all the pagan speculation wells up to try and fill a great void. This void which the Trinity seeks so desperately to fill is the canyon between God and man. But for those who value the message of the Bible above all else, this is a space which can only be filled by the teachings of Christ. As we have seen, in those teachings there is nothing but an undivided and unquestionable monotheism; the Trinity is not the God of Jesus.

The solemn conclusion of this book, to be considered justly in light of the preceding evidence, is that neither Jesus nor his earliest followers present him as identical to the one true God of Israel, but instead as the one true God's human son; a uniquely, supernaturally begotten man who was anointed and empowered by God to complete the saving work as God's agent, a man whom God raised from the dead and made the source of salvation for all who would obey him. The God of the Jewish Scriptures is not therefore the peculiar tri-personal being of post-Apostolic Trinitarian theology, but the monolithic uni-personal identity described by the faiths of unitarian Christians and Jews, the entity whom Jesus exclusively identified as his own God and Father. The Holy Spirit is likewise not a distinct third Person within God, but the power and personal influence of the Father, and in the post New Testament era, also of the glorified Jesus. The New Testament language relating this information, language which later Christianity has long identified as indicating Trinitarian principles, is actually reflective of deeply Jewish traditions found in the Old Testament and in Second Temple Jewish literature. The opinions of the New Testament writers have thus been gravely misinterpreted or otherwise misappropriated by the systematic interpretations of ancient philosophers, and it is their daring conclusions, though now hardly understood or agreed upon, which remain on the books in most

---

[1517] Athanasian Creed, c. 500 CE.

Christian circles today. But if all of these things can be so readily demonstrated, as they have been in this humble volume, what reason have we to continue to tangle with the abstruse systems of Christian dogma? In the final analysis, we are pressed to agree with Professor Kaiser that "The Church's doctrine of the Trinity would seem to be the farthest thing from [Jesus' and the writers of the New Testament's] minds," and we are further pressed to wonder "if it is even helpful to refer to such a dogma in order to grasp the theology of the New Testament."[1518] In reality, the New Testament is found to present not a Chalcedonian mystery, but a Human Christology set against the backdrop of Jewish monotheism and projected through the lens of the Hebraic law of agency. We are not then compelled to accept the Trinity dogma, as the Athanasian Creed claims. We are given a clear choice.

Our exacting criticism of the doctrine of the Trinity also finds its motivation, not in a fear of a theological framework that is merely difficult to understand, but in a fear that the proposed formulations, whether inherited from the pagans or not, do not present intelligible ideas at all. In light of our completed survey, we may only wonder if the modern Christian will care to extract himself from his present difficulty, if he will esteem the unspoiled testimony of the historical Jesus about God as the naked and necessary doctrine, or continue to hold the para-biblical confusion of antiquity as the essential companion of that message.

As it has been said, theology is a fortress, and no crack in a fortress may be accounted small.[1519] The devotee may do his very best to patch up the dogma's weaknesses, to fill in its holes with painful arguments which elicit more bickering about words than lasting resolution. But ultimately, new wine cannot be placed into old wine skins—a costly demolition and rebuilding is in order. As W. R. Inge once said, Platonic philosophy has become part of the "vital structure" of Christian theology. It will be impossible to excise Platonism from Christianity without tearing the religion to pieces.[1520] Yet the deconstruction of beloved dogma need not be entirely painful. It affords us the latitude of reflection, an opportunity to salvage and illuminate the best things about the Christian faith, the things which help all men to be more like Christ, and to discard the useless, confusing, non-biblical and detrimental things which restrain him. Regardless of social value, all that can be shaken, must be. What then remains of Christian

---

[1518] Christopher B. Kaiser, *The Doctrine of God* (Eugene: Wipf & Stock, 2001), p. 27.
[1519] Arthur Miller, *The Crucible*, 1953.
[1520] W. R. Inge, *The Philosophy of Plotinus* (London: Longmans, 1918), p. 12, 14.

doctrine is nothing less than the truth God himself has prescribed, and beyond that there is no greater treasure. As one poet opined:

> It is a pleasure to stand upon the shore and to see ships tossed upon the sea; a pleasure to stand in the window of a castle and to see a battle and the adventures thereof below: but no pleasure is comparable to the standing upon the vantage ground of truth, and to see the errors and wanderings and mists and tempests in the vale below.[1521]

Yet in the course of human history, nothing has been as widely valued as the comfort of the familiar. In the collision between truth and custom, custom has largely prevailed; it has had many persons, ages, and institutions to constitute its weight, and with its full force it has refused the advance of the most unpopular and costly facts. But how much more water must burst through the many cracks in the official dogma about God before the dam breaks? How loudly must the growing evidence be publicly declared? No matter how valuable that dam may be considered, no matter how many ages were spent in its construction and adoration, if it remains unsound, it will not restrain the surge of truth. In the end, it is the persons most concerned with such things, with direct confrontation with the evidence, who will be sought by the God of Jesus. As Christ himself promises:

> *The hour is coming, and now is, when the true worshippers shall worship the Father in spirit and in truth: for the Father seeks such to worship him. God is spirit: and they that worship him must worship him in spirit and in truth* (John 4:23-24).

[1521] Sir Francis Bacon, *Essays, Of Truth*, 1625.

SELECTED BIBLIOGRAPHY

Abbot, Ezra. *The Authorship of the Fourth Gospel, and Other Critical Essays*. Boston: Geo. Ellis, 1888.

Akin, Daniel L. *A Theology for the Church*. Nashville: B&H Publishing Group, 2007.

Amidon, Philip R. *The Church History of Rufinus of Aquileia*. London: OUP, 1997.

Anders, Max. *Holman Old Testament Commentary, Proverbs*. Nashville: B&H Publishing Group, 2005.

Anderson, Hugh. *New Century Bible Commentary on Mark*. Grand Rapids: Eerdmans, 1981.

Arndt, William F. and F. Wilbur Gingrich. *A Greek-English Lexicon of the New Testament and Other Early Christian Literature (The Bauer Lexicon)*. Chicago: University of Chicago Press, 1957.

Ashwin-Siejkowski, Piotr. *Clement of Alexandria: A Project of Christian Perfection*. New York: T & T Clark, 2008.

Ayres, Lewis. "Athanasius' Initial Defense of the Term homoousios: Rereading the De Decretis," *Journal of Early Christian Studies*, Vol. 12, No. 3, Fall 2004. John Hopkins University Press, 2004.

Bache, Samuel, Charles Clarke. *Examination of Objections Made to Unitarianism by the Rev. J.C. Miller, M.A.* London: Whitfield, Strand, 1854.

Bainton, Roland H. *Christendom: A Short History of Christianity and Its Impact on Western Civilization*, Vol. 1. New York: Harper & Row, 1964.

Barclay, William. *Jesus as They Saw Him*. Grand Rapids: Eerdmans, 1978.

Barnes, Timothy D. *Athanasius and Constantius: Theology and Politics in the Constantinian Empire*. Cambridge, Mass.: Harvard University Press, 1993.

Barnstone, Willis, Marvin Meyer, *The Gnostic Bible*. Boston: Shambhala, 2006.

Barrett, C.K. *Essays on John*. Philadelphia: Westminster, 1982.

Barrow, Isaac. *Defense of the Blessed Trinity; in Works*, Vol. 2. New York: John C. Riker, 1845.

Bauckham, Richard. *The Image of the Judeo-Christians in Ancient Jewish and Christian Literature*. Leiden: Brill, 2003.

Beale, G. K. *The Right Doctrines from the Wrong Texts*. Grand Rapids: Baker, 1994.

Beasley-Murray, George R. *World Biblical Commentary*, Vol. 36. New York: Thomas Nelson, 1999.

Beatrice, Pier Franco. "The Word 'Homoousios' from Hellenism to Christianity," *Church History*, Vol. 71, No 2. Cambridge: CUP, 2002.

BeDuhn, Jason David. *Truth in Translation: Accuracy and Bias in English Versions of the New Testament*. Lanham, University Press of America, 2003.

Bernhard, J.H. *A Critical and Exegetical Commentary on the Gospel According to St. John*. Edinburgh: T&T Clark., 1928.

Bernal, Martin. *Black Athena Writes Back*. London: Duke University Press, 2001.

Bernard, John Henry. *International Critical Commentary: St. John*, Vol. 1. Edinburgh: T&T Clark, 1999.

Bertram, Martin H. *On The Jews and Their Lies, Luther's Works, Volume 47*; Philadelphia: Fortress Press, 1971.

Beveridge, Bishop William. *Private Thoughts Upon Religion and Upon Christian Life*, Part II. Literary Licensing LLC, 1829.

Bigg, Charles. *International Critical Commentary on Peter and Jude*. Edinburgh: T & T Clark, 1910.

Blass, Friedrich. *A Greek Grammar of the New Testament and Other Early Literature*. Chicago: University of Chicago Press, 1961.

Boccaccini, Gabriele. *Enoch and the Messiah Son of Man: Revisiting the Book of Parables*. Grand Rapids: Eerdmans, 2007.

Boer, Harry R. *A Short History of the Early Church*. Grand Rapids: Eerdmans, 1976.

Bonwick, James. *Egyptian Belief and Modern Thought*. London: C. Kegan Paul & Co., 1878.

Boobyer, G. H. "Jesus as Theos in the New Testament," Bulletin of the John Rylands Library 1967-1968, Vol. 50. Manchester University Press, 1968.

Borella, Jean. *Secret of the Christian Way*. New York: SUNY Press, 2001.

Bowman, John Wick. *The Intention of Jesus*. London: SCM Press, 1945.

Bowman, Robert M., J. Ed Komoszewski. *Putting Jesus in His Place*. Grand Rapids: Kregal Publications, 2007.

Bromiley, Geoffrey W. *The International Standard Bible Encyclopedia,* Vol. IV. Grand Rapids: Eerdmans, 1995.

Brown, Colin. "Trinity and Incarnation," *Ex Auditu*, Vol. 7. Eugene: Wipf and Stock, 1991.

———. *The New International Dictionary of New Testament Theology*, Vol. 3. Regency Reference Library, 1979.

Bruce, F. F. *The Gospel & Epistles of John*. Eerdmans, 1983.

———. "Marius Victorinus and His Works," *The Evangelical Quarterly*, Vol. 18. 1946.

Bruner, Frederick Dale. *The Churchbook: Matthew 13-28*. Grand Rapids: Eerdmans, 1990.

Brunner, Emil. *Dogmatics,* Vol. 1. London: Lutterworth Press, 1949.

Bullinger, E. W. *A Critical Lexicon and Concordance to the English and Greek New Testament*. Samuel Bagster and Sons Ltd., London, Tenth Edition, 1971.

Bultmann, Rudolph. *Theology of the New Testament*, Vol. I. Waco: Baylor University Press, 2007 [1951]),

Burnap, George Washington. *Lectures On The Doctrines of Christianity*. Wm. R. Lucas & R.N. Wright, 1835.

Buzzard, Anthony F. *Jesus Was Not a Trinitarian*. McDonough: Restoration Fellowship, 2012.

———. *The One God, the Father, One Man Messiah Translation*. McDonough: Restoration Fellowship, 2015.

———. *Our Fathers Who Aren't In Heaven: The Forgotten Christianity of Jesus the Jew*. McDonough: Restoration Fellowship, 1995.

———., Charles F. Hunting. *The Doctrine of the Trinity: Christianity's Self-Inflicted Wound*. Lanham: International Scholars Publications, 1998.

Carrell, Peter R. *Jesus and the Angels: Angelology and the Christology of the Apocalypse of John*. Cambridge: CUP, 1997.

Carroll, James. *Constantine's Sword: The Church and the Jews*, A History. New York: Houghton Mifflin Company, 2002.

Carson, D. A. *The Gospel According to John*. Grand Rapids: Eerdmans, 1991.

Carson, Thomas. *The New Catholic Encyclopedia, Second Edition*. Farmington Hills: Gale, 2003.

Casey, Maurice. *From Jewish Prophet to Gentile God: The Origins and Development of New Testament Christology*. Louisville: Westminster John Knox Press, 1991.

———. "Monotheism, Worship and Christological Developments in Pauline Churches," *The Jewish Roots of Christological Monotheism*. Leiden: Brill, 1999.

Chadwick, Henry. *The Early Church*. New York: Penguin Books, 1967.

Charles, R. H. *The Book of Enoch, or, 1 Enoch*. Oxford: Clarendon Press, 1912.

Charlesworth, James H. *The Old Testament Pseudepigrapha*, Vol. 2. Peabody: Hendrickson Publishers, 1983.

Chilton, Bruce. Do *Jews, Christians, and Muslims Worship the Same God?* Nashville: Abingdon Press, 2012.

Christie, William. *Dissertations on the Unity of God in the Person of the Father*. Philadelphia: R.H. Small, 1828.

Clarke, Samuel. *The Works*. London: John & Paul Knapton, 1738.

Cole, Graham. *The God Who Became Human: A Biblical Theology of Incarnation*. Downer's Grove: IVP, 2013. p. 84.

Collins, Adela Yarbro, John Joseph Collins. *King and Messiah as Son of God: Divine, Human, and Angelic Messianic Figures in Biblical and Related Literature*. Grand Rapids: Eerdmans, 2008.

Collins, John. *The Scepter and the Star: The Messiahs of the Dead Sea Scrolls and Other Ancient Literature*. New York: Doubleday, 1995.

Collins, Raymond F. *First and Second Timothy and Titus: A Commentary*. Louisville: Westminster John Knox Press, 2002.

Cottrell, Jack. *What the Bible Says About God the Redeemer*. Eugene: Wipf and Stock Publishers, 1987.

Creed, J.M. *The Divinity of Jesus Christ.* London: Fontana, 1964.

Cremer, Hermann. *Biblico-Theological Lexicon of New Testament Greek.* Edinburgh: T & T Clark, 1878.

Crowe, Jerome. *From Jerusalem to Antioch: The Gospel Across Cultures.* Collegeville: The Liturgical Press, 1997.

Cullmann, Oscar. *The Christology of the New Testament,* Rev. Ed., trans, Shirley C. Guthrie and Charles A. M. Hall. Philadelphia: Westminster Press, 1963.

Cupitt, Don. *The Debate About Christ.* London: SCM Press, 1979.

Dalman, G. *Words of Jesus.* Edinburgh: T & T Clark, 1902.

David, Ben. *The Monthly Repository of Theology and General Literature,* Vol. 21. Hackney: Sherwood, Gilbert, and Piper, 1826.

Davies, W. D., Louis Finkelstein. *The Cambridge History of Judaism, Volume 4.* Cambridge: CUP, 1984.

Dewick, E. C. *Primitive Christian Eschatology, The Hulsean Prize Essay for 1908,* Cambridge: CUP, 1912.

Dollinger, John. *Hippolytus and Callistus.* Edinburgh: T & T Clark, 1876.

Drecoll, Volker Henning. "The Greek Text Behind the Parallel Sections in Zostrianos and Marius Victorinus," *Plato's Parmenides and Its Heritage,* Vol. 1. Atlanta: Society of Biblical Literature, 2010.

Duchesne, Louis. *Early History of the Christian Church,* Vol. 2. New York: Longmans, Green and Co., 1920.

Dunn, James. *Christ and the Spirit: Collected Essays of James D.G. Dunn, Volume 1.* Grand Rapids: Eerdmans, 1998.

———. *Christology in the Making.* Grand Rapids: Eerdmans, 1980.

———. *Did the First Christians Worship Jesus?* Louisville: Westminster John Knox Press, 2010.

———. *Neither Jew Nor Greek: A Contested Identity.* Grand Rapids: Eerdmans, 2015.

———. *The Theology of Paul the Apostle.* Grand Rapids: Eerdmans, 1998.

Durant, Will. *The Story of Civilization Vol. 2: The Life of Greece.* Simon & Schuster, 1966.

———. *The Story of Civilization Vol. 3: Caesar and Christ.* Simon & Schuster, 1944.

Easton, Burton. *The Apostolic Tradition of Hippolytus.* Cambridge: CUP, 1934.

Edwards, M. J. "Porphyry and the Intelligible Triad," *The Journal of Hellenic Studies,* Vol. 110. Society for the Promotion of Hellenic Studies, 1990.

Ehrenthal, Ferenc Frank. *Szekely Origins and Radical Faith: From Mongolia to Transylvania, the Birth of Unitarianism.* North Charleston: CreateSpace, 2014.

Ehrman, Bart. *How Jesus Became God: The Exaltation of a Jewish Preacher from Galilee.* New York: HarperOne, 2014.

———. *Lost Christianities: The Battles for Scripture and the Faiths We Never Knew.* New York: OUP, 2003.

Erickson, Millard J. *Christian Theology.* Grand Rapids: Baker Books, Second Edition, 1999.

———. *God in Three Persons: A Contemporary Interpretation of the Trinity.* Grand Rapids: Baker Publishing Group, 1995.

Esler, Philip F. *The Early Christian World, Vol. I-II.* London: Routledge, 2000.

Evans, Craig. *Word Biblical Commentary, Mark 34b.* Nashville: Thomas Nelson, 2001.

Ezigbo, Victor I. *Introducing Christian Theologies,* Vol. 1. Eugene: Wipf & Stock, 2013.

Farrar, Frederic. *Early Days of Christianity,* Vol. I. Boston: DeWolfe, Fiske & Company, 1882.

Fitzgerald, Allan, John C. Cavadini, ed. *Augustine Through the Ages: An Encyclopedia.* Grand Rapids: Eerdmans, 1999.

Fitzmyer, Joseph. *A Christological Catechism.* Costa Mesa: Paulist Press, 1991.

Flatt, J.F. "Dissertation on the Deity of Christ," *Biblical Repertory,* Vol. 1. Philadelphia: Peter Walker, 1829.

Fortman, Edmund J. *The Triune God.* Grand Rapids: Baker Book House, 1972.

Franzmann, Majella. *Jesus in the Manichaean Writings.* London: T & T Clark, 2003.

Freeman, Charles. *The Closing of the Western Mind.* New York: Vintage Books, 2002.

———. *AD 381.* New York: The Overlook Press, 2009.

Frend, W. H. C. *Rise of Christianity.* Philadelphia: Fortress Press, 1984.

Fuller, R. H. "Pre-existence Christology: Can We Dispense with It?" *Word and World 2*. St. Paul, MN: Luther Seminary, 1982.

Gallarte, Israel, Lautaro Lanzillotta. *Plutarch in the Religious and Philosophical Discourse of Late Antiquity*. Leiden: Koninklije Brill, 2012.

Garland, David E. *The NIV Application Commentary: Colossians, Philemon*. Grand Rapids: Zondervan, 1998.

Geivett, R. Douglas. Timothy R. Phillips, Dennis L. Okholm, Alister E. McGrath, Clark H. Pinnock, John Hick, W. Gary Phillips. *Four Views on Salvation in a Pluralistic World*. Grand Rapids: Zondervan, 1996.

Gibbon, Edward. *History of Christianity*. New York: Peter Eckler, 1891.

———. *The Decline and Fall of the Roman Empire*. London: Methuen & Co., 1902 (1776-1789).

Gier, N.F. *God, Reason, and the Evangelicals: Case Against Evangelical Rationalism*. Lanham, Maryland: Rowman & Littlefield, 1986.

Gilbert, George H. "An Important Unnoticed Argument in John Chapter 17," *The Biblical World*, Vol. 13, No. 5. Chicago: University of Chicago Press, 1899.

Giles, Kevin. *The Eternal Generation of the Son: Maintaining Orthodoxy in Trinitarian Theology*. IVP, 2012.

Goguel, Maurice. *Jesus and the Origins of Christianity*. New York: Harper, 1960.

Gore, Charles. *Belief in Christ*. New York: Charles Scribner's Sons, 1922.

Goulder, Michael. *Incarnation and Myth: the Debate Continued*. Grand Rapids: Eerdmans, 1979.

Graeser, Mark H., John A. Lynn, John W. Schoenheit. *One God & One Lord: Reconsidering the Cornerstone of the Christian Faith*. Indianapolis: Christian Educational Services, 2000.

Granerod, Gard. *Abraham and Melchizedek: Scribal Activity of Second Temple Times in Genesis 14 and Psalm 110, Vol 23*. Berlin: Walter de Gruyter, 2010.

Griffin, Svetla, Pauliina Remes. *The Routledge Handbook of Neoplatonism*. Routledge, 2014.

Griggs, C. Wilfred. *Early Egyptian Christianity: From Its Origins to 451 CE*. Leiden: Brill, 2000.

Groningen, Gerard. *First Century Gnosticism: Its Origin and Motifs*. Leiden: Brill, 1967.

Gruber, Maye Irwin. *Rashi's Commentary on Psalms*. Leiden: E.J. Brill, 2004.

Grudem, Wayne. *Systematic Theology: An Introductory to Biblical Doctrine*. Grand Rapids: Zondervan, 1994.

Guitton, Jean. *Great Heresies and Church Councils*. New York: Harper & Row, 1965.

Gundry, Robert H. "Style and Substance in 'The Myth of God Incarnate' according to Philippians 2:6-11," in *Crossing the Boundaries*. Leiden: Brill, 1994.

Guthrie, Shirley C. *Christian Doctrine*. Louisville: Westminster John Knox Press, 1994.

Gwynn, David M. *Athanasius of Alexandria: Bishop, Theologian, Ascetic, Father*. Oxford: OUP, 2012.

Haag, Herbert. "Son of God", *Concilium*. Norwich: SCM Press, 1996.

Haight, Roger. *Jesus: Symbol of God*. Maryknoll: Orbis Books, 1999.

Hanson, A. T. "Two Consciousnesses: The Modern Version of Chalcedon," *Scottish Journal of Theology*, Vol. 37. Cambridge: CUP, 1984.

———. *The Image of the Invisible God*. London: SCM Press, 1982.

Hanson, R. P. C. *The Search for the Christian Doctrine of God: The Arian Controversy, 318-381*. Edinburgh: T & T Clark, 1988.

Hare, Julius Charles. *Mission of the Comforter*, Vol. 1. Boston: Gould and Lincoln, 1877.

Harnack, Adolf. *History of Dogma*, Vol 1. London: Williams & Norgate, 1894.

———. *History of Dogma*, Vol. 2. New York: Dover Publications, 1961 [1901].

———. *Marcion: The Gospel of the Alien God*. Darmstadt: W.B., 1996 [1921].

Harris, Murray J. *Jesus as God: The New Testament Use of Theos in Reference to Jesus*. Eugene: Wipf & Stock Publishers, 1992.

Hart, Thomas N. *To Know and Follow Jesus*. New York: Paulist Press, 1984.

Harvey, A. E. *Jesus and the Constraints of History*. London: Duckworth, 1980.

Hastings, James. *Hasting's Dictionary of the Bible*. Grand Rapids: Baker Books, 1994.

Hefele, Charles Joseph. *A History of the Christian Councils From the Original Documents*. Edinburgh: T&T Clark, 1894.

Heppe, Heinrich. *Reformed Dogmatics*. Eugene: Wipf & Stock Publishers, 2007.

Hey, John. *Lectures in Divinity Delivered in the University of Cambridge*, Vol. 2. L.A.: HardPress, 2013.

Hick, John. *The Concept of Monotheism in Islam and Christianity, A Recent Development within Christian Monotheism*. Austria: Typostudio & Druckkunst Wie, 1982.

———. *The Metaphor of God Incarnate*. London: Westminster John Knox Press, 2005 [1993].

Hodgson, Leonard. *Christian Faith and Practice, Seven Lectures*. Oxford: Blackwell, 1952.

Hoffman, James B. *Sin and Life in the Kingdom of God*. Indianapolis, IN: Dog Ear Publishing, 2009.

Holder, Meir. *History of the Jewish People: From Yavneh to Pumbedisa*. New York: Mesorah Pub., 2004.

Holloway, Ross R. *Constantine and Rome*. New Haven: Yale University Press, 2004.

Holmen, Tom, Stanley E. Porter. *Handbook for the Study of the Historical Jesus*. Leiden: Brill, 2011.

Home, Thomas Hartwell. *A Concise History and Analysis of the Athanasian Creed*. London: T. Cadell, Strand, 1834.

Holmes, O.W. "Competing Concepts of the Cosmos in the Sixteenth and Seventeenth Centuries," *Phenomenology and the Human Positioning in the Cosmos*. London: Springer, 2012.

Hopkins, S.M. "The Death of Arius," *The Biblical Repository*. London: John Wiley, 1850.

Horbury, William. *Jews and Christians*. Edinburgh: Bloomsbury, 1998.

Hurtado, Larry W. "The Binitarian Pattern of Earliest Christian Devotion and Early Doctrinal Development," *The Place of Christ in Liturgical Prayer*. Collegeville: Liturgical Press, 2008.

———. *Lord Jesus Christ*. Grand Rapids: Eerdmans, 2003.

———. "The Binitarian Shape of Early Christian Worship," *The Jewish Roots of Christological Monotheism*. Leiden: Brill, 1999. p. 208.

Inge, W. R. *The Philosophy of Plotinus*. London: Longmans, 1918.

———. "The Permanent Influence of Neoplatonism upon Christianity," *The American Journal of Theology*, Vol. 4, No. 2. Chicago: The University of Chicago Press, 1900.

Jackson, T. *New Creation in Paul's Letters*. Tubingen: Mohr Siebeck, 2010.

Jacobovici, Simcha, Barrie Wilson. *The Lost Gospel*. New York: Pegasus Books, 2014.

Jenkins, John Philip. *Jesus Wars*. New York: HarperOne, 2011.

Jeremias, J. *New Testament Theology*. New York: Scribner's, 1971

Jervell, Jacob. *Jesus in the Gospels*. Minneapolis: Augsburg Publishing House, 1984.

Johnson, Aubrey R. *Sacral Kingship in Ancient Israel*. Cardiff: University of Wales Press, 1955.

Jowett, Benjamin. *The Dialogues of Plato*. New York: Charles Scribner's Sons, 1911.

Jurgens, William A., *The Faith of the Early Fathers, Volume 1*. Collegeville, MN: The Liturgical Press, 1970.

Kaiser, Christopher B. *The Doctrine of God: A Historical Survey*. Eugene: Wipf & Stock, 2001.

Kappelle, Robert. *Wisdom Revealed: The Message of Biblical Wisdom Literature, Then and Now*. Eugene: Wipf & Stock, 2014.

Kariatlis, Philip. "Dazzling Darkness: The Mystical or Theophanic Theology of St Gregory of Nyssa," *Phronema*, Vol. 27, No. 2. Redfern: St. Andrew's, 2012.

Keener, Craig S. *The Gospel of John: A Commentary*. Peabody: Hendrickson Publishers, 2003.

Kelly, J. N. D. *Early Christian Doctrines*, 5th edition. London: A&C Black, 1977.

———. *Early Christian Creeds*. London: Longman, 1972.

Kennard, Douglas Welker. *Messiah Jesus: Christology in His Day and Ours*. Oxford: Peter Lang, 2008.

Kirk, J. R. Daniel. "Mark's Son of Man and Paul's Second Adam," *Horizons in Biblical Theology*, Vol. 37. Leiden: Brill, 2015.

Klausner, Joseph. Jesus of Nazareth: His Life, Times, and Teachings. New York: Bloch, 1989.

Klijn, A. F. J., G. J. Reinink, *Patristic Evidence for Jewish Christian Sects*. Leiden: Brill, 1973.

Knapp, G. C. *Christian Theology*. London: Leonard Woods, 1831.

Knoch, Adolph Ernst. *Christ and Deity*. Birkenfeld: Concordant Publishing, 1958.

Kuschel, Karl Josef. *Born Before All Time?* New York: Crossroad, 1998.

Ladd, George Eldon, Donald Alfred Hagner. *A Theology of the New Testament*. Grand Rapids: Eerdmans, 1993.

Laird, Martin. *Gregory of Nyssa and the Grasp of Faith*. Oxford: OUP, 2004.

Lambert, Malcom. *Medieval Heresy: Popular Movements from Bogomil to Hus.* New York: Homes & Meier Publishers, 1977.

Lampe, G.W.H. *Explorations in Theology,* Vol. 8. SCM Press, 1981.

———. *God as Spirit.* Norwich: SCM Press, 1977.

Lamson, Alvan, Ezra Abbot. *The Church of the First Three Centuries.* Toronto: University of Toronto Libraries, 1875.

Lapide, Pinchas. *Jewish Monotheism and Christian Trinitarian Doctrine.* Philadelphia: Fortress, 1981.

Lardner, Nathaniel. *The Works of Nathaniel Lardner.* London: William Ball, 1893.

Latourette, Kenneth. *A History of Christianity,* Vol. 1. New York: HarperCollins, 1875.

Layton, Bentley. *The Gnostic Scriptures.* New York: Doubleday and Co., 1987.

Leftow, Brian. *God and Necessity.* Oxford: OUP, 2012.

Lewis, C.S. *Mere Christianity.* New York: HarperCollins, 1952.

Lim, Paul C.H. *Mystery Unveiled: The Crisis of the Trinity in Early Modern England.* London: OUP, 2012.

Lipschitz, Oded, Gary N. Knoppers, Rainer Albertz. *Judah and the Judeans in the Fourth Century B.C.E.* Warsaw: Eisenbrauns, 2007.

Loofs, Friedrich. *Guide to Studying the History of Dogma.* Niemeyer Verlag, 1951 [1890].

Mahoney, John. "The Legacy of Augustine," *The Making of Moral Theology: A Study of the Roman Catholic Tradition.* OUP, 1987.

Manchester, Peter. "The Noetic Triad in Plotinus, Marius Victorinus, and Augustine" in *Neoplatonism and Gnosticism.* Albany: SUNY Press, 1992.

Manson, Thomas Walter. *Studies in the Gospels and Epistles.* Manchester: University Press, 1962.

Marcus, Joel. "Son of Man as Son of Adam," *Revue Biblique,* Vol. 110. Paris, 2003.

Martin, Ralph P. *Epistle of Paul to the Philippians.* Grand Rapids: Eerdmans, 1987.

Matthews, W. R. *God in Christian Experience.* Whitefish: Kessinger Publishing, 2010 [1930].

———. *The Problem of Christ in the 20th Century.* Oxford: OUP, 1949.

Maurice Wiles, *The Remaking of Christian Doctrine, The Hulsean Lectures.* London: SCM Press, 1974.

McCready, Douglas. *He Came Down From Heaven: The Preexistence of Christ and the Christian Faith.* Downer's Grove: IL: IVP Academic, 2005.

McGrath, Alister E. *Christian Theology: An Introduction.* Oxford: Blackwell Publishing, 2011.

———. *Christianity's Dangerous Idea: The Protestant Revolution: A History from the Sixteenth Century to the Twenty-First.* New York: HarperOne, 2007.

McGrath, James F. "Johannine Christianity – Jewish Christianity?" *Koinonia* 8.1, 1996. pp. 1-20.

———. *The Only True God: Early Christian Monotheism in its Jewish Context.* Urbana and Chicago: The University of Illinois Press, 2009.

———. "Two Powers and Early Jewish and Christian Monotheism," *JBS,* Vol. 4, No. 1, 2004.

McKenzie, John L. *Dictionary of the Bible.* New York: Touchstone, 1995.

Mead, G. R. S. *Thrice-Great Hermes,* Vol. 1. Whitefish: Kessinger, 2002 [1906].

Metzger, Bruce, Michael Coogan. *The Oxford Companion to the Bible.* Oxford: OUP, 1993.

Meyer, H.A.W. *A Critical and Exegetical Handbook to the Epistles to the Philippians and the Colossians.* Edinburgh: T & T Clark, 1875.

Miller, Stephen. *The New American Commentary: Daniel.* Nashville: Broadman & Holman Pub., 1994.

Moffatt, James. *Jesus Christ the Same.* Abingdon-Cokesbury, 1945.

Moll, Sebastian. *The Arch-heretic Marcion.* Tubingen: Mohr Siebeck, 2010.

Moody, Dale. *The Word of Truth.* Grand Rapids: Eerdmans, 1981.

Morenz, Siegfried. *Egyptian Religion.* New York: Cornell, 1992.

Mowinckel, Sigmund. *He That Cometh.* Grand Rapids: Eerdmans, 2005 [1956].

Najovits, Simson. *Egypt, Trunk of the Tree,* Vol. 2. Algora Publishing, 2004.

Neander, August. *History of the Christian Religion and Church.* London: Wiley & Putnam, 1854.

Neusner, Jacob, William Scott Green (ed.). *Dictionary of Judaism in the Biblical Period.* Peabody: Hendrickson Publishers, 1996.

Newman, Albert Henry. *A Manual of Church History.* Philadelphia: The American Baptist Publication Society, 1899, rev. 1942.

Norton, Andrews. *A Statement of Reasons for Not Believing the Doctrines of Trinitarians.* Cambridge: Brown, Shattuck and Co., 1833.

Noth, Martin. "God, King and Nation," *The Laws in the Pentateuch and Other Studies.* Philadelphia: Fortress, 1966.

O'Brien, Carl Sean. *The Demiurge in Ancient Thought.* Cambridge: CUP, 2015.

O'Carroll, Michael. *Trinitas: A Theological Encyclopedia of the Holy Trinity.* Collegeville: Liturgical Press, 1987.

O'Dowd, Ryan. *The Wisdom of Torah: Epistemology in Deuteronomy and the Wisdom Literature.* Gottingen: Vandenhoeck & Ruprecht, 2009.

O'Hare, Patrick F. *The Facts About Luther.* Rockford: TAN Books, 1987.

Oden, Thomas C, Peter Gorday. *Colossians, 1-2 Thessalonians, 1-2 Timothy, Titus, Philemon.* New York: Fitzroy Dearborn Publishers, 2000.

Olson, Roger E. *The Story of Christian Theology.* Wheaton: IVP, 1999.

Ommanney, George. *A Critical Dissertation on the Athanasian Creed.* London: OUP, 1897.

Packer, J. I. *Knowing God.* Downers Grove, IL: IVP, 1993.

Pagels, Elaine. *Adam, Eve, and the Serpent.* New York: Vintage, 1989.

———. *The Gnostic Gospels.* New York: Vintage Books, 1979.

Paige, Lucius Robinson. *A Commentary on the New Testament,* Vol. 1. Boston: B. B. Mussey, 1849.

Paine, L. L. *A Critical History of the Evolution of Trinitarianism.* Boston: Houghton, Mifflin & Co., 1900.

———. *The Ethnic Trinities and Their Relations to the Christian Trinity.* New York: Houghton, Mifflin and Co., 1901.

Peake, Arthur Samuel. *A Commentary on the Bible.* New York: Thomas Nelson & Sons, 1920.

Pearson, Albert Birger. *Gnosticism and Christianity: In Roman and Coptic Egypt.* London: Continuum International Publishing Group, 2004.

Peppard, Michael. *The Son of God in the Roman World: Divine Sonship in Its Social and Political Context.* Oxford: OUP, 2011.

Pfafflin, Frederic. *Die Briefe des Neuen Testaments in der Sprache von heute.* Heilbronn: Salzer, 1993.

Pohlsander, Hans A. *Emperor Constantine.* London: Routledge, 2004.

Prestige, George Leonard. *God in Patristic Thought.* London: SPCK, 1952 (1936).

Priestley, Joseph. *The Theological Works of Joseph Priestley,* Vol. 6. G. Smallfield, 1786.

Pritz, Ray. *Nazarene Christianity.* Jerusalem: Hebrew University of Jerusalem Press, 1988.

Purves, G. T. *The Testimony of Justin Martyr to Early Christianity.* New York: Randolph and Co., 1889.

Quispel, Gilles. "Origen and Valentinian Gnosis," *Gnostica, Judaica, Catholica.* Leiden: Brill, 2008.

———. "Qumran, John and Jewish Christianity," *John and Qumran.* London: Geoffery Chapman, 1972.

Raisanen, Heikki. *The Rise of Christian Beliefs: The Thought World of Early Christians.* Minneapolis: Fortress Press, 2010.

Reade, William Winwood. *The Martyrdom of Man.* New York: Peter Eckler, 1890.

Reinecker, Fritz, Cleon Rogers. *Linguistic Key to the Greek New Testament.* Grand Rapids: Zondervan Publishing House, 1982.

Richardson, Cyril C. *The Doctrine of the Trinity: A Clarification of What it Attempts to Express.* Nashville: Abingdon Press, 1958.

Ridgley, Thomas. *A Body of Divinity,* Vol. I. Philadelphia: William W. Woodward, 1814.

Riesenfeld, H. "The Mythological Background of New Testament Christology," *The Background of the New Testament and Its Eschatology,* ed. W. D. Davies and D. Daube. Cambridge: CUP, 1956.

Robertson, A. T. *A Grammar of the Greek New Testament in the Light of Historical Research.* Nashville: Braodman Press, 1934.

———. *Word Pictures in the New Testament,* Vol. IV. Grand Rapids: Baker Book House, 1933.

Robertson, Nicoll. ed. *The Expositor's Greek Testament,* Vol. 1. Grand Rapids: Eerdmans, 1983.

Robinson, J. A. T. *The Human Face of God.* Philadelphia: Westminster Press, 1873.

———. *Twelve More New Testament Studies.* London: SCM Press, 1984.

Robinson, James M. ed. *The Nag Hammadi Library.* San Francisco: Harper and Row, 1988.

Roqueah, Dawid. *Justin Martyr and the Jews.* Leiden: Brill, 2001.

Rubenstein, Richard E. *When Jesus Became God: The Epic Fight Over Christ's Divinity in the Last Days of Rome.* New York: Harcourt Brace & Company, 1999.

Rudolph, Kurt. *Gnosis: The Nature and History of Gnosticism.* New York: Harper & Row, 1983.

Rusch, William G. *Ecumenical Reception: Its Challenge and Opportunity.* Grand Rapids: Eerdmans, 2007.

Russell, Bertrand. *History of Western Philosophy.* London: George Allen and Unwin Ltd., 1946.

Ruzica, Steven. *The Byzantine Theocracy.* Cambridge: CUP, 2004.

Ryrie, Charles C. *Basic Theology: A Popular Systematic Guide to Understanding Biblical Truth.* Chicago: Moody Publishers, 1999.

Sanders, J. N., B.A. Mastin. *Black's New Testament Commentaries: The Gospel According to Saint John.* London: Randomhouse Publishers, 1968.

Sanders, Jack T. *Schismatics, Sectarians, Dissidents, Deviants: The First One Hundred Years of Jewish-Christian Relations.* London: SCM Press, 1993.

Schaff, Philip, Alexander Roberts, James Donaldson, and Arthur Cleveland Coxe. *Nicene and Post-Nicene Fathers, Series II.* Grand Rapids: Eerdmans, 1885.

Schaff, Philip. *History of the Christian Church,* Vol 1. Grand Rapids: Eerdmans, 1985 [1882].

———. *History of the Christian Church,* Vol. 2. New York: Scribner's, 1914 [1884].

———. *The New Schaff-Herzog Encyclopedia of Religious Knowledge,* Vol. IX. Ed. Samuel Macauley Jackson, Grand Rapids: Baker Book House, 1957.

———. *History of the Christian Church.* Grand Rapids: Eerdmans, 1910.

Schimanowski, Gottfried. *Wisdom and Messiah.* Tubingen: Mohr Siebeck, 1985.

Schonfield, Hugh J. *The Original New Testament.* Rockport, MA: Element Books Ltd, 1985.

Schurer, Emil. *The History of The Jewish People In The Age Of Jesus Christ.* Edinburgh: T & T Clark, 1979.

Scott, Alan B. *Origen and the Life of the Stars.* Oxford: Clarendon Press, 1992.

Segal, Alan F. "Jewish Christianity," *Eusebius, Christianity, and Judaism.* Detroit: Wayne State University Press, 1992.

———. *Two Powers in Heaven: Early Rabbinc Reports About Christianity and Gnosticism,* Leiden: Brill, 2002.

Selwyn, E. G. *First Epistle of St. Peter.* Grand Rapids: Baker Book House, 1983.

Shepardson, Christine. *Anti-Judaism and Christian Orthodoxy: Ephrem's Hymns in Fourth-century Syria.* Washington D.C.: The Catholic University of America Press, 2008.

Shotwell, Willis. *The Biblical Exegesis of Justin Martyr.* London: SPCK, 1965.

Smith, Dustin, Charles Lee Irons, Danny Andre Dixon. *The Son of God: Three Views of the Identity of Jesus.* Eugene: Wipf & Stock, 2015.

Smith, John Pye. *Scripture Testimony to the Messiah,* Vol. II. Edinburgh: London: Hamilton & Co. Jackson & Walford, 1759.

Smith, Warren J. "The Fourth Century Fathers," *Oxford Handbook of the Trinity.* Oxford: OUP, 2011.

Smith, William. *A Dictionary of Greek and Roman Biography and Mythology.* London: John Murray, 1880.

Stauffer, Ethelbert. *New Testament Theology.* London: SCM Press, 1955.

Stec, David M. *The Targum of Psalms: Translated, with a Critical Introduction, Apparatus, and Notes.* London: T & T Clark, 2004.

Stein, Robert H. *The Method and Message of Jesus' Teaching.* London: Westminster John Knox Press, 1994.

Strong, Augustus H. *Systematic Theology.* Philadelphia: Judson Press, 1985.

Strong, James, John McClintock. *Cyclopaedia of Biblical, Theological, and Ecclesiastical Literature.* New York: Harper, 1891.

Studer, Basil. *Trinity and Incarnation: The Faith of the Early Church.* Minnesota: T&T Clark Ltd, 1993.

Tasker, R. V. G. *The Gospel According to St. John: Tyndale New Testament Commentaries.* 1960.

———. *Tyndale NT Commentaries: John.* Westmont: InverVarsity Press, 1983.

Temple, William. *Readings in St. John's Gospel.* London: Macmillan, 1933.

Thayer, Joseph Henry. *The New Thayer's Greek-English Lexicon of the New Testament.* Lafayette: Associated Publishers and Authors, 1979.

Thompson, Marianne Meyer. *Dictionary of Jesus and the Gospels.* Downer's Grove: IVP 1992.

———. *Colossians and Philemon.* Grand Rapids: Eerdmans, 2005.

Thompson, R. W. *Athanasius, Contra Gentes and De Incarnatione.* Oxford, 1971.

Thomsett, Michael. *The Inquisition: A History.* Jefferson: McFarland, 2010.

Tomline, George P. *Elements of Christian Theology,* Vol. 2. London: Luke Hansard & Sons, 1815.

Toom, Tarmo. *Classical Trinitarian Theology: A Textbook.* New York: T & T Clark, 2007.

Toon, Peter. *Our Triune God: A Biblical Portrait of the Trinity.* Vancouver: Regent College Pub., 1996.

Torrance, Thomas F. *The Christian Doctrine of God: One Being Three Persons.* London: T&T Clark, 1996

Tozer, A. W. *The Knowledge of the Holy.* New York: HarperOne, 1961.

Traketellis, Demetrius. *Pre-Existence of Christ in the Writings of Justin Martyr,* Scholars PR, 1976.

Turvasi, Francesco. *The Condemnation of Alfred Loisy and the Historical Method.* Rome: Storia E Letteratura, 1979.

Tuggy, Dale. "On Bauckham's Bargain," *Theology Today,* 70:2. Los Angeles: Sage, 2013. pp. 128-143.

Wallace, Daniel B. *Greek Grammar: Beyond the Basics.* Grand Rapids: Zondervan, 1996.

Warfield, B. B. "The Spirit of God in the Old Testament," *The Works of Benjamin B. Warfield.* New York: OUP, 1932.

Weigall, Arthur. *Paganism in Our Christianity.* Kessinger Publishing, 1928.

Wenham, Gordon J. *Word Biblical Commentary, Vol. 1: Genesis 1-15.* Nashville: Thomas Nelson, 1987.

Werner, Martin. *The Formation of Christian Doctrine.* London: A. & C. Black, 1957.

Whiteley, D. E. H. *The Theology of St. Paul.* Oxford: Blackwell, 1980.

Wiedemann, Alfred. *The Ancient Egyptian Doctrine of the Immortality of the Soul.* London: H. Grevel & Co., 1895.

Wiersbe, Warren. *Ephesians Through Revelation,* Vol. 2. David C. Cook, 2003.

Wilberding, James. *Plotinus' Cosmology: A Study of Ennead II.1 (40).* New York: OUP, 2006.

Wilbur, E. M. *A History of Unitarianism, Socinianism and its Antecedents.* Boston: Beacon Press, 1946.

Williams, Rowan. "Arius: Heresy and Tradition," *The Journal of Roman Studies,* Vol. 79. Society for the Promotion of Roman Studies, 1989.

———. *Arius: Heresy and Tradition.* London: Darton, Longman and Todd, 1987.

Williams, Stephen, Gerard Friell. *Theodosius: The Empire At Bay.* London: B T Batsford, 1994.

Wolfson, Henry A. *The Philosophy of the Church Fathers,* Vol. 1. Cambridge: HUP, 1964.

Wordsworth, C. *St. Hippolytus and the Church of Rome.* Oxford: Rivingtons, 1880.

Wright, C. J. "Jesus the Revelation of God," in *The Mission and Message of Jesus: An Exposition of the Gospels in the Light of Modern Research.* New York: E.P. Dutton and Co., 1953.

Wright, N. T. "Harpagmos and the Meaning of Philippians 2:5-11," *Journal of Theological Studies,* Vol. 37. Oxford: OUP, 1986.

———. *Jesus and the Victory of God.* Minneapolis: Fortress Press, 1996.

———. *Paul and the Faithfulness of God.* Minneapolis: Fortress Press, 2013.

———. "The Resurrection of Resurrection," *Bible Review,* Vol. 16, No. 4. Washington D.C.: Biblical Archaeology Society, 2000.

Wuest, Kenneth S. *Wuest's Word Studies from the Greek New Testament for the English Reader,* Vol. 1. Grand Rapids: Eerdmans, 1973.

Young, Robert. *Concise Commentary on the Holy Bible.* Grand Rapids: Baker, 1885.

Zahn-Harnack, Agnes. *Adolf von Harnack.* Berlin: Tempelhof & Bott, 1936.

Zeller, Eduard. *Outlines of the History of Greek Philosophy.* New York: Henry Holt, 1889.

———. *Plato and the Older Academy.* London: Longmans, Green, and Co., 1888.

Zizioulas, John D. "The Doctrine of the Holy Trinity: The Significance of the Cappadocian Contribution," *Trinitarian Theology Today.* Edinburgh: T & T Clark, 2000 [1995].

Zweig, Stefan. *The Right to Heresy; Castellio Against Calvin.* Boston: The Beacon Press, 1951.

Scripture Index

INDEX OF ANCIENT WORKS

SUBJECT INDEX